Congressional
Districts

IN THE 1970s

2nd Edition
September 1974

CONGRESSIONAL QUARTERLY

1414 22ND ST. N.W., WASHINGTON, D.C. 20037

Congressional Quarterly Inc.

Congressional Quarterly Inc., an editorial research service and publishing company, serves clients in the fields of news, education, business and government. It combines specific coverage of Congress, government and politics by Congressional Quarterly with the more general subject range of an affiliated service, Editorial Research Reports.

Congressional Quarterly was founded in 1945 by Henrietta and Nelson Poynter. Its basic periodical publication was and still is the CQ *Weekly Report*, mailed to clients every Saturday. A cumulative index is published quarterly.

The CQ *Almanac*, a compendium of legislation for one session of Congress, is published every spring. *Congress and the Nation* is published every four years as a record of government for one presidential term.

Congressional Quarterly also publishes paperback books on public affairs. These include the twice yearly *Guide to Current American Government* and such recent titles as *The Supreme Court, Justice and the Law* and *The Washington Lobby, 2nd Edition.*

CQ Direct Research is a consulting service which performs contract research and maintains a reference library and query desk for the convenience of clients.

Editorial Research Reports covers subjects beyond the specialized scope of Congressional Quarterly. It publishes reference material on foreign affairs, business, education, cultural affairs, national security, science and other topics of news interest. Service to clients includes a 6,000-word report four times a month bound and indexed semi-annually. Editorial Research Reports publishes paperback books in its fields of coverage. Founded in 1923, the service merged with Congressional Quarterly in 1956.

Congressional Districts in the 1970s, 2nd Edition, was organized and compiled by Senior Researcher Warden Moxley, assisted by Wayne Walker and Robert Healy.

Book Service Editor: Robert A. Diamond. Editorial Assistants: Janice L. Goldstein and Robert Healy.

Cover: Art Director Howard Chapman. Maps: Chapman, Sandra Katz, *St. Petersburg Times* Art Department, Bureau of Census.

Research Staff: Elizabeth Bowman, Kim W. Brace, Prudence Crewdson, Oliver W. Cromwell, James W. Lawrence, Andrea W. Loewenstein, August Maffry Jr., Margaret Thompson.

Production Manager: Donald R. Buck. Production assistance by Richard Butler.

Library of Congress Catalog No. 72-94078
International Standard Book No. 0-87187-063-0

TABLE OF CONTENTS

Congressional District Profiles

INTRODUCTION

Court Decision and 1970 Census
Led to Equitably Drawn House Districts

For the first time in history, voters in November 1972 elected representatives to the U.S. House from districts of nearly equal population within each state.

The change from malapportioned districts to equality sprung from two primary sources—the 1964 Supreme Court decision in *Wesberry v. Sanders* and the 1970 decennial census. *(Wesberry decision p. 234)*

The effect of the "one person, one vote" standard on congressional districts did not bring about immediate equality in districts in the years 1964-70. Following the *Wesberry* ruling, district lines were redrawn in 39 states. But most of the new districts were far from equal in population, since the only official population figures came from the 1960 census. Massive population shifts during the decade rendered most post-*Wesberry* efforts to achieve equality useless.

Following redistricting in 1971-72, based on the 1970 census, the result achieved was that House members elected in November 1972 to the 93rd Congress represented districts which differed only slightly in population from the state average. In 385 of the 435 districts, the district's variance was less than one percent from the state average district population.

By contrast, only nine of the districts in the 88th Congress (elected in 1962) deviated less than one percent from the state average; 81 were between one and five percent; 87 from five to ten percent; and in 236 districts, the deviation was ten percent or greater. Twenty-two House members were elected at large.

New California, Texas, New York Districts. The original redistricting plans for three states, California, Texas and New York, were successfully challenged in the courts. As a result, all of the California and Texas districts were redrawn and four districts in New York—the 12th, 13th, 14th and 15th—were changed. This second edition contains new profiles and statistics for these districts, and describes all 435 districts as they exist for the 1974 congressional elections.

Political Impact

For the 1972 congressional elections more than a dozen entirely new districts were created, and others had major changes in their boundary lines. Many of the changes tended to favor the Republicans because many of the new districts were placed in fast-growing Republican suburbs and because legislatures in several states drew the lines to partisan Republican advantage.

Forty-three representatives retired or were defeated in primary elections before the November 1972 elections. One of the principal reasons for these departures was the redrawing of district lines. Some incumbents found themselves in new districts and some in combined districts with other incumbents of their own or the opposition party.

A Congressional Quarterly study of the results of the November 1972 election showed that 17 of the 24 seats that moved into Republican hands in the election did so largely because of reapportionment and redistricting. Democrats won eight of their 14 new seats for these reasons. Redistricting also played a significant role in the defeat of House incumbents. Thirteen incumbents, eight Democrats and five Republicans were defeated. *(Details on the political impact of redistricting are described throughout this book at the beginning of each state profile.)*

About This Book

Congressional Districts in the 1970s, 2nd edition, represents a major effort by Congressional Quarterly to gather and analyze in a single volume information on the 435 districts from a variety of sources. The book provides:

• Descriptive and statistical profiles of the districts based on the 1970 census and subsequent reapportionment and redistricting.

• Maps of all states showing district lines. Where appropriate, additional maps of cities containing several districts are included.

• Official election returns for the 1972 elections together with comparisons with 1968 and 1970 results.

• Information on the major military, space, atomic energy facilities in each district—as well as lists of major industries, universities, newspapers and television stations in the district.

The major source of this book has been the Congressional District Data booklets, published by the Bureau of the Census from August to October 1972. Congressional Quarterly has rearranged the material appearing in these 50 booklets to facilitate comparisons and analyses by scholars, journalists and laymen in search of descriptive profiles of the 435 districts.

Definitions of the terms used throughout the book, a list of additional sources and general instructions on how to use the book appear on pages two to eight, written by Senior Researcher Warden Moxley, who is also author of the chapter on the history of reapportionment and redistricting.

Robert A. Diamond
Book Service Editor
September 1974

State Descriptions

The two-column boldface heading beginning each state description indicates the state's total of U.S. House seats based on the 1970 decennial census and subsequent reapportionment. The heading also includes the number of seats gained or lost with the phrase "no change" used when the number of seats remained the same. This phrase does not imply there was no change in district lines or the political balance of the state's congressional delegation.

The narrative description of each state highlights the congressional redistricting process for the state in 1971-72—the politics, intended impact and actual results of redistricting, as reflected in the 1972 congressional elections.

Information for each state is presented as follows:

• First, a series of statistical tables including election results, voting age population, income and occupation, education, and housing and residential patterns.

• Second, individual district profiles which include data on race and ethnic groups, cities, universities, military installations or activities, Atomic Energy Commission installations, NASA facilities, newspapers, commercial television stations, and plants and offices.

If a certain category is not listed in a congressional district profile, it means the district contains nothing in that category. For example, compare the 6th District of Alabama, p. 12 columns one and two, where no "Military Installations or Activities" category is listed, with the following 7th District which includes Craig Air Force Base near Selma.

The first table lists the 1972 winners of House seats in each district and their winning percentage. For example, see Alabama, p. 9, column 1. This table also includes the 1970 population of each district, and the percent variance of each district from the ideal district population.

Ideal District. The ideal district population is calculated by dividing the population of the state by the number of congressional districts. For example Alabama, with a state population of 3,444,165, is entitled to seven districts; the state population divided by seven is 492,024, rounded off. Under the "one person, one vote" rule of the U.S. Supreme Court, this is the figure toward which the legislators (or judges) drawing congressional district lines should aim. For example, see Alabama, p. 9 column one, bottom of first table. The percent by which each district varies from this ideal population is called the "percent variance" and is listed in the last column of the table.

Even if all states were to be redistricted in a manner creating districts exactly equal in population within each state, there would still be wide population variances between districts in different states.

If the population of the United States, minus the District of Columbia (202,478,788 in the 1970 Census) were divided by the number of congressional districts (435), the result would be an ideal congressional district population of 465,468. Two factors however, determine that congressional district populations will vary considerably from this figure, between states.

First, the Constitution provides that every state must be allocated at least one Representative. Thus, Alaska, with 302,173 persons, Wyoming with 332,416 and Vermont with 444,732 are each entitled to one Representa-

tive, even though their populations are well below the national ideal district figure.

Similarly Nevada with a population of 488,738, Delaware with 548,104 and North Dakota with 617,761 have only one Representative, even though their population is above the national ideal district number.

A second and more important factor causing variance between congressional districts on a national basis is that district boundaries may not cross state lines. Since state populations are not equally divisible by 465,468, the various remainders will cause the ideal congressional district to differ in population from state to state.

For example, Idaho has 713,008 persons. If the state were to receive one Representative, his district would consist of all 713,008 inhabitants, almost 250,000 above the national ideal district population. But with the two Representatives it in fact has, the Idaho districts would consist (ideally) of 356,504 persons each, more than 100,000 below the national figure. Actually, the two Idaho districts vary slightly from the ideal. *(p. 52)*

This pattern is repeated in all states. The state with the highest ideal congressional district population for the 1970s is Utah, with 529,637; the smallest is South Dakota with 333,129.

Maps of State. Maps of all states showing their congressional district boundaries are included. Maps of cities and counties divided between three or more congressional districts are provided where appropriate. For example, see Jefferson County, Alabama, including the city of Birmingham, p. 10. When the word "part" appears on the map, it indicates that only part of the district is shown, the remaining portion being outside the city or county pictured on the map. The word "part" appearing on a state map also indicates a district with non-contiguous parts.

ELECTION RESULTS, 1968-1972

Source: National Republican Congressional Committee and Congressional District Data booklets.

Figures for 1968 and 1970 are for congressional districts as constituted for the 1972 elections and not as they existed at the time of each election. Thus, the figures

---

Reapportionment Process

Regular and automatic reapportionment of the House was provided for by the Reapportionment Act of 1929, as amended in 1941. The Act requires the President to transmit to Congress, within the first week of the regular January session following every decennial census, the new apportionment based on census figures and computed according to a complex mathematical formula called the Method of Equal Proportions. Within 15 days of receipt of the President's message, the Clerk of the House automatically informs the executive of each state of the number of representatives his state is entitled to in the following Congress.

For an explanation of the Method of Equal Proportions and a history of reapportionment and redistricting, see appendix p. 221, 231.

reflect what the vote would have been in the districts had the district lines for 1972 been in force in 1968 and 1970—i.e., the votes were *reallocated* according to the new congressional district lines. In this way, it is possible to see the political history and trends within each current congressional district for the last three elections. The 1972 figures are the official returns in the new districts.

It should be noted that the 1968 and 1970 figures presented are strictly in terms of a party vote and are not necessarily comparable as a vote cast for a particular candidate—i.e., the total may represent votes cast for more than one Democratic or Republican candidate, where a district's boundary has been changed to include new areas.

When a district is footnoted with the phrase "No candidate in this district as constituted before redistricting," it means that no candidate of one of the major parties ran in the district in 1968 and/or 1970. Ballots cast for both parties appear for the years 1968 and/or 1970, however, because territory was gained from other districts in the 1971-72 redistricting in which candidates of both parties ran in 1968 and/or 1970.

For example, see Alabama's 4th District, p. 9, column one. There was no Republican candidate in the district in 1970. But for the 1972 elections, the district gained St. Clair and part of Jefferson Counties from another district in which a Republican House candidate had run in 1970. Hence, in the *reallocation* of the 1970 votes to conform with the 1972 district lines, 1,651 votes cast for the Republican candidate in St. Clair and Jefferson Counties in 1970 appear under the 4th District.

Votes are for Democratic and Republican candidates only. Since minor party totals are not included, percentages sometimes do not add to one hundred. When there was no major party opposition, a line is drawn in the space where the vote would have been recorded. For example, see Alabama, p. 9, column one, second table, where the fifth District had no Republican candidate in 1968 or 1970. The figures for the Democratic candidate are less than 100.0 percent because of minor or third party candidates.

In a few instances where candidates were endorsed by both major parties, or by a third party, footnotes are included to explain how votes have been recorded.

VOTING AGE POPULATION

Source: Congressional District Data booklets.

Voting age population includes all persons 18 or over —i.e., all potential voters, not just those registered. Of these potential voters, Congressional Quarterly calculated the percentage represented by 18, 19, and 20 year olds and those 65 and over.

The median age is that age which divides the voting age population into two equal groups, one half of the persons being older than the median age, one half being younger. For example of Voting Age Population table, see Alabama p. 9, column two, first table.

There are often some minor discrepancies in the addition of congressional district figures to the state total. These may be due to Census Bureau adjustments of the sample data for consistency with the official state apportionment population, or in some instances to rounding. In Alabama, for example, the total for the district voting age populations is slightly higher than the voting

---

Census Sampling Techniques

Total state and congressional district population are based on *complete* count census data. Census data for other categories—voting age, income and occupation, education, housing, race and ethnic groups—were derived from representative *samples* of the population, rather than complete count. The samples consisted of 5 percent, 15 percent, and 20 percent, depending on the subject covered. The sample data was adjusted by the Census Bureau to reflect the entire population. For a measure of the sampling variability of the sample data and for comment regarding reliability of the data, see the section "Accuracy of the Data" in *U.S. Census of Population, 1970, Vol. I, Characteristics of the Population*, Bureau of Census, Washington, D.C.

---

age population figure given for the state. *(For description of Census Bureau sampling, box above)*

INCOME AND OCCUPATION

Source: Congressional District Data booklets.

Median family income is the income level that divides families into two equal groups, with half having incomes above the median and the other half having incomes below the median.

Percentages of white collar, blue collar, service and farm workers, were calculated by Congressional Quarterly from the figures contained in the Congressional District Data booklets for each state. For example of Income and Occupation table, see Alabama, p. 9, column 2, second table.

The Census Bureau divides employed persons into twelve major categories. These categories are in turn grouped into the four major classifications of white collar, blue collar, service, and farm workers, as follows:

—White collar: professional, technical and kindred workers; managers and administrators, except farm; sales workers; clerical and kindred workers.

—Blue collar: craftsmen, foremen, and kindred workers; operatives, except transport (i.e., includes by and large persons who operate machines or tools); transport equipment operatives; laborers, except farm.

—Service workers: service workers, except private households; private household workers.

—Farm workers: farmers and farm managers; farm laborers and farm foremen.

For a full explanation of the criteria used in determining the various categories of workers, see the Bureau of the Census publication *1970 Census of Population Classified Index of Industries and Occupations*.

EDUCATION: SCHOOL YEARS COMPLETED

Source: Congressional District Data booklets.

Data on years of school completed refer to the adult population 25 years of age or over. Percentages were calculated by Congressional Quarterly from the Congressional District Data booklets.

The median number of school years completed divides adults 25 or older into two equal groups, one having completed more, the other less schooling than the median.

For example of Education table, see Alabama, p. 9, column two, third table.

HOUSING AND RESIDENTIAL PATTERNS

Source: Congressional District Data booklets.

Housing units are broken down into owner-occupied and renter-occupied units. Housing units include both individual houses and individual apartments. For example of Housing data table, see Alabama, p. 9, column two, fourth table.

The urban-suburban-nonmetropolitan breakdown is based on Standard Metropolitan Statistical Areas (SMSAs). SMSAs are defined by the Bureau of the Budget. Except in New England, an SMSA consists of a county or group of contiguous counties which contain at least one city of 50,000 inhabitants or more, or "twin cities" with a combined population of at least 50,000.

In addition to one county, or counties, containing such a city or cities, contiguous counties are included in an SMSA if they are socially and economically integrated with the city. In the New England states, SMSAs consist of towns and cities instead of counties.

For a detailed description of all criteria used in defining SMSAs, see Bureau of the Budget publication *Standard Metropolitan Statistical Areas: 1967.*

In the urban-suburban-nonmetropolitan breakdown, the urban category consists of the population of central cities in SMSAs; the suburban category consists of the population of all areas inside SMSAs but outside the central cities (that is, persons living in the metropolitan area outside the core city or cities); the nonmetropolitan category consists of the population outside of SMSAs. The "nonmetropolitan" areas include rural areas, small towns, and small urban areas—cities of under 50,000 and their environs. Percentages were calculated by Congressional Quarterly from the Congressional District Data booklets.

Some problems inevitably are present in any attempt to define uniformly urban-suburban-nonmetropolitan areas nationwide. In the particular method used by Congressional Quarterly in this book, the suburban category may be exaggerated in those SMSAs with relatively small central cities.

The Charleston, South Carolina SMSA for example, has a central city of only 66,945 persons, and an SMSA of 303,849. The population of the outer areas of such an SMSA tends to have only a loose political, economic and social connection with the central city.

However, if Congressional Quarterly had used an alternative and more restricted definition of suburban areas—such as the Census Bureau's "urbanized areas" category—the result would have been to under-represent suburban areas surrounding the larger cities.

For example, in the Illinois portion of the Chicago SMSA—all those counties which are socially and economically integrated with Chicago—the population is 6,-978,947. But in the Illinois portion of the Chicago urbanized area, there are 6,185,156, a difference of almost 800,000. These 800,000 persons are more likely to be oriented toward the city of Chicago, with its 3,366,957 persons and its large business and financial resources,

than the persons in the outlying areas of the Charleston SMSA are to be oriented toward Charleston.

In addition since suburban areas are growing everywhere, a method which exaggerated their size in some areas as of 1970 would seem less distorted than one which was more limiting and undercounted the suburbs in other areas.

Therefore, Congressional Quarterly used the whole counties contained in SMSAs rather than portions of counties. Even in the outlying rural or semirural areas of the SMSA counties, people will usually be oriented to the urban areas—through television and radio, newspapers, shopping at branch stores, election of county officials, payment of county taxes, etc.

Another problem is the definition of the term "suburban" itself. Twenty years ago, "suburban," at least in the popular mind, usually meant upper middle to upper income residential and shopping areas adjacent to large cities. Today, there is every possible variety of suburb—blue collar, white collar, black, low income, upper income, high density, low density. Consequently, whatever its particular population or income characteristics, a suburb is defined in this book as an urbanized or urban-oriented area surrounding a central city, and contained in a Standard Metropolitan Statistical Area.

District Profiles

Following the tabular material on all states provided in the tables described above, a description of the information contained in the district by district profiles follows.

There are a total of nine possible categories under each district heading:
- Race and Ethnic Groups.
- Cities, 1970 Population.
- Universities, Enrollment.
- AEC-Owned, Contractor-Operated Installations.
- NASA Facilities.
- Military Installations or Activities.
- Newspapers, Circulation.
- Commercial Television Stations, Affiliation.
- Plants and Offices, Products, Employment.

Every district will not necessarily include all nine categories. If a district has nothing in a category, the category heading is omitted. For example, see the 1st District of Alabama, page 10, column one, where there are no major AEC-Owned, Contractor-Operated Installations, NASA facilities, or major military installations or activities and hence, no category headings.

RACE AND ETHNIC GROUPS

Source: Congressional District Data booklets.

When numbers of blacks, Indians, Japanese, Chinese, and other racial groups exceed 2.5 percent in any congressional district, they are listed by Congressional Quarterly, with the percent of the district's population they represent. See for example Alabama, p. 10, column one, 1st District, which lists "Blacks, 32.7 per cent." Compare with Connecticut, p. 39, column one, 2nd District, where no racial group is listed by Congressional Quarterly because none exceeded 2.5 percent of the population.

(Continued on p. 6)

Source Materials on the 435 Congressional Districts

Congressional District Data booklets, 93rd Congress, one for each state, Bureau of the Census, Washington, D.C. 20233, published August through October, 1972, Texas published April 1974, California published May 1974.

Includes data on state, city and district populations and population variances between districts, voting age population, income and occupation, education, housing and residential patterns, race and ethnic data.

Election statistics for 1968 and 1970, carried in the Congressional District Data booklets, were prepared by the National Republican Congressional Committee (NRCC). The statistics represent House election returns *reallocated* according to 1972 congressional district lines.

Figures for five states—Arizona, Colorado, Louisiana, Michigan, and New York (1970) were not completed by the NRCC in time to be printed in the Congressional District Data booklets. They were obtained directly by Congressional Quarterly in draft form. Thus, there may be some minor differences between the final figures and the voting figures for these states published in this book.

Figures were not available for Oklahoma (1968 and 1970), New York (1968 and for some districts in 1970), and Washington (1968 and 1970).

Congressional Quarterly obtained the final 1972 House election returns from the Secretaries of State of all states and the Board of Elections of the District of Columbia.

U.S. Census of Population, 1970, Volume I, Characteristics of the Population, published by the Bureau of the Census, Washington, D.C. 20233.

Includes information on the reliability and sampling variability of the Census Bureau sample data; see section entitled "Accuracy of the Data."

1970 Census of the Population Classified Index of Industries and Occupations, Bureau of the Census, Washington, D.C. 20233.

Provides detailed information on the components of the major occupation groups—white collar, blue collar, service, farm workers.

Standard Metropolitan Statistical Areas: 1967, a Bureau of the Budget Publication (now Office of Management and Budget), 17th and Pennsylvania Ave. N.W., Washington, D.C. 20503.

Provides a detailed description of criteria used in defining Standard Metropolitan Statistical Areas (SMSAs).

Accredited Institutions of Higher Education, 1972-73, published for the Federation of Regional Accrediting Commissions for Higher Education by the American Council on Education, One Dupont Circle, Washington, D.C. 20036.

Includes name, location and enrollment of all accredited senior colleges that are members of the six regional accrediting associations.

Major Activities in the Atomic Energy Programs, United States Atomic Energy Commission, 1971, Washington, D.C. 20545.

Includes a listing of "Major AEC-Owned, Contractor-Operated Installations," and their addresses.

Official NASA Installation Addresses, a list of addresses for NASA facilities, obtained from the National Aeronautics and Space Administration, Washington, D.C. 20546, in December, 1971.

Principal Military Installations or Activities in the 50 States, official Pentagon list, published July, 1972. Department of Defense, The Pentagon, Washington, D.C. 20301.

Includes the name and location of the 486 principal military installations or activities in the United States, listed by state.

Newspaper Rates and Data, October 12, 1972, Vol. 54 No. 10, a monthly publication of the Standard Rate and Data Service Inc. (SRDS), 5201 Old Orchard Road, Skokie, Illinois 60076.

Includes names, addresses, and circulation figures for U.S. newspapers.

Newspaper Circulation Analysis, 1972-73 edition, Vol. 15, an annual publication of SRDS. Includes newspaper circulation figures by county.

Standard Rate and Data Service has developed and compiled much useful market data and advertising information in their publications. They include: market data by region, states, metro areas, counties and cities. (e.g., households, circulation, total retail sales, food and drug sales, consumer spendable income). None of this data is reproduced by Congressional Quarterly.

Spot Television Rates and Data, Sept. 15, 1972, Vol. 54, No. 9, a monthly publication of SRDS.

Includes call letters, addresses and network affiliations for television stations.

1972-73 Exclusive Television Market Areas of Dominant Influence in the United States, published by the American Research Bureau (ARB), 592 5th Ave., New York, New York 10036.

The television Area of Dominant Influence (ADI) is a concept developed by ARB. It consists of a geographic market design which defines each TV market exclusive of another based on measurable viewing patterns. An ADI is an area that consists of all counties in which the home market stations receive a preponderance of viewing. Each county in the U.S., excluding Alaska, is allocated exclusively to only one ADI; there is no overlap.

Congressional Quarterly does not reproduce the exact boundaries of any ADIs nor any of the market data from ARB or SRDS publications. Rather, Congressional Quarterly's purpose is to show what television stations are received in each congressional district.

Dun and Bradstreet, Washington Office, 2233 Wisconsin Ave. N.W., Washington, D.C. 20007. Computer listing of all plants and offices in the United States, employing more than 1,000 persons.

Includes information on number of persons employed at each plant or office, whether the plant or office is a subsidiary, division, branch, or headquarters, and the main product, products, or services.

Spanish heritage population is also included when the population in any district exceeds 2.5 percent. Identification of persons of Spanish heritage by the Census Bureau was done by various means, including: birthplace, birthplace of parents, language, surname, and direct query on origin and descent. The category includes Mexican-Americans, Puerto Ricans, Cubans, and others. See, for example, Arizona, p. 15, column one, 4th District, where there is a large Spanish heritage population.

The census category "foreign stock" is used for identification of ethnic groups.

Foreign stock includes the foreign-born, and the native born population of foreign or mixed parentage. As can be seen, this method severely limits the identification of the total number of any ethnic group because it does not include anyone further than the children born in the United States of at least one foreign born parent. Thus, those third and fourth generation Americans and beyond, who may identify themselves (or be identifiable) with a certain ethnic group, are not so listed by the Census Bureau. (Problems of identification caused by intermarriage between ethnic groups, reluctance to answer questionnaires calling for self-identification with an ethnic group, etc., have prevented the evolution of a better method of identifying ethnic population on a large scale.)

Because of this necessarily restricted nature of the census identification of ethnic groups, more recent immigrants, such as the Italian-Americans and Polish-Americans, are comparatively over-represented in the figures. Most of the latter groups came at the turn of the century and many of them and/or their children are still alive. On the other hand, the earlier groups, such as the Irish-Americans and German-Americans, many of whom came in the middle of the last century, are under-represented.

Nevertheless, the figures are valuable in that they help identify the *concentration* of particular ethnic groups in specific places. It should be noted, however, that even if a group as defined by the Census Bureau represents only three or four percent of a congressional district's population, with the inclusion of all those in the district who are third or fourth generation Americans and beyond, and their families, the group often is considerably more influential politically than the absolute figures indicate. The particular groups which are concentrated in a congressional district give a good idea of the ethnic composition of that district.

Each ethnic group representing more than 2.5 percent of a congressional district's population is listed under the category "Race and Ethnic Groups." For example, see Connecticut, p. 39, column one, 1st District, which has four foreign stock (ethnic) groups over 2.5 percent. However, if a congressional district has none or only one group over 2.5 percent, the top two are listed by Congressional Quarterly, no matter what the percentage they represent. For example, see Arizona, p. 14, column one, 1st District, where both foreign stock (ethnic) groups are below 2.5 percent. Percentages were calculated by Congressional Quarterly from the information contained in the Congressional District Data booklets.

Race, country of origin of foreign stock, and Spanish heritage population are listed by the Census Bureau *only* if the state total for the particular group is 25,000 or more (50,000 or more in California and New York).

Therefore there may be a few congressional districts which have a significant concentration of a racial or ethnic group which are not listed because the statewide population of that group does not exceed the figure set by the Census Bureau.

Blacks are excepted; they are listed by the Census Bureau for all states and congressional districts.

CITIES, 1970 POPULATION

Source: Congressional District Data booklets.

The Census Bureau lists all communities with 10,000 or more inhabitants by congressional district. Most, but not all, are cities. Congressional Quarterly has listed the top four communities, incorporated or unincorporated, in each congressional district. If there are less than four, all are listed.

When large portions of a city lie in different congressional districts, the total population in each district is listed. For example, see Arizona, p. 14-15, 1st, 3rd, and 4th Districts each have a portion of the city of Phoenix.

UNIVERSITIES, ENROLLMENT

Source: *Accredited Institutions of Higher Education, 1972-73.*

Congressional Quarterly located by congressional district all senior colleges and universities with a total enrollment of 1,000 or over as listed in *Accredited Institutions.* Technical, engineering, and fine arts colleges are included. Junior colleges are not included.

Most enrollment figures are as of the beginning of the 1971-72 school year. In a few instances, where enrollment figures for branch campuses are not available, the total enrollment figure for the university is listed, with the proper notation.

Congressional Quarterly lists the full name of the college or university, the community in which it is located, and the total enrollment. For example, see Alabama, p. 10, column one, 1st District, University of South Alabama (Mobile—5,440).

AEC, NASA, MILITARY FACILITIES

Sources: Atomic Energy Commission, National Aeronautics and Space Administration, Department of Defense.

Congressional Quarterly lists all installations and facilities in their respective congressional districts. The city listed as the location for each installation or facility is the city nearest the installation.

NEWSPAPERS, CIRCULATION

Sources: *Newspaper Rates and Data: Newspaper Circulation Analysis.*

Included under this heading are all daily newspapers with a circulation of 50,000 or more. Morning and evening editions of the same newspaper are not combined to reach the 50,000 figure. Only those that have morning or evening editions of 50,000 or more are listed, except where the circulation figure listed is "all day."

The papers are listed in the congressional district where they are published. In the case of a large city,

Gains and Losses in U.S. House Seats by State

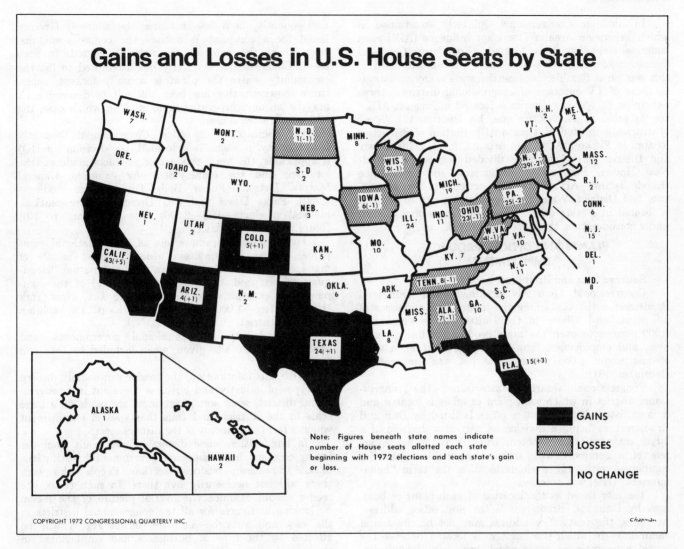

Note: Figures beneath state names indicate number of House seats allotted each state beginning with 1972 elections and each state's gain or loss.

GAINS

LOSSES

NO CHANGE

COPYRIGHT 1972 CONGRESSIONAL QUARTERLY INC.

Chapman

divided between congressional districts, newspapers published in that city are listed together in the congressional district containing a majority of the downtown business section of the city. The listing includes the name of the city, the name of the paper, and the circulation, as listed in *Newspaper Rates and Data*. Times of publication on which circulation figures are based are denoted by the following abbreviations: Morning—Morn; Evening—Eve; Morning Except Saturday—MxSat; Evening Except Saturday—ExSat; All Day—All Day. Sunday circulation is not used. For examples, see Alabama, p. 10, column one, 1st District, under **Newspapers, Circulation**, Mobile Press (ExSat—58,953); column two, 2nd District; Montgomery Advertiser (Morn—58,660).

A newspaper's circulation will often go beyond the confines of one congressional district. If a newspaper not published in a congressional district circulates in that district to the extent of at least 20,000 copies per day, it is noted with a phrase such as "Birmingham papers circulate in portions of district." For example, see Alabama, p. 12, column two, 7th District. The Standard Rate and Data Service (SRDS) publication, *Newspaper Circulation Analysis* lists, among other items, newspaper circulation by county, from which Congressional Quarterly determined the extent of circulation by congressional district.

COMMERCIAL TELEVISION STATIONS, AFFILIATION

Sources: *Spot Television Rates and Data; 1972-73 Exclusive Television Market Areas of Dominant Influence in the United States.*

Congressional Quarterly ascertained which congressional districts all commercial television stations are located in. They are listed by their call letters, with their address of record and network affiliation, as recorded in *Spot Television Rates and Data*. For example, KGUN-TV, Tucson (ABC), see Arizona, p. 14, column two, 2nd District. When stations are not affiliated with one of the three national networks, the word "None" is used. Spanish language stations are so designated.

Stations are listed by city. When a city is divided between congressional districts, all stations for that city are listed in the congressional district which includes a majority of the downtown business section. In a few of the largest cities, some stations may be physically located in a suburb. However, their broadcast range is over the same approximate area as stations in the central cities, and are therefore listed for convenience in the same district as the others for that central city.

In addition, Congressional Quarterly ascertained in which Television Area of Dominant Influence (ADI) each congressional district is located. (For description and definition of ADIs, see source box). The wording used in this section is flexible, because there are many variations in areas of TV coverage of congressional districts—three examples: (1) "Entire district is located in Phoenix ADI," see Arizona, p. 14, column one, 1st District. (2) "Most of district is located in Tucson ADI. Portion of district is located in Phoenix ADI," see Arizona, p. 14, column two, 2nd District. (3) "District is divided between Hartford-New Haven, Boston (Massachusetts) and Providence (Rhode Island) ADIs," see Connecticut, p. 39, column two, 2nd District. When the broadcasting city of an ADI is located in a state other than the congressional district under consideration, the state is identified.

PLANTS AND OFFICES, PRODUCTS, EMPLOYMENT

Source: Dun and Bradstreet

Congressional Quarterly obtained from Dun and Bradstreet a list containing the names and addresses of all plants and offices in the United States employing 1,000 persons or over, the main products or line of business, and employment figures for each location, a total of just under 4,000 entries. The list was prepared in December, 1971.

Congressional Quarterly ascertained the congressional district in which each plant or office is located and it is so listed. If the plant or office is listed by Dun and Bradstreet as being a division or part of a division of a larger company, this is noted; also if it is the headquarters of a company with more than one location. For companies with only a single location the term "headquarters" (HQ) was not used.

The city listed as the location of each plant or business by Dun and Bradstreet is the post office address. At times, the post office address may not be the actual community in which the business is located because the postal zone includes areas which cross city boundaries.

Consequently, in a few instances the address of record listed for a company is outside the congressional district where the company is actually located. In such cases, Congressional Quarterly has attempted to list the community where the plant is actually located; sometimes, however, this has been difficult to determine (it may be an unincorporated area, etc.), in which case, the address of record is used.

For each plant or office, Congressional Quarterly lists the city in which it is located, the division (or HQ) if applicable, the main product or products made at that location, and the employment—for example, General Motors, Detroit (Fisher Body Division—car bodies—1,700); Parke Davis and Co., Detroit (Pharmaceutical, medical products—HQ—2,300). See Michigan, p. 101, column one, 13th District.

For corporate headquarters of giant national companies, whose headquarters usually consist mostly of management and office workers, the designation "Headquarters" is used, omitting the product(s) of the company—for example, Colgate Palmolive Co., New York (Headquarters—1,000). See New York, p. 136, column one, 18th District.

State, county and municipal governments, and school boards are also given, when included by Dun and Bradstreet.

With this information, the reader can usually discern the types of industry and business prevalent in a congressional district, what sort of products are made on a large scale in the district, and thus the types of employment which affect the economy of the district most.

In large cities, some distortion will result from the listing of many businesses and governmental institutions in the downtown business section. People who work there will not necessarily live there. In such cases, the reader should examine the overall picture of the region by looking at figures for all the congressional districts in the city and suburbs—i.e., the entire region will be affected by the type of businesses and employment in the central city.

ALABAMA: SEVEN HOUSE SEATS, LOSS OF ONE

Alabama lost one House seat because of reapportionment. The state legislature, dominated by Democrats, sought to eliminate one of the three Republican incumbents. Rep. William L. Dickinson of the 2nd District was seen as the most vulnerable. *(Maps, p. 10 and 11)*

But a controversy arose over which district to place Dickinson in—the old 3rd, represented by George W. Andrews (D), dean of the Alabama congressional delegation, or the old 4th, represented by Bill Nichols (D). Andrews' death on Dec. 25, 1971, resolved the dilemma. His district was divided, with the seven counties in the southern part of the district combined with Dickinson's district and the five northern counties given to Nichols.

But despite the new district lines, Dickinson survived; adjustments in the state's five other districts did not alter the delegation's political balance.

Redistricting legislation passed the state Senate on Jan. 9, 1972, 30-3, and the House on Jan. 11, 81-13. Gov. George C. Wallace (D) signed the bill Jan. 19.

The U.S. District Court in Alabama, which had assumed jurisdiction of congressional redistricting when the legislature failed to approve a plan in 1971, approved the redistricting measure Jan. 22, 1972.

District	Member Elected 1972	Winning Percentage	1970 Population	Percent Variance
1	Jack Edwards (R)	76.5	491,747	—0.0562
2	William L. Dickinson (R)	54.8	491,676	—0.0707
3	Bill Nichols (D)	75.6	493,588	+ 0.3178
4	Tom Bevill (D)	69.6	492,196	+ 0.0349
5	Robert E. Jones (D)	74.2	489,771	—0.4579
6	John Buchanan (R)	59.8	493,045	+ 0.2075
7	Walter Flowers (D)	84.8	492,142	+ 0.0239

1970 State Population: 3,444,165
Ideal District Population: 492,024

Election Results, 1968-1972

Vote for U.S. Representative
(Adjusted to new district boundaries)

District	1968	1970	1972
1	71,035 R (55.8%)	72,721 R (60.0%)	104,606 R (76.5%)
	51,494 D (40.4%)	34,273 D (28.3%)	24,357 D (17.8%)
2	74,963 D (54.8%)	61,224 D (49.3%)	80,362 R (54.8%)
	46,650 R (34.1%)	49,107 R (39.5%)	60,769 D (41.5%)
3	100,250 D (84.3%)	78,997 D (82.3%)	100,045 D (75.6%)
	8,596 R (7.2%)	9,667 R (10.1%)	27,253 R (20.6%)
4	118,698 D (75.9%)	98,966 D (97.2%)	108,039 D (69.6%)
	32,164 R (20.6%)	1,651 R[1] (1.6%)	46,551 R (30.0%)
5	85,528 D (76.1%)	76,413 D (84.8%)	101,303 D (74.2%)
	—	—	33,352 R (24.4%)
6	70,171 R (54.1%)	50,421 R (54.7%)	91,499 R (59.8%)
	46,429 D (35.8%)	39,970 D (43.3%)	54,497 D (35.6%)
7	77,132 D (56.8%)	85,060 D (73.9%)	95,060 D (84.8%)
	17,740 R (13.1%)	14,296 R[1] (3.7%)	—
State	555,026 D (60.4%)	475,095 D (64.1%)	545,070 D (56.0%)
	247,438 R (26.9%)	188,050 R (25.4%)	383,623 R (39.4%)

1 No candidate in this district as constituted before redistricting.

Voting Age Population

District	Voting Age Population	Voting Age Population 18, 19, 20	Voting Age Population 65 and Over	Median Age of Voting Age Population
1	302,373	24,464 (8.1%)	43,304 (14.3%)	42.7
2	316,740	28,427 (9.0%)	47,822 (15.1%)	42.5
3	317,093	32,141 (10.1%)	45,769 (14.4%)	42.0
4	324,393	23,125 (7.1%)	53,573 (16.5%)	44.9
5	306,177	23,802 (7.8%)	35,433 (11.6%)	40.4
6	326,861	23,844 (7.3%)	51,045 (15.6%)	44.0
7	311,969	29,427 (9.4%)	50,067 (16.0%)	43.4
State	2,205,486	185,276 (8.4%)	327,017 (14.8%)	42.8

Income and Occupation

District	Median Family Income	White Collar Workers	Blue Collar Workers	Service Workers	Farm Workers
1	$7,305	41.0%	42.3%	14.2%	2.5%
2	6,749	41.5	40.0	14.1	5.4
3	6,817	33.8	50.1	13.6	2.5
4	6,350	31.3	53.2	10.3	5.2
5	8,271	46.5	38.1	12.0	3.4
6	8,683	51.5	34.2	14.0	0.3
7	6,806	38.1	43.3	15.3	3.3
State	7,263	40.7	42.8	13.3	3.2

Education: School Years Completed

District	Completed 4 years of High School	Completed 4 years of College	Completed 5 years or less of School	Median School years completed
1	40.3%	6.8%	14.3%	10.8
2	43.1	8.4	16.6	11.0
3	36.9	6.9	17.3	10.2
4	32.5	4.1	14.6	9.9
5	48.6	10.9	12.0	11.8
6	49.2	10.6	10.5	11.9
7	38.5	7.4	18.0	10.4
State	41.3	7.8	14.7	10.8

Housing and Residential Patterns

	Housing		Urban-Suburban-Nonmetropolitan Breakdown		
District	Owner Occupied Units	Renter Occupied Units	Urban	Suburban	Nonmetropolitan
1	68.7%	31.3%	38.6%	38.0%	23.4%
2	62.6	37.4	27.1	7.0	65.9
3	65.3	34.7	—	16.0	84.0
4	71.9	28.1	11.0	21.0	68.0
5	69.7	30.3	28.2	18.4	53.4
6	62.7	37.3	60.7	39.3	—
7	65.8	34.2	14.0	47.0	39.0
State	66.7	33.3	25.6	26.7	47.7

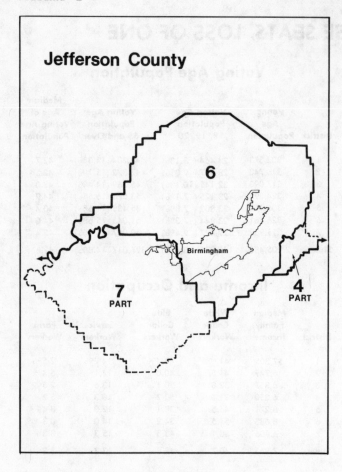

Jefferson County

6

7 PART

4 PART

Birmingham

1st District

(Southwest—Mobile)

Race and Ethnic Groups. Blacks 32.7 percent.

Cities, 1970 Population. Mobile 189,986, Prichard 41,644.

Universities, Enrollment. University of South Alabama (Mobile—5,440).

Newspapers, Circulation. Mobile Press (ExSat—58,953).

Commercial Television Stations, Affiliation. WALA-TV, Mobile (NBC); WKRG-TV, Mobile (CBS). Most of district is located in Mobile-Pensacola (Fla.) ADI. Portion of district is in Montgomery ADI.

Plants and Offices, Products, Employment.
International Paper Co., Mobile (Paper—2,200). **Scott Paper Co.,** Mobile (Paper—3,000). **Courtaulds North America Inc.,** Mobile (Men's neckwear, acrylic fibers—1,080). **Vanity Fair Mills Inc.,** Monroeville (Women's, children's wear—1,100). **Alabama Dry Dock and Shipbuilding Co.,** Mobile (Shipbuilding, repair—at least 3,500). **Teledyne Industries Inc.,** Mobile (Continental Motors Division—internal combustion engines—1,000).

2nd District

(Southeast—Montgomery, Dothan)

Race and Ethnic Groups. Blacks 29.8 percent.
Cities, 1970 Population. Montgomery 133,471, Dothan 36,733, Enterprise 15,591, Fort Rucker 14,242.
Universities, Enrollment. Alabama State University (Montgomery—2,704), Troy State University (Troy—6,082).
Military Installations or Activities. Fort Rucker; Gunter Air Force Base, Montgomery; Maxwell Air Force Base, Montgomery.
Newspapers, Circulation. Montgomery Advertiser (Morn—58,660).
Commercial Television Stations, Affiliation. WCOV-TV, Montgomery (CBS); WKAB-TV, Montgomery (None); WSFA-TV, Montgomery (NBC); WDHN-TV, Dothan (ABC); WTVY, Dothan (CBS primary, ABC). District is divided between Montgomery and Dothan ADIs. Small portion of district is in Mobile-Pensacola (Fla.) ADI.
Plants and Offices, Products, Employment.
Dorsey Trailers Inc., Elba (Trailers and truck bodies—(HQ)—1,050). **Page Aircraft Maintenance Inc.,** Fort Rucker (Aircraft service—4,000). **Alatex Inc.,** Andalusia (Men's shirts, work clothes—HQ—1,100). **Dan River Inc.,** Montgomery (Piece goods—1,000).

3rd District

(East—Anniston, Phenix City)

Race and Ethnic Groups. Blacks 31.3 percent.
Cities, 1970 Population. Anniston 31,508, Phenix City 25,281, Auburn 22,767, Opelika 19,027.
Universities, Enrollment. Auburn University (Auburn—16,046). Jacksonville State University (Jacksonville—5,749). Tuskegee Institute (Tuskegee—3,073).
Military Installations or Activities. Anniston Army Depot, Fort McClellan.
Commercial Television Stations, Affiliation. WHMA-TV, Anniston (CBS). In addition to Anniston ADI, district is divided between Birmingham, Montgomery, Columbus (Ga.) and Chattanooga (Tenn.) ADIs.
Plants and Offices, Products, Employment.
Mead Corp., Anniston (Alabama Pipe Co. Division—cast iron pipe fittings—2,000). **Indian Head Inc.,** Blue Mountain (Thread, twine, etc.—at least 1,000). **West Point Pepperell Inc.,** Fairfax (Cotton towels, fabrics, waste processing—2,040). **West Point Pepperell Inc.,** Lanett (Fabrics, bleaching, dying—1,700). **West Point Pepperell Inc.,** Langdale (Cotton fabrics—1,500). **Mount Vernon Mills,** Tallassee (Tallassee Mills Division—cotton fabrics—1,520). **Beaunit Corp.,** Childersburg (Wool yarn—1,000). **Beaunit Corp.,** Coosa Pines (Rayon yarn—1,200). **Ampex Corp.,** Opelika (Magnetic Tape Division—magnetic tape and accessories—1,200). **Uniroyal Inc.,** Opelika (U.S. Rubber Tire Co. Division—tires—1,130). **Kimberly-Clark Corp.,** Coosa Pines (Coosa River Newsprint Division—pulp and newsprint—1,400). **Russell Mills Inc.,** Alexander City (Clothing—HQ—4,200).

4th District

(North Central—Gadsden)

Race and Ethnic Groups. Blacks 8.5 percent.
Cities, 1970 Population. Gadsden 53,898, Cullman, 12,598, Jasper 10,795.
Commercial Television Stations, Affiliation. District is divided between Birmingham, Huntsville and Atlanta (Georgia) ADIs.
Plants and Offices, Products, Employment.
> **Bendix-Westinghouse Automotive Air Brake Co.,** Cullman (Hermetic motors, compressors, etc.—1,200). **Republic Steel Corp.,** Gadsden (Steel products—4,500). **Goodyear Tire and Rubber Co.,** Gadsden (Tires and tubes—at least 3,500). **Bowman Transportation Inc.,** Gadsden (Common carrier—2,300).

5th District

(North—Huntsville)

Race and Ethnic Groups. Blacks 13.3 percent.
Cities, 1970 Population. Huntsville 137,878, Decatur 38,044, Florence 34,031, Athens 14,360.
Universities, Enrollment. Alabama Agricultural and Mechanical University (Normal—2,129), Florence State University (Florence—3,425), University of Alabama in Huntsville (Huntsville—2,603).
Atomic Energy Facilities. Marshall Space Flight Center, Huntsville.
Military Installations or Activities. Redstone Arsenal, Huntsville.
Newspapers, Circulation. Huntsville Times (ExSat—54,426).
Commercial Television Stations, Affiliation. WAAY-TV, Huntsville (NBC); WHNT-TV, Huntsville (CBS); WMSL-TV, Huntsville (ABC). Most of district is in Huntsville-Decatur-Florence ADI. Part of district is in Chattanooga (Tennessee) ADI.
Plants and Offices, Products, Employment.
> **Reynolds Metals Co.,** Sheffield (Fabricating Division—aluminum sheets—3,000). **Reynolds Metals Co.,** Sheffield (Reduction Division—aluminum products—1,450). **Ford Motor Co.,** Sheffield (Aluminum Castings Division—automobile aluminum castings—1,100). **International Business Machines,** Huntsville (Business machines—1,800). **Boeing Co.,** Huntsville (Aircraft missiles—3,500). **General Electric Co.,** Huntsville (Electronic devices—1,100). **Brown Engineering Co.,** Huntsville (Electronic systems equipment—HQ—1,000). **M. Lowenstein & Sons Inc.,** Huntsville (Print fabrics—1,200). **Monsanto Co.,** Decatur (Chemicals—2,500). **Universal Oil Products Co.,** Decatur (Wolverine Tube Division—metal tubing—1,200).

6th District

(Birmingham)

Race and Ethnic Groups. Blacks 30.0 percent.
Cities, 1970 Population. Part of Birmingham 229,340, Homewood 21,395, Mountain Brook 19,595, Center Point 15,768.

Universities, Enrollment. Birmingham-Southern College (Birmingham—1,031), Samford University (Birmingham—2,973), University of Alabama in Birmingham (Birmingham—7,439).

Newspapers, Circulation. Birmingham News (Eve—176,550), Birmingham Post-Herald (Morn—76,038).

Commercial Television Stations, Affiliation. WAPI-TV, Birmingham (NBC); WBMG-TV, Birmingham (CBS); WBRC-TV, Birmingham (ABC). Entire district is in Birmingham ADI.

Plants and Offices, Products, Employment.
> **Alabama Power Co.,** Birmingham (Electric utility—HQ—1,000). **United States Steel Corp.,** Birmingham (Hot steel, pig iron—1,000). **Hayes International Corp.,** Birmingham (Aircraft modification, missiles—HQ—3,500). **Southern Railway Co. Inc.,** Birmingham (Railroad—1,000). **Baptist Medical Center,** Birmingham (Hospital—1,180). **Stockham Valves & Fittings Inc.,** Birmingham (Valves and fittings—HQ—1,850). **American Cast Iron Pipe Co.,** Birmingham (Cast iron pipe fittings—HQ—2,900). **Great Atlantic & Pacific Tea Co.,** Birmingham (Groceries—at least 2,000).

7th District

(West Central—Tuscaloosa, Birmingham suburbs)

Race and Ethnic Groups. Blacks 37.9 percent.

Cities, 1970 Population. Tuscaloosa 65,228, Bessemer 33,207, Selma 27,152, Fairfield 14,250.

Universities, Enrollment. Livingston University (Livingston—1,638), Miles College (Birmingham—1,280), University of Alabama in Tuscaloosa (Tuscaloosa—13,564), University of Montevallo (Montevallo—2,564).

Military Installations or Activities. Craig Air Force Base, Selma.

Newspapers, Circulation. Birmingham papers circulate in portions of district.

Commercial Television Stations, Affiliations. WCFT-TV, Tuscaloosa (CBS). Majority of district is located in Birmingham ADI. Portions of district are located in Meridian (Mississippi) ADI.

Plants and Offices, Products, Employment.
> **American Can Co.,** Butler (Marathon Southern Division—wood pulp—1,600). **United States Steel Corp.,** Fairfield (Tennessee Coal and Iron Division—steel products, chemicals, coal—14,000). **Pullman Inc.,** Bessemer (Pullman-Standard Division—railway car parts—2,300). **Mead Corp.,** Woodward (Woodward Division—pig iron, coke, chemicals—at least 10,000). **Central Foundry Co.,** Holt (Cast iron, pipes—1,600). **B. F. Goodrich Co.,** Tuscaloosa (Automobile and truck tires—1,200). **Gulf States Paper Corp.,** Tuscaloosa (Paper products—HQ—1,750).

ARIZONA: FOUR HOUSE SEATS, GAIN OF ONE

Arizona had two problems in trying to draw new congressional district boundaries. First, the legislature had to decide how to draw the new congressional district the state had been allocated through reapportionment. Second, the legislature was working under a court-ordered deadline of Nov. 1, 1971.

No compromise between parties was necessary, because both houses of the legislature were Republican-controlled, and the governor was a Republican. However, a controversy developed over whether or not the new district should be dominated by Maricopa County (Phoenix). The county already had a majority of the population in two of the three old districts.

The legislature decided to divide Maricopa County, which has 55 percent of the state's population, among all four districts. The new district, the 4th, was given the northeastern quadrant of the state along with Scottsdale and part of Phoenix. The 2nd District's share of Maricopa includes only 719 persons. The 1st District remains entirely within the county. Republicans are dominant in all but the 2nd District, which is centered around Democratic Pima County (Tucson).

The legislature met the court deadline. Approved by the state House Sept. 30, 1971, by a vote of 34-21, the legislation passed the Senate Oct. 11 by a vote of 18-12. Gov. Jack Williams signed the bill Oct. 21, 1971. Court approval was finally handed down March 8, 1972.

District	Member Elected 1972	Winning Percentage	1970 Population	Percent Variance
1	John J. Rhodes (R)	57.3	442,589	—0.1200
2	Morris K. Udall (D)	63.5	443,117	—0.0009
3	Sam Steiger (R)	63.0	443,201	+ 0.0180
4	John B. Conlan (R)	53.0	443,575	+ 0.1024
	1970 State Population:		1,772,482	
	Ideal District Population:		443,121	

Election Results, 1968-1972

Vote for U.S. Representative
(Adjusted to new district boundaries)

District	1968	1970	1972
1	76,932 R (67.4%)	64,351 R (65.4%)	80,453 R (57.3%)
	37,164 D (32.6%)	34,061 D (34.6%)	59,900 D (42.7%)
2	85,011 D (70.6%)	72,755 D (69.3%)	97,616 D (63.5%)
	35,427 R (29.4%)	31,126 R (29.6%)	56,188 R (36.5%)
3	66,477 R (62.6%)	55,106 R (60.4%)	90,710 R (63.0%)
	39.704 D (37.4%)	36,088 D (39.5%)	53,220 D (37.0%)
4	80,767 R (66.6%)	68,050 R (63.3%)	82,511 R (53.0%)
	40,576 D (33.4%)	39,302 D (36.6%)	73,309 D (47.0%)
State	260,663 R (56.2%)	218,506 R (54.3%)	309,862 R (52.2%)
	202,967 D (43.8%)	182,256 D (45.3%)	284,045 D (47.8%)

Voting Age Population

District	Voting Age Population	Voting Age Population 18, 19, 20	Voting Age Population 65 and Over	Median Age of Voting Age Population
1	289,806	25,834 (8.9%)	45,125 (15.6%)	42.0
2	286,937	26,289 (9.2%)	42,295 (14.7%)	42.0
3	273,740	22,728 (8.3%)	39,552 (14.4%)	41.5
4	273,765	20,373 (7.4%)	34,972 (12.8%)	42.6
State	1,124,327	95,261 (8.5%)	162,001 (14.4%)	42.0

Income and Occupation

District	Median Family Income	White Collar Workers	Blue Collar Workers	Service Workers	Farm Workers
1	$9,126	51.5%	32.5%	14.0%	2.0%
2	8,832	51.5	32.1	14.5	1.9
3	8,964	45.8	35.6	13.4	5.2
4	9,886	55.7	29.6	12.1	2.6
State	9,186	51.2	32.4	13.5	2.9

Education: School Years Completed

District	Completed 4 years of High School	Completed 4 years of College	Completed 5 years or less of School	Median School years completed
1	56.8%	11.9%	7.6%	12.2
2	61.0	14.6	7.1	12.3
3	54.7	9.7	8.1	12.2
4	59.8	14.0	8.4	12.3
State	58.1	12.6	7.8	12.3

Housing and Residential Patterns

	Housing		Urban-Suburban-Nonmetropolitan Breakdown		
District	Owner Occupied Units	Renter Occupied Units	Urban	Suburban	Nonmetropolitan
1	60.6%	39.4%	47.9%	52.1%	—
2	64.0	36.0	59.3	20.2	20.5%
3	69.7	30.3	35.6	25.7	38.7
4	67.4	32.6	48.0	9.0	43.0
State	65.3	34.7	47.7	26.8	25.5

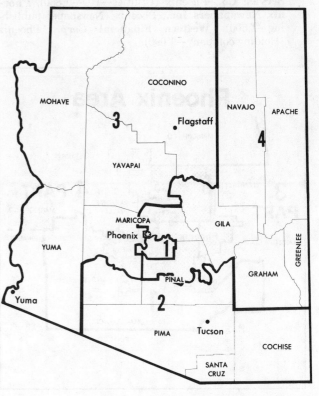

1st District

(Southern Phoenix, Tempe, Mesa)

Race and Ethnic Groups. Blacks 5.8 percent. Spanish heritage population 16.8 percent. Canadian stock 1.5 percent, German stock 1.5 percent.

Cities, 1970 Population. Part of Phoenix 211,792, Mesa 62,760, Tempe 62,707, part of Scottsdale 48,884.

Universities, Enrollment. Arizona State University (Tempe—30,319), Maricopa Technical College (Phoenix—5,683), Phoenix College (Phoenix—5,473).

Military Installations or Activities. Williams Air Force Base, Chandler.

Newspapers, Circulation. Phoenix newspapers circulate throughout district. They include: Arizona Republic (Morn—200,467), Phoenix Gazette (Eve—117,968).

Commercial Television Stations, Affiliation. Entire district is located in Phoenix ADI. Phoenix stations include: KOOL-TV, Phoenix (CBS); KPAZ-TV, Phoenix (None); KPHO-TV, Phoenix (None), KTAR-TV, Phoenix (NBC); KTVK-TV, Phoenix (ABC).

Plants and Offices, Products, Employment.

Motorola Inc., Phoenix (Semi-Conductor Division—semi-conductors—12,000). **Motorola Inc.**, Phoenix (Semi-Conductor Division—industrial controls—2,000). **Motorola Inc.**, Mesa (Integrated Circuit Center—integrated circuits—3,500). **Motorola Inc.**, Scottsdale (Government Electronics Division—radio and television transmitting, signaling and detection equipment—2,800). **The Garrett Corp.**, Phoenix (Airesearch Manufacturing Co. of Arizona Division—gas turbine engines—4,000). **Talley Industries Inc.**, Mesa (Aerospace devices, timing devices, plastic manufacturing, etc.—HQ—1,600). **Arizona Public Service Co.**, Phoenix (Utilities—HQ—1,850). **Phoenix Newspapers Inc.**, Phoenix (Newspaper publishing—1,500). **Western Financial Corp.**, Phoenix (Holding company—1,090).

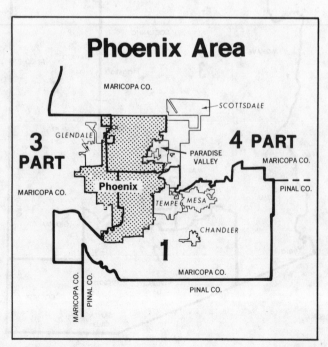

Phoenix Area

2nd District

(South—Tucson)

Race and Ethnic Groups. Blacks 2.8 percent. Spanish heritage population 27.2 percent. Canadian stock 1.6 percent, German stock 1.6 percent.

Cities, 1970 Population. Tucson 262,826, Douglas 12,457.

Universities, Enrollment. University of Arizona (Tucson—26,910).

Military Installations or Activities. Fort Huachuca, Douglas; Davis-Monthan Air Force Base, Tucson; Gila Bend Air Force Auxiliary Field, Gila Bend.

Newspapers, Circulation. Tucson newspapers circulate throughout district. They include: Tucson Star (Morn—57,271), Tucson Citizen (Eve—60,706). In addition, Phoenix newspapers circulate in portion of district.

Commercial Television Stations, Affiliation. Most of district is located in Tucson ADI. Portion of district is located in Phoenix ADI. Tucson stations include: KGUN-TV, Tucson (ABC); KOLD-TV, Tucson (CBS); KVOA-TV, Tucson (NBC); KZAZ-TV, Tucson (None).

Plants and Offices, Products, Employment.

Phelps Dodge Corp., Bisbee (Copper mining and smelting—1,700). **Phelps Dodge Corp.**, Ajo (Copper mining and smelting—1,250). **American Smelting & Refining Co.**, Tucson (Copper mining—1,000). **Anaconda Co.**, Sahuarita (Copper mining—1,370). **Duval Sierrita Corp.**, Sahuarita (Copper mining—1,250). **Magma Copper Co.**, San Manuel (Copper mining and smelting—2,600). **Hughes Aircraft Co.**, Tucson (Missiles—3,000). **Textron Inc.**, Tucson (Bell Aerospace Division—engineering—1,000). **Mountain States Telephone & Telegraph Co.**, Tucson (Telephone and telegraph—1,400). **Federated Department Stores**, Tucson (Levys—department store—1,000). **Tucson Medical Center Inc.**, Tucson (Hospital—1,400).

3rd District

(North and West—Western Phoenix, Glendale, Yuma)

Race and Ethnic Groups. Spanish heritage population 18.6 percent. American Indians 3.9 percent. German stock 1.5 percent, Canadian stock 1.4 percent.

Cities, 1970 Population. Part of Phoenix, 157,933, Glendale 36,236, Yuma 28,952, Flagstaff 26,068.

Universities, Enrollment. Northern Arizona University (Flagstaff—9,869).

Military Installations or Activities. Navajo Army Depot, Flagstaff; Yuma Proving Ground, Yuma; Marine Corps Air Station, Yuma; Luke Air Force Base, Phoenix.

Newspapers, Circulation. Phoenix newspapers circulate in major portion of district.

Commercial Television Stations, Affiliation. Major portion of district is located in Phoenix ADI. Portion located in Flagstaff ADI. Stations include: KOAL-TV, Flagstaff (NBC); KBLU-TV, Yuma (NBC).

Plants and Offices, Products, Employment.

Reynolds Metals Co., Phoenix (Rolled and extruded aluminum—1,600). **Goodyear Aerospace**

Corp., Litchfield Park (Aircraft parts—2,500). **Western Electric Co.**, Phoenix (Steel wire and cable—1,250). **Spring City Knitting Co. Inc.**, Glendale (Men's and boys' underwear—1,600).

4th District

(East—Northern Phoenix)

Race and Ethnic Groups. Spanish heritage population 12.6 percent. American Indians 13.9 percent. Canadian stock 1.4 percent, German stock 1.2 percent.

Cities, 1970 Population. Part of Phoenix 212,826, part of Scottsdale 18,986, Casa Grande 10,627.

Newspapers, Circulation. Phoenix newspapers circulate in major portion of district.

Commercial Television Stations, Affiliation. Major portion of district is located in Phoenix ADI. Portion located in Tucson ADI.

Plants and Offices, Products, Employment.

Inspiration Consolidated Copper Co., Inspiration (Copper mining and smelting—at least 1,600). **Kennecott Copper Corp.**, Hayden (Ray Mines Division—copper mining and smelting—2,000). **Phelps Dodge Corp.**, Morenci (Copper mining and smelting—2,350). **Magma Copper Co.**, Superior (Copper mining and smelting—1,200). **General Electric Co.**, Phoenix (Electronic computers—1,050). **Sperry Rand Corp.**, Phoenix (Engineering, laboratory and scientific instruments—3,000).

ARKANSAS: FOUR HOUSE SEATS, NO CHANGE

Arkansas enacted its congressional redistricting bill in January 1971, the first state to do so. The bill passed the state Senate Jan. 21 by a vote of 27-5 and the state House on Jan. 26 by a vote of 89-0. It was signed by Gov. Dale Bumpers (D) on Jan. 28. (Map p. 17)

However, some state legislators expressed dissatisfaction with the legislation. State Sen. Bill Walmsley (D) and State Rep. Paul Henry (D), both of Batesville (Independence County), criticized the plan and said they believed it would be declared unconstitutional because of the population variance between the largest and smallest districts.

Furthermore, the Arkansas Republican party threatened a lawsuit to test the plan's constitutionality. The variance between the largest (2nd) and smallest (1st) districts was 3.1 percent, compared with 23.2 percent between the largest (3rd) and smallest (1st) before redistricting.

In the face of this criticism, the Arkansas Legislature passed a new redistricting bill reducing the variance from 3.1 percent to 0.26 percent. The 1st District remains the smallest, but the largest is now the 4th.

The new bill passed the state Senate 29-0 on Feb. 24, 1971, and the House on March 12 by a vote of 60-8. Gov. Bumpers signed the bill March 22.

The main feature of the legislation was to transfer several counties in north central Arkansas from the 2nd and 3rd Districts to the underpopulated 1st. Other adjustments to the 2nd, 3rd and 4th Districts were slight.

District	Member Elected 1972	Winning Percentage	1970 Population	Percent Variance
1	Bill Alexander (D)	—[1]	479,893	—0.1936
2	Wilbur D. Mills (D)	—[1]	481,120	+0.0615
3	John Paul Hammerschmidt (R)	77.3	481,106	+0.0586
4	Ray Thornton (D)	—[1]	481,176	+0.0732
	1970 State Population:	1,923,295		
	Ideal District Population:	480,824		

[1] No votes tabulated where candidate was unopposed.

Election Results, 1968-1972

Vote for U.S. Representative
(Adjusted to new district boundaries)

District	1968	1970	1972
1	81,768 D (68.1%)	1,846 R[2]	—[1]
	38,301 R (31.9%)	1,683 D[2]	—
2	—[1]	—[1]	—[1]
3	107,644 R (68.3%)	103,782 R (68.6%)	144,571 R (77.3%)
	50,011 D (31.7%)	47,477 D (31.4%)	42,481 D (22.7%)
4	12,110 R[2]	9,904 R[2]	—[1]
	8,156 D[2]	8,519 D[2]	—
State	158,055 R[3]	115,543 R[3]	144,571 R[3]
	139,935 D[3]	57,679 D[3]	42,841 D[3]

[1] No votes tabulated in districts where candidate was unopposed.
[2] Figures represent vote cast in counties transferred by redistricting from two-candidate districts. Percentages not applicable.
[3] Excludes votes for unopposed candidates because tabulation not required by law. Percentages not applicable.

Voting Age Population

District	Voting Age Population	Voting Age Population 18, 19, 20	Voting Age Population 65 and Over	Median Age of Voting Age Population
1	303,439	23,178 (7.6%)	57,771 (19.0%)	45.9
2	316,730	24,263 (7.7%)	49,409 (15.6%)	43.0
3	330,976	24,483 (7.4%)	68,684 (20.8%)	46.9
4	313,564	24,302 (7.8%)	62,237 (19.8%)	46.7
State	1,264,709	96,226 (7.6%)	238,101 (18.8%)	45.6

Glossary and Sources

For a complete explanation of all terms used in this book and a list of source material, consult the details included in the Introduction.

Income and Occupation

District	Median Family Income	White Collar Workers	Blue Collar Workers	Service Workers	Farm Workers
1	$5,381	34.5%	39.9%	12.7%	12.9%
2	7,484	46.1	36.5	13.1	4.3
3	6,057	38.4	42.5	12.6	6.5
4	6,191	36.0	44.2	13.8	6.0
State	6,271	39.0	40.7	13.1	7.2

Education: School Years Completed

District	Completed 4 years of High School	Completed 4 years of College	Completed 5 years or less of School	Median School years completed
1	29.4%	4.9%	22.3%	8.8
2	50.0	9.0	9.6	12.0
3	41.9	6.6	9.3	10.8
4	38.0	5.9	16.1	10.4
State	39.9	6.7	14.2	10.5

Housing and Residential Patterns

	Housing		Urban-Suburban-Nonmetropolitan Breakdown		
District	Owner Occupied Units	Renter Occupied Units	Urban	Suburban	Nonmetropolitan
1	59.8%	40.2%	—	10.0%	90.0%
2	66.0	34.0	40.0%	27.2	32.8
3	71.1	28.9	13.1	8.7	78.2
4	69.4	30.6	16.4	8.3	75.3
State	66.7	33.3	17.4	13.5	69.1

1st District

(East—Jonesboro, West Memphis)

Race and Ethnic Groups. Blacks 23.1 percent.

Cities, 1970 Population. Jonesboro 27,026, West Memphis 25,929, Blytheville 25,186, Forrest City 12,521.

Universitites, Enrollment. Arkansas State University (Jonesboro—7,092).

Military Installations or Activities. Blytheville Air Force Base, Blytheville.

Commercial Television Stations, Affiliation. KAIT-TV, Jonesboro (ABC). Most of district is divided between Jonesboro ADI, Memphis (Tennessee) ADI and Little Rock ADI. Small portion of district is located in Springfield (Missouri) ADI.

Plants and Offices, Products, Employment.
Warwick Electronics Inc., Forrest City (Television, stereos—at least 1,900). **Singer Co.**, Trumann (Wood Products Division—sewing machine cabinets and stools—1,750). **American Greetings Corp.**, Osceola (Greeting cards, party goods—1,500). **Emer-**

son **Electric Co.**, Paragould (Emerson Electric Motors—electric motors—1,350). **Frolic Footwear Inc.** Jonesboro (Women's shoes —1,200).

2nd District

(Central—Little Rock)

Race and Ethnic Groups. Blacks 16.3 percent.

Cities, 1970 Population. Little Rock 132,482, North Little Rock 60,040, Jacksonville 19,832, Benton 16,621.

Universitites, Enrollment. Harding College (Searcy—2,060), State College of Arkansas (Conway—4,499), University of Arkansas at Little Rock (Little Rock—4,535).

Military Installations or Activities. Little Rock Air Force Base, Jacksonville.

Newspapers, Circulation. Little Rock Arkansas Democrat (ExSat—70,042), Little Rock Arkansas Gazette (MxSat—112,439).

Commercial Television Stations, Affiliation. Entire district is located in Little Rock ADI. Little Rock stations include: KARK-TV, Little Rock (NBC); KATV, Little Rock (ABC); KTHV, Little Rock (CBS).

Plants and Offices, Products, Employment.
Aluminum Company of America, Bauxite (Aluminum production—1,410). **Reynolds Metals Co.**, Bauxite (Aluminum production—1,200). **Timex Corp.**, Little Rock (Watches, cameras—3,320). **Controls Company of America**, Jacksonville (Industrial controls—1,100). **Teletype Corp.**, Little Rock (Telegraph apparatus—1,200). **Kellwood Co.**, Little Rock (Ottenheimer Manufacturing Co.—women's and girls' apparel—1,500). **Safeway Stores Inc.**, Little Rock (Groceries—1,520). **Baptist Medical Center**, Little Rock (Hospital—1,290).

3rd District

(West—Fort Smith, Hot Springs)

Race and Ethnic Groups. Blacks 2.6 percent.

Cities, 1970 Population. Fort Smith 62,802, Hot Springs 35,631, Fayetteville 30,639, Springdale 16,562.

Universities, Enrollment. Arkansas Polytechnic College (Russellville—2,525), University of Arkansas, Fayetteville (Fayetteville—12,131).

Commercial Television Stations, Affiliation. KFPW-TV, Fort Smith (NBC, CBS, ABC, all per program); KFSA-TV, Fort Smith (CBS primary, NBC, ABC per program); KGTO-TV, Fayetteville (NBC per program). In addition to Fort Smith ADI, portions of district are located in Little Rock, Tulsa (Oklahoma), Springfield (Missouri), and Joplin (Missouri)-Pittsburg (Kansas) ADIs.

Plants and Offices, Products, Employment.
Tyson Foods Inc., Springdale (Poultry processing, prepared animal feeds—2,000). **Ralston Purina Co.**, Rogers (Gold Bond Poultry Co.—poultry processing—2,000). **ITT Continental Baking Co. Inc.**, Russellville (Morton Frozen Food Division—frozen dinners—1,000). **Campbell Soup Co.**, Fayetteville (Canning—1,250). **Weyerhaeuser Co. Inc.**, Hot Springs

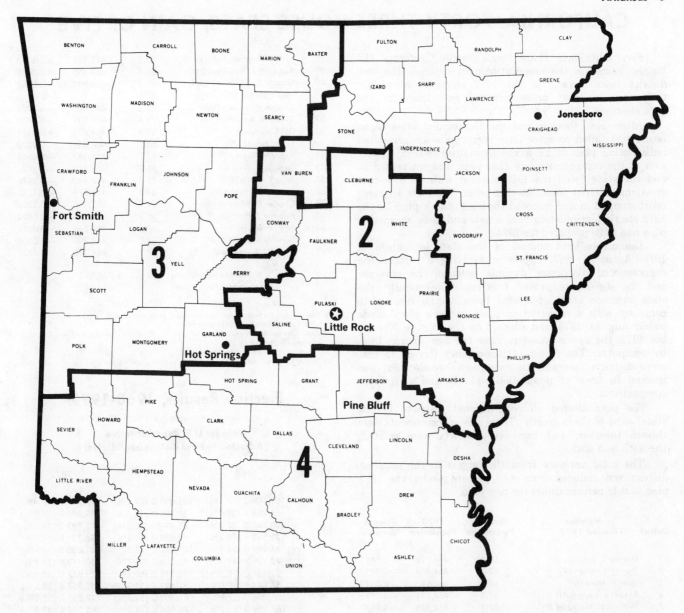

National Park (Dierks Division—lumber, millwork, insulation, gypsum—3,000). **Desoto Inc.**, Fort Smith (Ward Furniture Division—bedroom furniture—1,350). **Whirlpool Corp.**, Fort Smith (Refrigeration equipment—2,000). **Walton Enterprises Inc.**, Bentonville (Retailing general merchandise, holding company—1,200). **Arkansas Best Corp.**, Fort Smith (Diversified holding company—2,360).

4th District

(South—Pine Bluff)

Race and Ethnic Groups. Blacks 31.3 percent.
Cities, 1970 Population. Pine Bluff 57,295, El Dorado 25,283, Texarkana 21,795, Camden 15,159.
Universities, Enrollment. University of Arkansas, Pine Bluff (Pine Bluff—2,656), Henderson State College (Arkadelphia—3,300), Ouachita Baptist University (Arkadelphia—1,377), Southern State College (Magnolia—2,050), University of Arkansas at Monticello (Monticello—1,958).
Military Installations or Activities. Pine Bluff Arsenal.
Commercial Television Stations, Affiliation. KTVE, El Dorado (NBC primary, ABC). In addition to Monroe (Louisiana)-El Dorado ADI, major portion of district is located in Little Rock ADI; portion of district is located in Shreveport (Louisiana)-Texarkana (Texas) ADI.
Plants and Offices, Products, Employment.
 International Paper Co., Pine Bluff (Southern Kraft Division—paper mill—1,350). **Potlatch Forests Inc.**, Warren (Southern Division—Wood Products Group—lumber—1,450). **Georgia-Pacific Corp.**, Crossett (Plywood, chemicals, paper mill—3,250). **Cooper Tire and Rubber Co.**, Texarkana (Tires—1,000). **St. Louis Southwestern Railway Co.**, Pine Bluff (Railway and maintenance—1,500).

CALIFORNIA: FORTY-THREE HOUSE SEATS, GAIN OF FIVE

Five additional House seats made California the biggest gainer in the reapportionment process. The new district lines drawn for the 1972 elections were only temporary; a court order required new lines for the 1974 elections.

After Gov. Reagan and the Democratic state legislature had failed to agree on a compromise congressional redistricting plan in 1971, the legislature passed its version of the compromise late that year. Reagan vetoed it, and the state faced the 1972 election with no new congressional district lines. At that point, the state supreme court stepped in and imposed the legislature's plan for the 1972 election, stipulating that a new and more acceptable plan had to be prepared for 1974.

Democrats kept control of the state legislature in 1972. Again in 1973, efforts at evolving a compromise congressional districting formula between the governor and the legislature proved fruitless. Consequently, the state supreme court appointed three special masters to come up with a redistricting plan. In their plan, made public Aug. 31, 1973, and adopted by the court in November 1973, the special masters drew the new district lines by computer. The factor of incumbency (trying to preserve districts favorable to incumbents' re-election) was ignored in favor of population equality and geographic compactness.

The plan altered all congressional districts in the state, some of them greatly. Three sets of incumbents were thrown together, and two new districts were created, the 24th and 35th.

The total variance from the largest to the smallest district was reduced from 4.69 percent under the 1972 plan to 0.45 percent under the new plan.

District	Member Elected 1972	Winning Percentage[1]	1970 Population	Percent Variance
1	Harold T. Johnson (D)	68.4	464,028	—0.0891
2	Don H. Clausen (R)	62.3	464,334	—0.0232
3	John E. Moss (D)	69.9	464,541	+ 0.0213
4	Robert L. Legget (D)	67.4	464,171	—0.0583
5	William S. Mailliard (R)[1]	52.1	463,523	—0.1978
6	Phillip Burton (D)	81.8	463,521	—0.1983
7	Jerome R. Waldie (D)	77.6	464,283	—0.0342
8	Ronald V. Dellums (D)	55.9	462,953	—0.3205
9	Fortney H. (Pete) Stark (D)	52.9	464,934	+ 0.1059
10	Don Edwards (D)	72.3	463,419	—0.2202
11	Leo J. Ryan (D)	60.5	464,187	—0.0549
12	Paul N. McCloskey Jr. (R)	54.6	463,161	—0.2758
13	Charles S. Gubser (R)	64.6	466,988	+ 0.5481
14	John J. McFall (D)	100.0	464,656	+ 0.0460
15	B. F. Sisk (D)	79.1	465,631	+ 0.2560
16	Burt L. Talcott (R)	54.0	465,345	+ 0.1944
17	Robert B. (Bob) Mathias	66.4	465,492	+ 0.2260
18	William M. Ketchum (R)	52.7	463,813	—0.1354
19	Charles M. Teague (R)*[2]	73.8	465,095	+ 0.1405
20	Barry M. Goldwater Jr. (R)	57.4	466,149	+ 0.3675
21	James C. Corman (D)	67.6	464,934	+ 0.1059
22	Carlos J. Moorhead (R)	57.4	464,760	+ 0.0684
23	Thomas M. Rees (D)	68.6	464,026	—0.0895
24	No Incumbent		465,475	+ 0.2224
25	Edward R. Roybal (D)	68.4	464,972	+ 0.1141
26	John H. Rousselot (R)	70.1	464,122	—0.0688
27	Alphonzo Bell (R)	60.7	464,100	—0.0736
28	Yvonne Brathwaite Burke (D)	73.2	465,182	+ 0.1593
29	Augustus F. Hawkins (D)	82.9	464,125	—0.0682
30	George E. Danielson (D)[3]	62.7	464,892	+ 0.0968
	Chet Holifield (D)	67.2		
31	Charles H. Wilson (D)	52.3	463,470	—0.2092
32	Glenn M. Anderson (D)	74.8	466,639	+ 0.4730
33	Del Clawson (R)	61.4	464,494	+ 0.0111
34	Craig Hosmer (R)	65.9	464,336	—0.0228
35	Victor V. Veysey (R)[4]	62.7	464,185	—0.0553
36	George E. Brown Jr. (D)	55.9	463,898	—0.1171
37	Jerry L. Pettis (R)	75.0	462,640	—0.3879
38	Richard T. Hanna (D)	67.1	463,879	—0.1212
39	Charles E. Wiggins (R)	64.9	463,836	—0.1304
40	Andrew J. Hinshaw (R)	65.7	464,254	—0.0404
41	Bob Wilson (R)	67.8	464,046	—0.0852
42	Lionel Van Deerlin (D)	74.0	464,208	—0.0503
43	Clair W. Burgener (R)	67.5	464,325	—0.0251

1970 State Population:	19,971,022
Ideal District Population	464,442

1 Percentage of the vote for representative received in 1972 election in districts as constituted before Nov. 1973 redistricting.
2 Rep. Charles M. Teague (R) died Jan. 1, 1974. He was replaced by Robert J. Lagomarsino March 13, 1974.
3 Incumbents thrown together in redistricting.
4 Victor V. Veysey moved into the 30th District when his old 43rd District was abolished.

Election Results, 1968-1972

Vote for U.S. Representative
(Adjusted to new district boundaries)

District	1968	1970	1972
1	101,109 D (59.1%)	121,658 D (77.2%)	140,707 D (68.4%)
	66,764 R (39.0%)	31,731 R (20.1%)	59,886 R (29.1%)
2	38,941 D (23.3%)	62,491 D (38.5%)	75,785 D (34.5%)
	122,583 R (73.2%)	99,685 R (61.5%)	136,137 R (62.0%)
3	91,969 D (54.8%)	105,237 D (61.8%)	147,800 D (70.9%)
	72,329 R (43.1%)	62,506 R (36.7%)	60,178 R (28.9%)
4	81,861 D (58.3%)	90,593 D (68.1%)	119,862 D (69.4%)
	54,744 R (39.0%)	41,591 R (31.3%)	52,957 R (30.6%)
5	66,956 D (37.8%)	81,000 D (51.4%)	117,535 D (57.9%)
	107,959 R (60.9%)	76,504 R (48.6%)	85,216 R (42.0%)
6	79,707 D (50.5%)	79,755 D (58.9%)	105,742 D (67.2%)
	75,710 R (47.9%)	55,697 R (41.1%)	51,616 R (32.8%)
7	122,402 D (75.4%)	117,467 D (76.7%)	148,859 D (76.7%)
	36,631 R (22.6%)	35,610 R (23.3%)	44,807 R (23.1%)
8	117,781 D (61.5%)	114,460 D (61.0%)	127,798 D (56.6%)
	62,184 R (32.4%)	71,279 R (38.0%)	87,217 R (38.6%)
9	102,050 D (64.9%)	99,226 D (67.1%)	99,867 D (54.1%)
	54,879 R (34.9%)	48,340 R (32.7%)	82,665 R (44.8%)
10	71,952 D (56.7%)	82,033 D (68.6%)	113,871 D (68.9%)
	54,874 R (43.2%)	34,794 R (29.1%)	47,959 R (29.0%)
11	34,466 D (20.7%)	32,977 D (22.2%)	106,284 D (57.2%)
	130,758 R (78.4%)	115,817 R (77.8%)	72,070 R (38.8%)
12	54,038 D (33.4%)	63,560 D (42.7%)	77,370 D (41.0%)
	105,355 R (65.1%)	83,885 R (56.3%)	105,968 R (56.1%)
13	49,796 D (34.8%)	58,020 D (41.1%)	74,800 D (38.7%)
	91,626 R (64.0%)	81,134 R (57.5%)	118,195 R (61.2%)
14	85,019 D (54.8%)	97,509 D (65.5%)	132,961 D (82.0%)
	69,098 R (44.6%)	48,640 R (32.7%)	28,335 R (17.5%)
15	85,602 D (62.2%)	87,944 D (69.0%)	101,189 D (68.9%)
	49,952 R (36.3%)	36,585 R (28.7%)	45,765 R (31.1%)
16	1,605 D[1] (1.2%)	41,432 D (32.0%)	81,670 D (42.8%)
	123,515 R (94.0%)	85,071 R (65.5%)	103,989 R (54.5%)

District	1968	1970	1972
17	58,156 D (42.9%)	61,437 D (48.3%)	95,302 D (59.0%)
	74,603 R (55.0%)	62,939 R (49.4%)	65,638 R (40.6%)
18	49,298 D (32.1%)	52,749 D (38.2%)	62,789 D (37.0%)
	102,435 R (66.7%)	83,052 R (60.2%)	102,421 R (60.2%)
19	50,623 D (33.3%)	60,311 D (42.3%)	67,814 D (35.0%)
	100,852 R (66.7%)	80,940 R (56.7%)	125,240 R (64.6%)
20	45,983 D (31.2%)	48,771 D (33.5%)	67,814 D (33.6%)
	101,594 R (68.8%)	93,942 R (64.6%)	133,520 R (66.2%)
21	89,896 D (55.4%)	83,283 D (57.5%)	111,679 D (63.1%)
	69,771 R (43.0%)	59,463 R (41.1%)	60,947 R (34.4%)
22	52,575 D (26.7%)	49,090 D (28.6%)	81,334 D (41.1%)
	142,079 R (72.3%)	120,315 R (69.9%)	116,259 R (58.7%)
23	103,128 D (48.7%)	95,338 D (49.2%)	141,722 D (60.1%)
	103,963 R (49.1%)	92,515 R (49.2%)	88,910 R (37.7%)
24	103,285 D (53.8%)	93,775 D (57.1%)	118,749 D (63.1%)
	85,767 R (44.7%)	67,094 R (40.8%)	62,583 R (33.3%)
25	67,367 D (61.8%)	57,563 D (67.3%)	72,538 D (70.4%)
	40,043 R (36.8%)	27,012 R (31.6%)	27,582 R (26.8%)
26	53,442 D (28.8%)	55,860 D (34.4%)	70,544 D (37.0%)
	132,018 R (71.1%)	103,660 R (63.8%)	117,760 R (61.8%)
27	52,081 D (28.3%)	53,227 D (31.5%)	82,697 D (37.9%)
	128,574 R (69.9%)	108,064 R (63.9%)	129,407 R (59.3%)
28	106,884 D (64.5%)	106,813 D (74.3%)	114,667 D (68.9%)
	54,665 R (33.0%)	35,363 R (24.6%)	48,531 R (29.2%)
29	96,942 D (71.0%)	83,998 D (74.1%)	101,908 D (82.4%)
	35,566 R (26.0%)	29,419 R (29.0%)	18,151 R (14.7%)
30	73,241 D (62.0%)	76,638 D (54.7%)	92,927 D (66.2%)
	44,305 R (37.5%)	62,508 R (44.6%)	41,804 R (29.8%)
31	78,675 D (55.5%)	76,174 D (65.0%)	91,150 D (66.9%)
	59,973 R (42.3%)	39,750 R (34.0%)	40,987 R (30.1%)
32	56,475 D (40.4%)	61,289 D (50.1%)	93,441 D (63.1%)
	80,991 R (57.9%)	58,673 R (47.9%)	53,214 R (35.9%)
33	72,083 D (45.8%)	72,752 D (51.1%)	83,266 D (44.8%)
	82,726 R (52.6%)	69,208 R (48.6%)	97,147 R (52.3%)
34	58,917 D (31.8%)	56,659 D (34.2%)	86,620 D (41.4%)
	123,948 R (66.8%)	106,565 R (64.3%)	118,555 R (56.6%)
35	48,704 D (32.8%)	47,498 D (35.7%)	58,665 D (35.5%)
	99,149 R (66.7%)	83,124 R (62.5%)	105,256 R (63.6%)
36	84,785 D (59.4%)	61,245 D (49.2%)	78,701 D (51.3%)
	55,082 R (38.6%)	61,849 R (49.8%)	74,756 R (48.7%)
37	58,500 D (39.6%)	42,472 D (31.4%)	47,588 D (28.4%)
	87,170 R (59.0%)	92,241 R (68.1%)	119,949 R (71.6%)
38	68,148 D (49.9%)	66,101 D (53.4%)	95,980 D (58.7%)
	68,278 R (50.0%)	55,528 R (44.9%)	62,600 R (38.3%)
39	49,552 D (31.0%)	49,594 D (33.7%)	76,368 D (38.2%)
	108,964 R (68.2%)	94,980 R (64.6%)	122,589 R (61.4%)
40	34,811 D (24.5%)	43,474 D (30.8%)	70,863 D (32.0%)
	103,760 R (73.1%)	93,970 R (66.5%)	147,468 R (66.6%)
41	56,272 D (31.9%)	45,710 D (28.8%)	75,349 D (34.1%)
	120,220 R (68.0%)	106,281 R (66.9%)	141,481 R (64.0%)
42	77,211 D (63.6%)	75,658 D (70.5%)	99,983 D (71.4%)
	44,241 R (36.4%)	28,082 R (26.2%)	39,727 R (28.4%)
43	55,007 D (35.6%)	50,680 D (34.0%)	71,203 D (31.8%)
	96,548 R (62.6%)	93,778 R (63.0%)	147,195 R (65.7%)
State	3,808,934 R (54.4%)	3,124,147 D (49.4%)[1]	4,209,586 D (51.9%)
	3,085,320 D (44.1%)	3,095,405 R (49.0%)[1]	3,760,094 R (46.3%)

1 Includes all absentee votes some of which are omitted in the district-by-district tabulation.

Voting Age Population

District	Voting Age Population	Voting Age Population 18-19-20	Voting Age Population 65 and Over	Median Age of Voting Age Population
1	309,307	22,552 (7.3%)	51,394 (16.6%)	44.8
2	312,543	22,733 (7.3%)	56,758 (18.2%)	45.4
3	301,436	22,393 (7.4%)	35,009 (11.6%)	41.3
4	298,163	29,190 (10.9%)	31,045 (11.6%)	38.9

District	Voting Age Population	Voting Age Population 18-19-20	Voting Age Population 65 and Over	Median Age of Voting Age Population
5	349,078	20,558 (5.9%)	54,404 (15.6%)	41.7
6	348,666	23,735 (6.8%)	62,431 (17.9%)	45.5
7	292,999	21,520 (7.3%)	32,177 (11.0%)	41.5
8	347,089	29,502 (8.5%)	57,413 (16.5%)	42.7
9	310,443	23,929 (7.7%)	38,676 (12.5%)	42.0
10	287,310	23,846 (8.3%)	29,195 (10.2%)	38.0
11	314,699	21,573 (6.9%)	34,732 (11.0%)	42.1
12	313,373	26,108 (8.3%)	30,737 (9.8%)	39.4
13	274,741	19,587 (7.1%)	21,982 (8.0%)	38.1
14	307,521	23,068 (7.5%)	48,437 (15.8%)	44.7
15	298,220	24,487 (8.2%)	46,694 (15.7%)	43.0
16	321,762	37,753 (11.7%)	50,354 (15.6%)	40.3
17	291,566	24,583 (8.4%)	39,640 (13.6%)	41.7
18	289,370	21,734 (7.5%)	36,747 (12.7%)	42.4
19	303,850	28,542 (9.4%)	42,022 (13.8%)	40.5
20	279,457	21,686 (7.8%)	21,483 (7.7%)	39.4
21	302,757	23,724 (7.8%)	30,674 (10.1%)	41.0
22	333,392	19,663 (5.9%)	60,479 (18.1%)	46.3
23	352,470	24,306 (6.9%)	52,750 (15.0%)	44.6
24	387,505	16,907 (4.4%)	88,331 (22.8%)	47.8
25	308,242	25,703 (8.3%)	49,027 (15.9%)	41.4
26	311,861	20,434 (6.6%)	50,007 (16.0%)	44.4
27	327,515	20,674 (6.3%)	37,864 (11.6%)	41.7
28	330,374	22,450 (6.8%)	44,954 (13.6%)	41.7
29	290,498	21,068 (7.3%)	41,818 (14.4%)	42.3
30	286,191	22,312 (7.8%)	31,203 (10.9%)	40.6
31	290,480	22,497 (7.7%)	27,927 (9.6%)	39.7
32	317,720	25,464 (8.0%)	47,884 (15.1%)	40.8
33	286,848	24,480 (8.5%)	23,122 (8.1%)	40.1
34	319,024	22,555 (7.1%)	43,739 (13.7%)	42.6
35	286,709	26,080 (9.1%)	31,572 (11.0%)	40.1
36	291,212	24,392 (8.4%)	39,899 (13.7%)	40.9
37	312,732	22.854 (7.3%)	64,615 (20.7%)	46.0
38	275,161	21,599 (7.8%)	22,484 (8.2%)	38.2
39	290,804	24,651 (8.4%)	26,391 (9.1%)	40.0
40	318,229	40,055 (12.6%)	42,264 (13.3%)	37.8
41	328,006	37,373 (11.4%)	42,494 (13.0%)	39.9
42	309,319	40,716 (13.2%)	32,356 (10.5%)	35.3
43	299,994	21,151 (7.1%)	54,483 (18.2%)	44.5
State	13,297,263	1,059,174 (8.0%)	1,806,489 (13.6%)	41.6

Income and Occupation

District	Median Family Income	White Collar Workers	Blue Collar Workers	Service Workers	Farm Workers
1	$ 8,681	45.3%	32.7%	15.5%	6.5%
2	9,474	47.1	33.8	15.2	3.9
3	11,019	62.2	24.8	12.3	0.7
4	9,556	50.5	29.8	14.4	5.3
5	12,010	68.9	16.6	13.9	0.6
6	10,606	57.5	26.2	16.0	0.3
7	11,826	51.8	35.1	12.4	0.7
8	11,401	65.5	21.8	12.4	0.3
9	11,309	52.2	34.9	12.3	0.6
10	11,095	46.8	40.3	11.9	1.0
11	13,062	59.0	29.3	11.4	0.3
12	13,418	64.9	23.8	10.6	0.7
13	12,972	60.0	28.5	10.3	1.2
14	9,348	43.7	33.5	14.3	8.5
15	7,930	43.0	30.7	14.4	11.9
16	9,384	47.4	28.2	15.9	8.5
17	8,672	45.8	27.8	12.6	13.8
18	9,300	44.5	32.4	13.5	9.6
19	10,241	52.2	28.8	14.2	4.8
20	13,583	61.4	26.0	10.2	2.4

District	Median Family Income	White Collar Workers	Blue Collar Workers	Service Workers	Farm Workers
21	11,440	54.7	34.1	10.9	0.3
22	11,741	61.7	26.9	11.2	0.2
23	14,141	74.4	16.2	9.3	0.1
24	10,137	69.1	20.2	10.7	0.0
25	7,804	38.6	48.0	13.2	0.2
26	11,668	59.0	30.4	10.3	0.3
27	13,625	66.7	22.8	10.3	0.2
28	9,942	53.7	31.1	14.8	0.4
29	7,359	35.3	46.3	18.2	0.2
30	10120	41.9	47.7	10.0	0.3
31	10,042	43.6	43.7	12.4	0.3
32	9,873	45.6	40.7	13.3	0.4
33	12,340	53.4	36.2	10.0	0.4
34	11,831	57.3	31.5	10.9	0.3
35	11,265	52.0	33.9	12.3	1.8
36	9,407	47.5	36.6	14.0	1.9
37	8,794	49.3	30.1	15.6	5.0
38	11,367	48.3	38.8	12.1	0.8
39	12,749	60.1	28.4	11.0	0.5
40	12,093	63.9	22.8	12.5	0.8
41	11,118	64.2	22.9	12.6	0.3
42	8,960	46.6	35.7	17.0	0.7
43	9,995	51.7	30.1	13.0	5.2
State	10,729	54.4	30.8	12.6	2.2

District	Completed 4 years of High School	Completed 4 years of College	Completed 5 years or less of School	Median school Years
35	62.5	12.2	4.4	12.4
36	55.9	9.3	6.3	12.2
37	59.7	10.8	6.0	12.3
38	61.2	8.3	4.2	12.3
39	71.7	16.5	2.7	12.6
40	76.3	20.6	2.2	12.8
41	71.5	18.3	2.6	12.6
42	56.2	8.2	6.2	12.2
43	63.2	13.6	5.8	12.4
State	62.6	13.4	5.7	12.4

Education: School Years Completed

District	Completed 4 years of High School	Completed 4 years of College	Completed 5 years or less of School	Median School Years
1	58.3%	9.1%	4.8%	12.3
2	60.1	10.4	4.7	12.3
3	68.6	14.6	4.6	12.5
4	60.9	11.2	5.2	12.3
5	73.1	23.6	4.3	12.8
6	57.7	13.9	9.6	12.3
7	64.3	13.2	4.6	12.4
8	69.3	25.9	5.6	12.7
9	61.7	9.6	5.1	12.3
10	56.8	9.1	7.6	12.2
11	70.6	14.6	3.4	12.6
12	75.0	26.4	3.3	12.8
13	71.8	19.0	4.0	12.7
14	51.4	8.0	9.2	12.1
15	73.5	8.0	11.7	11.8
16	61.9	13.6	7.2	12.4
17	52.5	10.2	11.8	12.1
18	53.6	8.6	8.7	12.1
19	65.7	14.8	5.9	12.5
20	73.8	17.8	3.4	12.7
21	63.9	10.4	4.8	12.4
22	68.5	16.0	3.2	12.6
23	76.5	24.1	2.9	12.9
24	66.3	16.5	5.6	12.5
25	38.6	6.0	18.6	10.3
26	65.7	14.5	3.7	12.5
27	75.3	23.2	3.8	12.8
28	62.9	11.8	5.5	12.4
29	41.9	3.1	10.7	11.1
30	48.5	5.2	8.1	11.8
31	54.9	5.8	5.6	12.1
32	55.0	8.1	6.1	12.2
33	64.8	10.7	3.1	12.4
34	67.3	13.6	2.8	12.5

Housing and Residential Patterns

	Housing		Urban-Suburban-Nonmetropolitan Breakdown		
District	Owner Occupied Units	Renter Occupied Units	Urban	Suburban	Nonmetro-politan
1	64.2%	35.8%	00.0%	18.7%	81.3%
2	64.5	35.5	18.5	41.7	39.8
3	62.5	37.5	44.1	55.9	—
4	57.9	42.1	25.3	62.9	11.8
5	35.6	64.4	54.5	45.5	—
6	40.6	59.4	100.0	—	—
7	67.8	32.2	—	100.0	—
8	44.3	55.7	50.0	50.0	—
9	59.4	40.6	27.8	72.2	—
10	60.4	39.6	35.0	65.0	—
11	61.0	39.0	—	100.0	—
12	56.8	43.2	3.4	96.6	—
13	72.3	27.7	58.2	41.8	—
14	62.3	37.7	23.5	55.9	20.6
15	57.1	42.9	34.1	35.2	32.7
16	56.5	43.5	18.2	35.2	46.6
17	63.7	36.3	14.5	35.2	50.3
18	61.0	39.0	15.0	77.2	7.8
19	56.3	43.7	19.8	41.7	51.8
20	74.2	25.8	41.9	58.1	—
21	55.9	44.1	96.4	3.6	—
22	51.1	48.3	11.7	88.3	—
23	44.3	55.7	88.2	11.8	—
24	22.4	77.6	98.2	1.8	—
25	32.0	68.0	82.0	18.0	—
26	61.3	38.7	—	100.0	—
27	47.6	52.4	25.1	74.9	—
28	37.6	62.4	69.8	30.2	—
29	37.6	62.4	56.7	43.3	—
30	56.5	43.5	—	100.0	—
31	51.1	48.9	6.8	93.2	—
32	44.6	55.4	65.6	34.4	—
33	72.0	28.0	—	100.0	—
34	62.6	37.4	42.1	57.9	—
35	66.3	33.7	13.8	86.2	—
36	62.1	37.9	46.0	54.0	—
37	64.7	35.3	6.6	93.4	—
38	65.9	34.1	55.7	44.3	—
39	63.7	36.3	32.8	67.2	—
40	60.1	39.9	7.4	92.6	—
41	52.5	47.5	88.8	11.2	—
42	52.1	47.9	53.1	46.9	—
43	67.5	32.5	8.6	75.3	—
State	55.0	45.0	36.3	56.4	7.3

1st District

(North—Chico)

Race and Ethnic Groups. Spanish heritage population 6.2 percent. Canadian stock 1.7 percent. German stock 1.5 percent.

Cities, 1970 Population. Chico 19,607, Roseville 18,044, Redding 16,682, Paradise 14,607.

Universities, Enrollment. California State University, Chico (Chico—12,935).

Military Installations or Activities. Sierra Army Depot, Herlong; Beale Air Force Base, Marysville.

Newspapers, Circulation. Sacramento newspapers circulate in portions of the district.

Commercial Television Stations, Affiliaions. Most of district located in Chico-Redding ADI. Portions are located in Medford (Ore.), Reno (Nev.) and Sacramento-Stockton ADIs.

Plants and Offices, Products, Employment.
Kimberly-Clark Corp., Anderson (Forest Products Division—pulp and paper—1,000). **Diamond National Corp.**, Red Bluff (Sawmill—1,230).

2nd District

(North Coast—Santa Rosa, Eureka)

Race and Ethnic Groups. Spanish heritage population 6.2 percent. Italian stock 2.4 percent. Canadian stock 2.2 percent.

Cities, 1970 Population. Santa Rosa 49,868, Napa 35,947, Petaluma 24,867, Eureka 24,334.

Universities, Enrollment. California State College, Sonoma (Sonoma—6,971), California State University, Humbolt (Arcata—6,360), Pacific Union College (Angwin—1,977).

Military Installations or Activities. Naval Security Group (Skaggs Island), Sonoma; Klamath Air Force Station, Requa; Point Arena Air Force Station, Point Arena.

Newspapers, Circulation. Santa Rosa Press Democrat (ExSat—50,752).

Commercial Television Stations, Affiliation. Most of district located in Eureka ADI. Small portion of district located in San Francisco ADI.

Plants and Offices, Products, Employment.
Georgia-Pacific Corp., Samoa (Lumber—1,500). **Simpson Timber Co.**, Arcata (Forest products—1,700). **Boise-Cascade Corp.**, Fort Bragg (Union Lumber Division—lumber products—1,000). **Kaiser Steel Corp.**, Napa (Steel fabricating—1,300).

3rd District

(Sacramento)

Race and Ethnic Groups. Blacks 5.4 percent. Spanish heritage population 9.2 percent. Canadian stock 2.0 percent. German stock 1.8 percent.

Cities, 1970 Population. Sacramento (part) 204,875, Arden-Arcade 52,261, Carmichael 37,795, Parkway-Sacramento South 28,704.

Universities, Enrollment. California State University, Sacramento (Sacramento—20,045).

Military Installations or Activities. Sacramento Army Depot, Sacramento.

Newspapers, Circulation. Sacramento Bee (Eve—177,685), Sacramento Union (MxSat—97,715).

Commercial Television Stations, Affiliation. Entire district is located in Sacramento-Stockton ADI. KCRA-TV, Sacramento (NBC); KOVR-TV, Stockton (ABC); KTXL, Sacramento (CBS, ABC on a per program basis); KXTV, Sacramento (CBS).

Plants and Offices, Products, Employment.
Aerojet-General Corp., Sacramento (Propulsion systems—8,000). **Sacramento Municipal Utilities District**, Sacramento (Electric utility—1,100). **Pacific Telephone and Telegraph**, Sacramento (Telephone company—4,500). **Campbell Soup Co.**, Sacramento (Cannery—1,800). **Broadway-Hale Stores Inc.**, Sacramento (Weinstock's—department store—1,000). **Safeway Stores Inc.**, Sacramento (Super S Stores Division—groceries and general merchandise—1,000).

4th District

(Lower Sacramento Valley—Vallejo)

Race and Ethnic Groups. Blacks 6.2 percent. Spanish heritage population 11.4 percent. Canadian stock 1.6 percent. German stock 1.6 percent.

Cities, 1970 Population. Vallejo 66,872, Sacramento (part) 50,725, Fairfield 44,442, North Highlands 32,057.

Universities, Enrollment. University of California, Davis (Davis—13,981).

Military Installations or Activities. Naval Schools Command, Vallejo; Mare Island Naval Shipyard, Vallejo; McClellan Air Force Base, Sacramento; Travis Air Force Base, Fairfield.

Newspapers, Circulation. Sacramento and San Francisco newspapers circulate in portions of the district.

Commercial Television Stations, Affiliation. A major part of the district is located in the Sacramento-Stockton ADI. A small portion of the district is located in the San Francisco ADI.

5th District

(Northwest San Francisco—Marin County)

Race and Ethnic Groups. Black 10.0 percent. Spanish heritage population 6.6 percent. German stock 3.1 percent. British stock 3.0 percent. Italian stock 2.8 percent.

Cities, 1970 Population. San Francisco (part) 252,456, San Rafael 39,033, Novato 30,900, Mill Valley 13,007.

Universities, Enrollment. San Francisco Art Institute, (San Francisco—6,311).

Military Installations or Activities. Presidio of San Francisco, San Francisco; Hamilton Air Force Base, San Rafael; Mill Valley Air Force Station, Mill Valley.

(Continued on p. 24)

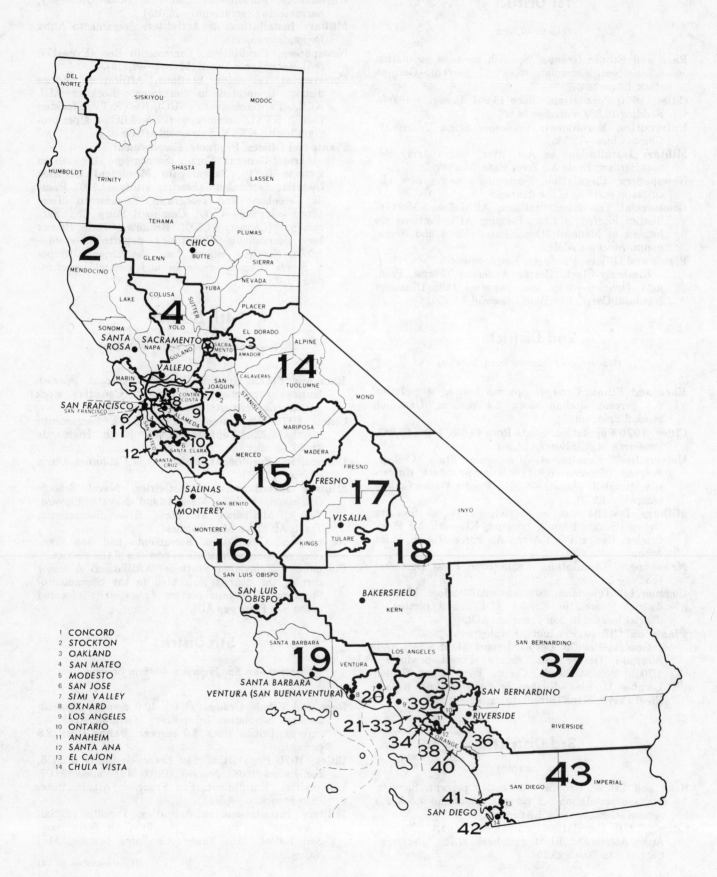

1 CONCORD
2 STOCKTON
3 OAKLAND
4 SAN MATEO
5 MODESTO
6 SAN JOSE
7 SIMI VALLEY
8 OXNARD
9 LOS ANGELES
10 ONTARIO
11 ANAHEIM
12 SANTA ANA
13 EL CAJON
14 CHULA VISTA

SAN FRANCISCO COUNTY

5th District also includes
Marin County and a portion
of Sonoma County
See State map.

PACIFIC OCEAN

5
PART

6

SAN
FRANCISCO
BAY

SAN FRANCISCO

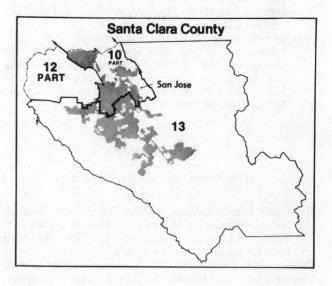

Santa Clara County

12
PART

10
PART

San Jose

13

SAN FRANCISCO BAY AREA

LAKE

COLUSA

2

4

SUTTER

PLACER

SONOMA

SANTA
ROSA

YOLO

SACRAMENTO

NAPA

EL DORADO

SOLANO

SACRA-
MENTO

3

AMADOR

VALLEJO

MARIN

5

CALAVERAS

SAN
JOAQUIN

STANISLAUS

14

San Francisco

1

CONTRA
COSTA

8

7

2

3

ALAMEDA

9

6

4

11

SAN MATEO

5

6

10

SANTA CLARA

12

MERCED

SANTA
CRUZ

13

See state map for
key to numbered cities.

15

(Continued from p. 21)

Newspapers, Circulation. San Francisco newspapers circulate throughout district.

Commercial Television Stations, Affiliation. Entire district is located in San Francisco ADI.

Plants and Offices, Products, Employment.

    Fireman's Fund Insurance Co., San Francisco (Insurance—HQ—1,320). **California State Automobile Assn.**, San Francisco (Automobile association—HQ—1,000). **Pacific Gas and Electric Co.**, San Rafael (Gas and electric utility—1,000).

6th District

(Eastern and Southern San Francisco)

Race and Ethnic Groups. Blacks 11.8 percent. Spanish heritage population 18.0 percent. Chinese 8.5 percent. Filipino 4.1 percent. Italian stock 4.7 percent. Irish stock 2.6 percent. German stock 2.5 percent.

Cities, 1970 Population. San Francisco (part) 463,521.

Universities, Enrollment. California State University, San Francisco (San Francisco—22,450), Golden Gate College (San Francisco—4,499).

Military Installations or Activities. Naval Schools Command (Treasure Island), San Francisco; Treasure Island Naval Station, San Francisco; Hunters Point Naval Shipyard, San Francisco.

Newspapers, Circulation. San Francisco Chronicle (MxSat—457,015), San Francisco Examiner (ExSat—182,164).

Commercial Television Stations, Affiliation. Entire district is located in San Francisco ADI. KBHK-TV, San Francisco (None); KEMO-TV, San Francisco (None—Spanish); KGO-TV, San Francisco (ABC); KPIX-TV, San Francisco (CBS); KRON-TV, San Francisco (NBC).

Plants and Offices, Products, Employment.

    Bechtel Corp., San Francisco (Heavy construction—HQ—4,000). **Bethlehem Steel Corp.**, San Francisco (Ship Building Division—ship repairs—1,100). **Standard Oil Co. of California**, San Francisco (Petroleum production and refining—HQ—3,000), **Del Monte Corp.**, San Francisco (Canning—HQ—1,300). **Schlage Lock Co.**, San Francisco (Door locks and closers—HQ—1,600). **San Francisco Newspaper Printing Co.**, San Francisco (Newspaper publishing—1,500). **General Services Administration**, San Francisco (Printing office—1,000). **Southern Pacific Transportation Co.**, San Francisco (Railroad—HQ—3,700). **Trans World Airlines Inc.**, San Francisco (Airline—2,000). **Yellow Cab Co.**, San Francisco (Taxicab company—1,400). **California Motor Transport Co.**, San Francisco (Motor carrier—1,020). **United Parcel Service Inc.**, San Francisco (Delivery service—1,700). **Western Union Telegraph Co.**, San Francisco (Telegraph company—1,500). **Pacific Gas & Electric Co.**, San Francisco (Gas and electric utility—HQ—2,000). **Pacific Telephone & Telegraph Co.**, San Francisco (Telephone and telegraph company—HQ—2,000). **Broadway-Hale Stores Inc.**, San Francisco (Emporium—department store—1,900). **R. H. Macy & Co. Inc.**, San Francisco (Department store—1,000). **Fairmont**

Hotel Co., San Francisco (Hotel—1,000). **Stevens California Enterprises Inc.**, San Francisco (Caterers—2,090). **Bankamerica Corp.**, San Francisco (Holding company—HQ—2,000). **Metropolitan Life Insurance Co.**, San Francisco (Insurance—1,750).

7th District

(Most of Contra Costa County)

Race and Ethnic Groups. Blacks 8.5 percent. Spanish heritage population 8.5 percent. Italian stock 2.1 percent. Canadian stock 2.0 percent.

Cities, 1970 Population. Concord 84,284, Richmond 78,360, Walnut Creek 39,466, Antioch 27,747.

Military Installations or Activities. Naval Weapons Station, Concord.

Newspapers, Circulation. San Francisco newspapers circulate throughout district.

Commercial Television Stations, Affiliation. Parts of district are located in San Francisco and Sacramento ADIs.

Plants and Offices, Products, Employment.

    Chevron Chemical Co., Richmond (Laboratory—1,500). **Standard Oil Co. of California**, Richmond (Refinery—2,800). **California & Hawaiian Sugar Co.**, Crockett (Cane sugar refinery—1,500). **Shell Oil Co.**, Martinez (Refinery—1,000). **United States Steel Corp.**, Pittsburg (Steel and iron products—3,000). **Crown Zellerback Corp.**, Antioch (Paper products—1,000). **Contra Costa County**, Martinez (County government—4,500).

8th District

(Northern Alameda County—Berkeley, Oakland)

Race and Ethnic Groups. Blacks 20.9 percent. Spanish heritage population 7.1 percent. Chinese 3.4 percent. British stock 2.3 percent. Canadian stock 2.3 percent.

Cities, 1970 Population. Oakland (part) 231,424, Berkeley 116,232, El Cerrito 25,070, Lafayette 20,524.

Universities, Enrollment. California College of Arts and Crafts (Oakland—1,529), Mills College (Oakland—1,040), Saint Mary's College (Moraga—1,265), University of California, Berkeley (Berkeley—27,712).

AEC-Owned, Contractor-Operated Facilities. E. O. Lawrence Radiation Laboratory, Berkeley.

Military Installations or Activities. Oakland Army Base, Oakland; Naval Supply Center, Oakland.

Newspapers, Circulation. Oakland Tribune (ExSat—192,102). San Francisco newspapers also circulate in district.

Commercial Television Stations, Affiliation. Entire district located in San Francisco ADI. KTVU, Oakland (None).

Plants and Offices, Products, Employment.

    Shell Oil Co., Oakland (Research center—1,400). **Southern Pacific Co.**, Oakland (Railroad—20,000). **Tribune Publishing Co.**, Oakland (Newspaper publishing—1,200). **East Bay Municipal Utility District**, Oakland (Utility—1,100). **City of Berkeley**, Berkeley (City government—1,880). **Montgomery Ward and Co. Inc.**, Oakland (Department Store—2,400). **Owens-Illinois Inc.**, Oakland (Glass containers—1,800).

9th District

(Southern Oakland—Eastern Alameda County)

Race and Ethnic Groups. Blacks 13.7 percent. Spanish heritage population 12.4 percent. Italian stock 2.1 percent. Portuguese stock 2.1 percent.

Cities, 1970 Population. Oakland (part) 129,368, Alameda 70,990, San Leandro 68,745, Castro Valley 44,844.

Universities, Enrollment. California State University, Hayward (Hayward—15,750).

AEC-Owned, Contractor-Operated Facilities. E. O. Lawrence Radiation Laboratory, Livermore.

Military Installations or Activities. Naval Air Rework Facility, Alameda; Naval Air Station, Alameda; Naval Hospital, Oakland.

Newspapers, Circulation. Oakland newspaper circulates throughout district. San Francisco newspapers circulate in portions of district.

Commercial Television Stations, Affiliation. Entire district is located in San Francisco ADI.

Plants and Offices, Products, Employment.
De Laval Turbine California Inc., Oakland (Engines, industrial machinery—1,000). **Caterpiller Tractor Co.**, San Leandro (Motor vehicle parts and accessories—1,200). **Singer Co.**, San Leandro (Friden division—office machinery and equipment—2,600). **Sandia Corp.**, Livermore (Research laboratory—1,000). **National Can Corp.**, Oakland (Fruitvale Canning Co. Division—cannery—1,300). **Western Electric Co. Inc.**, San Leandro (Warehouse, repair shop—1,200).

10th District

(San Jose, Fremont, Hayward)

Race and Ethnic Groups. Spanish heritage population 25.5 percent. Italian stock 2.6 percent.

Cities, 1970 Population. San Jose (part) 162,147, Fremont 101,099, Hayward (part) 84,447, Milpitas 27,358.

Universities, Enrollment. California State University, San Jose (San Jose—30,608).

Newspapers, Circulation. San Jose Mercury (Morn—131,416), San Jose News (Eve—75,420).

Commercial Television Stations, Affiliation. Entire district is located in San Francisco ADI. KGSC-TV, San Jose (None); KNTV, San Jose (None).

Plants and Offices, Products, Employment.
Pacific States Steel Corp., Union City (American Forge Co. Divison—steel mill—1,100). **Pacific Car & Foundry Co.**, Newark (Peterbuilt Motors Co. Division—trucks—1,200). **Ford Motor Co.**, Milpitas (Automobile and truck assembly—3,800). **General Motors Corp.**, Fremont (Automobile assembly—5,700). **FMC Corp.**, San Jose (Motor vehicles,

allied equipment—2,900). **FMC Corp.**, San Jose (Headquarters—4,800). **Del Monte Corp.**, San Jose (Cannery—1,000). **Northwest Publications Inc.**, San Jose (Newspaper publishing—1,300). **Pacific Telephone and Telegraph Co.**, San Jose (Telephone company—3,500). **San Jose Hospital & Health Center Inc.**, San Jose (Hospital—1,000).

11th District

(San Francisco suburbs)

Race and Ethnic Groups. Spanish heritage population 14.2 percent. Italian stock 4.3 percent. German stock 2.9 percent. Canadian stock 2.8 percent. British stock 2.6 percent.

Cities, 1970 Population. San Mateo 79,127, Daly City 67,332, South San Francisco 46,606, Redwood City (part) 44,196.

Universities, Enrollment. College of Notre Dame (Belmont—1,152).

Newspapers, Circulation. San Francisco newspapers circulate throughout district.

Commercial Television Stations, Affiliation. Entire district is located in San Francisco ADI.

Plants and Offices, Products, Employment.
Textron Inc., Belmont (Dalmo Victor Co. Division —Locomotives, railroad and streetcars—1,200). **Ampex Corp.**, Redwood City (Radios, televisions, electronic equipment—1,700). **Ampex Corp.**, Redwood City (Headquarters—3,450). **Pan American World Airways Inc.**, South San Francisco (Airline—3,400). **United Air Lines Inc.**, South San Francisco (Airline—8,000). **Western Air Lines Inc.**, South San Francisco (Airline—1,000). **GTE Lenkurt Inc.**, San Carlos (Communications equipment—HQ—2,800).

12th District

(Southern San Mateo County—
Northwestern Santa Clara County)

Race and Ethnic Groups. Blacks 4.3 percent. Spanish heritage population 10.8 percent. Canadian stock 2.5 percent. British stock 2.5 percent.

Cities, 1970 Population. Sunnyvale (part) 92,947, Santa Clara 87,293, Palo Alto 55,657, Mountain View 50,804.

Universities, Enrollment. Stanford University (Palo Alto—12,479), University of Santa Clara (Santa Clara—6,085).

AEC-Owned, Contractor-Operated Facilities. Stanford Linear Accelerator Center, Palto Alto.

NASA Facilities. Ames Research Center (Moffett Field), Mountain View.

Military Installations or Activities. Moffett Field Naval Air Station, Mountain View.

Newspapers, Circulation. San Jose newspapers circulate in district. San Francisco newspapers circulate in portion of district.

Commercial Television Stations, Affiliation. Entire district is located in San Francisco ADI.

Plants and Offices, Products, Employment.

Westinghouse Electric Corp., Sunnyvale (Marine turbines, missile launchers—2,600). **United Aircraft Corp.**, Sunnyvale (Rocket engines—1,500). **Space Ordnance Systems Inc.**, Sunnyvale (Explosive devices—1,000). **National Semiconductor Corp.**, Santa Clara (Transistors, integrated circuits—HQ—1,100). **Raytheon Co.**, Mountain View (Semiconductor components—1,200). **Fairchild Camera & Instrument Corp.**, Mountain View (Photographic equipment and supplies—HQ—1,500). **Fairchild Camera & Instrument Corp.**, Mountain View (Controls—3,460). **Fairchild Camera & Instrument Corp.**, Mountain View (Electronic products—1,000). **Fairchild Camera & Instrument Corp.**, Mountain View (Electronic products—1,000). **Hewlett-Packard Co.**, Palo Alto (Electronic equipment—HQ—6,300). **Hewlett-Packard Co.**, Santa Clara (Laboratory instruments—1,000). **Singer-General Precision Systems Inc.**, Sunnyvale (Electronic products, computers—1,100). **Varian Associates**, Palo Alto (Electronic equipment, tubes—HQ—3,000). **Sylvania Electric Products**, Mountain View (Electronic components—2,000). **Signetics Corp.**, Sunnyvale (Electronic components—1,500). **Western Electric Co.**, Sunnyvale (Regional headquarters—1,850). **Stanford Research Institute**, Menlo Park (Educational and scientific research—2,500). **Lockheed Missiles and Space Co.**, Sunnyvale (Missile and space systems—HQ—13,600). **Memorex Corp.**, Santa Clara (Recording devices, tape—HQ—1,300).

13th District

(Most of Santa Clara County)

Race and Ethnic Groups. Spanish heritage population 15.7 percent. Italian stock 2.7 percent. Canadian stock 2.3 percent.

Cities, 1970 Population. San Jose (part) 271,639, Saratoga 27,421, Los Gatos 27,421, Campbell 25,197.

Newspapers, Circulation. San Jose and San Francisco newspapers circulate in district.

Commercial Television Stations, Affiliation. Entire district is located in San Francisco ADI.

Plants and Offices, Products, Employment.

Pacific Telephone and Telegraph, San Jose (Telephone company—1,000). **International Business Machines Corp.**, San Jose (Computers—6,000). **General Electric Co.**, San Jose (Nuclear powered motors —3,500). **International Business Machines Corp.**, San Jose (Development laboratory—1,000). **International Business Machines Corp.**, Campbell (Processing, supplies—at least 2,000).

14th District

(Lower San Joaquin Valley—Stockton)

Race and Ethnic Groups. Blacks 3.7 percent. Spanish heritage population 15.5 percent. Italian stock 2.3 percent. German stock 1.5 percent.

Cities, 1970 Population. Stockton 107,429, Lodi 28,683, Tracy 14,720, Manteca 13,888.

Universities, Enrollment. University of the Pacific (Stockton—4,444).

Military Installations or Activities. Sharpe Army Depot, Lathrop; Naval Communication Station, Stockton.

Newspapers, Circulation. Stockton Record (Eve—53,800).

Commercial Television Stations, Affiliation. Most of district is located in Sacramento-Stockton ADI. Portions of district are located in Reno (Nev.) ADI.

Plants and Offices, Products, Employment.

Norris Industries Inc., Riverbank (Shell casings—1,300). **Tillie Lewis Foods Inc.**, Stockton (Cannery—at least 1,000).

15th District

(Middle San Joaquin Valley— Fresno, Modesto)

Race and Ethnic Groups. Blacks 5.7 percent. Spanish heritage population 20.8 percent. Italian stock 1.5 percent. Russian stock 1.1 percent.

Cities, 1970 Population. Fresno (part) 98,822, Modesto (part) 60,046, Merced 22,698, Madera 16,064.

Universities, Enrollment. California State College, Stanislaus (Turlock—4,036).

Military Installations or Activities. Castle Air Force Base, Merced.

Newspapers, Circulation. Modesto Bee (ExSat—50,544), Fresno Bee (Eve—112,095).

Commercial Television Stations, Affiliation. Entire district is located in Fresno ADI. KAIL-TV, Fresno (None); KFSN-TV, Fresno (CBS); KJEO, Fresno (ABC); KMJ-TV, Fresno (NBC); KLOC-TV, Fresno (None—Spanish).

Plants and Offices, Products, Employment.

E. and J. Gallo Winery Inc., Modesto (Winery—1,600).

16th District

(Central Coast—Salinas, Monterey)

Race and Ethnic Groups. Blacks 3.2 percent. Spanish heritage population 17.6 percent. German stock 2.2 percent. Canadian stock 2.0 percent.

Cities, 1970 Population. Salinas 58,568, Seaside 35,742, Santa Cruz 31,897, San Luis Obispo 27,880.

Universities, Enrollment. California Polytechnic State University, San Luis Obispo (San Luis Obispo—12,343); Naval Postgraduate School (Monterey—1,766); University of California, Santa Cruz (Santa Cruz—4,396).

Military Installations or Activities. Presidio of Monterey, Monterey; Fort Ord, Monterey; Naval Postgraduate School, Monterey; Almedan Air Force Base, Almaden.

Commercial Television Stations, Affiliation. Entire district is located in Salinas-Monterey ADI. KMST, Monterey (CBS); KSBW-TV, Salinas (NBC); KSBY-TV, San Luis Obispo (NBC).

17th District

(Upper San Joaquin Valley—Fresno, Visalia)

Race and Ethnic Groups. Spanish heritage population 24.5 percent. Russian stock 1.5 percent. Canadian stock 1.0 percent.

Cities, 1970 Population. Fresno (part) 67,399, Visalia 27,320, Tulare 16,091, Hanford 15,208.

Universities, Enrollment. California State University, Fresno (Fresno—18,537).

Military Installations or Activities. Naval Air Station, Lemoore.

Newspapers, Circulation. Fresno newspaper circulates in district.

Commercial Television Stations, Affiliation. Entire district located in Fresno ADI. KMPH-TV, Visalia (None).

18th District

(South Central—Bakersfield)

Race and Ethnic Groups. Blacks 4.8 percent. Spanish heritage population 15.5 percent. Canadian stock 1.2 percent. British stock 1.1 percent.

Cities, 1970 Population. Bakersfield 69,677, Lancaster 32,646, Oildale 21,049, Delano 14,593.

Universities, Enrollment. California State College, Bakersfield (Bakersfield—2,599).

NASA Facilities. Flight Research Center, Edwards.

Military Installations or Activities. Naval Weapons Center, China Lake; Air Force Plant 42, Palmdale; Boron Air Force Station, Boron; Edwards Air Force Base, Edwards.

Newspapers, Circulation. Bakersfield Californian (Eve—53,550).

Commercial Television Stations, Affiliation. Bakersfield ADI covers part of district. Most of district is located in Los Angeles ADI. Small portion of district is located in Fresno ADI. KBAK-TV, Bakersfield (CBS); KERO-TV, Bakersfield (NBC); KJTV, Bakersfield (ABC).

19th District

(South Central Coast—Santa Barbara)

Race and Ethnic Groups. Spanish heritage population 19.8 percent. Canadian stock 2.3 percent. British stock 2.2 percent.

Cities, 1970 Population. Santa Barbara 70,337, Ventura, (San Buenaventura) 57,157, Oxnard 66,667, Santa Maria 32,808.

Universities, Enrollment. University of California, Santa Barbara (Santa Barbara—12,916).

NASA Facilities. KSC Western Test Range, Lompoc.

Military Installations or Activities. Vandenberg Air Force Base, Lompoc.

Newspapers, Circulation. Los Angeles newspapers circulate in most of district.

Commercial Television Stations, Affiliation. Entire district is located in Santa Barbara-Santa Maria ADI. KEYT, Santa Barbara (ABC); KCOY-TV, Santa Maria (CBS).

20th District

(Southern Ventura County—West Los Angeles)

Race and Ethnic Groups. Spanish heritage population 11.1 percent. Canadian stock 2.9 percent. British stock 2.1 percent.

Cities, 1970 Population. Los Angeles (part) 191,955, Simi Valley 57,175, Thousand Oaks 36,252, Camarillo 19,477.

Universities, Enrollment. California Lutheran College (Thousand Oaks—1,286).

AEC-Owned, Contractor-Operated Facilities. Liquid Metal Engineering Center, Canoga Park.

Military Installations or Activities. Naval Air Station, Point Mugu; Naval Construction Battalion, Port Heuneme; Pacific Missile Range, Point Mugu.

Newspapers, Circulation. Los Angeles newspapers circulate throughout district.

Commercial Television Stations, Affiliation. Entire district is located in Los Angeles ADI.

Plants and Offices, Products, Employment.
Northrop Corp., Newbury Park (Target drones —1,500). **Bunker Ramo Corp.,** Thousand Oaks (Line control information systems—1,200). **North American Rockwell,** Canoga Park (Nuclear reactors, aircraft engines—1,400). **Teledyne Inc.,** Northridge (Electronics components—1,100). **Minnesota Mining and Manufacturing Co.,** Camarillo (Recorders and tape—1,100).

21st District

(Northwest Los Angeles—San Fernando valley)

Race and Ethnic Groups. Blacks 3.6 percent. Spanish heritage population 17.3 percent. Canadian stock 3.0 percent. Russian stock 2.9 percent.

Cities, 1970 Population. Los Angeles (part) 448,420, San Fernando 16,514.

Universities, Enrollment. California State University, Northridge (Northridge—25,918).

Newspapers, Circulation. Los Angeles newspapers circulate throughout district.

Commercial Television Stations, Affiliation. Entire district is located in Los Angeles ADI.

Plants and Offices, Products, Employment.
ITT-Gilfillan Inc., Van Nuys (Electronic equipment, research and development—1,700). **General Motors Corp.,** Van Nuys (Motor vehicles—2,500). **Lockheed Aircraft Corp.,** Van Nuys (Missile systems—at least 1,010). **The Bendix Corp.,** North Hollywood (Dynamic controls, radar—1,400). **The Bendix Corp.,** San Fernando (Radar guidance devices—1,000). **CCI Aerospace Corp.,** Van Nuys (Aircraft instruments—1,500). **RCA Corp.,** Van Nuys (Computers—1,500). **Litton Systems Inc.,** Van Nuys (Air data equipment—3,000).

22nd District

(Central Los Angeles—Glendale, Pasadena)

Race and Ethnic Groups. Blacks 6.5 percent. Spanish heritage population 9.9 percent. Canadian stock 3.3 percent. British stock 2.9 percent. German stock 2.5 percent.

Cities, 1970 Population. Glendale 132,691, Pasadena (part) 103,400, Burbank 88,838, Los Angeles (part) 54,361.

Universities, Enrollment. California Institute of Technology (Pasadena—1,504). Pasadena College (Pasadena—1,329).

NASA Facilities. Jet Propulsion Laboratory, Pasadena; NASA Pasadena Office, Pasadena.

Newspapers, Circulation. Los Angeles newspapers circulate throughout district.

Commercial Television Stations, Affiliation. Entire district is located in Los Angeles ADI. KHOF, Glendale (None).

Plants and Offices, Products, Employment.

Lockheed Aircraft Corp., Burbank (Headquarters —10,000). **Walter Kidde and Co. Inc.**, (Morrison Industries Division—safety and security equipment— 1,800). **International Telephone and Telegraph Corp.**, Glendale (Automatic temperature controls— 1,500). **Singer-General Precision Inc.**, Glendale (Kear Fott Division—electronic computing equipment—1,200). **Walt Disney Productions**, Burbank (Motion picture production, amusement parks— 1,500). **City of Pasadena**, Pasadena (City government—1,800).

23rd District

(Los Angeles—Beverly Hills)

Race and Ethnic Groups. Spanish heritage population 7.1 percent. Russian stock 7.9 percent. Canadian stock 3.6 percent. German stock 2.9 percent. Polish stock 3.4 percent. British stock 3.0 percent.

Cities, 1970 Population. Los Angeles (part) 409,176, Beverly Hills 33,706, West Hollywood (part) 21,109.

Universities, Enrollment. Mount St. Mary's College (Los Angeles—1,201), University of California, Los Angeles (Los Angeles—27,891).

Newspapers, Circulation. Los Angeles newspapers circulate throughout district.

Commercial Television Stations, Affiliation. Entire district is located in Los Angeles ADI.

Plants and Offices, Products, Employment.

Bomaine Corp., Los Angeles (Holding company, railroad—4,280). **Data Products Corp.**, Woodland Hills (Computer accessories—HQ—1,000). **Twentieth Century Fox Film Corp.**, Los Angeles (Motion picture production, distribution—2,000). **Everest and Jennings International**, Los Angeles (Wheel chairs, holding company—1,200). **Chanco Medical Industries**, Los Angeles (Holding company, hospitals— 3,000). **National Medical Enterprises**, Beverly Hills (Hospitals, convalescent homes—1,250). **United Convalescent Hospitals Inc.**, Los Angeles (Holding company, hospitals—1,400). **Associated Hosts Inc.**, Beverly Hills (Holding company, restaurants—1,400).

24th District

(Los Angeles—North Hollywood)

Race and Ethnic Groups. Blacks 5.5 percent. Spanish heritage population 16.2 percent. Russian stock 6.2 percent. Polish stock 3.2 percent. Japanese 2.9 percent. Canadian stock 2.8 percent. German stock 2.8 percent. British stock 2.7 percent.

Cities, 1970 Population. Los Angeles (part) 456,981, West Hollywood (part) 8,494.

Universities, Enrollment. Art Center College of Design (Los Angeles—1,062).

Newspapers, Circulation. Los Angeles newspapers circulate throughout district.

Commercial Television Stations, Affiliation. Entire district is located in Los Angeles ADI.

Plants and Offices, Products, Employment.

Farmers Underwriters Assn., Los Angeles (Legal services and insurance—5,000). **Pacific Indemnity Co.**, Los Angeles (Insurance—1,440). **William J. Burns International**, Los Angeles (Detective, security agency—1,800). **Paramount Pictures Corp.**, Los Angeles (Motion picture production, records—2,000). **Universal City Studios Inc.**, North Hollywood (Motion picture and television production—HQ—5,000). **Columbia Broadcasting System Inc.**, North Hollywood (Motion picture production—1,000). **MCA Inc.**, North Hollywood (Television motion picture production, records—HQ—2,500). **Technicolor Inc.**, Los Angeles (Photographic equipment, film—2,000). **Carnation Co.**, Los Angeles (Headquarters—1,000). **Du Pars Ltd.**, Studio City (Restaurants—1,000). **System Auto Parks Inc.**, Los Angeles (Holding company—1,000). **Karls Shoe Stores Ltd.**, Los Angeles (Shoe stores—1,400). **Childrens Hospital of Los Angeles**, Los Angeles (Hospital—1,300). **Interpace Corp.**, Los Angeles (Ceramic products—1,250).

25th District

(Central Los Angeles)

Race and Ethnic Groups. Blacks 5.1 percent. Spanish heritage population 60.3 percent. Italian stock 1.5 percent. Canadian stock 1.2 percent.

Cities, 1970 Population. East Los Angeles (part), 83,853, Los Angeles (part) 381,119.

Universities, Enrollment. California State University, Los Angeles (Los Angeles—25,134), Occidental College (Los Angeles—1,879), Woodbury College (Los Angeles—1,242).

Newspapers, Circulation. Los Angeles Times (Morn— 1,006,021), Los Angeles Herald-Examiner (ExSat— 106,160).

Commercial Television Stations, Affiliation. Entire district is located in Los Angeles ADI. KABC-TV, Los Angeles (ABC); KBSC-TV, Los Angeles (None); KCOP-TV, Los Angeles (None); KHJ-TV, Los Angeles (None); KLXA-TV, Los Angeles (None—Spanish); KNBC, Los Angeles (NBC); KNXT, Los Angeles (CBS); KTLA, Los Angeles (None); KTTV, Los Angeles (None); KWHY-TV, Los Angeles (None).

Plants and Offices, Products, Employment.

The Ralph M. Parsons Co., Los Angeles (Heavy construction, engineering—15,000). **Turner & Mc-**

LOS ANGELES COUNTY

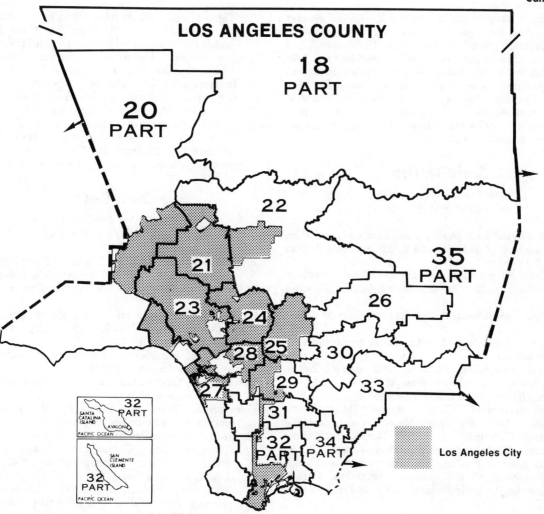

Los Angeles City

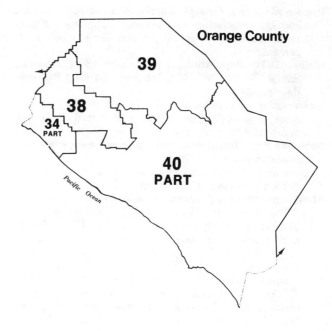

Orange County

Kee, Los Angeles (General contracting—at least 1,000). **Union Oil Co. of California**, Los Angeles (Headquarters—1,200). **Lockheed Aircraft International Inc.**, Los Angeles (Aircraft equipment—1,450). **Continental Can Co. Inc.**, Los Angeles (Metal containers—1,100). **Norris Industries Inc.**, Los Angeles (Metal stamping, ovens—HQ—2,500). **Carnation Co.**, Los Angeles (Milk, ice cream—1,420). **The Times-Mirror Co.**, Los Angeles (Newspaper publishing—HQ—4,000). **Pacific Telephone & Telegraph Co.**, Los Angeles (Telephone company—2,000). **Yellow Cab Co.**, Los Angeles (Taxi service, holding company—1,600). **Airportransit of California**, Los Angeles (Transportation—1,600). **Kinney National Services**, Los Angeles (Cleaning, maintenance contractor—1,500). **Los Angeles Biltmore Hotel Co.**, Los Angeles (Hotel—1,000). **Equitable Life Assurance Society of the United States**, Los Angeles (Insurance—3,000). **Title Insurance & Trust Co.**, Los Angeles (Insurance—HQ—2,100). **Pacific Mutual Life Insurance Co.**, Los Angeles (Insurance—1,500). **Western Bancorporation**, Los Angeles (Holding company—HQ—1,000). **City of Los Angeles**, Los Angeles (City government—45,000). **Hospital of the Good Samaritan**, Los Angeles (Hospital—1,000). **Foremost-McKesson Inc.**, Los Angeles

(Continued on p. 30)

(Continued from p. 29)

(Foremost Dairies—milk processing—1,700). **Hearst Corp.**, Los Angeles (Newspaper publishing—1,500). **Automobile Club of Southern California**, Los Angeles (Headquarters—1,400). **Occidental Life Insurance Co. of California**, Los Angeles (Insurance —HQ—3,000). **The Service Group Inc.**, Los Angeles (Holding company—1,800). **Lutheran Hospital Society of Southern California**, Los Angeles (Hospital—1,000). **General Host Co.**, Los Angeles (Bakery products—2,500).

26th District

(East Central Los Angeles—
Alhambra, Arcadia, Azusa)

Race and Ethnic Groups. Spanish heritage population 15.4 percent. Canadian stock 3.0 percent. Italian stock 2.3 percent.

Cities, 1970 Population. Alhambra 62,105, Baldwin Park (part) 46,829, Arcadia (part) 44,498, Glendora 31,263.

Universities, Enrollment. Azusa Pacific College (Azusa—1,039).

Newspapers, Circulation. Los Angeles newspapers circulate in district.

Commercial Television Stations, Affiliation. Entire district is located in Los Angeles ADI.

Plants and Offices, Products, Employment.

Aerojet-General Corp., Azusa (Microelectric systems—3,000). **Bell and Howell Co.**, Pasadena (Electronic instruments—1,150). **Burroughs Corp.**, Pasadena (Data processing systems—2,400). **C. F. Braun and Co.**, Alhambra (Contractors and engineers—1,500). **Vinnell Corp.**, Alhambra (Heavy construction, highway building—at least 4,000).

27th District

(Pacific Coast—Santa Monica)

Race and Ethnic Groups. Blacks 39.8 percent. Spanish heritage population 12.2 percent. Japanese 4.2 percent. Canadian stock 2.0 percent. German stock 1.6 percent.

Cities, 1970 Population. Los Angeles (part) 116,624, Santa Monica 87,544, Torrance 64,964, Redondo Beach 55,541.

Universities, Enrollment. Loyola University of Los Angeles (Los Angeles—3,822), Marymount College at Loyola University (Los Angeles—1,161).

Newspapers, Circulation. Los Angeles newspapers circulate throughout district.

Commercial Television Stations, Affiliation. Entire district is located in Los Angeles ADI.

Plants and Offices, Products, Employment.

The Aerospace Corp., El Segundo (Research and development—HQ—1,000). **North American Rockwell Corp.**, Los Angeles (Aircraft—13,000). **TRW Inc.**, Redondo Beach (Missile controls—10,300). **Hughes Aircraft Co.**, El Segundo (Guidance systems, computing equipment—2,500). **Hughes Aircraft Co.**, El Segundo (Guidance systems, computing equipment—3,200). **International Rectifier Corp.**, El Segundo (Electric products—1,200). **The Flying**

Tiger Corp., Los Angeles (Holding company, plane service—HQ—1,200). **Western Air Lines Inc.**, Los Angeles (Air carrier—HQ—3,000). **McCulloch Corp.**, Los Angeles (Power saws, aircraft engines—HQ—1,100). **Hughes Tool Co.**, Culver City (Helicopters, armament—4,500). **Hughes Aircraft Co.**, Culver City (Headquarters—10,000). **Ampex Corp.**, Venice (Computer equipment—1,200). **Sav-On Drugs Inc.**, Venice (Drug stores—3,000). **Systems Development Corp.**, Santa Monica (Computer systems research—HQ—2,000). **McDonnell Douglas Corp.**, Santa Monica (Missile and space systems—18,000).

28th District

(Western Los Angeles County—
Culver City, Inglewood)

Race and Ethnic Groups. Blacks 39.8 percent. Spanish heritage population 12.2 percent. Japanese 4.2 percent. Canadian stock 2.0 percent. German stock 1.6 percent.

Cities, 1970 Population. Los Angeles (part) 324,706, Inglewood (part) 87,466, Culver City 31,358, Viewpark-Windsor Hills 12,271.

Universities, Enrollment. University of Southern California (Los Angeles—18,884).

Newspapers, Circulation. Los Angeles newspapers circulate throughout district.

Commercial Television Stations, Affiliation. Entire district is located in Los Angeles ADI.

Plants and Offices, Products, Employment.

Ampex Corp., Culver City (Computer Products Division—electronic components—1,300). **Metro-Goldwyn-Mayer Inc.**, Culver City (Motion picture production, records—HQ—1,500). **General Health Services Inc.**, Culver City (Holding company, hospitals—1,000).

29th District

(South Los Angeles—Huntington Park, Watts)

Race and Ethnic Groups. Blacks 59.1 percent. Spanish heritage population 15.2 percent. British stock 0.8 percent. German stock 0.8 percent.

Cities, 1970 Population. Los Angeles (part) 263,303, South Gate 56,910, Florence-Graham 42,895, Huntington Park 33,813.

Universities, Enrollment. Pepperdine University (Los Angeles—2,802).

Newspapers, Circulation. Los Angeles newspapers circulate throughout district.

Commercial Television Stations, Affiliation. Entire district is located in Los Angeles ADI.

Plants and Offices, Products, Employment.

General Motors Corp., South Gate (Automobile assembly—3,000). **Goodyear Tire & Rubber Co.**, Los Angeles (Tires, rubber products—1,800). **Bethlehem Steel Corp.**, Los Angeles (Steel mill, bolts and nuts—2,000). **Bechtel Corp.**, Los Angeles (Heavy construction—1,150). **Borg-Warner Corp.**, Los Angeles (Byron-Jackson Pump Division—centrifugal pumps—1,000). **Flintkote Co.**, Los Angeles (Pioneer Division—building supplies—1,000). **Norris Industries Inc.**, South Gate (Weiser Co. Division—locks —1,400). **Aluminum Co. of America**, Los Angeles (Rome Cable Divison—aluminum—2,000). **American Building Maintenance Co. Inc.**, Los Angeles (Building maintenance—1,700). **Arcata Graphics Corp.**, Los Angeles (Printing—1,100). **Owens-Illinois Inc.**, Los Angeles (Glass and plastic containers—1,100).

30th District

(Los Angeles County—El Monte, Monterey Park

Race and Ethnic Groups. Spanish heritage population 42.2 percent. Canadian stock 1.7 percent. German stock 1.3 percent.

Cities, 1970 Population. El Monte (part) 69,547, Pico Rivera 54,207, Monterey Park 49,131, Montebello 42,838.

Newspapers, Circulation. Los Angeles newspapers circulate in district.

Commercial Television Stations, Affiliation. Entire district is located in Los Angeles ADI.

Plants and Offices, Products, Employment.

Aerojet-General Corp., El Monte (Rocket motors, propellants—HQ-2,500). **Hoffman Electronics Corp.**, El Monte (Communications systems—HQ—1,100). **Southern California Edison**, Rosemead (Electric systems). **United States Steel Corp.**, Los Angeles (Fabricated steel—1,000). **Chrysler Corp.**, Los Angeles (Automobile assembly—1,500). **Ford Motor Co.**, Pico Rivera (Automobile assembly—2,680). **Uniroyal Inc.**, Los Angeles (Tires, rubber processing, chemicals—1,300). **B. F. Goodrich Co.**, Los Angeles (Tires, rubber—administrative office—7,000). **Union Pacific Railroad Co.**, Los Angeles (Railroad —1,350). **Mattel Inc.**, Industry (Toys—at least 1,200).

31st District

(Southern Los Angeles County— Hawthorne, Compton)

Race and Ethnic Groups. Blacks 27.8 percent. Spanish heritage population 14.9 percent. Japanese 3.3 percent. Canadian stock 1.8 percent. British stock 1.4 percent.

Cities, 1970 Population. Compton (part) 78,857, Hawthorne 53,578, Lynwood 43,677, Gardena 41,366.

Newspapers, Circulation. Los Angeles newspapers circulate throughout district.

Commercial Television Stations, Affiliation. Entire district is located in Los Angeles ADI.

Plants and Offices, Products, Employment.

Max Factor and Co., Hawthorne (Cosmetics— 1,000). **Mattel Inc.**, Hawthorne (Holding company, toys—HQ—3,520). **Standard Brands Paint Co.**, Torrance (Holding company, paint—1,240). **Continental Device Corp.**, Hawthorne (Semi-conductors —HQ—1,100). **Garrett Corp.**, Torrance (Aircraft

control systems—3,000). **Western Gear Corp.**, Lynwood (Gears, machinery, aircraft equipment— 1,600). **National Cash Register Co.**, Hawthorne (Electronic data processing equipment—2,500). **Philco-Ford Corp.**, Lawndale (Electronic communication devices—1,500). **TRW Inc.**, Lawndale (Semi-conductors—1,000).

32nd District

(Southern Los Angeles County— Carson, Torrance)

Race and Ethnic Groups. Blacks 7.5 percent. Spanish heritage population 17.9 percent. Canadian stock 2.1 percent. British stock 2.0 percent.

Cities, 1970 Population. Long Beach 164,346, Los Angeles (part) 141,899, Carson (part) 71,048, Torrance (part) 34,506.

Universities, Enrollment. California State College, Dominguez Hills (Dominguez Hills—3,628).

Military Installations or Activities. Fort McArthur, San Pedro; Long Beach Naval Shipyard, Long Beach; Naval Station, Long Beach; Naval Supply Center, Long Beach; Navy Fuel Depot, San Pedro.

Newspapers, Circulation. Torrance South Bay Breeze (Eve—64,271), Long Beach Independent (MxSat— 55,429), Long Beach Press-Telegram (ExSat—106,160).

Commercial Television Stations, Affiliation. Entire district is located in Los Angeles ADI.

Plants and Offices, Products, Employment.

Atlantic Richfield Co., Wilmington (Petroleum refinery—1,700). **Harvey Aluminum Inc.**, Torrance (Headquarters—1,500). **Todd Shipyards Corp.**, San Pedro (Shipbuilding—1,000). **McDonnell Douglas Corp.**, Torrance (Aircraft controls, parts—5,100). **Robertshaw Controls Inc.**, Long Beach (Grayson Controls Division—thermal control devices—1,300). **Ralston Purina Co.**, San Pedro (Van Camp Sea Food Co. Division—cannery—1,500).

33rd District

(Eastern Los Angeles County— Downey, Norwalk, Whittier)

Race and Ethnic Groups. Spanish heritage population 18.4 percent. Canadian stock 2.7 percent. British stock 1.8 percent.

Cities, 1970 Population. Norwalk 91,329, Downey 88,498, Whittier (part) 71,714, South Whittier 46,531.

Universities, Enrollment. Biola College (La Miranda— 1,628), Whittier College (Whittier—2,363).

Newspapers, Circulation. Los Angeles newspapers circulate in district.

Commercial Television Stations, Affiliation. Entire district is located in Los Angeles ADI.

Plants and Offices, Products, Employment.

Carrier Corp., LaPuente (Day and Night Manufacturing Co. Division—air conditioning equipment— 2,000). **North American Rockwell Corp.**, Downey (Spacecraft launchers—8,800).

34th District

(Los Angeles County, North Coastal
Orange County—Long Beach)

Race and Ethnic Groups. Spanish heritage population 8.4 percent. Canadian stock 3.0 percent. British stock 2.4 percent.

Cities, 1970 Population. Long Beach (part) 195,590, Lakewood 83,262, Huntington Beach (part) 58,267.

Universities, Enrollment. California State University, Long Beach (Long Beach—28,667).

Military Installations or Activities. Naval Hospital, Long Beach; Naval Weapons Station, Seal Beach.

Newspapers, Circulation. Los Angeles newspapers circulate throughout district.

Commercial Television Stations, Affiliation. Entire district is located in Los Angeles ADI.

Plants and Offices, Products, Employment.
McDonnell-Douglas Corp., Long Beach (Aircraft—2,000). **McDonnell-Douglas Corp.,** Huntington Beach (Missile and space systems—6,000). **Specialty Restaurants Corp.,** Long Beach (Holding company, restaurants—1,500).

35th District

(Los Angeles County—Covina,
Pomona, West San Bernardino)

Race and Ethnic Groups. Blacks 3.5 percent. Spanish heritage population 15.0 percent. Canadian stock 2.6 percent. British stock 1.8 percent.

Cities, 1970 Population. Pomona (part) 87,296, West Covina (part) 67,464, Ontario 64,096, Upland 32,546.

Universities, Enrollment. California State Polytechnic University, Pomona (Pomona—10,368). The Claremont Colleges (Claremont—total enrollment 5,144).

Newspapers, Circulation. San Gabriel Valley Tribune (Eve—81,920), Los Angeles and San Bernardino papers also circulate in portions of district.

Commercial Television Stations, Affiliation. Entire district is located in Los Angeles ADI.

Plants and Offices, Products, Employment.
American Hospital Supply Corp., Irwindale (Disposable hospital supplies—1,250). **General Dynamics Corp.,** Pomona (Missiles—4,000). **General Electric Co.,** Ontario (Electric housewares—1,000). **Lockheed Aircraft Corp.,** Ontario (Aircraft overhauling and modification—1,500).

36th District

(Riverside, San Bernardino)

Race and Ethnic Groups. Blacks 6.6 percent. Spanish heritage population 17.9 percent. Canadian stock 2.0 percent. German stock 1.5 percent.

Cities, 1970 Population. Riverside 139,865, San Bernardino (part) 73,736, Rialto 28,510, Corona 27,525.

Universities, Enrollment. University of California, Riverside (Riverside—6,168).

Military Installations or Activities. March Air Force Base, Riverside.

Newspapers, Circulation. Riverside Enterprise (MxSat—53,011), San Bernardino Sun (MxSat—66,709).

Commercial Television Stations, Affiliation. Entire district is located in Los Angeles ADI.

Plants and Offices, Products, Employment.
Atchison Topeka and Santa Fe Railway Co., San Bernardino (Railroad—3,000). **Bourns Inc.,** Riverside (Electrical measuring instruments—HQ—1,300). **Kaiser Steel Corp.,** Fontana (Blast furnace, steel fabricating—8,300). **County of San Bernardino,** San Bernardino (County government—4,700). **Rohr Corp.,** Riverside (Aircraft assemblies—1,600).

37th District

(San Bernardino County—Riverside County)

Race and Ethnic Groups. Blacks 3.0 percent. Spanish heritage population 15.0 percent. Canadian stock 2.1 percent. German stock 2.0 percent.

Cities, 1970 Population. Redlands 36,312. San Bernardino (part) 30,623, Palm Springs 20,877. Yucaipa 19,230.

Universities, Enrollment. California State College, San Bernardino (San Bernardino—3,656); Loma Linda University, Loma Linda Campus (Loma Linda—3,574).

Military Installations or Activities. Marine Corps Base, Twenty-Nine Palms; Marine Corps Supply Center, Barstow; George Air Force Base, Victorville; Norton Air Force Base, San Bernardino.

Newspapers, Circulation. Riverside and San Bernardino newspapers circulate in portions of district.

Commercial Television Stations, Affiliation. Most of district is located in Los Angeles ADI. Parts of district are located in Palm Springs and Phoenix (Ariz.) ADIs. KMIR-TV, Palm Springs (NBC); KPLM-TV, Palm Springs (ABC).

Plants and Offices, Products, Employment.
Atchison Topeka and Santa Fe Railway Co., Barstow (Railroad—1,000). **Continental Telephone Co. of California,** Victorville (Telephone company—1,400). **Deutsch Co.,** Banning (Electronic connectors, relays—1,000). **Kaiser Steel Corp.,** Eagle Mountain (Iron ore mining—1,250). **Petrolane Inc.,** Colton (Stater Bros. Markets Division—grocery stores—1,250).

38th District

(Orange County—Buena Park, Westminster)

Race and Ethnic Groups. Spanish heritage population 15.6 percent. Canadian stock 2.6 percent. British stock 1.8 percent.

Cities, 1970 Population. Santa Ana 121,229, Garden Grove (part), 117,805, Buena Park (part) 58,866, Westminster (part) 56,744.

Newspapers, Circulation. Santa Ana Register (MxSat—60,400; ExSat 114,187).

Commercial Television Stations, Affiliation. Entire district is located in Los Angeles ADI.

Plants and Offices, Products, Employment.

AMF Voit Inc., Santa Ana (Rubber sporting goods —1,180). International Telephone and Telegraph Corp., Santa Ana (ITT Cannon Electric Division— electric connectors—1,100). State Farm Fire and Casualty Co., Santa Ana (Insurance—1,070). Knotts Berry Farm, Buena Park (Amusement park, restaurant—1,500).

39th District

(North Orange County—Anaheim, Fullerton)

Race and Ethnic Groups. Spanish heritage population 11.1 percent. Canadian stock 2.9 percent. German stock 2.0 percent.

Cities, 1970 Population. Anaheim (part) 146,527, Fullerton 85,656, Orange 77,056, La Habra 41,172.

Universities, Enrollment. California State University, Fullerton (Fullerton—16,100); Chapman College (Orange—4,935).

Newspapers, Circulation. Santa Ana newspaper circulates in district. Los Angeles newspapers circulate in most of district.

Commercial Television Stations, Affiliation. Entire district is located in Los Angeles ADI.

Plants and Offices, Products, Employment.

LTV Ling Altec Inc., Anaheim (Electronic systems equipment—1,000). North American Rockwell Corp., Anaheim (Communications and computing equipment—10,000). Northrop Corp., Anaheim (Ground support, testing equipment—2,000). Beckman Instruments Inc., Fullerton (Precision instruments—HQ— 2,000). Baker Industries Inc., Fullerton (Holding company—1,200). Walt Disney Productions, Anaheim (Disneyland—2,300). Standard Oil Co. of California, La Habra (Southern Division Headquarters—1,000). First American Financial Corp., Santa Ana (Holding company—1,000). City of Anaheim, Anaheim (City government—1,000).

40th District

(Southern Orange County—part of San Diego County, Newport Beach)

Race and Ethnic Groups. Spanish heritage population 8.4 percent. Canadian stock 3.1 percent. British stock 2.5 percent.

Cities, 1970 Population. Costa Mesa 73,038, Huntington Beach (part) 57,657, Newport Beach 49,551, Oceanside (part) 35,698.

Universities, Enrollment. University of California, Irvine (Irvine—6,523).

Military Installations or Activities. Marine Corps Air Facility, Santa Ana; Marine Corps Air Station (El Toro), Santa Ana; Marine Corps Base (Camp Pendleton), Oceanside; Naval Hospital, Oceanside.

Newspapers, Circulation. Santa Ana and Los Angeles newspapers circulate in portions of the district.

Commercial Television Stations, Affiliation. District divided between Los Angeles and San Diego ADIs.

Plants and Offices, Products, Employment.

Allstate Insurance Co., Santa Ana (Insurance— 1,500). Burroughs Corp., Mission Viejo (Computers —1,600). Philco-Ford Corp., Newport Beach (Electronic communications and detection systems— 2,500). Collins Radio Co., Newport Beach (Data communication equipment—1,800). Avco Financial Services Inc., Newport Beach (Holding company— 1,000).

41st District

(San Diego—North)

Race and Ethnic Groups. Spanish heritage population 8.8 percent. Canadian stock 2.8 percent. British stock 2.3 percent.

Cities, 1970 Population. San Diego (part) 412,062, La Mesa 39,190.

Universities, Enrollment. California State University, San Diego (San Diego—32,493); United States International University, California Western Campus (San Diego—total enrollment 4,108); University of San Diego, College for Men (San Diego—1,501).

Military Installations or Activities. Fleet Anti-Submarine Warfare School, San Diego; Fleet Anti-Air Warfare Training Center, San Diego; Naval Air Station, Miramar; Naval Undersea Warfare Center, San Diego; Naval Training Center, San Diego; Naval Recruit Training Command, San Diego; Naval Electronics Laboratory, San Diego.

Newspapers, Circulation. San Diego newspapers circulate in district.

Commercial Television Stations, Affiliation. Entire district is located in San Diego ADI.

Plants and Offices, Products, Employment.

General Dynamics Corp., San Diego (Missiles— 13,500). General Dynamics Corp., San Diego (Convair Division—aircraft—5,800). Teledyne Industries Inc., San Diego (Target drones—3,810). International Harvester Co. Inc., San Diego (Solar Division —gas turbine engines—3,000). Cubic Corp., San Diego (Electronic aircraft systems, computer equipment—1,400). Royal Inns of America Inc., San Diego (Motels—3,000).

42nd District

(San Diego—South)

Race and Ethnic Groups. Blacks 11.0 percent. Spanish heritage population 19.0 percent. Canadian stock 1.6 percent. British stock 1.4 percent.

Cities, 1970 Population. San Diego (part) 246,424, Chula Vista 68,220, National City 43,400, Imperial Beach 20,382.

Military Installations or Activities. Marine Corps Recruit Depot, San Diego; Naval Air Rework Facility, San Diego; Naval Air Station (North Island), San Diego; Naval Amphibious Base (Coronado), San Diego; Naval Amphibious School (Coronado), San

Diego; Naval Air Station (Ream Field), Imperial Beach; Naval Communication Station, San Diego; Naval Hospital, San Diego; Naval Public Works Center, San Diego; Naval Station, San Diego; Naval Supply Center, San Diego.

Newspapers, Circulation. San Diego Union (Morn—168,554), San Diego Tribune (Eve—119,996).

Commercial Television Stations, Affiliation. Entire district is located in San Diego ADI. KCST-TV, San Diego (None); KFMD-TV, San Diego (CBS); KGTV, San Diego (NBC); XETV, San Diego (ABC).

Plants and Offices, Products, Employment.

Ratner Manufacturing Co., San Diego (Men's clothing—HQ—1,850). **Pacific Southwest Airlines,** San Diego (Holding company, air carrier—HQ—1,000). **National Steel & Shipbuilding Co.,** San Diego (Ship construction and repair—3,700). **Rohr Corp.,** Chula Vista (Headquarters—6,000). **Pacific Telephone & Telegraph Co.,** San Diego (Telephone Company—4,100). **Westward Realty Co.,** San Diego (Holding company—2,000). **City of San Diego,** San Diego (City government—at least 5,200).

43rd District

(San Diego—Imperial County)

Race and Ethnic Groups. Spanish heritage population 16.1 percent. Canadian stock 2.2 percent. British stock 1.8 percent.

Cities, 1970 Population. El Cajon 51,941, San Diego (part) 40,098, Escondido 36,745, Vista (part) 24,294.

Universities, Enrollment. University of California, San Diego (La Jolla—6,178).

Military Installations or Activities. Naval Air Facility, El Centro; Mt. Laguna Air Force Base, Mt. Laguna.

Newspapers, Circulation. San Diego newspapers circulate in most of district.

Commercial Television Stations, Affiliation. District divided between San Diego and Los Angeles ADIs.

Plants and Offices, Products, Employment.

Intermark Investing Inc., La Jolla (Holding company—2,500). **Singer-General Precision Inc.,** San Marcos (Computers, circuit boards—1,000).

COLORADO: FIVE HOUSE SEATS, GAIN OF ONE

Colorado Republicans, in control of the governorship and both houses of the state legislature, designed new congressional district boundaries that they hoped might result in a four-to-one advantage for their party in the state's House delegation. *(Map p. 36)*

Republicans designed in their favor the new 5th District seat, which the state gained through reapportionment after the 1970 census. It contains suburban counties east of Denver and Republican areas of El Paso County (Colorado Springs) as well as several rural eastern counties. Republicans carried the district easily in the November 1972 elections.

Former Rep. James D. (Mike) McKevitt (R) of the 1st District in Denver was strengthened when about 73,000 residents of the city's heavily Democratic west side were attached to a suburban district west of the city. However, McKevitt was defeated in an upset by Rep. Patricia Schroeder (D).

Rep. Wayne N. Aspinall (D) of the 4th District was weakened when 19 counties in the southwest quadrant of the state were removed from his district. Of his 1970 winning margin of 14,075 votes, 11,273 were provided by these counties. Aspinall picked up new territory on the eastern end of his district, about evenly divided politically. Aspinall was defeated for renomination in the primary Sept. 12, 1972, and the Republicans captured the seat in November.

The state's other Democratic representative, Frank E. Evans of the 3rd District, retained a district relatively favorable to his re-election, although changed geographically. Evans had threatened to run against Sen. Gordon Allott (R) if his chances for re-election to the House were too badly damaged by the Republican remappers. Evans won re-election easily.

Thus, Republicans emerged from the 1972 elections with a three-to-two advantage—gaining the new 5th District and the old 4th, but losing the 1st.

Glossary and Sources

For a complete explanation of all terms used in this book and a list of source material, consult the details included in the Introduction.

Several traditions were broken by the Republicans in drawing the new lines. Denver, Adams and El Paso Counties were all divided among congressional districts. And the Western Slope, containing the entire sparsely populated western half of the state, was divided almost in half, the northern part remaining in the 4th District and the southern half attached to the 3rd District. A Republican state senator cast the deciding vote in approving the division of the Western Slope, arguing that this would give the west a chance to elect two representatives instead of one.

The redistricting bill passed the state Senate April 10, 1972, by a vote of 18-15 and the state House April 20, 33-29. The bill became law on May 11 without the governor's signature.

District	Member Elected 1972	Winning Percentage	1970 Population	Percent Variance
1	Patricia Schroeder (D)	51.6	441,881	+ 0.0971
2	Donald G. Brotzman (R)	66.3	439,399	—0.4650
3	Frank E. Evans (D)	66.3	442,217	+ 0.1732
4	James T. Johnson (R)	51.0	442,024	+ 0.1295
5	William L. Armstrong (R)	62.3	441,738	+ 0.0647

1970 State Population: 2,207,259
Ideal District Population: 441,452

Election Results, 1968-1972

Vote for U.S. Representative
(Adjusted to new district boundaries)

District	1968	1970	1972
1	73,319 D (44.1%)	75,337 R (53.0%)	101,832 D (51.6%)
	72,672 R (43.7%)	62,727 D (44.2%)	93,733 R (47.5%)
2	92,869 R (59.7%)	77,233 R (60.6%)	132,562 R (66.3%)
	58,789 D (37.8%)	48,996 D (38.5%)	66,817 D (33.4%)
3	92,745 D (59.3%)	83,468 D (65.5%)	107,511 D (66.3%)
	63,712 R (40.7%)	41,141 R (32.3%)	54,556 R (33.7%)
4	76,678 D (50.0%)	62,617 D (50.5%)	94,994 R (51.0%)
	76,608 R (49.9%)	61,305 R (49.5%)	91,151 D (49.0%)
5	76,488 R (59.3%)	56,422 R (52.6%)	104,214 R (62.3%)
	52,318 D (40.6%)	49,765 D (46.4%)	60,948 D (36.5%)
State	392,779 R (50.3%)	317,696 R (49.9%)	480,059 R (52.6%)
	362,164 D (46.4%)	310,117 D (48.7%)	428,259 D (46.9%)

Voting Age Population

District	Voting Age Population	Voting Age Population 18, 19, 20	Voting Age Population 65 and Over	Median Age of Voting Age Population
1	311,132	26,468 (8.5%)	52,391 (16.8%)	42.6
2	278,168	25,536 (9.2%)	27,806 (10.0%)	38.7
3	282,445	26,655 (9.4%)	41,928 (14.8%)	41.5
4	282,392	28,779 (10.2%)	38,730 (13.7%)	40.2
5	274,958	23,818 (8.7%)	27,135 (9.9%)	39.2
State	1,429,241	131,256 (9.2%)	188,091 (13.2%)	40.4

Income and Occupation

District	Median Family Income	White Collar Workers	Blue Collar Workers	Service Workers	Farm Workers
1	$ 9,977	61.1%	23.8%	14.7%	0.4%
2	11,201	59.7	28.0	11.4	0.9
3	7,578	43.3	32.8	16.3	7.6
4	8,992	47.0	30.0	14.0	9.0
5	10,278	55.5	28.5	13.3	2.7
State	9,553	53.9	28.3	13.9	3.9

Education: School Years Completed

District	Completed 4 years of High School	Completed 4 years of College	Completed 5 years or less of School	Median School years completed
1	64.3%	17.4%	4.4%	12.5
2	70.0	19.2	2.7	12.6
3	53.9	8.7	7.4	12.1
4	62.0	12.8	4.3	12.4
5	69.4	16.3	2.4	12.5
State	63.9	14.9	4.2	12.4

Housing and Residential Patterns

District	Housing Owner Occupied Units	Housing Renter Occupied Units	Urban-Suburban-Nonmetropolitan Breakdown Urban	Suburban	Nonmetropolitan
1	49.6%	50.4%	98.9%	1.1%	—
2	67.0	33.0	16.7	83.3	—
3	69.7	30.3	27.7	17.2	55.1%
4	67.8	32.2	—	19.7	80.3
5	66.2	33.8	25.5	68.3	6.2
State	63.4	36.6	33.9	37.8	28.3

1st District

(Denver)

Race and Ethnic Groups. Blacks 10.4 percent. Spanish heritage population 13.6 percent. German stock 2.2 percent, Russian stock 1.6 percent.

Cities, 1970 Population. Part of Denver 437,108.

Universities, Enrollment. Metropolitan State College (Denver—6,853), Regis College (Denver—1,414), University of Colorado, Denver Center (Denver—6,987), University of Denver (Denver—9,119).

Military Installations or Activities. Lowry Air Force Base, Denver; Air Force Accounting and Finance Center, Denver.

Newspapers, Circulation. Denver newspapers circulate throughout district. They include: Denver Post (Ex Sat—252,867), Rocky Mountain News (Morn—208,441).

Commercial Television Stations, Affiliation. Entire district is located in Denver ADI. Denver stations include: KBTV, Denver (ABC); KMGH-TV, Denver (CBS); KOA-TV, Denver (NBC); KWGN, Denver (None).

Plants and Offices, Products, Employment.
The Gates Rubber Company, Denver (Tires, rubber industrial products—HQ—7,060). **Stearns-Roger Corp.**, Denver (Engineering, industrial controls—HQ—1,500). **United Airlines Inc.**, Denver (Airline—3,000). **Frontier Airlines Inc.**, Denver (Airline—HQ—1,500). **Denver and Rio Grande Western Railroad**, Denver (Railroad—HQ—3,400). **May Department Stores Co.**, Denver (Department store—2,400). **Montgomery Ward and Co.**, Denver (Mail order, general merchandise—2,500). **The Denver Post**, Denver (Newspaper publisher—HQ—1,500). **Public Service Company of Colorado**, Denver (Utility—HQ—1,000). **Mountain States Telephone and Telegraph Co.**, Denver (Telephone and telegraph communication—HQ—3,300). **Western Electric Co. Inc.**, Denver (Telephone equipment—at least 1,000). **National Tea Co.**, Denver (Millers Super Market Division—groceries—1,500). **Samsonite Corp.**, Denver (Luggage, furniture, toys—HQ—3,700). **Keebler Co.**, Denver (Bakery—1,000).

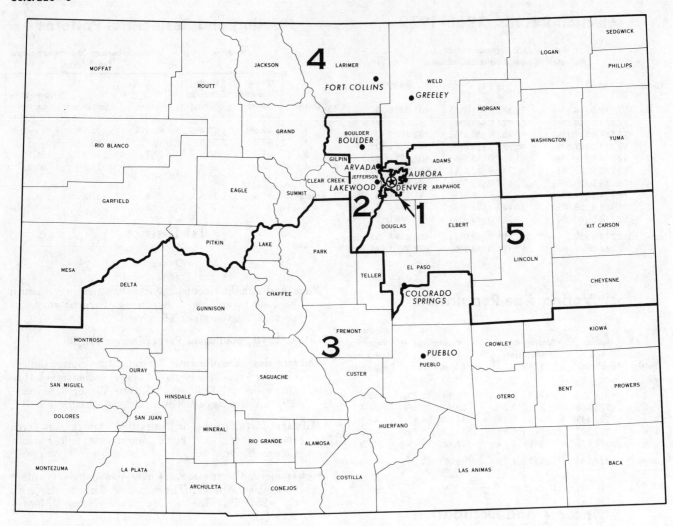

2nd District

(Western Denver Suburbs, Boulder)

Race and Ethnic Groups. Spanish heritage population 9.8 percent. German stock 1.8 percent, British stock 1.4 percent.

Cities, 1970 Population. Lakewood 92,993, part of Denver 73,385, Boulder 67,070, part of Arvada 45,395.

Universities, Enrollment. Colorado School of Mines (Golden—1,699), University of Colorado (Boulder—31,712).

AEC-Owned, Contractor-Operated Installations: Rocky Flats Plant, Rocky Flats.

Newspapers, Circulation. Denver newspapers circulate throughout district.

Commercial Television Stations, Affiliation. Entire district is located in Denver ADI.

Plants and Offices, Products, Employment.

Ball Brothers Research Corp. Boulder (Communications equipment, electronic instruments—HQ—1,230). **International Business Machines Corp.,** Boulder (Systems Manufacturing Division—electronic computing equipment—4,000). **Dow Chemical Co.,** Golden (Rocky Flats Division—defense materiel—

3,200). **Adolph Coors Co.,** Golden (Brewery—HQ—2,140). **Coors Porcelain Co.,** Golden (Laboratory and industrial products—HQ—2,150).

3rd District

(South—Pueblo)

Race and Ethnic Groups. Spanish heritage population 23.0 percent. German stock 1.7 percent, British stock 0.9 percent.

Cities, 1970 Population. Pueblo 97,565, part of Colorado Springs 24,777, Fort Carson 19,421, Security-Widefield 15,315.

Universities, Enrollment. Adams State College (Alamosa—2,936), Fort Lewis College (Durango—2,315), Southern Colorado State College (Pueblo—6,344), Western State College of Colorado (Gunnison—3,194).

Military Installations or Activities. Fort Carson, Colorado Springs; Pueblo Army Depot; Ent Air Force Base, Colorado Springs; Peterson Field, Colorado Springs.

Newspapers, Circulation. Colorado Springs newspaper circulates in portion of district.

Commercial Television Stations, Affiliation. KOAA-TV, Pueblo (NBC). Majority of district is located in Colorado Springs-Pueblo ADI. Portions of district are located in Denver, Grand Junction, Albuquerque (New Mexico), and Wichita-Hutchinson (Kansas) ADIs.

4th District

(North—Fort Collins, Greeley)

Race and Ethnic Groups. Spanish heritage population 9.8 percent. Russian stock 2.5 percent, German stock 2.0 percent.

Cities, 1970 Population. Fort Collins 43,365, Greeley 38,900, North Glenn 27,985, Grand Junction 20,167.

Universities, Enrollment. Colorado State University (Fort Collins—17,608), University of Northern Colorado (Greeley—10,756).

Newspapers, Circulation. Denver newspapers circulate in portion of district.

Commercial Television Stations, Affiliation. KREX-TV, Grand Junction (CBS, NBC, ABC). Major portion of district is located in Denver ADI. Portions of district are located in Grand Junction, Salt Lake City (Utah), Cheyenne (Wyoming), and Wichita-Hutchinson (Kansas) ADIs.

Plants and Offices, Products, Employment.
Hewlett-Packard Co., Loveland (Electronic measuring equipment—1,500). Monfort of Colorado Inc., Greeley (Cattle production, meat processing, holding company—HQ—1,600).

5th District

(Eastern and Southern Denver Suburbs Colorado Springs)

Race and Ethnic Groups. Spanish heritage population 8.6 percent. German stock 2.1 percent, British stock 1.3 percent.

Cities, 1970 Population. Part of Colorado Springs 110,339, part of Aurora 74,886, Englewood 33,697, Littleton 26,397.

Universities, Enrollment. Colorado College (Colorado Springs—1,820), United States Air Force Academy (Colorado Springs—4,201), University of Colorado-Colorado Springs Center (Colorado Springs—2,312).

Military Installations or Activities. Fitzsimons General Hospital, Denver; Rocky Mountain Arsenal, Denver.

Newspapers, Circulation. Colorado Springs Gazette Telegraph (Eve—52,048). In addition, Denver newspapers circulate in major portion of district.

Commercial Television Stations, Affiliation. KKTV, Colorado Springs (CBS); KRDO-TV, Colorado Springs (ABC). District is divided between Colorado Springs-Pueblo and Denver ADIs. In addition, small portion of district is located in Wichita-Hutchinson (Kansas) ADI.

Plants and Offices, Products, Employment.
Western Electric Co. Inc., Aurora (Telephone and telegraph apparatus—1,500). Western Electric Co. Inc., Denver (Telephone equipment—at least 1,000). Norwalk Truck Lines Inc., Littleton (Trucking—1,200). Red Top Inc., Englewood (Janitorial services—HQ—2,200).

CONNECTICUT: SIX HOUSE SEATS, NO CHANGE

On July 18, 1972, Connecticut became the last state to redistrict when a federal court imposed new congressional district lines. The court adopted a plan submitted by John M. Bailey, the Democratic state chairman. His plan differed only slightly from one approved in 1971 by the Democratic state legislature and vetoed by Republican Gov. Thomas J. Meskill. *(Map p. 38)*

What to do with the city of Bridgeport was the main point of contention. Republicans wanted it removed from the 4th District to make the district securely Republican. Democrats wanted to leave it in to give them a fighting chance of capturing the district.

The plan approved left the city in the 4th District, as the Democrats wanted, and transferred three Republican towns from the 4th District to the 5th. In other parts of the state, only slight shifts in the political balance of the districts occured. The new district lines split town lines for the first time in state history. The five towns involved are Portland, Westport, Somors, Clinton and Newtown.

District	Member Elected 1972	Winning Percentage	1970 Population	Percent Variance
1	William R. Cotter (D)	56.9	505,418	+ 0.0094
2	Robert H. Steele (R)	65.9	505,493	+ 0.0243
3	Robert N. Giaimo (D)	53.3	505,293	—0.0152
4	Stewart B. McKinney (R)	63.1	505,366	—0.0007
5	Ronald A. Sarasin (R)	51.2	505,316	—0.0106
6	Ella T. Grasso (D)	60.2	505,331	—0.0077

1970 State Population: 3,032,217
Ideal District Population: 505,370

Election Results, 1968-1972

Vote for U.S. Representative
(Adjusted to new district boundaries)

District	1968	1970	1972
1	130,634 D (61.0%)	94,644 D (48.6%)	130,701 D (56.9%)
	82,892 R (38.7%)	94,361 R (48.5%)	96,188 R (41.9%)
2	99,120 D (54.4%)	84,949 R (52.9%)	142,094 R (65.9%)
	81,865 R (45.0%)	75,744 D (47.1%)	73,400 D (34.1%)
3	112,091 D (54.1%)	97,106 D (54.4%)	121,217 D (53.3%)
	88,112 R (42.5%)	76,306 R (42.7%)	106,313 R (46.7%)
4	101,218 R (50.2%)	93,570 R (55.7%)	135,883 R (63.1%)
	98,462 D (48.8%)	72,999 D (43.5%)	79,515 D (36.9%)
5	108,607 D (53.6%)	95,964 D (52.6%)	117,578 R (51.2%)
	93,240 R (46.0%)	84,590 R (46.4%)	112,142 D (48.8%)
6	122,630 R (61.6%)	95,066 D (51.0%)	140,290 D (60.2%)
	76,364 D (38.4%)	91,177 R (48.9%)	92,783 R (39.8%)
State	625,278 D (51.8%)	531,523 D (49.7%)	690,839 R (51.1%)
	569,957 R (47.2%)	524,953 R (49.0%)	657,265 D (48.7%)

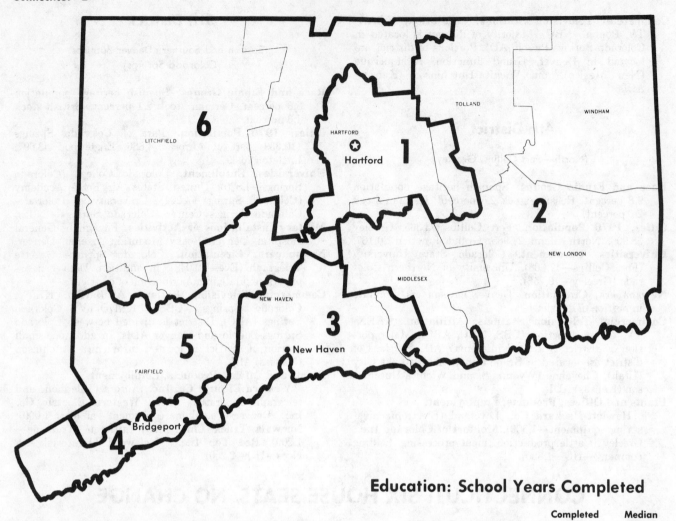

Voting Age Population

District	Voting Age Population	Voting Age Population 18, 19, 20	Voting Age Population 65 and Over	Median Age of Voting Age Population
1	343,525	23,993 (7.0%)	52,703 (15.3%)	44.4
2	330,238	28,730 (8.7%)	44,350 (13.4%)	40.8
3	341,026	24,220 (7.1%)	50,047 (14.7%)	43.8
4	341,274	22,946 (6.7%)	50,841 (14.9%)	45.1
5	326,738	20,419 (6.2%)	47,411 (14.5%)	44.4
6	325,876	20,560 (6.3%)	45,079 (13.8%)	43.3
State	2,007,938	140,716 (7.0%)	290,116 (14.4%)	43.6

Income and Occupation

District	Median Family Income	White Collar Workers	Blue Collar Workers	Service Workers	Farm Workers
1	$12,031	57.7%	30.8%	10.9%	0.6%
2	10,885	47.5	39.3	11.9	1.3
3	11,463	53.3	35.4	10.9	0.4
4	12,692	55.9	32.6	11.3	0.2
5	12,200	50.5	39.5	9.5	0.5
6	11,898	49.5	40.1	9.4	1.0
State	11,808	52.5	36.2	10.7	0.6

Education: School Years Completed

District	Completed 4 years of High School	Completed 4 years of College	Completed 5 years or less of School	Median School years completed
1	56.8%	13.6%	6.7%	12.2
2	53.7	11.7	5.1	12.1
3	56.8	13.3	5.2	12.2
4	57.2	17.2	6.3	12.3
5	56.1	13.6	6.3	12.2
6	55.6	12.3	5.7	12.2
State	56.0	13.7	5.9	12.2

Housing and Residential Patterns

	Housing		Urban-Suburban-Nonmetropolitan Breakdown		
District	Owner Occupied Units	Renter Occupied Units	Urban	Suburban	Nonmetro-politan
1	54.2%	45.8%	32.6%	65.8%	1.6%
2	65.9	34.1	14.5	36.1	49.4
3	62.3	37.7	27.2	62.3	10.5
4	56.4	43.6	68.3	31.7	—
5	68.0	32.0	42.5	38.8	18.7
6	68.7	31.3	26.4	50.6	23.0
State	62.5	37.5	35.2	47.4	17.4

1st District

(Central—Hartford)

Race and Ethnic Groups. Blacks 10.2 percent. Spanish heritage population 2.9 percent. Italian stock 6.7 percent, Canadian stock 5.6 percent, Polish stock 3.7 percent, Irish stock 2.7 percent.
Cities, 1970 Population. Hartford 158,017.
Universities, Enrollment. Trinity College (Hartford—1,995), University of Hartford (West Hartford—8,902).
Newspapers, Circulation. Hartford Courant (Morn—174,752), Hartford Times (ExSat—131,898).
Commercial Television Stations, Affiliation. Entire district is located in Hartford-New Haven ADI. Hartford stations include: WHCT-TV, Hartford (None); WHNB-TV, West Hartford (NBC); WTIC-TV, Hartford (CBS). New Haven station: WTNH-TV, New Haven (ABC).
Plants and Offices, Products, Employment.
Travelers Corp., Hartford (Insurance, holding company—HQ—7,000). Aetna Life & Casualty Co., Hartford (Insurance, holding company—HQ—23,000). Connecticut Mutual Life Insurance Co., Hartford (Insurance—HQ—2,900). Phoenix Mutual Life Insurance Co., Hartford (Insurance—HQ—1,000). Hartford Fire Insurance Co., Hartford (Insurance—HQ—2,000). Security-Connecticut Life Insurance Co., Hartford (Insurance—1,000). United Aircraft Corp., East Hartford (Aircraft, aircraft equipment—HQ—23,000). Kaman Corp., Bloomfield (Aerospace parts, electrical equipment—HQ—2,050). Combustion Engineering Inc., Windsor (Optimum Controls Division—aeronautical parts—2,500). Chandler-Evans Inc., West Hartford (Aerospace control systems, components, etc.—1,800). Pratt & Whitney Inc., West Hartford (Machine tools, gauges—HQ—1,100). Stanadyne Inc., Windsor (Fuel injection pumps—HQ—1,500). Arrow-Hart Inc., Hartford (Electrical devices, switches—HQ—2,020). Emhart Corp., Berlin (Hardware Division—builders hardware—3,000). Litton Industries Inc., Hartford (Royal Products Division—typewriters—5,600). Colt's Firearms Group, Hartford (Firearms—HQ—1,200). Fuller Brush Co., East Hartford (Household specialities—HQ—1,200). Sanitas Service Corp., Hartford (Building maintenance, holding company—6,000). May Department Stores Co., Hartford (G. Fox & Co.—department store—1,500). St. Francis Hospital Corp., Hartford (Hospital—1,320).

2nd District

(East—New London)

Race and Ethnic Groups. Canadian stock 5.7 percent, Italian stock 4.1 percent, Polish stock 3.1 percent.
Cities, 1970 Population. Norwich 41,467, Middletown 36,933, New London 31,632, Willimantic 14,414.
Universities, Enrollment. Connecticut College (New London—1,767), Eastern Connecticut State College (Willimantic—2,791), United States Coast Guard Academy (New London—1,000); University of Connecticut (Storrs—21,253); Wesleyan University (Middletown—1,881).
Military Installations or Activities. Naval Submarine Base, Groton; Naval Underseas Research and Development Center, New London (HQ in Newport, Rhode Island); Naval Submarine School, New London.
Newspapers, Circulation. Hartford newspapers circulate in portions of district.
Commercial Television Stations, Affiliation. District is divided between Hartford-New Haven, Boston (Massachusetts) and Providence (Rhode Island) ADIs.
Plants and Offices, Products, Employment.
Pervel Industries Inc., Plainfield (Plastic film—HQ—1,140). American Thread Co., Willimantic (Threads—1,500). King-Seeley Thermos Co., Taftville (Vacuum containers—1,500). King-Seely Thermos Co., Norwich (Hardware, canvas products—1,050). General Dynamics Corp., Groton (Shipbuilding—12,000). Pfizer Inc., Groton (Medicinal chemicals—2,360).

3rd District

(South—New Haven)

Race and Ethnic Groups. Blacks 8.8 percent. Italian stock 10.4 percent, Polish stock 2.5 percent.
Cities, 1970 Population. New Haven 137,739, West Haven 52,860, Milford 50,867.
Universities, Enrollment. Quinnipiac College (Hamden—2,975), Southern Connecticut State College (New Haven—12,727), University of New Haven (West Haven—5,120), Yale University (New Haven—9,245).
Newspapers, Circulation. New Haven Register (ExSat—109,545).
Commercial Television Stations, Affiliation. Entire district is located in Hartford-New Haven ADI. New Haven station: WTNH-TV, New Haven (ABC).
Plants and Offices, Products, Employment.
United Aircraft Corp., North Haven (Pratt & Whitney Division—aircraft engines—5,500). Emerson Electric Co., Milford (U.S. Electrical Motor Division—motors—1,000). Raybestos-Manhattan Inc., Stratford (Raybestos Division—automotive, industrial products—1,000). American Cyanamid Co., Wallingford (Industrial chemicals—1,170). Armstrong Rubber Co., West Haven (Eastern Division—tires, tubes—1,100). Walter Kidde & Co., New Haven (Sargent & Co. Division—locks, hardware—1,100). Warner-Lambert Co., Milford (Shick Safety Razor Co. Division—razors, shaving preparations—at least 1,000). Olin Corp., New Haven (Winchester-Western Division—sporting arms—4,830). Consolidated Foods Corp., New Haven (Gant Shirt Makers Division—men's shirts—1,400). Alliance Medical Industries, Stratford (Medical products, holding company—2,100). Southern New England Telephone Co., New Haven (Telephone company—at least 1,010).

4th District

(Southwest—Bridgeport, Stamford)

Race and Ethnic Groups. Blacks 9.9 percent. Spanish heritage population 4.8 percent. Italian stock 8.4 percent, Polish stock 2.8 percent, British stock 2.8 percent.

Cities, 1970 Population. Bridgeport 156,754, Stamford 108,997, Norwalk 79,297.

Newspapers, Circulation. New York City newspapers circulate throughout district.

Universities, Enrollment. Fairfield University (Fairfield —2,284), Sacred Heart University (Bridgeport— 2,042), University of Bridgeport (Bridgeport—8,318).

Commercial Television Stations, Affiliation. Entire district is located in New York City ADI.

Plants and Offices, Products, Employment.
United Aircraft Corp., Norwalk (Norden Division —Research & Development—3,000). **Burndy Corp.**, Norwalk (Electrical connectors, tools, accessories— HQ—1,230). **Condec Corp.**, Old Greenwich (Electrical generators—HQ—1,700). **National Distillers & Chemical Corp.**, Bridgeport (Bridgeport Brass Co. Division—brass, copper, bronze products—1,000). **White Consolidated Industries Inc.**, Bridgeport (Bullard Co. Division—machine tools, iron castings— 2,000). **American Can Co.**, Greenwich (Headquarters—1,800). **Dictaphone Corp.**, Bridgeport (Business Machines Division—office machines, recording equipment—1,100). **General Electric Co.**, Bridgeport (Electric fans, heating equipment, etc.—1,800). **Sperry Rand Corp.**, Bridgeport (Remington Electric Shaver Division—electric shavers—1,500). **Remington Arms Co. Inc.**, Bridgeport (Firearms, ammunition—HQ—2,300). **Pitney-Bowes Inc.**, Stamford (Mailing equipment—HQ—3,800). **Consolidated Foods Corp.**, Old Greenwich (Electrolux Division— vacuum cleaners—1,200). **Perkin-Elmer Corp.**, Norwalk (Optical, scientific instruments—HQ— 1,000). **Warnaco Inc.**, Bridgeport (Women's apparel, paper boxes, etc.—HQ—1,100).

5th District

(Southwest—Danbury, Meriden, Waterbury)

Race and Ethnic Groups. Blacks 3.7 percent. Italian stock 9.1 percent, Canadian stock 4.0 percent, Polish stock 3.1 percent.

Cities, 1970 Population. Waterbury 107,928, Meriden 55,905, Danbury 50,732, Shelton 27,168.

Universities, Enrollment. Western Connecticut State College (Danbury—4,372).

Commercial Television Stations, Affiliation. District is divided between New York City and Hartford-New Haven ADI.

Plants and Offices, Products, Employment.
International Silver Co., Meriden (Silverware— 4,300). **Scovill Manufacturing Co.**, Waterbury (Brass, aluminum mill products, fabricated metal products, etc.—HQ—5,000). **Anaconda American Brass Co.**, Ansonia (Copper & brass mill products —1,100). **Anaconda American Brass Co.**, Waterbury (Copper & brass mill products—HQ—1,500). **Chase Brass & Copper Co. Inc.**, Waterville (Chase Metal Works—brass, copper products—1,100). **American Chain & Cable Co. Inc.**, Waterbury (Bristol Division —industrial screws—1,500). **Insilco Corp.**, Meriden (Silverware, paint, holding company—HQ—1,100). **USM Corp.**, Ansonia (Farrel Division—Machinery, gears—1,700). **USM Corp.**, Derby (Farrel Division —special industrial machinery—1,700). **Barden Corp.**, Danbury (Precision ball bearings, etc.—HQ —1,000). **Perkin-Elmer Corp.**, Danbury (Optical instruments—1,250). **Uniroyal Inc.**, Naugatuck (Naugatuck Chemical Division—chemicals—4,500). **Uniroyal Inc.**, Naugatuck (Naugatuck Footwear Division—footwear—3,000). **B. F. Goodrich Co.**, Shelton (Sponge products—2,000). **Timex Corp.**, Middlebury (Watches, timing instruments, etc.—HQ —2,000). **Allied Stores Corp.**, Trumbull (D. M. Read Co.—department store—1,200). **Waterbury Hospital Corp.**, Waterbury (Hospital—1,000).

6th District

(Northwest—Bristol, New Britain)

Race and Ethnic Groups. Italian stock 6.5 percent, Canadian stock 5.3 percent, Polish stock 5.2 percent.

Cities, 1970 Population. New Britain 83,441, Bristol 55,487, Torrington 31,952.

Universities, Enrollment. Central Connecticut State College (New Britain—12,318).

Newspapers, Circulation. Hartford newspapers circulate in portion of district.

Commercial Television Stations, Affiliation. Nearly entire district is in Hartford-New Haven ADI. Small portion of district is located in New York City ADI.

Plants and Offices, Products, Employment.
United Aircraft Corp., Windsor Locks (Airplane propellers—5,700). **United Aircraft Corp.**, Southington (Pratt & Whitney Division—engine parts— 2,500). **Associated Spring Corp.**, Bristol (Springs, wire forms—HQ—1,700). **Textron Inc.**, New Britain (Fafnir Bearing Co.—bearings—8,800). **General Motors Corp.**, Bristol (Ball bearings—3,000). **Torrington Co.**, Torrington (Bearings, needles—HQ— 3,000). **New Britain Machine Co.**, New Britain (Machine, hand tools—HQ—1,200). **Stanley Works**, New Britain (Hardware, hand and power tools, etc. —HQ—6,000). **Torin Corp.**, Torrington (Air handling devices—HQ—1,100). **General Electric Co.**, Plainville (Electric switches—2,000). **Emhart Corp.**, New Britain (Hardware, locks, cabinets—at least 1,010). **Allstate Insurance Co.**, Farmington (Insurance—1,000).

FLORIDA: FIFTEEN HOUSE SEATS, GAIN OF THREE

Florida was the second biggest gainer in the redistribution of congressional districts after the 1970 census. Its three new seats were surpassed only by California's five. *(Maps p. 43 and 45)*

After considerable maneuvering and infighting, the state legislature finally passed a redistricting bill April 7, 1972. It was favorable to the state's nine Democratic and three Republican incumbents and divided the three new districts between the parties—one favorable to the Democrats, one favorable to the Republicans and one a tossup. Orange County (Orlando) legislators fought hard against the bill, because it divided their county three ways.

Redistricting was passed by the House, 66-34, and the Senate accepted the House bill, 30-17. Gov. Reubin Askew (D) signed the legislation April 26, 1972. The plan distributed the new districts as follows:

• One in the Miami area, the 13th, consisting of a northern portion of Dade County and a small piece of Broward County. This district is predominantly Democratic.

• One in central Florida, the 5th, including western Orange County and northern Pinellas County. Republicans hoped to capture this seat, but the Democrats came up with an unusually strong candidate and won it.

• One in the south central part of the state, the 10th, stretching from the Gulf Coast on the west to the Atlantic Coast on the east. Rated a tossup, the Republicans carried it handily in November.

District	1968	1970	1972
3	91,299 D (80.1%)	463 D (52.1%)[3]	101,441 D (82.0%)
	22,682 R (19.9%)	426 R (47.9%)[3]	22,219 R (18.0%)
4	78,401 D (62.2%)	48,860 D (61.0%)	92,451 D (55.9%)
	47,652 R (37.8%)	31,280 R (39.0%)	72,960 R (44.1%)
5	62,795 R (65.3%)	62,179 R (59.9%)	97,902 R (55.5%)
	33,366 D (34.7%)	41,561 D (40.1%)	78,468 D (44.5%)
6	88,956 R (100.0%)	92,547 R (67.5%)	156,150 R (76.0%)
		44,507 D (32.5%)	49,399 D (24.0%)
7	71,977 D (62.9%)	69,364 D (72.9%)	91,931 D (68.0%)
	42,374 R (37.1%)	25,774 R (27.1%)	43,343 R (32.0%)
8	73,421 D (58.2%)	62,035 D (58.3%)	89,068 D (57.8%)
	52,695 R (41.8%)	44,365 R (41.7%)	64,920 R (42.2%)
9	80,187 R (62.0%)	82,019 R (75.1%)	—[4]
	49,178 D (38.0%)	27,123 D (24.9%)	—[4]
10	65,392 D (50.3%)	64,745 D (55.4%)	113,461 R (62.0%)
	64,689 D (49.7%)	52,197 R (44.6%)	69,502 D (38.0%)
11	72,262 D (56.5%)	78,728 D (70.2%)	116,157 D (60.2%)
	55,659 R (43.5%)	33,385 R (29.8%)	76,739 R (39.8%)
12	78,310 R (64.2%)	65,787 R (60.2%)	110,750 R (62.8%)
	43,630 D (35.8%)	43,542 D (39.8%)	65,526 D (37.2%)
13	75,580 D (68.2%)	28,226 D (62.3%)	92,258 D (61.6%)
	35,300 R (31.8%)	17,104 R (37.7%)	57,418 R (38.4%)
14	67,966 D (71.1%)	20,000 D (72.9%)	75,131 D (67.6%)
	27,604 R (28.9%)	7,431 R (27.1%)	35,935 R (32.4%)
15	70,963 D (60.6%)	54,449 D (71.5%)	89,961 D (56.8%)
	46,043 R (39.4%)	21,692 R (28.5%)	68,320 R (43.2%)
State	1,011,779 D (57.2%)[1]	681,415 D (54.5%)[1,2]	1,011,383 D (52.4%) [2]
	757,907 R (42.8%)[1]	568,518 R (45.5%)[1]	920,117 R (47.6%) [2]

1 Includes some absentee votes omitted in the district-by-district tabulation.
2 Excludes votes for unopposed candidates not required by law to be tabulated.
3 No candidate in this district as constituted before redistricting.
4 No votes tabulated where candidates were unopposed.

District	Member Elected 1972	Winning Percentage	1970 Population	Percent Variance
1	Robert L. F. Sikes (D)	—[1]	452,562	—0.0150
2	Don Fuqua (D)	—[1]	452,633	+ 0.0006
3	Charles E. Bennett (D)	82.0%	452,841	+ 0.0466
4	Bill Chappell Jr. (D)	55.9%	452,076	—0.1223
5	William D. Gunter Jr. (D)	55.5%	452,965	+ 0.0740
6	C. W. Bill Young (R)	76.0%	452,615	—0.0033
7	Sam Gibbons (D)	68.0%	452,820	+ 0.0419
8	James A. Haley (D)	57.8%	451,776	—0.1886
9	Louis Frey Jr. (R)	—[1]	452,923	+ 0.0647
10	L. A. (Skip) Bafalis (R)	62.0%	452,848	+ 0.0481
11	Paul G. Rogers (D)	60.2%	452,170	—0.1016
12	J. Herbert Burke (R)	62.8%	453,053	+ 0.0934
13	William Lehman (D)	61.6%	452,817	+ 0.0413
14	Claude Pepper (D)	67.6%	452,663	+ 0.0072
15	Dante B. Fascell (D)	56.8%	452,681	+0.0112

1970 State Population: 6,789,443
Ideal District Population: 452,630

1 No votes tabulated where candidates were unopposed.

Election Results, 1968-1972

Vote for U.S. Representative
(Adjusted to new district boundaries)

District	1968	1970	1972
1	108,704 D (84.9%)	83,324 D (81.3%)	—[4]
	19,266 R (15.1%)	19,141 R (18.7%)	—[4]
2	82,594 D (97.8%)	5,793 D (66.2%)[3]	—[4]
	1,891 R (2.2%)[3]	2,960 R (33.8%)[3]	—[4]

Voting Age Population

District	Voting Age Population	Voting Age Population 18, 19, 20	Voting Age Population 65 and Over	Median Age of Voting Age Population
1	285,964	26,481 (9.3%)	29,326 (10.3%)	38.7
2	297,700	35,356 (11.9%)	39,087 (13.1%)	39.0
3	291,939	27,683 (9.5%)	34,526 (11.8%)	40.1
4	306,056	20,348 (6.6%)	67,962 (22.2%)	47.7
5	312,247	17,279 (5.5%)	83,856 (26.9%)	50.9
6	348,038	14,711 (4.2%)	134,123 (38.5%)	58.6
7	301,617	23,822 (7.9%)	47,356 (15.7%)	43.0
8	314,457	18,893 (6.0%)	84,232 (26.8%)	50.5
9	291,371	24,024 (8.2%)	37,102 (12.7%)	41.3
10	316,783	15,148 (4.8%)	86,657 (27.4%)	52.6
11	321,567	17,021 (5.3%)	86,368 (26.9%)	51.3
12	322,037	16,856 (5.2%)	74,607 (23.2%)	48.8
13	309,809	19,886 (6.4%)	55,095 (17.8%)	46.1
14	340,089	18,600 (5.5%)	72,473 (21.3%)	48.5
15	311,512	23,298 (7.5%)	58,462 (18.8%)	43.7
State	4,671,112	319,413 (6.8%)	991,148 (21.2%)	46.6

Income and Occupation

District	Median Family Income	White Collar Workers	Blue Collar Workers	Service Workers	Farm Workers
1	$ 7,621	48.1%	35.7%	14.6%	1.6%
2	7,071	48.3	28.2	16.2	7.3
3	8,252	49.6	34.5	15.0	0.9

District	Median Family Income	White Collar Workers	Blue Collar Workers	Service Workers	Farm Workers
4	7,719	51.0	29.6	15.3	4.1
5	6,910	43.7	34.9	14.4	7.0
6	7,657	54.9	27.9	16.7	0.5
7	8,256	49.4	36.0	12.9	1.7
8	7,341	43.1	35.3	13.7	7.9
9	10,267	59.8	26.6	12.4	1.2
10	7,323	43.3	33.2	14.5	9.0
11	8,995	49.0	30.6	16.1	4.3
12	9,717	52.8	31.2	15.3	0.7
13	9,411	49.0	34.4	16.2	0.4
14	8,203	45.4	37.4	16.8	0.4
15	9,909	59.6	24.4	13.9	2.1
State	8,261	49.8	32.0	15.0	3.2

Education: School Years Completed

District	Completed 4 years of High School	Completed 4 years of College	Completed 5 years or less of School	Median School years completed
1	52.1%	9.5%	9.9%	12.1
2	46.0	13.0	16.7	11.3
3	48.2	7.7	9.9	11.8
4	54.4	10.1	7.5	12.1
5	47.7	8.0	8.2	11.7
6	53.0	10.0	4.8	12.1
7	50.3	8.9	8.7	12.0
8	50.6	10.0	8.2	12.0
9	66.0	14.2	4.3	12.5
10	52.1	9.9	7.3	12.1
11	55.2	11.3	7.3	12.2
12	56.1	9.9	5.4	12.2
13	50.8	7.9	7.6	12.0
14	46.6	9.6	11.2	11.4
15	59.1	14.5	8.4	12.3
State	52.6	10.3	8.2	12.1

Housing and Residential Patterns

	Housing		Urban-Suburban-Nonmetropolitan Breakdown		
District	Owner Occupied Units	Renter Occupied Units	Urban	Suburban	Nonmetropolitan
1	69.2%	30.8%	13.2%	40.5%	46.3%
2	66.7	33.3	30.1	15.8	54.1
3	66.6	33.4	95.4	0.0	4.6
4	74.3	25.7	21.4	2.3	76.3
5	76.9	23.1	6.2	51.8	41.9
6	76.4	23.6	47.8	52.2	0.0
7	72.8	27.2	61.3	38.7	0.0
8	74.5	25.5	0.0	8.3	91.7
9	68.3	31.7	15.6	33.6	50.8
10	75.3	24.7	0.0	6.1	93.9
11	69.8	30.2	12.7	87.3	0.0
12	71.6	28.4	54.1	45.9	0.0
13	69.1	30.9	8.5	91.5	0.0
14	40.5	59.5	58.0	42.0	0.0
15	55.6	44.4	7.8	80.6	11.6
State	68.6	31.4	28.8	39.8	31.4

1st District

(Northwest—Pensacola, Panama City)

Race and Ethnic Groups. Blacks 14.4 percent. British stock 0.8 percent, German stock 0.7 percent.

Cities, 1970 Population. Pensacola 59,573, Panama City 32,126, West Pensacola 20,834, Fort Walton Beach 19,995.

Universities, Enrollment. University of West Florida (Pensacola—3,843).

Military Installations or Activities. Naval Air Station, Pensacola; Naval Air Rework Facility, Pensacola; Naval Air Station, Saufley Field, Pensacola; Naval Air Station, Whiting Field, Milton; Naval Aerospace Medical Center, Pensacola; Naval Communications Training Center, Pensacola; Naval Air Station, Ellyson Field, Pensacola; Naval Coastal Systems Laboratory, Panama City; Naval Public Work Center, Pensacola; Eglin AF Auxiliary Field 2, Niceville; Eglin AF Auxiliary Field 3, Crestview; Eglin AF Auxiliary Field 9, Fort Walton Beach; Eglin Air Force Base, Valparaiso; Tyndall Air Force Base, Springfield.

Newspapers, Circulation. Pensacola Journal (MxSat—64,494).

Commercial Television Stations, Affiliation. WEAR-TV, Pensacola (ABC); WJHG-TV, Panama City (NBC primary, ABC). Most of district is divided between Mobile (Alabama)-Pensacola and Panama City ADIs. A small portion of district is located in Dothan (Alabama) ADI.

Plants and Offices, Products, Employment.
International Paper Co., Panama City (Paper products—1,030). St. Regis Paper Co., Cantonment (Kraft Divison—paper, fiber, veneer—1,000). Monsanto Co., Pensacola (Chemstrand Co.—nylon yarns—5,500). Vitro Corp. of America, Fort Walton Beach (Electronic equipment—1,500).

2nd District

(North—Tallahassee, Gainesville)

Race and Ethnic Groups. Blacks 28.0 percent. Canadian stock 0.5 percent, German stock 0.5 percent.

Cities, 1970 Population. Tallahassee 71,921, Gainesville 64,498, Lake City 10,573.

Universities, Enrollment. Florida Agricultural and Mechanical University (Tallahassee—4,944), Florida State University (Tallahassee—18,367), University of Florida (Gainesville 23,672).

Commercial Television Stations, Affiliation. WCJB, Gainesville (NBC); WCTV, Tallahassee (CBS, ABC; offices also in Thomasville, Georgia). Most of district is divided between Tallahassee, Gainesville and Jacksonville ADIs. In addition, small portions of district are located in Panama City, Orlando-Daytona Beach and Dothan (Alabama) ADIs.

3rd District

(Northeast—Jacksonville)

Race and Ethnic Groups. Blacks 26.0 percent. British stock 0.7 percent, Canadian stock 0.6 percent.

Cities, 1970 Population. Part of Jacksonville 432,204.

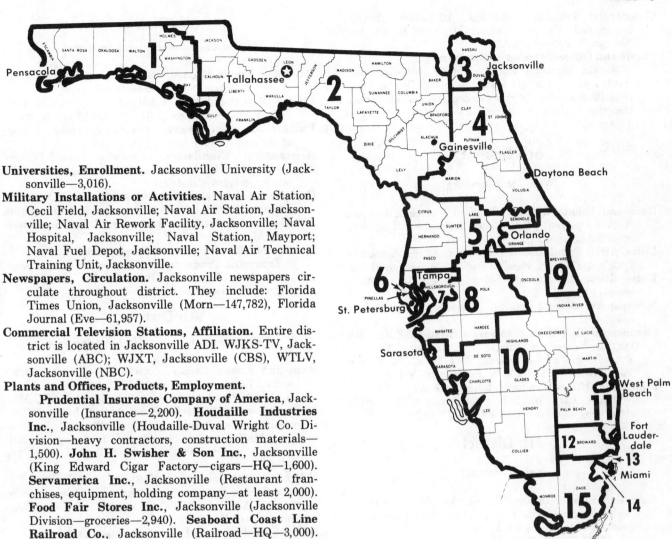

Universities, Enrollment. Jacksonville University (Jacksonville—3,016).

Military Installations or Activities. Naval Air Station, Cecil Field, Jacksonville; Naval Air Station, Jacksonville; Naval Air Rework Facility, Jacksonville; Naval Hospital, Jacksonville; Naval Station, Mayport; Naval Fuel Depot, Jacksonville; Naval Air Technical Training Unit, Jacksonville.

Newspapers, Circulation. Jacksonville newspapers circulate throughout district. They include: Florida Times Union, Jacksonville (Morn—147,782), Florida Journal (Eve—61,957).

Commercial Television Stations, Affiliation. Entire district is located in Jacksonville ADI. WJKS-TV, Jacksonville (ABC); WJXT, Jacksonville (CBS), WTLV, Jacksonville (NBC).

Plants and Offices, Products, Employment.
    Prudential Insurance Company of America, Jacksonville (Insurance—2,200). **Houdaille Industries Inc.**, Jacksonville (Houdaille-Duval Wright Co. Division—heavy contractors, construction materials—1,500). **John H. Swisher & Son Inc.**, Jacksonville (King Edward Cigar Factory—cigars—HQ—1,600). **Servamerica Inc.**, Jacksonville (Restaurant franchises, equipment, holding company—at least 2,000). **Food Fair Stores Inc.**, Jacksonville (Jacksonville Division—groceries—2,940). **Seaboard Coast Line Railroad Co.**, Jacksonville (Railroad—HQ—3,000). **Florida Publishing Co.**, Jacksonville (Newspaper publishing—1,000). **City of Jacksonville**, Jacksonville (City government—6,000). **City Coach Lines Inc.**, Jacksonville (Transit company, holding company—1,250).

4th District

(Northeast—Daytona Beach)

Race and Ethnic Groups. Blacks 15.4 percent. British stock 1.7 percent, German stock 1.7 percent.

Cities, 1970 Population. Part of Jacksonville 96,834, Daytona Beach 45,301, Ocala 22,570, Ormond Beach 14,055.

Universities, Enrollment. Bethune-Cookman College (Daytona Beach—1,219), Embry-Riddle Aeronautical University (Daytona Beach—1,755), Stetson University (DeLand—3,034).

Military Installations or Activities. Jacksonville Air Force Station.

Newspapers, Circulation. Jacksonville and Orlando newspapers circulate in portions of district.

Commercial Television Stations, Affiliation. WESH-TV, Daytona Beach (NBC). District is divided between Jacksonville and Orlando-Daytona Beach ADIs.

Plants and Offices, Products, Employment.
    Hudson Pulp and Paper Corp., Palatka (Paper—2,500). **General Electric Co.**, Daytona Beach (Electronic components—1,600).

5th District

(West Central—Parts of Clearwater and Orlando)

Race and Ethnic Groups. Blacks 16.0 percent. German stock 2.2 percent, British stock 1.8 percent.

Cities, 1970 Population. Part of Orlando 28,286, part of Clearwater 21,363, part of Dunedin 17,740, Pine Hills 13,892.

Universities, Enrollment. Saint Leo College (St. Leo—1,153).

Newspapers, Circulation. Orlando and St. Petersburg newspapers circulate in portions of district.

Commercial Television Stations, Affiliation. District is divided between Orlando-Daytona Beach and Tampa-St. Petersburg ADIs.

Plants and Offices, Products, Employment.

Martin Marietta Corp., Orlando (Missiles, electronic communciations systems—5,500). **Buena Vista Distribution Co.**, Winter Garden (Buena Vista Construction Division—general contractor—at least 1,000).

6th District

(West—St. Petersburg)

Race and Ethnic Groups. Blacks 7.7 percent. German stock 4.1 percent, British stock 3.7 percent, Canadian stock 3.5 percent.

Cities, 1970 Population. St. Petersburg 216,136, part of Clearwater 30,286, Pinellas Park 22,242, Largo 21,963.

Universities, Enrollment. Eckerd College (St. Petersburg—1,112).

Newspapers, Circulation. St. Petersburg Times (Morn—186,544).

Commercial Television Stations, Affiliation. Entire district is located in Tampa-St. Petersburg ADI. St. Petersburg stations include: WLCY-TV, St. Petersburg (ABC); WTOG-TV, St. Petersburg (None).

Plants and Offices, Products, Employment.

Webbs City Inc., St. Petersburg (Department store, drug store, supermarket—HQ—1,180).

7th District

(West—Tampa)

Race and Ethnic Groups. Blacks 13.4 percent. Spanish heritage population 11.6 percent. Italian stock 1.8 percent, German stock 1.3 percent.

Cities, 1970 Population. Tampa 277,736, Sweetwater Creek 19,556, Brandon 12,830, University 10,009.

Universities, Enrollment. University of South Florida (Tampa—17,428), University of Tampa (Tampa—2,449).

Military Installations or Activities. MacDill Air Force Base, Tampa.

Newspapers, Circulation. Tampa Tribune (Morn—171,110).

Commercial Television Stations, Affiliation. Entire district is located in Tampa-St. Petersburg ADI. Tampa stations include: WFLA-TV, Tampa (NBC); WTVT, Tampa (CBS).

Plants and Offices, Products, Employment

Honeywell Inc., Tampa (Electronic components—1,600). **American Can. Co.**, Tampa (Metal cans—1,000). **Cities Service Co.**, Gibsonton (Tampa Agruchemical Operations—fertilizer—1,100). **Havatampa Cigar Corp.**, Tampa (Cigars—1,000). **Polymer International Corp.**, Tampa (Interpak Division—plastic packaging material, bags, twine—1,020). **Seaboard Coast Line Railroad Co.**, Tampa (Railroad—1,000). **Winn-Dixie Stores Inc.**, Tampa (Kwik Chek Supermarkets—groceries—1,000). **General Telephone Co. of Florida**, Tampa (Telephone company—HQ—3,000).

8th District

(West Central—Lakeland, Sarasota)

Race and Ethnic Groups. Blacks 13.9 percent. German stock 1.7 percent, Canadian stock 1.5 percent.

Cities, 1970 Population. Lakeland 41,552, part of Sarasota 38,933, Bradenton 21,041, Winter Haven 16,137.

Universities, Enrollment. Florida Southern College (Lakeland—1,480).

Newspapers, Circulation. Sarasota Herald-Tribune (Morn—52,841). In addition, Tampa papers circulate in portions of district.

Commercial Television Stations, Affiliation. WXLT-TV, Sarasota (ABC). (Sarasota does not form a separate ADI; entire district is located in Tampa-St. Petersburg ADI.)

Plants and Offices, Products, Employment.

Tropicana Products Inc., Bradenton (Citrus products—HQ—1,700). **Continental Oil Co.**, Pierce (Agrico Chemical Co. Division—fertilizer—1,100).

9th District

(East Central—Part of Orlando, Melbourne)

Race and Ethnic Groups. Blacks 8.4 percent. British stock 1.7 percent, German stock 1.6 percent.

Cities, 1970 Population. Part of Orlando 70,667, Melbourne 40,294, Titusville 30,501, Merritt Island 29,220.

Universities, Enrollment. Florida Institute of Technology (Melbourne—2,119), Florida Technological University (Orlando—4,906), Rollins College (Winter Park—3,547).

Military Installations or Activities. Naval Training Device Center, Orlando; Naval Training Center, Orlando; McCoy Air Force Base, Orlando; Patrick Air Force Base, Cocoa Beach.

NASA Facilities. John F. Kennedy Space Center.

Newspapers, Circulation. Today, Cocoa (Morn—52,943), Orlando Sentinel (Morn—142,736).

Commercial Television Stations, Affiliation. Entire district is located in Orlando-Daytona Beach ADI. Orlando stations include: WDBO-TV, Orlando (CBS); WFTV, Orlando (ABC).

Plants and Offices, Products, Employment.

Boeing Co., Cape Kennedy (Research and development—3,250). **North American Rockwell Corp.**, Cocoa Beach (Space Division—space engineering and equipment—1,020). **General Electric Co.**, Cape Kennedy (Apollo Systems Dept.—engineering, consulting—1,500). **Federal Electric Corp.**, Cocoa Beach (Electrical contracting work—1,360). **Bendix Corp.**, Orlando (Electrical Component Division—electrical components—at least 2,000). **Bendix Corp.**, Titusville (Signal and detection equipment—1,800). **Radiation Inc.**, Melbourne (Electronic data and communications systems, etc.—HQ—4,200).

10th District

(South Central—Fort Pierce, Fort Myers)

Race and Ethnic Groups. Blacks 13.8 percent. German stock 2.3 percent, British stock 2.0 percent.

Cities, 1970 Population. Fort Pierce 29,699, Fort Myers 27,324, Naples 12,030, Vero Beach 11,896.

Newspapers, Circulation. Palm Beach papers circulate in portion of district.

Commercial Television Stations, Affiliation. Most of district is divided between Fort Myers, West Palm Beach, and Tampa-St. Petersburg ADIs. In addition, small portion of district is located in Orlando-Daytona Beach ADI. Fort Myers stations include: WBBH-TV, Fort Myers (NBC); WINK-TV, Fort Myers (CBS). Fort Pierce station: WTVX, Fort Pierce (CBS). (Fort Pierce does not form a separate ADI; area is included in West Palm Beach ADI.)

Plants and Offices, Products, Employment.

    United States Sugar Corp., Clewiston (Raw sugar, cattle ranch—at least 1,180). **Piper Aircraft Corp.**, Vero Beach (Aircraft development—1,100).

11th District

(Southeast—West Palm Beach, Pompano Beach)

Race and Ethnic Groups. Blacks 17.5 percent. Spanish heritage population 3.4 percent. German stock 2.8 percent, British stock 2.8 percent, Canadian stock 2.7 percent.

Cities, 1970 Population. Part of West Palm Beach 57,482 (includes all but 27 residents of West Palm Beach), Pompano Beach 37,830, Boca Raton 28,632, Lake Worth 23,795.

Universities, Enrollment. Florida Atlantic University (Boca Raton—5,732).

Newspapers, Circulation. Palm Beach Post (MxSat—64,432). In addition, Miami papers circulate in district.

Commercial Television Stations, Affiliation. Entire district is located in West Palm Beach ADI. West Palm Beach stations include: WEAT-TV, West Palm Beach (ABC); WPTV, Palm Beach (NBC).

Plants and Offices, Products, Employment.

    International Business Machines Corp., Boca Raton (Data processing equipment—1,600). **United Aircraft Corp.**, West Palm Beach (Pratt and Whitney Aircraft Division—aircraft engines—5,300). **RCA Corp.**, West Palm Beach (Electronic Components—2,800). **Southern Bell Telephone and Telegraph Co.**, West Palm Beach (Telephone service—1,010).

12th District

(Southeast—Fort Lauderdale, Hollywood)

Race and Ethnic Groups. Blacks 11.7 percent. Spanish heritage population 2.7 percent. Italian stock 3.7 percent, German stock 3.0 percent, Canadian stock 3.0 percent, British stock 2.5 percent.

Cities, 1970 Population. Part of Fort Lauderdale 139,134 (includes all but 26 residents of Fort Lauderdale), part of Hollywood 105,890 (includes all but 829 residents of Hollywood), part of Miramar 23,859 (includes all but 328 residents of Miramar), part of Plantation 23,041 (includes all but 445 residents of Plantation).

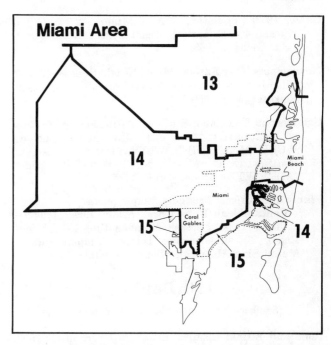

Newspapers, Circulation. Fort Lauderdale News (ExSat—103,645). In addition, Miami newspapers circulate in district.

Commercial Television Stations, Affiliation. WKID, Dania (None—national and Dade Co. sales office in Miami). Entire district is located in Miami ADI.

13th District

(Northern Miami and Suburbs)

Race and Ethnic Groups. Blacks 18.2 percent. Spanish heritage population 13.3 percent. Russian stock 4.0 percent, Italian stock 2.7 percent.

Cities, 1970 Population. Part of Hialeah 56,155, part of Miami 37,746, part of North Miami 29,782, part of North Miami Beach 29,769 (includes all but 916 residents of North Miami Beach).

Universities, Enrollment. Barry College (Miami—1,248).

Newspapers, Circulation. Miami newspapers circulate throughout district.

Commercial Television Stations, Affiliation. Entire district is located in Miami ADI.

Plants and Offices, Products, Employment.

    Keller Industries Inc., Miami (Aluminum windows—HQ—1,000). **Ecological Science Corp.**, Miami (Water, heating, air conditioning equipment—HQ—2,030). **GAC Properties Inc.**, Miami (Land developer—HQ—1,200). **Suave Shoe Corp.**, Hialeah (Shoes—1,900). **Lums Inc.**, Miami (Holding company, food franchises—3,000). **Food Fair Stores Inc.**, Miami (General offices, groceries—7,000).

14th District

(Central Miami and Suburbs)

Race and Ethnic Groups. Blacks 15.2 percent. Spanish heritage population 41.1 percent. Russian stock 4.5 percent, Polish stock 1.7 percent.

Cities, 1970 Population. Part of Miami 262,705, part of Hialeah 46,028, part of Miami Beach 41,880, part of Coral Gables 27,668.

Newspapers, Circulation. Miami Herald (Morn—426,889), Miami News (ExSat—81,893), Miami Beach Sun-Reporter (Morn—50,000).

Commercial Television Stations, Affiliation. Entire district is located in Miami ADI. Miami stations include: WCKT, Miami (NBC); WLTV, Miami (Spanish station); WCIX-TV, Miami (None); WPLG-TV, Miami (ABC); WTVJ, Miami (CBS).

Plants and Offices, Products, Employment.
Fontainbleau Hotel Corp., Miami Beach (Hotel—at least 1,000). **Storer Broadcasting Co.,** Miami Radio, TV broadcasting, holding company—1,200). **Mount Sinai Hospital,** Miami (Hospital—2,000).

15th District

(Southern Miami and Suburbs, Monroe County)

Race and Ethnic Groups. Blacks 10.7 percent. Spanish heritage population 13.7 percent. Russian stock 4.7 percent, Polish stock 2.1 percent.

Cities, 1970 Population. Part of Miami Beach 45,144, Kendall 35,389, part of Miami 35,151, Key West 27,295.

Universities, Enrollment. University of Miami 15,754.

Military Installations or Activities. Fleet Sonar School, Key West; Naval Security Group Activities, Homestead; Naval Air Station, Key West; Naval Hospital, Key West; Naval Station, Key West; Homestead Air Force Base, Homestead; Richmond Air Force Station, Perrine.

Newspapers, Circulation. Miami newspapers circulate throughout district.

Commercial Television Stations, Affiliation. Entire district is located in Miami ADI.

Plants and Offices, Products, Employment.
AO Industries, Coral Gables (Rubber and metal products, boat manufacturing and repair—1,300). **Ryder System Inc.,** Miami (Transportation and distribution services, holding company—HQ—5,950). **Winn-Dixie Stores Inc.,** Miami (Groceries—3,000). **Miami Herald Publishing Co. Inc.,** Miami (Newspaper publishing—HQ—1,500). **Dade County Metropolitan Govt.,** Miami (County government—25,000).

GEORGIA: 10 HOUSE SEATS, NO CHANGE

The Georgia legislature passed a congressional redistricting bill in October 1971 after a bitter conflict over the composition of districts in the Atlanta area. Blacks had wanted a district likely to elect a black but were disappointed in their hopes. Consequently, attorneys for the NAACP filed suit against the plan in federal district court. *(Map p. 48)*

The legislature's plan provided for a newly drawn 5th District, covering the northern two-thirds of Fulton County and including most of Atlanta but containing only a 35 to 37 percent black population, according to black spokesmen. Previously, the 5th District contained a population 39.5 percent black. Theoretically Fulton County has enough blacks to create a congressional district that would be 50 percent black.

But instead of being consolidated in an Atlanta-Fulton County district, large numbers of blacks—about 60,000—were placed in the neighboring 6th District to the south.

This led directly to the blacks' suit in federal court, charging an attempt to "undermine and destroy" black voting strength in Atlanta.

Meanwhile, the Justice Department was also reviewing the plan under provisions of the Voting Rights Act of 1965. Before the courts could act, on Feb. 17, 1972, the department announced its own disapproval of the redistricting plan, because of apparent racial gerrymandering in the 5th and 6th Districts.

Subsequently, the Georgia legislature redrew the boundary between the two districts to increase the black population of the 5th District to 44.2 percent. Andrew Young (D), a black, was elected to the House from the district in November 1972.

A second major controversy surrounding the original passage of the redistricting bill in October 1971 involved the effort of legislators from central Georgia to create a new district in that part of the state. They were only partially successful. Instead, the state legislature drew an 8th District that snakes its way from the Florida line northward to within 60 miles of Rockdale County, in the Atlanta metropolitan area of north Georgia.

The original redistricting plan was passed by the state House on October 8, 1971, by a vote of 120 to 64. The state Senate had acted on Sept. 30 by a vote of 36 to 11. Gov. Jimmy Carter (D) signed the legislation Oct. 14.

The revision of boundaries between the 5th and 6th Districts was acted on by the state House Feb. 29, 1972, by a vote of 156 to 28. The Senate concurred 43 to 4 on March 8 and Gov. Carter signed the new legislation March 16.

District	Member Elected 1972	Winning Percentage	1970 Population	Percent Variance
1	Ronald B. (Bo) Ginn (D)	100.0	456,354	—0.567
2	Dawson Mathis (D)	100.0	460,450	+ 0.325
3	Jack Brinkley (D)	100.0	460,749	+ 0.390
4	Ben B. Blackburn (R)	75.9	459,335	+ 0.087
5	Andrew Young (D)	52.8	460,589	+ 0.355
6	John J. Flynt Jr. (D)	100.0	455,810	—0.686
7	John W. Davis (D)	58.3	460,095	+ 0.248
8	W. S. (Bill) Stuckey (D)	62.4	458,097	—0.188
9	Phil M. Landrum (D)	100.0	457,247	—0.373
10	Robert G. Stephens Jr. (D)	100.0	460,829	+ 0.408

1970 State Population: 4,589,575
Ideal District Population: 458,958

Election Results, 1968-1972

Vote for U.S. Representative
(Adjusted to new district boundaries)

District	1968	1970	1972
1	78,317 D (71.5%)	70,026 D (100.0%)	55,256 D (100.0%)
	31,155 R (28.5%)	—	—
2	88,229 D (100.0%)	72,223 D (93.1%)	65,997 D (100.0%)
	—	5,376 R (6.9%)	—
3	69,849 D (100.0%)	66,568 D (100.0%)	71,756 D (100.0%)
4	68,275 R (61.2%)	75,745 R (67.8%)	103,155 R (75.9%)
	43,302 D (38.8%)	36,034 D (32.2%)	32,731 D (24.1%)
5	68,746 D (51.4%)	63,349 R (51.3%)	72,289 D (52.8%)
	64,916 R (48.6%)	60,114 D (48.7%)	64,495 R (47.2%)
6	73,357 D (74.4%)	66,169 D (70.6%)	70,586 D (100.0%)
	24,820 R (25.6%)	27,501 R (29.4%)1	
7	73,919 D (100.0%)	63,441 D (71.8%)	59,031 D (58.3%)
		24,957 R (28.2%)	42,265 R (41.7%)
8	83,595 D (94.4%)1	76,613 D (100.0%)	71,283 D (62.4%)
	4,963 R (5.6%)1	—	42,986 R (37.6%)
9	90,004 D (100.0%)	68,605 D (71.2%)	71,801 D (100.0%)
	—	27,684 R (28.8%)	—
10	80,840 D (100.0%)	73,720 D (98.6%)	68,096 D (100.0%)
	—	1,021 R (1.4%)1	—
State	750,538 D (79.4%)	653,513 D (74.3%)	638,826 D (71.6%)
	194,129 R (20.6%)	225,633 R (25.7%)	252,901 R (28.4%)

1 No candidate in this district as constituted before redistricting.

Voting Age Population

District	Voting Age Population	Voting Age Population 18, 19, 20	Voting Age Population 65 and Over	Median Age of Voting Age Population
1	288,360	25,819 (9.0%)	38,691 (13.4%)	41.6
2	283,487	25,371 (8.9%)	42,285 (14.9%)	42.5
3	292,612	29,696 (10.1%)	33,937 (11.6%)	38.9
4	293,108	22,310 (7.6%)	25,110 (8.6%)	38.3
5	313,414	28,358 (9.0%)	42,714 (13.6%)	40.8
6	287,876	22,924 (8.0%)	32,571 (11.3%)	39.5
7	294,345	20,415 (6.9%)	32,416 (11.0%)	40.1
8	291,540	23,921 (8.2%)	44,235 (15.1%)	43.9
9	294,562	23,009 (7.8%)	38,858 (13.1%)	41.0
10	299,272	35,905 (12.0%)	37,458 (12.5%)	38.8
State	2,938,518	257,709 (8.8%)	368,221 (12.5%)	40.5

Income and Population

District	Median Family Income	White Collar Workers	Blue Collar Workers	Service Workers	Farm Workers
1	$ 7,102	39.2%	40.3%	15.2%	5.3%
2	6,238	35.5	38.3	14.3	11.9
3	7,550	41.1	40.2	40.4	3.3
4	11,750	65.5	25.4	8.9	0.2
5	9,050	37.3	28.4	33.9	0.4
6	9,284	43.7	44.3	10.6	1.4
7	9,223	42.7	46.7	9.4	1.1
8	6,836	37.1	41.5	15.0	6.4
9	7,657	33.7	53.4	8.9	3.9
10	7,307	38.7	43.5	14.7	3.1
State	8,165	43.7	40.0	12.8	3.5

Education: School Years Completed

District	Completed 4 years of High School	Completed 4 years of College	Completed 5 years or less of School	Median School years completed
1	38.6%	7.5%	16.9%	10.6
2	33.4	6.5	21.4	9.9
3	41.8	8.4	16.5	10.9
4	60.5	17.7	6.0	12.4
5	51.2	16.5	11.7	12.1
6	39.9	6.8	12.2	10.9
7	38.3	6.8	13.1	10.6
8	32.6	6.4	20.1	9.8
9	30.6	5.2	16.5	9.6
10	38.5	9.9	17.2	10.5
State	40.6	9.2	15.1	10.8

Housing and Residential Patterns

District	Housing Owner Occupied Units	Housing Renter Occupied Units	Urban	Suburban	Nonmetropolitan
1	59.7%	40.3%	26.0%	15.2%	58.8%
2	59.1	40.9	15.8	3.7	80.5
3	57.9	42.1	33.5	22.1	44.4
4	64.0	36.0	16.0	80.0	4.0
5	41.8	58.2	87.2	12.8	—
6	65.7	34.3	5.0	43.1	51.9
7	69.8	30.2	—	53.8	46.2
8	62.2	37.8	26.7	4.6	68.7
9	72.1	27.9	—	15.8	84.2
10	60.4	39.6	13.0	22.2	64.8
State	61.1	38.9	22.3	27.4	50.3

1st District

(Southeast—Savannah, Brunswick)

Race and Ethnic Groups. Blacks 33.6 percent.

Cities, 1970 Population. Savannah 118,366, Brunswick 19,589, Statesboro 14,619.

Universities, Enrollment. Armstrong State College (Savannah—2,712), Georgia Southern College (Statesboro—6,156), Savannah State College (Savannah—2,444).

Military Installations or Activities. Hunter Army Airfield, Savannah; Fort Stewart, Savannah; Naval Air Station, Glynco; Naval Air Technical Training Center, Glynco.

Newspapers, Circulation. Savannah Press (Eve—56,504).

Commercial Television Stations, Affiliation. WJCL-TV, Savannah (ABC); WSAV-TV, Savannah (NBC); WTOC-TV, Savannah (CBS). Most of district is divided between Savannah and Augusta ADIs. Part of district is in Jacksonville (Fla.) ADI.

Plants and Offices, Products, Employment.

American Argo Corp., Swainsboro (Knitted shirts, underwear—1,110). Seaboard Coastline Railroad, Savannah (Railroad—1,000). Hercules Inc., Brunswick (Powder division—explosives—1,000). Grum-

(Continued on p. 49)

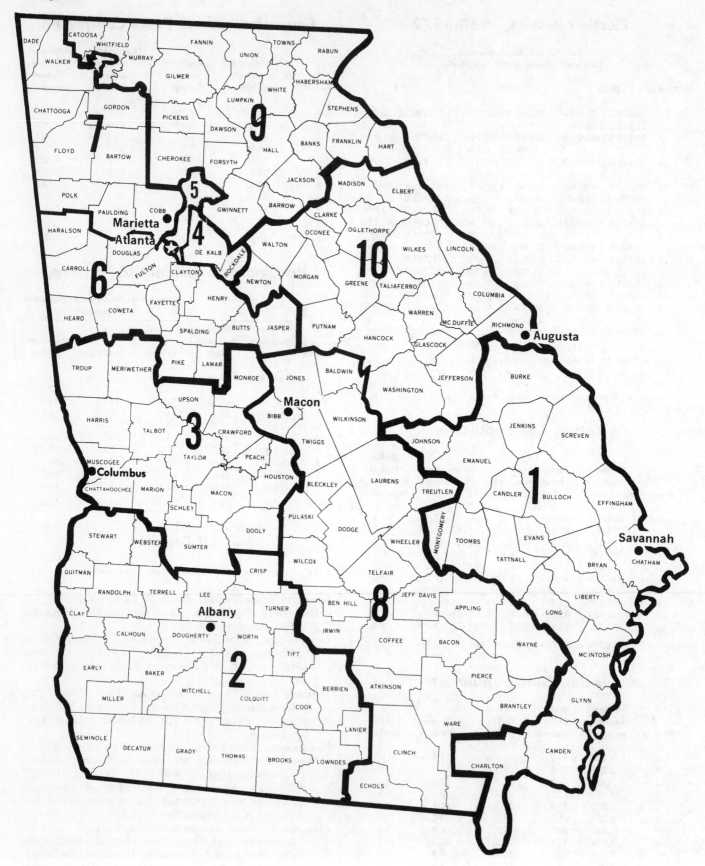

(Continued from p. 47)
man Aerospace Corp., Savannah (Aircraft—1,000). **Brunswick Pulp & Paper Co.**, Brunswick (Paper—1,100). **Union Camp Corp.**, Savannah (Paper bags, corrugated boxes—8,000). **Gilman Paper Co.**, St. Marys (Paper bags, linings—1,750).

2nd District

(Southwest—Albany)

Race and Ethnic Groups. Blacks 36.8 percent.

Cities, 1970 Population. Albany 72,635, Valdosta 32,507, Thomasville 18,158, Moultrie 14,296.

Universities, Enrollment. Albany State College (Albany—1,926), Valdosta State College (Valdosta—3,232).

Military Installations or Activities. Marine Corps Supply Center, Albany; Naval Air Station, Albany; Moody Air Force Base, Valdosta.

Commercial Television Stations, Affiliation. WALB-TV, Albany (NBC primary, ABC). District is divided between Albany, Columbus, Tallahassee (Fla.), and Dothan (Ala.) ADIs.

Plants and Offices, Products, Employment.
Great Northern Nekoosa Corp., Cedar Springs (Paper mill—1,000). **Coats & Clark Inc.**, Albany (Wool yarn, thread—1,470).

3rd District

(West Central—Columbus)

Race and Ethnic Groups. Blacks 32.0 percent.

Cities, 1970 Population. Columbus 154,098, Warner Robins 33,430, Fort Benning 27,302, La Grange 23,301.

Universities, Enrollment. Columbus College (Columbus—3,814), Fort Valley State College (Fort Valley—2,373). Georgia Southwestern College (Americus—2,383).

Military Installations or Activities. Fort Benning.

Commercial Television Stations, Affiliation. WRBL-TV, Columbus (CBS), WTVM-TV, Columbus (ABC), WYEA-TV, Columbus (NBC). Most of district is located in Columbus ADI. Parts of district are located in Macon and Atlanta ADIs.

Plants and Offices, Products, Employment.
Toms Foods Ltd., Columbus (Potato chips, candy—HQ—1,000). **B. F. Goodrich Co.**, Thomaston (Textile products division—tire cord—2,000). **Deering Milliken Inc.**, La Grange (Textiles—2,500). **West Point-Pepperell Inc.**, Columbus (Textiles—1,000). **Fieldcrest Mills Inc.**, Columbus (Towels and other dry goods—1,470). **Bibb Manufacturing Co. Inc.**, Columbus (Yarn—1,450). **Bibb Manufacturing Co. Inc.**, Columbus (Cotton fabric—2,200). **Swift Textiles Inc.**, Columbus (Cotton, synthetic goods—HQ—1,350).

4th District

(Atlanta Suburbs)

Race and Ethnic Groups. Blacks 14.5 percent.

Cities, 1970 population. Part of Atlanta 73,553, Decatur 21,903.

Universities, Enrollment. Emory University (Atlanta—5,897).

Military Installations or Activities. Atlanta Army Depot.

Newspapers, Circulation. Atlanta papers circulate throughout district.

Commercial Television Stations, Affiliation. Entire district is located in Atlanta ADI.

Plants and Offices, Products, Employment.
General Motors Corp., Atlanta (Assembly division—automobiles—2,300). **General Motors Corp.**, Doraville (Assembly division—automobiles—3,500).

5th District

(Atlanta)

Race and Ethnic Groups. Blacks 44.2 percent.

Cities, 1970 Population. Part of Atlanta 401,635.

Universities, Enrollment. Atlanta University (Atlanta—1,048), Clark College (Atlanta—1,182), Georgia Institute of Technology (Atlanta—8,125), Georgia State University (Atlanta—16,044), Morehouse College (Atlanta—1,227), Morris Brown College (Atlanta—1,527), Oglethorpe University (Atlanta—1,051), Spelman College (Atlanta—1,119).

Military Installations or Activities. Fort McPherson, Atlanta.

Newspapers, Circulation. Atlanta Constitution (Morn—212,391), Atlanta Journal (Eve—257,961).

Commercial Television Stations, Affiliation. WAGA-TV, Atlanta (CBS); WHAE-TV, Atlanta (None); WQXI-TV, Atlanta (ABC); WSB-TV, Atlanta (NBC); WTCG-TV (NBC per program). Entire district is located in Atlanta ADI.

Plants and Offices, Products, Employment.
Coca-Cola Co., Atlanta (Soft drinks—HQ—1,380). **National Biscuit Co.**, Atlanta (Bakery—1,000). **Great Atlantic & Pacific Tea Co.**, Atlanta (Retail groceries, meats and bakery products—2,750). **Richs Inc.**, Atlanta (Department store—HQ—1,000). **R. H. Macy & Co. Inc.**, Atlanta (Department store—1,500). **Atlanta Newspapers Inc.**, Atlanta (Newspaper publishing—1,800). **Southern Security Services Inc.**, Atlanta (Detective agency—1,000). **Oxford Building Services**, Atlanta (Janitor service and landscaping—HQ—1,500). **Orkin Exterminating Co. Inc.**, Atlanta (Exterminating, alarm system maintenance—7,000). **Georgia International Life Insurance**, Atlanta (Insurance—1,410). **Oxford Builders Inc.**, Atlanta (Operative builders—1,000). **Southern Bell Telephone & Telegraph Co.**, Atlanta (Telephone communication—HQ—13,500). **Western Electric Co. Inc.**, Atlanta (Telephone equipment—2,300). **American Telephone & Telegraph**, Atlanta (Telephone communication—1,000). **Allied Products Corp.**, Atlanta (Cotton Mills division—textiles—1,800). **The Lovable Co.**, Atlanta (Women's undergarments—HQ—1,600). **Cluett Peabody & Co. Inc.**, Atlanta (Men's shirts—1,690). **Georgia Railroad**, Atlanta (Railroad—1,050). **Atlanta & West Point Railroad Co.**, Atlanta (Railroad—1,150). **Atlantic Steel Co.**, Atlanta (Steel products—HQ—1,530).

6th District

(West Central—Atlanta Suburbs)

Race and Ethnic Groups. Blacks 19.4 percent.

Cities, 1970 Population. East Point 39,324, Griffin 22,823, part of Atlanta 22,697, Forest Park 20,104.

Universities, Enrollment. West Georgia College (Carrollton—6,114).

Newspapers, Circulation. Atlanta papers circulate throughout the district.

Commercial Television Stations, Affiliation. Entire district is located in Atlanta ADI.

Plants and Offices, Products, Employment.
Eastern Air Lines, Atlanta (Air transportation—3,000). **Southern Airways Inc.**, Atlanta (Air transportation—HQ—1,080). **Ford Motor Co.**, Hapeville (Assembly division—passenger automobiles—3,500). **William L. Bonnell Co.**, Newnan (Aluminum extruding, mouldings—HQ—1,200). **Southwire Co. Inc.**, Carrollton (Wire cable—HQ—1,940). **The Kroger Co.**, East Point (Wholesale groceries—2,200). **Bremen-Bowden Investment Co.**, Bowdon (Men's suits —1,300). **William Carter Co. Inc.** Barnesville (Men's and boys' underwear, playwear—1,000). **Dundee Mills Inc.**, Griffin (Towels and cotton goods —HQ—1,800).

7th District

(Northwest—Rome, Atlanta Suburbs)

Race and Ethnic Groups. Blacks 7.3 percent.

Cities, 1970 Population. Rome 30,734, Marietta 27,196, Smyrna 19,143.

Universities, Enrollment. Southern Technical Institute (Marietta—1,627).

Military Installations or Activities. Atlanta Naval Air Station, Marietta; Dobbins Air Force Base, Marietta.

Newspapers, Circulation. Atlanta papers circulate in most of district.

Commercial Television Stations, Affiliation. Most of district is located in Atlanta ADI. Part of district is located in Chattanooga (Tenn.) ADI.

Plants and Offices, Products, Employment.
Lockheed Aircraft Corp., Marietta (Aircraft—19,000). **General Electric Co.**, Rome (Power distribution, specialty transformers—19,000). **Klopman Mills Inc.**, Shannon (Broad woven textiles—1,500). **West Point-Pepperell Inc.**, Lindale (Cotton goods —1,500). **Crystal Springs Textile Inc.**, Chickamauga (Cotton goods—1,100). **Riegel Textile Corp.**, Trion (Cotton goods—2,500). **E. T. Barwick Industries Inc.**, La Fayette (Rugs, carpeting—2,500). **E. T. Barwick Industries Inc.**, Kensington (Tufted carpet—1,500). **Trend Mills Inc.**, Rome (Tufted carpet—HQ—1,000).

8th District

(South Central—Macon, Waycross)

Race and Ethnic Groups. Blacks 31.0 percent.

Cities, 1970 Population. Macon 122,441, Waycross 18,999, Dublin 15,089, Midway-Hardwick 14,049.

Universities, Enrollment. Georgia College (Milledgeville—2,330), Mercer University (Macon—1,903).

Military Installations or Activities. Robins Air Force Base, Macon.

Newspapers, Circulation. Macon Telegraph (Morn—50,223).

Commercial Television Stations, Affiliation. WCWB-TV, Macon (NBC); WMAZ-TV, Macon (CBS and ABC). District is divided between Macon, Albany, Savannah and Jacksonville (Fla.) ADIs.

Plants and Offices, Products, Employment.
Seaboard Coast Line Railroad, Waycross (Railroad—1,300). **Armstrong Cork Co.**, Macon (Acoustical tile, insulation—1,350). **J. P. Stevens Co. Inc.**, Milledgeville (Dyes, wool—1,000). **J. P. Stevens Co. Inc.**, Dublin (Dyes, fabrics—1,400).

9th District

(Northeast—Gainsville)

Race and Ethnic Groups. Blacks 6.3 percent.

Cities, 1970 Population. Gainsville 15,471, part of Dalton 15,333.

Universities, Enrollment. North Georgia College (Dahlonega—1,366).

Newspapers, Circulation. Atlanta papers circulate in portions of district.

Commercial Television Stations, Affiliation. Most of district is located in Atlanta ADI. Parts of district are located in Chattanooga (Tenn.) and Greenville (S.C.)-Spartanburg (S.C.)-Asheville (N.C.) ADIs.

Plants and Offices, Products, Employment.
Western Electric Co. Inc., Norcross (Cable wire—3,000). **Chadbourn Inc.**, Winder (Men's work and leisure clothes—2,000). **Coats & Clark Inc.**, Toccoa (Cotton and synthetic threads—1,500). **Johnson & Johnson**, Gainsville (Textile products—1,000). **Carolyn Products Inc.**, Dalton (Chenille products—1,100).

10th District

(North Central—Athens, Augusta)

Race and Ethnic Groups. Blacks 32.8 percent.

Cities, 1970 Population. Augusta 59,839, Athens 44,323, Fort Gordon 15,582, Covington 10,418.

Universities, Enrollment. Augusta College (Augusta—2,973); University of Georgia (Athens—21,298).

Military Installations or Activities. Fort Gordon, Augusta; Navy Supply Corps School, Athens.

Newspapers, Circulation. Atlanta papers circulate in portion of district.

Commercial Television Stations, Affiliation. WJBF-TV, Augusta (ABC primary and NBC); WRDW-TV, Augusta (CBS and NBC). Most of district is divided between Augusta and Atlanta ADIs. Part of district is located in Greenville (S.C.)-Spartanburg (S.C.)-Asheville (N.C.) ADI.

Plants and Offices, Products, Employment.
Bibb Manufacturing Co., Porterdale (Fabrics—1,200). **Uniroyal Inc.**, Thomson (Rubber footwear —1,100).

HAWAII: TWO HOUSE SEATS, NO CHANGE

Hawaii did not redraw its congressional district lines after the 1970 census. The state's two districts were established in July, 1969; previously, the two representatives were elected on an at-large basis. *(Map p. 52)*

Hawaii was required by an act of Congress in 1967 to establish separate districts for the 1970 elections. The two-district alignment was passed by the legislature and signed by Gov. John A. Burns (D) on July 14, 1969.

In establishing the new districts, the state took the unprecedented step of drawing its congressional districts on the basis of "one voter, one vote" instead of "one man, one vote." Rather than using the total population as a base for congressional constituencies, the state decided to use only registered voters as the basis for its districts.

The districting was based on a 1968 registered voter list of 274,199 Hawaiians. Registered voters comprised only about 38 percent of the state's total population and considerably less than the number of Hawaiians of voting age (now 493,852).

The primary reason for the departure from tradition was the large number of military personnel and dependents in the state. Many of these people are counted as residents of Hawaii for census purposes but do not vote there. Thus there is a potential for the establishment of districts particularly in and around military reservations, where there might be a large population but a limited number of voters.

District	Member Elected 1972	Winning Percentage	1970 Population	Percent Variance
1	Spark M. Matsunaga (D)	54.7	362,119	—5.9326
2	Patsy T. Mink (D)	57.1	407,794	+ 5.9323

1970 State Population: 769,913
Ideal District Population: 384,957

Election Results, 1968-1972

Vote for U.S. Representative
(Adjusted to new district boundaries)

District	1968	1970	1972
1	81,009 D (66.1%)	85,411 D (72.9%)	73,826 D (54.7%)
	40,150 R (32.8%)	31,764 R (27.1%)	61,138 R (45.3%)
2	75,165 D (65.7%)	91,038 D (100.0%)	79,856 D (57.1%)
	38,192 R (33.4%)	—	60,043 R (42.9%)
State	156,174 D (65.9%)	176,449 D (84.7%)	153,682 D (55.9%)
	78,342 R (33.1%)	31,764 R (15.3%)	121,181 R (44.1%)

Voting Age Population

District	Voting Age Population	Voting Age Population 18, 19, 20	Voting Age Population 65 and Over	Median Age of Voting Age Population
1	250,544	22,609 (9.0%)	23,005 (9.2%)	38.1
2	243,257	21,169 (8.7%)	21,365 (8.8%)	38.4
State	493,852	43,784 (8.9%)	44,377 (9.0%)	38.3

Income and Occupation

District	Median Family Income	White Collar Workers	Blue Collar Workers	Service Workers	Farm Workers
1	$12,491	55.3%	28.6%	15.7%	0.4%
2	10,848	44.0	34.4	15.2	6.4
State	11,552	49.9	31.4	15.4	3.3

Education: School Years Completed

District	Completed 4 years of High School	Completed 4 years of College	Completed 5 years or less of School	Median School years completed
1	66.5%	17.2%	8.0%	12.5
2	57.3	10.8	12.4	12.2
State	61.9	14.0	10.2	12.3

Housing and Residential Patterns

District	Housing Owner Occupied Units	Housing Renter Occupied Units	Urban	Suburban	Nonmetropolitan
1	40.5%	59.5%	89.9%	10.1%	—
2	53.6	46.4	—	65.8	34.2%
State	46.9	53.1	42.3	39.6	18.1

1st District

(Honolulu)

Race and Ethnic Groups. Japanese 3.4 percent. Chinese 10.4 percent. Filipino 8.9 percent.

Cities, 1970 Population. Honolulu 324,964, part of Aiea 6,228.

Universities, Enrollment. Chaminade College of Honolulu (Honolulu—1,574), University of Hawaii (Honolulu—22,118).

Military Installations or Activities. Fort Shafter Military Reservation, Honolulu; Schoefield Barracks, Honolulu; Tripler Army Hospital, Honolulu; Camp H. M. Smith, Honolulu; Naval Air Station (Barbers Point), Honolulu; Hickam Air Force Base, Honolulu.

Newspapers, Circulation. Honolulu Advertiser (Morn—75,416), Honolulu Star-Bulletin (Eve—127,500).

Commercial Television Stations, Affiliation. KGMB-TV, Honolulu (CBS); KHON-TV, Honolulu (NBC); KHVH-TV, Honolulu (ABC); KIKU-TV, Honolulu (None). Entire district located in Honolulu ADI.

Plants and Offices, Products, Employment.
Hilton-Burns Hotels Co. Inc., Honolulu (Hotel—1,220). **Hawaiian Telephone Co.**, Honolulu (Telephone company—1,500). **Crown Corp.**, Honolulu

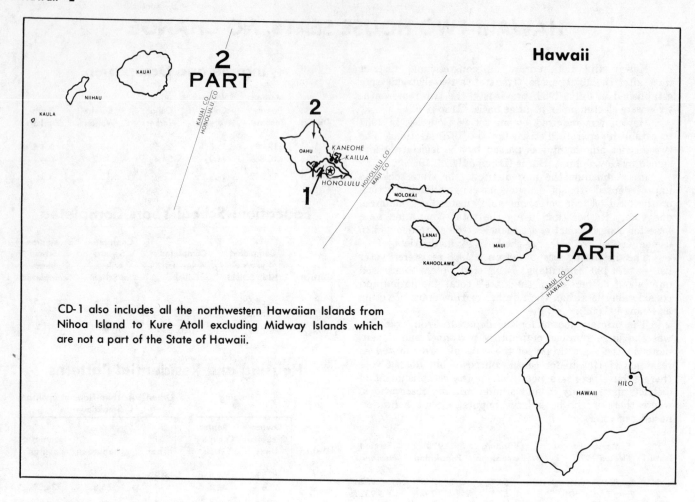

Hawaii

CD-1 also includes all the northwestern Hawaiian Islands from Nihoa Island to Kure Atoll excluding Midway Islands which are not a part of the State of Hawaii.

(Holding company, men's and women's apparel—1,160). **Telecheck International Inc.,** Honolulu (Holding company, houseboats—1,000).

2nd District

(Honolulu Suburbs and Outer Islands)

Race and Ethnic Groups. Japanese 25.4 percent. Filipino 15.7 percent. Chinese 3.7 percent.

Cities, 1970 Population. Kailua 33,887, Kaneohe 29,956, Hilo 26,440, Waipahu 22,868.

Universities, Enrollment. Church College of Hawaii (Laie—1,299).

Military Installations or Activities. Fleet Operations and Control Center, Kunia; Marine Barracks, Pearl Har-

bor; Marine Corps Air Station (Kanohe Bay), Kailua; Naval Communication Station, Wahiawa; Naval Station, Pearl Harbor; Naval Ammunition Depot, Lualualei; Naval Submarine Base, Pearl Harbor; Naval Supply Center, Pearl Harbor; Navy Public Works Center, Pearl Harbor; Pearl Harbor Naval Shipyard; Wheeler Air Force Base, Wahiawa.

Newspapers, Circulation. Honolulu newspapers circulate in portion of district.

Commercial Television Stations, Affiliation. Entire district located in Honolulu ADI.

Plants and Offices, Products, Employment.

Alexander and Baldwin Inc., Puunene (Hawaiian Commercial & Sugar Co.—sugar and molasses—1,300).

IDAHO: TWO HOUSE SEATS, NO CHANGE

Only the shift of one county and part of another was necessary to bring Idaho's two congressional districts close to the ideal population. *(Map p. 53)*

The state Senate passed a redistricting bill April 7, 1971, by a vote of 34-1 and the House followed suit April 8 by a vote of 65-5. Gov. Cecil D. Andrus (D) signed the bill April 13.

Neither of the state's two incumbent Republican representatives—James A. McClure of the 1st District and Orval Hansen of the 2nd District—was endangered by the redistricting.

McClure was elected to the U.S. Senate in November 1972 and his district remained in Republican hands. Hansen was easily re-elected.

The city of Boise, capital of Idaho, is split between the districts for the first time. The variance between the two districts is 0.1990 percent.

District	Member Elected 1972	Winning Percentage	1970 Population	Percent Variance
1	Steven D. Symms (R)	55.6	356,859	+ 0.0995
2	Orval Hansen (R)	69.2	356,149	—0.0995

1970 State Population: 713,008
Ideal District Population: 356,504

Election Results, 1968-1972

Vote for U.S. Representative
(Adjusted to new district boundaries)

District	1968	1970	1972
1	80,892 R (58.8%)	69,262 R (58.0%)	85,270 R (55.6%)
	56,577 D (41.2%)	50,206 D (42.0%)	68,106 D (44.4%)
2	75,007 R (53.9%)	74,681 R (65.0%)	102,537 R (69.2%)
	59,681 D (42.9%)	37,409 D (32.6%)	40,081 D (27.0%)
State	155,899 R (56.4%)	143,943 R (61.4%)	187,807 R (62.3%)
	166,258 D (42.0%)	87,615 D (37.4%)	108,187 D (35.9%)

Voting Age Population

District	Voting Age Population	Voting Age Population 18, 19, 20	Voting Age Population 65 and Over	Median Age Voting Age Population
1	229,576	18,914 (8.2%)	36,475 (15.9%)	44.1
2	218,459	19,796 (9.1%)	31,346 (14.3%)	42.4
State	448,082	38,706 (8.6%)	67,844 (15.1%)	43.3

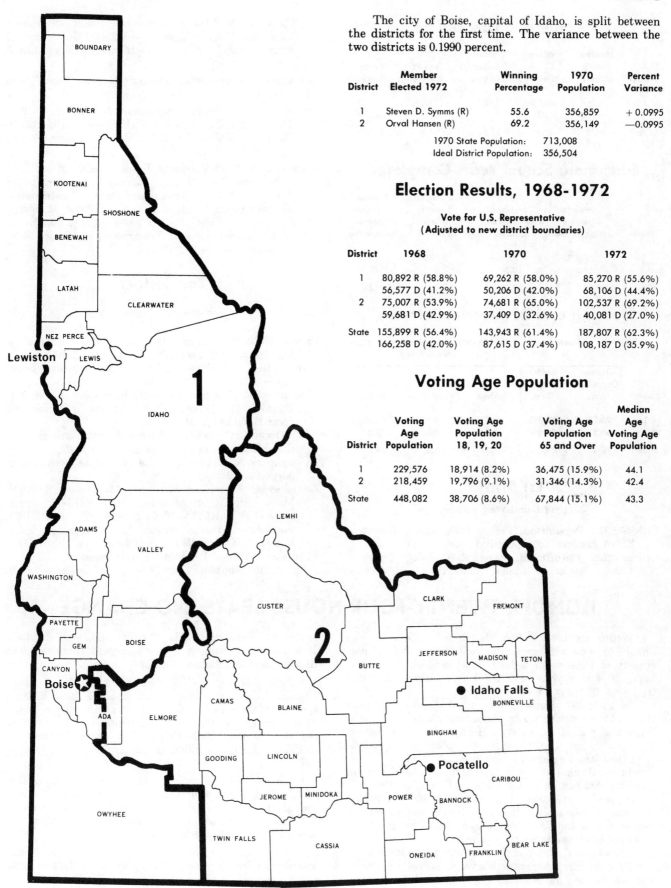

Income and Occupation

District	Median Family Income	White Collar Workers	Blue Collar Workers	Service Workers	Farm Workers
1	$8,466	43.5%	34.3%	13.7%	8.5%
2	8,280	42.7	30.6	12.5	14.2
State	8,381	43.1	32.5	13.1	11.3

Education: School Years Completed

District	Completed 4 years of High School	Completed 4 years of College	Completed 5 years or less of School	Median School years completed
1	57.6%	9.7%	3.5%	12.2
2	61.5	10.3	3.0	12.3
State	59.5	10.0	3.2	12.3

Housing and Residential Patterns

	Housing		Urban-Suburban-Nonmetropolitan Breakdown		
District	Owner Occupied Units	Renter Occupied Units	Urban	Suburban	Nonmetropolitan
1	70.7%	29.3%	14.7%	9.5%	75.8%
2	69.5	30.5	6.3	0.9	92.8
State	70.1	29.9	10.5	5.2	84.3

1st District

(North and West—Boise)

Cities, 1970 Population. Part of Boise 52,463, Lewiston 25,964, Nampa 20,685, Coeur d'Alene 16,163.

Universities, Enrollment. Boise State College (Boise—8,300), College of Idaho (Caldwell—1,024), Lewis- Clark State College (Lewiston—1,282), Northwest Nazarene College (Nampa—1,114), University of Idaho (Moscow—7,935), North Idaho College (Coeur d'Alene—1,206).

Newspapers, Circulation. Idaho Statesman, Boise (Morn —55,843).

Commercial Television Stations, Affiliation. KBOI-TV, Boise (CBS, ABC); KTVB, Boise (NBC, ABC). Portions of district located in Boise, Spokane (Wash.) and Yakima (Wash.) ADIs.

Plants and Offices, Products, Employment.
Potlatch Forests Inc., Lewiston (Lumber, paper products—2,140). **Dworshak Dam Constructors**, Ahsahka (Dam builders, on site—1,040). **J. R. Simplot Co.**, Caldwell (Frozen foods—1,500). **Mountain States Telephone and Telegraph Co.**, Boise (Telephone company—1,620).

2nd District

(East—Pocatello, Idaho Falls)

Cities, 1970 Population. Pocatello 40,247, Idaho Falls 35,965, part of Boise 22,435, Twin Falls 22,030.

Universities, Enrollment. Idaho State University (Pocatello—6,862).

Military Installations or Activities. Naval Nuclear Training Unit, Idaho Falls; Mountain Home Air Force Base, Mountain Home.

AEC Owned, Contractor-Operated Installations. National Reactor Testing Station, Idaho Falls.

Newspapers, Circulation. Boise newspaper circulates in portion of district.

Commercial Television Stations, Affiliation. KID-TV, Idaho Falls (CBS primary, ABC); KIFI-TV, Idaho Falls (NBC); KMTV, Twin Falls (CBS, ABC, NBC). Portions of district located in Boise, Idaho Falls-Pocatello, Twin Falls and Salt Lake City (Utah) ADIs.

Plants and Offices, Products, Employment.
J. R. Simplot Co., Pocatello (Fertilizer—1,600).

ILLINOIS: TWENTY-FOUR HOUSE SEATS, NO CHANGE

During its 1971 session, the Illinois legislature was unable to pass a congressional redistricting bill. Consequently, a three-judge federal panel stepped in and on Sept. 21 of that year instituted a new congressional district map. *(Maps p. 58, 61)*

In their 2-1 decision, the judges approved a plan similar to one drawn up by three Republican state legislators and passed by the state House but not the Senate. The two judges who supported the plan were Republicans, the dissenting judge a Democrat.

Political analysts said the map was designed to give Republicans 15 of the state's 24 seats in the U.S. House. Both parties held 12 seats as a result of the 1970 elections. In November 1972 the Republicans picked up two seats—in the 3rd District and 10th District—for a new total of 14, one below their expectations.

Features and results of the plan were the following:

• Chicago Rep. Abner J. Mikva, a liberal Democrat, was moved into an overwhelmingly black district repre- sented by Rep. Ralph H. Metcalfe (D), who is black. Mikva chose to run in a newly created suburban 10th district north of Chicago, and lost.

• Reps. George Collins and Frank Annunzio, both Chicago Democrats, were tossed into the same district, the 7th. Collins ran in the 7th, Annunzio moved to the 11th, vacated by Rep. Roman Pucinski (D) who ran for the U.S. Senate. Both Collins and Annunzio were re-elected. Collins was killed in an airplane crash Dec. 8, 1972.

• Rep. George E. Shipley (D), from the downstate 22nd District, lost Democratic areas in the shuffle and picked up several largely Republican counties. Nevertheless, Shipley bucked the Republican redistricters and was re-elected in November 1972.

• Rep. Leslie C. Arends, dean of House Republicans, was moved into a new district, the 15th. He had little trouble winning re-election, however.

District	Member Elected 1972	Winning Percentage	1970 Population	Percent Variance
1	Ralph H. Metcalfe (D)	91.4	462,434	—0.1399
2	Morgan F. Murphy (D)	75.0	464,792	+ 0.3692
3	Robert P. Hanrahan (R)	62.3	461,180	—0.4107
4	Edward J. Derwinski (R)	70.5	464,452	+ 0.2958
5	John C. Kluczynski (D)	72.8	465,990	+ 0.6279
6	Harold R. Collier (R)	61.2	461,360	—0.3718
7	George W. Collins (D)[1]	82.8	464,283	+ 0.2593
8	Dan Rostenkowski (D)	74.0	459,902	—0.6867
9	Sidney R. Yates (D)	68.3	463,991	+ 0.1962
10	Samuel H. Young (R)	51.6	462,121	—0.2075
11	Frank Annunzio (D)	53.3	461,079	—0.4325
12	Philip M. Crane (R)	74.2	461,054	—0.4379
13	Robert McClory (R)	61.5	463,096	+ 0.0030
14	John N. Erlenborn (R)	72.8	464,029	+ 0.2044
15	Leslie C. Arends (R)	57.2	462,969	—0.0244
16	John B. Anderson (R)	71.9	461,719	—0.2943
17	George M. O'Brien (R)	55.6	462,943	—0.0300
18	Robert H. Michel (R)	64.8	463,155	+ 0.0157
19	Tom Railsback (R)	100.0	462,085	—0.2152
20	Paul Findley (R)	68.8	464,551	+ 0.3172
21	Edward R. Madigan (R)	54.8	464,693	+ 0.3478
22	George E. Shipley (D)	56.5	464,121	+ 0.2243
23	Melvin Price (D)	75.1	462,960	—0.0263
24	Kenneth J. Gray (D)	93.7	465,017	+ 0.4178

1970 State Population: 11,113,976
Ideal District Population: 463,082

1 Died Dec. 8, 1972.

Election Results, 1968-1972

Vote for U.S. Representative
(Adjusted to new district boundaries)

District	1968	1970	1972
1	148,583 D (84.9%)	115,941 D (90.5%)	136,755 D (91.4%)
	26,397 R (15.0%)	12,124 R (9.5%)	12,877 R (8.6%)
2	109,811 D (58.1%)	98,310 D (72.5%)	115,306 D (75.0%)
	79,330 R (41.9%)	37,366 R (27.5%)	38,391 R (25.0%)
3	124,675 R (64.4%)	82,988 R (53.8%)	128,329 R (62.3%)
	69,020 D (35.6%)	71,275 D (46.2%)	77,814 D (37.7%)
4	114,824 R (67.2%)	88,932 R (63.2%)	141,402 R (70.5%)
	55,936 D (32.8%)	51,786 D (36.8%)	59,057 D (29.5%)
5	121,870 D (66.6%)	111,601 D (75.5%)	121,278 D (72.8%)
	61,253 R (33.4%)	36,151 R (24.5%)	45,264 R (27.2%)
6	132,793 R (64.5%)	103,192 R (63.5%)	124,486 R (61.2%)
	73,226 D (35.5%)	59,200 D (36.5%)	79.002 D (38.8%)
7	125,247 D (85.3%)	99,744 D (89.0%)	95,018 D (82.8%)
	21,582 R (14.7%)	12,383 R (11.0%)	19,758 R (17.2%)
8	114,571 R (65.9%)	102,130 D (75.6%)	110,457 D (74.0%)
	59,320 R (34.1%)	32,888 R (24.4%)	38,758 R (26.0%)
9	123,719 D (61.9%)	119,628 D (74.4%)	131,777 D (68.3%)
	76,256 R (38.1%)	41,268 R (25.6%)	61,083 R (31.7%)
10	146,767 R (68.8%)	95,714 R (54.5%)	120,681 R (51.6%)
	66,562 D (31.2%)	80,088 D (45.6%)	113,222 D (48.4%)
11	129,886 D (56.6%)	134,718 D (71.3%)	118,637 D (53.3%)
	99,728 R (43.4%)	54,234 R (28.7%)	103,773 R (46.7%)
12	119,414 R (75.9%)	86,294 R (66.4%)	152,938 R (74.2%)
	37,993 D (24.1%)	43,756 D (33.6%)	53,055 D (25.8%)
13	101,823 R (71.0%)	72,867 R (65.3%)	98,201 R (61.5%)
	41,620 D (29.0%)	38,723 D (34.7%)	61,537 D (38.5%)
14	129,306 R (75.7%)	99,463 R (70.7%)	154,794 R (72.8%)
	41,530 D (24.3%)	41,276 D (29.3%)	57,874 D (27.2%)
15	122,995 R (67.8%)	94,496 R (67.8%)	111,022 R (57.2%)
	58,299 D (32.1%)	44,886 D (32.2%)	82,925 D (42.8%)
16	115,838 R (67.8%)	87,735 R (67.0%)	129,640 R (71.9%)
	55,095 D (32.2%)	43,167 D (49.2%)	50,649 D (28.1%)
17	100,720 R (61.9%)	72,886 R (57.7%)	100,175 R (55.6%)
	61,959 D (38.0%)	53,487 D (42.3%)	79,840 D (44.4%)

District	1968	1970	1972
18	112,681 R (60.1%)	91,374 R (65.6%)	124,407 R (64.8%)
	74,866 D (39.9%)	47,853 D (34.4%)	67,514 D (35.2%)
19	125,017 R (65.3%)	98,543 R (68.4%)	138,123 R (100.0%)
	66,373 D (34.7%)	45,447 D (31.6%)	—
20	123,608 R (59.7%)	109,432 R (61.5%)	148,419 R (68.8%)
	83,387 D (40.3%)	68,528 D (38.5%)	67,445 D (31.2%)
21	104,707 R (64.3%)	75,915 R (60.9%)	99,966 R (54.8%)
	58,040 D (35.7%)	48,716 D (39.1%)	82,523 D (45.2%)
22	118,388 R (55.2%)	94,990 R (50.8%)	124,589 D (56.5%)
	95,985 D (44.8%)	92,038 D (49.2%)	90,390 R (41.0%)
23	114,295 D (71.0%)	89,094 D (73.7%)	121,682 D (75.1%)
	46,775 R (29.0%)	31,712 R (26.3%)	40,428 R (24.9%)
24	122,899 D (55.2%)	117,722 D (61.7%)	138,867 D (93.7%)
	99,543 R (44.8%)	73,176 R (38.3%)	—
State	2,363,740 R (53.5%)	1,819,114 D (51.9%)	2,223,305 R (50.7%)
	2,050,772 D (46.5%)	1,686,123 R (48.1%)	2,146,823 D (49.0%)

Voting Age Population

District	Voting Age Population	Voting Age Population 18, 19, 20	Voting Age Population 65 and Over	Median Age of Voting Age Population
1	301,472	20,994 (7.0%)	41,417 (13.7%)	42.1
2	301,794	20,861 (6.9%)	45,390 (15.0%)	43.8
3	299,760	20,765 (6.9%)	38,894 (13.0%)	44.8
4	287,590	18,871 (6.6%)	29,017 (10.1%)	42.0
5	304,866	23,137 (7.6%)	41,593 (13.6%)	44.3
6	325,798	20,768 (6.3%)	49,867 (15.3%)	45.3
7	275,240	25,067 (9.1%)	32,261 (11.7%)	39.3
8	308,656	21,547 (7.0%)	46,152 (15.0%)	42.8
9	363,790	20,757 (5.7%)	71,484 (19.6%)	44.7
10	304,620	20,343 (6.7%)	39,241 (12.9%)	44.1
11	339,864	19,629 (5.8%)	65,045 (19.1%)	48.7
12	266,733	16,147 (6.1%)	19,240 (7.2%)	39.1
13	295,003	34,970 (11.9%)	34,715 (11.8%)	39.6
14	281,611	19,888 (7.1%)	26,654 (9.5%)	40.8
15	302,405	29,043 (9.6%)	47,220 (15.6%)	42.5
16	293,297	20,302 (6.9%)	45,069 (15.4%)	43.1
17	287,159	20,543 (7.2%)	37,552 (13.1%)	41.7
18	304,976	21,564 (7.1%)	52,381 (17.2%)	44.6
19	306,387	27,266 (8.9%)	53,283 (17.4%)	44.6
20	308,817	21,122 (6.8%)	61,546 (19.9%)	46.8
21	317,262	44,012 (13.9%)	43,629 (13.8%)	38.3
22	313,377	22,209 (7.1%)	65,342 (20.9%)	47.4
23	292,272	21,515 (7.4%)	41,202 (14.1%)	43.1
24	323,960	26,078 (8.0%)	68,116 (21.0%)	47.2
State	7,306,649	557,305 (7.6%)	1,096,321 (15.0%)	43.3

Income and Occupation

District	Median Family Income	White Collar Workers	Blue Collar Workers	Service Workers	Farm Workers
1	$ 8,373	45.7%	35.3%	18.7%	0.3%
2	11,147	48.0	39.3	12.6	0.1
3	12,762	52.7	36.9	10.3	0.1
4	13,451	55.7	35.5	8.7	0.1
5	9,881	40.0	46.6	13.3	0.1
6	12,700	55.3	35.9	8.7	0.1
7	7,536	35.1	49.3	15.4	0.2
8	9,867	39.3	49.1	11.5	0.1
9	10,966	64.5	24.7	10.7	0.1
10	16,576	73.9	18.0	8.0	0.1

Illinois - 3

District	Median Family Income	White Collar Workers	Blue Collar Workers	Service Workers	Farm Workers
11	12,005	53.6	36.7	9.7	—
12	15,173	67.3	24.7	7.6	0.4
13	11,994	46.9	40.1	11.6	1.4
14	14,527	64.8	26.7	8.1	0.4
15	10,619	41.2	41.4	12.2	5.2
16	10,668	40.7	43.3	11.1	4.9
17	11,286	41.4	43.2	12.4	3.0
18	10,096	43.6	38.4	38.2	4.8
19	9,579	39.3	38.9	14.0	7.8
20	9,269	46.1	33.0	14.2	6.7
21	10,043	51.2	29.1	14.7	5.0
22	8,350	36.7	40.2	13.4	9.7
23	9,872	44.6	41.5	12.6	1.3
24	7,501	38.0	40.2	14.8	7.0
State	10,957	49.1	36.7	11.8	2.4

Education: School Years Completed

District	Completed 4 years of High School	Completed 4 years of College	Completed 5 years or less of School	Median School years completed
1	46.3%	10.1%	9.5%	11.5
2	48.7	7.4	7.0	11.8
3	56.0	7.6	4.2	12.2
4	62.4	13.0	3.3	12.4
5	35.1	3.4	10.3	10.2
6	54.6	10.4	4.7	12.2
7	31.2	5.7	16.3	9.7
8	35.4	4.6	11.9	10.1
9	56.4	16.6	6.0	12.3
10	76.4	27.0	2.2	12.9
11	46.7	6.9	6.7	11.5
12	76.3	22.3	2.2	12.7
13	57.4	11.0	3.9	12.2
14	74.2	20.8	2.0	12.6
15	55.7	8.7	3.8	12.2
16	52.6	7.8	4.4	12.1
17	51.3	7.5	5.4	12.0
18	53.3	8.6	4.0	12.1
19	53.7	7.5	3.4	12.1
20	51.2	7.9	4.7	12.0
21	59.7	14.7	3.5	12.3
22	46.8	5.9	4.2	11.4
23	44.2	6.6	7.1	11.1
24	40.3	6.0	7.4	10.1
State	52.6	10.3	5.7	12.1

Housing and Residential Patterns

District	Owner Occupied Units	Renter Occupied Units	Urban	Suburban	Nonmetropolitan
1	22.2%	77.8%	100.0%	—	—
2	56.4	43.6	100.0	—	—
3	74.3	25.7	27.0	73.0%	—
4	79.1	20.9	—	100.0	—
5	43.0	57.0	100.0	—	—
6	60.0	40.0	—	100.0	—

District	Owner Occupied Units	Renter Occupied Units	Urban	Suburban	Nonmetropolitan
7	16.9	83.1	100.0	—	—
8	33.7	66.3	100.0	—	—
9	14.5	85.5	100.0	—	—
10	72.5	27.5	—	100.0	—
11	53.1	46.9	100.0	—	—
12	79.4	20.6	—	100.0	—
13	68.8	31.2	—	100.0	—
14	79.5	20.5	—	100.0	—
15	68.4	31.6	—	32.7	67.3%
16	68.5	31.5	31.9	36.4	31.7
17	71.3	28.7	—	71.7	28.3
18	71.3	28.7	27.4	40.4	32.2
19	71.0	29.0	20.9	26.7	52.4
20	70.6	29.4	19.7	30.8	49.5
21	63.4	36.6	53.0	30.7	16.3
22	74.4	25.6	—	0.8	99.2
23	69.4	30.6	—	100.0	—
24	74.1	25.9	—	—	100.0
State	59.4	40.6	36.6	43.5	19.9

1st District

(Chicago—South Side)

Race and Ethnic Groups. Blacks 88.9 percent. Russian stock 0.6 percent, German stock 0.6 percent.
Cities, 1970 Population. Part of Chicago 462,434.
Universities, Enrollment. University of Chicago (Chicago—8,497).
Newspapers, Circulation. Chicago newspapers circulate throughout district.
Commercial Television Stations, Affiliation. Entire district is located in Chicago ADI.
Plants and Offices, Products, Employment.
   General Motors Corp., Chicago (Electro-Motive Division—diesel locomotives—1,250). **Verson Allsteel Press Co.**, Chicago (Machine tools—HQ—1,200).

2nd District

(Chicago—South Side)

Race and Ethnic Groups. Blacks 39.7 percent. Spanish heritage population 5.2 percent. Polish stock 4.2 percent, Italian stock 2.4 percent.
Cities, 1970 Population. Part of Chicago 464,792.
Newspapers, Circulation. Chicago newspapers circulate throughout district.
Commercial Television Stations, Affiliation. Entire district is located in Chicago ADI.
Plants and Offices, Products, Employment.
   International Harvester Co., Chicago (Roller bearings, coil springs—2,500). **International Harvester Co.**, Chicago (Wisconsin Steel Works—carbon steel, pig iron—4,700). **Ford Motor Co.**, Chicago (Auto assembly—4,200). **American Can Co.**, Chicago (Canco Division—tin containers—2,000).

Continental Can Co. Inc., Chicago (White Cap & Bond Division—boxcard folding cartons—1,100). **Sherwin-Williams Co.**, Chicago (Martin Senour Paint Co. Division—paints, varnishes, etc.—1,800). **Interlake Inc.**, Chicago (Iron and Steel Division—steel products—2,100). **Borg-Warner Corp.**, Chicago (Borg-Warner Health Products Division—health products—1,000).

3rd District

(Chicago—Southwest Suburbs)

Race and Ethnic Groups. Blacks 5.3 percent. Polish stock 4.0 percent, Irish stock 3.2 percent, German stock 2.9 percent, Italian stock 2.8 percent.
Cities, 1970 Population. Part of Chicago 124,384, Oak Lawn 60,350, part of Harvey 33,743, Calumet City 32,958.
Universities, Enrollment. Saint Xavier College (Chicago—1,103).
Newspapers, Circulation. Chicago newspapers circulate throughout district.
Commercial Television Stations, Affiliation. Entire district is located in Chicago ADI.
Plants and Offices, Products, Employment.
Allis-Chalmers Corp., Harvey (Engines—1,200). **Allis-Chalmers Corp.**, Harvey (Engines, lift trucks—2,330). **Whiting Corp.**, Harvey (Industrial equipment, metal and chemical processing—HQ—1,200). **Wyman-Gordon Co.**, Harvey (Midwest Division—iron and steel forgings—1,600). **United States Steel Corp.**, Chicago (U.S. Steel Products Division—steel drums and vials—11,000). **Rheem Mfg. Co. Inc.**, Chicago (Environmental Products Group—household products, wrapping material—1,200). **Tootsie Roll Industries Inc.**, Chicago (Confectionaries—1,000). **Consolidated Freightways Corp.**, Chicago (Truck terminal—1,000).

4th District

(Chicago Suburbs—South and Southwest)

Race and Ethnic Groups. Blacks 3.9 percent. Polish stock 3.1 percent, German stock 2.9 percent, Italian stock 2.7 percent.
Cities, 1970 Population. South Stickney 29,862, part of Park Forest 21,976, Westchester 19,999, part of Brookfield 18,353.
Newspapers, Circulation. Chicago newspapers circulate throughout district.
Commercial Television Stations, Affiliation. Entire district is located in Chicago ADI.
Plants and Offices, Products, Employment.
General Motors Corp., LaGrange (Locomotives—10,000). **General Motors Corp.**, Willow Springs (Fisher Body Division—auto bodies and components—3,550). **International Harvester Co.**, Broadview (Parts Division—farm equipment and machinery—1,000). **C. F. Braun and Co.**, Lemont (Heavy construction—3,000). **Reynolds Metals Co.**, LaGrange (Aluminum products—2,800). **CPC International**, Argo (Moffett Technical Center—milling and refin-

ing—2,700). **CPC International**, Summit (Liquid resin—3,000). **Minnesota Mining and Manufacturing Co.**, Argo (3M Co. Division—pressure sensitizers—1,100). **Szabo Food Service Inc.**, Lyons (Automatic vending and merchandising—HQ—7,000 total employment). **Bunker Ramo Corp.**, LaGrange (Amphenol Connector Division—connectors—1,800).

5th District

(Chicago—Central)

Race and Ethnic Groups. Blacks 31.1 percent. Spanish heritage population 5.9 percent. Polish stock 9.5 percent, Italian stock 2.4 percent.
Cities, 1970 Population. Part of Chicago 465,990.
Universities, Enrollment. Chicago State University (Chicago—5,806), Illinois Institute of Technology (Chicago—7,067).
Newspapers, Circulation. Chicago newspapers circulate throughout district.
Commercial Television Stations, Affiliation. Entire district is located in Chicago ADI.
Plants and Offices, Products, Employment.
Continental Can Co. Inc., Chicago (Metal cans, containers—1,100). **Union Carbide Corp.**, Chicago (Food Products Divison—food casings—1,500). **Central Steel and Wire Co.**, Chicago (Metal products—HQ—1,500). **Singer Co.**, Chicago (Household goods—2,800). **Swift and Co.**, Chicago (Meat packing—1,500). **Campbell Soup Co.**, Chicago (Canned food—2,000). **William Wrigley Jr. Co.**, Chicago (Chewing gum—at least 1,010). **Maryland Cup Corp.**, Chicago (Food products—1,400). **Johnson and Johnson**, Chicago (Vetco Division—surgical supplies—1,000). **Varco Inc.**, Chicago (Business forms—1,000). **Illinois Institute of Technology Research Institute**, Chicago (Technological research—1,200). **Michael Reese Hospital and Medical Center**, Chicago (Hospital—2,000).

6th District

(Cook County—Northwest Suburbs)

Race and Ethnic Groups. Blacks 2.9 percent. Italian stock 7.0 percent, Polish stock 4.2 percent, German stock 3.9 percent, Czechoslovakian stock 3.9 percent.
Cities, 1970 Population. Cicero 67,129, Oak Park 62,587, Berwyn 52,558, Maywood 30,068.
Universities, Enrollment. Concordia Teachers College (River Forest—1,666), Rosary College (River Forest—1,300).
Military Installations or Activities. Troop Carrier Squadron and Air National Guard Base, O'Hare International Airport, Chicago.
Newspapers, Circulation. Chicago newspapers circulate throughout district.
Commercial Television Stations, Affiliation. Entire district is located in Chicago ADI.
Plants and Offices, Products, Employment.
GTE Automatic Electric Inc., Melrose Park (Communications and electronic apparatus—HQ—11,000). **Western Electric Co. Inc.**, Cicero (Tele-

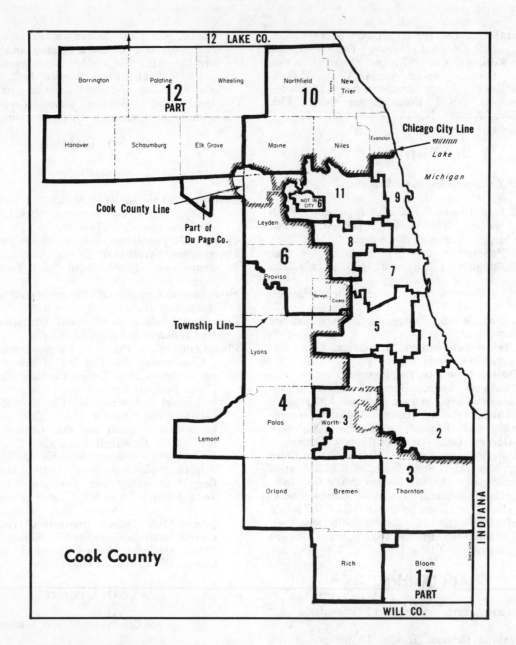

12 LAKE CO.

Barrington | Palatine | Wheeling | Northfield | New Trier
12 PART
Hanover | Schaumburg | Elk Grove | Maine | Niles

10

Chicago City Line

Lake Michigan

Evanston

11

NOT IN CITY **6**

9

Cook County Line

Leyden

Part of Du Page Co.

8

6

Proviso

7

Township Line

Berwyn | Cicero

Lyons

5

1

4

Palos | Worth **3**

2

Lemont

3

Orland | Bremen | Thornton

INDIANA

State Line

Cook County

Rich | Bloom

17 PART

WILL CO.

phone equipment—22,000). **General Electric Co.**, Cicero (Hotpoint Division—refrigeration equipment —3,900). **General Electric Co.**, Cicero (Hotpoint Division—electric ranges, refrigerators—at least 1,010). **Stanadyne Inc.**, Bellwood (Chicago Division —screw machine products, auto parts and equipment—at least 1,300). **Taylor Forge Inc.**, Cicero (Forging products—1,200). **Danly Machine Corp.**, Cicero (Stampings, presses, dies—HQ—1,800). **Illinois Tool Work Inc.**, Itasca (Shake Proof Division— machine tools—1,000). **Borg-Warner Corp.**, Bellwood (Spring Division—auto parts and equipment— 1,000). **International Harvester Co.**, Melrose Park (Construction Equipment Division—construction equipment—4,700). **Skil Corp.**, Melrose Park (Nordon Die Casting Division—construction machinery and equipment—1,000). **Zenith Radio Corp.**, Melrose Park (Cathode rays and tubes—5,000). **Wilson Sporting Goods Co.**, River Grove (Sporting and athletic goods—HQ—1,500). **Alberto-Culver Co.**, Melrose Park (Toiletries, cosmetics—2,900). **Standard Brands Inc.**, Franklin Park (Curtiss Candy Co. Division—candy—2,000). **Miehle-Goss-Dexter Inc.**, Cicero (Goss Co. Division—printing—1,750). **Trans World Airlines Inc.**, O'Hare International Airport, Chicago (Air transport—1,500).

7th District

(Chicago—Downtown, West Side)

Race and Ethnic Groups. Blacks 54.9 percent. Spanish heritage population 16.6 percent. Polish stock 4.1 percent, Italian stock 2.3 percent.
Cities, 1970 Population. Part of Chicago 464,283.
Universities, Enrollment. DePaul University (Chicago— 9,404), Loyola University (Chicago—14,752 total enrollment, part in 9th District), Roosevelt University

(Chicago—7,049), University of Illinois at Chicago Circle (Chicago—19,955), Schools of the Art Institute of Chicago (Chicago—1,464).

Newspapers, Circulation. Chicago newspapers circulate throughout district. They include: Chicago Daily News (ExSat—449,148), Chicago Sun-Times (MxSat—552,423), Chicago Today (ExSat—453,130), Chicago Tribune (Morn—746,596).

Commercial Television Stations, Affiliation. Entire district is located in Chicago ADI. Chicago stations include: WBBM-TV, Chicago (CBS); WCIU-TV, Chicago (Spanish station); WFLD-TV, Chicago (None); WGN-TV, Chicago (None); WLS-TV, Chicago (ABC); WMAQ-TV, Chicago (NBC); WSNS-TV, Chicago (None).

Plants and Offices, Products, Employment. (Note: District includes downtown business section of Chicago.)

International Harvester Co., Chicago (Headquarters—1,000). **Amoco International Oil Co.**, Chicago (Headquarters—1,000). **American Oil Co.**, Chicago (Headquarters—3,500). **Standard Oil Company of Indiana**, Chicago (Headquarters—1,600). **Sears, Roebuck and Co.**, Chicago (Headquarters—3,500). **Swift and Co.**, Chicago (Headquarters—1,200). **Hilton Hotels Corp.**, Chicago (Headquarters—1,000). **Pick Hotels Corp.**, Chicago (Headquarters—3,000). **CNA Financial Corp.**, Chicago (Insurance, holding company—14,500). **Continental Insurance Co.**, Chicago (Insurance—5,000). **Zurich American Life Insurance Co.**, Chicago (Insurance—HQ—2,000). **Marlennan Corp.**, Chicago (Insurance, holding company—6,500). **First Chicago Corp.**, Chicago (Banking, holding company—4,820). **Chicago Title and Trust Co.**, Chicago (Title insurance, holding company—HQ—1,000). **Trans Union Corp.**, Chicago (Tank cars, holding company—5,790). **Atlantic Richfield Co.**, Chicago (Petroleum products wholesalers—1,000). **FMC Corp.**, Chicago (Trucks, tractors, trailers—4,600). **American Can Co.**, Chicago (Canco Division—industrial supplies—1,900). **Union Special Machine Co.**, Chicago (Sewing machines—HQ—1,200). **Joseph T. Ryerson and Son Inc.**, Chicago (Metal products—HQ—2,500). **TRW Inc.**, Chicago (Chinch Manufacturing Division—electrical components—1,000). **REA Express Inc.**, Chicago (Railway express agency—1,000). **Western Union Telegraph Co.**, Chicago (Telegraph communications—1,100). **Spector Industries Inc.**, Chicago (Common carrier, holding company—4,750). **United Parcel Service Inc.**, Chicago (Common carrier—1,000). **Penn Central Transportation Co.**, Chicago (Chicago Headquarters Division—rail transportation—2,000). **Checker Taxi Co. Inc.**, Chicago (Taxi transportation—3,000). **Yellow Cab Co.**, Chicago (Taxicab service—3,000). **Consolidated Leasing Corp. of America**, Chicago (Renting and leasing transportation equipment, etc., holding company—HQ—1,700). **Illinois Central Railroad**, Chicago (Railroad—HQ—2,000). **Baltimore and Ohio, Chicago Terminal**, Chicago (Railroad—1,300). **Chicago, Milwaukee, St. Paul and Pacific Railroad Co.**, Chicago (Railroad—HQ—14,000 total employment). **Chicago and Northwestern Railway Co.**, Chicago (Railroad—HQ—2,000). **MGD**

Graphic Systems Inc., Chicago (Miehle Co. Division—printing presses—1,300). **Tribune Co.**, Chicago (Newspaper publisher, holding company—21,000). **R. R. Donnelley and Sons Co.**, Chicago (Commercial printing—HQ—1,000). **Field Enterprises Inc.**, Chicago (Newspaper publisher—HQ—2,000). **Field Enterprises Educational**, Chicago (Book publishers—1,000). **Follett Corp.**, Chicago (Books, textbooks, school supplies—1,100). **Encyclopedia Britannica Inc.**, Chicago (Publishers—HQ—1,500). **Belscot Retailers Inc.**, Chicago (Clothing wholesaler and retailer, holding company—1,200). **Marshall Field and Co.**, Chicago (Department store—HQ—1,000). **Goldblatt Brothers Inc.**, Chicago (Department store—HQ—1,950). **Carson Pirie Scott and Co.**, Chicago (Department stores, holding company—HQ—1,000). **Wieboldt Stores Inc.**, Chicago (Department stores—HQ—1,600). **Sherman House Corp.**, Chicago (Hotel—1,000). **Palmer House Co.**, Chicago (Hotel—1,600). **Drake Hotel Inc.**, Chicago (Hotel—1,000). **William J. Burns International Detective Agency**, Chicago (Detective agency—2,000). **Kane Service Inc.**, Chicago (Detective agency—1,500). **Leo Burnett Co. Inc.**, Chicago (Advertising—HQ—1,280). **Arthur Andersen and Co.**, Chicago (Public accountants—HQ—1,400). **Interstate United**, Chicago (Holding company, vending machine operators—HQ—9,000). **Gale Industries Inc.**, Chicago (Holding company—2,000). **J. R. Thompson Co.**, Chicago (Restaurants, holding company—3,500). **ABC Great States Inc.**, Chicago (Motion picture theaters, holding company—1,100). **Brunswick Corp.**, Chicago (Sporting goods—HQ—1,000). **Joanna Western Mills Co.**, Chicago (Kaywood Division—window shades—HQ—1,000). **Allied Radio Corp.**, Chicago (Wholesale and retail, radio parts—HQ—1,400). **City of Chicago**, Chicago (Municipal government—42,000). **Cook County**, Chicago (County government—20,000). **City of Chicago Board of Education**, Chicago (School system—36,400). **Illinois Bell Telephone Co.**, Chicago (Telephone company—HQ—8,000). **Peoples Gas Light and Coke Co.**, Chicago (Gas distribution—HQ—1,000). **Commonwealth Edison Co.**, Chicago (Electric utility—HQ—2,500). **Presbyterian St. Luke's Hospital Inc.**, Chicago (Hospital—4,300). **Mt. Sinai Hospital and Medical Center**, Chicago (Hospital—1,000).

8th District

(Chicago—North Central)

Race and Ethnic Groups. Blacks 18.1 percent. Spanish heritage population 13.3 percent. Polish stock 8.6 percent, Italian stock 6.2 percent, German stock 3.2 percent.

Cities, 1970 Population. Part of Chicago 459,902.

Newspapers, Circulation. Chicago newspapers circulate throughout district.

Commercial Television Stations, Affiliation. Entire district is located in Chicago ADI.

Plants and Offices, Products, Employment.

Zenith Radio Corp., Chicago (Radios, TVs, electronic equipment—at least 1,010). **Zenith Radio**

Corp., Chicago (Radio, TV, electronic equipment—3,100). **Zenith Radio Corp.**, Chicago (Headquarters—4,500). **Admiral Corp.**, Chicago (Headquarters—1,000).**Admiral Corp.**, Chicago (Electronic components—1,800). **Motorola Inc.**, Chicago (Communications Division—communications equipment—1,000). **Wells-Gardner Electronics Corp.**, Chicago (Radio and television equipment—1,000). **General Electric Co.**, Chicago (Hotpoint Division—electric household appliances—at least 1,010). **American Home Products Corp.**, Chicago (Ecko Housewares Co. Division—household products, equipment—1,000). **Intercraft Industries Corp.**, Chicago (Metal and wood frames—HQ—1,300). **Seeburg Corp. of Delaware**, Chicago (Coin operated phonographs, vending machines—HQ—1,800). **Sunbeam Corp.**, Chicago (Electrical appliances—HQ—4,500).**Commonwealth United Corp.**, Chicago (Juke boxes, holding company—4,600). **Continental Can Co. Inc.**, Chicago (Metal cans, containers—1,100). **Dana Corp.**, Chicago (Victor Division—metal gaskets—1,000). **Pettibone Corp.**, Chicago (Machinery and equipment—HQ—1,350). **American Gage and Machine Co.**, Chicago (Simpson Electric Co. Division—machine tools—3,000). **Beatrice Foods Co.**, Chicago (Burney Brothers Division—bakery goods—1,900). **John Morrell and Co.**, Chicago (Meat products—1,500). **Mars Inc.**, Chicago (M and M Mars Division—candy—1,600). **American Home Products Corp.**, Chicago (E. J. Brach and Son Division—candy—3,000). **John Conrad and Associates**, Chicago (Business and management consulting services—1,680). **Chicago Rawhide Mfg. Co.**, Chicago (Leather and fabricated rubber products—HQ—1,000). **Helene Curtis Industries Inc.**, Chicago (Cosmetics, hair preparations—HQ—1,400). **Gamble Department Stores Inc.**, Chicago (Department store, holding company—1,920). **Aldens Inc.**, Chicago (Mail order—HQ—4,700). **St. Anne's Hospital of Chicago**, Chicago (Hospital—1,000).

9th District

(Chicago—Northeast, Lake Shore)

Race and Ethnic Groups. Blacks 4.7 percent. Spanish heritage population 8.7 percent. Russian stock 6.0 percent, German stock 4.6 percent, Polish stock 3.3 percent.

Cities, 1970 Population. Part of Chicago 463,991.

Universities, Enrollment. Loyola University (Chicago—14,752 total enrollment, part in 7th District), Mundelein College (Chicago—1,362).

Newspapers, Circulation. Chicago newspapers circulate throughout district.

Commercial Television Stations, Affiliation. Entire district is located in Chicago ADI.

Plants and Offices, Products, Employment.

Scholl Inc., Chicago (Orthopedic supplies and shoes—HQ—1,500). **Stewart-Warner Corp.**, Chicago (Measuring and testing instruments and equipment, etc.—HQ—4,000). **S & C Electric Co.**, Chicago (Electrical equipment—1,050). **Appleton Electric Co.**, Chicago (Wiring devices, light fixtures—

HQ—1,150). **Kemper Insurance Group**, Chicago (Insurance—HQ—1,700). **Combined Insurance Co. of America**, Chicago (Insurance—HQ—1,130). **A. C. Nielsen Co.**, Chicago (Marketing research—HQ—1,000). **Oscar Mayer and Co.**, Chicago (Processed meat products—1,700). **Chicago Rawhide Mfg. Co.**, Chicago (Oil seals—1,000). **St. Joseph's Hospital**, Chicago (Hospital—1,200). **Edgewater Hospital Inc.**, Chicago (Hospital—1,100).

10th District

(Cook County—Northern Suburbs)

Race and Ethnic Groups. Blacks 3.0 percent. Russian stock 4.4 percent, German stock 4.3 percent, Polish stock 3.7 percent.

Cities, 1970 Population. Evanston 79,910, Skokie 68,597, part of DesPlaines 44,750, part of Park Ridge 35,158.

Universities, Enrollment. National College of Education (Evanston—3,088), Northwestern University (Evanston—15,006).

Military Installations or Activities. Naval Air Station, Glenview.

Newspapers, Circulation. Chicago newspapers circulate throughout district.

Commercial Television Stations, Affiliation. Entire district is located in Chicago ADI.

Plants and Offices, Products, Employment.

Bell and Howell, Lincolnwood (Motion picture, photographic equipment, etc.—HQ—3,300).**Warwick Electronics**, Niles (Radios, TVs, tape recorders—HQ—1,400). **Honeywell Inc.**, Morton Grove (Commercial Division—automatic temperature controls—at least 1,000). **Apeco Corp.**, Evanston (Photocopy equipment—HQ—1,000). **International Telephone and Telegraph Co.**, Morton Grove (ITT Bell and Gossett Division—industrial pumps and heating equipment—1,150). **Teletype Corp.**, Skokie (Printing, telephone, telegraph equipment—HQ—6,000). **Baxter Laboratories Inc.**, Morton Grove (Pharmaceutical products, holding company—HQ—10,000). **G. D. Searle and Co.**, Skokie (Pharmaceuticals—5,000). **Avon Products Inc.**, Morton Grove (Cosmetics, perfumes—1,000). **Allstate Insurance Co.**, Northbrook (Insurance—HQ—1,500). **Crane Packing Co.**, Morton Grove (Sales and packaging equipment—HQ—1,400). **Cook Electric Co.**, Morton Grove (Electrical equipment—1,000). **Signode Corp.**, Glenview (Tools and machinery—1,100). **Vapor Corp.**, Niles (Heating equipment, temperature controls, etc.—HQ—1,900). **Marshall Field and Co.**, Skokie (Department store—1,800).. **Marx Industrial Maintenance**, DesPlaines (Janitorial and protection services—HQ—1,750). **Universal Oil Products Company**, Des Plaines (Petroleum, petrochemical technological services—HQ—2,000).

11th District

(Chicago—Northwest)

Race and Ethnic Groups. Polish stock 10.1 percent, German stock 7.2 percent, Italian stock 5.2 percent, Russian stock 3.1 percent.

(Continued on p. 62)

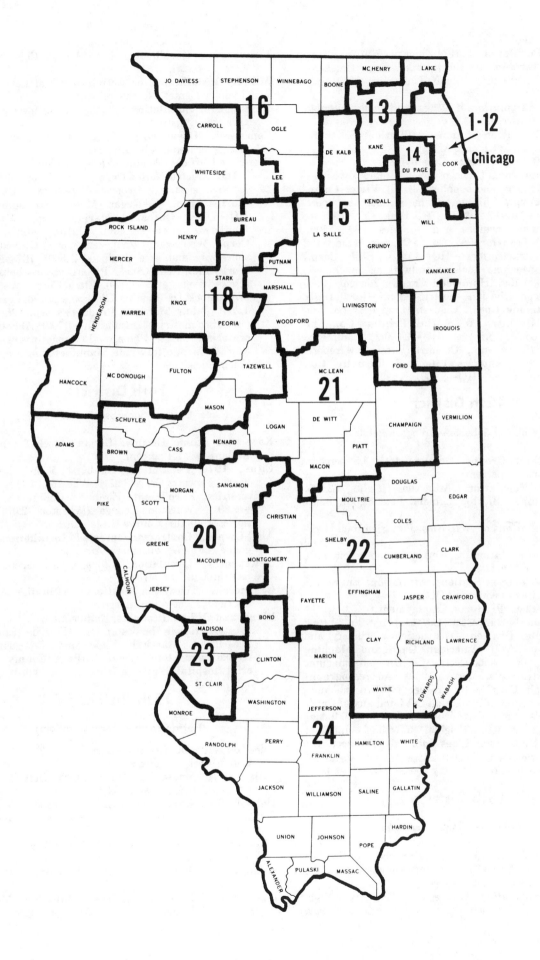

Cities, 1970 Population. Part of Chicago 461,079.

Universities, Enrollment. North Park College (Chicago—1,294), Northeastern Illinois University (Chicago—7,764).

Newspapers, Circulation. Chicago newspapers circulate throughout district.

Commercial Television Stations, Affiliation. Entire district is located in Chicago ADI.

Plants and Offices, Products, Employment.

Swingline Inc., Chicago (Wilson Jones Division—office machinery and supplies—1,110). **Victor Comptometer Corp.**, Chicago (Business machines, sporting goods—HQ—2,200). **A. B. Dick Co.**, Chicago (Duplicating machines and supplies—HQ—2,500). **Advance Transformer Co.**, Chicago (Electrical products, transformers—HQ—1,000). **Skil Corp.**, Chicago (Machine tools, metalworking machinery, etc.—HQ—1,100). **Hammond Corp.**, Chicago (Hammond Organ Division—electric organs—1,000). **Bally Manufacturing Corp.**, Chicago (Coin operated machines—HQ—1,000). **W. F. Hall Printing Co.**, Chicago (Books, printing—HQ—2,400). **Commerce Clearing House Inc.**, Chicago (Public law reports—HQ—1,200). **Bankers Life and Casualty Co.**, Chicago (Insurance—HQ—3,000).

12th District

(Outer Chicago Suburbs—Arlington Heights)

Race and Ethnic Groups. German stock 3.5 percent, Italian stock 2.3 percent.

Cities, 1970 Population. Arlington Heights 62,905, Mount Prospect 37,018, Highland Park 32,057, Palatine 25,919.

Military Installations or Activities. Fort Sheridan, Highwood.

Newspapers, Circulation. Chicago newspapers circulate throughout district.

Commercial Television Stations, Affiliation. Entire district is located in Chicago ADI.

Plants and Offices, Products, Employment.

International Harvester Co., Libertyville (Frank Hough Mfg. Division—construction machinery and equipment—2,020). **American Gage and Machine Co.**, Elgin (Simpson Electric Co. Division—machine tools, instruments, gages 3,000). **Addressograph-Multigraph Corp.**, Mt. Prospect (Office machines and equipment—1,650). **Union Oil Company of California**, Palatine (Petroleum refining—1,500). **Ampex Corp.**, Arlington Heights (Recording equipment—1,050). **United Air Lines Inc.**, Mt. Prospect (Air transportation—HQ—3,500). **Kitchens of Sara Lee Inc.**, Deerfield (Frozen bakery goods—HQ—1,700).

13th District

(Northeast—Elgin, Waukegan)

Race and Ethnic Groups. Blacks 4.8 percent. Spanish heritage population 3.1 percent. German stock 3.6 percent, Polish stock 1.3 percent.

Cities, 1970 Population. Waukegan 65,179, part of Elgin 50,318, North Chicago 47,215, Carpentersville 23,989.

Universities, Enrollment. Lake Forest College (Lake Forest—1,223).

Military Installations or Activities. Great Lakes Naval Training Center, North Chicago.

Newspapers, Circulation. Chicago newspapers circulate throughout district.

Commercial Television Stations, Affiliation. Entire district is located in Chicago ADI.

Plants and Offices, Products, Employment.

Oak Electro-Netics Corp., Crystal Lake (Electronic and electrical devices—HQ—3,000). **Outboard Marine Corp.**, Waukegan (Motors and equipment—HQ—5,000). **Outboard Marine Corp.**, Waukegan (Outboard motors—2,400). **United States Steel Corp.**, Waukegan (Waukegan Works Cyclone Division—wire and wire products—1,500). **Illinois Tool Works Inc.**, Elgin (Shake Proof Division—bolts, nuts, screws, rivets, etc.—1,000). **Eltra Corp.**, Woodstock (Woodstock Die Casting Division—zinc die casting—1,250). **Johns Manville Products Corp.**, Waukegan (Building materials, insulation—1,700). **Abbott Laboratories**, North Chicago (Pharmaceuticals—HQ—5,500). **Chicago Rawhide Manufacturing Co.**, Elgin (Elgin Division—oil seals—1,500).

14th District

(Outer Chicago Suburbs—DuPage County)

Race and Ethnic Groups. German stock 3.7 percent, Italian stock 2.1 percent.

Cities, 1970 Population. Elmhurst 50,484, Lombard 35,992, Downers Grove 32,719, Wheaton 31,419.

Universities, Enrollment. Elmhurst College (Elmhurst—2,891), Wheaton College (Wheaton—2,079), Illinois Benedictine College (Lisle—1,022).

AEC-Owned, Contractor-Operated Installations. Argonne National Laboratory, Argonne.

Newspapers, Circulation. Chicago newspapers circulate throughout district.

Commercial Television Stations, Affiliation. Entire district is located in Chicago ADI.

Plants and Offices, Products, Employment.

International Harvester Co., Hinsdale (Engineering—1,200). **Marshall Field and Co.**, Hinsdale (Department store—1,300). **DuPage County Memorial Hospital**, Elmhurst (Hospital—1,300).

15th District

(North Central—Aurora, DeKalb)

Race and Ethnic Groups. German stock 3.1 percent, Italian stock 1.2 percent.

Cities, 1970 Population. Aurora 74,820, DeKalb 32,927, Ottawa 18,606, Streator 15,589.

Universities, Enrollment. Aurora College (Aurora—1,094), Northern Illinois University (DeKalb—24,667).

AEC-Owned, Contractor-Operated Facilities. National Accelerator Laboratory, Batavia.

Newspapers, Circulation. Chicago Newspapers circulate in portion of district.

Commercial Television Stations, Affiliation. Most of district is located in Chicago ADI. Small portions of district are located in Peoria and Springfield-Decatur-Champaign ADIs.

Plants and Offices, Products, Employment.

Libbey-Owens-Ford Co., Ottawa (Glass—1,800). **Owens-Illinois Inc.**, Streator (Glass containers—2,500). **Barber-Greene Co.**, Aurora (Construction machinery and equipment, etc.—HQ—1,560).**Caterpillar Tractor Co. Inc.**, Aurora (Tractors—4,000). **Lyon Metal Products Inc.**, Montgomery (Metal products—1,000). **Lyon Metal Products Inc.**, Aurora (Metal products—HQ—1,000). **G. W. Murphy Industries Inc.**, Geneva (Portable tools—1,000).**Thor Power Tool Co.**, Aurora (Power and pneumatic tools—HQ—1,000). **General Time Corp.**, Peru (Westclox Division—timing devices—2,000). **Western Electric Co.**, Montgomery (Telephone equipment—2,860). **GTE Automatic Electric Inc.**, Genoa (Switchboard equipment—1,700).

16th District

(Northwest—Rockford, Freeport)

Race and Ethnic Groups. Blacks 4.2 percent. German stock 2.9 percent, Swedish stock 2.9 percent.

Cities, 1970 Population. Rockford 147,224, Freeport 27,740, Dixon 18,149, North Park 15,673.

Universities, Enrollment. Rockford College (Rockford—1,433).

Newspapers, Circulation. Rockford Star (MxSat—56,034).

Commercial Television Stations, Affiliation. Most of district is located in Rockford ADI. Rockford stations include: WCEE-TV, Rockford (CBS); WREX-TV, Rockford (ABC); WTVO, Rockford (NBC). In addition, portions of district are located in Chicago and Davenport (Iowa)-Rock Island-Moline ADIs.

Plants and Offices, Products, Employment.

Sundstrand Corp., Rockford (Aircraft parts, machine tools etc.—HQ—2,200). **Sundstrand Corp.**, Rockford (Aircraft missile parts—3,320).**Sundstrand Corp.**, Belvidere (Machine tools—1,100). **Chrysler Corp.**, Belvidere (Auto assembly—5,500). **Admiral Corp.**, Harvard (Television sets—1,900). **Admiral Corp.**, Dixon (TV, stereo equipment—1,000).**Ingersoll Milling Machine Co.**, Rockford (Metal cutting machinery—1,500). **Greenlee Bros. and Co.**, Rockford (Metal working machine tools—HQ—1,150). **Atwood Vacuum Machine Co. Inc.**, Rockford (Automatic hardware—HQ—1,000). **Amerock Corp.**, Rockford (Cabinets, hardware—HQ—1,900). **Keystone Consolidated Industries.**, Rockford (Hardwood products, metal dies—1,500).**Barber-Colman Co.**, Rockford (Textile machinery and equipment—HQ—2,000. **Barber-Colman Co.**, Rockford (Textile machinery and equipment—2,100).**Rockford Products Corp.**, Rockford (Screw products—HQ—1,500). **Woodward Governor Co.**, Rockford (Aircraft parts—HQ—1,000). **Honeywell Inc.**, Freeport (Micro Switch Division—switches and motors—3,000). **Kelly Springfield Tire Co.**, Freeport (Tires—1,300). **Kable Printing Co.**, Mount Morris (Commercial printing—HQ—1,450).

17th District

(Northeast—Joliet, Kankakee)

Race and Ethnic Groups. Blacks 8.7 percent. Spanish heritage population 2.8 percent. German stock 2.5 percent, Italian stock 2.3 percent.

Cities, 1970 Population. Joliet 78,675, Chicago Heights 40,860, Kankakee 30,898, Romeoville 12,679.

Universities, Enrollment. Lewis College (Lockport—2,536), Olivet Nazarene College (Kankakee—1,805).

Newspapers, Circulation. Chicago newspapers circulate in portions of district.

Commercial Television Stations, Affiliation. Majority of district is located in Chicago ADI. Portion of district is located in Springfield-Decatur-Champaign ADI.

Plants and Offices, Products, Employment.

Caterpillar Tractor Co., Joliet (Earth moving equipment—6,000). **Ford Motor Co.**, Chicago Heights (Metal Stamping Division—auto stampings—5,000). **Uniroyal Inc.**, Joliet (Explosives—8,200). **United States Steel Corp.**, Joliet (Metal rods, wire products—1,500). **Roper Corp.**, Bradley (Lawn mowers, chain saws—1,150). **General Foods Corp.**, Kankakee (Animal feed—at least 1,000). **Elgin, Joliet and Eastern Railway Co.**, Joliet (Railroad—1,500).

18th District

(West Central—Peoria, Pekin)

Race and Ethnic Groups. Blacks 3.6 percent. German stock 2.5 percent, British stock 1.0 percent.

Cities, 1970 Population. Peoria 126,956, Galesburg 36,288, Pekin 31,295, East Peoria 18,528.

Universities, Enrollment. Bradley University (Peoria—5,703), Knox College (Galesburg—1,439).

Newspapers, Circulation. Peoria Journal Star (ExSat—60,541).

Commercial Television Stations, Affiliation. Most of district is located in Peoria ADI. Peoria stations include: WEEK-TV, East Peoria (NBC); WMBD-TV, Peoria (CBS); WRAU-TV, Creve Coeur (ABC). In addition, portions of district are located in Quincy-Hannibal (Missouri) and Davenport (Iowa)-Rock Island-Moline ADIs.

Plants and Offices, Products, Employment.

Caterpillar Tractor Co., Peoria (Construction and earth moving equipment, tractors, etc.—HQ—20,000). **Caterpillar Tractor Co.**, Morton (Construction equipment—1,800). **Caterpillar Tractor Co.**, Mossville (Diesel engines—2,400). **CPC International Inc.**, Pekin (Corn Industrial Division—wet corn milling—1,050). **Hiram Walker and Sons**, Peoria (Distilled liquor—1,600). **Westinghouse Air Brake Co.**, Peoria (Construction machinery and equipment—1,800). **Outboard Marine Corp.**, Galesburg (Gale Products Division—machinery and equipment—2,200). **Admiral Corp.**, Galesburg (Midwest Manufacturing Division—air conditioners, refrigerators, freezers—3,000).

19th District

(West—Moline, Rock Island)

Race and Ethnic Groups. German stock 2.1 percent, Swedish stock 1.9 percent.

Cities, 1970 Population. Rock Island 50,275, Moline 46,337, East Moline 20,765, Macomb 19,653.

Universities, Enrollment. Augustana College (Rock Island—2,261), Monmouth College (Monmouth—1,178), Western Illinois University (Macomb—13,711).

Military Installations or Activities. Savanna Army Depot, Savanna; Rock Island Arsenal, Rock Island.

Commercial Television Stations, Affiliation. Most of district is located in Davenport (Iowa)—Rock Island-Moline ADI. Stations include: WHBF-TV, Rock Island (CBS); WQAD-TV, Moline (ABC). In addition, small portion of district is located in Quincy-Hannibal (Missouri) ADI.

Plants and Offices, Products, Employment.

Deere and Co., Moline (Farm implements—HQ—9,000). **Deere and Co.,** Moline (John Deere Planter Works—farm implements—at least 1,010). **Deere and Co.,** Moline (John Deere Plow Works—farm implements—1,100). **Deere and Co.,** East Moline (John Deere East Moline Works—farm implements—4,200). **Deere and Co.,** East Moline (John Deere Foundry—farm implements—1,000). **International Harvester Co.,** East Moline (Farm equipment—2,950). **International Harvester Co.,** Rock Island (Farmall Works—tractors—4,000). **International Harvester Co.,** Canton (Canton Works Division—farm implements and machinery—at least 1,600). **J. I. Case Co.,** Rock Island (Engine and transmission equipment—1,000). **General Electric Co.,** Morrison (Automatic controls—1,850). **Russell, Birdsall, and Ward Bolt and Nut Co.,** Rock Falls (Bolts and nuts—1,300). **Northwestern Steel and Wire Co.,** Sterling (Steel wire and wire products—HQ—3,860). **Luckey Stores Inc.,** Rock Island (Groceries, meat, baked goods—1,800). **Luckey Stores Inc.,** Milan (Groceries and meat—4,500).

20th District

(West Central—Springfield, Quincy)

Race and Ethnic Groups. Blacks 3.8 percent. German stock 2.3 percent, Italian stock 1.2 percent.

Cities, 1970 Population. Springfield 91,563, Quincy 45,266, Alton 39,681, Jacksonville 20,543.

Universities, Enrollment. Quincy College (Quincy—2,164).

Newspapers, Circulation. Illinois State Journal, Springfield (MxSat—54,986).

Commercial Television Stations, Affiliation. District is divided between Springfield-Decatur-Champaign, Quincy-Hannibal (Missouri), and St. Louis (Missouri) ADIs. Springfield station: WICS, Springfield (NBC). Quincy stations include: KHQA-TV, Quincy (CBS primary); WGEM-TV, Quincy (NBC).

Plants and Offices, Products, Employment.

Gardner-Denver Co., Quincy (Mining machinery and equipment—HQ—1,400). **Gardner-Denver Co.,** Quincy (Mining machinery and equipment—1,180). **Firestone Tire and Rubber Co.,** Quincy (Electric Wheel Co.—motor vehicle, trailer parts and accessories—1,200). **Sangamo Electric Co.,** Springfield (Electric power products and equipment—HQ—2,000). **Motorola Inc.,** Quincy (Radio and TV sets—1,000). **Owens-Illinois Inc.,** Alton (Glass Containers—2,600). **Allis-Chalmers Manufacturing Co.,** Springfield (Farm machinery and equipment—4,300). **Mobil Oil Corp.,** Jacksonville (Chemical products—1,200). **Laclede Steel Co.,** (Iron and steel—2,800). **Franklin Life Insurance Co.,** Springfield (Insurance—1,280). **Illinois Bell Telephone,** Springfield (Telephone company—1,660).

21st District

(Central—Bloomington, Decatur, Champaign, Urbana)

Race and Ethnic Groups. Blacks 5.0 percent. German stock 2.2 percent, British stock 0.8 percent.

Cities, 1970 Population. Decatur 90,724, Champaign 56,633, Bloomington 39,964, Urbana 32,763.

Universities, Enrollment. Illinois State University (Normal—17,930), Illinois Wesleyan University (Bloomington—1,727), Millikin University (Decatur—1,755), University of Illinois (Urbana—33,835).

Military Installations or Activities. Chanute Air Force Base, Rantoul.

Commercial Television Stations, Affiliation. District is divided between Springfield-Decatur-Champaign and Peoria ADIs. Decatur station: WAND, Decatur (ABC). Champaign stations include: WCIA, Champaign (CBS); WICD, Champaign (NBC).

Plants and Offices, Products, Employment.

State Farm Mutual Automobile Insurance Co., Bloomington (Insurance—HQ—1,300). **Mueller Co.,** Decatur (Brass and iron valves—HQ—1,000). **Wagner Castings Co.,** Decatur (Malleable iron and castings—1,250). **Caterpillar Tractor Co.,** Decatur (Construction machinery and equipment, engines—4,300). **General Electric Co.,** Decatur (Audio Products Dept.—phonograph parts—1,500). **A.E. Staley Manufacturing Co.,** Decatur (Soybean and corn products, chemicals—HQ—2,400). **Jewel Companies Inc.,** Champaign (Eisner Food Store Division—wholesale groceries—1,800).

22nd District

(Southeast—Danville)

Race and Ethnic Groups. German stock 1.1 percent, British stock 0.5 percent.

Cities, 1970 Population. Danville 42,686, Mattoon 19,516, Charleston 16,320, Taylorville 10,789.

Universities, Enrollment. Eastern Illinois University (Charleston—8,893).

Commercial Television Stations, Affiliation. District is divided between Springfield-Decatur-Champaign ADI and Terre-Haute (Indiana) ADI. Small portions of district are located in Evansville (Indiana) ADI and St. Louis (Missouri) ADI.

Plants and Offices, Products, Employment.
General Motors Corp., (Central Foundary Division—gray iron—2,500). **General Electric Co.**, Danville (Fluorescent lamp equipment—1,100). **General Electric Co.**, Mattoon (Electric lamps—1,200). **Fedders Corp.**, Effingham (Norge Division—gas and electric ranges—1,500). **Borg-Warner Corp.**, Effingham (Air conditioning, drying, heating appliances—1,420). **National Distillers and Chemical Corp.**, Tuscola (Alcoholic beverages—1,200).

23rd District

(Southwest—East St. Louis, Belleville)

Race and Ethnic Groups. Blacks 15.0 percent. German stock 1.8 percent, British stock 0.7 percent.
Cities, 1970 Population. East St. Louis 69,957, Belleville 41,914, Granite City 40,492, Cahokia 20,658.
Universities, Enrollment. Belleville Area College (Belleville—4,913).
Military Installations or Activities. Scott Air Force Base, Belleville.
Newspapers, Circulation. St. Louis newspapers circulate in district.
Commercial Television Stations, Affiliation. Entire district is located in St. Louis (Missouri) ADI.
Plants and Offices, Products, Employment.
Monsanto Co., Monsanto (Chemicals—2,500). **Shell Oil Co.**, Wood River (Petroleum refinery—

2,200). **Granite City Steel Co.**, Granite City (Steel wire—HQ—4,800). **General Steel Industries Inc.**, Granite City (Castings Division—iron foundry transportation equipment—at least 1,500). **Amsted Industries Inc.**, Granite City (Steel casting—1,000). **Indian Head Inc.**, East St. Louis (Obear-Nester Glass Division—glass products—1,200). **A. O. Smith Corp.**, Granite City (Auto frames—1,400).

24th District

(South—Carbondale)

Race and Ethnic Groups. Blacks 3.9 percent. German stock 1.4 percent, Italian stock 0.6 percent.
Cities, 1970 Population. Carbondale 22,816, Mount Vernon 16,067, Centralia 15,055, Marion 11,676.
Universities, Enrollment. Southern Illinois University (Carbondale—24,543), Southern Illinois University (Edwardsville—14,266).
Commercial Television Stations, Affiliation. WSIL-TV, Harrisburg (ABC). District is divided between St. Louis (Missouri) ADI and Paducah (Kentucky)-Cape Girardeau (Missouri)-Harrisburg ADI.
Plants and Offices, Products, Employment.
Norge-Fedders Corp., Herrin (Norge Division—washing machines—1,400). **Spartan Printing Co.**, Sparta (Printing—1,500). **Old Ben Coal Corp.**, Benton (Coal mine—1,100). **Consolidated Foods Corp.**, Centralia (Hollywood Brands Division—candy—1,700).

INDIANA: ELEVEN HOUSE SEATS, NO CHANGE

A redistricting bill designed to benefit the Republicans passed the Indiana Senate April 16, 1971, by a vote of 26-20. Later the same day, the House concurred in the Senate bill by a voice vote, and the Governor signed it the same night. *(Map p. 67)*

Designed by State Rep. Jack N. Smitherman, Republican chairman of the House Reapportionment Committee, the redistricting plan was checked through a telephone hookup to a Chicago computer, according to the *Indianapolis News.* The computer was fed 1970 census figures for Indiana as well as voting results for all precincts in the state.

Politically, the plan was based on returns in the 1970 race for Secretary of State. Since the Republicans lost that contest, it was believed that precinct election figures would reflect a rock-bottom Republican vote. Moreover, in this race, the basic vote of the party would not be distorted, as in a well-publicized issue oriented contest such as that for the U.S. Senate. This basic Republican strength could be expected to expand in a normal Republican year.

The 1st, 3rd and 9th Districts were made relatively safe for their incumbent Democratic representatives, Ray J. Madden, John Brademas and Lee H. Hamilton, respectively. Likewise, Republican Representatives Earl F. Landgrebe, Elwood Hillis and William G. Bray of the 2nd, 5th and 6th Districts were put in relatively strong positions. All six representatives were re-elected in November 1972.

But two Democratic representatives, Andrew Jacobs Jr. of the 11th District and J. Edward Roush of the 4th District, saw their 1970 margins of victory wiped out by redistricting. Roush survived, but Jacobs was defeated.

The state's remaining three districts—the 7th, 8th and 10th—underwent no significant political alteration.

District	Member Elected 1972	Winning Percentage	1970 Population	Percent Variance
1	Ray J. Madden (D)	56.9	471,761	—0.0828
2	Earl F. Landgrebe (R)	54.7	472,460	+ 0,0652
3	John Brademas (D)	55.2	471,849	—0.0641
4	J. Edward Roush (D)	51.5	472,678	+ 0.1114
5	Elwood Hillis (R)	64.1	471,921	—0.0489
6	William G. Bray (R)	64.8	471,595	—0.1179
7	John T. Myers (R)	61.6	472,041	—0.0235
8	Roger H. Zion (R)	63.4	472,175	+ 0.0048
9	Lee H. Hamilton (D)	62.9	472,321	+ 0.0357
10	David W. Dennis (R)	57.2	472,335	+ 0.0387
11	William H. Hudnut III (R)	51.2	472,533	+ 0.0806

1970 State Population: 5,193,669
Ideal District Population: 472,152

Glossary and Sources

For a complete explanation of all terms used in this book and a list of source material, consult the details included in the Introduction.

Election Results, 1968-1972

Vote for U.S. Representative
(Adjusted to new district boundaries)

District	1968	1970	1972
1	95,340 D (56.0%)	77,818 D (64.8%)	95,873 D (56.9%)
	74,461 R (43.8%)	42,284 R (35.2%)	72,662 R (43.1%)
2	107,549 R (58.3%)	82,488 R (53.2%)	110,406 R (54.7%)
	76,791 D (41.7%)	72,511 D (46.8%)	91,533 D (45.3%)
3	99,848 D (55.0%)	90,474 D (59.9%)	103,949 D (55.2%)
	81,731 R (45.0%)	60,460 R (40.1%)	81,369 R (43.2%)
4	96,557 R (52.7%)	80,846 D (51.2%)	100,327 D (51.5%)
	86,633 D (47.3%)	77,068 R (48.8%)	94,492 R (48.5%)
5	110,044 R (59.0%)	85,416 R (52.6%)	124,692 R (64.1%)
	76,464 D (41.0%)	77,067 D (47.4%)	69,746 D (35.9%)
6	105,609 R (61.6%)	82,650 R (56.8%)	112,525 R (64.8%)
	65,894 D (38.4%)	62,745 D (43.2%)	61,070 D (35.2%)
7	113,690 R (59.8%)	93,395 R (56.4%)	128,688 R (61.6%)
	76,368 D (40.2%)	72,109 D (43.7%)	80,145 D (38.4%)
8	115,986 R (54.4%)	97,322 R (52.0%)	133,850 R (63.4%)
	97,407 D (45.6%)	89,860 D (48.0%)	77,371 D (36.6%)
9	102,806 D (54.2%)	104,291 D (61.5%)	122,698 D (62.9%)
	86,860 R (45.8%)	65,326 R (38.5%)	72,325 R (37.1%)
10	100,983 R (54.8%)	83,743 R (52.6%)	106,798 R (57.2%)
	83,355 D (45.2%)	75,594 D (47.4%)	79,756 D (42.8%)
11	101,591 R (55.1%)	78,637 R (51.0%)	95,839 R (51.2%)
	82,900 D (44.9%)	75,526 D (49.0%)	91,238 D (48.8%)
State	1,095,061 R (53.7%)	878,841 D (50.9%)	1,133,646 R (53.7%)
	943,806 D (46.3%)	848,789 R (49.1%)	973,706 D (46.1%)

Voting Age Population

District	Voting Age Population	Voting Age Population 18, 19, 20	Voting Age Population 65 and Over	Median Age of Voting Age Population
1	292,093	22,880 (7.8%)	32,858 (11.2%)	42.2
2	305,346	32,583 (10.7%)	41,661 (13.6%)	40.3
3	306,820	26,453 (8.6%)	44,270 (14.4%)	43.0
4	298,921	23,390 (7.8%)	44,506 (14.9%)	42.3
5	303,137	21,957 (7.2%)	44,460 (14.7%)	42.6
6	295,350	21,568 (7.3%)	37,467 (12.7%)	41.1
7	325,503	37,203 (11.4%)	56,640 (17.4%)	42.3
8	309,861	22,632 (7.3%)	56,376 (18.2%)	45.4
9	299,509	20,280 (6.8%)	46,940 (15.7%)	43.1
10	306,176	26,859 (8.8%)	46,013 (15.0%)	42.3
11	303,733	22,005 (7.2%)	43,099 (14.2%)	42.6
State	3,346,442	277,803 (8.3%)	494,293 (14.8%)	42.5

Income and Occupation

District	Median Family Income	White Collar Workers	Blue Collar Workers	Service Workers	Farm Workers
1	$10,706	37.1%	50.4%	12.4%	0.1%
2	10,377	41.9	40.6	12.2	5.3
3	10,606	44.3	42.6	11.7	1.4
4	10,443	43.7	41.6	11.2	3.5
5	10,314	41.5	43.8	12.1	2.6
6	10,497	45.3	41.9	11.0	1.8
7	8,808	42.2	39.2	13.7	4.9
8	8,557	38.2	44.0	13.1	4.7
9	9,001	36.7	47.1	11.4	4.8
10	9,635	37.4	46.4	12.0	4.2
11	10,785	53.2	33.3	13.2	0.3
State	9,966	42.1	42.7	12.2	3.0

Education: School Years Completed

District	Completed 4 years of High School	Completed 4 years of College	Completed 5 years or less of School	Median School years completed
1	46.9%	6.0%	8.8%	11.6
2	59.2	10.5	3.1	12.2
3	52.7	8.7	4.5	12.1
4	57.8	8.4	3.5	12.2
5	57.0	9.8	3.6	12.2
6	51.3	7.0	4.5	12.0
7	54.4	9.8	3.8	12.1
8	48.7	6.6	4.5	11.8
9	45.9	5.8	5.4	11.4
10	51.6	6.9	4.4	12.1
11	57.4	12.1	4.6	12.2
State	52.9	8.3	4.6	12.1

Housing and Residential Patterns

District	Housing — Owner Occupied Units	Housing — Renter Occupied Units	Urban	Suburban	Nonmetropolitan
1	64.3%	35.7%	70.0%	30.0%	—
2	74.3	25.7	13.6	51.2	35.2%
3	76.4	23.6	26.7	25.3	48.0
4	75.3	24.7	37.6	21.7	40.7
5	72.3	27.7	25.4	17.1	57.5
6	70.0	30.0	53.6	46.4	—
7	72.6	27.4	14.9	29.3	55.8
8	75.4	24.6	29.4	12.3	58.3
9	75.8	24.2	—	34.1	65.9
10	73.4	26.6	15.1	27.1	57.8
11	58.6	41.4	93.1	6.9	—
State	71.7	28.3	34.5	27.4	38.1

1st District

(Northwest—East Chicago, Gary, Hammond)

Race and Ethnic Groups. Blacks 23.7 percent. Spanish heritage population 7.3 percent.

Cities, 1970 Population. Gary 175,313, Hammond 107,778, East Chicago 46,998, Highland 24,964.

Universities, Enrollment. Indiana University Northwest (Gary—4,516), Purdue University, Calumet Campus (Hammond—4,640), Saint Joseph's Calumet College (East Chicago—1,605).

Newspapers, Circulation. Gary Post-Tribune (Eve—74,590), Hammond Times (ExSat—67,959). In addition, Chicago newspapers circulate in district.

Commercial Television Stations, Affiliation. Entire district is located in Chicago ADI.

Plants and Offices, Products, Employment.
Inland Steel Co., East Chicago (Steel—20,500). **United States Steel Corp.**, Gary (American Bridge Divison—steel—1,200). **United States Steel Corp.**, Gary (Gary Ellwood Works—steel form composition —1,000). **United States Steel Corp.**, Gary (Gary Works—steel, steel products—27,000). **Youngstown**

(Continued on p. 68)

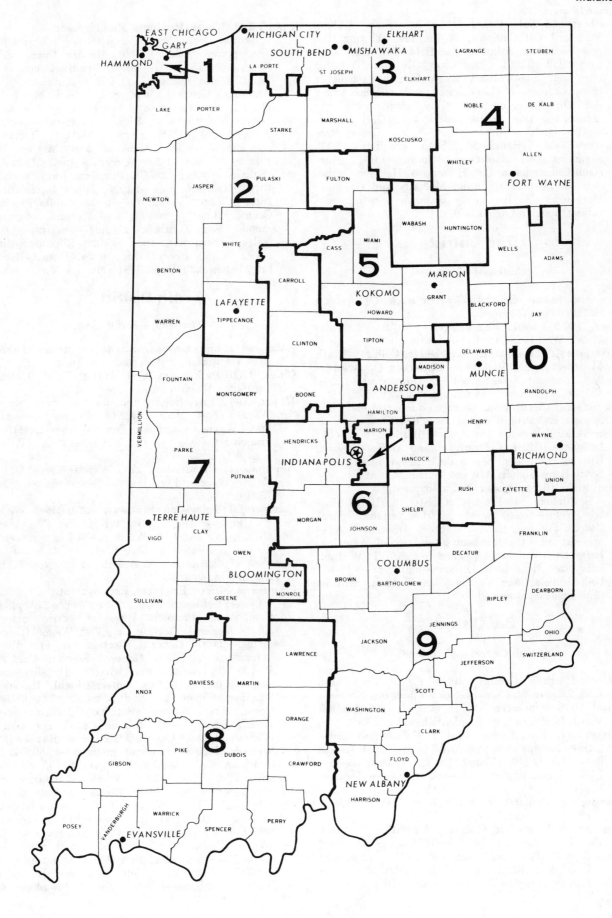

Sheet and Tube Co., East Chicago (Steel—10,500). **Standard Oil Company of Indiana**, Whiting (Research—2,700). **Atlantic Richfield Co.**, East Chicago (Oil—2,500). **American Oil Co.**, Whiting (Refining—2,450). **Blaw Knox Co.**, East Chicago (East Chicago Works—foundry and mill machinery —1,760). **Anderson Co.**, Gary (Auto parts and accessories—HQ—1,100). **Budd Co.**, Gary (Automotive Division—auto bodies—2,120). **Lever Brothers Co.**, Hammond (Soap products—1,500). **Simmons Co.**, Hammond (Bedding—1,600). **Morrison Construction Co.**, Hammond (Heavy construction—at least 1,000). **Rand McNally and Co. Inc.**, Hammond (W. B. Conkey Division—printing, publishing, bookbinding—1,240).

2nd District

(Northwest—Lafayette)

Race and Ethnic Groups. German stock 1.9 percent, British stock 0.7 percent.

Cities, 1970 Population. Lafayette 44,936, Valparaiso 19,462, West Lafayette 19,149, Portage 19,086.

Universities, Enrollment. Manchester College (North Manchester—1,410), Purdue University (Lafayette—35,372), Saint Joseph's College (Rensselaer—1,197), Valparaiso University (Valparaiso—4,703).

Newspapers, Circulation. Chicago, Hammond and Gary newspapers circulate in portions of district.

Commercial Television Stations, Affiliation. WLFI-TV, Lafayette (CBS). Lafayette has no ADI of its own. District is divided between Chicago (Illinois) ADI, South Bend-Elkhart ADI and Indianapolis ADI.

Plants and Offices, Products, Employment.
 Bethlehem Steel Corp., Chesterton (Burns Harbor Plant—rolled steel—6,000). **National Steel Corp.**, Portage (Midwest Steel Division—steel—at least 1,650). **Aluminum Company of America**, Lafayette (Aluminum products—2,200). **TRW Inc.**, Lafayette (Ross Gear Division—auto parts—1,140). **United Telephone Company of Indiana**, Warsaw (Telephone company—1,300).

3rd District

(North Central—South Bend)

Race and Ethnic Groups. Blacks 6.3 percent. Polish stock 2.6 percent, German stock 2.1 percent.

Cities, 1970 Population. South Bend 125,823, Elkhart 43,601, Michigan City 39,280, Mishawaka 35,459.

Universities, Enrollment. Goshen College (Goshen—1,258), Indiana University at South Bend (South Bend—4,803), St. Mary's College (Notre Dame—1,789), University of Notre Dame (Notre Dame—8,237).

Newspapers, Circulation. South Bend Tribune (Eve—116,388).

Commercial Television Stations, Affiliation. WNDU-TV, South Bend (NBC); WSBT-TV, South Bend (CBS); WSJV-TV, Elkhart (ABC). Most of district is located in South Bend-Elkhart ADI. Portion of district is located in Chicago (Illinois) ADI.

Plants and Offices, Products, Employment.
 Bendix Corp., South Bend (Energy Control Division—power brakes—3,500). **Bendix Corp.**, South Bend (Aircraft parts—4,000). **Bendix Corp.**, South Bend (Auto parts, electrical equipment—2,800). **American General Corp.**, South Bend (Motor vehicles—1,900). **Reliance Electric Co.**, Mishawaka (Dodge Manufacturing Division—transmission equipment—1,760). **CTS Corp.**, Elkhart (Electronic components—5,250). **Henkels and McCoy Inc.**, Elkhart (Cables—1,200). **Uniroyal Inc.**, Mishawaka (Fabrics, rubber—2,500). **Pullman Inc.**, Michigan City (Railroad cars—1,100). **Host International Inc.**, Elkhart (Restaurants—1,300). **Riblet Products Corp.**, Elkhart (Housing products and equipment, mobile home chassis, holding company—1,000). **Miles Laboratories Inc.**, Elkhart (Pharmaceuticals —HQ—2,700). **Poor Sisters of St. Francis Hospital**, Mishawaka (Hospital—1,000).

4th District

(Northeast—Fort Wayne)

Race and Ethnic Groups. Blacks 4.1 percent. German stock 1.8 percent, British stock 0.5 percent.

Cities, 1970 Population. Fort Wayne 177,590, Huntington 16,203, Wabash 13,368.

Universities, Enrollment. Indiana University at Fort Wayne (Fort Wayne—3,990), Purdue University, Fort Wayne Campus (Fort Wayne—2,441), St. Francis College (Fort Wayne—2,226), TriState College (Angola—1,605).

Newspapers, Circulation. Fort Wayne Journal-Gazette (Morn—66,267), Fort Wayne News-Sentinel (Eve—75,419).

Commercial Television Stations, Affiliation. WANE-TV, Fort Wayne (CBS); WKJG-TV, Fort Wayne (NBC); WPTA, Fort Wayne (ABC). Nearly entire district is located in Fort Wayne ADI. Small portions of district are located in South Bend-Elkhart ADI and Indianapolis ADI.

Plants and Offices, Products, Employment.
 General Electric Co., Fort Wayne (Appliance Components Products Division—electric motors—2,860). **General Electric Co.**, Fort Wayne (Electric motors—2,000). **General Electric Co.**, Fort Wayne (Transformers—1,700). **General Electric Co.**, Fort Wayne (Industrial Drive System Division—small electric motors—1,200). **International Harvester Co.**, Fort Wayne (Heavy duty trucks—5,600). **Dana Corp.**, Fort Wayne (Salisbury Division—motor vehicle parts—2,000). **Zollner Corp.**, Fort Wayne (Pistons—1,500). **General Tire and Rubber Co.**, Wabash (Industrial rubber products—1,480). **B. F. Goodrich Co.**, Woodburn (Tires—1,170). **Babcock and Wilcox Co.**, Mount Vernon (Nuclear energy equipment—1,200). **International Telephone and Telegraph**, Fort Wayne (ITT Aerospace/Optical Division—radio and TV transmitting, signaling, detection equipment—1,000). **Magnavox Co.**, Fort Wayne (Radios, radar, etc.—2,200). **Lincoln National Life Insurance**, Fort Wayne (Insurance—HQ —2,000). **Transport Motor Express Inc.**, Fort Wayne (Trucking—1,200). **General Telephone Co.**

of Indiana, Fort Wayne (Telephone company—HQ—2,000). **Sears, Roebuck and Co.**, Fort Wayne (Department stores—1,000).

5th District

(North Central—Anderson, Kokomo, Marion)

Race and Ethnic Groups. Blacks 6.4 percent. German stock 0.9 percent, British stock 0.6 percent.

Cities, 1970 Population. Part of Anderson 68,530 (includes all but 2,347 residents of Anderson), part of Indianapolis 51,405, Kokomo 44,057, Marion 39,849.

Universities, Enrollment. Anderson College (Anderson—1,754), Butler University (Indianapolis—4,363), Indiana University at Kokomo (Kokomo—1,715), Taylor University (Upland—1,418).

Military Installations or Activities. Grissom Air Force Base, Peru.

Newspapers, Circulation. Indianapolis newspapers circulate in portion of district.

Commercial Television Stations, Affiliation. Nearly entire district is located in Indianapolis ADI. Small portion of district is located in South Bend-Elkhart ADI.

Plants and Offices, Products, Employment.
General Motors Corp., Anderson (Guide Lamp Division—automobile electrical equipment—5,300). **General Motors Corp.**, Anderson (Delco-Remy Division—electrical equipment, storage batteries—17,500). **General Motors Corp.**, Kokomo (Delco Radio Division—radios, controls—8,500). **General Motors Corp.**, Marion (Fisher Body Division—auto bodies—5,000). **Chrysler Corp.**, Kokomo (Kokomo Casting Division—power transmissions—4,000). **Continental Steel Corp.**, Kokomo (Steel and steel products—2,590). **Cabot Corp.**, Kokomo (Stellite Division—special alloys—2,500). **Firestone Tire and Rubber Co.**, Noblesville (Industrial rubber products—1,700). **General Tire and Rubber Co.**, Marion (Chemical Plastics Division—industrial plastic products—1,700). **Owens-Illinois Inc.**, Gas City (Glass Container Division—glass containers—1,000). **Dana Corp.**, Marion (Marion Division—motor vehicle parts—1,280). **RCA Corp.**, Marion (TV Picture Tube Division—TV picture tubes—2,960). **Essex International Inc.**, Logansport (RBM Controls Division—industrial controls—1,000).

6th District

(Central—Indianapolis Suburbs)

Race and Ethnic Groups. Blacks 3.7 percent. German stock 0.9 percent, British stock 0.5 percent.

Cities, 1970 Population. Part of Indianapolis 252,808, Speedway 15,119, Shelbyville 15,070, Franklin 11,436.

Universities, Enrollment. Indiana Central College (Indianapolis—2,469).

Newspapers, Circulation. Indianapolis newspapers circulate throughout district.

Commercial Television Stations, Affiliation. Entire district is located in Indianapolis ADI.

Plants and Offices, Products, Employment.
FMC Corp., Indianapolis (Link Belt Co., Ewart Plant—machinery—3,000). **FMC Corp.**, Indianapolis (Link Belt Co. Bearing Plant—bearings—1,100). **Chrysler Corp.**, Indianapolis (Foundry—1,200). **General Motors Corp.**, Indianapolis (Allison Division—aircraft engines, tank bodies—16,000). **Carrier Corp.**, Indianapolis (Bryant Air Conditioning Co. Division—air conditioning equipment—2,300). **Dow Chemical Co.**, Indianapolis (Pharmaceuticals—1,150). **Eli Lilly and Co.**, Indianapolis (Drugs and pharmaceuticals—HQ—12,000). **Amsted Industries Inc.**, Indianapolis (Diamond Chain Co. Division—power transmission chains—1,400). **National Distillers and Chemical Corp.**, Indianapolis (Bridgeport Brass Division—mill products—1,500). **Economy Finance Corp.**, Indianapolis (Installment loans—1,020). **Great Atlantic and Pacific Tea Co.**, Indianapolis (Groceries—2,300). **Sears, Roebuck and Co. Inc.**, Indianapolis (Department stores—2,100).

7th District

(West—Terre Haute, Bloomington)

Race and Ethnic Groups. German stock 0.8 percent, British stock 0.8 percent.

Cities, 1970 Population. Terre Haute 70,335, Bloomington 42,787, Frankfort 14,899, Crawfordsville 13,846.

Universities, Enrollment. DePauw University (Greencastle—2,274), Indiana State University (Terre Haute—16,274), Indiana University (Bloomington—30,368, 1970 enrollment), Rose-Hulman Institute of Technology (Terre Haute—1,138).

Commercial Television Stations, Affiliation. WTHI-TV, Terre Haute (CBS primary, ABC); WTWO, Terre Haute (NBC primary, ABC; also CBS on per program basis). District is divided between Terre Haute and Indianapolis ADIs.

Plants and Offices, Products, Employment.
Harrison Steel Casting Co. Inc., Attica (Foundry—1,200). **P. R. Mallory and Co. Inc.**, Frankfort (Mallory Controls Co.—control switches—1,000). **General Electric Co.**, Bloomington (Hotpoint Division—electric appliances—1,300). **RCA Corp.**, Bloomington (Consumer Electronic Division—televisions and appliances—7,700). **Tarzian Sarkes Inc.**, Bloomington (TV parts, broadcasting equipment—HQ—1,300). **Columbia Broadcasting System**, Terre Haute (Columbia Records Division—phonograph records—2,400). **R. R. Donnelley and Sons Co.**, Crawfordsville (Lakeside Press—printing—2,400).

8th District

(Southwest—Evansville)

Race and Ethnic Groups. Blacks 2.6 percent. German stock 1.1 percent, British stock 0.3 percent.

Cities, 1970 Population. Evansville 138,673, Vincennes 19,865, Bedford 13,140, Washington 11,357.

Universities, Enrollment. University of Evansville (Evansville—5,393).

Military Installations or Activities. Naval Ammunition Depot, Crane.

Newspapers, Circulation. Evansville Courier (Morn—65,860).

Commercial Television Stations, Affiliation. WEHT-TV, Evansville (CBS); WFIE-TV, Evansville (NBC); WTVW, Evansville (ABC). Most of district is located in Evansville ADI. Portions of district are located in Terre Haute ADI and Louisville (Kentucky) ADI.

Plants and Offices, Products, Employment.

Whirlpool Corp., Evansville (Air conditioners and dehumidifiers—3,000). **Whirlpool Corp.**, Evansville (Refrigerators, air conditioners—1,000). **Whirlpool Corp.**, Evansville (Refrigerators, freezers—5,500). **General Motors Corp.**, Bedford (Central Foundry Division—foundry—1,110). **Aluminum Company of America**, Newburgh (Alcoa Warrick Operations—aluminum—2,600). **Admiral Corp.**, Orleans (Televisions, radios, stereos—1,300). **AMF Inc.**, Princeton (Potter and Brumfield Division—electric relays—2,300). **Bluss and Laughlin Industries**, Evansville (Faultless Caster Division—furniture casters and furniture hardware—1,000). **Mead Johnson and Co.**, Evansville (Pharmaceuticals, infant foods—1,800).

9th District

(Southeast—Columbus, New Albany)

Race and Ethnic Groups. German stock 0.8 percent, British stock 0.3 percent.

Cities, 1970 Population. New Albany 38,406, Columbus 27,298, Jeffersonville 19,931, Connersville 17,629.

Universities, Enrollment. Hanover College (Hanover—1,031), Indiana University Southeast (Jeffersonville—2,408).

Military Installations or Activities. Jefferson Proving Ground (Army), Madison.

Newspapers, Circulation. Louisville (Kentucky) papers circulate in portions of district.

Commercial Television Stations, Affiliation. District is divided between Indianapolis ADI, Louisville (Kentucky) ADI and Cincinnati (Ohio) ADI.

Plants and Offices, Products, Employment.

Cummins Engine Co. Inc., Columbus (Diesel engines, parts, accessories—HQ—8,500). **Hamilton Cosco Inc.**, Columbus (Furniture, household equipment, holding company—2,400). **Cosco Household Products Inc.**, Columbus (Metal household furniture—1,400). **Hillenbrand Industries Inc.**, Batesville (Hospital equipment, caskets, holding company—1,350). **Philco-Ford Corp.**, Connersville (Refrigeration Products Division—automobile air conditioners—3,000). **Design and Manufacturing Corp.**, Connersville (Dishwashers—1,000). **Jeffboat Inc.**, Jeffersonville (Shipbuilding and repair—1,000). **Mead Corp.**, Columbus (Woodward Division—grey iron castings—1,000). **Colgate-Palmolive Co.**, Jeffersonville (Soap, toilet preparations—

1,150). **Olin Corp.**, Charlestown (Indiana Ammunition Plant—ammunition—5,000).

10th District

(East—Muncie, Richmond)

Race and Ethnic Groups. Blacks 2.6 percent. German stock 0.6 percent, British stock 0.4 percent.

Cities, 1970 Population. Muncie 69,159, Richmond 44,027, New Castle 21,223.

Universities, Enrollment. Ball State University (Muncie—19,403), Earlham College (Richmond—1,155).

Commercial Television Stations, Affiliation. Majority of district is located in Indianapolis ADI. Portions of district are located in Fort Wayne ADI, Dayton (Ohio) ADI and Cincinnati (Ohio) ADI.

Plants and Offices, Products, Employment.

General Motors Corp., Muncie (Chevrolet Motor Division—auto parts—2,400). **General Motors Corp.**, Muncie (Chevrolet Muncie Division—auto parts—3,300). **Chrysler Corp.**, New Castle (Auto parts—2,500). **National Automatic Tool Co. Inc.**, Richmond (Machine tools, industrial machinery—1,000). **Sheller-Globe Corp.**, Union City (Hardy Division—metal castings, screw machine products—1,000). **Borg-Warner Corp.**, Muncie (Warner Gear Division—mechanical transmission equipment—4,000). **AVCO Corp.**, Richmond (Electronics and Ordnance Division—missile control systems, ammunition—2,000). **Belden Corp.**, Richmond (Electric wire, cable—1,650). **Westinghouse Electric Corp.**, Muncie (Transformers—1,900). **Anchor Hocking Corp.**, Winchester (Glass products—1,100). **Kerr Glass Manufacturing Corp.**, Dunkirk (Packaging Products Division—glass containers—1,200). **Marhoefer Packing Co. Inc.**, Muncie (Meat packer—HQ—1,200).

11th District

(Central—Indianapolis)

Race and Ethnic Groups. Blacks 22.4 percent. German stock 1.3 percent, British stock 0.7 percent.

Cities, 1970 Population. Part of Indianapolis 440,103, Lawrence 16,565, part of Beech Grove 13,322 (includes all but 146 residents of Beech Grove).

Universities, Enrollment. Indiana University-Purdue University at Indianapolis (Indianapolis—14,605).

Military Installations or Activities. Fort Benjamin Harrison, Indianapolis.

Newspapers, Circulation. Indianapolis Star (Morn—223,697), Indianapolis News (Eve—178,246).

Commercial Television Stations, Affiliation. WRTV, Indianapolis (NBC); WISH-TV, Indianapolis (CBS); WLWI-TV, Indianapolis (ABC); WTTV, Indianapolis-Bloomington (None). Entire district is located in Indianapolis ADI.

Plants and Offices, Products, Employment.

RCA Corp., Indianapolis (RCA Victor Record Division—phonograph records—2,000). **RCA Corp.**,

Indianapolis (TV sets—4,000). **Western Electric Co. Inc.**, Indianapolis (Telephone and telegraph apparatus —7,500). **General Motors Corp.**, Indianapolis (Chevrolet Indianapolis Division—auto parts, assemblies —4,000). **Chrysler Corp.**, Indianapolis (Indianapolis Electric Plant—automobile electrical equipment— 3,500). **Ford Motor Co.**, Indianapolis (Chassis and Transmission Division—automobile parts—4,500). **Wallace-Murray Corp.**, Indianapolis (Schwitzer Division—automobile parts and equipment—1,700). **International Harvester Co.**, Indianapolis (Truck engines, farm equipment—3,000). **Penn Central Transportation Co.**, Beech Grove (Railroad—1,600). **P. R. Mallory and Co. Inc.**, Indianapolis (Electronic and metallurgical components—HQ—1,950).

Mutual Hospital Insurance Inc., Indianapolis (Insurance—1,100). **United Parcel Service Inc.**, Indianapolis (Delivery service—1,000). **American Janitorial Service Corp.**, Indianapolis (Janitorial services—1,190). **Indiana Bell Telephone Co. Inc.**, Indianapolis (Telephone company—HQ—5,000). **The William H. Block Co.**, Indianapolis (Department stores—HQ—1,200). **Kroger Co.**, Indianapolis (Grocery stores—3,360). **L. S. Ayres and Co.**, Indianapolis (Department stores—HQ—1,000). **National Tea Co. Inc.**, Indianapolis (Standard Grocery Division—groceries—4,000). **Indianapolis Newspapers Inc.**, Indianapolis (Newspaper publishing—1,800). **State of Indiana**, Indianapolis (State government—25,000 total employment).

IOWA: SIX HOUSE SEATS, LOSS OF ONE

Faced with the necessity of eliminating one of the state's seven congressional seats, the Iowa Legislature turned to the University of Iowa computer center for help. The center came up with 12 possible plans, all of them adhering to county lines.

One of these plans (plan 12) formed the basis of the final bill, which placed Representatives John H. Kyl (R) of the old 4th District and Neal Smith (D) of the old 5th District together.

The redistricting bill passed the state Senate Feb. 18, 1971, by a vote of 37-11 and the state House Feb. 25 by a vote of 62-34. Gov. Robert Ray (R) signed it March 5, 1971.

The population variance between the largest and smallest districts is 0.648 percent.

Despite the small population variance, some doubt was expressed that the new districts could survive a test of their constitutionality. State Attorney General Richard

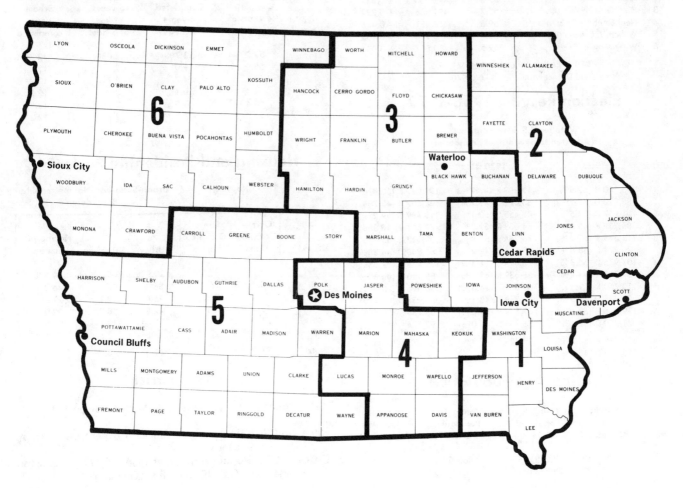

Turner (R), whose job it would have been to defend the districts in federal court, said he doubted the courts would uphold them.

One consideration in any court challenge would have been the fact that several of the other plans developed by the computer had smaller variances between largest and smallest districts. Thus, it could have been argued that several other feasible plans came closer to mathematical equality. However, no serious court challenge developed and the new districts stood for the 1972 elections.

Under the realignment, three districts were designed to be strongly Republican: the 3rd, represented by H.R. Gross (R); the new 5th, represented by William J. Scherle (R), and the 6th, represented by Wiley Mayne (R).

Republicans also held a moderate advantage in the 1st District, whose incumbent Rep. Fred Schwengel (R) was nevertheless defeated. Rep. John C. Culver (D) saw little change in his 2nd District, where he was re-elected easily in 1972.

In the counties constituting the new 4th District, where Smith and Kyl were placed, the Democratic vote for Representative in November 1970 was 21,455 greater than the Republican vote, giving Smith an edge. He was overwhelmingly re-elected in 1972.

District	Member Elected 1972	Winning Percentage	1970 Population	Percent Variance
1	Edward Mezvinsky (D)	53.4	471,260	+ 0.089
2	John C. Culver (D)	59.2	471,933	+ 0.232
3	H. R. Gross (R)	55.7	471,886	+ 0.222
4	Neal Smith (D)	59.6	468,881	−0.416
5	William J. Scherle (R)	55.3	470,214	−0.133
6	Wiley Mayne (R)	52.5	470,867	+ 0.006

1970 State Population: 2,825,041
Ideal District Population: 470,840

Election Results, 1968-1972

Vote for U.S. Representative
(Adjusted to new district boundaries)

District	1968	1970	1972
1	96,160 R (52.8%)	63,999 R (49.9%)	107,099 D (53.4%)
	85,790 D (47.2%)	63,021 D (49.2%)	91,609 R (45.7%)
2	101,937 D (54.5%)	82,455 D (60.1%)	115,489 D (59.2%)
	85,239 R (45.5%)	54,638 R (39.8%)	79,667 R (40.8%)
3	115,645 R (62.0%)	76,264 R (57.8%)	109,113 R (55.7%)
	70,871 D (38.0%)	55,696 D (42.2%)	86,848 D (44.3%)
4	107,976 D (56.8%)	77,094 D (57.3%)	125,431 D (59.6%)
	81,995 R (43.2%)	55,639 R (41.4%)	85,156 R (40.4%)
5	110,750 R (59.5%)	68,369 R (56.3%)	108,596 R (55.3%)
	75,235 D (40.5%)	52,389 D (43.1%)	87,937 D (44.7%)
6	119,086 R (62.4%)	69,519 R (55.0%)	103,284 R (52.5%)
	71,720 D (37.6%)	56,855 D (45.0%)	93,574 D (47.5%)
State	608,875 R (54.2%)	388,428 R (49.8%)	616,378 D (51.5%)
	513,529 D (45.8%)	387,510 D (49.7%)	577,425 R (48.3%)

Voting Age Population

District	Voting Age Population	Voting Age Population 18, 19, 20	Voting Age Population 65 and Over	Median Age of Voting Age Population
1	309,977	27,272 (8.8%)	52,865 (17.1%)	42.7
2	297,578	23,870 (8.0%)	52,463 (17.6%)	43.8
3	307,394	24,143 (7.9%)	59,142 (19.2%)	46.0
4	312,536	23,729 (7.6%)	56,219 (18.0%)	44.8
5	313,539	26,687 (8.5%)	65,589 (20.9%)	46.2
6	305,065	22,188 (7.3%)	64,151 (21.0%)	47.4
State	1,846,089	147,891 (8.0%)	350,422 (19.0%)	45.2

Income and Occupation

District	Median Family Income	White Collar Workers	Blue Collar Workers	Service Workers	Farm Workers
1	$9,594	44.8%	32.6%	14.3%	8.3%
2	9,511	41.3	34.2	12.8	11.7
3	8,911	39.7	32.2	13.8	14.3
4	9,589	51.0	30.0	13.6	5.4
5	8,338	40.2	28.4	14.0	17.4
6	8,314	39.7	28.0	14.0	18.3
State	9,017	42.9	30.9	13.7	12.5

Education: School Years Completed

District	Completed 4 years of High School	Completed 4 years College	Completed 5 years or less of School	Median School years completed
1	59.7%	11.7%	2.6%	12.3
2	58.6	9.0	2.7	12.2
3	58.8	7.7	2.7	12.2
4	61.4	10.1	3.0	12.3
5	58.4	8.5	2.6	12.2
6	56.9	7.8	2.9	12.2
State	59.0	9.1	2.8	12.2

Housing and Residential Patterns

District	Housing		Urban-Suburban-Nonmetropolitan Breakdown		
	Owner Occupied Units	Renter Occupied Units	Urban	Suburban	Nonmetropolitan
1	68.9%	31.1%	20.9%	9.4%	69.7%
2	73.7	26.3	36.7	17.1	46.2
3	73.4	26.6	16.0	12.2	71.8
4	72.1	27.9	42.8	18.2	39.0
5	71.9	28.1	—	18.5	81.5
6	70.3	29.7	18.3	3.6	78.1
State	71.7	28.3	22.4	13.2	64.4

1st District

(Southeast—Davenport, Burlington, Iowa City)

Race and Ethnic Groups. Blacks 1.5 percent. German stock 3.1 percent.

Cities, 1970 Population. Davenport 98,477, Burlington 32,444, Iowa City 46,850, Muscatine 22,470.

Universities, Enrollment. University of Iowa (Iowa City—20,604), Parsons College (Fairfield—1,669), St. Ambrose College (Davenport—1,410), Grinnell College (Grinnell—1,261), Marycrest College (Davenport—1,061).

AEC-Owned, Contractor-Operated Installations. Burlington AEC Plant, Burlington.

Newspapers, Circulation. Davenport Times-Democrat (All day—60,205).

Commercial Television Stations, Affiliation. WOC-TV, Davenport (NBC). Most of district is divided between Davenport-Rock Island (Illinois)-Moline (Illinois) ADI and Cedar Rapids-Waterloo ADI. Small portions of district are located in Quincy (Illinois)-Hannibal (Missouri) ADI, Des Moines ADI and Ottumwa-Kirksville (Missouri) ADI.

Plants and Offices, Products, Employment.

J. I. Case Co., Burlington (Construction machinery and equipment—1,110). **J. I. Case Co.**, Bettendorf (Farm implements—1,000). **Caterpillar Tractor Co.**, Bettendorf (Construction equipment—1,200). **Caterpillar Tractor Co.**, Davenport (Construction equipment—1,030). **Oscar Mayer & Co.**, Davenport (Meat packing—1,600). **Grain Processing Corp.**, Muscatine (Alcohol and corn milling—1,110). **Amana Refrigeration Inc.**, Amana (Refrigeration and home freezing equipment—1,400). **Sheller-Globe Corp.**, Keokuk (Rubber molded products—1,000). **Aluminum Company of America**, Bettendorf (Aluminum—3,210). **Mason & Hanger Silas Mason Co.**, Burlington (Ammunition—3,600).

2nd District

(Northeast—Cedar Rapids, Dubuque)

Race and Ethnic Groups. Blacks 0.5 percent. German stock 3.9 percent.

Cities, 1970 Population. Cedar Rapids 110,642, Dubuque 62,313, Clinton 34,719, Marion 18,028.

Universities, Enrollment. Luther College (Decorah—2,083), Loras College (Dubuque—1,586), Upper Iowa College (Fayette—1,188), Coe College (Cedar Rapids—1,108), University of Dubuque (Dubuque—1,070).

Newspapers, Circulation. Cedar Rapids Gazette (Ex-Sat—75,832).

Commercial Television Stations, Affiliation. KCRG-TV, Cedar Rapids (ABC); WMT-TV, Cedar Rapids (CBS). Most of district is located in Cedar Rapids-Waterloo ADI. Small portion of district is located in Davenport-Rock Island (Illinois)-Moline (Illinois) ADI.

Plants and Offices, Products, Employment.

Deere & Co., Dubuque (Farm implements and tractors—4,000). **FMC Corp.**, Cedar Rapids (Construction machinery—1,400). **Iowa Manufacturing Co.**, Cedar Rapids (Construction machinery—1,100). **Standard Brands Inc.**, Clinton (Corn processing—1,500). **Penick & Ford Ltd.**, Cedar Rapids (Corn products—1,100). **Dubuque Packing Co.**, Dubuque (Meat packing—3,100). **Wilson-Sinclair Co.**, Cedar Rapids (Meat packing—2,500). **E. I. du Pont de Nemours & Co.**, Clinton (Cellulosic films—1,400). **Square D Co.**, Cedar Rapids (Electric devices—1,000).

Collins Radio Co., Cedar Rapids (Transmitting, signalling and detection equipment—7,000).

3rd District

(North Central—Waterloo)

Race and Ethnic Groups. Blacks 1.6 percent. German stock 5.3 percent.

Cities, 1970 Population. Waterloo 75,594, Mason City 30,498, Cedar Falls 29,510, Marshalltown 26,372.

Universities, Enrollment. University of Northern Iowa (Cedar Falls—10,534), Wartburg College (Waverly—1,404).

Newspapers, Circulation. Waterloo Courier (ExSat—53,986).

Commercial Television Stations, Affiliation. KWWL-TV Waterloo (NBC); KGLO-TV, Mason City (CBS). Most of district is divided between Cedar Rapids-Waterloo ADI and Rochester (Minnesota)-Mason City-Austin (Minnesota) ADI. Portion of district is located in Des Moines ADI.

Plants and Offices, Products, Employment.

Deere & Co., Waterloo (Farm implements, tractors—7,500). **White Farm Equipment Co.**, Charles City (Farm machinery—1,000). **Rath Packing Co.**, Waterloo (Meat packing—4,000). **Armour & Co.**, Mason City (Meat packing—1,400). **Fisher Controls Co.**, Marshalltown (Automatic controls—1,100). **Rite Way Plumbing Co.**, Marshalltown (Plumbing contractors—5,000). **Chamberlain Manufacturing Corp.**, Waterloo (Ordnance material—1,080).

4th District

(South Central—Des Moines, Ottumwa)

Race and Ethnic Groups. Blacks 2.7 percent. German stock 1.2 percent.

Cities, 1970 Population. Des Moines 200,772, Ottumwa 29,695, West Des Moines 16,441, Newton 15,588.

Universities, Enrollment. Drake University (Des Moines—7,586), Central College (Pella—1,226).

Newspapers, Circulation. Des Moines Register (Morn—244,050), Des Moines Tribune (Eve—107,429).

Commercial Television Stations, Affiliation. KRNT-TV, Des Moines (CBS). WHO-TV, Des Moines (NBC); KTVO-TV, Ottumwa (primarily ABC). Most of district is located in Des Moines ADI. Small portions of district are located in Ottumwa - Kirksville (Missouri) ADI and Davenport-Rock Island (Illinois)-Moline (Illinois) ADI.

Plants and Offices, Products, Employment.

Massey-Ferguson Inc., Des Moines (Farm machinery, tractors—1,100). **Deere & Co.**, Des Moines (Farm implements—2,200). **Deere & Co.**, Ottumwa (Farm implements—1,500). **John Morrell & Co.**, Ottumwa (Meat packing—2,630). **Meredith Corp.**, Des Moines (Periodical and book publishing—2,260). **Meredith Corp.**, Des Moines (Magazine publishing—1,300). **Des Moines Register Tribune**, Des Moines (Newspaper publishing—1,070). **Bankers Life Co.**, Des Moines (Life insurance—1,000). **Yonk-**

er Brothers Inc., Des Moines (Department store—2,000). **Iowa Power & Light Co.**, Des Moines (Gas, electric utility—1,000). **Northwestern Bell Telephone Co.**, Des Moines (Telephone company—2,500). **Firestone Tire & Rubber Co.**, Des Moines (Tires—2,400). **Armstrong Rubber Co.**, Des Moines (Tires—1,750). **Maytag Co.**, Newton (Washing machines, dryers—3,500).

5th District

(Southwest—Council Bluffs)

Race and Ethnic Groups. Blacks 0.3 percent. German stock 2.6 percent.

Cities, 1970 Population. Council Bluffs 60,617, Ames 39,718, Boone 12,474.

Universities, Enrollment. Iowa State University (Ames—19,620), Graceland College (Lamoni—1,295), Simpson College (Indianola—1,001).

AEC-Owned, Contractor-Operated Installations. Ames Laboratory, Ames.

Newspapers, Circulation. Des Moines and Omaha, Nebraska papers circulate in portions of district.

Commercial Television Stations, Affiliation. WOI-TV, Ames (ABC). District is divided between Des Moines and Omaha (Nebraska) ADIs.

6th District

(Northwest—Sioux City, Fort Dodge)

Race and Ethnic Groups. Blacks 0.4 percent. German stock 5.5 percent.

Cities, 1970 Population. Sioux City 85,986, Fort Dodge 31,285, Spencer 10,285.

Universities, Enrollment. Morningside College (Sioux City—1,645), Briar Cliff College (Sioux City—1,131), Westmar College (LeMars—1,074).

Newspapers, Circulation. Sioux City Journal (Morn—67,938).

Commercial Television Stations, Affiliations. KCAU-TV, Sioux City (ABC); KMEG-TV, Sioux City (CBS); KTIV-TV, Sioux City (NBC); KVFD-TV, Fort Dodge (NBC). Most of district is located in Sioux City ADI. Portions of district are located in Omaha (Nebraska) ADI, Des Moines ADI, Rochester (Minnesota)-Mason City-Austin (Minnesota) ADI, and Sioux Falls (South Dakota) ADI.

Plants and Offices, Products, Employment.
Winnebago Industries Inc., Forest City (Motor homes—1,100). **Zenith Radio Corp. of Iowa**, Sioux City (Radios, phonographs, TV—1,200).

KANSAS: FIVE HOUSE SEATS, NO CHANGE

No major revisions were necessary in the realignment of congressional districts in Kansas. A redistricting measure passed the Kansas House on March 9, 1971, by a vote of 87-30 and the state Senate March 24 by a vote of 24-15. Gov. Robert Docking (D) expressed his dissatis-faction with the bill by letting it become law without his signature.

Kansas City was split for the first time, but only because the city extended its boundary westward, not because of any change in the district line.

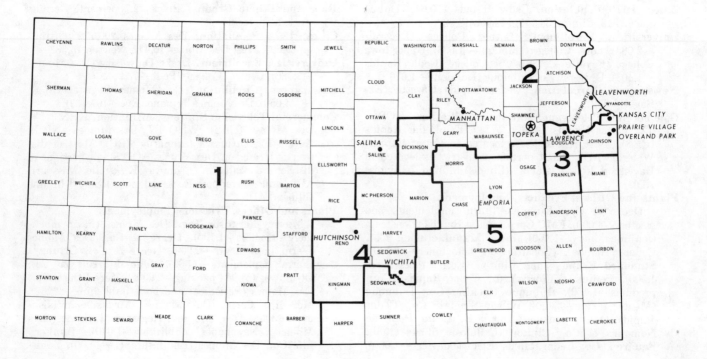

In other parts of the state, a few counties were shifted between districts to bring their populations closer to the ideal.

None of the districts saw any major changes in their economic, social or political makeup.

District	Member Elected 1972	Winning Percentage	1970 Population	Percent Variance
1	Keith G. Sebelius (R)	77.2	447,787	—0.4506
2	William L. Roy (D)	60.6	454,028	+ 0.9368
3	Larry Winn Jr. (R)	71.0	449,743	—0.0157
4	Garner E. Shriver (R)	73.2	450,487	+ 0.1496
5	Joe Skubitz (R)	72.3	447,026	—0.6198

1970 State Population: 2,249,071
Ideal District Population: 449,814

Election Results, 1968-1972

Vote for U.S. Representative
(Adjusted to new district boundaries)

District	1968	1970	1972
1	100,470 R (53.6%)	93,846 R (57.2%)	145,712 R (77.2%)
	86,999 D (46.4%)	69,843 D (42.5%)	40,678 D (21.6%)
2	101,634 R (66.8%)	75,532 D (53.0%)	106,276 R (60.6%)
	50,526 D (33.2%)	63,055 R (44.2%)	65,071 R (37.1%)
3	94,318 R (63.0%)	69,428 R (52.9%)	122,358 R (71.0%)
	55,508 D (37.0%)	60,166 D (45.8%)	43,777 D (25.4%)
4	98,459 R (64.7%)	82,320 R (63.4%)	120,120 R (73.2%)
	53,694 D (35.2%)	45,052 D (34.7%)	40,753 D (24.8%)
5	112,852 R (64.2%)	98,855 R (65.0%)	128,639 R (72.3%)
	62,824 D (35.7%)	53,155 D (34.9%)	49,169 D (27.6%)
State	507,733 R (62.1%)	407,504 R (56.6%)	581,900 R (66.2%)
	309,551 D (37.8%)	303,748 D (42.2%)	280,653 D (32.0%)

Voting Age Population

District	Voting Age Population	Voting Age Population 18, 19, 20	Voting Age Population 65 and Over	Median Age of Voting Population
1	295,484	20,650 (7.0%)	62,503 (21.2%)	47.7
2	307,573	31,487 (10.2%)	49,970 (16.2%)	40.7
3	291,688	26,861 (9.2%)	36,978 (12.7%)	40.5
4	297,075	24,727 (8.3%)	45,686 (15.4%)	42.8
5	307,987	23,141 (7.5%)	71,427 (23.2%)	48.5
State	1,499,851	126,861 (8.5%)	266,642 (17.8%)	44.0

Income and Occupation

District	Median Family Income	White Collar Workers	Blue Collar Workers	Service Workers	Farm Workers
1	$ 7,820	40.5%	26.6%	14.2%	18.7%
2	8,680	48.7	30.2	13.8	7.3
3	10,928	58.2	29.4	10.9	1.5
4	9,097	50.9	31.9	13.7	3.5
5	7,450	40.0	35.8	13.9	10.3
State	8,690	47.8	30.7	13.3	8.2

Education: School Years Completed

District	Completed 4 years of High School	Completed 4 years of College	Completed 5 years or less of School	Median School years completed
1	58.2%	9.1%	2.9%	12.2
2	60.7	11.6	3.0	12.3
3	65.0	17.2	3.6	12.5
4	62.1	12.0	3.1	12.3
5	54.1	7.7	3.8	12.1
State	59.9	11.4	3.3	12.3

Housing and Residential Patterns

District	Housing — Owner Occupied Units	Renter Occupied Units	Urban	Suburban	Nonmetro-politan
1	71.9%	28.1%	—	—	100.0%
2	65.7	34.3	27.5%	14.4%	58.1
3	68.8	31.2	—	82.6	17.4
4	65.5	34.5	61.4	8.5	30.1
5	73.2	26.8	—	16.7	83.3
State	69.1	30.9	17.9	24.4	57.7

1st District

(West—Salina)

Race and Ethnic Groups. German stock 2.5 percent.

Cities, 1970 Population. Salina 37,702, Great Bend 15,721, Hays 15,523, Garden City 14,758.

Universities, Enrollment. Fort Hays Kansas State College (Hays—6,144).

Commercial Television Stations, Affiliation. KTVC, Ensign (CBS); KGLD, Garden City (NBC); KUPK, Garden City (ABC); KCKT, Great Bend (ABC); KAYS, Hays (CBS, ABC). Major portion of district located in Wichita-Hutchinson ADI. Portions located in Topeka ADI and Lincoln-Hasting-Kearney (Nebraska) ADI.

2nd District

(Northeast—Topeka, Kansas City Suburbs)

Race and Ethnic Groups. Blacks 6.0 percent. Spanish heritage population 2.6 percent. German stock 2.7 percent.

Cities, 1970 Population. Topeka 124,924, Manhattan 27,552, Leavenworth 25,144, part of Kansas City 23,252.

Universities, Enrollment. Kansas State University (Manhattan—14,789), Washburn University of Topeka (Topeka—5,196), Benedictine College (Atchison—1,288).

Military Installations or Activities. Fort Leavenworth, Leavenworth; Fort Riley, Junction City; Forbes Air Force Base, Topeka.

Newspapers, Circulation. Topeka Capital (Morn—62,775). Kansas City, Mo., newspapers circulate in major portions of district.

Commercial Television Stations, Affiliation. KTSB, Topeka (NBC primary); WIBW-TV, Topeka (CBS primary; ABC). Major portions of district located in Topeka and Kansas City (Missouri) ADIs. Portion located in Wichita-Hutchinson ADI.

Plants and Offices, Products, Employment.

Goodyear Tire and Rubber Co., Topeka (Tires—3,600). **Atchison, Topeka and Santa Fe Railroad**, Topeka (Railroad terminal and hospital—4,000). **Southwestern Bell Telephone Co.**, Topeka (Telephone company—1,300). **Menninger Foundation**, Topeka (Hospital, psychiatric research—1,000).

3rd District

(East—Kansas City)

Race and Ethnic Groups. Blacks 8.2 percent. German stock 1.3 percent.

Cities, 1970 Population. Part of Kansas City 145,692, Overland Park 77,291, Lawrence 45,831, Prairie Village 28,259.

Universities, Enrollment. University of Kansas (Lawrence—20,043).

Newspapers, Circulation. Kansas City, Mo., newspapers circulate throughout district.

Commercial Television Stations, Affiliation. Entire district located in Kansas City (Missouri) ADI.

Plants and Offices, Products, Employment.

Phillips Petroleum Co., Kansas City (Refinery—1,200). **Hercules Inc.**, Sunflower (Explosives—2,800). **General Motors Corp.**, Kansas City (Automobile assembly—4,500). **Fairbanks Morse & Co.**, Kansas City (Pumps, motor controls—1,000). **Certain-Teed Products Corp.**, Kansas City (Fiberglass insulation—1,020). **Owens-Corning Fiberglass Corp.**, Kansas City (Fiberglass insulation—1,000). **Proctor & Gamble Manufacturing Co.**, Kansas City (Soap, detergent—at least 1,000). **Union Pacific Railroad Co.**, Kansas City (Railroad—1,100).

4th District

(Central—Wichita)

Race and Ethnic Groups. Blacks 6.5 percent. German stock 1.6 percent.

Cities, 1970 Population. Wichita 276,660, Hutchinson 36,880, Newton 15,437, McPherson 10,849.

Universities, Enrollment. Wichita State University (Wichita—13,034).

Military Installations or Activities. McConnell Air Force Base, Wichita.

Newspapers, Circulation. Wichita Eagle (MxSat—127,-604), Wichita Beacon (ExSat—59,022).

Commercial Television Stations, Affiliation. KAKE-TV, Wichita (ABC); KARD-TV, Wichita (NBC); KTVH, Wichita (CBS). Entire district located in Wichita-Hutchinson ADI.

Plants and Offices, Products, Employment.

Boeing Co., Wichita (Aircraft, missiles—5,000). **Beech Aircraft Corp.**, Wichita (Aircraft—HQ—at least 4,000). **Cessna Aircraft Co.**, Wichita (Aircraft and parts—HQ—3,200). **Cessna Aircraft Co.**, Wichita (Military aircraft division—hydraulic controls—4,000). **Cessna Aircraft Co.**, Hutchinson (Industrial Products Division—hydraulic equipment—1,000). **Hesston Corp. Inc.**, Hesston (Farm equipment—1,400). **Coleman Co. Inc.**, Wichita (Camping trailers and other camping equipment, air conditioning equipment—HQ—1,000). **Cudahy Co.**, Wichita (Meat packing—1,090). **Southwestern Bell Telephone Co.**, Wichita (Telephone company—1,300). **Unified School District No. 259**, Wichita (Public schools—5,950). **City of Wichita**, Wichita (City government—1,800).

5th District

(Southeast—Emporia, Pittsburg)

Race and Ethnic Groups. German stock 1.5 percent.

Cities, 1970 Population. Emporia 23,342, Pittsburg 20,184, Coffeyville 15,072, Arkansas City 13,400.

Universities, Enrollment. Kansas State College of Pittsburg (Pittsburg—5,894). Kansas State Teachers College (Emporia—7,112).

Newspapers, Circulation. Wichita newspapers circulate in most of district. Kansas City, Mo., newspapers circulate in portion of district.

Commercial Television Stations, Affiliation. KOAM-TV, Pittsburg (NBC). Portions of district located in Joplin (Missouri)-Pittsburg ADI, Wichita-Hutchinson (ADI), Kansas City (Missouri) ADI, Topeka ADI and Tulsa (Oklahoma) ADI.

Plants and Offices, Products, Employment.

Day and Zimmerman Inc., Parsons (Ammunition—1,600).

KENTUCKY: SEVEN HOUSE SEATS, NO CHANGE

Kentucky's congressional delegation was unaffected by reapportionment, remaining at seven. But adjustments in district lines were necessary, especially in the Louisville and Covington-Newport areas in order to equalize population differences. *(Map p. 79)*

The newly elected Kentucky legislature began consideration of congressional redistricting shortly after convening in January 1972. The bill ultimately passed reportedly was worked out by the congressional delegation in Washington, with the state's senior representative, Carl D. Perkins (D), reportedly playing a major role. It maintained the 5-2 political balance in favor of the Democrats.

During consideration of the bill, a major controversy developed concerning the 4th District, which stretches from the Louisville suburbs northeast along the Ohio River to Covington-Newport. The district was overpopulated by 25.4 percent, according to the 1970 census.

To reduce this overpopulation, two methods were possible—take areas in the Jefferson County (Louisville) area out of the district or split the northern Kentucky counties of Kenton (Covington) and Campbell (Newport). After lengthy debate, the latter method was chosen, over the strong objections of northern Kentucky legislators, who wanted to keep the area intact. The final legislation provided for the transfer of Pendleton and Grant Counties and the southern portions of Campbell and Kenton Counties from the 4th to the 6th District.

The redistricting bill passed the House Jan. 28, 1972, by a vote of 75-18. The state Senate concurred Feb. 18, 26-7. Gov. Wendell Ford (D) signed the bill Feb. 23.

District	Member Elected 1972	Winning Percentage	1970 Population	Percent Variance
1	Frank A. Stubblefield (D)	64.8	460,754	+ 0.1852
2	William H. Natcher (D)	61.5	459,416	—0.1056
3	Romano L. Mazzoli (D)	62.1	460,340	+ 0.0952
4	M. G. (Gene) Snyder (R)	73.8	458,896	—0.2187
5	Tim Lee Carter (R)	73.5	459,586	—0.0687
6	John B. Breckinridge (D)	52.4	460,521	+ 0.1345
7	Carl D. Perkins (D)	61.9	459,798	—0.0226

1970 State Population: 3,219,311
Ideal District Population: 459,902

Election Results, 1968-1972

Vote for U.S. Representative
(Adjusted to new district boundaries)

District	1968	1970	1972
1	73,422 D (97.6%)	28,266 D (100.0%)	81,456 D (64.8%)
	1,763 R (2.4%)[1]	—	42,286 R (33.7%)
2	64,387 D (56.7%)	20,621 D (100.0%)	75,871 D (61.5%)
	49,074 R (43.3%)	—	47,436 R (38.5%)
3	72,218 R (55.6%)	52,651 R (48.6%)	86,810 D (62.1%)
	57,696 D (44.4%)	52,375 D (48.4%)	51,634 R (37.0%)
4	81,033 R (64.4%)	68,323 R (66.9%)	110,902 R (73.8%)
	44,732 D (35.6%)	33,827 D (33.1%)	39,332 D (26.2%)
5	95,886 R (69.9%)	52,607 R (75.1%)	109,264 R (73.5%)
	39,371 D (28.7%)	17,442 D (24.9%)	39,301 D (26.5%)
6	67,375 D (52.4%)	38,482 D (56.3%)	76,185 D (52.4%)
	59,927 R (46.6%)	29,866 R (43.7%)	68,012 R (46.8%)
7	92,061 D (62.1%)	55,983 D (75.2%)	94,840 D (61.9%)
	55,948 R (37.8%)	18,501 R (24.8%)	58,286 R (38.1%)
State	440,894 D (51.0%)[2]	247,522 D (52.3%)	493,795 D (50.1%)
	420,983 R (48.7%)	222,813 R (47.0%)	487,820 R (49.5%)

1 *No Republican candidate in this district as constituted before redistricting.*
2 *Includes absentee votes not distributed in district-by-district tabulation.*

Voting Age Population

District	Voting Age Population	Voting Age Population 18, 19, 20	Voting Age Population 65 and Over	Median Age of Voting Age Population
1	313,146	26,283 (8.4%)	60,561 (19.3%)	45.7
2	299,840	36,230 (12.1%)	43,055 (14.4%)	39.7
3	306,898	24,696 (8.0%)	49,756 (16.2%)	44.0
4	284,798	19,536 (6.9%)	37,159 (13.0%)	41.7
5	298,587	26,562 (8.9%)	54,097 (18.1%)	45.0
6	305,560	25,898 (8.5%)	44,596 (14.6%)	41.4
7	291,423	24,167 (8.3%)	48,595 (16.7%)	44.1
State	2,100,218	183,360 (8.7%)	337,806 (16.1%)	43.1

Income and Occupation

District	Median Family Income	White Collar Workers	Blue Collar Workers	Service Workers	Farm Workers
1	$ 6,788	33.6%	45.8%	12.8%	7.8%
2	7,042	34.5	42.5	12.1	10.9
3	8,902	44.1	41.6	14.1	0.2
4	10,359	50.8	37.4	10.3	1.5
5	4,660	32.8	43.2	11.8	12.2
6	8,678	45.8	33.9	12.9	7.4
7	5,528	34.4	47.5	11.6	6.5
State	7,439	40.2	41.2	12.3	6.3

Education: School Years Completed

District	Completed 4 years of High School	Completed 4 years of College	Completed 5 years or less of School	Median School years completed
1	37.7%	5.2%	12.3%	9.9
2	39.0	6.6	12.6	9.8
3	41.6	7.7	8.1	10.9
4	50.4	10.4	5.4	12.0
5	24.6	5.2	22.9	8.5
6	48.2	10.6	8.8	11.7
7	28.3	4.9	19.6	8.7
State	38.5	7.2	12.8	9.9

Housing and Residential Patterns

	Housing		Urban-Suburban-Nonmetropolitan Breakdown		
District	Owner Occupied Units	Renter Occupied Units	Urban	Suburban	Nonmetropolitan
1	71.6%	28.4%	—	7.8%	92.2%
2	68.8	31.2	11.0%	6.3	82.7
3	57.4	42.6	78.6	21.4	—
4	72.4	27.6	—	92.9	7.1
5	68.0	32.0	—	—	100.0
6	62.6	37.4	23.5	27.2	49.3
7	68.3	31.7	6.4	5.0	88.6
State	66.9	33.1	17.1	22.9	60.0

1st District

(West—Paducah)

Race and Ethnic Groups. Blacks 9.0 percent.
Cities, 1970 Population. Paducah 31,610, Henderson 22,958, Hopkinsville 21,239, Madisonville 15,324.
Universities, Enrollment. Murray State University (Murray—7,331).
Military Installations or Activities. Fort Campbell.
Commercial Television Stations, Affiliation. WPSD-TV, Paducah (NBC); WDXR-TV, Paducah (None). District is divided between Paducah-Cape Girardeau (Missouri)-Harrisburg (Illinois) ADI, Evansville (Indiana) ADI and Nashville (Tennessee) ADI.

Plants and Offices, Products, Employment.
Merit Clothing Co., Mayfield (Men's suits and slacks—HQ—1,400). General Tire & Rubber Co., Mayfield (Tires—1,000). Union Carbide Corp., Paducah (Union Carbide Chemical Co.—inorganic chemicals—1,200). Island Creek Coal Co., Madisonville (West Kentucky Coal Co. Division—coal mining—2,000). Island Creek Coal Co., Morganfield (Coal mining—1,250).

2nd District

(West Central—Owensboro)

Race and Ethnic Groups. Blacks 6.0 percent.
Cities, 1970 Population. Owensboro 50,344, Fort Knox 37,522, Bowling Green 36,272, Elizabethtown 11,754.
Universities, Enrollment. Western Kentucky University (Bowling Green—11,922).
Military Installations or Activities. Fort Knox.
Newspapers, Circulation. Louisville papers circulate in portions of district.
Commercial Television Stations, Affiliation. WBKO-TV, Bowling Green (ABC), Bowling Green has no ADI of its own. Most of district is located in Louisville ADI. Parts of district are located in Evansville (Indiana) ADI and Nashville (Tennessee) ADI.
Plants and Offices, Products, Employment.
Union Underwear Co. Inc., Bowling Green (Men's and boys' underwear—1,000). Southwire Co. Inc., Hawesville (Southwire Rod and Cable Mill— wire cable—1,000). Cutler-Hammer Inc., Bowling Green (Electric supplies—1,150). General Electric Co., Owensboro (Electronic Department, Tube Division— light bulbs, radio and television tubes—2,700).

3rd District

(Louisville and Suburbs)

Race and Ethnic Groups. Blacks 19.9 percent.
Cities, 1970 Population. Louisville 361,930, Shively 19,268.
Universities, Enrollment. Bellarmine College (Louisville—1,655), Southern Baptist Theological Seminary (Louisville—1,083), Spalding College (Louisville—1,067), University of Louisville (Louisville—10,468).
Military Installations or Activities. Naval Ordnance Stations, Louisville.
Newspapers, Circulation. Louisville Courier-Journal (Morn —233,472), Louisville Times (Eve —170,926).
Commercial Television Stations, Affiliation. WAVB-TV, Louisville (NBC); WHAS-TV, Louisville (CBS); WLKY-TV, Louisville (ABC); WDRB-TV, Louisville (None). Entire district is located in Louisville ADI.
Plants and Offices, Products, Employment.
B.F. Goodrich Co., Louisville (Automobile tires, chemical supplies—1,010). Ford Motor Co., Louisville (Automobile and truck assembly—4,120). International Harvester Co., Louisville (Louisville

Works—motor trucks, engines, farm machinery—4,850). Chevron Oil Co., Louisville (Standard Oil Co., Kentucky Division— petroleum refining, petroleum products—1,200). American Air Filter Co., Inc., Louisville (Heating and air conditioning equipment—HQ—2,200). Brown & Williamson Tobacco, Louisville (Cigarettes—HQ—6,300). Philip Morris Inc., Louisville (Tobacco products—2,500). Loews Theatres Inc., Louisville (Lorillard Division—tobacco products—1,300). Brown-Forman Distillers Corp., Louisville (Distilled, rectified and blended liquors—HQ—1,000). Courier-Journal & Louisville Times Co., Louisville (Newspaper publishing—1,400). Fawcett Printing Corp., Louisville (Printing—1,720). Celanese Coatings Co., Louisville (Paints, varnishes, synthetic resins and brushes—HQ—1,000). American Standard Inc., Louisville (Plumbing fixtures, plastics—1,850). Capital Holding Corp., Louisville (Holding company—HQ—1,250). Commonwealth Life Insurance Co., Louisville (Life insurance—HQ—1,250). Louisville & Nashville Railroad, Louisville (Railroad—HQ—6,500). Belknap Inc., Louisville (Hardware, furniture, floor covering—HQ—1,230). Sears Roebuck & Co., Louisville (Department store—1,120). Associated Dry Goods Corp., Louisville (Department store—1,100). E. I. du Pont de Nemours & Co., Louisville (Elastomer Chemicals Division—neoprene, freon—1,500). South Central Bell Telephone Co., Louisville (Telephone communication—3,200). Louisville Gas & Electric Co., Louisville (Public utility—3,010).

4th District

(North—Louisville Suburbs, Covington, Newport)

Cities, 1970 Population. Part of Covington 51,927, (all but 408 residents of Covington) Newport 25,923, Valley Station 24,649, part of Pleasure Ridge Park 19,000.
Universities, Enrollment. Thomas More College (Fort Mitchell—1,812).
Newspapers, Circulation. Kentucky Post & Times-Star (Eve—58,713, an edition of the Cincinnati Post & Times-Star). Louisville papers circulate in portions of district.
Commercial Television Stations, Affiliation. District is divided between Louisville and Cincinnati (Ohio) ADIs.
Plants and Offices, Products, Employment.
Ford Motor Co., Louisville (Truck assembly—3,500). Interlake Inc., Newport (Steel products—1,600). Franciscan Sisters of the Poor, Covington (St. Elizabeth Hospital—1,000).

5th District

(Southeast)

Race and Ethnic Groups. Blacks 3.0 percent.
Cities, 1970 Population. Richmond 16,847, Middlesborough 12,159, Somerset 10,427.

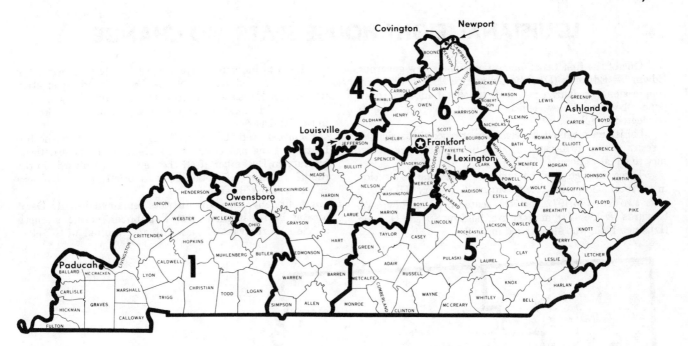

Universities, Enrollment. Asbury College (Wilmore —1,091), Berea College (Berea—1,448), Cumberland College (Williamsburg—1,807), Eastern Kentucky University (Richmond—10,170).

Military Installations or Activities. Lexington-Blue Grass Army Depot, Richmond.

Commercial Television Stations, Affiliation. District is divided between Louisville ADI, Lexington ADI, Nashville (Tennessee) ADI and Knoxville (Tennesee) ADI.

Plants and Offices, Products, Employment.
    Union Underwear Co. Inc., Campbellsville (Men's and boys' underwear—3,150).

6th District

(North Central—Lexington, Frankfort)

Race and Ethnic Groups. Blacks 8.7 percent.

Cities, 1970 Population. Lexington 108,336, Frankfort 21,395, Winchester 13,427, Danville 11,563.

Universities, Enrollment. Georgetown College (George—town—1,300), Kentucky State University (Frankfort—1,970), University of Kentucky (Lexington—20,455).

Newspapers, Circulation. Lexington Herald (MxSat—53,841).

Commercial Television Stations, Affiliation. WBLG-TV, Lexington (ABC); WKYT-TV, Lexington (CBS); WBLX-TV, Lexington (NBC). District is divided between Lexington ADI, Louisville ADI and Cincinnati (Ohio) ADI.

Plants and Offices, Products, Employment.
    International Business Machines, Lexington (Office Products Division—electric typewriters, dictating equipment—5,750). **Square D. Co.**, Lexing-ton (Distribution Equipment Division—switches and controls—1,600). **Cowden Manufacturing Co.**, Lexington (Work clothing—2,400).

7th District

(East—Ashland)

Cities, 1970 Population. Ashland 29,286.

Universities, Enrollment. Morehead State University (Morehead—6,255).

Commercial Television Stations, Affiliation. WKYH-TV, Hazard (NBC). Hazard has no separate ADI. Most of district is located in Charleston-Huntington (W.Va.) ADI. Parts of district are in Lexington ADI, Cincinnati (Ohio) ADI, and Bristol-Kingsport-Johnson City (Tenn.) ADI.

Plants and Offices, Products, Employment.
    Chesapeake & Ohio Railway Co., Russell (Maintenance and repair of railroad freight cars—1,430). **Island Creek Coal Co.**, Price (Coal, general store —1,100). **Armco Steel Corp.**, Ashland (Ashland works—steel sheets—4,650). **Ashland Oil Inc.**, Ashland (Refined petroleum, carbon black—HQ—1,200). **Ashland Oil Inc.**, Catlettsburg (Paving mixtures and blocks—2,290). **A. O. Smith Corp.**, Mt. Sterling (Electric Motor Division—electric motors—1,000). **Emerson Electric Co.**, Maysville (Browning Manufacturing Co. Division—power transmission equipment—1,000).

Glossary and Sources

For a complete explanation of all terms used in this book and a list of source material, consult the details included in the Introduction.

LOUISIANA: EIGHT HOUSE SEATS, NO CHANGE

One of the first tasks facing Louisiana's new governor, Edwin W. Edwards (D), who took office May 9, 1972, was congressional redistricting. Redistricting had been postponed because a new legislature and governor were to be elected in February 1972.

Louisiana retained its eight congressional districts as a result of the 1970 census, but adjustments were necessary to equalize population.

Three districts had no incumbent seeking re-election in 1972—the 3rd, where Rep. Patrick T. Caffery (D) retired after two terms in 1972; the 7th vacated by Gov. Edwin W. Edwards (D 1965-72); and the 8th, held by Speedy O. Long (D) since 1965, who also retired in 1972.

Reports indicated an effort was made in drawing the new lines to aid friends of the Edwards administration who sought House seats in two of these three districts:

• Gov. Edwards' former law partner, John B. Breaux, in the 7th District.

• Former Rep. Gillis W. Long (D 1963-65) in the 8th District. Long ran third in the Democratic gubernatorial primary in December 1971, then endorsed Edwards in the runoff. In early 1972, Long served briefly in an advisory capacity with Edwards.

Politically, all eight districts remained heavily Democratic in registration. But Republican voting strength in the suburbs west of New Orleans resulted in the elec-

tion of the first GOP representative from the state in this century.

In north Louisiana, conservative Democratic representatives have been able to forestall a swing to Republican congressional voting by their personal popularity.

Under provisions of the 1965 Voting Rights Act, the state's new congressional districts had to receive the approval of the Justice Department. The department posed no objections.

The redistricting bill passed the state House of Representatives May 30, 1972, by a vote of 76-18, and the state Senate May 31, 30-8. Edwards signed the bill June 1.

District	Member Elected 1972	Winning Percentage	1970 Population	Percent Variance
1	F. Edward Hebert (D)	100.0	454,873	—0.1152
2	Hale Boggs (D) [1]	100.0	454,772	—0.1374
3	David C. Treen (R)	54.0	455,575	+ 0.388
4	Joe D. Waggonner Jr. (D)	100.0	455,272	—0.0276
5	Otto E. Passman (D)	100.0	455,205	—0.0423
6	John R. Rarick (D)	100.0	456,178	+ 0.1712
7	John B. Breaux (D)	100.0	455,014	—0.0843
8	Gillis W. Long (D)	68.5	456,291	+ 0.1960

1 Disappeared on plane trip Oct. 16, 1972. Seat declared vacant Jan. 3, 1973.

1970 State Population: 3,643,180
Ideal District Population: 455,398

Election Results, 1968-1972

Vote for U.S. Representative
(Adjusted to new district boundaries)

District	1968	1970	1972
1	77,597 D (95.0%)	69,033 D (87.5%)	78,156 D (100.0%)
	4,101 R (5.0%) [1,2]	891 R (1.1%) [1]	—
2	66,094 D (60.5%) [3]	54,042 D (70.7%)	68,093 D (100.0%)
	43,220 R (39.5%)	18,170 R (23.8%)	—
3	38,831 D (54.3%) [4]	42,839 D (98.4%)	71,090 R (54.0%)
	32,745 R (45.7%) [1]	642 R (1.5%) [1]	60,521 D (46.0%)
4	65,593 D (100.0%)	46,924 D (100.0%)	74,397 D (100.0%)
	—	—	—
5	40,577 D (100.0%)	35,045 D (100.0%)	64,027 D (100.0%)
	—	—	—
6	84,788 D (78.5%) [5]	30,159 D (100.0%) [5]	84,275 D (100.0%)
	23,106 R (21.4%)	—	—
7	83,032 D (90.1%) [6]	29,500 D (100.0%) [6]	71,901 D (100.0%)
	9,091 R (9.8%)	—	—
8	55,132 D (90.4%) [7]	21,269 D (100.0%) [7]	72,607 D (68.5%)
	5,750 R (9.6%) [1]	—	15,517 R (14.7%)
State	511,644 D (76.1%)	328,811 D (90.5%)	573,977 D (84.6%)
	160,809 R (23.9%)	21,236 R (5.8%)	86,607 R (12.8%)

1 No Republican candidate in district as constituted before redistricting.
2 Estimated for Orleans Parish.
3 Estimated.
4 Estimated for St. Martin Parish.
5 Estimated for Livingston and West Feliciana Parishes.
6 Estimated for Allen and St. Martin Parishes.
7 Estimated for Allen, Livingston, Rapides and West Feliciana Parishes.

Voting Age Population

District	Voting Age Population	Voting Age Population 18, 19, 20	Voting Age Population 65 and Over	Median Age of Voting Age Population
1	280,698	23,241 (8.3%)	35,159 (12.5%)	42.1
2	296,023	24,802 (8.4%)	45,709 (15.4%)	42.7
3	265,937	21,450 (8.1%)	25,303 (9.5%)	38.9
4	294,034	32,412 (11.0%)	44,519 (15.1%)	41.2
5	284,312	28,891 (10.2%)	49,462 (17.4%)	44.2
6	283,665	30,619 (10.8%)	33,199 (11.7%)	39.6
7	273,150	25,079 (9.2%)	34,198 (12.5%)	41.2
8	270,179	22,505 (8.3%)	40,340 (14.9%)	42.6
State	2,248,095	209,019 (9.3%)	307,944 (13.7%)	41.5

Income and Occupation

District	Median Family Income	White Collar Workers	Blue Collar Workers	Service Workers	Farm Workers
1	$8,655	52.1%	34.0%	13.5%	0.4%
2	7,611	46.8	34.7	18.2	0.3
3	9,146	49.9	36.7	11.4	2.0
4	7,336	44.0	37.3	16.7	2.0
5	5,762	39.9	36.7	16.5	6.9
6	8,230	48.0	34.3	15.1	2.6
7	7,197	42.3	37.5	14.9	5.3
8	6,092	36.1	39.3	17.2	7.4
State	7,527	45.2	36.2	5.4	3.2

Education: School Years Completed

District	Completed 4 years of High School	Completed 4 years of College	Completed 5 years or less of School	Median School years completed
1	45.3%	9.7%	11.4%	11.3
2	39.9	9.5	14.8	10.5
3	46.0	9.3	17.1	11.3
4	46.3	9.3	14.3	11.5
5	36.5	8.0	19.5	10.1
6	50.0	12.6	13.1	12.0
7	40.4	8.2	22.4	10.2
8	33.3	5.6	25.6	9.2
State	42.2	9.0	17.2	10.8

Housing and Residential Patterns

District	Housing Owner Occupied Units	Renter Occupied Units	Urban	Suburban	Nonmetropolitan
1	58.3%	41.7%	69.1%	25.3%	5.6%
2	39.5	60.5	61.4	38.6	—
3	69.3	30.7	—	35.5	64.5
4	66.5	33.5	40.0	24.5	35.5
5	68.6	31.4	12.4	13.0	74.6
6	68.3	31.7	36.4	26.1	37.5
7	70.9	29.1	32.4	23.9	43.7
8	66.8	33.2	—	—	100.0
State	63.1	36.9	31.5	23.3	45.2

1st District

(Southeast—New Orleans)

Race and Ethnic Groups. Blacks 31.2 percent. Spanish heritage population 4.0 percent.

Cities, 1970 Population. Part of New Orleans 314,547, Slidell 16,331.

Universities, Enrollment. Louisiana State University (New Orleans—12,985), Southern University (New Orleans—1,598).

Military Installations or Activities. Naval Air Station, New Orleans; Naval Support Activity, New Orleans.

NASA Installations. Michoud Assembly Facility, New Orleans.

Newspapers, Circulation. New Orleans papers circulate throughout district.

Commercial Television Stations, Affiliation. Entire district is located in New Orleans ADI.

Plants and Offices, Products, Employment.
    Kaiser Aluminum and Chemical Corp., Chalmette (Aluminum—2,620). **Avondale Shipyards Inc.,** New Orleans (Ship construction and repair—HQ—7,720). **Boeing Co.,** New Orleans (Space vehicles—1,030). **Chrysler Corp.,** New Orleans (Space Division—missile systems—1,000). **Haspel Brothers Inc.,** New Orleans (Men's clothing—1,300).

2nd District

(Jefferson Parish—New Orleans)

Race and Ethnic Groups. Blacks 39.7 percent. Spanish heritage population 4.3 percent.

Cities, 1970 Population. Part of New Orleans 279,028, Marrero 28,949, Gretna 24,955, Jefferson Heights 16,462.

Universities, Enrollment. Loyola University (New Orleans—4,981), Tulane University (New Orleans—8,732), Xavier University of Louisiana (New Orleans—1,554).

Newspapers, Circulation. New Orleans Times-Picayune (Morn—208,236), New Orleans States-Item (ExSat—130,188).

Commercial Television Stations, Affiliation. WDSU-TV, New Orleans (NBC); WGNO-TV, New Orleans (CBS, NBC, ABC); WVUE, New Orleans (ABC); WWL-TV, New Orleans (CBS). Entire district is located in New Orleans ADI.

Plants and Offices, Products, Employment.
    Boh Brothers Construction Co. Inc., New Orleans (Heavy construction—at least 1,200). **Shell Oil Co.,** New Orleans (Crude petroleum and natural gas—1,500). **Ocean Drilling & Exploration,** New Orleans (Drilling oil and gas wells—1,101). **Freemont Minerals Co.,** New Orleans (Crude petroleum and gas—1,500). **Lykes-Youngstown Corp.,** New Orleans (Holding company, deep sea transportation, steel products—33,200). **Avondale Shipyards Inc.,** Westwego (Avoncraft Division ship construction—7,720). **D. H. Holmes Co. Ltd.,** New Orleans (Department store—HQ—1,300.) **City Stores Co.,** New Orleans (Department store—1,800). **The Times-Picayune Publishing Co.,** New Orleans (Newspaper publishing—1,100). **Southern Baptist Hospital Inc.,** New Orleans (Hospital—1,200). **City of New Orleans,** New Orleans (City government—8,000).

3rd District

(South Central—Metairie)

Race and Ethnic Groups. Blacks 14.8 percent.

Cities, 1970 Population. Part of Metairie 131,695, Houma 30,936, New Iberia 30,189, Kenner 29,952.

Universities, Enrollment. Nicholls State University (Thibodeaux—5,411).

Newspapers, Circulation. New Orleans newspapers circulate in portions of district.

Commercial Television Stations, Affiliation. KHMA-TV, Houma (None). Houma has no separate ADI. Most of district is located in New Orleans ADI. Parts of district are in Baton Rouge and Lafayette ADIs.

Plants and Offices, Products, Employment.
    T. L. James & Co. Inc., Kenner (Road construction, dredging—1,500). **J. Ray McDermott & Co. Inc.,** Morgan City (Fabricated steel, shipyard—1,500). **J. Ray McDermott & Co., Inc.,** Amelia (Excavating and foundation work—1,400). **Loffland Brothers Drilling Co.,** New Iberia (Drilling oil and gas wells—1,060). **Tidewater Marine Services,** Morgan City (Holding company, marine transportation—1,650).

4th District

(Northwest—Shreveport)

Race and Ethnic Groups. Blacks 31.2 percent.

Cities, 1970 Population. Shreveport 182,280, Bossier City 41,750, South Fort Polk 15,600, Minden 13,996.

Military Installations or Activities. Fort Polk, Leesville; Barksdale Air Force Base, Shreveport.

Newspapers, Circulation. Shreveport Times (Morn—92,137).

Commercial Television Stations, Affiliation. KSLA-TV, Shreveport (CBS); KTAL-TV, Shreveport (NBC); KTBS-TV, Shreveport (ABC). Most of district is located in Shreveport-Texarkana ADI. Portion of district is located in Alexandria ADI.

Plants and Offices, Products, Employment.
    Kast Metals Corp., Shreveport (Steel castings—HQ—1,000). **AMF Beaird Inc.,** Shreveport (Oil field machinery and equipment—1,350). **International Paper Co.,** Springhill (Southern Kraft division—building paper and building board—1,800). **Sperry Rand Corp.,** Minden (Louisiana Army ammunition plant—ammunition—3,000). **Western Electric Co. Inc.,** Shreveport (Telephone apparatus—4,000). **South Central Bell Telephone Co.,** Shreveport (Telephone communication—1,170).

5th District

(North—Monroe)

Race and Ethnic Groups. Blacks 34.5 percent.
Cities, 1970 Population. Monroe 56,374, Ruston 17,365, Natchitoches 15,974, West Monroe 14,868.
Universities, Enrollment. Grambling College (Grambling—3,913), Louisiana Tech University (Ruston—8,135), Northeast Louisiana University (Monroe—8,810), Northwestern State University of Louisiana (Natchitoches—6,268).
Newspapers, Circulation. Shreveport newspaper circulates in portion of district.
Commercial Television Stations, Affiliation. KNOE-TV, Monroe (CBS primary, ABC); KTVE-TV, Monroe (NBC primary, ABC). Most of district is in Monroe-El Dorado (Arkansas) ADI. Parts of district are in Shreveport-Texarkana (Texas), Alexandria, and Jackson (Mississippi) ADIs.
Plants and Offices, Products, Employment.
   Continental Can Co. Inc., Hodge (Paper mill, paper products—1,630). **Olinkraft Inc.,** West Monroe (Kraft paper—HQ—2,300).

6th District

(East Central—Baton Rouge)

Race and Ethnic Groups. Blacks 29.7 percent.
Cities, 1970 Population. Baton Rouge 165,847, Scotlandville 22,540, Bogalusa 18,398, Hammond 12,478.
Universities, Enrollment. Louisiana State University and Agricultural and Mechanical College (Baton Rouge—21,486), Southeastern Louisiana University (Hammond 5,790), Southern University and Mechanical College (Baton Rouge—8,315).
Newspapers Circulation. Baton Rouge Advocate (Morn—60,388).
Commercial Television Stations, Affiliation. WAFB-TV, Baton Rouge (CBS primary, ABC); WBRZ, Baton Rouge (NBC primary); WRBT, Baton Rouge (ABC). Major portion of district is located in Baton Rouge ADI. Portion of district is located in New Orleans ADI.
Plants and Offices, Products, Employment.
   Ethyl Corp., Baton Rouge (Ethyl Visqueen Division—tetraethyl lead, industrial chemicals—3,000). **Humble Oil & Refining Co.,** Baton Rouge (Pe-

troleum refining—2,860). **Allied Chemical Corp.,** Baton Rouge (Industrial Chemical Division—alkalies and chlorine 1,000). **Crown Zellerbach Corp.,** Bogalusa (Paper, fiberboard, boxes—2,500). **Nichols Construction Corp.,** Baton Rouge (Industrial contractor—1,500). **Barnard & Burke Industrial Corp.,** Baton Rouge (General contractors, industrial fabricated pipe—1,420)

7th District

(Southwest—Lake Charles, Lafayette)

Race and Ethnic Groups. Blacks 21.1 percent.
Cities, 1970 Population. Lake Charles 78,342, Lafayette 69,288, Crowley 16,175, Sulphur 13,611.
Universities, Enrollment. McNeese State University (Lake Charles—6,025), University of Southwestern Louisiana (Lafayette—10,654).
Commercial Television Stations, Affiliation. KATC-TV, Lafayette (ABC); KLFY-TV, Lafayette (CBS); KLNI-TV, Lafayette (NBC); KPLC-TV, Lake Charles (NBC). District is divided between Lake Charles, Lafayette and Alexandria ADIs.
Plants and Offices, Products, Employment.
   Cities Service Oil Co., Lake Charles (Petroleum refining—2,600). **Continental Oil Co.,** Westlake (Petroleum terminal—1,800). **PPG Industries Inc.,** Lake Charles (Organic chemicals—1,000). **Gulf Menhaden Co. Inc.,** Cameron (Fish oil—2,000).

8th District

(Central—Alexandria)

Race and Ethnic Groups. Blacks 36.2 percent.
Cities, 1970 Population. Alexandria 41,540, Opelousas 20,147, Eunice 11,287.
Military Installations or Activities. England Air Force Base, Alexandria.
Newspapers, Circulation. Baton Rouge and New Orleans newspapers circulate in portions of district.
Commercial Television Stations, Affiliation. KALB-TV, Alexandria (NBC). District is divided between Alexandria, Baton Rouge, Lafayette and New Orleans ADIs.
Plants and Offices, Products, Employment.
   Dow Chemical Co. Inc., Plaquemine (Chemicals, plastics—1,150).

MAINE: TWO HOUSE SEATS, NO CHANGE

Maine did not change the boundaries of its two congressional districts following the 1970 census. *(Map p. 84)*

When the 1970 population figures were published, it was found that the variance in population between the two districts was only 0.4630 percent.

This was actually a considerably smaller variance than when the districts were originally drawn in 1961 on the basis of the 1960 census. At that time, the variance between the two was set at 4.3 percent.

Thus, a progressive population shift in the 1960s from one district to another automatically resulted in a

minimal variance and eliminated the necessity to redraw district lines.

District	Member Elected 1972	Winning Percentage	1970 Population	Percent Variance
1	Peter N. Kyros (D)	59.4	495,681	—0.2315
2	William S. Cohen (R)	54.4	497,982	+ 0.2315

1970 State Population: 993,663
Ideal District Population: 496,832

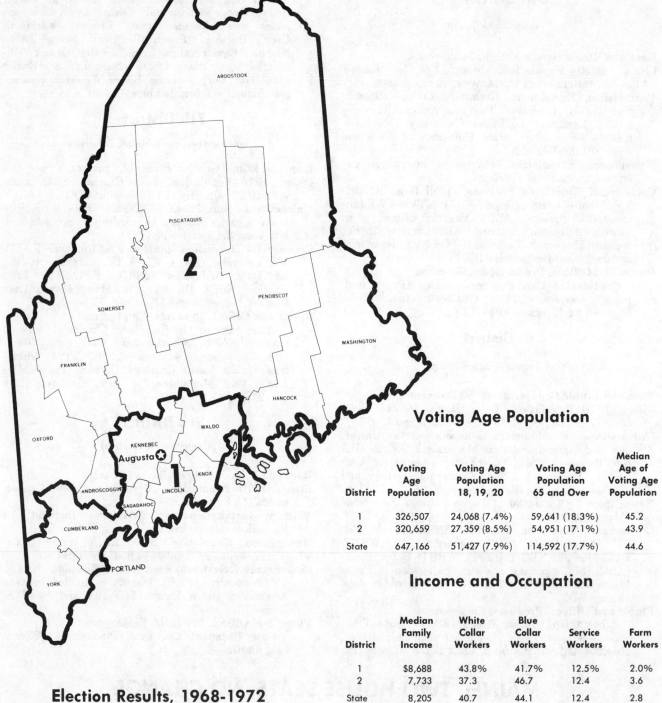

Voting Age Population

District	Voting Age Population	Voting Age Population 18, 19, 20	Voting Age Population 65 and Over	Median Age of Voting Age Population
1	326,507	24,068 (7.4%)	59,641 (18.3%)	45.2
2	320,659	27,359 (8.5%)	54,951 (17.1%)	43.9
State	647,166	51,427 (7.9%)	114,592 (17.7%)	44.6

Income and Occupation

District	Median Family Income	White Collar Workers	Blue Collar Workers	Service Workers	Farm Workers
1	$8,688	43.8%	41.7%	12.5%	2.0%
2	7,733	37.3	46.7	12.4	3.6
State	8,205	40.7	44.1	12.4	2.8

Election Results, 1968-1972

Vote for U.S. Representative
(Adjusted to new district boundaries)

District	1968	1970	1972
1	113,501 D (56.6%)	99,483 D (59.2%)	129,408 D (59.4%)
	86,959 R (43.4%)	68,671 R (40.8%)	88,588 R (40.6%)
2	102,369 D (55.7%)	96,235 D (64.2%)	106,280 R (54.4%)
	81,398 R (44.3%)	53,642 R (35.8%)	89,135 R (45.6%)
State	215,870 D (56.2%)	195,718 D (61.5%)	218,543 D (52.9%)
	168,347 R (43.8%)	122,313 R (38.5%)	194,868 R (47.1%)

Education: School Years Completed

District	Completed 4 years of High School	Completed 4 years of College	Completed 5 years or less of School	Median School years completed
1	58.1%	9.6%	3.4%	12.2
2	51.3	7.1	5.2	12.0
State	54.7	8.4	4.3	12.1

Housing and Residential Patterns

	Housing		Urban-Suburban-Nonmetropolitan Breakdown		
District	Owner Occupied Units	Renter Occupied Units	Urban	Suburban	Nonmetro-politan
1	68.8%	31.2%	13.1%	15.5%	71.4%
2	71.3	28.3	13.2	1.3	85.5
State	70.0	30.0	13.2	8.4	78.4

1st District

(South—Portland, Augusta)

Race and Ethnic Groups. Canadian stock 11.5 percent.
Cities, 1970 Population. Portland 65,116, South Portland 23,294, Augusta 21,945, Biddeford 19,983.
Universities, Enrollment. Bowdoin College (Brunswick—1,034), Colby College (Waterville—1,572), University of Maine at Portland-Gorham (Portland—6,107).
Military Installations or Activities. Naval Air Station, Brunswick.
Newspapers, Circulation. Portland Press-Herald (Morn—52,615).
Commercial Television Stations, Affiliation. WCSH-TV, Portland (NBC); WGAN-TV, Portland (CBS). Most of district located in Portland-Poland Springs ADI. Portion located in Bangor ADI.
Plants and Offices, Products, Employment.
Bath Iron Works Corp., Bath (Shipbuilding—3,200). **Maremont Corp.,** Saco (Machine guns—1,000). **Martin Marietta Corp.,** Thomaston (Dragon Cement Co. Division—cement—2,300). **Scott Paper Co.,** Westbrook (S.D. Warren Co. Division—paper—3,000). **Scott Paper Co.,** Waterville (Pulp and paper products—1,400). **Keyes Fibre Co.,** Waterville (Pulp, paperboard, plastics products—HQ—1,000). **Fairchild Camera & Instrument Corp.,** South Portland (Fair-

child Semiconductor Division—transistors—2,000). **West Point-Pepperell Inc.,** Biddeford (Pepperell Manufacturing Co. Division—fabrics—1,500). **Valles Steak House,** Portland (Restaurants, holding company—1,650).

2nd District

(North—Lewiston, Bangor)

Race and Ethnic Groups. Canadian stock 16.0 percent.
Cities, 1970 Population. Lewiston 41,779, Bangor 33,168, Auburn 24,151, Presque Isle 11,452.
Universities, Enrollment. Bates College (Lewiston—1,237), University of Maine at Farmington (Farmington—1,624), University of Maine at Orono (Orono—9,486), University of Maine at Presque Isle (Presque Isle—1,170).
Military Installations or Activities. Naval Radio Station Cutler, East Machias; Naval Security Group Activity, Winter Harbor; Bucks Harbor Air Force Station, Bucks Harbor; Charleston Air Force Station, Charleston; Loring Air Force Base, Limestone; Caswell Air Force Station, Caswell.
Newspapers, Circulation. Bangor News (Morn—77,194).
Commercial Television Stations, Affiliation. WABI-TV, Bangor (CBS); WEMT, Bangor (ABC); WLBZ-TV, Bangor (NBC); WMTW-TV, Poland Springs (ABC); WAGM-TV, Presque Isle (CBS, ABC, NBC on per program basis). Portions of district located in Bangor ADI, Portland-Poland Springs ADI and Presque Isle ADI.
Plants and Offices, Products, Employment.
Fraser Paper Ltd., Madawaska (Paper—1,000). **Ethyl Corp.,** Rumford (Papermill—1,200). **Great Northern Nekoosa Corp.** Millinocket (Papermill—1,300). **Scoa Industries Inc.,** Skowhegan (Norrwock Shoe Division—shoes—1,000). **Scoa Industries Inc.,** Norridgewock (Norrwock Shoe Division—shoes—1,800). **Bates Manufacturing Co.,** Lewiston (Fabrics, holding company—2,500). **J.S. Industries Inc.,** Presque Isle (Holding company—1,500).

MARYLAND: EIGHT HOUSE SEATS, NO CHANGE

In an attempt to avoid a repeat of the bitter redistricting struggle of 1966, when the Legislature failed to agree on new district lines and the courts had to draw them instead, a special redistricting task force was formed in Maryland following the 1970 census. Gov. Marvin Mandel (D) and State House Speaker Thomas Hunter Lowe (D) appointed the 11-member panel which produced a plan March 4, 1971. *(Map p. 87)*

With several alterations and amendments, the task force proposals were enacted into law. The Maryland House passed the redistricting bill on April 5, 1971, by a vote of 86-39 and the Senate followed suit on April 7 by a vote of 29-12.

The basic strategy proposed by the special redistricting panel was to shift a congressional district from the Baltimore area to the Washington suburbs. As originally proposed, the plan would have placed Rep. Clarence D.

Long (D) of the suburban Baltimore County 2nd District and Rep. Paul S. Sarbanes (D) of the old 4th District in Baltimore City in the same district.

However, the Legislature instead put Sarbanes with another Baltimore City Representative, Edward A. Garmatz (D), in the new 3rd District. Garmatz retired and Sarbanes was re-elected.

District lines in the Washington suburbs were drawn to favor the congressional aspirations of two prominent Democratic politicians in the state. Newspaper reports speculated that Maryland Secretary of State Fred L. Wineland might run in the newly-created district, the 4th, and State Sen. Edward T. Conroy, chairman of the special task force which drew the new lines, might oppose Rep. Lawrence J. Hogan (R) in Prince Georges County (5th District). Wineland did not run; Conroy ran, but was defeated in November 1972.

Elsewhere in the state, the 7th District in Baltimore City was constructed to make it safe for the state's first black representative, Parren J. Mitchell (D). Other districts retained their basic character and proved relatively safe for the incumbents.

District	Member Elected 1972	Winning Percentage	1970 Population	Percent Variance
1	William O. Mills (R)	70.5	489,455	—0.1723
2	Clarence D. Long (D)	65.8	491,331	+ 0.2102
3	Paul S. Sarbanes (D)	69.7	490,851	+ 0.1123
4	Marjorie S. Holt (R)	59.4	495,249	+1.0093
5	Lawrence J. Hogan (R)	62.9	482,721	—1.5457
6	Goodloe E. Byron (D)	64.8	491,839	+ 0.3138
7	Parren J. Mitchell (D)	80.0	487,832	—0.5033
8	Gilbert Gude (R)	63.9	493,121	+ 0.5753

1970 State Population: 3,922,399
Ideal District Population: 490,300

Election Results, 1968-1972

Vote for U.S. Representative
(Adjusted to new district boundaries)

District	1968	1970	1972
1	78,174 R (62.6%)	72,717 R (66.6%)	86,326 R (70.5%)
	46,726 D (37.4%)	35,988 D (33.0%)	36,139 D (29.5%)
2	95,383 D (64.0%)	85,247 D (62.5%)	123,346 D (65.8%)
	53,690 R (36.0%)	50,974 R (37.4%)	64,119 R (34.2%)
3	87,697 D (66.5%)	70,957 D (67.5%)	93,093 D (69.7%)
	44,255 R (33.5%)	34,128 R (32.5%)[1]	40,442 R (30.3%)
4	54,572 R (54.3%)	44,475 R (53.3%)	87,534 R (59.4%)
	45,873 D (45.7%)	38,537 D (46.2%)	59,877 D (40.6%)
5	63,403 R (52.6%)	56,790 R (58.8%)	90,016 R (62.9%)
	57,053 D (47.4%)	39,774 D (41.2%)	53,049 D (37.1%)
6	73,954 R (54.5%)	60,831 R (50.9%)	107,283 R (64.8%)
	61,799 D (45.5%)	57,001 D (47.7%)	58,259 R (35.2%)
7	70,463 D (84.9%)	68,105 D (83.0%)	83,749 D (80.0%)
	12,544 R (15.1%)	13,957 R (17.0%)	20,876 R (20.0%)
8	98,797 R (60.7%)	94,678 R (63.5%)	137,287 R (63.9%)
	63,961 D (39.3%)	54,480 D (36.5%)	77,551 D (36.1%)
State	535,839 D (52.6%)	452,546 D (51.1%)	634,087 D (52.0%)
	483,829 R (47.4%)	430,300 R (48.6%)	584,859 R (48.0%)

1 No Republican candidate in this district as constituted before redistricting.

Voting Age Population

District	Voting Age Population	Voting Age Population 18, 19, 20	Voting Age Population 65 and Over	Median Age of Voting Age Population
1	309,590	25,163 (8.1%)	45,569 (14.7%)	41.4
2	323,500	22,089 (6.8%)	34,982 (10.8%)	42.6
3	338,666	24,242 (7.2%)	57,272 (16.9%)	45.6
4	310,819	25,753 (8.3%)	22,898 (7.4%)	37.7
5	306,845	29,060 (9.5%)	21,598 (7.0%)	34.9
6	322,820	23,585 (7.3%)	45,470 (14.1%)	42.9
7	311,039	25,963 (8.3%)	45,067 (14.5%)	42.7
8	312,886	20,270 (6.5%)	30,321 (9.7%)	41.9
State	2,536,223	196,097 (7.7%)	300,210 (11.8%)	41.2

Income and Occupation

District	Median Family Income	White Collar Workers	Blue Collar Workers	Service Workers	Farm Workers
1	$ 8,925	41.9%	39.8%	12.7%	5.6%
2	12,140	59.0	32.1	8.3	0.6
3	10,022	53.4	35.3	11.2	0.1
4	11,892	60.0	28.4	10.7	0.9
5	12,286	66.4	23.2	10.1	0.3
6	9,749	46.3	38.9	11.4	3.4
7	7,841	36.5	40.4	22.8	0.3
8	17,102	79.0	13.2	7.4	0.4
State	11,057	55.8	31.1	11.7	1.4

Education: School Years Completed

District	Completed 4 years of High School	Completed 4 years of College	Completed 5 years or less of School	Median School years completed
1	42.4%	8.4%	9.1%	11.1
2	53.0	13.1	5.3	12.1
3	39.1	8.2	9.0	10.6
4	60.0	13.6	4.8	12.3
5	67.0	18.1	3.4	12.5
6	47.3	9.7	6.7	11.6
7	31.1	6.5	15.0	9.8
8	80.3	34.1	2.5	13.2
State	52.3	13.9	7.0	12.1

Housing and Residential Patterns

District	Housing Owner Occupied Units	Renter Occupied Units	Urban-Suburban-Nonmetropolitan Breakdown Urban	Suburban	Nonmetropolitan
1	67.3%	32.7%	—	34.5%	65.5%
2	68.7	31.3	5.2%	94.8	—
3	57.1	42.9	80.0	20.0	—
4	61.4	38.6	—	100.0	—
5	49.6	50.4	—	100.0	—
6	68.4	31.6	—	40.2	59.8
7	35.2	64.8	100.0	—	—
8	62.7	37.3	—	100.0	—
State	58.8	41.2	23.1	61.2	15.7

1st District

(Eastern Shore—Salisbury, Aberdeen)

Race and Ethnic Groups. Blacks 19.4 percent. German stock 1.1 percent, British stock 0.7 percent.
Cities, 1970 Population. Salisbury 15,252, Aberdeen 12,375, Cambridge 11,595.
Universities, Enrollment. Salisbury State College (Salisbury—1,984).
Military Installations or Activities. Aberdeen Proving Ground/Edgewood Arsenal (Army), Aberdeen; Naval

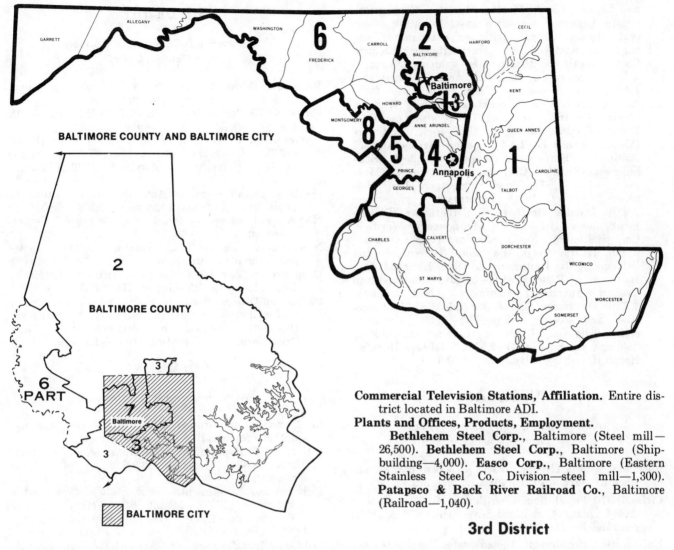

BALTIMORE COUNTY AND BALTIMORE CITY

BALTIMORE COUNTY

BALTIMORE CITY

Air Test Center, Patuxent River; Naval Ordnance Station, Indian Head.

Commercial Television Stations, Affiliation. WBOC-TV, Salisbury (ABC, CBS, NBC). Portions of district located in Baltimore and Salisbury ADIs.

Plants and Offices, Products, Employment.
    Bechtel Corp., Newburg (Heavy construction—1,500). **Dresser Industries Inc.**, Salisbury (Petroleum Equipment Division—dispensing pumps—1,000). **Bata Shoe Co. Inc.**, Belcamp (Leather and rubber footwear—HQ—2,800).

2nd District

(North—Baltimore Suburbs)

Race and Ethnic Groups. Blacks 3.1 percent. Russian stock 3.7 percent, Polish stock 2.2 percent.

Cities, 1970 Population Dundalk 85,248, part of Towson 51,308, Essex 38,104, Parkville 33,928.

Universities, Enrollment. Goucher College (Towson—1,050).

Newspapers, Circulation. Baltimore newspapers circulate throughout district.

Commercial Television Stations, Affiliation. Entire district located in Baltimore ADI.

Plants and Offices, Products, Employment.
    Bethlehem Steel Corp., Baltimore (Steel mill—26,500). **Bethlehem Steel Corp.**, Baltimore (Shipbuilding—4,000). **Easco Corp.**, Baltimore (Eastern Stainless Steel Co. Division—steel mill—1,300). **Patapsco & Back River Railroad Co.**, Baltimore (Railroad—1,040).

3rd District

(Baltimore South and East, Baltimore suburbs)

Race and Ethnic Groups. Blacks 12.6 percent. German stock 2.5 percent, Italian stock 2.5 percent.

Cities, 1970 Population. Part of Baltimore 392,484, part of Catonsville 31,717, part of Towson 26,430, Arbutus 22,659.

Universities, Enrollment. Johns Hopkins University (Baltimore—9,632), Loyola College (Baltimore—1,270), Morgan State College (Baltimore—4,889), Towson State College (Towson—8,174).

Newspapers, Circulation. Baltimore News-American (ExSat—207,219), Baltimore Sun (MxSat—171,050; ExSat 198,830).

Commercial Television Stations, Affiliation. WBAL-TV, Baltimore (NBC); WJZ-TV, Baltimore (ABC); WMAR-TV, Baltimore (CBS); WBFF-TV, Baltimore (None). Entire district located in Baltimore ADI.

Plants and Offices, Products, Employment.
    Armco Steel Corp., Baltimore (Steel mill—1,500). **American Smelting and Refining Co.**, Baltimore (Copper refining—1,200). **Maryland Shipbuilding & Drydock Co.**, Baltimore (Shipbuilding—2,700). **Bethlehem Steel Corp.**, Baltimore (Shipbuilding

and repair—2,300). **Martin Marietta Corp.**, Baltimore (Aircraft, aerospace systems—2,900). **General Motors Corp.**, Baltimore (Automobile and truck assembly—6,000). **Westinghouse Electric Corp.**, Baltimore (Underwater weapons systems—1,400). **Koppers Co. Inc.**, Baltimore (Piston rings—1,400). **Anchor-Hocking Corp.**, Baltimore (Carr-Lowery Division—glass containers—1,250). **Western Electric Co. Inc.**, Baltimore (Cable, wiring devices—7,000). **Continental Can Co. Inc.**, Baltimore (Metal containers—1,500). **Lever Brothers Co.**, Baltimore (Soaps and detergents—1,250). **Schluderberg-Kurdle Co. Inc.**, Baltimore (Meat packer—HQ—1,600). **Food Fair Stores Inc.**, Baltimore (Pantry Pride Supermarkets—groceries—7,000). **Hutzler Brothers Co.**, Baltimore (Department stores—HQ—1,200). **Montgomery Ward & Co.**, Baltimore (Mail order department stores—2,500). **Hearst Corp.**, Baltimore (Newspaper publishing—1,000). **Baltimore & Ohio Railroad Co.**, Baltimore (Railroad—HQ—3,000). **Metropolitan Transit Authority**, Baltimore (Local transit—1,770). **Baltimore Gas & Electric Co.**, Baltimore (Gas and electric utility—HQ—1,550). **Commercial Credit Co.**, Baltimore (Commercial banking, holding company—HQ—2,500). **Johns Hopkins Hospital**, Baltimore (Hospital—4,200).

4th District

(Anne Arundel County, Southern Prince Georges County)

Race and Ethnic Groups. Blacks 10.5 percent. German stock 1.7 percent, British stock 1.2 percent.

Cities, 1970 Population. Glen Burnie 38,354, Annapolis 29,444, part of Suitland-Silver Hill 27,525, Hillcrest Heights 24,699.

Universities, Enrollment. United States Naval Academy (Annapolis—4,310).

Military Installations or Activities. Fort Meade, Odenton; United States Naval Academy, Annapolis; Reconnaissance Technical Support Center (Navy), Suitland; Naval Air Facility, Camp Springs; Naval Hospital, Annapolis; National Security Agency (Navy), Odenton; Naval Station, Annapolis; Naval Oceanographic Office, Suitland; Naval Ship Research and Development Center, Annapolis; Andrews Air Force Base, Camp Springs.

Newspapers, Circulation. Washington, D.C., newspapers circulate throughout district. Baltimore papers circulate in portion of district.

Commercial Television Stations, Affiliation. Portions of district located in Baltimore and Washington, D.C. ADIs.

Plants and Offices, Products, Employment.
Westinghouse Electric Corp., Baltimore (Electric aircraft systems—4,000). **Westinghouse Electric Corp.**, Baltimore (Radar systems communication—2,800). **Enjay Chemical Co.**, Odenton (Enjay Fibers & Laminates Co. Division—plastics, synthetic fibers—1,000).

5th District

(Washington, D.C., Suburbs—Northern Prince Georges County)

Race and Ethnic Groups. Blacks 15.6 percent. Italian stock 1.5 percent, German stock 1.3 percent.

Cities, 1970 Population. Chillum 35,756, Bowie 35,402, College Park 26,492, Takoma Park 18,538.

Universities, Enrollment. Bowie State College (Bowie—2,353), Columbia Union College (Takoma Park—1,003), University of Maryland (College Park—36,028).

Military Installations or Activities. Naval Ordnance Laboratory, White Oak (part also in 8th district).

NASA Facilities. Goddard Space Flight Center, Greenbelt.

Newspapers, Circulation. Washington, D.C., newspapers circulate throughout district.

Commercial Television Stations, Affiliation. Entire district located in Washington, D.C., ADI.

Plants and Offices, Products, Employment.
Washington Suburban Sanitary Commission, Hyattsville (Sanitation services—1,500). **Dart Drug Corp.**, Landover (Drug stores—1,100).

6th District

(West—Hagerstown, Cumberland)

Race and Ethnic Groups. Blacks 4.3 percent. German stock 0.9 percent, British stock 0.9 percent.

Cities, 1970 Population. Hagerstown 35,867, Cumberland 29,824, Frederick 23,597, part of Catonsville 23,178.

Universities, Enrollment. Bowie State College (Bowie (Frostburg—2,736), Mount Saint Mary's College (Emmitsburg—1,149), Western Maryland College (Westminster—2,325).

Military Installations or Activities. Fort Detrick, Frederick, Fort Ritchie, Cascade.

Newspapers, Circulation. Baltimore newspapers circulate in portion of district.

Commercial Television Stations, Affiliation. WHAG-TV, Hagerstown (NBC). Hagerstown has no separate ADI. Portions of district are in Baltimore, Johnstown-Altoona (Penn.) and Wash., D.C., ADIs.

Plants and Offices, Products, Employment.
Westvaco Corp., Westernport (Paper mill—2,200). **Mack Trucks Inc.**, Hagerstown (Truck engines—3,000). **Fairchild Hiller Corp.**, Hagerstown (Aircraft and space systems—1,400). **Kelly-Springfield Tire Co.**, Cumberland (Tires, tubes, automobile accessories—HQ—2,800). **PPG Industries Inc.**, Cumberland (Glass—1,240). **Black & Decker Manufacturing Co. Inc.**, Hampstead (Portable electric tools—3,000). **Celanese Corp.**, Cumberland

Glossary and Sources

For a complete explanation of all terms used in this book and a list of source material, consult the details included in the Introduction.

(Acetate yarns—3,000). **Sagner Inc.,** Frederick (Men's clothing—HQ—1,000). **Hercules Inc.,** Cumberland (Research and development—1,100). **Carborundum Co. Inc.,** Hagerstown (Pangborn Division—blast cleaning and dust control equipment—1,000). **Potomac Edison Co.,** Frederick (Electric utility—at least 1,500).

7th District

(Balitmore—West and Central)

Race and Ethnic Groups. Blacks 74.0 percent. Russian stock 0.8 percent, German stock 0.7 percent.
Cities, 1970 Population. Part of Baltimore 487,832.
Universities, Enrollment. Coppin State College (Baltimore—2,488), Maryland Institute, College of Art (Baltimore—1,051), University of Baltimore (Baltimore—4,855).
Newspapers, Circulation. Baltimore newspapers circulate throughout district.
Commercial Television Stations, Affiliation. Entire district located in Baltimore ADI.
Plants and Offices, Products, Employment.
   Londontown Manufacturing Co., Baltimore (Rainwear—HQ—1,100). **A.S. Abell Co.,** Baltimore (Newspaper publishing, television broadcasting—1,600). **Monumental Life Insurance Co.,** Baltimore (Insurance—1,660).

8th District

(Washington, D.C, Suburbs—Silver Spring)

Race and Ethnic Groups. Blacks 3.7 percent. Spanish heritage population 3.0 percent. Russian stock 2.9 percent, German stock 1.8 percent.
Cities, 1970 Population. Silver Spring 77,547, Bethesda 71,753, Wheaton 66,241, Rockville 41,586.
Military Installations or Activities. Naval Ship Research and Development Center, Carderock; National Naval Medical Center, Bethesda; Naval Ordnance Laboratory, White Oak (part also in 5th district).
NASA Facilities. AEC-NASA Space Nuclear Systems Office, Germantown.
Newspapers, Circulation. Washington, D.C. newspapers circulate throughout district.
Commercial Television Stations, Affiliation. Entire district located in Washington, D.C. ADI.
Plants and Offices, Products, Employment.
   Computer Sciences Corp., Silver Spring (Data processing services—1,300). **International Business Machines Corp.,** Gaithersburg (Laboratory—2,000). **Vitro Corp. of America,** Wheaton (Electronic research—3,000). **Quality Courts Motels Inc.,** Silver Spring (Motel franchises—1,200). **Johns Hopkins University Applied Physics Laboratory,** Silver Spring (Scientific research—2,000).

MASSACHUSETTS: TWELVE HOUSE SEATS, NO CHANGE

Two incumbent representatives, a Democrat and a Republican, were hurt politically by Massachusetts congressional redistricting. One was first-term Rep. Louise Day Hicks (D), nationally known candidate for mayor of Boston in 1967 and 1971. The other was Hastings Keith (R) of West Bridgewater in Plymouth County.

The redistricting plan was devised by a 21-member joint legislative committee headed by a Democratic state senator. With the exception of Hicks and Keith, the legislation generally favored the incumbents. The bill passed the state Senate on Oct. 28, 1971, by a vote of 22-13 and the state House on Oct. 29, 150-67. Gov. Francis W. Sargent (R) signed it Nov. 12, 1971. *(Maps p. 91, 94)*

The major changes in House district lines were in the Boston area. Boston lost population over the last decade, while the suburbs gained. Thus, Rep. Hicks, whose 9th District previously was contained entirely within the city, saw her district expand to take in seven suburban communities southwest of the city. These areas were less favorable to her candidacy.

Keith, of the 12th District, fared no better. West Bridgewater, with several surrounding communities, was transferred to the 10th District, represented by Margaret M. Heckler (R). In addition, some Democrats were added to the 12th District, making it even more marginal for Keith, who won by only 1,522 votes in 1970.

Rep. Hicks was defeated for re-election and Rep. Keith retired.

District	Member Elected 1972	Winning Percentage	1970 Population	Percent Variance
1	Silvio O. Conte (R)	99.9	469,438	−0.9829
2	Edward P. Boland (D)	100.0	472,270	−0.3855
3	Harold D. Donohue (D)	99.9	469,443	−0.9818
4	Robert F. Drinan (D)	48.8	476,130	+ 0.4286
5	Paul W. Cronin (R)	53.5	473,154	−0.1991
6	Michael J. Harrington (D)	64.1	475,885	+ 0.3769
7	Torbert H. Macdonald (D)	67.7	476,565	+ 0.5203
8	Thomas P. O'Neill Jr. (D)	88.7	474,090	−0.0016
9	John Joseph Moakley (D) [1]	43.2	473,680	−0.0881
10	Margaret M. Heckler (R)	100.0	477,054	+ 0.6234
11	James A. Burke (D)	100.0	475,789	+ 0.3566
12	Gerry E. Studds (D)	50.3	475,672	+ 0.3319

1 *Elected as Independent.*

1970 State Population:	5,689,170
Ideal District Population:	474,098

Election Results, 1968-1972

Vote for U.S. Representative
(Adjusted to new district boundaries)

District	1968	1970	1972
1	131,972 R (92.6%)	106,301 R (91.2%)	159,282 R (99.9%)
	10,267 D (7.2%)[1]	10,281 D (8.8%)[1]	—
2	116,555 D (66.8%)	97,887 D (83.3%)	137,616 D (100.0%)
	56,852 R (32.6%)	17,922 R (15.2%)	—

District	1968	1970	1972
3	123,757 D (65.2%)	89,686 D (54.4%)	156,703 D (99.9%)
	63,202 R (33.3%)	62,298 R (37.8%)	—
4	88,020 D (51.2%)	69,561 D (46.2%)	99,977 D (48.8%)
	48,172 R (28.0%)	55,657 R (37.0%)	93,927 R (45.8%)
5	105,168 R (56.9%)	104,411 R (62.7%)	110,970 R (53.5%)
	71,216 D (38.5%)	59,527 D (35.8%)	92,847 D (44.7%)
6	132,936 R (65.8%)	111,996 D (62.0%)	139,697 D (64.1%)
	69,110 D (34.2%)	68,521 R (38.0%)	78,381 R (35.9%)
7	118,469 D (59.8%)	109,604 D (65.6%)	135,193 D (67.7%)
	79,739 R (40.2%)	57,401 R (34.4%)	64,357 R (32.3%)
8	121,275 D (79.7%)	109,240 D (84.6%)	142,470 D (88.7%)
	25,728 R (16.9%)[1]	17,063 R (13.2%)[1]	—
9	102,495 D (73.3%)	77,133 D (62.5%)	67,143 D (41.1%)[2]
	37,242 R (26.7%)	32,609 R (26.4%)	23,177 R (14.2%)
10	125,238 R (67.3%)	91,691 R (55.4%)	161,708 R (100.0%)
	60,739 D (32.7%)	73,671 D (44.6%)	—
11	150,828 D (92.9%)	128,503 D (91.4%)	154,397 D (100.0%)
	11,484 R (7.1%)[1]	8,183 R (5.8%)[1]	—
12	153,457 R (99.9%)	90,395 D (50.6%)	117,753 D (50.3%)
	—	88,168 R (49.4%)	116,547 R (49.7%)
State	1,032,731 D (50.2%)	1,027,484 D (57.1%)	1,243,796 D (57.6%)
	971,190 R (47.2%)	710,225 R (39.4%)	808,349 R (37.4%)

1 No candidate in this district as constituted before redistricting.
2 Moakley (Ind.) 70,571.

Voting Age Population

District	Voting Age Population	Voting Age Population 18, 19, 20	Voting Age Population 65 and Over	Median Age of Voting Age Population
1	319,341	32,669 (9.6%)	53,025 (14.4%)	44.1
2	309,850	22,923 (7.4%)	50,551 (16.3%)	45.1
3	306,517	23,544 (7.7%)	51,567 (16.8%)	44.5
4	327,734	29,942 (9.1%)	52,591 (16.0%)	42.9
5	295,533	20,220 (6.8%)	43,683 (14.8%)	43.1
6	315,514	21,125 (6.7%)	56,743 (18.0%)	45.5
7	318,742	21,939 (6.9%)	53,107 (16.7%)	45.3
8	360,054	38,579 (10.7%)	60,683 (16.8%)	39.4
9	317,432	28,495 (9.0%)	54,565 (17.2%)	43.5
10	309,517	22,742 (7.3%)	47,693 (15.4%)	44.1
11	312,465	21,361 (6.8%)	54,960 (17.6%)	45.5
12	310,193	18,469 (6.0%)	57,556 (18.6%)	46.0
State	3,802,869	301,988 (7.9%)	636,724 (16.7%)	44.2

Income and Occupation

District	Median Family Income	White Collar Workers	Blue Collar Workers	Service Workers	Farm Workers
1	$10,311	48.6%	36.2%	13.8%	1.4%
2	10,268	45.3	41.8	12.2	0.7
3	10,863	48.7	38.0	12.8	0.5
4	12,409	61.8	26.7	11.1	0.4
5	11,532	52.1	36.4	11.0	0.5
6	10,904	51.8	35.6	12.3	0.4
7	11,406	56.4	32.2	11.1	0.2
8	10,317	62.6	24.6	12.8	0.1
9	10,144	55.0	28.3	16.6	0.2
10	10,747	45.9	41.4	11.9	0.8
11	11,052	54.2	33.2	12.4	0.2
12	10,132	48.2	38.2	12.9	0.7
State	10,833	52.7	34.2	12.5	0.5

Education: School Years Completed

District	Completed 4 years of High School	Completed 4 years of College	Completed 5 years or less of School	Median School years completed
1	56.1%	11.5%	4.7%	12.2
2	51.5	8.8	6.1	12.1
3	54.9	10.0	5.1	12.2
4	67.3	21.1	4.5	12.5
5	59.2	13.8	5.1	12.3
6	61.1	11.8	4.4	12.3
7	61.8	10.7	4.7	12.3
8	60.3	18.2	6.3	12.3
9	57.8	12.7	7.0	12.2
10	51.6	11.4	8.1	12.1
11	61.8	8.9	4.2	12.3
12	57.7	11.6	6.6	12.2
State	58.5	12.6	5.6	12.3

Housing and Residential Patterns

	Housing		Urban-Suburban-Nonmetropolitan Breakdown		
District	Owner Occupied Units	Renter Occupied Units	Urban	Suburban	Nonmetro-politan
1	62.2%	37.8%	22.8%	38.2%	38.9%
2	62.8	37.2	48.8	28.2	23.0
3	62.0	38.0	37.6	36.1	26.3
4	56.9	43.1	16.0	70.9	13.1
5	64.6	35.4	34.1	57.5	8.4
6	61.6	38.4	9.9	71.5	18.8
7	60.5	39.5	0.0	100.0	0.0
8	30.2	69.8	34.5	65.5	—
9	39.5	60.5	70.4	29.6	—
10	65.7	34.3	20.3	55.3	24.4
11	60.1	39.9	49.0	51.0	0.0
12	69.4	30.6	21.4	47.4	31.2
State	57.5	42.5	30.4	54.3	15.3

1st District

(West—Berkshires, Pittsfield, Holyoke)

Race and Ethnic Groups. Canadian stock 6.5 percent, Polish stock 5.2 percent, Italian stock 3.4 percent.

Cities, 1970 Population. Pittsfield 57,116, Holyoke 50,025, Westfield 31,429, Northampton 29,633.

Universities, Enrollment. Amherst College (Amherst—1,227), Mount Holyoke College (South Hadley—1,919), North Adams State College (North Adams—2,450), Smith College (Northampton—2,794), University of Massachusetts (Amherst—22,505), Westfield State College (Westfield—2,667), Williams College (Williamstown—1,592).

Newspapers, Circulation. Springfield newspapers circulate in portions of district.

Commercial Television Stations, Affiliation. Most of district is located in Springfield ADI. Portion of district is located in Albany (New York) ADI.

Plants and Offices, Products, Employment.
    General Electric Co., Pittsfield (Power trans-

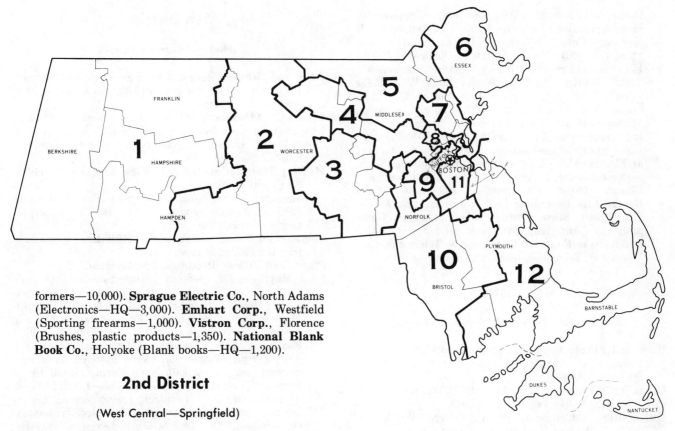

formers—10,000). **Sprague Electric Co.**, North Adams (Electronics—HQ—3,000). **Emhart Corp.**, Westfield (Sporting firearms—1,000). **Vistron Corp.**, Florence (Brushes, plastic products—1,350). **National Blank Book Co.**, Holyoke (Blank books—HQ—1,200).

2nd District

(West Central—Springfield)

Race and Ethnic Groups. Blacks 4.7 percent. Canadian stock 8.9 percent, Polish stock 5.3 percent, Italian stock 3.1 percent.

Cities, 1970 Population. Springfield 163,934, Chicopee 66,696, Southbridge Center 14,265, Webster Center 12,437.

Universities, Enrollment. American International College (Springfield—2,761), Springfield College (Springfield—2,692), Western New England College (Springfield—3,586).

Military Installations or Activities. Westover Air Force Base, Chicopee Falls.

Newspapers, Circulation. Springfield Union (Morn—79,279), Springfield News (Eve—92,153).

Commercial Television Stations, Affiliation. WHYN-TV, Springfield (ABC); WWLP-TV, Springfield (NBC). In addition to Springfield ADI, portion of district is located in Boston ADI.

Plants and Offices, Products, Employment.

L. S. Starrett Co., Athol (Precision tools, saws, knives, etc—HQ—1,100). **UTD Corp.**, Athol (Cutting tools—HQ—1,000). **Moore Drop Forging Company**, Springfield (Forgings, tools—HQ—2,000). **A. G. Spalding & Bros. Inc.**, Chicopee (Sporting goods—HQ—2,000). **Bangor Punta Operations Inc.**, Springfield (Firearms—1,400). **Buxton Inc.**, Springfield (Leather goods, cases, belts—HQ—1,100). **General Instrument Corp.**, Chicopee (F. W. Sickles Division—electrical accessories—1,000). **Uniroyal Inc.**, Chicopee (Fisk Tire & Rubber Division—tires—1,950). **Ambac Industries Inc.**, Springfield (American Bosch Division—fuel injection systems—1,500). **Monsanto Co.**, Indian Orchard (Hydrocarbons &

Polymers Division—plastics—2,050). **American Optical Corp.**, Southbridge (Ophthalmic, Optical products—HQ—4,500). **Massachusetts Mutual Life Insurance Co.**, Springfield (Insurance—HQ—2,500). **Milton Bradley Co.**, East Longmeadow (Games, school supplies—HQ—1,500).

3rd District

(Central—Worcester)

Race and Ethnic Groups. Canadian stock 8.0 percent, Italian stock 5.1 percent, Irish stock 3.4 percent.

Cities, 1970 Population. Worcester 176,596, Marlborough 27,935, Hudson Center 14,162, Milford Center 13,739.

Universities, Enrollment. Assumption College (Worcester—1,054), Clark University (Worcester—3,228), College of the Holy Cross (Worcester—2,492), Worcester Polytechnic Institute (Worcester—2,476), Worcester State College (Worcester—3,919).

Newspapers, Circulation. Worcester Telegram (Morn—57,640), Worcester Gazette (Eve—92,450).

Commercial Television Stations, Affiliation. WSMW-TV, Worcester (NBC). Worcester has no separate ADI. Entire district is included in Boston ADI.

Plants and Offices, Products, Employment.

Wyman-Gordon Co., North Grafton (Metal Forgings—1,100). **Wyman-Gordon Co.**, Worcester (Metal forgings—HQ—1,800). **United States Steel Corp.**, Worcester (Cables & wires—1,500). **Avco**

Corp., Westborough (Avco Bay State Abrasives Division—grinding wheels—1,100). **Crompton & Knowles Corp.,** Worcester (Textile, plastics, machinery—1,400). **North American Rockwell Corp.,** Hopedale (Draper Division—textile machinery—2,200). **Whitin Machine Works Inc.,** Whitinsville (Textile machinery, parts—1,400). **Norton Co.,** Worcester (Abrasives products—HQ—4,500). **Cincinnati Milacron-Heald Corp.,** Worcester (Grinding, boring machinery—1,150). **RCA Corp.,** Marlborough (Info Systems Division—computers—1,500). **General Electric Co.,** Ashland (Specialty Appliance Dept.—electric clocks, timers—1,500). **Colonial Press Inc.,** Clinton (Offset litho printing—HQ—1,000). **Paul Revere Life Insurance Co.,** Worcester (Insurance—HQ—1,000). **State Mutual Life Assurance Company of America,** Worcester (Insurance—HQ—1,350). **New England Telephone & Telegraph Co.,** Worcester (Telephone, telegraph services—1,370).

4th District

(East Central—Newton, Waltham, Fitchburg)

Race and Ethnic Groups. Canadian stock 10.8 percent, Italian stock 4.9 percent, Russian stock 4.8 percent, Irish stock 3.0 percent.

Cities, 1970 Population. Newton 91,085, Waltham 61,590, Fitchburg 43,349, Leominster 32,943.

Universities, Enrollment. Bentley College (Waltham—3,437), Boston College (Chestnut Hill—11,111), Brandeis University (Waltham—2,247), Fitchburg State College (Fitchburg—3,167), Framingham State College (Framingham—4,452), Newton College of the Sacred Heart (Newton—1,007).

Military Installations or Activities. Fort Devens, Ayer.

Newspapers, Circulation. Boston newspapers circulate in major portion of district.

Commercial Television Stations, Affiliation. Entire district is located in Boston ADI.

Plants and Offices, Products, Employment.

Raytheon Co., Waltham (Electronic guidance components—2,300). **Raytheon Co.,** Waltham (Microwave tubes—2,450). **Raytheon Co.,** Wayland (Electronic equipment—2,000). **Raytheon Co.,** Sudbury (Communications equipment—2,000). **Honeywell Information Systems Inc.,** Framingham (Digital computer components—2,000). **Honeywell Inc.,** Waltham (Electronic computing equipment—1,250). **Digital Equipment Corp.,** Maynard (Digital computers—HQ—3,800). **GTE Sylvania Inc.,** Waltham (Tube semi-conductors—5,000). **Polaroid Corp.,** Waltham (Photographic film—2,200). **Weyerhaeuser Co.,** Fitchburg (Weyerhaeuser Co. Paper Division—paper products—1,200). **Dennison Manufacturing Co.,** Framingham (Paper products, allied machinery—HQ—2,500). **General Electric Co.,** Fitchburg (Steam turbines—1,100). **Wallace-Murray Corp.,** Fitchburg (Simonds Saw & Steel Division—machine knives—1,200). **Foster Grant Co. Inc.,** Leominster (Plastic products, powders—HQ—1,500). **Perini Corp. & Gordon H. Ball,** Framingham (Dam construction—1,000). **General Motors Corp.,** Framingham (Autos—3,000).

5th District

(North—Lawrence, Lowell)

Race and Ethnic Groups. Canadian stock 10.1 percent, Italian stock 4.2 percent, British stock 3.4 percent, Irish stock 3.1 percent.

Cities, 1970 Population. Lowell 94,247, Lawrence 66,912.

Universities, Enrollment. Lowell State College (Lowell—1,894), Lowell Technological Institute (Lowell—6,891).

Military Installations or Activities. Laurence G. Hanscom Field, Bedford.

Newspapers, Circulation. Lowell Sun (Eve—53,434). In addition, Boston newspapers circulate in major portion of district.

Commercial Television Stations, Affiliation. Entire district is included in Boston ADI.

Plants and Offices, Products, Employment.

Raytheon Co., Bedford (Missile Systems Division—electronic equipment—11,300). **Raytheon Co.,** Andover (Missile Systems Division—electronic equipment—3,700). **Raytheon Co.,** Lowell (Missile Systems Division—electronic equipment—2,800). **Raytheon Co.,** Lexington (Headquarters—1,000). **Avco Corp.,** Wilmington (Avco Systems Division—systems analysis—2,000). **Avco Corp.,** Lowell (Avco Systems Division—systems analysis—1,000). **EG & G Inc.,** Bedford (Research, development, manufacture, service of electronic and nucleonic systems, etc.—HQ—1,000). **Itex Corp.,** Lexington (Mechanical measuring controls—HQ—2,600). **Compugraphic Corp.,** Wilmington (Photo typesetting machinery—HQ—1,000). **Mitre Corp.,** Bedford (Systems engineering—HQ—1,400). **Malden Mills Inc.,** Lawrence (Pile fabrics—HQ—1,500). **Tyer Rubber Corp.,** Andover (Rubber footwear, industrial goods—1,000). **Courier-Citizen Co.,** Lowell (Uniform Printing Supply Co. Division—books, special forms—1,100).

6th District

(Northeast—Lynn, Peabody)

Race and Ethnic Groups. Canadian stock 10.3 percent, Italian stock 4.0 percent, Irish stock 3.1 percent, British stock 2.7 percent.

Cities, 1970 Population. Lynn 90,279, Peabody 48,081, Haverhill 46,133, Salem 40,543.

Universities, Enrollment. Merrimack College (North Andover—2,846), Salem State College (Salem—7,304).

Newspapers, Circulation. Boston newspapers circulate in major portion of district.

Commercial Television Stations, Affiliation. Entire district is located in Boston ADI.

Plants and Offices, Products, Employment.

Western Electric Co. Inc., North Andover (Telephone, telegraph apparatus—10,000). **General Electric Co.,** Lynn (Aircraft engines—7,000). **General Electric Co.,** Lynn (Steam generators—6,200). **General Electric Co.,** Lynn (Instruments & meters—3,500). **GTE Sylvania Inc.,** Salem (Incandescent lamps—1,000). **GTE Sylvania Inc.**, Salem (Lighting equipment—1,000). **USM Corp.**, Beverly (Industrial machinery & equipment—2,320).

7th District

(Northeast—Boston Suburbs)

Race and Ethnic Groups. Italian stock 11.7 percent, Canadian stock 9.0 percent, Irish stock 4.2 percent, Russian stock 2.7 percent, British stock 2.5 percent.

Cities, 1970 Population. Medford 64,412, Malden 56,130, Revere 43,161, Everett 42,480.

Universities, Enrollment. Tufts University (Medford—5,560).

Military Installations or Activities. Naval Hospital, Chelsea.

Newspapers, Circulation. Boston newspapers circulate throughout district.

Commercial Television Stations, Affiliation. Entire district is located in Boston ADI.

Plants and Offices, Products, Employment.
   Transitron Electronic Corp., Wakefield (Electronic components—HQ—1,000). **Itek Corp.**, Burlington (Electronic, optical systems—1,150). **Microwave Associates Inc.**, Burlington (Communications equipment—1,720). **American Optical Corp.**, Chelsea (Cool Ray Division—sunglasses—1,000). **RCA Corp.**, Burlington (Research instruments, associated equipment—1,600). **General Electric Co.**, Everett (Jet engines—1,600).

8th District

(Boston, Boston Suburbs, Cambridge)

Race and Ethnic Groups. Italian stock 9.8 percent, Canadian stock 7.5 percent, Irish stock 6.2 percent.

Cities, 1970 Population. Part of Boston 163,742, Cambridge 100,411, Somerville 88,748.

Universities, Enrollment. Boston University (Boston—24,568), Emerson College (Boston—1,879), Harvard University (Cambridge—20,796), Radcliffe College (Cambridge—enrollment included in Harvard figure), Massachusetts Institute of Technology (Cambridge—7,717), University of Massachusetts at Boston (Boston—4,853).

Military Installations or Activities. Boston Naval Shipyard, Army Materiel and Mechanical Research Center, Watertown.

AEC-Owned, Contractor-Operated Installations. Cambridge Electron Accelerator.

Newspapers, Circulation. Boston newspapers circulate throughout district.

Commercial Television Stations, Affiliation. Entire district is located in Boston ADI.

Plants and Offices, Products, Employment.
   New England Mutual Life Insurance Co., Boston (Insurance—HQ—2,000). **John Hancock Mutual Life Insurance Co.**, Boston (Insurance—HQ—8,000). **Honeywell Inc.**, Boston (Electronic data processing components—1,700). **Polaroid Corp.**, Cambridge (Photo, polaroid equipment—HQ—2,250). **American Biltrite Rubber Co.**, Cambridge (Industrial, mechanical rubber—1,000). **TRW Inc.**, Cambridge (Carr Fastener Co.—T Nuts, metal fasteners—1,000). **Ashland Oil Inc.**, Cambridge (Warren Brothers Co. Division—paving contractor—5,000). **Helme Products, Inc.**, Boston (Schrafft Candy Co. Division—candy—at least 1,200). **H. P. Hood & Sons Inc.**, Boston (Dairy products, frozen orange juice—HQ—2,000). **American Airlines Inc.**, Boston (Air transportation—1,500). **United Parcel Service Inc.**, Watertown (Common carrier—1,700).

9th District

(Boston and Suburbs)

Race and Ethnic Groups. Blacks 19.9 percent. Spanish heritage population 3.0 percent. Irish stock 7.1 percent, Italian stock 5.3 percent, Canadian stock 5.3 percent.

Cities, 1970 Population. Part of Boston 333,265.

Universities, Enrollment. Boston State College (Boston 8,290), Emmanuel College (Boston—1,333), Massachusetts College of Art (Boston—1,212), Northeastern University (Boston—34,150), Simmons College (Boston—2,585), Suffolk University (Boston—5,710).

Military Installations or Activities. Boston Naval Station.

Newspapers, Circulation. Boston newspapers circulate throughout district. Boston newspapers include: Boston Globe (MxSat—236,884, ExSat 178,045), Boston Herald Traveler-Record American (MxM—334,874).

Commercial Television Stations, Affiliation. Entire district is located in Boston ADI. Boston stations include: WBZ-TV, Boston (NBC); WCVB-TV, Needham (ABC); WNAC-TV, Boston (CBS); WSBK-TV, Boston (NBC per program basis); WKBG-TV, Cambridge (None).

Plants and Offices, Products, Employment.
   Prudential Insurance Company of America, Boston (Insurance—1,500). **Employers Group Associates**, Boston (Insurance, holding company—HQ—at least 2,000). **GTE Sylvania Inc.**, Needham Heights (Electronic systems—1,000). **Northrop Corp.**, Norwood (Electronics Division—precision gyroscopes—1,100). **Stone & Webster Engineering**, Boston (Consulting engineers—1,700). **Aberthaw Construction Co.**, Boston (General building contractor—HQ—1,200). **Jordan Marsh Co.**, Boston (Department store—HQ—9,000). **Green Shoe Manufacturing Co.**, Boston (Children's shoes—HQ—1,500). **Globe Newspaper Co.**, Boston (Publisher—1,800). **Hearst Corp.**, (Publisher—1,200).

10th District

(Southeast—Fall River)

Race and Ethnic Groups. Canadian stock 8.0 percent, Portuguese stock 5.7 percent, British stock 3.1 percent.

Cities, 1970 Population. Fall River 96,935, Taunton 43,758, Attleboro 32,908.

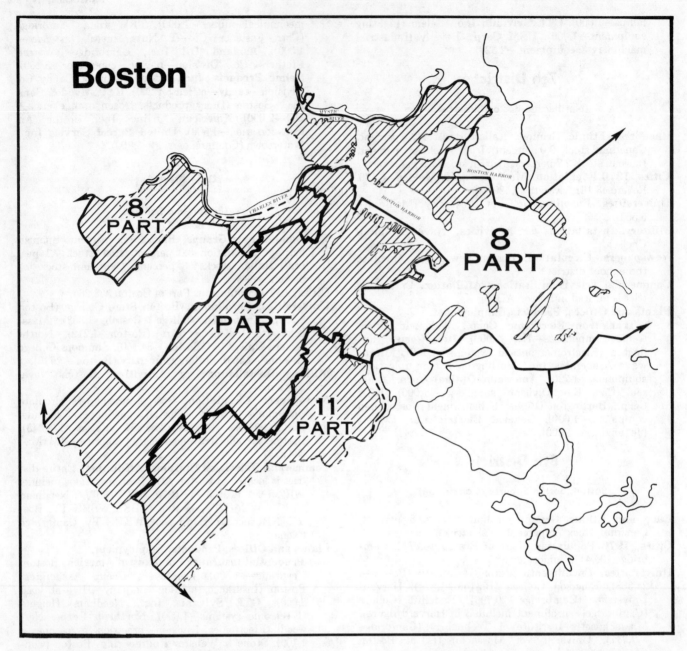

Boston

Universities, Enrollment. Babson College (Babson Park—1,599), Bridgewater State College (Bridgewater—6,792), Stonehill College (North Easton—1,905), Wellesley College (Wellesley—1,872), Wheaton College (Norton—1,217).

Military Installations or Activities. Natick Laboratories, Natick.

Newspapers, Circulation. Boston and Brockton papers circulate in major portions of district.

Commercial Television Stations, Affiliation. District is divided between Boston and Providence (Rhode Island) ADIs.

Plants and Offices, Products, Employment.

Honeywell Inc., Wellesley Hills (Data processing, electronic equipment—6,000). **Raytheon Co.**, North Dighton (Equipment Division—Electronic equipment—2,000). **Texas Instruments Inc.**, At-tleboro (Industrial controls, electrical contacts, etc.—HQ—3,700). **Foxboro Co.**, Foxborough (Recording, control instruments—HQ—4,500). **L. G. Balfour Co.**, Attleboro (Jewelry, insignia, etc.—HQ—1,600). **Swank Inc.**, Attleboro (Men's jewelry, leather accessories, toiletries, etc.—HQ—1,100). **Providence Pile Fabric,** Fall River (Holding comany, fabrics—HQ—1,100). **ITT Continental Baking Co. Inc.**, Natick (Breads, cakes, etc.—1,300).

11th District

(East—Boston, Brockton, Quincy)

Race and Ethnic Groups. Irish stock 7.3 percent, Canadian stock 7.1 percent, Italian stock 5.7 percent, British stock 3.0 percent, Russian stock 2.8 percent.

Cities, 1970 Population. Part of Boston 144,562, Brockton 88,774, Quincy 87,703.

Newspapers, Circulation. Brockton Enterprise & Times (Eve 53,474). In addition, Boston newspapers circulate throughout district.

Commercial Television Stations, Affiliation. Entire district is located in Boston ADI

Plants and Offices, Products, Employment.

Westinghouse Electric Corp., Boston (Sturtevant Division—industrial fans—1,000). **General Dynamics Corp.**, Quincy (Quincy Shipbuilding Division—shipbuilding—9,000). **Randy Manufacturing Co. Inc.**, Randolph (Canvas, rubber footwear—1,000).

12th District

(Southeast—New Bedford, Cape Cod)

Race and Ethnic Groups. Canadian stock 6.9 percent, Portuguese stock 5.4 percent, British stock 3.8 percent.

Cities, 1970 Population. New Bedford 101,735.

Universities, Enrollment. Southeastern Massachusetts University (North Dartmouth—4,857).

Military Installations or Activities. Naval Air Station, South Weymouth; Naval Facility, Nantucket; North Truro Air Force Station.

Newspapers, Circulation. Boston, Brockton and Quincy newspapers circulate in portions of district.

Commercial Television Stations, Affiliation. WTEV-TV, New Bedford (ABC). New Bedford has no separate ADI. Most of district is in Boston ADI. Small portion is in Providence (R.I.) ADI.

Plants and Offices, Products, Employment.

Acushnet Co., New Bedford (Rubber, plastic products, gold equipment—HQ—2,000). **Gulf Western Precision Engineering**, New Bedford (Morse Cutting Tools—1,100). **Chamberlain Manufacturing Corp.** New Bedford (Artillery shells—1,050).

MICHIGAN: NINETEEN HOUSE SEATS, NO CHANGE

Democrats hoped to benefit from new congressional district lines in Michigan, drawn by a federal judge May 12, 1972, after the state legislature had failed to act.

Based on the new lines, Democrats hoped to pick up at least one and perhaps two seats. From 1967, Republicans controlled the Michigan House delegation 12 to 7, even though Democrats usually polled more popular votes in House races statewide. *(Map p. 98)*

Both districts were in the Detroit metropolitan area. In the 2nd District, incumbent Republican Marvin L. Esch had Democratic areas in northwestern Wayne County added to his district, while retaining the liberal student community in Ann Arbor and losing Republican areas to the south and west.

North of Detroit, Republican incumbent William S. Broomfield received a heavily Democratic district, the 18th, consisting of communities in southeastern Oakland County and southwestern Macomb County. He decided to move to the 19th District and successfully challenged his Republican colleague, Rep. Jack H. McDonald, for renomination.

Because of internal Democratic dissension, however, Republicans were able to keep both the 2nd and 18th Districts.

In other parts of the state, districts remained in the hands of the party of the incumbent. Although the homes of Representatives Edward Hutchinson (R), Guy Vander Jagt (R), Elford A. Cederberg (R) and Jack H. McDonald (R) were transferred to other districts, they ran in their old districts—the 4th, 9th, 10th and 19th, respectively.

District	Member Elected 1972	Winning Percentage	1970 Population	Percent Variance
1	John Conyers Jr. (D)	88.4	467,636	+ 0.1126
2	Marvin L. Esch (R)	56.0	466,852	—0.0552
3	Garry Brown (R)	59.2	467,546	+ 0.0933
4	Edward Hutchinson (R)	67.3	467,140	+ 0.0064
5	Gerald R. Ford (R)	61.1	467,543	+ 0.0926
6	Charles E. Chamberlain (R)	50.6	467,536	+ 0.0911

District	Member Elected 1972	Winning Percentage	1970 Population	Percent Variance
7	Donald W. Riegle Jr. (R) [1]	70.1	466,287	—0.1761
8	James Harvey (R)	59.3	467,206	+ 0.0205
9	Guy Vander Jagt (R)	69.4	467,245	+ 0.0289
10	Elford A. Cederberg (R)	66.7	467,547	+ 0.0935
11	Philip E. Ruppe (R)	69.4	467,547	+ 0.0935
12	James G. O'Hara (D)	50.8	467,543	+ 0.0926
13	Charles C. Diggs Jr. (D)	85.6	465,076	—0.4354
14	Lucien N. Nedzi (D)	54.9	467,603	+ 0.1055
15	William D. Ford (D)	65.8	466,608	—0.1074
16	John D. Dingell (D)	68.1	467,168	+ 0.0124
17	Martha W. Griffiths (D)	66.4	467,544	+ 0.0929
18	Robert J. Huber (R)	52.6	465,916	—0.2556
19	William S. Broomfield (R)	70.4	467,540	+ 0.0920

1 Switched to Democratic party February 27, 1973

1970 State Population: 8,875,083

Ideal District Population: 467,110

Election Results, 1968-1972

Vote for U.S. Representative
(Adjusted to new district boundaries)

District	1968	1970	1972
1	150,858 D (95.3%)	116,087 D (88.4%)	131,353 D (88.4%)
	7,171 R (4.5%) [1]	14,674 R (11.2%)	16,096 R (10.8%)
2	76,181 R (52.2%)	74,588 R (60.0%)	103,321 R (56.0%)
	68,808 D (47.1%)	49,641 D (39.9%)	79,762 D (43.3%)
3	106,112 R (64.9%)	77,849 R (56.1%)	110,082 R (59.2%)
	57,306 D (35.1%)	60,806 D (43.9%)	74,114 D (39.9%)
4	100,434 R (63.8%)	76,134 R (62.1%)	111,185 R (67.3%)
	56,794 D (36.1%)	46,433 D (37.9%)	54,141 D (32.7%)
5	107,435 R (62.8%)	89,870 R (61.3%)	118,027 R (61.1%)
	63,457 D (37.1%)	56,640 D (38.6%)	72,782 D (37.7%)
6	99,812 R (63.8%)	83,563 R (61.8%)	97,666 R (50.6%)
	56,629 D (36.2%)	51,578 D (38.2%)	95,209 D (49.4%)
7	97,832 R (59.8%)	92,690 R (68.9%)	114,656 R (70.1%)
	65,685 D (40.2%)	39,859 D (29.6%)	48,883 D (29.9%)
8	104,674 R (66.3%)	83,902 R (62.5%)	100,597 R (59.3%)
	53,243 D (33.7%)	50,217 D (37.4%)	66,873 D (39.4%)

District	1968	1970	1972
9	113,144 R (67.5%) 2	94,077 R (64.0%)	132,268 R (69.4%)
	54,600 D (32.5%)	52,291 D (35.6%)	56,236 D (29.5%)
10	107,569 R (69.3%) 2	85,970 R (63.5%)	121,368 R (66.7%)
	47,759 D (30.7%)	49,383 D (36.5%)	56,149 D (30.9%)
11	106,677 R (60.0%)	94,922 R (61.8%)	135,786 R (69.4%)
	71,220 D (40.0%)	58.603 D (38.2%)	58,334 D (29.8%)
12	80,753 D (56.6%)	78,457 D (61.9%)	83,351 D (50.8%)
	61,513 R (43.1%)	47,683 R (37.6%)	80,667 R (49.2%)
13	120,676 D (87.0%)	100,237 D (83.8%)	97,562 D (85.6%)
	18,069 R (13.0%)	19,311 R (16.1%)	15,180 R (13.3%)
14	127,125 D (65.1%)	100,993 D (72.2%)	93,923 D (54.9%)
	68,045 R (34.8%)	38,508 R (27.5%)	77,273 R (45.1%)
15	91,872 D (70.2%)	85,885 D (78.9%)	97,054 D (65.8%)
	39,035 R (29.8%)	23,023 R (21.1%)	48,504 R (32.9%)
16	121,984 D (73.9%)	119,704 D (79.1%)	110,715 D (68.1%)
	42,722 R (25.9%)	31,687 R (20.9%)	48,414 R (29.7%)
17	112,213 D (59.6%)	84,351 D (58.1%)	123,331 D (66.4%)
	75,625 R (40.2%)	60,546 R (41.7%)	60,337 R (32.5%)
18	78,864 D (51.4%)	67,613 D (50.6%)	95,053 D (52.6%)
	73,807 R (48.1%)	65,523 R (49.0%)	85,580 D (47.4%)
19	101,115 R (65.6%)	87,000 R (65.2%)	123,697 R (70.4%)
	52,837 D (34.3%)	45,700 D (34.3%)	50,355 D (28.6%)
State	1,532,683 D (50.2%)	1,314,478 D (51.3%)	1,710,177 R (52.5%)
	1,514,143 R (49.6%)	1,241,520 R (48.5%)	1,535,707 D (46.9%)

1 No Republican candidate in this district as constituted before redistricting.
2 Estimated for Benzie County

Voting Age Population

District	Voting Age Population	Voting Age Population 18, 19, 20	Voting Age Population 65 and Over	Median Age of Voting Age Population
1	309,222	23,721 (7.7%)	46,597 (15.1%)	43.0
2	300,070	37,451 (12.5%)	27,030 (9.0%)	36.5
3	300,291	30,025 (10.0%)	38,719 (12.9%)	40.6
4	296,266	21,713 (7.3%)	46,623 (15.7%)	43.6
5	291,530	24,895 (8.5%)	43,668 (15.0%)	42.2
6	306,178	38,599 (12.6%)	36,388 (11.9%)	37.8
7	278,297	22,102 (7.9%)	30,751 (11.0%)	40.1
8	284,881	21,706 (7.6%)	40,630 (14.3%)	42.6
9	285,896	21,708 (7.6%)	44,281 (15.5%)	43.6
10	293,147	29,715 (10.1%)	44,289 (15.1%)	41.9
11	300,322	24,625 (8.2%)	54,379 (18.1%)	45.8
12	281,627	21,071 (7.5%)	31,015 (11.0%)	40.8
13	302,022	24,319 (8.1%)	53,188 (17.6%)	44.6
14	320,248	21,240 (6.6%)	53,590 (16.7%)	47.2
15	273,824	20,486 (7.5%)	20,121 (7.3%)	38.4
16	308,293	24,153 (7.8%)	41,332 (13.4%)	45.1
17	309,325	21,942 (7.1%)	46,170 (14.9%)	45.7
18	287,662	18,836 (6.5%)	26,868 (9.3%)	39.9
19	282,089	21,157 (7.5%)	29,511 (10.5%)	41.3
State	5,611,114	469,458 (8.4%)	755,098 (13.5%)	42.1

Income and Occupations

District	Median Family Income	White Collar Workers	Blue Collar Workers	Service Workers	Farm Workers
1	$ 9,997	40.9%	41.7%	17.2%	0.2%
2	12,908	53.4	32.7	13.0	0.9
3	10,913	45.8	38.9	13.3	2.0
4	9,693	36.8	47.4	11.7	4.1
5	10,550	45.9	40.0	12.3	1.8
6	11,105	50.0	34.2	13.8	2.0

District	Median Family Income	White Collar Workers	Blue Collar Workers	Service Workers	Farm Workers
7	11,207	37.3	50.1	12.0	0.6
8	10,270	38.5	44.5	12.9	4.1
9	9,474	36.9	46.5	13.0	3.6
10	9,299	40.7	40.6	14.4	4.3
11	7,884	41.3	39.6	16.5	2.6
12	12,003	45.4	42.3	11.2	1.1
13	7,770	32.0	47.7	30.1	0.2
14	12,394	49.8	39.1	11.0	0.1
15	12,460	41.8	47.0	10.9	0.3
16	11,800	43.1	44.5	12.3	0.1
17	13,449	57.8	31.4	10.7	0.1
18	13,627	56.6	34.5	8.8	0.1
19	13,405	53.2	35.1	11.1	0.6
State	11,029	44.9	40.8	12.8	1.5

Education: School Years Completed

District	Completed 4 years of High School	Completed 4 years of College	Completed 5 years or less of School	Median School years completed
1	46.0%	7.8%	9.1%	11.5
2	63.0	18.9	3.6	12.4
3	58.0	10.9	3.2	12.2
4	51.8	7.5	5.0	12.1
5	54.6	9.5	3.4	12.1
6	59.6	13.4	3.3	12.3
7	52.0	7.3	4.2	12.1
8	49.2	6.4	5.3	11.9
9	48.1	7.0	3.9	11.8
10	52.9	9.1	3.5	12.1
11	50.5	7.1	5.6	12.0
12	55.1	7.4	3.7	12.1
13	31.7	4.4	14.2	10.0
14	49.1	8.7	7.3	11.9
15	51.7	6.6	4.3	12.1
16	45.4	6.8	8.2	11.4
17	61.2	12.8	3.9	12.3
18	62.8	12.4	3.4	12.3
19	62.0	16.2	3.4	12.4
State	52.8	9.4	5.2	12.1

Housing and Residential Patterns

District	Housing		Urban-Suburban-Nonmetropolitan Breakdown		
	Owner Occupied Units	Renter Occupied Units	Urban	Suburban	Nonmetro-politan
1	61.7%	38.3%	92.4%	7.6%	—
2	69.9	30.1	21.4	78.6	—
3	76.2	23.8	18.6	43.7	37.7%
4	77.0	23.0	—	—	100.0
5	76.3	23.7	42.2	46.3	11.5
6	70.9	29.1	37.6	54.5	7.9
7	77.9	22.1	41.5	56.5	2.0
8	79.6	20.4	30.2	45.1	24.7
9	81.5	18.5	13.3	47.9	38.8
10	80.5	19.5	—	11.1	88.9
11	77.2	22.8	—	—	100.0
12	80.2	19.8	—	73.6	26.4
13	35.8	64.2	100.0	—	—

	Housing		Urban-Suburban-Nonmetropolitan Breakdown		
District	Owner Occupied Units	Renter Occupied Units	Urban	Suburban	Nonmetro- politan
14	80.5	19.5	46.5	53.5	—
15	82.0	18.0	—	100.0	—
16	73.4	26.6	28.9	71.1	—
17	81.3	18.7	56.2	43.8	—
18	78.4	21.6	—	100.0	—
19	80.4	19.6	—	95.3	4.7
State	74.4	25.6	27.8	48.9	23.3

1st District

(Detroit—North Central, Highland Park)

Race and Ethnic Groups. Blacks 70.0 percent. Canadian stock 2.5 percent, Polish stock 2.4 percent.

Cities, 1970 Population. Part of Detroit 432,127, Highland Park 35,509.

Universities, Enrollment. Marygrove College (Detroit—1,102), Mercy College of Detroit (Detroit—1,620), University of Detroit (Detroit—9,597).

Newspapers, Circulation. Detroit newspapers circulate throughout district.

Commercial Television Stations, Affiliation. Entire district is located in Detroit ADI.

Plants and Offices, Products, Employment.

Chrysler Corp., Highland Park (Headquarters—5,000). **Chrysler Corp.**, Detroit (Automotive trim—14,000). **Chrysler Corp.**, Detroit (Auto stampings—1,100). **General Motors Corp.**, Detroit (Detroit Diesel Engine Division—diesel engines—8,000). **General Motors Corp.**, Detroit (Chevrolet Motor Division—automotive gear—at least 1,000). **Ford Motor Co.**, Detroit (Ford Tractor Operations—tractors—1,000). **Lear Siegler Inc.**, Detroit (Automotive Division—auto parts—2,000). **Massey-Ferguson Inc.**, Detroit (Transmissions, axles—1,000). **Darin & Armstrong Inc.**, Detroit (General contractor—2,000).

2nd District

(Southeast—Ann Arbor, Livonia)

Race and Ethnic Groups. Blacks 4.6 percent. Canadian stock 4.1 percent, German stock 2.1 percent.

Cities, 1970 Population. Part of Livonia 106,982, Ann Arbor 99,703, Ypsilanti 29,474, Monroe 23,871.

Universities, Enrollment. Eastern Michigan University (Ypsilanti—21,217), University of Michigan (Ann Arbor—39,986).

Newspapers, Circulation. Detroit newspapers circulate throughout most of district.

Commercial Television Stations, Affiliation. Entire district is in Detroit ADI.

Plants and Offices, Products, Employment.

General Motors Corp., Livonia (Car bodies—1,820). **General Motors Corp.**, Livonia (Auto bumpers, springs—2,200). **General Motors Corp.**, Ypsilanti (Autos—1,500). **General Motors Corp.**, Ypsilanti (Hydra-matic Division—Car, truck transmissions—7,000). **General Motors Corp.**, Ypsilanti (Fisher Body Division—auto bodies—2,800). **Ford Motor Co.**, Plymouth (Auto heaters—1,500). **Ford Motor Co.**, Livonia (Auto transmissions—6,500). **Ford Motor Co.**, Ypsilanti (General Parts Division—auto parts—5,650). **Ford Motor Co.**, Ypsilanti (Auto parts, accessories—4,570). **Ford Motor Co.**, Monroe (Auto parts—1,500). **Ford Motor Co.**, Saline (General Parts Division—auto parts—2,500). **Bendix Corp.**, Ann Arbor (Aerospace Systems Division—aerospace systems—1,000). **Consolidated Packaging Corp.**, Monroe (Corrugated boxes, sheets—1,700). **Burroughs Corp.**, Plymouth (Accounting machines, computers—4,900). **Kroger Co.**, Livonia (Food products—5,000).

3rd District

(South Central—Kalamazoo, Battle Creek)

Race and Ethnic Groups. Blacks 4.7 percent. Dutch stock 1.9 percent, Canadian stock 1.6 percent.

Cities, 1970 Population. Kalamazoo 85,702, Battle Creek 38,950, Portage 33,501, Albion 12,118.

Universities, Enrollment. Albion College (Albion—1,782), Kalamazoo College (Kalamazoo—1,360), Western Michigan University (Kalamazoo—21,846).

Newspapers, Circulation. Kalamazoo Gazette (Eve—57,699). In addition, Lansing newspapers circulate in a portion of district.

Commercial Television Stations, Affiliation. WZKO-TV, Kalamazoo (CBS); WUHQ-TV, Battle Creek (ABC). Most of district is in Grand Rapids-Kalamazoo ADI. In addition, a portion of district is in Lansing ADI.

Plants and Offices, Products, Employment.

General Foods Corp., Battle Creek (Carton & Container Division—cartons, containers—1,200). **General Foods Corp.**, Battle Creek (Post Division—cereals, etc.—1,000). **Kellogg Co.**, Battle Creek (Cereals—HQ—4,200). **Upjohn Co.**, Kalamazoo (Drug products—HQ—5,000). **Eaton Corp.**, Kalamazoo (Transmission Division—truck transmissions—1,500). **Eaton Corp.**, Battle Creek (Eaton Valve Division—valves, gears, etc.—1,800). **Eaton Corp.**, Marshall (Marshall Plant Fluid Power Division—automotive equipment—1,000). **General Motors Corp.**, Kalamazoo (Fisher Body Division—auto body components—3,000). **Checker Motors Corp.**, Kalamazoo (Taxicabs & cars—HQ—6,390). **Brown Co. Inc.**, Kalamazoo (Rigid & flexible packaging—3,550). **Clark Equipment Co.**, Battle Creek (Industrial Truck Division—lift trucks, tractors, etc.—2,400).

4th District

(South—Benton Harbor, Adrian)

Race and Ethnic Groups. Blacks 6.2 percent. German stock 2.6 percent, Canadian stock 1.3 percent.

Cities, 1970 Population. Adrian 20,377, Benton Harbor 16,477, Niles 12,985, St. Joseph 11,039.

Commercial Television Stations, Affiliation. Portions of district are in Detroit, Lansing, Grand Rapids-Kalamazoo, South Bend-Elkhart (Indiana) and Chicago (Illinois) ADIs.

Plants and Offices, Products, Employment.

Whirlpool Corp., St. Joseph (Washers, washer-dryers—2,500). **Tecumseh Products Co.**, Tecumseh (Refrigeration, air conditioning systems—HQ—3,300). **Rudy Manufacturing Co.**, Dowagiac (Con-densers—HQ—1,100). **V-M Corp.**, Benton Harbor (Radio, TV sets—1,000). **Heath Co.**, St. Joseph (Radio, TV testing equipment, sets, etc.—1,250). **Clark Equipment Co.**, Buchanan (Vehicle parts, machinery, equipment—HQ—12,000). **Bendix Corp.**, St. Joseph (Hydraulic Division—1,250). **Auto Specialties Mfg. Co.**, St. Joseph (Motor Vehicle parts—HQ—1,900). **Simplicity Pattern Co. Inc.**, Niles (Patterns—2,400). **Kirsch Co.**, Sturgis (Drapery, hardware, accessories—HQ—1,450).

5th District

(West Central—Grand Rapids)

Race and Ethnic Groups. Blacks 5.1 percent. Dutch stock 6.7 percent, Polish stock 1.9 percent.

Cities, 1970 Population. Grand Rapids 197,439, Wyoming 56,541, Kentwood 20,287, East Grand Rapids 12,549.

Key

Small numbers on map indicate the names of the following cities and places:

1 PONTIAC
2 STERLING HEIGHTS
3 ROSEVILLE
4 ST. CLAIR SHORES
5 WARREN
6 ROYAL OAK
7 SOUTHFIELD
8 LIVONIA
9 DEARBORN HEIGHTS
10 DEARBORN
11 LINCOLN PARK
12 WESTLAND
13 TAYLOR
14 ANN ARBOR
15 YPSILANTI

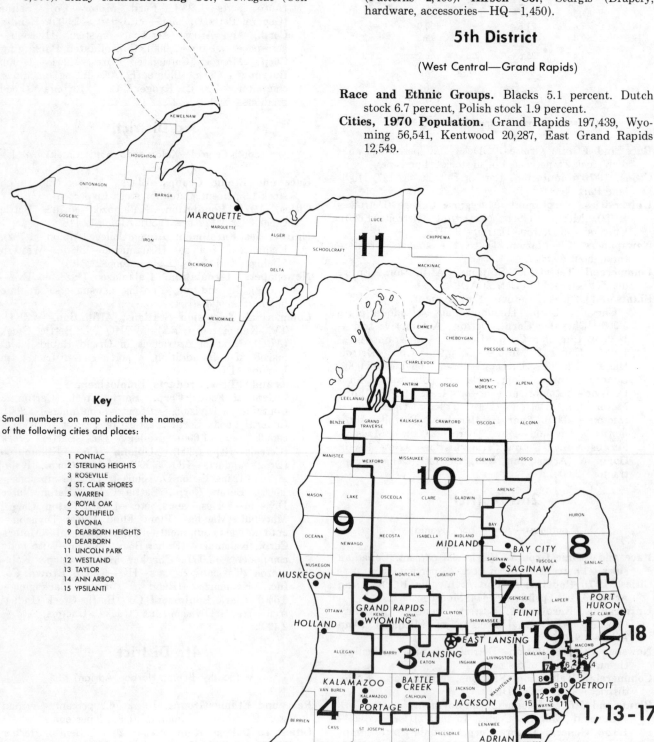

Universities, Enrollment. Aquinas College (Grand Rapids—1,422), Calvin College (Grand Rapids—3,306).

Newspapers, Circulation. Grand Rapids Press (Eve—129,520).

Commercial Television Stations, Affiliation. WOTV, Grand Rapids (NBC); WZZM-TV, Grand Rapids (ABC). Most of district is in Grand Rapids-Kalamazoo ADI; small part is in Lansing ADI.

Plants and Offices, Products, Employment.

General Motors Corp., Grand Rapids (Fisher Body #1—car bodies—3,000). **General Motors Corp.**, Grand Rapids (Fisher Body #2—auto upholstery—2,300). **General Motors Corp.**, Grand Rapids (Diesel Equipment Division—diesel fuel injectors, etc.—2,100). **Chrysler Corp.**, Lyons (Lyons Trim Plant—auto trim—1,050). **Lear Siegler Inc.**, Grand Rapids (Instrument Division—electric, aerospace products—2,600). **Gibson Products Corp.**, Belding (Air conditioners—1,060). **Kelvinator Inc.**, Grand Rapids (Household, commercial appliances—HQ—2,200). **McInerney Spring & Wire Co.**, Grand Rapids (Cushion springs, trim—1,000). **Steelcase Inc.**, Grand Rapids (Metal office furniture—HQ—2,700). **American Seating Co.**, Grand Rapids (Public Seating Division—institutional furniture—HQ—1,220). **Amway Corp.**, Ada (Home & personal cleaning products—1,600). **Wolverine World Wide Inc.**, Rockford (Shoes, belts, gloves—HQ—1,200). **Butterworth Hospital**, Grand Rapids (Hospital—1,200). **Michigan Bell Telephone Co.**, Grand Rapids (Telephone company—1,100).

6th District

(Central—Lansing, Jackson)

Race and Ethnic Groups. Blacks 4.9 percent. Canadian stock 2.4 percent, German stock 1.8 percent.

Cities, 1970 Population. Part of Lansing 130,458, East Lansing 47,583, Jackson 45,527.

Universities, Enrollment. Michigan State University (East Lansing—43,888).

Newspapers, Circulation. Lansing State-Journal (Eve—78,411).

Commercial Television Stations, Affiliation. WILX-TV, Onondaga (NBC); WJIM-TV, Lansing (CBS). District is divided between Lansing and Detroit ADIs.

Plants and Offices, Products, Employment.

General Motors Corp., Lansing (Oldsmobile Division—passenger cars—16,000). **General Motors Corp.**, Lansing (Oldsmobile Division—bumpers, axle shafts—3,800). **General Motors Corp.**, Lansing (Fisher Body Division—car bodies—4,900). **Diamond Reo Trucks Inc.**, Lansing (Trucks—2,000). **Motor Wheel Corp.**, Lansing (Vehicular parts, air conditioners, etc.—HQ—3,000). **Kelsey-Hayes Co.**, Jackson (Auto parts, brakes—1,400). **Clark Equipment Co.**, Jackson (Transmission Division—transmissions—2,500). **Goodyear Tire & Rubber Co.**, Jackson (Tires—1,700). **Aeroquip Corp.**, Jackson (Flexible hose line fittings—HQ—1,300). **Auto Owners Insurance Co. Inc.**, Lansing (Insurance—4,180). **American Central Corp.**, Lansing (Land

developer—2,000). **Consumers Power Co.**, Jackson (Public utility—HQ—2,200).

7th District

(East Central—Flint)

Race and Ethnic Groups. Blacks 13.0 percent. Canadian stock 3.3 percent, British stock 1.6 percent.

Cities, 1970 Population. Flint 193,459.

Universities, Enrollment. General Motors Institute (Flint—3,075), University of Michigan, Flint Campus (Flint—1,819).

Newspapers, Circulation. Flint Journal (Eve—113,447).

Commercial Television Stations, Affiliation. WJRT-TV, Flint (ABC). Entire district is located in Flint-Saginaw-Bay City ADI.

Plants and Offices, Products, Employment.

General Motors Corp., Flint (Buick Motor Division—autos—4,500). **General Motors Corp.**, Flint (AC Spark Plug Division—spark plugs, etc.—13,000). **General Motors Corp.**, Flint (Chevrolet Motor Division—autos—5,120). **General Motors Corp.**, Flint (Chevrolet Motor Division—autos—4,500). **General Motors Corp.**, Flint (Chevrolet Motor Division—autos assembly—3,800). **General Motors Corp.**, Flint (Chevrolet Motor Division—autos—9,000). **General Motors Corp.**, Flint (Fisher Body Division—auto equipment, trim, accessories—7,400). **General Motors Corp.**, Flint (Fisher Body Division—car and commercial bodies—4,000). **General Motors Corp.**, Flint (Fisher Body Division—car and commercial bodies—21,000). **General Motors Corp.**, Grand Blanc (Fisher Body Division—car and commercial bodies—3,490). **General Motors Corp.**, Swartz Creek (GM Parts Division—auto parts—4,000).

8th District

(East—Bay City, Saginaw)

Race and Ethnic Groups. Blacks 6.0 percent. Spanish heritage population 3.0 percent. Canadian stock 3.9 percent, German stock 3.3 percent.

Cities, 1970 Population. Saginaw 91,793, Bay City 49,435.

Universities, Enrollment. Saginaw Valley College (University Center—2,124).

Military Installations or Activities. Port Austin Air Force Station, Port Austin.

Newspapers, Circulation. Saginaw News (Eve—57,915).

Commercial Television Stations, Affiliation. WEYI-TV, Saginaw (CBS); WNEM-TV, Saginaw (NBC). Most of district is located in Flint-Saginaw-Bay City ADI. Portion of district is located in Detroit ADI.

Plants and Offices, Products, Employment.

General Motors Corp., Saginaw (Grey iron, aluminum castings—3,000). **General Motors Corp.**, Saginaw (Chevrolet Motor Division—auto transmissions, equipment—1,300). **General Motors Corp.**, Saginaw (Chevrolet Motor Division—grey iron, castings—8,000). **General Motors Corp.**, Bay City (Chevrolet Motor Division—assembly plant—3,800). **General Motors Corp.**, Saginaw (Saginaw Steering Gear Division—auto parts—8,400). **General Motors**

Corp., Saginaw (Saginaw Steering Gear Division—auto parts—1,200). **General Motors Corp.**, Saginaw (Chevrolet-Saginaw Foundries—iron foundry—1,600). **Eaton Corp.**, Saginaw (Precision Products Division—auto parts—1,300). **Eltra Corp.**, Bay City (Prestolite Division—ignition systems—1,000). **Baker Perkins Inc.**, Saginaw (Baking, chemical processing machinery—1,000).

9th District

(West—Muskegon)

Race and Ethnic Groups. Blacks 4.3 percent. Dutch stock 4.2 percent, German stock 2.0 percent.

Cities, 1970 Population. Muskegon 44,642, Holland 26,343, Norton Shores 22,437, Muskegon Heights 17,308.

Universities, Enrollment. Grand Valley State College (Allendale—4,174), Hope College (Holland—2,101).

Military Installations or Activities. Empire Air Force Station, Empire.

Newspapers, Circulation. Grand Rapids paper circulates in portion of district.

Commercial Television Stations, Affiliation. Most of district is located in Grand Rapids-Kalamazoo ADI. Portion of district is located in Traverse City-Cadillac ADI.

Plants and Offices, Products, Employment.

Textron Inc., Muskegon (Campbell, Wyant, and Cannon Foundry Division—gray iron foundry—2,100). **Howmet Corp.**, Whitehall (Misco Division—cast & coatings—1,000). **General Electric Co.**, Holland (Hermetic motors—1,000). **Sealed Power Corp.**, Muskegon (Piston rings, pistons, cylinder sleeves, etc.—HQ—2,100). **Teledyne Industries Inc.**, Muskegon (Teledyne Continental Motors Division—internal combustion engines—1,800). **Brunswick Corp.**, Muskegon (Bowling Division—bowling equipment—1,200). **Scott Paper Co.**, Muskegon (S.D. Warren Co. Division—paper—1,000). **Shaw-Walker Co.**, Muskegon (Metal office furniture and equipment—HQ—1,100).

10th District

(North Central—Midland)

Race and Ethnic Groups. Canadian stock 3.0 percent, German stock 1.9 percent.

Cities, 1970 Population. Part of Midland 34,889, Mount Pleasant 20,485, Traverse City 18,032, Owosso 17,163.

Universities, Enrollment. Alma College (Alma—1,328), Central Michigan University (Mt. Pleasant—16,931), Ferris State College (Big Rapids—9,161).

Commercial Television Stations, Affiliation. WGTU-TV, Traverse City (ABC); WPBN-TV, Traverse City (NBC); WWTV, Cadillac (CBS). District is divided between Traverse City-Cadillac ADI and Flint-Saginaw-Bay City ADI.

Plants and Offices, Products, Employment.

Dow Chemical Co., Midland (Headquarters—10,800). **Dow Corning Corp.**, Midland (Silicon compounds—HQ—2,500). **Gibson Products Corp.**, Greenville (Gibson International Co. Division—household appliances—HQ—2,600). **Universal Electric Co.**, Owosso (Electric motors—HQ—1,000).

11th District

(Upper Peninsula)

Race and Ethnic Groups. Canadian stock 4.8 percent, Finnish stock 4.6 percent.

Cities, 1970 Population. Marquette 21,973, Escanaba 15,384, Sault Ste. Marie 15,289, Alpena 13,809.

Universities, Enrollment. Lake Superior State College (Sault Ste. Marie—1,712), Michigan Technological University (Houghton—5,002), Northern Michigan University (Marquette—12,906).

Military Installations or Activities. K. I. Sawyer Air Force Base, Marquette; Sault Ste. Marie Air Force Station, Sault Ste. Marie; Wurtsmith Air Force Base, Oscoda.

Commercial Television Stations, Affiliation. WLUC-TV, Marquette (CBS; ABC per program basis); WWUP-TV, Sault Ste. Marie (CBS, satellite to WWTV, Cadillac); WTOM-TV, Cheboygan (NBC, satellite to WPBN-TV, Traverse City). Portions of district are included in Traverse City-Cadillac, Marquette, Green Bay (Wisconsin) and Duluth (Minn.)-Superior (Wisconsin) ADIs.

Plants and Offices, Products, Employment.

National Gypsum Co., Alpena (Huron Cement Division—cement—1,000). **Cleveland-Cliffs Iron Co.**, Ishpeming (Humbolt Mining Co.—iron mining—2,000). **White Pine Copper Co.**, White Pine (Mining & smelting copper ores—3,000).

12th District

(Southeast—Part of Macomb County, Port Huron)

Race and Ethnic Groups. Canadian stock 6.7 percent, German stock 3.0 percent, Italian stock 2.7 percent.

Cities, 1970 Population. St. Clair Shores 88,120, Roseville 60,629, Port Huron 35,843, Mount Clemens 20,489.

Universities, Enrollment. Oakland University (Rochester—7,069).

Newspapers, Circulation. Macomb Daily, Mount Clemens (Eve—53,465). In addition, Detroit newspapers circulate throughout most of district.

Commercial Television Stations, Affiliation. Entire district is located in Detroit ADI.

Plants and Offices, Products, Employment.

Ford Motor Co., Mount Clemens (Industrial and Chemical Products Division—paint, chemical products—1,000). **Ford Motor Co.**, Utica (Utica Trim Plant—auto trim—3,500). **Ford Motor Co.**, Utica (Auto parts—7,790). **Lear Siegler**, Rochester (National Twist Drill and Tool Division—cutting tools—at least 1,000). **Mueller Brass Co.**, Port Huron (Non-ferrous metal products—HQ—2,000). **Cross Co.**, Fraser (Cross-Fraser Division—automation machines, assembly machines, etc.—1,800). **Sears Roebuck & Co.**, Roseville (Department store—1,200).

13th District

(Downtown Detroit)

Race and Ethnic Groups. Blacks 65.8 percent. Canadian stock 2.1 percent, Polish stock 1.9 percent.
Cities, 1970 Population. Part of Detroit 465,076.
Universities, Enrollment. Detroit Institute of Technology (Detroit—1,086), Wayne State University (Detroit—36,765).
Newspapers, Circulation. Detroit newspapers circulate throughout district. They include: Detroit Free Press (Morn—583,508), Detroit News (Eve—653,698).
Commercial Television Stations, Affiliation. Entire district is located in Detroit ADI. Detroit television stations include: WJBK-TV, Southfield (CBS); WKBD-TV, Southfield (None); WWJ-TV, Detroit (NBC); WXON-TV, Walled Lake (None); WXYZ-TV, Southfield (ABC).
Plants and Offices, Products, Employment. (Note: District includes downtown business section of Detroit.)
  General Motors Corp., Detroit (Dies, machine parts—1,000). **General Motors Corp.**, Detroit (Fisher Body Division—car bodies—1,700). **General Motors Corp.**, Detroit (Cadillac Motor Car Division—10,000). **General Motors Corp.**, Detroit (Headquarters—7,400). **General Motors Corp.**, Detroit (Assembly Division—auto assembly—1,000). **Chrysler Corp.**, Detroit (Automotive stamping—5,000). **Chrysler Corp.**, Detroit (Jefferson Assembly Plant—auto assembly—4,630). **Budd Co.**, Detroit (Automotive Division—auto body & wheel components—3,800). **Parke Davis & Co.**, Detroit (Pharmaceutical, medical products—HQ—2,300). **Federal-Mogul Corp.**, Detroit (Roller, ball, sleeve bearings—2,000). **Federal-Mogul Corp.**, Detroit (Roller bearings—2,400). **Uniroyal Inc.**, Detroit (Rubber products—4,000). **Burroughs International Co.**, Detroit (Holding company—general business machines and equipment—7,000). **Stroh Brewery Co.**, Detroit (Beer, ice cream—1,420). **Evening News Association Inc.**, Detroit (Newspaper publishing, TV station—HQ—3,350). **Knight Newspapers Inc.**, Detroit (Publishing—1,500). **Michigan Mutual Liability Co.**, Detroit (Insurance—4,300). **Grand Trunk Western Railroad Co.**, Detroit (Railroad company—HQ—1,560). **J. L. Hudson Co.**, Detroit (Department stores—HQ—3,000). **S. S. Kresge Co.**, Detroit (Department stores—HQ—11,000). **Detroit Edison Co.**, Detroit (Electric utility—HQ—2,500). **Michigan Consolidated Gas Co.**, Detroit (Public utility—HQ—1,250). **Michigan Bell Telephone Co.**, Detroit (Phone company—HQ—3,000).

14th District

(Northeast Detroit, Hamtramck,
Grosse Pointe, Warren)

Race and Ethnic Groups. Blacks 3.0 percent. Polish stock 8.7 percent, Italian stock 5.6 percent, Canadian stock 5.6 percent, German stock 4.0 percent.
Cities, 1970 Population. Part of Detroit 217,452, part of Warren 87,724, East Detroit 45,900, Hamtramck 27,268.
Military Installations or Activities. Detroit Arsenal.
Newspapers, Circulation. Detroit newspapers circulate throughout district.
Commercial Television Stations, Affiliation. Entire district is located in Detroit ADI.
Plants and Offices, Products, Employment.
  Chrysler Corp., Warren (Stamping Division—auto stamping—3,100). **Chrysler Corp.**, Warren (Warren Truck Assembly Division—truck assembly—10,000). **Chrysler Corp.**, Detroit (Axle Division—axles and brake parts—1,650). **Chrysler Corp.**, Detroit (Hamtramck Assembly Plant—auto assembly—7,000). **Chrysler Corp.**, Detroit (Winfield Foundry—forgings—1,000). **Chrysler Corp.**, Detroit (Engines and parts—3,000). **Chrysler Corp.**, Detroit (Car Assembly Group—autos—3,500). **Chrysler Corp.**, Center Line (Defense engineering—1,000). **Champion Spark Plug Co.**, Detroit (Ceramic Division—spark plug insulators—1,200). **Jones & Laughlin Steel Corp.**, Warren (Iron and steel—1,600). **General Electric Co.**, Warren (Metallurgical products—1,800). **Chatham Super Markets Inc.**, Warren (Groceries—2,500).

15th District

(Southwestern Wayne County)

Race and Ethnic Groups. Blacks 5.1 percent. Canadian stock 5.1 percent, Polish stock 2.9 percent.
Cities, 1970 Population. Westland 86,615, Dearborn Heights 80,046, Taylor 70,050, Garden City 41,882.
Newspapers, Circulation. Detroit newspapers circulate throughout district.
Commercial Television Stations, Affiliation. Entire district is located in Detroit ADI.
Plants and Offices, Products, Employment.
  Sargent Industries of Michigan Inc., Wayne (Truck and bus bodies, trailers, machinery, etc.—HQ—1,000). **Ford Motor Co.**, Wayne (Autos—4,000). **Kelsey-Hayes Co.**, Romulus (Auto parts, etc.—HQ—2,500).

16th District

(Dearborn, South Detroit and Suburbs)

Race and Ethnic Groups. Blacks 8.5 percent. Spanish heritage population 3.2 percent. Polish stock 6.5 percent, Canadian stock 5.2 percent, Italian stock 2.8 percent.
Cities, 1970 Population. Part of Detroit 134,940, Dearborn 104,244, Lincoln Park 53,069, Wyandotte 41,103.
Newspapers, Circulation. Detroit newspapers circulate throughout district.
Commercial Television Stations, Affiliation. Entire district is located in Detroit ADI.
Plants and Offices, Products, Employment.
  Ford Motor Co., Dearborn (Headquarters—3,400). **Ford Motor Co.**, Dearborn (Steel Division

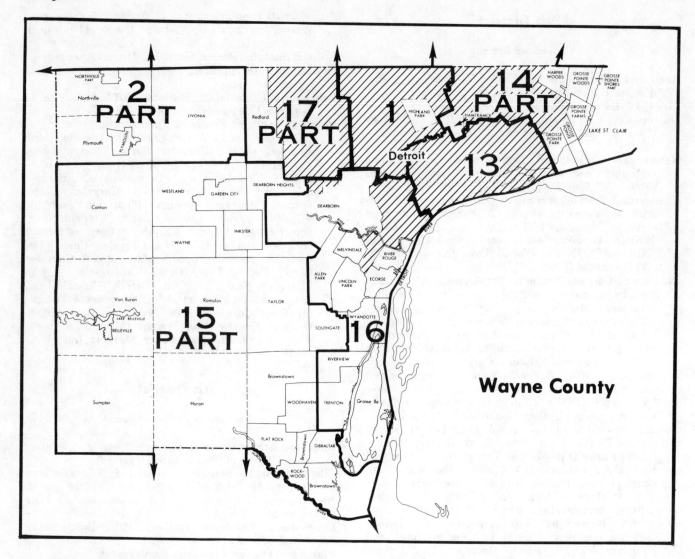

Wayne County

—steel—6,500). **Ford Motor Co.**, Dearborn (Metal Stamping Division—metal stampings—6,500). **Ford Motor Co.**, Dearborn (Frame and Axle Division—auto frames—3,070). **Ford Motor Co.**, Dearborn (Foundry Division—iron castings—3,800). **Ford Motor Co.**, Dearborn (Tools, dies—1,400). **Ford Motor Co.**, Dearborn (Autos—4,600). **Ford Motor Co.**, Dearborn (Glass Division—glass—1,000). **Ford Motor Co.**, Dearborn (Auto assembly—1,530). **Ford Motor Co.**, Trenton (Autos—4,500). **Chrysler Corp.**, Dearborn (Detroit Universal Division—steering shafts—1,300). **Chrysler Corp.**, Trenton (Trenton Engine Plant—engines and parts—4,800). **General Motors Corp.**, Detroit (Fisher Body Ternsted Division—auto parts, trim, accessories—3,350). **General Motors Corp.**, Detroit (Fisher Body Division—car bodies—5,000). **Dana Corp.**, Detroit (Midwest Frame Division—auto frames—1,000). **Kelsey-Hayes Co.**, Detroit (Auto hubs, drums—2,100). **Firestone Tire & Rubber Co.**, Wyandotte (Firestone Steel Products Division—wheels, rims, metal stampings—1,000). **McLouth Steel Corp.**, Trenton (Rolled strip steel—3,300). **Whitehead & Kales Co.**, Detroit (Structural steel—HQ—1,000).

National Steel Corp., Ecorse (Great Lakes Steel Division—steel—12,000). **BASF Wyandotte Corp.**, Wyandotte (Basic organic chemical products—HQ—2,300).

17th District

(Northwest Detroit and Suburbs)

Race and Ethnic Groups. Canadian stock 8.2 percent, Polish stock 4.4 percent, British stock 3.9 percent, German stock 2.5 percent, Russian stock 2.5 percent.

Cities, 1970 Population. Part of Detroit 262,575, Southfield 69,117, Farmington 13,397.

Universities, Enrollment. Lawrence Institute of Technology (Southfield—4,107).

Newspapers, Circulation. Detroit newspapers circulate throughout district.

Commercial Television Stations, Affiliation. Entire district is located in Detroit ADI.

Plants and Offices, Products, Employment.

American Motors Corp., Detroit (Headquarters—2,500). **Massey-Ferguson Inc.**, Detroit (North American Tractor Assembly—farm machinery—1,200).

18th District

(Detroit Suburbs—Southeast Oakland County,
Southwest Macomb County)

Race and Ethnic Groups. Canadian stock 7.1 percent, Polish stock 3.9 percent, British stock 3.2 percent, Italian stock 2.5 percent.
Cities, 1970 Population. Part of Warren 91,340, Royal Oak 85,496, Sterling Heights 61,391, Troy 39,313.
Newspapers, Circulation. Royal Oak Tribune (Eve 59,658). In addition, Detroit newspapers circulate throughout district.
Commercial Television Stations, Affiliation. Entire district is located in Detroit ADI.
Plants and Offices, Products, Employment.
General Motors Corp., Warren (Chevrolet Motor Division—axles, wheels—3,500). **Chrysler Corp.**, Warren (Sterling Stamping Plant—metal stampings —4,000). **Chrysler Corp.**, Center Line (Tanks, missile components—1,140). **Chrysler Corp.**, Warren (Missile Plant—guided missiles—3,400). **LTV Aerospace Corp.**, Warren (Vought Missiles and Space Division—missiles, space vehicles—1,200). **TRW Inc.**, Warren (Michigan Division—link, suspension parts—1,500). **Sperry Rand Corp.**, Troy (Vickers Division—business machines, instruments—1,200).

William Beaumont Hospital, Royal Oak (Hospital —at least 1,100).

19th District

(Detroit Suburbs—Part of Oakland County,
Eastern Livingston County)

Race and Ethnic Groups. Blacks 5.1 percent. Canadian stock 5.2 percent, British stock 2.3 percent.
Cities, 1970 Population. Pontiac 85,345, Birmingham, 26,183, Drayton Plains 16,592, Beverly Hills 13,600.
Newspapers, Circulation. Oakland Press, Pontiac (Eve— 76,303). In addition, Detroit newspapers circulate throughout district.
Commercial Television Stations, Affiliation. Entire district is located in Detroit ADI.
Plants and Offices, Products, Employment.
General Motors Corp., Pontiac (Pontiac Motor Division—autos—18,000). **General Motors Corp.**, Pontiac (Fisher Body Division—car and commercial bodies—3,400). **General Motors Corp.**, Pontiac (GMC Truck and Coach Division—trucks and buses— 12,000). **Ford Motor Co.**, Wixom (Automotive Assembly Division—autos—6,000). **County of Oakland**, Pontiac (County government—5,000).

MINNESOTA: EIGHT HOUSE SEATS, NO CHANGE

Neither party was able to dominate the drawing of new congressional districts in Minnesota, because the majority Conservative (Republican) faction in the nominally nonpartisan legislature was confronted with Democratic Gov. Wendell R. Anderson's veto power.

Consequently, a bill was drafted by the majority faction creating relatively safe districts for all the state's eight incumbent representatives. The bill passed the state House May 21, 1971, by a vote of 97-37 and the state Senate on the same day, 56-11. Anderson signed it June 7.

Hennepin County, which includes Minneapolis and its western suburbs, was divided among four congressional districts. Previously, the county had been divided into only two districts. The new plan gives two predominantly nonmetropolitan districts (2nd and 6th) slices of population from Hennepin County to make up their population deficits.

Other Minneapolis-St. Paul suburban counties were attached to nonurban districts in a similar manner— Anoka County to the 8th District and Washington County to the 1st. *(Map p. 105)*

District	Member Elected 1972	Winning Percentage	1970 Population	Percent Variance
1	Albert H. Quie (R)	70.7	473,918	—0.3607
2	Ancher Nelsen (R)	57.1	476,647	+ 0.2129
3	Bill Frenzel (R)	62.9	472,662	—0.6248
4	Joseph E. Karth (D)	72.4	473,902	—0.3641
5	Donald M. Fraser (D)	65.8	479,280	+ 0.7665
6	John M. Zwach (R)	51.0	476,748	+ 0.2342
7	Bob Bergland (D)	59.0	472,753	—0.6057
8	John A. Blatnik (D)	75.9	479,159	+ 0.7411

1970 State Population: 3,805,069
Ideal District Population: 475,634

Election Results, 1968-1972

Vote for U.S. Representative
(Adjusted to new district boundaries)

District	1968	1970	1972
1	119,436 R (66.1%)	100,967 R (64.2%)	142,698 R (70.7%)
	61,219 D (33.9%)	56,271 D (35.8%)	59,106 D (29.3%)
2	119,951 R (62.1%)	108,832 R (63.7%)	124,350 R (57.1%)
	73,282 D (37.9%)	62,045 D (36.3%)	93,433 D (42.9%)
3	118,489 R (66.3%)	85,515 R (53.5%)	132,568 R (69.9%)
	60,293 D (33.7%)	74,417 D (46.5%)	66,070 D (31.3%)
4	112,684 D (62.1%)	113,502 D (74.9%)	138,292 D (72.4%)
	68,727 R (37.9%)	38,091 R (25.1%)	52,786 R (27.6%)
5	113,824 D (56.1%)	90,845 D (57.5%)	135,108 D (65.8%)
	87,744 R (43.3%)	66,378 R (42.0%)	50,014 R (24.4%)
6	112,770 R (56.9%)	96,186 R (53.8%)	114,537 R (51.0%)
	85,383 D (43.1%)	81,168 D (45.4%)	109,955 D (49.0%)
7	105,438 R (51.3%)	101,007 R (53.8%)	133,067 R (59.0%)
	99,898 D (48.7%)	86,576 D (46.1%)	92,283 R (41.0%)
8	124,953 D (64.5%)	130,380 D (73.9%)	161,823 D (75.9%)
	68,654 R (35.5%)	46,035 R (26.1%)	51,314 R (24.1%)
State	801,209 R (52.2%)	709,635 D (53.0%)	896,854 D (53.1%)
	731,536 D (47.7%)	628,590 R (46.9%)	760,620 R (45.0%)

Voting Age Population

District	Voting Age Population	Voting Age Population 18, 19, 20	Voting Age Population 65 and Over	Median Age of Voting Age Population
1	291,518	24,150 (8.3%)	46,681 (16.0%)	42.1
2	296,981	24,406 (8.2%)	50,442 (17.0%)	43.2
3	286,987	21,182 (7.4%)	25,069 (8.7%)	39.1

District	Voting Age Population	Voting Age Population 18, 19, 20	Voting Age Population 65 and Over	Median Age of Voting Age Population
4	307,407	27,612 (9.0%)	48,142 (15.7%)	41.5
5	343,509	33,855 (9.9%)	65,324 (19.0%)	42.3
6	294,465	24,262 (8.2%)	58,642 (19.9%)	46.0
7	302,098	23,137 (7.7%)	67,040 (22.2%)	48.4
8	293,802	21,317 (7.3%)	47,818 (16.3%)	44.0
State	2,416,815	199,932 (8.3%)	409,200 (16.9%)	43.2

Income and Occupation

District	Median Family Income	White Collar Workers	Blue Collar Workers	Service Workers	Farm Workers
1	$10,272	46.1%	30.4%	14.5%	9.0%
2	9,703	43.0	32.7	12.5	11.8
3	13,248	63.7	25.9	10.2	0.2
4	11,306	56.2	30.4	13.2	0.2
5	10,323	54.9	30.3	14.7	0.1
6	7,984	37.5	29.8	13.4	19.3
7	7,089	39.0	27.5	15.2	18.3
8	9,393	41.2	41.7	14.2	2.9
State	9,928	48.6	30.9	13.4	7.1

Education: School Years Completed

District	Completed 4 years of High School	Completed 4 years of College	Completed 5 years or less of School	Median School years completed
1	58.8%	11.2%	2.9%	12.3
2	55.8	10.0	3.1	12.2
3	77.1	19.1	1.2	12.7
4	62.5	14.2	3.1	12.4
5	59.6	12.8	3.0	12.3
6	48.0	7.0	3.8	11.5
7	45.2	6.7	5.4	10.9
8	55.0	8.1	4.1	12.1
State	57.6	11.1	3.3	12.2

Housing and Residential Patterns

	Housing		Urban-Suburban-Nonmetropolitan Breakdown		
District	Owner Occupied Units	Renter Occupied Units	Urban	Suburban	Nonmetro-politan
1	76.5%	23.5%	11.4%	42.7%	45.9%
2	77.0	23.0	—	18.6	81.4
3	75.2	24.8	3.9	96.1	—
4	62.4	37.6	65.4	34.6	—
5	50.6	49.4	86.7	13.3	—
6	77.8	22.2	—	5.6	94.4
7	79.1	20.9	6.3	3.6	90.1
8	78.1	21.9	21.0	46.0	33.0
State	71.5	28.5	24.4	32.5	43.1

1st District

(Southeast—Rochester, Winona)

Race and Ethnic Groups. German stock 4.0 percent, Norwegian stock 2.0 percent.

Cities, 1970 Population. Rochester 53,793, Winona 26,396, South St. Paul 24,994, West St. Paul 18,831.

Universities, Enrollment. Carleton College (Northfield—1,600), St. Olaf College (Northfield—2,650), Winona State College (Winona—4,261).

Newspapers, Circulation. Minncapolis newspapers circulate in major portion of district.

Commercial Television Stations, Affiliation. KROC-TV, Rochester (NBC). Portions of district located in Minneapolis-St. Paul ADI, Rochester-Austin-Mason City (Iowa) ADI, and La Crosse (Wisconsin)-Eau Claire (Wisconsin) ADI.

Plants and Offices, Products, Employment.
Andersen Corp., Bayport (Wooden window units—1,200). **3M Co.,** Hastings (Chemicals, photographic equipment and supplies—1,450). **International Business Machines Corp.,** Rochester (Data processing equipment—4,100). **Mayo Clinic,** Rochester (Hospital—3,000).

2nd District

(Southcentral—Mankato)

Race and Ethnic Groups. German stock 4.9 percent, Norwegian stock 2.1 percent.

Cities, 1970 Population. Mankato 30,866, Austin 25,008, Burnsville 19,812, Albert Lea 19,400.

Universities, Enrollment. Gustavus Adolphus College (St. Peter—1,918), Mankato State College (Mankato—13,232).

Newspapers, Circulation. Minneapolis newspapers circulate in portion of district.

Commercial Television Stations, Affiliation. KAUS-TV, Austin (ABC); KEYC-TV, Mankato (CBS). Portions of district located in Minneapolis-St. Paul ADI, Mankato ADI and Rochester-Austin-Mason City (Iowa) ADI.

Plants and Offices, Products, Employment.
3M Co., Hutchinson (Magnetic tape—2,000). **Tonka Corp.,** Mound (Metal toys—1,700). **George A. Hormel & Co.,** Austin (Meat packer—HQ—3,900). **Wilson & Co. Inc.,** Albert Lea (Meat packer—1,000).

3rd District

(Minneapolis Suburbs)

Race and Ethnic Groups. Swedish stock 2.8 percent, Norwegian stock 2.2 percent.

Cities, 1970 Population. Bloomington 82,037, St. Louis Park 48,943, Richfield 47,293, Edina 44,079.

Newspapers, Circulation. Minneapolis newspapers circulate throughout district.

Commercial Television Stations, Affiliation. Entire district located in Minneapolis-St. Paul ADI.

Plants and Offices, Products, Employment.
Honeywell Inc., Hopkins (Ammunition—3,000).
Thermo King Corp., Bloomington (Commercial refrigeration equipment—HQ—1,500). **Control Data Corp.**, Bloomington (Computer equipment—1,300). **General Mills Inc.**, Minneapolis (Flour and other mill products, cereals—HQ—1,000). **Gamble-Skogmo Inc.**, St. Louis Park (Wholesale, retail auto and home supplies—HQ—1,000). **Super Valu Stores Inc.**, Hopkins (Groceries—HQ—2,000). **Red Owl Stores Inc.**, Hopkins (Groceries—HQ—1,000). **Northwest Airlines Inc.**, Minneapolis-St. Paul International Airport (Airline—HQ—at least 1,000). **North Central Airlines Inc.**, Richfield (Airline—HQ—1,200).

Prudential Insurance Company of America, St. Louis Park (Insurance—1,100). **Premium Service Corp.**, Golden Valley (Management company—3,000).

4th District

(St. Paul)

Race and Ethnic Groups. German stock 3.4 percent, Swedish stock 2.5 percent.
Cities, 1970 Population. St. Paul 309,989, Roseville 34,526, Maplewood 25,215, White Bear Lake 23,367.
Universities, Enrollment. Bethel College (St. Paul—1,044), College of St. Catherine (St. Paul—1,367), College of St. Thomas (St. Paul—2,488), Hamline College (St. Paul—1,283), Macalester College (St. Paul—2,097).
Newspapers, Circulation. St. Paul Dispatch (Eve—127,837), St. Paul Pioneer Press (Morn—107,085).

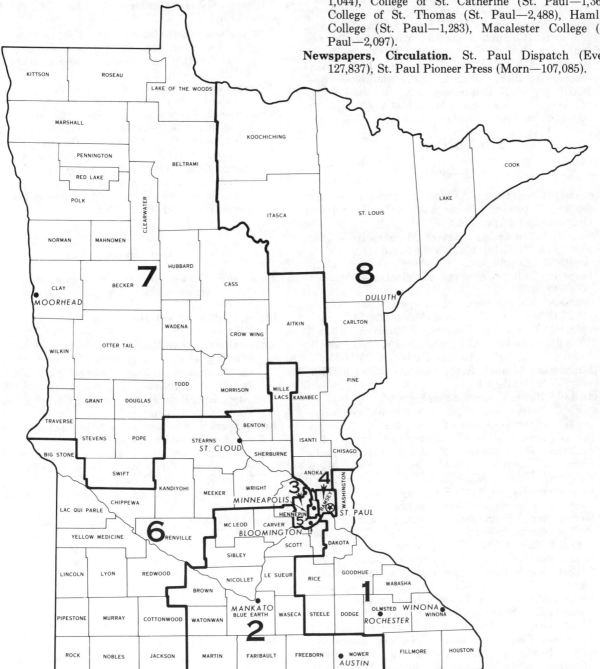

Commercial Television Stations, Affiliation. Entire district located in Minneapolis-St. Paul ADI.
Plants and Offices, Products, Employment.

Honeywell Inc., St. Paul (Ordnance Division—miscellaneous ordnance—1,800). **Ford Motor Co.,** St. Paul (Automobile assembly—2,300). **American Hoist & Derrick Co.,** St. Paul (Hoists and derricks—HQ—1,800). **Whirlpool Corp.,** St. Paul (Refrigeration and air conditioning equipment—2,000). **Hoerner Waldorf Corp.,** St. Paul (Corrugated shipping cartons—HQ—1,700). **3M Co.,** St. Paul (Headquarters—1,000). **3M Co.,** St. Paul (Tape—1,500). **Control Data Corp.,** St. Paul (Computers—2,000). **Sperry Rand Corp.,** St. Paul (Univac Division—computers and equipment—1,570). **Sperry Rand Corp.,** St. Paul (Univac Division—computers—4,360). **Sperry Rand Corp.,** St. Paul (Computers—1,500). **Minnesota Fabrics Inc.,** St. Paul (Fabrics—1,000). **Theodore Hamm Brewing Co.,** St. Paul (Beer—HQ—1,500). **Burlington Northern Inc.,** St. Paul (Railroad—HQ—1,000). **St. Paul Companies Inc.,** St. Paul (Holding company, insurance—HQ—2,000). **City of St. Paul,** St. Paul (City government—3,280).

5th District

(Minneapolis)

Race and Ethnic Groups. Blacks 3.9 percent. Swedish stock 5.0 percent, Norwegian stock 3.7 percent, German stock 2.7 percent.
Cities, 1970 Population. Part of Minneapolis 415,683, Fridley 29,189, Columbia Heights 23,975.
Universities, Enrollment. Augsburg College (Minneapolis—1,616), University of Minnesota (Minneapolis—68,336).
Newspapers, Circulation. Minneapolis Star (Eve—257,838), Minneapolis Tribune (Morn—229,342).
Commercial Television Stations, Affiliation. KMSP-TV, Minneapolis (ABC); KSTP-TV, Minneapolis (NBC); WCCO-TV, Minneapolis (CBS); WTCN-TV, Minneapolis (None). Entire district located in Minneapolis-St. Paul ADI.
Plants and Offices, Products, Employment.

FMC Corp., Minneapolis (Northern Ordnance—naval ordnance—3,300). **Graco Inc.,** Minneapolis (Pumps—HQ—1,000). **Honeywell Inc.,** Minneapolis (Headquarters—17,500). **Control Data Corp.,** Minneapolis (Headquarters—2,000). **Munsingwear Inc.,** Minneapolis (Men's, women's underwear—HQ—1,000). **Pillsbury Co.,** Minneapolis (Headquarters—1,600). **International Multifoods Corp.,** Minneapolis (Flour, grain and feed, food products, holding company—HQ—1,000). **Associated Dry Goods Corp.,** Minneapolis (Powers Dry Goods Co. Division—department store—1,020). **Target Stores Inc.,** Minneapolis (Discount department stores—HQ—1,000). **G & K Services Inc.,** Minneapolis (Garment and linen rental—1,170). **Minneapolis Star & Tribune Co.,** Minneapolis (Newspaper publishing—2,300). **Northwestern Bell Telephone Co.,** Minneapolis (Telephone company—5,300). **Northern States Power Co.,** Minneapolis (Electric, gas, steam, telephone utility—HQ—1,500).

Investors Stock Fund, Minneapolis (Mutual fund company 2,600). **Investors Diversified Service,** Minneapolis (Management investment company—HQ—1,350). **Northwest Bancorporation,** Minneapolis (Holding company—7,000). **First Bank System Inc.,** Minneapolis (Bank holding company—6,100).

6th District

(Southwest and Central—St. Cloud)

Race and Ethnic Groups. German stock 5.8 percent, Norwegian stock 3.0 percent, Swedish stock 2.5 percent.
Cities, 1970 Population. St. Cloud 39,699, Willmar 12,872.
Universities, Enrollment. St. Cloud State College (St. Cloud—9,965), St. John's University (Collegeville—1,604), Southwest Minnesota State College (Marshall—3,136).
Newspapers, Circulation. Minneapolis newspapers circulate in portion of district.
Commercial Television Stations, Affiliation. Portions of district located in Minneapolis-St. Paul ADI, Alexandria ADI, Mankato ADI and Sioux Falls (South Dakota)-Mitchell (South Dakota) ADI.
Plants and Offices, Products, Employment.

Franklin Manufacturing Co., St. Cloud (Household appliances—HQ—1,190). **Fingerhut Corp., Corp.,** St. Cloud (Plastics—1,220).

7th District

(Northwest—Moorhead)

Race and Ethnic Groups. Norwegian stock 6.6 percent, German stock 4.1 percent, Swedish stock 3.7 percent.
Cities, 1970 Population. Moorhead 29,687, Fergus Falls 12,443, Brainerd 11,667, Bemidji 11,457.
Universities, Enrollment. Bemidji State College (Bemidji—4,839), Concordia College (Moorhead—2,402), Moorhead State College (Moorhead—5,160), University of Minnesota, Morris (Morris—1,719).
Military Installations or Activities. Baudette Air Force Station, Baudette.
Newspapers, Circulation. Minneapolis newspapers circulate in portion of district.
Commercial Television Stations, Affiliation. KCMT, Alexandria (NBC, ABC on per program basis). Portions of district located in Alexandria ADI, Fargo (North Dakota) ADI and Duluth-Superior (Wisconsin) ADI.
Plants and Offices, Products, Employment.

Textron Inc., Roseau (Polaris Industries Division—snowmobiles—1,500). **Arctic Enterprises Inc.,** Thief River Falls (Snow vehicles—HQ—2,200).

8th District

(Northeast—Duluth)

Race and Ethnic Groups. Swedish stock 4.7 percent, Finnish stock 3.7 percent, Norwegian stock 2.9 percent.

Cities, 1970 Population. Duluth 100,590, Coon Rapids 30,513, Blaine 20,709, Hibbing 16,074.

Universities, Enrollment. University of Minnesota, Duluth (Duluth—5,712).

Military Installations or Activities. Finland Air Force Station, Finland.

Newspapers, Circulation. Duluth News-Tribune (Morn—55,502). Minneapolis newspapers circulate in portion of district.

Commercial Television Stations, Affiliation. KDAL-TV, Duluth (CBS); WDIO-TV, Duluth (ABC); WDSM-TV, Duluth (NBC). Portions of district located in Duluth-Superior (Wisconsin) ADI and Minneapolis-St. Paul ADI.·

Plants and Offices, Products, Employment.
Federal Cartridge Corp., Anoka (Hoffman Engineering Co. Division—small arms ammunition—2,000). **Erie Mining Co.,** Hoyt Lakes (Rickands Mather & Co.—iron mining—2,800). **Hanna Mining Co.,** Hibbing (Iron mining—1,800). **Reserve Mining Co.,** Silver Bay (Iron mining—HQ—1,600). **Reserve Mining Co.,** Babbitt (Iron mining—13,700). **Boise Cascade International,** International Falls (Minnesota & Ontario Paper Co. Division—pulp and paper mill—2,500). **Northwest Paper Co.,** Cloquet (Paper mill—HQ—1,550). **Conwed Corp.,** Cloquet (Insulation materials, wood—1,100). **Duluth Mesabi Iron Range Railway Co.,** Duluth (Railroad—1,580).

MISSISSIPPI: FIVE HOUSE SEATS, NO CHANGE

Relatively minor changes were made in Mississippi's five congressional districts as a result of redistricting legislation. The 1st and 4th Districts were not changed. One county was shifted from the 3rd to the 2nd District.

The most substantial change occurred in southern Mississippi, where the 5th District, which includes the fast-growing Gulf Coast area, lost four counties to the 3rd District. *(Map p. 108)*

All district numbers were changed except the 5th. The old 1st became the 2nd, the old 2nd became the 1st, the old 3rd became the 4th and the old 4th became the 3rd.

The main political impact lay in the split in the Mississippi delta region, with its heavy black concentrations. In the 1966 redistricting, the delta was divided among three congressional districts. The new plan continues the division, giving the 1st, 2nd and 3rd Districts parts of the delta.

The redistricting bill passed the Mississippi House Feb. 17, 1972, by a vote of 85-31. The state Senate concurred Feb. 23 by a vote of 27-20. Gov. William Waller (D) signed the bill March 1.

District	Member Elected 1972	Winning Percentage	1970 Population	Percent Variance
1	Jamie L. Whitten (D)	100.0	433,825	—2.1554%
2	David R. Bowen (D)	61.9	440,689	—0.6073
3	G.V. (Sonny) Montgomery (D)	100.0	445,713	+ 0.5257
4	Thad Cochran (R)	47.8	444,704	+ 0.2981
5	Trent Lott (R)	55.3	451,981	+ 1.9394

1970 State Population:	2,216,912
Ideal District Population:	443,382

Election Results, 1968-1972

Vote for U.S. Representative
(Adjusted to new district boundaries)

District	1968	1970	1972
1	71,260 D (100.0%)	51,689 D (86.5%)	87,526 D (100.0%)
	—	—	—
2	78,272 D (98.5%)	45,618 D (100.0%)	69,892 D (61.9%)
	1,174 R¹(1.5%)	—	39,117 R (34.7%)
3	87,887 D (73.0%)	72,604 D (98.5%)	105,722 D (100.0%)
	32,509 R (27.0%)	—	—

District	1968	1970	1972
4	82,896 D (100.0%)	50,527 D (63.7%)	67,655 R (47.8%)
	—	28,847 R (36.3%)	62,148 D (44.0%)
5	94,706 D (100.0%)	48,755 D (90.5%)	77,826 R (55.3%)
	—	—	62,101 D (44.2%)
State	415,021 D (92.5%)	269,193 D (86.2%)	387,389 D (65.9%)
	33,683 R (7.5%)	28,847 R (9.2%)	184,598 R (31.4%)

¹ *No candidate in this district as constituted before redistricting*

Voting Age Population

District	Voting Age Population	Voting Age Population 18, 19, 20	Voting Age Population 65 and Over	Median Age of Voting Age Population
1	267,605	23,864 (8.9%)	47,416 (17.7%)	44.4
2	265,625	25,542 (9.6%)	45,822 (17.3%)	43.8
3	275,629	22,166 (8.0%)	50,645 (18.4%)	45.5
4	274,966	24,868 (9.0%)	43,069 (15.7%)	43.3
5	283,911	29,625 (10.4%)	36,048 (12.7%)	40.0
State	1,367,736	126,065 (9.2%)	223,000 (16.3%)	43.3

Income and Occupation

District	Median Family Income	White Collar Workers	Blue Collar Workers	Service Workers	Farm Workers
3	$5,577	33.5%	45.0%	12.3%	9.2%
2	5,446	36.6	39.5	15.1	8.8
3	5,320	33.4	43.7	13.4	9.5
4	6,802	46.6	34.9	15.4	3.1
5	7,053	42.2	42.7	13.3	1.8
State	6,068	38.6	41.1	13.9	6.4

Glossary and Sources

For a complete explanation of all terms used in this book and a list of source material, consult the details included in the Introduction.

Education: School Years Completed

District	Completed 4 years of High School	Completed 4 years of College	Completed 5 years or less of School	Median School years completed
1	34.3%	6.5%	19.2%	9.7
2	36.0	7.9	20.6	9.9
3	36.6	5.8	18.2	10.2
4	48.5	11.4	13.8	11.8
5	49.2	8.7	11.0	11.9
State	41.0	8.1	16.5	10.7

Housing and Residential Patterns

	Housing		Urban-Suburban-Nonmetropolitan Breakdown		
District	Owner Occupied Units	Renter Occupied Units	Urban	Suburban	Nonmetropolitan
1	64.0%	36.0%	—	—	100.0%
2	60.6	39.4	—	—	100.0
3	70.3	29.7	—	9.9%	90.1
4	65.9	34.1	34.6%	13.7	51.7
5	70.2	29.8	19.8	10.0	70.2
State	66.3	33.7	11.0	6.8	82.2

1st District

(North—Clarksdale)

Race and Ethnic Groups. Blacks 35.5 percent.

Cities, 1970 Population. Clarksdale 21,673, Tupelo 20,471, Oxford 13,915, Corinth 11,572.

Universities, Enrollment. University of Mississippi (University, near Oxford—7,823).

Newspapers, Circulation. Memphis (Tennessee) papers circulate throughout district.

Commercial Television Stations, Affiliation. Most of district is located in Memphis (Tennessee) ADI. In addition, two counties of district form Tupelo ADI. Tupelo station: WTWV, Tupelo (NBC).

Plants and Offices, Products, Employment.
U.S. Industries Inc., Grenada (Round the Clock Hosiery Division—women's hosiery—1,200).

2nd District

(North Central—Greenville, Columbus)

Race and Ethnic Groups. Blacks 45.9 percent.

Cities, 1970 Population. Greenville 39,648, Columbus 25,795, Greenwood 22,400, Cleveland 13,345.

Universities, Enrollment. Delta State College (Cleveland—3,211), Mississippi State College for Women (Columbus—2,591), Mississippi State University (State College, near Starkville—10,068), Mississippi Valley State College (Itta Bena—2,410).

Military Installations or Activities. Columbus Air Force Base.

Commercial Television Stations, Affiliation. Most of district is divided between Columbus and Greenwood ADIs. In addition, small portions of district are located in Jackson and Meridian ADIs. Columbus station: WCBI-TV, Columbua (CBS, ABC per program). Greenwood station: WABG-TV, Greenwood-Greenville (ABC).

Plants and Offices, Products, Employment.
Ambac Industries Inc., Columbus (Mississippi Division—auto accessories—1,200). Babcock and Wilcox Co., West Point (Boilers, furnaces—1,200). Baxter Laboratories Inc., Cleveland (Travenol Laboratories—pharmaceuticals—1,000).

3rd District

(South Central—Meridian)

Race and Ethnic Groups. Blacks 40.4 percent.

Cities, 1970 Population. Meridian 45,083, Yazoo City 10,796, Canton 10,503.

Military Installations or Activities. Naval Air Station, Meridian.

Commercial Television Stations, Affiliation. Most of district is divided between Jackson and Meridian ADIs. In addition, small portion of district is located in Laurel-Hattiesburg ADI and Columbus ADI. Meridan station: WTOK-TV, Meridian (CBS primary, ABC program).

Plants and Offices, Products, Employment.
Universal Manufacturing Corp., Mendenhall (Transformers—1,400).

4th District

(Southwest—Jackson, Vicksburg)

Race and Ethnic Groups. Blacks 43.1 percent.

Cities, 1970 Population. Jackson 153,968, Vicksburg 25,586, Natchez 19,704, McComb 11,833.

Universities, Enrollment. Alcorn Agricultural and Mechanical College (Lorman—2,677), Jackson State College (Jackson—5,058), Millsaps College (Jackson—996), Mississippi College (Clinton—2,415).

Newspapers, Circulation. Jackson Clarion-Ledger (Morn—60,041).

Commercial Television Stations, Affiliation. Most of district is located in Jackson ADI. Small portions of district are located in Monroe (Louisiana) ADI, Baton Rouge (Louisiana) ADI and New Orleans (Louisiana) ADI. Jackson stations: WAPT-TV, Jackson (ABC); WJTV, Jackson (CBS); WLBT, Jackson (NBC).

Plants and Offices, Products, Employment.
Armstrong Rubber Co., Natchez (Southern Division—tires and tubes—1,400). Presto Manufacturing Co., Jackson (Household appliances—1,000). City of Jackson, Jackson (City government—2,000).

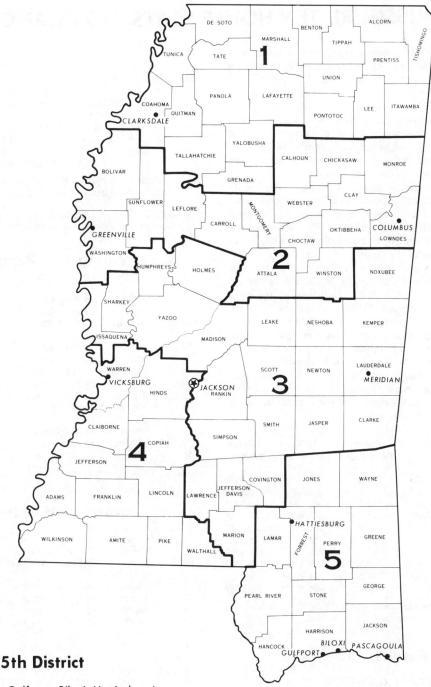

5th District

(Southeast—Gulfport, Biloxi, Hattiesburg)

Race and Ethnic Groups. Blacks 19.4 percent.

Cities, 1970 Population. Biloxi 48,486, Gulfport 40,787, Hattiesburg 38,274, Pascagoula 27,471.

Universities, Enrollment. University of Southern Mississippi (Hattiesburg—10,868).

Military Installations or Activities. Keesler Air Force Base, Biloxi; Naval Construction Batallion Center, Gulfport.

NASA Facilities. Mississippi Test Facility, Bay St. Louis.

Commercial Television Stations, Affiliation. District is divided between Gulfport-Biloxi-Pascagoula ADI, Laurel-Hattiesburg ADI, New Orleans (Louisiana) ADI and Mobile (Alabama) ADI. Biloxi station: WLOX-TV, Biloxi (ABC). Hattiesburg station: WDAM-TV, Hattiesburg (NBC, ABC).

Plants and Offices, Products, Employment.

Litton Systems Inc., Pascagoula (Ingalls Shipbuilding Division—shipbuilding—11,000). **Masonite Corp.**, Laurel (Fibre boards—2,000). **International Paper Co.**, Moss Point (Paper and pulpwood—1,620). **Stirling Homex Corp.**, Gulfport (Prebuilt apartments—2,000). **Puritan Fashions Inc.**, Hattiesburg (Men's trousers—1,220).

MISSOURI: TEN HOUSE SEATS, NO CHANGE

On Feb. 22, 1972, congressional redistricting was taken out of the hands of the Missouri legislature by a three-judge federal court. Because the legislature had been unable to agree upon a plan, the court imposed one of its own. *(Map p. 112)*

The court plan closely resembled one adopted by the Missouri house the previous year. It protected all 10 of the state's incumbents and maintained control of the City of St. Louis over two congressional districts, giving the separate St. Louis County control of only one.

A redistricting measure approved by the state Senate in 1971 would have shifted control of one district from St. Louis City to St. Louis County and would have created a suburban Republican district. The failure of the two houses of the legislature to reconcile their differences led to the intervention of the court.

The one controversial aspect of the court's plan was the transfer of Jefferson County, a St. Louis suburban area, to the 10th District. The 10th traditionally had been dominated by the southeast Missouri "boot-heel" area, but the new Jefferson County area constituted 22 percent of the district's population, based on the 1970 census. Moreover the county's population was expected to grow rapidly, giving it ever-increasing weight in the district.

In its decision, the court left open the possibility that if the legislature were to enact a suitable plan, it could supersede the court's map. But the legislators made little further effort in this regard.

District	Member Elected 1972	Winning Percentage	1970 Population	Percent Variance
1	William (Bill) Clay (D)	64.0	468,056	+ 0.0675
2	James W. Symington (D)	63.5	468,808	+ 0.2283
3	Leonor K. Sullivan (D)	69.3	467,544	−0.0419
4	William J. Randall (D)	57.4	466,940	−0.1710
5	Richard Bolling (D)	62.8	467,457	−0.0605
6	Jerry Litton (D)	54.6	469,642	+ 0.4066
7	Gene Taylor (R)	63.7	466,699	−0.2225
8	Richard H. Ichord (D)	62.1	467,532	−0.0444
9	William L. Hungate (D)	66.5	467,990	+ 0.0534
10	Bill D. Burlison (D)	64.3	466,731	−0.2157

1970 State Population: 4,677,399
Ideal District Population: 467,740

Election Results, 1968-1972

Vote for U.S. Representative
(Adjusted to new district boundaries)

District	1968	1970	1972
1	104,571 D (66.9%)	74,104 D (80.7%)	95,098 D (64.0%)
	51,640 R (33.1%)	12,666 R (13.8%)	53,596 R (36.0%)
2	89,903 D (50.1%)	80,032 D (57.5%)	134,332 D (63.5%)
	89,336 R (49.8%)	55,890 R (40.2%)	77,192 R (36.5%)
3	118,352 D (68.7%)	86,696 D (69.3%)	124,365 D (69.3%)
	53,670 R (31.2%)	38,098 R (30.4%)	30,523 R (30.4%)
4	97,504 D (56.9%)	74,793 D (59.8%)	108,131 D (57.4%)
	73,777 R (43.1%)	50,280 R (40.2%)	80,228 R (42.6%)
5	101,821 D (64.6%)	61,077 D (60.9%)	93,812 D (62.8%)
	55,727 R (35.4%)	38,397 R (38.3%)	53,257 R (35.6%)
6	104,385 D (54.3%)	74,782 D (53.8%)	110,047 D (54.6%)
	87,952 R (45.7%)	63,573 R (45.7%)	91,610 R (45.4%)
7	118,885 R (63.6%)	89,676 R (99.4%)	132,780 R (63.7%)
	68,160 D (36.4%)	539 D (0.6%)[1]	75,613 D (36.3%)
8	84,591 D (53.5%)	71,337 D (59.8%)	112,556 D (62.1%)
	73,166 R (46.3%)	47,394 R (39.7%)	68,580 R (37.9%)
9	95,051 D (54.1%)	87,629 D (65.2%)	132,150 D (66.5%)
	80,629 R (45.9%)	45,539 R (33.9%)	66,528 R (33.5%)
10	91,634 D (57.1%)	74,839 D (60.0%)	106,301 D (64.3%)
	68,604 R (42.8%)	49,784 R (40.0%)	59,083 R (35.7%)
State	968,733 D (55.9%)[2]	692,026 D (57.8%)	1,092,405 D (59.6%)
	763,399 R (44.0%)[2]	493,557 R (41.2%)	737,377 R (40.2%)

1 No candidate in this district as constituted before redistricting.
2 Includes absentee ballots not included in district-by-district tabulation.

Voting Age Population

District	Voting Age Population	Voting Age Population 18, 19, 20	Voting Age Population 65 and Over	Median Age of Voting Age Population
1	307,366	24,888 (8.1%)	58,304 (19.0%)	45.5
2	300,143	20,588 (6.9%)	34,903 (11.6%)	42.3
3	326,362	21,122 (6.5%)	65,079 (19.9%)	47.3
4	313,759	22,706 (7.2%)	58,090 (18.5%)	44.6
5	316,425	21,742 (6.9%)	58,455 (18.5%)	44.7
6	318,184	22,936 (7.2%)	63,548 (20.0%)	45.9
7	322,247	24,382 (7.6%)	67,034 (20.8%)	47.0
8	317,211	41,898 (13.2%)	49,680 (15.7%)	40.0
9	295,782	19,055 (6.4%)	50,487 (17.1%)	43.6
10	300,675	21,151 (7.0%)	56,065 (18.6%)	45.7
State	3,118,165	240,458 (7.7%)	561,652 (18.0%)	44.7

Income and Occupation

District	Median Family Income	White Collar Workers	Blue Collar Workers	Service Workers	Farm Workers
1	$ 8,485	45.7%	32.8%	21.2%	0.3%
2	12,597	62.6	28.3	8.9	0.2
3	10,199	52.1	35.8	11.9	0.2
4	8,740	42.2	38.3	11.5	8.0
5	9,727	52.7	32.3	14.7	0.3
6	8,507	42.8	35.3	11.6	10.3
7	6,832	40.8	39.6	12.7	6.9
8	7,743	45.5	36.6	12.4	5.5
9	9,573	44.8	35.9	11.2	8.1
10	7,048	36.3	44.1	12.3	7.3
State	8,908	46.9	35.7	12.8	4.6

Education: School Years Completed

District	Completed 4 years of High School	Completed 4 years of College	Completed 5 years or less of School	Median School years completed
1	40.8%	9.7%	10.2%	10.7
2	61.4	17.3	3.2	12.4
3	41.2	7.5	6.7	10.6
4	53.0	7.5	3.9	12.1

District	Completed 4 years of High School	Completed 4 years of College	Completed 5 years or less of School	Median School years completed
5	55.3	10.0	5.7	12.2
6	54.2	7.7	3.3	12.1
7	48.1	6.7	5.6	11.7
8	46.3	10.9	6.5	11.2
9	52.3	7.9	3.7	12.1
10	35.3	5.1	13.0	9.4
State	48.8	9.0	6.2	11.8

Housing and Residential Patterns

	Housing		Urban-Suburban-Nonmetropolitan Breakdown		
District	Owner Occupied Units	Renter Occupied Units	Urban	Suburban	Nonmetropolitan
1	45.8%	54.2%	65.8%	34.2%	—
2	76.2	23.8	—	100.0	—
3	54.6	45.4	67.2	32.8	—
4	73.3	26.7	1.6	47.0	51.4%
5	56.5	43.5	92.7	7.3	—
6	72.8	27.2	29.8	21.8	48.4
7	74.3	25.7	25.7	7.1	67.2
8	70.7	29.3	12.5	23.7	63.8
9	78.9	21.1	—	48.9	51.1
10	71.4	28.6	—	22.6	77.4
State	67.2	32.8	29.5	34.6	35.9

1st District

(North St. Louis and Western Suburbs)

Race and Ethnic Groups. Blacks 54.3 percent. German stock 1.8 percent, Italian stock 0.7 percent.

Cities, 1970 Population. Part of St. Louis 307,917, part of University City 30,294, Richmond Heights 13,794, Maplewood 12,770.

Universities, Enrollment. University of Missouri, St. Louis (St. Louis—10,487), Washington University (St. Louis—11,197).

Newspapers, Circulation. St. Louis Globe Democrat (MxSat—298,209), St. Louis Post-Dispatch (ExSat—332,162).

Commercial Television Stations, Affiliation. KDNL-TV, St. Louis (None); KMOX-TV, St. Louis (CBS); KPLR-TV, St. Louis (None); KSD-TV, St. Louis (NBC); KTVI-TV, St. Louis (ABC). Entire district is located in St. Louis ADI.

Plants and Offices, Products, Employment.
General Steel Industries Inc., St. Louis (St. Louis Car Co. Division—railroad cars, street cars—1,000). **General Motors Corp.**, St. Louis (Ammunition—2,600). **General Motors Corp.**, St. Louis (Automobile bodies—8,000). **ACF Industries Inc.**, St. Louis (Carter Carburetor Division—fuel systems—1,500). **Century Electric Co.**, St. Louis (Century Foundry—motors and generators, iron foundry—HQ—1,500). **Emerson Electric Co.**, St. Louis (Headquarters—1,500). **Wagner Electric Corp.**, St. Louis (Motors and generators—5,000). **Central Moloney Inc.**, St. Louis (Moloney Electric Co. Division—transformers—1,100). **McGraw-Edison Co.**, St. Louis (Bussmann Manufacturing Division—electric fuses—1,000). **Mallinckrodt Chemical Works**, St. Louis (Medical, industrial chemicals—HQ—1,500). **Brown Shoe Co. Inc.**, St. Louis (Headquarters—1,500). **Krey Packing Co.**, St. Louis (Meat packing—HQ—1,000). **L. B. Price Mercantile Co.**, St. Louis (Home furnishings—1,600). **Pulitzer Publishing Co.**, St. Louis (Newspaper publishing, radio and television broadcasting—2,100). **Southwestern Bell Telephone Co.**, St. Louis (Telephone company—HQ—10,000). **Union Electric Co.**, St. Louis (Electricity, gas and steam distribution—HQ—1,000). **Laclede Gas Co.**, St. Louis (gas distribution—HQ—1,500). **Norfolk & Western Railway Co.**, St. Louis (Railroad—at least 1,000). **Chase Hotel Inc.**, St. Louis (Chase-Park Plaza Hotel—1,100). **Barnes Hospital**, St. Louis (Hospital—3,700).

2nd District

(St. Louis Suburbs)

Race and Ethnic Groups. Blacks 4.0 percent. German stock 2.2 percent, Italian stock 2.0 percent.

Cities, 1970 Population. Kirkwood 31,885, Overland 24,906, part of Ferguson 23,380, Bridgeton 19,914.

Newspapers, Circulation. St. Louis newspapers circulate throughout district.

Commercial Television Stations, Affiliation. Entire district is located in St. Louis ADI.

Plants and Offices, Products, Employment.
Ford Motor Co., Hazelwood (Automobiles—3,300). **Chrysler Corp.**, Valley Park (Automobiles—2,600). **McDonnell Douglas Corp.**, St. Louis (Headquarters—37,000). **Hussman Refrigeration Co.**, Hazelwood (Commercial refrigeration equipment—HQ—2,700). **Boise Cascade Corp.** Hazelwood (Fibre bodied containers—1,580). **Monsanto Co.**, St. Louis (Headquarters—4,500). **Senack Shoes Inc.**, St. Louis (Shoe stores—1,000). **World Color Press Inc.**, Hazelwood (Magazine printing—HQ—1,400). **Sears Roebuck & Co.**, St. Ann (Department store—1,000). **Ozark Airlines Inc.**, St. Louis (Airline—HQ—1,500). **BHC Investment Co.**, St. Louis (Motels, restaurant—1,000).

3rd District

(Southern St. Louis and Suburbs)

Race and Ethnic Groups. Blacks 5.6 percent. German stock 4.1 percent, Italian stock 2.0 percent.

Cities, 1970 Population. Part of St. Louis 314,352, Lemay 39,824, Afton 23,961, Concord 21,290.

Universities, Enrollment. Harris Teachers College (St. Louis—1,156), St. Louis University (St. Louis—9,398), Webster College (St. Louis—1,665).

Military Installations or Activities. Aeronautical Chart and Information Center, St. Louis (Air Force).

Newspapers, Circulation. St. Louis newspapers circulate throughout district.

Commercial Television Stations, Affiliation. Entire district is located in St. Louis ADI.

Key: small numbers on map indicate the names of the following cities and places:

1	FLORRELL HILLS	22	PINE LAWN
2	COUNTRY CLUB HILLS	23	UPLANDS PARK
3	NORWOOD COURT	24	ARBOR TERRACE
4	BERDELL HILLS	25	BEVERLY HILLS
5	NORMANDY	26	VELDA VILLAGE
6	COOL VALLEY	27	VELDA VILLAGE HILLS
7	BEL-RIDGE	28	GLEN ECHO PARK
8	ACHUERMANN HEIGHTS	29	GREENDALE
9	EDMUNDSON	30	HILLSDALE
10	MARY RIDGE	31	HANLEY HILLS
11	BRIDGETON TERRACE	32	MACKENZIE
12	VINITA TERRACE	33	MARBOROUGH
13	SYCAMORE HILLS	34	WILBUR PARK
14	CHARLACK	35	LAKESHIRE
15	MARGONA VILLAGE	36	ST. GEORGE
16	BEL-NOR	37	BELLA VILLA
17	BELLERIVE	38	PEERLESS PARK
18	PASADENA PARK	39	WINCHESTER
19	PASADENA HILLS	30	COUNTRY LIFE ACRES
20	NORTHWOODS	41	CRYSTL LAKE PARK
21	GOODFELLOW TERRACE		

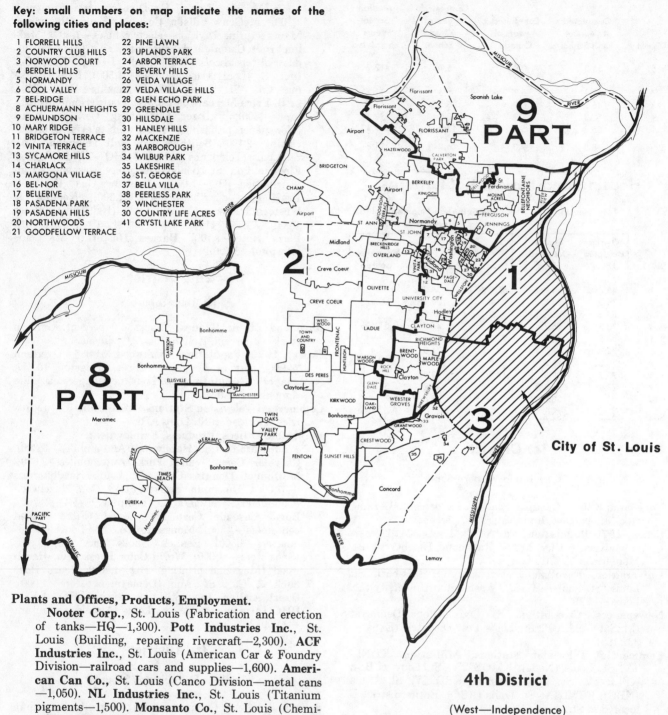

City of St. Louis

Plants and Offices, Products, Employment.

Nooter Corp., St. Louis (Fabrication and erection of tanks—HQ—1,300). **Pott Industries Inc.**, St. Louis (Building, repairing rivercraft—2,300). **ACF Industries Inc.**, St. Louis (American Car & Foundry Division—railroad cars and supplies—1,600). **American Can Co.**, St. Louis (Canco Division—metal cans —1,050). **NL Industries Inc.**, St. Louis (Titanium pigments—1,500). **Monsanto Co.**, St. Louis (Chemicals—1,900). **Swank Inc.**, St. Louis (Prince Gardner Division—wallets, leather goods—1,000). **Ralston Purina Co.**, St. Louis (Headquarters—1,000). **Swift & Co.**, St. Louis (Meat packing—1,800). **Anheuser-Busch Inc.**, St. Louis (Beer—HQ—5,000). **Missouri Pacific Railroad Co.**, St. Louis (Headquarters— 2,000). **Terminal Railroad Assn. of St. Louis**, St. Louis (Terminal company—2,790). **Sverdrup & Parcel Associates**, St. Louis (Consulting engineers—HQ —1,000). **American Transit Co.** St. Louis (Holding company—2,500). **General American Life Insurance Co. Inc.**, St. Louis (Insurance—HQ—1,100).

4th District

(West—Independence)

Race and Ethnic Groups. German stock 1.4 percent, Italian stock 0.2 percent.

Cities, 1970 Population. Independence 111,631, Sedalia 22,856, part of Raytown 16,813, Lee's Summit 16,252.

Universities, Enrollment. Central Missouri State University (Warrensburg—12,572).

Military Installations or Activities. Whiteman Air Force Base, Knobnoster; Richard-Gebaur Air Force Base, Grandview (part also in 5th District).

Newspapers, Circulation. Kansas City newspapers circulate in major portion of district.

Commercial Television Stations, Affiliation. Portions of district are located in Kansas City ADI, Columbia-Jefferson City ADI, Springfield ADI and Joplin-Pittsburg (Kansas) ADI.

Plants and Offices, Products, Employment.

Remington Arms Co. Inc., Independence (Small arms ammunition—3,400). **Western Electric Co. Inc.**, Lee's Summit (Telephone equipment—5,200).

5th District

(Kansas City)

Race and Ethnic Groups. Blacks 24.0 percent. Spanish heritage population 2.7 percent. German stock 1.3 percent, Italian stock 1.1 percent.

Cities, 1970 Population. Part of Kansas City 433,204, Grandview 17,424, part of Raytown 16,829.

Universities, Enrollment. Rockhurst College (Kansas City—2,415), University of Missouri, Kansas City (Kansas City—9,894).

Military Installations or Activities. Richards-Gebaur Air Force Base, Grandview (part also in 4th District.)

AEC-Owned, Contractor-Operated Installations. Kansas City Plant, Kansas City.

Newspapers, Circulation. Kansas City Star (Eve—319,328), Kansas City Times (Morn—336,679).

Commercial Television Stations, Affiliation. KMBA-TV, Kansas City (None); KCMO-TV, Kansas City (CBS); KMBC-TV, Kansas City (ABC); WDAF-TV, Kansas City (NBC). Entire district is located in Kansas City ADI.

Plants and Offices, Products, Employment.

Armco Steel Corp., Kansas City (Steel rods, bars, wire—3,700). **General Motors Corp.**, Kansas City (Automobile bodies—1,750). **Bendix Corp.**, Kansas City (Instruments, electronic devices—7,500). **Parkview-Gem Inc.**, Kansas City (Holding company, drug stores—HQ—1,400). **Montgomery Ward & Co.**, Kansas City (Department store—2,000). **R. H. Macy & Co. Inc.**, Kansas City (Department store—1,100). **Sears Roebuck & Co.**, Kansas City (Department store—1,000). **Hallmark Cards Inc.**, Kansas City (Greeting cards—HQ—5,000). **Kansas City Star Co.**, Kansas City (Newspaper publishing—1,740). **Trans World Airlines Inc.**, Kansas City (Airline—1,000). **Norfolk & Western Railway Co.**, Kansas City (Railroad—2,500). **Kansas City Terminal Railway Co.**, Kansas City (Terminal company—at least 1,000). **American Telephone and Telegraph Co.**, Kansas City (Telephone company—1,420). **Topsy's International Inc.**, Kansas City (Snack bars—1,000). **Vendo Co.**, Kansas City (Vending machines—HQ—1,000). **ISC Industries Inc.**, Kansas City (Holding company—1,800). **Old Security Life Insurance Co. Inc.**, Kansas City (Insurance—HQ—1,000).

6th District

(Northwest—St. Joseph)

Race and Ethnic Groups. German stock 1.2 percent, Italian stock 0.3 percent.

Cities, 1970 Population. St. Joseph 73,037, part of Kansas City 66,749, Gladstone 23,045, Kirksville 15,374.

Universities, Enrollment. Missouri Western College (St. Joseph—2,884), Northeast Missouri State University (Kirksville—6,819), Northwest Missouri State University (Maryville—5,632), William Jewell College (Liberty—1,089).

Newspapers, Circulation. Kansas City newspapers circulate in portion of district.

Commercial Television Stations, Affiliation. KQTV, St. Joseph (ABC). Portions of district are located in Kansas City ADI, St. Joseph ADI, Omaha (Nebraska) ADI and Ottumwa (Iowa)-Kirksville ADI.

Plants and Offices, Products, Employment.

Pacific Car and Foundry Co., Kansas City (Trucks, special vehicles—1,100). **Ford Motor Co.**, Kansas City (Automobile bodies—2,000).

7th District

(Southwest—Springfield, Joplin)

Race and Ethnic Groups. German stock 0.8 percent, Italian stock 0.1 percent.

Cities, 1970 Population. Springfield 119,999, Joplin 39,227, Carthage 11,056.

Universities, Enrollment. Drury College (Springfield—2,469), Evangel College (Springfield—1,228), Missouri Southern State College (Joplin—3,158), School of the Ozarks (Point Lookout—1,115), Southwest Baptist College (Bolivar—1,160), Southwest Missouri State University (Springfield—9,478).

Commercial Television Stations, Affiliation. KODE-TV, Joplin (ABC); KUHI-TV, Joplin (CBS); KMTC, Springfield (ABC primary); KOLR, Springfield (CBS primary); KYTV, Springfield (NBC; ABC on per program basis). District is divided between Joplin-Pittsburg (Kansas) ADI and Springfield ADI.

Plants and Offices, Products, Employment.

Sperry Rand Corp., Joplin (Vickers Division—hydraulic pumps—1,300). **Springday Co.**, Springfield (Rubber transmission belts—1,400). **Zenith Radio Corp.**, Springfield (Televisions—3,000). **Owens-Illinois Inc.**, Springfield (Lilly Tulip Cup Division—paper containers—1,800). **St. Louis-San Francisco Railway Co.**, Springfield (Railroad—2,500). **City of Springfield**, Springfield (City government—1,120).

8th District

(Central—Columbia)

Race and Ethnic Groups. Blacks 2.7 percent. German stock 1.6 percent, Italian stock 0.2 percent.

Cities, 1970 Population. Columbia 58,594, Fort Leonard Wood 33,870, Jefferson City 32,271, Rolla 13,306.

Universities, Enrollment. Lincoln University (Jefferson City—2,620), Stephens College (Columbia—2,052), University of Missouri, Columbia (Columbia—21,942), University of Missouri, Rolla (Rolla—5,829).

Military Installations or Activities. Fort Leonard Wood, Waynesville.

Newspapers, Circulation. St. Louis newspapers circulate in portion of district.

Commercial Television Stations, Affiliation. KCBJ-TV, Columbia (ABC); KOMU-TV, Columbia (NBC

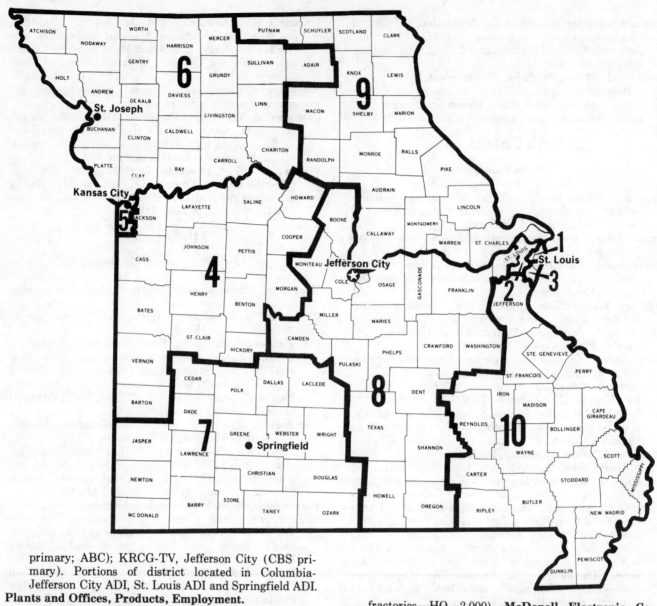

primary; ABC); KRCG-TV, Jefferson City (CBS primary). Portions of district located in Columbia-Jefferson City ADI, St. Louis ADI and Springfield ADI.

Plants and Offices, Products, Employment.

    Meramec Mining Co., Sullivan (Iron milling—1,040).

9th District

(Northeast—Florissant)

Race and Ethnic Groups. Blacks 2.6 percent. German stock 1.5 percent, Italian stock 0.6 percent.

Cities, 1970 Population. Florissant 65,999, St. Charles 31,830, Hannibal 18,541, Spanish Lake 15,712.

Universities, Enrollment. William Woods College (Fulton—1,200).

Newspapers, Circulation. St. Louis newspapers circulate in portion of district.

Commercial Television Stations, Affiliation. Portions of district are located in Ottumwa (Iowa)-Kirksville ADI, Quincy (Illinois)-Hannibal ADI, Columbia-Jefferson City ADI and St. Louis ADI.

Plants and Offices, Products, Employment.

    A. P. Green Refractories Co., Mexico (Clay re-

fractories—HQ—2,000). **McDonell Electronic Co.**, St. Charles (Electronic equipment—HQ—1,500).

10th District

(Southeast—Cape Girardeau)

Race and Ethnic Groups. Blacks 5.4 percent. German stock 0.7 percent, Italian stock 0.1 percent.

Cities, 1970 Population. Cape Girardeau 30,918, Poplar Bluff 16,653, Sikeston 14,642.

Universities, Enrollment. Southeast Missouri State University (Cape Girardeau—7,554).

Commercial Television Stations, Affiliation. KFVS-TV, Cape Girardeau (CBS). Portions of district are located in St. Louis ADI, Memphis (Tennessee) ADI, Paducah (Kentucky)-Cape Girardeau-Harrisburg (Illinois) ADI and Jonesboro (Arkansas) ADI.

Plants and Offices, Products, Employment.

    St. Joe Minerals Corp., Bonne Terre (Lead and zinc mining—1,500). **PPG Industries Inc.**, Crystal City (Paint, glass, chemicals—1,400).

MONTANA: TWO HOUSE SEATS, NO CHANGE

Montana legislators had an easy time in drawing new lines for their two congressional districts. The old districts varied only 1.8 percent from the ideal population.

This small disparity was reduced by transferring Teton County (population 6,116) from the 1st to the 2nd District. The legislation passed the state Senate Feb. 12, 1971, by a vote of 53-0. The House concurred Feb. 24, 78-20, and Gov. Forrest H. Anderson (D) signed the bill on March 3.

Because of Teton County's small size, its transfer from one district to another did not affect the political balance in either district.

District	Member Elected 1972	Winning Percentage	1970 Population	Percent Variance
1	Richard G. Shoup (R)	53.7	347,447	+ 0.0697
2	John Melcher (D)	76.1	346,962	—0.0700

1970 State Population: 694,409
Ideal District Population: 347,205

Election Results 1968-1972

Vote for U.S. Representative
(Adjusted to new district boundaries)

District	1968	1970	1972
1	73,487 D (53.7%)	62,974 R (50.5%)	88,373 R (53.7%)
	63,271 R (46.3%)	61,668 D (49.5%)	76,073 D (46.3%)
2	85,479 R (67.5%)	79,589 D (63.8%)	114,524 D (76.1%)
	41,239 D (32.5%)	45,166 R (36.2%)	36,063 R (23.9%)
State	148,750 R (56.5%)	141,257 D (56.6%)	190,597 D (60.5%)
	114,726 D (43.5%)	108,140 R (43.4%)	124,436 R (39.5%)

Voting Age Population

District	Voting Age Population	Voting Age Population 18, 19, 20	Voting Age Population 65 and Over	Median Age of Voting Age Population
1	223,324	20,324 (9.1%)	35,153 (15.7%)	43.6
2	217,251	16,128 (7.4%)	33,609 (15.5%)	43.6
State	440,583	36,457 (8.3%)	68,765 (15.6%)	43.6

Income and Occupation

District	Median Family Income	White Collar Workers	Blue Collar Workers	Service Workers	Farm Workers
1	$8,576	45.5%	31.5%	15.3%	7.7%
2	8,436	45.2	25.2	14.1	15.5
State	8,510	45.3	28.4	14.7	11.6

Education: School Years Completed

District	Completed 4 years of High School	Completed 4 years of College	Completed 5 years or less of School	Median School years completed
1	59.6%	11.9%	3.7%	12.3
2	58.8	10.1	4.0	12.3
State	59.2	11.0	3.8	12.3

Housing and Residential Patterns

	Housing		Urban-Suburban-Nonmetropolitan Breakdown		
District	Owner Occupied Units	Renter Occupied Units	Urban	Suburban	Nonmetropolitan
1	66.7%	33.3%	—	—	100.0%
2	64.7	35.3	35.1%	13.7%	51.2
State	65.7	34.3	17.5	6.8	75.6

1st District

(West—Missoula, Butte)

Race and Ethnic Groups. American Indians 3.0 percent.

Cities, 1970 Population. Missoula 29,368, Butte 23,424, Helena 22,703, Bozeman 18,648.

Universities, Enrollment. Carroll College (Helena—1,079), Montana State University (Bozeman—8,113), University of Montana (Missoula—8,800), Western Montana College (Dillon—1,008).

Military Installations or Activities. Kalispell Air Force Station, Kalispell.

Commercial Television Stations, Affiliation. KXLF-TV, Butte (CBS primary; ABC); KBLL-TV, Helena (NBC, ABC); KGVO-TV, Missoula (NBC, ABC). Majority of district is located in Missoula-Butte ADI. Portions of district are located in Helena ADI, Great Falls ADI, Spokane (Washington) ADI and Salt Lake City (Utah) ADI.

Plants and Offices, Products, Employment.
Anaconda Co., Anaconda (Zinc smelting and refining—2,500). **Anaconda Co.**, Butte (Copper mining—1,200). **Anaconda Co.**, Butte (Copper mining—1,060). **St. Regis Paper Co.**, Libby (J. Neils Lumber Co. Division—sawmill, planing mill, plywood—1,180).

2nd District

(East—Billings, Great Falls)

Race and Ethnic Groups. American Indians 4.6 percent.

Cities, 1970 Population. Billings, 61,654, (Great Falls 60,162, Havre 10,492.

Universities, Enrollment. College of Great Falls (Great Falls—1,031), Eastern Montana College (Billings—3,480), Northern Montana College (Havre—1,330).

Military Installations or Activities. Malstrom Air Force Base, Great Falls; Havre Air Force Station, Havre; Opheim Air Force Station, Opheim.

Commercial Television Stations, Affiliation. KOOK-TV, Billings (CBS primary, NBC on per program basis); KULR-TV, Billings (ABC, NBC); KXGN-TV, Glendive (CBS; NBC on per program basis); KRTV, Great Falls (NBC, CBS); KFBB-TV, Great Falls (ABC; NBC on per program basis); KYUS-TV, Miles City (NBC). Majority of district is divided between Billings ADI and Great Falls ADI. Portions of district are located in Glendive ADI, Minot (North Dakota)-Bismarck (North Dakota) ADI, Dickinson (North Dakota) ADI and Rapid City (South Dakota) ADI.

Plants and Offices, Products, Employment.
Anaconda Co., Great Falls (Copper and zinc rolling, drawing and extruding—1,620).

NEBRASKA: THREE HOUSE SEATS, NO CHANGE

No redistricting was necessary in Nebraska following the 1970 census because the population variances between the state's largest and smallest districts was only 0.1535 percent.

As in the case of Maine, population shifts between districts during the 1970s actually resulted in the districts becoming more equal in population. Based on the 1960 census, there was a 19.6502 percent variance between the largest and smallest districts.

District	Member Elected 1972	Winning Percentage	1970 Population	Percent Variance
1	Charles Thone (R)	64.2	494,335	—0.0529
2	John Y. McCollister (R)	63.9	495,095	+ 0.1006
3	Dave Martin (R)	69.6	494,361	—0.0477

	1970 State Population:	1,483,791
	Ideal District Population:	494,597

Election Results, 1968-1972

Vote for U.S. Representative
(Adjusted to new district boundaries)

District	1968	1970	1972
1	97,697 R (54.1%)	79,131 R (50.6%)	126,789 R (64.2%)
	78,374 D (43.4%)	36,240 D (23.2%)	70,570 D (35.8%)
2	87,683 R (55.2%)	69,671 R (51.9%)	114,669 R (63.9%)
	71,254 D (44.8%)	64,520 D (48.0%)	64,696 D (36.1%)
3	123,838 R (67.8%)	93,705 R (59.5%)	133,607 R (69.6%)
	58,728 D (32.2%)	63,698 D (47.4%)	58,378 D (30.4%)
State	309,218 R (59.2%)	242,507 R (54.1%)	375,065 R (66.0%)
	208,356 D (39.9%)	164,458 D (36.7%)	193,644 D (34.0%)

Voting Age Population

District	Voting Age Population	Voting Age Population 18, 19, 20	Voting Age Population 65 and Over	Median Age of Voting Age Population
1	335,859	31,576 (9.4%)	67,946 (20.2%)	45.2
2	312,613	25,586 (8.2%)	44,639 (14.3%)	40.8
3	325,644	22,581 (6.9%)	70,909 (21.8%)	47.7
State	974,141	79,739 (8.2%)	183,538 (18.8%)	44.5

Glossary and Sources

For a complete explanation of all terms used in this book and a list of source material, consult the details included in the Introduction.

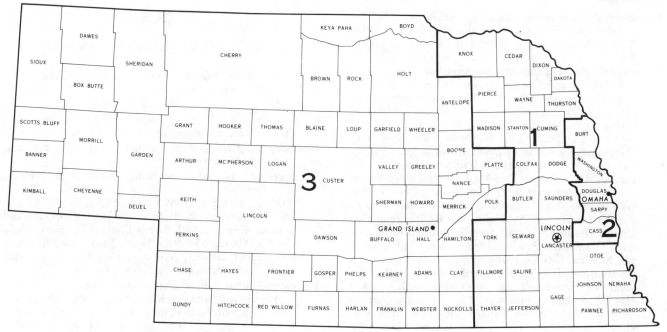

Income and Occupation

District	Median Family Income	White Collar Workers	Blue Collar Workers	Service Workers	Farm Workers
1	$ 8,203	42.6%	7.3%	14.9%	15.2%
2	10,163	52.9	30.9	13.8	2.4
3	7,549	37.9	27.0	13.9	21.2
State	8,562	44.4	28.4	14.2	13.0

Education: School Years Completed

District	Completed 4 years of High School	Completed 4 years of College	Completed 5 years or less of School	Median School years completed
1	58.2%	9.8%	3.3%	12.2
2	63.8	12.4	3.5	12.4
3	56.2	7.0	3.2	12.2
State	59.3	9.6	3.4	12.3

Housing and Residential Patterns

	Housing		Urban-Suburban-Nonmetropolitan Breakdown		
District	Owner Occupied Units	Renter Occupied Units	Urban	Suburban	Nonmetro-politan
1	67.8%	32.2%	30.3%	6.4%	63.3%
2	62.1	37.9	70.4	21.4	8.2
3	69.0	31.0	—	—	100.0
State	66.4	33.6	33.5	9.3	57.2

1st District

(East Central—Lincoln)

Race and Ethnic Groups. German stock 5.6 percent.

Cities, 1970 Population. Lincoln 149,596, Fremont 22,974, Norfolk 16,512, Beatrice 12,395.

Universities, Enrollment. Concordia Teachers College (Seward—1,737), Nebraska Wesleyan University (Lincoln—1,177), Peru State College (Peru—1,001), University of Nebraska (Lincoln—21,541), Wayne State College (Wayne—2,668).

Newspapers, Circulation. Omaha newspapers circulate in portion of district.

Commercial Television Stations, Affiliation. KOLN-TV, Lincoln (CBS). Portions of district are located in Lincoln-Hastings-Kearney ADI, Omaha ADI and Sioux City (Iowa) ADI.

Plants and Offices, Products, Employment.

Goodyear Tire & Rubber Co., Lincoln (Fabricated rubber products—1,800). **Iowa Beef Processors Inc.**, Dakota City (Meat packing—HQ—1,000). **City of Lincoln**, Lincoln (City government—2,000). **State of Nebraska**, Lincoln (State government—25,000).

2nd District

(East—Omaha)

Race and Ethnic Groups. Blacks 7.4 percent. German stock 2.8 percent.

Cities, 1970 Population. Omaha 348,302, Bellevue 19,511.

Universities, Enrollment. Creighton University (Omaha—4,172), University of Nebraska at Omaha (Omaha—12,711).

Military Installations or Activities. Offutt Air Force Base, Omaha.

Newspapers, Circulation. Omaha World-Herald (MxSat—129,477; ExSat—117,724). Omaha newspapers circulate throughout district.

Commercial Television Stations, Affiliation. KETV, Omaha (ABC); KMTV, Omaha (NBC); WOW-TV, Omaha (CBS). Entire district is located in Omaha ADI.

Plants and Offices, Products, Employment.

Sperry Rand Corp., Omaha (Vickers Division—hydraulic products—2,000). **Western Electric Co.**, Omaha (Switchgear equipment—7,000). **Western Electric Co.**, Omaha (Installation and distribution of switchgear equipment—1,000). **Wilson & Co.**, Omaha (Meat packing—at least 1,000). **Faberge Inc.**, Omaha (Tip Top Products Division—hair accessories—1,100). **Pamida Inc.**, Omaha (Wholesale general merchandise —1,400). **Supermarkets Interstate Inc.**, Omaha (Grocery stores—2,300). **Safeway Stores Inc.**, Omaha (Grocery stores—1,500). **Union Pacific Railroad Co.**, Omaha (Railroad—1,000). **Omaha Public Power District**, Omaha (Electricity distribution—1,340). **Northern Natural Gas Co.**, Omaha (Gas transmission and distribution—HQ—1,000). **Northwestern Bell Telephone Co.**, Omaha (Telephone company—HQ—3,000). **Mutual of Omaha Insurance Co.**, Omaha (Insurance —HQ—3,080). **United Benefit Life Insurance Co.**, Omaha (Insurance—HQ—1,400). **Bishop Clark Memorial Hospital**, Omaha (Hospital—1,400).

3rd District

(Central and West—Grand Island, Hastings)

Race and Ethnic Groups. German stock 4.3 percent.

Cities, 1970 Population. Grand Island 31,257, Hastings 23,535, North Platte 19,440, Kearney 19,174.

Universities, Enrollment. Chadron State College (Chadron—2,428), Kearney State College (Kearney—5,783).

Newspapers, Circulation. Omaha newspapers circulate in portion of district.

Commercial Television Stations, Affiliation. KHAS-TV, Hastings (NBC); KHOL-TV, Kearney (ABC); KOMC, McCook (NBC); KNOP-TV, North Platte (NBC). Portions of district are located in Lincoln-Hasting-Kearney ADI, North Platte ADI, Sioux Falls (South Dakota)-Mitchell (South Dakota) ADI, Rapid City (South Dakota) ADI, Cheyenne (Wyoming) ADI and Wichita (Kansas)-Hutchinson (Kansas) ADI.

Plants and Offices, Products, Employment.

Mason and Hanger Silas Mason Co., Grand Island (Ammunition—1,400). **Land O' Lakes Inc.**, Columbus (Al Fa Meal Division—dehydrated alfalfa —1,230).

NEW HAMPSHIRE: TWO HOUSE SEATS, NO CHANGE

No major controversy arose when new congressional district lines were first drawn by the New Hampshire legislature in the fall of 1971. The state's two districts had varied by only 2.4 percent from the ideal district population, so only minor adjustments were necessary.

A redistricting bill passed both the state Senate and the state House on Sept. 28, 1971, by voice vote. It was signed by Gov. Walter R. Peterson (R) on Sept. 29.

Among the minor adjustments made by the bill was the transfer of several townships in southern Coos County from the 2nd to the 1st District. In early 1972, however, objections were raised over the splitting of Coos County and a new redistricting bill placed the Coos County townships back in the 2nd District. The new redistricting legislation became law March 1, 1972.

District	Member Elected 1972	Winning Percentage	1970 Population	Percent Variance
1	Louis C. Wyman (R)	72.9	367,075	—0.4787
2	James C. Cleveland (R)	67.6	370,606	+ 0.4785
	1970 State Population:		737,681	
	Ideal District Population:		368,841	

Election Results, 1968-1972

Vote for U.S. Representative
(Adjusted to new district boundaries)

District	1968	1970	1972
1	91,919 R (64.3%)	73,227 R (67.4%)	115,732 R (72.9%)
	51,027 D (35.7%)	35,372 D (32.6%)	42,996 D (27.1%)
2	96,959 R (69.3%)	73,162 R (69.6%)	107,021 R (67.6%)
	42,874 D (30.7%)	31,884 D (30.4%)	51,259 D (32.4%)
State	188,878 R (66.8%)	146,389 R (68.5%)	222,753 R (70.3%)
	93,901 D (33.2%)	67,256 D (31.5%)	94,255 D (29.7%)

Voting Age Population

District	Voting Age Population	Voting Age Population 18, 19, 20	Voting Age Population 65 and Over	Median Age of Voting Age Population
1	239,396	19,023 (7.9%)	38,773 (16.2%)	43.2
2	243,259	20,297 (8.3%)	39,673 (16.3%)	43.3
State	482,655	39,320 (8.1%)	78,446 (16.3%)	43.2

Income and Occupation

District	Median Family Income	White Collar Workers	Blue Collar Workers	Service Workers	Farm Workers
1	$9,631	44.5%	42.4%	12.1%	1.0%
2	9,736	44.6	41.9	12.1	1.4
State	9,682	44.6	42.1	12.1	1.2

Education: School Years Completed

District	Completed 4 years of High School	Completed 4 years of College	Completed 5 years or less of School	Median School years completed
1	57.1%	10.5%	3.3%	12.2
2	58.0	11.2	3.5	12.2
State	57.6	10.9	3.4	12.2

1st District

(East—Manchester)

Race and Ethnic Groups. Canadian stock 12.9 percent.

Cities, 1970 Population. Manchester 87,754, Portsmouth 26,188, Dover 21,046, Rochester 17,938.

Universities, Enrollment. University of New Hampshire (Durham—10,517), St. Anselm's College (Manchester—1,674).

Military Installations or Activities. Naval Disciplinary Command, Portsmouth; Naval Hospital, Portsmouth; Portsmouth Naval Shipyard, Portsmouth; Pease Air Force Base, Portsmouth.

Newspapers, Circulation. Manchester Union Leader (All day—62,861).

Commercial Television Stations, Affiliation. WMUR-TV, Manchester (ABC). Manchester has no ADI of its own. Majority of district is located in Boston (Massachusetts) ADI. Portion of district is located in Portland (Maine)-Poland Springs (Maine) ADI.

Plants and Offices, Products, Employment.

Melville Shoe Corp., Manchester (J. F. McElwain Co. Division—shoes—1,250). **Davidson Rubber Co. Inc.**, Dover (Synthetic rubber products—1,600). **Scott & Williams Inc.**, Laconia (Knitting machines—1,000). **Sanders Associates Inc.**, Manchester (Electronic equipment—1,000). **Moore Business Forms Inc.**, Dover (Kidder Machinery Division—printing and paper industry machinery—1,120).

2nd District

(West—Nashua, Concord)

Race and Ethnic Groups. Canadian stock 13.3 percent.

Cities, 1970 Population. Nashua 55,820, Concord 30,022, Keene 20,467, Berlin 15,256.

Universities, Enrollment. Dartmouth College (Hanover—3,279), Franklin Pierce College (Rindge—1,077), Keene State College (Keene—2,706), New England College (Henniker—1,190), Plymouth State College (Plymouth—2,637).

Newspapers, Circulation. Manchester and Boston (Mass.) newspapers circulate in portion of district.

Commercial Television Stations, Affiliation. WRLH-TV, Lebanon (NBC on per program basis). Lebanon has no ADI of its own. Majority of district is located in Boston (Massachusetts) ADI. Portion of district is located in Portland (Maine)-Poland Springs (Maine) ADI.

Plants and Offices, Products, Employment.

Brown Co., Berlin (Pulp and paper products—1,920). **Nashua Corp.**, Nashua (Gubelman Charts Division—HQ—specialized paper products—1,500). **Improved Machinery Inc.**, Nashua (Paper industry machinery—1,200). **Joy Manufacturing Co.**, Claremont (Mining machinery—1,000). **MPB Corp.**, Keene (Ball bearings—HQ—1,000). **Sanders Associates Inc.**, Nashua (Electronic systems and equipment, research and development—HQ—5,900). **Granite State Rubber Co.**, Berlin (Rubber footwear—1,100). **Melville Shoe Corp.**, Nashua (J. F. McElwain Co. Division—shoes—1,100). **Rumford Press Inc.**, Concord (Commercial printing, bookbinding—1,000).

Housing and Residential Patterns

District	Housing		Urban-Suburban-Nonmetropolitan Breakdown		
	Owner Occupied Units	Renter Occupied Units	Urban	Suburban	Nonmetropolitan
1	66.7%	33.3%	23.9%	7.5%	68.6%
2	69.8	30.2	15.1	8.3	76.6
State	68.2	31.8	19.5	7.9	72.6

NEW JERSEY: FIFTEEN HOUSE SEATS, NO CHANGE

Despite three and a half months' effort, the New Jersey Legislature failed to pass a congressional redistricting bill by a court-ordered April 12, 1972, deadline. Within an hour after the deadline's expiration, the three-judge federal court imposed its own congressional district lines, based on the Republican plan passed earlier by the state Senate. *(Map p. 123)*

The main impact of the redistricting was to eliminate a Democratic urban district in the Bayonne-Jersey City area and to create a new Republican-oriented suburban-rural district in the northern and western part of the state. This threw two incumbents into the same district—Cornelius E. Gallagher (D) of Bayonne and Dominick V. Daniels (D) of Jersey City. Gallagher was indicted April 10, 1972, on charges of income tax evasion, perjury and conspiracy. He ran third in the Democratic congressional primary June 6, 1972.

The new district elected a Republican, giving that party a gain of one seat in the delegation.

Another result of the new plan was the reconstitution of the 10th District, which was redrawn to include all Newark, East Orange, Harrison and Glen Ridge, producing a district about 51.8 percent black. The incumbent, Peter W. Rodino Jr. (D), was reportedly considering running in the neighboring 11th District, represented by Joseph G. Minish (D). But on April 24, 1972, he announced his candidacy for re-election in the 10th. He won the June 6 primary against three black opponents.

Twelve of the state's 21 counties were divided by the new map, compared with seven under the old plan. However, the cities of Newark and Jersey City now lie wholly within their respective congressional districts; previously they were divided.

With the exception of the Republican gain in the new northwestern district, the party balance remained the same. All the remaining 14 districts had voting majorities favoring the incumbent party, based on the 1970 congressional vote within the newly aligned district boundaries.

Election Results, 1968-1972

Vote for U.S. Representative
(Adjusted to new district boundaries)

District	1968	1970	1972
1	105,967 R (58.4%)	83,251 R (61.4%)	97,650 R (52.5%)
	73,505 D (40.5%)	51,928 D (38.3%)	87,492 D (47.1%)
2	106,272 R (56.7%)	82,983 R (53.4%)	133,096 R (65.7%)
	80,668 D (43.0%)	71,866 D (46.4%)	69,374 D (34.3%)
3	99,681 D (57.5%)	77,187 D (53.8%)	103,893 D (53.0%)
	73,032 R (42.2%)	63,533 R (44.3%)	92,285 R (47.0%)
4	88,821 D (56.3%)	73,414 D (59.4%)	98,206 D (58.0%)
	68,471 R (43.4%)	49,116 R (39.7%)	71,030 R (42.0%)
5	120,501 R (65.7%)	92,293 R (63.4%)	127,310 R (62.0%)
	60,139 D (32.3%)	51,437 D (35.3%)	78,076 D (38.0%)
6	108,911 R (65.5%)	65,701 R (52.4%)	123,610 R (62.8%)
	56,774 D (34.1%)	57,030 D (45.5%)	71,113 D (36.1%)
7	120,812 R (59.6%)	89,444 R (55.6%)	124,365 R (58.0%)
	79,664 D (39.3%)	71,235 D (44.3%)	85,712 D (39.9%)
8	103,831 D (60.9%)	78,637 D (61.1%)	104,381 D (63.1%)
	65,750 R (38.6%)	50,077 R (38.9%)	61,073 R (36.9%)
9	100,700 R (49.3%)	92,460 D (55.7%)	119,543 D (55.8%)
	97,846 D (47.9%)	71,837 D (43.2%)	94,747 R (44.2%)
10	90,992 D (71.5%)	66,321 D (75.9%)	94,308 D (79.7%)
	33,537 R (26.3%)	20,923 R (24.0%)	23,949 R (20.3%)
11	115,154 D (55.0%)	94,997 D (59.3%)	120,277 D (57.5%)
	92,202 R (44.0%)	65,245 R (40.7%)	82,957 R (39.7%)
12	127,121 R (65.2%)	89,111 R (58.0%)	127,690 R (63.5%)
	64,665 D (33.1%)	62,804 D (40.9%)	72,758 D (36.1%)
13	105,010 R (59.3%)	76,207 R (53.8%)	109,640 R (55.7%)
	70,669 D (39.9%)	64,358 D (45.4%)	84,492 D (42.9%)
14	110,061 R (59.2%)	97,518 R (72.1%)	103,089 R (61.2%)
	58,315 R (31.4%)	34,758 R (25.7%)	57,683 R (34.3%)
15	97,428 D (55.1%)	87,596 D (63.2%)	98,155 D (52.3%)
	77,164 R (43.6%)	50,249 R (36.3%)	89,400 R (47.7%)
State	1,363,765 R (50.5%)	1,098,788 D (52.3%)	1,416,485 R (50.0%)
	1,289,898 D (47.8%)	984,728 R (46.9%)	1,390,869 D (49.1%)

District	Member Elected 1972	Winning Percentage	1970 Population	Percent Variance
1	John E. Hunt (R)	52.5	478,002	+ 0.0259
2	Charles W. Sandman Jr. (R)	65.7	478,126	+ 0.0518
3	James J. Howard (D)	53.0	475,599	— 0.4768
4	Frank Thompson Jr. (D)	58.0	478,045	+ 0.0349
5	Peter H.B. Frelinghuysen (R)	62.0	478,007	+ 0.0269
6	Edwin B. Forsythe (R)	62.8	478,137	+ 0.0541
7	William B. Widnall (R)	58.0	479,999	+ 0.4438
8	Robert A. Roe (D)	63.1	478,369	+ 0.1027
9	Henry Helstoski (D)	55.8	478,427	+ 0.1148
10	Peter W. Rodino Jr. (D)	79.7	478,217	+ 0.0709
11	Joseph G. Minish (D)	57.5	475,297	— 0.5400
12	Matthew J. Rinaldo (R)	63.5	477,887	+ 0.0018
13	Joseph J. Maraziti (R)	55.7	478,164	+ 0.0598
14	Dominick V. Daniels (D)	61.2	477,939	+ 0.0127
15	Edward J. Patten (D)	52.3	477,949	+ 0.0148

1970 State Population: 7,168,164

Ideal District Population 477,878

Voting Age Population

District	Voting Age Population	Voting Age Population 18, 19, 20	Voting Age Population 65 and Over	Median Age of Voting Age Population
1	306,376	21,951 (7.2%)	40,932 (13.4%)	43.2
2	324,432	18,916 (5.8%)	69,652 (21.5%)	48.2
3	308,309	21,617 (7.0%)	52,793 (17.1%)	43.9
4	315,122	32,680 (10.4%)	36,440 (11.6%)	40.1
5	311,559	21,057 (6.8%)	36,620 (11.8%)	42.6
6	298,622	17,218 (5.8%)	39,813 (13.3%)	42.8
7	318,425	19,942 (6.3%)	41,878 (13.2%)	45.0
8	326,680	20,419 (6.3%)	50,832 (15.6%)	45.0
9	335,979	18,810 (5.6%)	50,348 (15.0%)	46.0
10	308,839	22,515 (7.3%)	43,633 (14.1%)	41.7
11	340,671	20,629 (6.1%)	59,213 (17.4%)	47.3
12	326,210	18,874 (5.8%)	48,548 (14.9%)	46.0
13	305,329	19,034 (6.2%)	41,446 (13.6%)	42.9
14	334,733	22,922 (6.8%)	53,889 (16.1%)	45.4
15	315,352	24,989 (7.9%)	32,710 (10.4%)	41.7
State	4,777,221	321,542 (6.7%)	699,024 (14.6%)	44.1

Income and Occupation

District	Median Family Income	White Collar Workers	Blue Collar Workers	Service Workers	Farm Workers
1	$10,314	45.7%	41.9%	11.4%	1.0%
2	9,039	42.5	40.8	14.8	1.9
3	11,291	56.4	30.7	12.3	0.6
4	11,086	49.3	38.4	11.5	0.8
5	14,218	64.5	25.8	9.2	0.5
6	11,689	59.5	30.5	9.4	0.6
7	14,257	65.0	26.5	8.3	0.2
8	10,783	46.0	43.6	10.1	0.3
9	12,428	57.9	33.5	8.4	0.1
10	8,300	38.5	46.1	15.2	0.2
11	12,508	60.2	29.5	10.2	0.1
12	12,787	56.3	33.8	9.7	0.2
13	11,731	51.6	37.0	9.7	1.7
14	9,607	45.4	42.7	11.8	0.1
15	11,793	49.1	40.9	9.8	0.2
State	11,403	52.7	36.1	10.7	0.5

Education: School Years Completed

District	Completed 4 years of High School	Completed 4 years of College	Completed 5 years or less of School	Median School years completed
1	44.6%	7.0%	7.2%	11.3
2	43.5	6.1	8.2	11.1
3	59.2	13.7	5.0	12.3
4	51.6	10.2	7.2	12.1
5	69.0	24.5	3.9	12.6
6	59.9	13.3	3.9	12.3
7	64.2	18.0	3.8	12.4
8	42.5	7.9	10.1	10.9
9	52.8	12.2	6.2	12.1
10	37.7	6.1	12.9	10.5
11	56.2	14.6	5.7	12.2
12	58.7	15.2	6.1	12.3
13	58.9	12.6	3.9	12.3
14	37.1	5.7	11.1	10.3
15	53.1	10.2	12.1	12.1
State	52.5	11.8	6.8	12.1

Housing and Residential Patterns

	Housing		Urban-Suburban-Nonmetropolitan Breakdown		
District	Owner Occupied Units	Renter Occupied Units	Urban	Suburban	Nonmetro-politan
1	72.4%	27.6%	—	100.0%	—
2	69.6	30.4	28.7%	46.7	24.6%
3	69.5	30.5	—	——	100.0
4	66.8	33.2	21.9	45.2	32.9
5	71.7	28.3	—	53.9	46.1
6	77.9	22.1	—	78.2	21.8
7	74.2	25.8	—	100.0	—
8	52.2	47.8	59.0	41.0	—
9	55.1	44.9	—	100.0	—
10	22.7	77.3	80.0	20.0	—

	Housing		Urban-Suburban-Nonmetropolitan Breakdown		
District	Owner Occupied Units	Renter Occupied Units	Urban	Suburban	Nonmetro-politan
11	56.7	43.3	—	100.0	—
12	62.7	37.3	—	100.0	—
13	76.4	23.6	—	69.2	30.8
14	28.9	71.1	54.5	45.5	—
15	66.4	33.6	—	9.1	90.9
State	60.9	39.1	16.3	60.6	23.1

1st District

(Southwest—Camden)

Race and Ethnic Groups. Blacks 12.5 percent. Italian stock 5.4 percent, British stock 2.0 percent.

Cities, 1970 Population. Camden 102,553, Bellmawr 15,618, Gloucester City 14,717, Haddonfield 13,118.

Universities, Enrollment. Glassboro State College (Glassboro—11,335).

Military Installations or Activities. Gibbsboro Air Force Station, Gibbsboro.

Newspapers, Circulation. Camden Courier-Post (Eve—124,014). Philadelphia newspapers also circulate throughout district.

Commercial Television Stations, Affiliation. Entire district is located in Philadelphia ADI.

Plants and Offices, Products, Employment.
Campbell Soup Co., Camden (Headquarters—1,300). Campbell Soup Co., Camden (Canning—3,360). RCA Corp., Camden (Defense Communications System Division—communications systems—3,700). Columbia Broadcasting System, Pitman (CBS Records—records—1,500). Owens Corning Fiberglass Corp., Barrington (Fiberglass insulation—1,200). E. I. du Pont de Nemours & Co., Gibbstown (Explosives—1,700). Mobil Oil Corp., Paulsboro (Petroleum refining—1,300).

2nd District

(South—Atlantic City, Vineland)

Race and Ethnic Groups. Blacks 13.1 percent. Italian stock 5.4 percent, German stock 2.6 percent.

Cities, 1970 Population. Atlantic City 47,867, Vineland 47,621, Millville 21,286, Bridgeton 20,426.

Military Installations or Activities. Naval Air Station, Lakehurst.

Newspapers, Circulation. Atlantic City Press (Morn—63,162). In addition Philadelphia papers circulate in portion of district.

Commercial Television Stations, Affiliation. WCMC-TV, Wildwood (NBC). Wildwood has no separate ADI. Most of district is located in Philadelphia ADI. Portion of district is located in New York City ADI.

Plants and Offices, Products, Employment.
Lenox China Inc., Pomona (China—1,300). Wheaton Industries, Millville (Wheaton Glass Co. Division—HQ—glass containers and machinery—

3,000). **Owens-Illinois Inc.,** Bridgeton (Glass Container Division—glass containers—2,500). **Owens-Illinois Inc.,** Vineland (Consumers & Technical Parts Division—scientific glassware—2,200). **Kerr Glass Manufacturing Corp.,** Millville (Glass containers—1,240). **Anchor Hocking Corp.,** Salem (Glass containers—1,300). **E.I. du Pont de Nemours & Co.,** Deepwater (Chambers Works—elastomer, organic chemicals—6,500). **Seabrook Farms Co. Inc.,** Bridgeton (Frozen foods—at least 1,000).

3rd District

(Central Coast—Long Branch, Asbury Park)

Race and Ethnic Groups. Blacks 8.2 percent. Italian stock 4.8 percent, German stock 3.1 percent, British stock 3.0 percent.

Cities, 1970 Population. Long Branch 31,773, Lakewood 17,873, Asbury Park 16,533, Point Pleasant 15,968.

Universities, Enrollment. Monmouth College (West Long Branch—5,020).

Military Installations or Activities. Fort Monmouth, Oceanport.

Newspapers, Circulation. Asbury Park Press (Eve-83,510). In addition, New York City papers circulate in portions of district.

Commercial Television Stations, Affiliation. Entire district is located in New York City ADI.

Plants and Offices, Products, Employment.
Harvard Industries Inc., Farmingdale (Electronic devices, equipment, engineering—HQ—1,000). **Bell Telephone Laboratories,** Holmdel (Telephone lab—5,000). **Owens-Illinois Corp.,** Holmdel (Lily Tulip Cup Division—sanitary food containers—2,000). **Monmouth Medical Center,** Long Branch (Hospital—1,400).

4th District

(Central—Trenton)

Race and Ethnic Groups. Blacks 13.0 percent. Italian stock 5.4 percent, Polish stock 3.5 percent, German stock 2.5 percent.

Cities, 1970 Population. Trenton 104,534, Old Bridge 25,167, Mercerville-Hamilton Square 24,453, Fort Dix 23,016.

Universities, Enrollment. Rider College (Trenton—5,920).

Military Installations or Activities. Fort Dix, Wrightstown (part); McGuire Air Force Base, Wrightstown.

Newspapers, Circulation. Trenton Times (ExSat—78,665), Trentonian (Morn—57,187).

Commercial Television Stations, Affiliation. District is divided between Philadelphia and New York City ADIs.

Plants and Offices, Products, Employment.
CF & I Steel Corp., Roebling (Metal products—2,000). **Thiokol Chemical Corp.,** Trenton (Panelyte Industrial Division—rocket propellant—1,000). **Thiokol Chemical Corp.,** Trenton (Plastics—1,000). **De-Laval Turbine Inc.,** Trenton (Steam turbines—2,300). **General Motors Corp.,** Trenton (Fisher Body Ternstedt Division—hardware trim & accessories—at least

2,000). **Circle F Industries Inc.,** Trenton (Electric wiring devices—HQ—at least 1,700). **McGraw Hill Inc.,** Hightstown (F. W. Dodge Division—special publications—2,000).

5th District

(North Central—Morristown, Princeton)

Race and Ethnic Groups. Blacks 3.4 percent. Italian stock 6.1 percent, German stock 3.2 percent, British stock 2.9 percent, Polish stock 2.8 percent.

Cities, 1970 Population. North Plainfield 21,795, Morristown 17,661, Madison 16,709, Middlesex 15,037.

Universities, Enrollment. Drew University (Madison—1,691), Princeton University (Princeton—5,400), Farleigh Dickinson University (Madison Branch Campus—Madison—enrollment not available—see main campus listing, 9th District).

AEC-Owned, Contractor-Operated Facilities. Princeton-Pennsylvania Accelerator, Princeton Plasma Physics Lab, Princeton.

Newspapers, Circulation. Bridgewater Courier-News, Somerville (Eve—59,961). In addition, New York City and Newark papers circulate in portion of district.

Commercial Television Stations, Affiliation. Nearly entire district is located in New York City ADI. Small portion is located in Philadelphia ADI.

Plants and Offices, Products, Employment.
Warner-Lambert Co., Morris Plains (Headquarters—2,300). **Ortho Pharmaceutical Corp.,** Raritan (Pharmaceuticals—1,700). **Ethicon Inc.,** Somerville (Surgical supplies—HQ—2,000). **Allied Chemical Corp.,** Morristown (Industrial Chemical Division—industrial chemicals, plastics—3,200). **Research-Cottrell Inc.,** Bound Brook (Precipitation equipment—HQ—1,000). **RCA Corp.,** Princeton (David Sarnoff Research Center—research laboratories—1,500). **RCA Corp.,** Somerville (RCA Semiconductors Division—semiconductors—2,470). **Automatic Switch Co.,** Florham Park (Automatic switches, etc.—HQ—1,390). **Foster Wheeler Corp.,** Livingston (Headquarters—1,600). **Johns Manville Products Corp.,** Manville (Asbestos building products—1,500). **Vornado Inc.,** Hanover (Warehouse—1,000). **Educational Testing Service,** Princeton (Educational testing—1,000).

6th District

(South Central)

Race and Ethnic Groups. Blacks 4.5 percent. Italian stock 4.5 percent, German stock 2.9 percent, British stock 2.5 percent.

Cities, 1970 Population. Collingswood 17,425, Moorestown-Lenola 14,192, Marlton 10,209.

Military Installations or Activities. Fort Dix (part).

Newspapers, Circulation. Camden and Philadelphia papers circulate throughout most of district.

Commercial Television Stations, Affiliation. Major portion of district is located in Philadelphia ADI. Portion of district is located in New York City ADI.

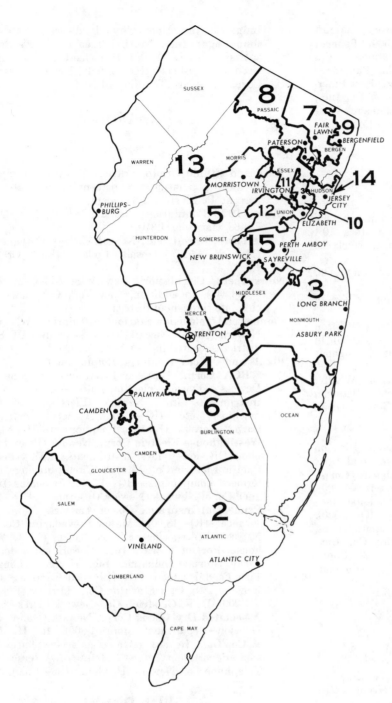

Key

Small numbers on map indicate the
names of the following cities and places:

1 Clifton

2 Passaic

3 Newark

Plants and Offices, Products, Employment.

RCA Corp., Moorestown (Electronic communications systems—2,700). **Toms River Chemical Corp.**, Toms River (Chemicals and dyes—1,370). **Lehigh Press Inc.**, Pennsauken (Offset printing—1,030).

7th District

(North—Fair Lawn, Hackensack)

Race and Ethnic Groups. Blacks 3.1 percent. Italian stock 8.7 percent, German stock 4.5 percent, Polish stock 2.9 percent, British stock 2.7 percent.

Cities, 1970 Population. Fair Lawn 39,267, Hackensack 37,007, Paramus 30,439, Ridgewood 28,474.

Universities, Enrollment. Farleigh Dickinson University (Teaneck Branch Campus—Teaneck—enrollment not available, see main campus listing, 9th District).

Newspapers, Circulation. Bergen County Record, Hackensack (ExSat—153,804). In addition New York City newspapers circulate throughout district.

Commercial Television Stations, Affiliation. Entire district is located in New York City ADI.

Plants and Offices, Products, Employment.

Terminal Construction Corp., Woodridge (Construction—1,000). **Ford Motor Co.**, Mahwah (Autos, trucks, tractors—5,000). **Bendix Corp.**, Hasbrouck

Heights (Navigation and Control Division—aircraft navigation and control equipment—6,500). **Federal Electric Corp.**, Paramus (Communications equipment—HQ—1,000). **National Biscuit Co.**, Fair Lawn (Biscuits, etc.—1,500). **Grand Union Co.**, East Paterson (Headquarters—1,000). **R. H. Macy & Co. Inc.**, Paramus (Department store—1,400). **Hackensack Hospital Association,** Hackensack (Hospital—1,400).

8th District

(North—Paterson)

Race and Ethnic Groups. Blacks 10.5 percent. Spanish heritage population 4.1 percent. Italian stock 10.1 percent, Polish stock 5.4 percent, German stock 3.0 percent, Russian stock 2.5 percent.
Cities, 1970 Population. Paterson 144,848, Clifton 82,448, Passaic 55,131, Garfield 30,698.
Universities, Enrollment. William Paterson College of New Jersey (Wayne—7,139).
Newspapers, Circulation. Herald-News, Passaic-Clifton (ExSat—94,837), Paterson News (All day—75,606). In addition, New York City papers circulate throughout district.
Commercial Television Stations, Affiliation. WXTV, Paterson (Spanish language broadcasts). Paterson has no separate ADI. Entire district is located in New York City ADI.
Plants and Offices, Products, Employment.
Raybestos-Manhattan, Passaic (Passaic Division—industrial rubber products—1,300). **Uniroyal Inc.**, Passaic (Rubber products—2,000). **Felsway Corp.**, Paterson (Footwear, handbags, hosiery, etc.—1,000). **American Cynamid Co.**, Wayne (Headquarters—1,500). **Shulton Inc.**, Clifton (Toiletries—HQ—1,500). **Yardley of London Inc.**, Paterson (Perfumes, soaps, toiletries—HQ—1,080). **Continental Can Co. Inc.**, Paterson (Metal containers warehouse—1,200). **Popular Services Inc.**, Passaic (Mail order general merchandise—HQ—1,700).

9th District

(North—Union City, Bergenfield)

Race and Ethnic Groups. Italian stock 12.3 percent, German stock 5.1 percent, Irish stock 2.7 percent, Polish stock 2.6 percent, British stock 2.5 percent.
Cities, 1970 Population. Union City 56,806, Bergenfield 32,315, Fort Lee 29,725, Englewood 24,282.
Universities, Enrollment. Farleigh Dickinson University (Rutherford—20,130 total enrollment).
Newspapers, Circulation. Hudson Dispatch, Union City (Morn—55,834). In addition, newspapers from Hackensack and New York City circulate in portions of district.
Commercial Television Stations, Affiliation. Entire district is located in New York City ADI.
Plants and Offices, Products, Employment.
Becton, Dickinson & Co., East Rutherford (Medical, surgical instruments—HQ—1,800). **Lever Bros. Co.**, Edgewater (Soap, dentrifices—1,000). **Olla**

Industries Inc., Union City (Handbags—1,400). **Jonathan Logan Inc.**, North Bergen (Women's dresses, sportswear—HQ—1,200). **Prentice-Hall Inc.**, Englewood (Publishers—HQ—2,000). **Nelson Resource Corp.**, Secaucus (Trucking—1,500).

10th District

(Newark)

Race and Ethnic Groups. Blacks 51.8 percent. Spanish heritage population 5.8 percent. Italian stock 6.8 percent, Polish stock 1.8 percent.
Cities, 1970 Population. Newark 382,381, East Orange 75,468, Harrison 11,810.
Universities, Enrollment. Newark College of Engineering (Newark—4,527), Upsala College (East Orange—1,954).
Newspapers, Circulation. Newark Star-Ledger (MxSat—343,844). In addition, New York City newspapers circulate throughout district.
Commercial Television Stations, Affiliation. WNJV-TV, Newark (None). Newark has no separate ADI. Entire district is located in New York City ADI.
Plants and Offices, Products, Employment.
RCA Corp., Harrison Electronic Components & Devices Division—electron tubes—4,000). **Weston Instruments Inc.**, Newark (Electrical, electronic machinery etc.—HQ—1,500). **General Instrument Corp.**, Newark (Electrical equipment—HQ—1,000). **Westinghouse Electric Corp.**, Newark (Relay Instrument Division—relays, instruments—1,650). **Federal Pacific Electric Co.**, Newark (Circuit breakers, transformers, components—HQ—1,750). **Firemens Insurance Co. of Newark**, Newark (Insurance—HQ—2,000). **Prudential Insurance Co. of America**, Newark (Insurance—HQ—18,000). **Maher Stevedoring Co. Inc.**, Newark (Stevedoring—at least 2,000). **I T O Warehouse, Port of Newark Inc.**, Newark (Stevedoring—1,000). **Sternco Industries Inc.**, Harrison (Long Life Fish Food Products Co.—fish food, supplies, aquariums—1,150). **Otis Elevator Co.**, Harrison (Elevators—1,200). **B. F. Goodrich Co.**, Newark (Tires—6,000). **Associated Dry Goods Corp.**, Newark (Hahne & Co. Division—department store—1,500). **R. H. Macy & Co. Inc.**, Newark (Bamberger's New Jersey Division—department store—3,500). **New Jersey Bell Telephone Co.**, Newark (Headquarters—2,500).

11th District

(Essex County—Newark suburbs)

Race and Ethnic Groups. Blacks 6.7 percent. Italian stock 11.1 percent, Polish stock 3.9 percent, Russian stock 3.6 percent, German stock 3.4 percent, British stock 3.1 percent.
Cities, 1970 Population. Irvington 59,739, Bloomfield 52,002, Montclair 44,030, West Orange 43,782.
Universities, Enrollment. Bloomfield College (Bloomfield—1,698), Montclair State College (Upper Montclair—10,453), Seton Hall University (South Orange—9,609).
Newspapers, Circulation. Newark and New York City newspapers circulate throughout district.

Commercial Television Stations, Affiliation. Entire district is located in New York City ADI.

Plants and Offices, Products, Employment.

Bankers National Life Insurance Co., Montclair (Insurance—1,020). **International Telephone & Telegraph Corp.**, Nutley (Communications equipment—1,900). **International Telephone & Telegraph Corp.**, Nutley (ITT Defense Space Group Division—communications equipment—3,000). **Hoffman-La Roche Inc.**, Nutley (Pharmaceuticals, medicine, chemicals—HQ—5,000). **Walter Kidde & Co. Inc.**, Belleville (Aerospace testing, medical instruments—1,300). **Lummus Co.**, Bloomfield (Designing, engineering, construction—HQ—2,500). **General Precision Systems Inc.**, Little Falls (Precision products—at least 1,010). **Mountainside Hospital**, Montclair (Hospital—1,200).

12th District

(Union County)

Race and Ethnic Groups. Blacks 11.5 percent. Italian stock 6.9 percent, Polish stock 4.1 percent, German stock 3.9 percent, Russian stock 2.9 percent, British stock 2.5 percent.

Cities, 1970 Population. Elizabeth 112,701, Plainfield 46,867, Westfield 33,716, Rahway 29,104.

Universities, Enrollment. Newark State College (Union—12,059).

Newspapers, Circulation. Elizabeth Journal (ExSat—66,524). In addition, Newark and New York City newspapers circulate throughout district.

Commercial Television Stations, Affiliation. Entire district is located in New York City ADI.

Plants and Offices, Products, Employment.

Amerace Esna Corp., Union (Elastic Stop Nut Division—nuts, gages, devices—1,300). **Phelps Dodge Copper Products**, Elizabeth (American Copper Products Division—copper products—1,000). **Lockheed Electronics Inc.**, Plainfield (Military electronic systems—HQ—1,000). **Thomas & Betts Corp.**, Elizabeth (Electric devices—HQ—1,000). **General Motors Corp.**, Clark (Motor vehicle bearings—3,000). **Schering Corp.**, Union (Ethical drug products—1,350). **CIBA-Geigy Corp.**, Summit (CIBA Pharmaceutical Division—pharmaceuticals—2,000). **Merck & Co. Inc.**, Rahway (Chemicals & pharmaceuticals—HQ—3,000). **Simmons Co.**, Elizabeth (Bedding—1,200). **Singer Co.**, Elizabeth (North Atlantic Consumer Products Division—sewing machines—1,050). **Topper Corp.**, Elizabeth (Toys & dolls—HQ—2,500). **Bell Telephone Laboratories**, Murray Hill (Developmental research—HQ—3,800). **Pall Trincor Corp.**, Union (Machinery—1,030). **Good Deal Warehouse Corp.**, Elizabeth (Groceries warehouse—1,000). **Wakefern Food Corp.**, Elizabeth (Wholesale groceries—HQ—at least 1,190).

13th District

(West—Phillipsburg)

Race and Ethnic Groups. Italian stock 4.4 percent, German stock 3.6 percent, British stock 2.7 percent.

Cities, 1970 Population. Phillipsburg 17,847, Dover 15,037.

Universities, Enrollment. Trenton State College (Trenton—10,929).

Military Installations or Activities. Picatinny Arsenal, Dover.

Newspapers, Circulation. Trenton and New York City newspapers circulate in major portions of district.

Commercial Television Stations, Affiliation. District is divided between Philadelphia and New York City ADIs.

Plants and Offices, Products, Employment.

Howmet Corp., Dover (Microcast Division—high temperature castings, steel alloys—1,000). **Ingersoll-Rand Co.**, Phillipsburg (Pumps, compressors—4,500). **Amerace Esna Corp.**, Butler (Molded Products Division—rubber, plastic products—1,850). **Pacific Vegetable Oil Corp.**, Boonton (Drew Chemical Division—foods & chemicals—1,500).

14th District

(Hudson County—Jersey City)

Race and Ethnic Groups. Blacks 12.7 percent. Spanish heritage population 6.0 percent. Italian stock 10.5 percent, Polish stock 4.9 percent, Irish stock 3.5 percent, British stock 2.5 percent.

Cities, 1970 Population. Jersey City 260,505, Bayonne 72,749, Hoboken 45,385, West New York 40,641.

Universities, Enrollment. Jersey City State College (Jersey City—9,157), Saint Peter's College (Jersey City—4,561), Stevens Institute of Technology (Hoboken—2,340).

Military Installations or Activities. Military Ocean Terminal, Bayonne.

Newspapers, Circulation. Jersey Journal (Eve—91,863). In addition, New York City newspapers circulate throughout district.

Commercial Television Stations, Affiliation. Entire district is located in New York City ADI.

Plants and Offices, Products, Employment.

Western Electric Co. Inc., Kearny (Telephone equipment—14,000). **National Union Electric Corp.**, Jersey City (Emerson & Motorola Division—TV, radios—1,500). **Maidenform Inc.**, Bayonne (Women's wear—1,150). **General Foods Corp.**, Hoboken (Coffee processing—at least 1,000). **Bethlehem Steel Corp.**, Hoboken (Ship repair—1,000). **City of Jersey City**, Jersey City (Municipal government—4,260).

15th District

(Central—New Brunswick, Perth Amboy)

Race and Ethnic Groups. Blacks 6.0 percent. Italian stock 5.4 percent, Polish stock 5.4 percent, Hungarian stock 3.5 percent, German stock 2.6 percent.

Cities, 1970 Population. New Brunswick 41,860, Linden 41,412, Perth Amboy 38,781, Sayreville 32,512.

Universities, Enrollment. Rutgers University (New Brunswick—36,869 total enrollment).

Newspapers, Circulation. Home News, New Brunswick (Eve—60,139); News Tribune, Perth Amboy-Woodbridge (Eve—56,492). In addition, Elizabeth and New York City newspapers circulate in major portions of district.

Commercial Television Stations, Affiliation. Entire district is located in New York City ADI.

Plants and Offices, Products, Employment.

Esso Research Engineering Co., Linden (Petrochemical research & development—HQ—1,800). **GAF Corp.**, Linden (Dyestuff & Chemical Division—dyes and chemicals—1,450). **Humble Oil & Refining Co.**, Linden (Petrochemical refinery—1,000). **Amerada Hess Corp.**, Woodbridge (Hess Oil Co. Division—administrative offices—1,500). **Hercules Inc.**, Parlin (Petroleum products—1,000). **International Smelting & Refining Co.**, Perth Amboy (Raritan Copper Works—copper & nonferrous metals—1,250). **American Smelting & Refining Co. Inc.**, Perth Amboy (Federated Metals Division—Nonferrous metal refining—1,550). **Triangle Conduit & Cable Co.**, New Brunswick (Wires, cables, conductors, etc.—HQ—1,000). **United States Metals Refining Co.**, Carteret (Non-ferrous metals—1,800). **National Lead Co.**, South Amboy (Titanium Division—titanium—1,600). **General Motors Corp.**, Linden (GM Assembly Division—auto assembly—4,500). **General Motors Corp.**, New Brunswick (Delco-Remy Division—automotive electrical equipment—1,000). **Ford Motor Co.**, Metuchen (Motor vehicles—3,030). **Westinghouse Electric Corp.**, Edison (Portable Products Division—radios, phonographs, recorders—at least 1,000). **RCA Corp.**, Woodbridge (Tubes—2,100). **Fedders Corp.**, Edison (Heating & air conditioning units—HQ—2,500). **E.R. Squibb & Sons Inc.**, New Brunswick (Pharmaceuticals—2,070). **Johnson & Johnson**, New Brunswick (Medical supplies—HQ—4,000). **Ronson Corp.**, Woodbridge (lighters, electric appliances, etc.—HQ—7,200). **Revlon Inc.**, Edison (Cosmetic products—4,000). **Sunshine Biscuits Inc.**, Sayreville (Biscuits, crackers—1,100). **R. H. Macy & Co. Inc.**, Edison (Bamberger's New Jersey Division—department stores—1,000). **New Jersey Turnpike Authority**, New Brunswick (Highway authority—HQ—at least 1,000).

NEW MEXICO: TWO HOUSE SEATS, NO CHANGE

New Mexico did not change its congressional district boundaries after the 1970 census. *(Map p. 127)*

The state had traditionally elected its U.S. House members at large—one from 1912 to 1942 and two members from 1942 to 1968. In the latter year, the state established two separate House districts, in accordance with federal legislation passed in 1967. The legislation prohibited at-large elections of House members except in states having only one member.

When 1970 census figures became available, it was found that each district varied only 0.6171 percent from the ideal district population for the state. Consequently, it was considered that no change in boundaries was necessary.

District	Member Elected 1972	Winning Percentage	1970 Population	Percent Variance
1	Manuel Lujan Jr. (R)	55.7	511,135	+ 0.6171
2	Harold Runnels (D)	72.2	504,865	—0.6171
	1970 State Population:		1,016,000	
	Ideal District Population:		508,000	

Election Results, 1968-1972

Vote for U.S. Representative
(Adjusted to new district boundaries)

District	1968	1970	1972
1	88,517 R (52.8%)	91,187 R (57.6%)	118,403 R (55.7%)
	78,117 D (46.7%)	64,598 D (40.8%)	94,239 D (44.3%)
2	71,857 R (50.5%)	64,518 D (50.8%)	116,152 D (72.2%)
	69,858 D (49.1%)	61,074 R (48.1%)	44,784 R (27.8%)
State	160,374 R (51.8%)	152,261 R (53.4%)	210,391 D (56.3%)
	147,975 D (47.8%)	129,116 D (45.3%)	163,187 R (43.7%)

Voting Age Population

District	Voting Age Population	Voting Age Population 18, 19, 20	Voting Age Population 65 and Over	Median Age of Voting Age Population
1	309,656	26,456 (8.5%)	36,257 (11.7%)	40.5
2	297,921	27,505 (9.2%)	34,573 (11.6%)	40.1
State	607,575	53,961 (8.9%)	70,830 (11.7%)	40.3

Income and Occupation

District	Median Family Income	White Collar Workers	Blue Collar Workers	Service Workers	Farm Workers
1	$8,187	57.4%	25.7%	14.8%	2.1%
2	7,551	45.2	34.6	14.6	5.6
State	7,845	51.5	30.0	14.7	3.8

Education: School Years Completed

District	Completed 4 years of High School	Completed 4 years of College	Completed 5 years or less of School	Median School years completed
1	59.7%	15.3%	9.1%	12.3
2	50.5	10.0	13.4	12.0
State	55.2	12.7	11.2	12.2

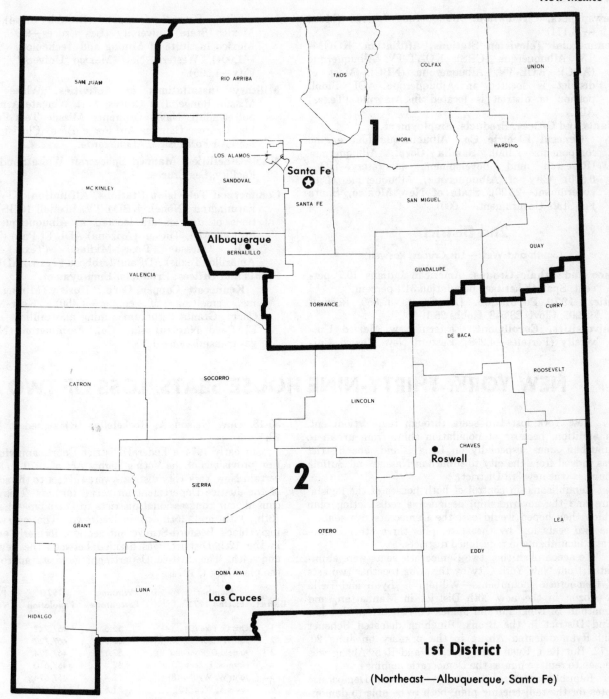

1st District

(Northeast—Albuquerque, Santa Fe)

Race and Ethnic Groups. American Indians 3.4 percent.
Spanish heritage population 48.9 percent.

Cities, 1970 Population. Albuquerque 243,793, Santa Fe
41,174, South Valley 29,648, Los Alamos 11,312.

Universities, Enrollment. College of Santa Fe (Santa
Fe—1,264), New Mexico Highlands University (Las
Vegas—2,655), University of Albuquerque (Albuquerque—2,919), University of New Mexico (Albuquerque—19,451).

Military Installations or Activities. Kirtland Air Force
Base/Sandia Base, Albuquerque.

AEC-Owned, Contractor-Operated Installations. Los
Alamos Scientific Laboratory, Los Alamos; Sandia
Laboratories, Albuquerque.

Housing and Residential Patterns

	Housing		Urban-Suburban-Nonmetropolitan Breakdown		
District	Owner Occupied Units	Renter Occupied Units	Urban	Suburban	Nonmetropolitan
1	67.6%	32.4%	47.7%	14.1%	38.2%
2	65.2	34.8	—	—	100.0
State	66.4	33.6	24.0	7.1	68.9

127

Newspapers, Circulation. Albuquerque Journal (Morn —73,171).

Commercial Television Stations, Affiliation. KGGM-TV, Albuquerque (CBS); KOAT-TV, Albuquerque (ABC); KOB-TV, Albuquerque (NBC). Most of district is located in Albuquerque ADI. Small portion of district is located in Amarillo (Texas) ADI.

Plants and Offices, Products, Employment.

General Electric Co., Albuquerque (Jet engine components—1,160). **Sandia Corp.**, Albuquerque (Research and development laboratory—HQ—6,500). **City of Albuquerque**, Albuquerque (City government—2,720). **State of New Mexico**, Santa Fe (State Government—3,000).

2nd District

(South and West—Las Cruces, Roswell)

Race and Ethnic Groups. American Indians 10.7 percent. Spanish heritage population 31.1 percent.

Cities, 1970 Population. Las Cruces 37,850, Roswell 33,902, Clovis 28,548, Hobbs 26,104.

Universities, Enrollment. Eastern New Mexico University (Portales—4,298), Eastern New Mexico University, Roswell Campus (Roswell—1,044), New Mexico State University (Las Cruces—9,075), New Mexico Institute of Mining and Technology (Socorro—1,004), Western New Mexico University (Silver City—1,505).

Military Installations or Activities. White Sands Missile Range, Las Cruces; Fort Wingate Army Depot, Gallup; Naval Ordnance Missile Test Facility, Las Cruces; Cannon Air Force Base, Clovis; Holloman Air Force Base, Alamagordo.

NASA Facilities. Manned Spacecraft White Sands Test Facility, Las Cruces.

Commercial Television Stations, Affiliation. KIVA-TV, Farmington (None); KBIM-TV, Roswell (CBS). Portions of district are located in Albuquerque ADI, Roswell ADI, Tucson (Arizona) ADI, El Paso (Texas) ADI, Odessa (Texas)-Midland (Texas) ADI, Amarillo (Texas) ADI and Lubbock (Texas) ADI.

Plants and Offices, Products, Employment.

Kennecott Copper Corp., Hurley (Mining, milling, smelting of copper—1,450). **Kerr-McGee Corp.**, Grants (Uranium mining and milling—1,100). **El Paso Natural Gas Co.**, Farmington (Natural gas transmission—1,100).

NEW YORK: THIRTY-NINE HOUSE SEATS, LOSS OF TWO

New York lost two seats through reapportionment. In addition, because of population shifts from urban to suburban areas, especially on Long Island, one district was moved from the city to suburban Nassau and Suffolk counties (the new 3rd District).

Republicans, in control of both houses of the legislature and the governorship, designed a redistricting plan which they hoped would cost the Democrats five seats—the two seats lost by the state, plus three other Democratic incumbents in redesigned districts.

To accomplish this, two Democratic seats were eliminated from New York City by throwing together two sets of Democratic incumbents—William F. Ryan and Bella S. Abzug in the new 20th District in Manhattan, and Jonathan B. Bingham and James H. Scheuer in the new 22nd District in the Bronx. Bingham defeated Scheuer and Ryan defeated Abzug in the primary on June 20, 1972. But Rep. Ryan died Sept. 17 and Rep. Abzug was chosen to replace him as the Democratic nominee.

Republicans were anxious to get some Democratic votes for the redistricting plan, both to be able to demonstrate its "bipartisan" support in the event of a court challenge and to ensure its passage by a large margin. Consequently, in drawing the new lines, they were careful to preserve the two predominantly black districts and the one Puerto Rican district in New York City.

Organization Democratic politicians in the city were also reportedly permitted to draw lines for the new Democratic districts within their respective areas, provided they did not challenge any Republican districts on their borders. Thus it appeared to be no accident that the two sets of incumbents thrown together in the city were reform anti-organization Democrats.

The bill went through the state legislature March 9, 1972, passing the Assembly 88-57 and the Senate 35-18. Gov. Nelson A. Rockefeller (R) signed it March 28.

In early 1974 a Federal District Court, applying certain provisions of the Voting Rights Act of 1970, held that certain New York City districts were subject to the scrutiny of the Justice Department for racial fairness. This ruling caused four congressional districts in Brooklyn—the 12th, 13th, 14th and 15th—to be redrawn. The overwhelmingly black Bedford-Stuyvesant section, formerly entirely in the 12th District, was divided between the new 12th and 14th. The Justice Department gave its approval to the plan July 1, 1974.

District	Member Elected 1972	Winning Percentage	1970 Population	Percent Variance
1	Otis G. Pike (D)	52.5	467,742	+ 0.0036
2	James R. Grover Jr. (R)	65.8	467,722	—0.0006
3	Angelo D. Roncallo (R)	53.1	467,894	+ 0.0361
4	Norman F. Lent (R)	62.4	467,610	—0.0245
5	John W. Wydler (R)	62.4	467,694	—0.0066
6	Lester L. Wolff (D)	51.5	467,602	—0.0262
7	Joseph P. Addabbo (D)	75.0	467,449	—0.0590
8	Benjamin S. Rosenthal (D)	64.7	467,691	—0.0072
9	James J. Delaney (D)	93.4	467,207	—0.1107
10	Mario Biaggi (D)	93.9	474,745	+ 1.5008
11	Frank J. Brasco (D)	63.9	469,790	+ 0.4414
12	Shirley Chisholm (D)	87.9	465,195	—0.5409
13	Bertram L. Podell (D)	65.1	470,242	+ 0.5381
14	John J. Rooney (D)	53.9	467,517	—0.0444
15	Hugh L. Carey (D)	52.1	467,453	—0.0581
16	Elizabeth Holtzman (D)	65.6	466,756	—0.2071
17	John M. Murphy (D)	60.3	467,656	—0.0147
18	Edward I. Koch (D)	69.9	467,533	—0.0410
19	Charles B. Rangel (D)	96.0	466,876	—0.1815
20	Bella S. Abzug (D)	55.7	468,667	+ 0.2014
21	Herman Badillo (D)	86.9	462,030	—1.2175
22	Jonathan B. Bingham (D)	76.5	466,931	—0.1697

District	Member Elected 1972	Winning Percentage	1970 Population	Percent Variance
23	Peter A. Peyser (R)	50.4	467,778	+ 0.0113
24	Ogden R. Reid (D)	52.2	468,148	+ 0.0904
25	Hamilton Fish Jr. (R)	71.7	467,859	+ 0.0286
26	Benjamin A. Gilman (R)	47.8	467,424	—0.0643
27	Howard W. Robison (R)	62.2	467,980	+ 0.0545
28	Samuel S. Stratton (D)	80.0	467,219	—0.1081
29	Carleton J. King (R)	69.9	467,767	+ 0.0089
30	Robert C. McEwen (R)	66.0	467,920	+ 0.0416
31	Donald J. Mitchell (R)	51.0	467,717	—0.0017
32	James M. Hanley (D)	57.2	467,826	+ 0.0215
33	William F. Walsh (R)	71.4	467,610	—0.0245
34	Frank Horton (R)	72.1	467,461	—0.0564
35	Barber B. Conable Jr. (R)	67.9	467,415	—0.0662
36	Henry P. Smith III (R)	57.3	467,761	+ 0.0076
37	Thaddeus J. Dulski (D)	72.2	467,759	+ 0.0072
38	Jack F. Kemp (R)	73.2	467,761	+ 0.0076
39	James F. Hastings (R)	71.9	467,859	+ 0.0286

1970 State Population: 18,241,266
Ideal District Population: 467,725

Election Results, 1968-1972

Vote for U.S. Representative
(Adjusted to new district boundaries)

District	1968	1970	1972
1	Not Available	74,341 D (53.4%) [1]	102,628 D (52.5%)
		64,884 R (46.6%) [2]	72,133 R (36.9%)
2	NA	66,856 R (58.0%) [2]	99,348 R (65.8%)
		48,416 D (42.0%) [1]	49,454 D (32.7%)
3	NA	93,655 R (60.2%) [2]	103,620 R (53.1%)
		59,043 D (38.0%) [1]	73,429 D (37.6%)
4	NA	90,816 R (51.6%) [2]	125,422 R (62.4%)
		76,697 D (43.6%) [1]	72,280 D (35.9%)
5	NA	98,350 R (54.0%) [2]	133,332 R (62.4%)
		73,184 D (40.2%) [1]	67,709 D (31.7%)
6	NA	Not Available	109,620 D (51.5%) [1]
			103,038 R (48.5%) [2]
7	NA	NA	103,110 D (75.0%) [1]
			28,296 R (20.6%)
8	NA	NA	110,293 D (64.7%) [1]
			60,166 R (35.3%) [2]
9	NA	NA	141,323 D (93.4%) [4]
10	NA	NA	130,200 D (93.9%) [4]
			—
11	NA	NA	87,869 D (63.9%)
			43,105 R (31.3%) [2]
12 [†]	NA	NA	57,821 D (87.9%) [1]*
			6,373 R (9.7%)
13 [†]	NA	NA	113,294 D (65.1%) *
			44,293 R (25.5%)
14 [†]	NA	NA	45,515 D (53.9%) [2] *
			14,813 R (17.5%)
15 [†]	NA	NA	77,019 D (52.1%) *
			63,446 R (43.0%)
16	NA	NA	96,984 D (65.6%)
			33,828 R (22.9%)
17	NA	NA	92,252 D (60.3%)
			60,812 R (39.7%) [2]
18	NA	NA	125,117 D (69.9%) [1]
			52,379 R (29.3%) [2]
19	NA	NA	104,427 D (96.0%) [3]
			—
20	NA	NA	85,558 D (55.7%)
			18,024 R (11.8%)

District	1968	1970	1972
21	NA	39,405 D (90.4%) [1]	48,441 D (86.9%) [1]
		2,722 R (6.2%)	6,366 R (11.4%)
22	NA	100,871 D (77.9%) [1,2]	107,448 D (76.5%) [1]
		19,315 R (14.9%) [2]	33,045 R (23.5%) [2]
23	NA	81,327 D (48.4%) [1,2]	99,737 D (50.4%) [2]
		60,915 R (36.2%)	98,335 D (49.6%) [1]
24	NA	105,026 D (61.5%)	107,979 D (52.2%) [1]
		37,965 D (22.2%) [2]	98,818 R (47.8%) [2]
25	NA	91,616 R (58.5%) [1,2]	144,386 R (71.7%) [2]
		55,068 D (35.1%) [1]	54,271 D (26.9%)
26	NA	67,269 R (46.9%) [2]	90,922 R (47.8%)
		66,453 D (46.4%) [1]	74,906 D (39.3%)
27	NA	100,991 R (66.0%) [2]	114,902 R (62.2%)
		49,745 D (32.5%) [1]	55,076 D (29.8%)
28	NA	135,856 D (67.2%) [1]	182,395 D (80.0%)
		66,308 R (32.8%) [1,2]	45,623 R (20.0%) [2]
29	NA	111,120 R (62.1%) [1,2]	148,170 R (69.9%) [2]
		66,335 D (37.1%) [1]	63,920 D (30.1%) [1]
30	NA	101,245 R (72.1%) [1,2]	114,193 R (66.0%) [2]
		39,230 D (27.9%) [1]	58,788 D (34.0%) [1]
31	NA	101,177 R (64.5%) [1]	98,454 R (51.0%) [2]
		54,924 D (35.1%)	75,513 D (39.1%) [2]
32	NA	79,183 R (50.8%) [2]	111,481 D (57.2%) [2]
		76,148 D (48.8%)	83,451 R (42.8%)
33	NA	109,632 R (60.6%) [2]	132,139 R (71.4%)
		71,238 D (39.4%) [1]	53,039 D (28.6%)
34	NA	118,101 R (70.3%)	142,803 R (72.1%)
		37,918 D (22.5%) [1]	46,509 D (23.5%)
35	NA	105,984 R (67.5%)	127,298 R (67.9%)
		44,359 D (28.2%)	53,321 D (28.4%)
36	NA	100,398 R (64.1%) [2]	110,238 R (57.3%) [2]
		55,657 D (35.5%) [1]	82,095 D (42.7%) [1]
37	NA	103,704 D (72.3%) [1]	114,605 D (72.2%) [1]
		39,802 R (27.7%) [2]	44,103 R (27.8%) [2]
38	NA	92,822 R (54.4%) [2]	156,967 R (73.2%) [2]
		76,782 D (45.1%) [1]	57,585 D (26.8%) [1]
39	NA	109,256 R (71.2%) [2]	126,147 R (71.9%) [2]
		44,224 D (28.8%) [1]	49,253 D (28.1%)
State	NA	Figures incomplete	3,340,862 D (50.5%) [5]
			2,980,190 R (45.1%) [6]

1 Includes vote received on Liberal party line.
2 Includes vote received on Conservative party line.
3 Includes vote received on Republican and Liberal party lines.
4 Includes vote received on Republican and Conservative party lines.
5 Includes Liberal, Conservative and Republican votes when Democratic candidate was placed on ballot of one or more of those parties.
6 Includes Liberal or Conservative votes when Republican candidate was placed on ballot of either of those parties.
7 No candidate in this district as constituted before redistricting.
8 Includes votes received on minor party line other than Conservative or Liberal.
* Vote for representative in district as constituted in 1972. Reallocated figures for 1974 boundaries not available.
† Based on Census Bureau preliminary figures, Sept. 1974.

Voting Age Population

District	Voting Age Population	Voting Age Population 18, 19, 20	Voting Age Population 65 and Over	Median Age of Voting Age Population
1	283,761	18,531 (6.5%)	39,408 (13.9%)	41.0
2	279,580	17,502 (6.3%)	33,829 (12.1%)	41.2
3	285,637	20,815 (7.3%)	29,444 (10.3%)	42.8
4	293,550	23,623 (8.0%)	28,998 (9.9%)	43.3
5	318,059	22,792 (7.2%)	47,530 (14.9%)	46.5
6	332,795	22,198 (6.7%)	50,004 (15.0%)	47.1
7	335,013	20,342 (6.1%)	54,802 (16.4%)	45.6
8	356,244	20,113 (5.6%)	52,514 (14.7%)	45.5
9	355,996	18,265 (5.1%)	71,616 (20.1%)	48.7
10	341,443	23,580 (6.9%)	59,921 (17.5%)	45.8
11	311,828	22,992 (7.4%)	44,484 (14.3%)	43.7

District	Voting Age Population	Voting Age Population 18, 19, 20	Voting Age Population 65 and Over	Median Age of Voting Age Population
12 †	272,829	23,201 (8.5%)	30,231 (11.1%)	38.7
13 †	357,114	20,600 (5.8%)	78,929 (22.1%)	50.4
14 †	302,882	24,897 (8.2%)	35,785 (11.8%)	39.1
15 †	337,671	20,678 (6.1%)	63,396 (18.8%)	46.8
16	340,807	21,439 (6.3%)	61,531 (18.1%)	46.7
17	323,051	24,194 (7.5%)	45,490 (14.1%)	41.9
18	402,153	15,655 (3.9%)	73,629 (18.3%)	44.0
19	329,557	20,017 (6.1%)	53,315 (16.2%)	43.3
20	372,673	19,881 (5.3%)	74,023 (19.9%)	45.1
21	265,265	22,444 (8.5%)	27,667 (10.4%)	37.4
22	345,184	20,837 (6.0%)	73,351 (21.2%)	47.0
23	329,731	21,767 (6.6%)	53,493 (16.2%)	46.0
24	325,161	20,260 (6.2%)	52,294 (16.1%)	46.0
25	300,066	18,679 (6.2%)	46,191 (15.4%)	42.8
26	294,241	20,168 (6.9%)	41,684 (14.2%)	42.2
27	312,753	31,986 (10.2%)	49,526 (15.8%)	42.7
28	320,901	23,965 (7.5%)	56,418 (17.6%)	46.0
29	303,516	23,374 (7.7%)	52,915 (17.4%)	44.7
30	295,125	30,251 (10.3%)	48,088 (16.3%)	43.1
31	308,640	21,962 (7.1%)	55,568 (18.0%)	46.1
32	306,328	33,378 (10.9%)	43,743 (14.3%)	41.5
33	300,539	22,098 (7.4%)	50,350 (16.8%)	44.6
34	312,348	22,747 (7.3%)	51,504 (16.5%)	44.2
35	296,584	21,538 (7.3%)	40,686 (13.7%)	41.5
36	302,579	23,993 (7.9%)	43,375 (14.3%)	44.3
37	321,700	26,503 (8.2%)	59,844 (18.6%)	46.0
38	294,008	20,472 (7.0%)	36,533 (12.4%)	43.2
39	304,263	25,913 (8.5%)	54,292 (17.8%)	45.2
State	12,371,748	873,642 (7.1%)	1,966,956 (15.9%)	44.2

Income and Occupation

District	Median Family Income	White Collar Workers	Blue Collar Workers	Service Workers	Farm Workers
1	$11,643	55.1%	30.4%	13.4%	1.1 %
2	11,938	49.1	37.0	13.7	0.2
3	14,396	62.0	26.5	11.3	0.2
4	14,376	63.2	25.9	10.8	0.1
5	14,102	65.0	24.2	10.7	0.1
6	14,483	67.9	21.9	10.1	0.1
7	11,317	59.3	27.1	13.4	0.2
8	12,244	67.7	22.9	9.3	0.03
9	10,657	53.4	34.0	12.5	0.03
10	9,988	51.8	33.9	14.2	0.1
11	10,834	57.5	31.4	11.0	0.1
12 †	6,432	37.9	44.8	17.9	0.2
13 †	10,294	64.2	28.1	7.7	0.03
14 †	6,874	46.3	37.2	16.1	0.1
15 †	9,629	53.8	34.6	11.6	0.04
16	10,504	64.1	24.7	11.1	0.1
17	10,632	56.5	28.2	15.2	0.1
18	14,853	79.3	9.9	10.7	0.02
19	6,712	48.9	26.7	24.3	0.1
20	9,743	63.5	22.0	14.4	0.1
21	5,613	37.0	41.7	21.2	0.1
22	8,850	57.6	28.6	13.7	0.1
23	12,693	62.0	26.0	11.8	0.2
24	13,577	62.8	23.9	13.0	0.3
25	11,885	55.6	29.7	13.4	1.3
26	11,632	52.7	32.0	13.7	1.6
27	9,904	50.9	31.9	14.5	2.7
28	10,764	58.2	29.4	11.9	0.5
29	9,621	47.0	38.1	12.2	2.7
30	8,584	41.4	37.2	15.6	5.8

District	Median Family Income	White Collar Workers	Blue Collar Workers	Service Workers	Farm Workers
31	9,388	43.9	39.0	13.2	3.9
32	10,416	53.1	31.8	11.8	3.3
33	9,851	45.7	37.1	13.9	3.3
34	12,082	54.3	33.5	10.9	1.3
35	11,528	45.8	39.9	11.8	2.5
36	10,702	46.9	39.6	12.1	1.4
37	8,845	41.6	42.1	16.2	0.1
38	11,583	52.4	36.2	10.4	1.0
39	8,936	42.6	39.5	13.7	4.2
State	10,609	55.2	30.8	13.0	1.0

Education: School Years Completed

District	Completed 4 years of High School	Completed 4 years of College	Completed 5 years or less of School	Median School years completed
1	59.8%	12.9%	4.1%	12.3
2	55.1	8.1	4.5	12.1
3	67.2	17.6	3.7	12.5
4	66.8	15.1	2.9	12.4
5	61.9	15.4	4.5	12.4
6	63.6	18.3	4.4	12.4
7	52.4	10.5	6.8	12.1
8	58.9	14.0	6.1	12.3
9	41.6	6.1	8.3	10.8
10	41.0	5.5	10.9	10.7
11	48.0	7.1	8.7	11.7
12 †	29.2	1.87	16.6	9.6
13 †	44.7	8.0	11.6	11.2
14 †	37.0	7.1	14.4	10.3
15 †	40.0	6.4	11.6	10.5
16	50.7	9.5	8.2	12.0
17	48.4	11.4	11.0	11.8
18	71.9	33.6	5.6	13.0
19	40.0	10.2	14.4	10.6
20	54.4	18.9	8.4	12.2
21	26.3	1.9	19.5	9.2
22	44.2	7.1	10.5	11.1
23	58.8	16.3	6.7	12.3
24	62.8	21.4	6.5	12.4
25	60.6	14.6	4.9	12.3
26	58.9	14.0	5.7	12.3
27	59.1	13.0	3.5	12.3
28	56.9	13.4	5.2	12.2
29	52.7	9.5	3.8	12.1
30	49.9	8.3	3.9	12.0
31	49.3	8.3	5.6	11.9
32	61.0	14.5	3.2	12.3
33	54.5	10.2	4.8	12.1
34	56.5	15.9	6.4	12.2
35	55.8	9.7	4.5	12.2
36	54.6	9.8	4.5	12.1
37	38.4	6.3	8.7	10.6
38	58.9	13.0	3.2	12.3
39	54.9	8.8	3.4	12.2
State	52.7	11.9	7.2	12.1

† *Based on Census Bureau preliminary figures, Sept. 1974.*

Glossary and Sources

For a complete explanation of all terms used in this book and a list of source material, consult the details included in the Introduction.

Housing and Residential Patterns

District	Housing Owner Occupied Units	Renter Occupied Units	Urban-Suburban-Nonmetropolitan Breakdown Urban	Suburban	Nonmetro-politan
1	82.9%	17.1%	—	100.0%	—
2	83.0	17.0	—	100.0	—
3	85.7	14.3	—	100.0	—
4	86.6	13.4	—	100.0	—
5	74.6	25.4	—	100.0	—
6	68.0	32.0	53.6%	46.4	—
7	43.6	56.4	100.0	—	—
8	32.4	67.6	100.0	—	—
9	34.2	65.8	100.0	—	—
10	28.3	71.7	100.0	—	—
11	48.5	51.5	100.0	—	—
12 †	13.8	86.2	100.0	—	—
13 †	25.9	74.1	100.0	—	—
14 †	12.3	87.7	100.0	—	—
15 †	26.6	73.4	100.0	—	—
16	30.9	69.1	100.0	—	—
17	38.6	61.4	100.0	—	—
18	8.7	91.3	100.0	—	—
19	5.1	94.9	100.0	—	—
20	5.2	94.8	100.0	—	—
21	4.7	95.3	100.0	—	—
22	9.7	90.3	100.0	—	—
23	44.7	55.3	34.2	65.8	—
24	48.8	51.2	—	100.0	—
25	69.8	30.2	—	25.6	74.4%
26	68.1	31.9	—	49.2	50.8
27	68.0	32.0	13.7	43.6	42.7
28	60.5	39.5	41.5	51.8	6.7
29	70.3	29.7	13.5	46.6	39.9
30	71.9	28.1	—	19.9	80.1
31	68.7	31.3	30.3	43.6	26.1
32	68.1	31.9	21.9	47.4	30.7
33	68.0	32.0	20.3	26.7	53.0
34	63.9	36.1	37.7	62.3	—
35	71.2	28.8	25.7	51.1	23.2
36	71.1	28.9	6.8	93.2	—
37	44.6	55.4	92.0	8.0	—
38	77.3	22.7	—	100.0	—
39	72.9	27.1	—	0.5	99.5
State	47.3	52.7	51.1	35.4	13.5

† Based on Census Bureau preliminary figures, Sept. 1974.

1st District

(Eastern Long Island)

Race and Ethnic Groups. Blacks 3.5 percent. Italian stock 7.0 percent, German stock 3.8 percent, British stock 2.5 percent.

Cities, 1970 Population. Part of Commack 19,052, South Stony Brook 15,417, Hauppauge 14,051, Holbrook-Holtsville 12,173.

Universities, Enrollment. State University of New York at Stony Brook (Stony Brook—10,697), Long Island University, Southampton Center (Southampton—1,416).

Military Installations or Activities. Montauk Air Force Station, Montauk.

AEC-Owned, Contractor-Operated Facilities. Brookhaven National Laboratory, Upton.

Newspapers, Circulation. New York City and Long Island newspapers circulate throughout district.

Commercial Television Stations, Affiliation. Entire district is located in New York City ADI.

Plants and Offices, Products, Employment.
Grumman Aerospace Corp., Calverton, Long Island (Aircraft, aerospace equipment—3,000).

2nd District

(Long Island—Western Suffolk County)

Race and Ethnic Groups. Blacks 3.5 percent. Italian stock 8.9 percent, German stock 3.5 percent.

Cities, 1970 Population. North Babylon 39,787, Central Islip 36,400, Deer Park 32,617, Lindenhurst 28,382.

Universities, Enrollment. Dowling College (Oakdale—1,800).

Newspapers, Circulation. New York City and Long Island newspapers circulate throughout district.

Commercial Television Stations, Affiliation. Entire district is located in New York City ADI.

Plants and Offices, Products, Employment.
Dero Industries Inc., Huntington (Electronic components—3,000).

3rd District

(Long Island—Eastern Nassau and Northwestern Suffolk Counties)

Race and Ethnic Groups. Blacks 5.4 percent. Italian stock 8.5 percent, German stock 3.7 percent, Russian stock 2.7 percent, British stock 2.5 percent.

Cities, 1970 Population. Plainview 33,135, Huntington Station 28,689, Massapequa 26,782, Glen Cove 25,733.

Newspapers, Circulation. New York City and Long Island newspapers circulate throughout district.

Commercial Television Stations, Affiliation. Entire district is located in New York City ADI.

Plants and Offices, Products, Employment.
Hazeltine Corp., Greenlawn (Electronic devices—HQ—1,100). Fairchild Industries Inc., Farmingdale (Republic Aviation Division—aircraft and equipment—at least 1,000). Litton Systems Inc., Farmingdale (Litcomb Division—radio, TV equipment—1,000). Eltra Corp., Plainview (Mergenthaler Linotype Co. Division—type setting equipment—1,000).

4th District

(Long Island—Eastern and Southern Nassau County)

Race and Ethnic Groups. Blacks 3.4 percent. Italian stock 6.9 percent, Russian stock 4.5 percent, German stock 3.7 percent, Polish stock 2.9 percent, Irish stock 2.5 percent.

Cities, 1970 Population. Levittown 65,840, Hicksville 48,377, Freeport 40,684, Oceanside 35,591.

Universities, Enrollment. Long Island University, C. W. Post Center (Greenvale—11,445), New York Institute of Technology (Old Westbury—5,207).

Newspapers, Circulation. New York City and Long Island papers circulate throughout district.

Commercial Television Stations, Affiliation. Entire district is located in New York City ADI.

Plants and Offices, Products, Employment.
Horn Construction Co. Inc., Merrick (Heavy construction—HQ—1,000).

5th District

(Long Island—Central and Southwestern Nassau County)

Race and Ethnic Groups. Blacks 8.5 percent. Italian stock 9.0 percent, Russian stock 5.4 percent, German stock 4.2 percent, Polish stock 3.5 percent, Irish stock 2.5 percent.

Cities, 1970 Population. Valley Stream 40,225, Hempstead 39,150, Long Beach 32,980, Franklin Square 32,011.

Universities, Enrollment. Adelphi University (Garden City—7,858), Hofstra University (Hempstead—12,616), Molloy College (Rockville Centre 1,161).

Newspapers, Circulation. Newsday, Garden City (Eve—440,765). In addition, New York City newspapers circulate throughout district.

Commercial Television Stations, Affiliation. Entire district is located in New York City ADI.

Plants and Offices, Products, Employment.
Doubleday and Co. Inc., Garden City (Publishing—HQ—2,000). **ITT Avis Inc.**, Garden City (Car and truck rental and leasing, holding company—HQ—7,010). **Wetsons Corp.**, Valley Stream (Restaurant franchises, holding company—1,000). **Aurora Products Corp.**, West Hempstead (Toys—HQ—1,100). **Triangle Maintenance Corp.**, Hempstead (Service and maintenance—1,000). **DIC Concrete Corp.**, Elmont (Concrete construction—2,500).

6th District

(Northeast Queens and Northwestern Nassau Counties)

Race and Ethnic Groups. Italian stock 9.7 percent, Russian stock 5.4 percent, German stock 4.8 percent, Polish stock 4.3 percent, Irish stock 3.1 percent, British stock 2.6 percent.

Cities, 1970 Population. Part of New York City 250,439, Mineola 21,808, North New Hyde Park 18,127, Port Washington 15,820.

Newspapers, Circulation. New York City and Long Island newspapers circulate throughout district.

Commercial Television Stations, Affiliation. Entire district is located in New York City ADI.

Plants and Offices, Products, Employment.
Seabrook Foods Inc., Great Neck (Frozen foods—1,100). **Skouras Theaters Corp.**, Great Neck (Theaters—1,500).

7th District

(Southern Queens—Ozone Park, Jamaica)

Race and Ethnic Groups. Blacks 36.5 percent. Italian stock 6.9 percent, Russian stock 5.1 percent, Polish stock 3.9 percent, German stock 3.8 percent.

Cities, 1970 Population. Part of New York City 467,449.

Universities, Enrollment. York College (Jamaica—2,707).

Military Installations or Activities. Naval Hospital, St. Albans.

Newspapers, Circulation. Long Island Press, Jamaica (Eve—390,998). New York City newspapers circulate throughout district.

Commercial Television Stations, Affiliation. Entire district is located in New York City ADI.

Plants and Offices, Products, Employment.
Ideal Toy Corp., Hollis (Games, toys, dolls—HQ—1,600). **Allied Stores of New York Inc.**, Jamaica (Department stores—2,000). **Long Island Railroad Co.**, Jamaica (Railroad—6,830).

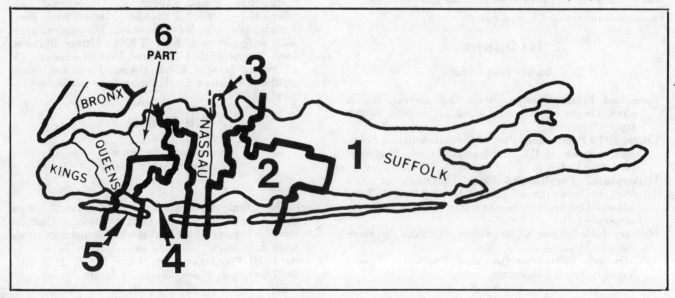

8th District

(Central and Northern Queens—Flushing)

Race and Ethnic Groups. Blacks 4.4 percent. Italian stock 8.3 percent, Russian stock 8.2 percent, Polish stock 5.6 percent, Irish stock 3.6 percent, German stock 3.6 percent, Austrian stock 3.1 percent.
Cities, 1970 Population. Part of New York City 467,691.
Universities, Enrollment. Queens College (Flushing—27,075), St. John's University (Jamaica—13,735).
Newspapers, Circulation. New York City newspapers circulate throughout district.
Commercial Television Stations, Affiliation. Entire district is located in New York City ADI.
Plants and Offices, Products, Employment.
　　Roto Broil Corp. of America., Long Island City (Household appliances, holding company—at least 1,200).

9th District

(Western Queens—Long Island City,
Maspeth, Glendale)

Race and Ethnic Groups. Italian stock 13.6 percent, German stock 8.1 percent, Irish stock 4.9 percent, Polish stock 3.1 percent, Russian stock 2.5 percent.
Cities, 1970 Population. Part of New York City 467,207.
Newspapers, Circulation. New York City newspapers circulate throughout district.
Commercial Television Stations, Affiliation. Entire district is located in New York City ADI.
Plants and Offices, Products, Employment.
　　Cerro Corp., Maspeth (Electric wires and cables—1,000). Slattery Associates Inc., Maspeth (Heavy construction—1,500). Neptune Meter Co., Long Island City (Meters—1,000). Bulova Watch Co. Inc., Astoria (Clocks and watches—2,820). Pickwick International Inc., Long Island City (Records musical instruments, retail music stores, holding company—HQ—1,000). Associated Retail Stores Inc., Long Island City (Women's and children's apparel—1,350). Bestform Foundations Inc., Long Island City (Garments—HQ—2,490). Barricini Inc., Long Island City (Candy—1,000).

10th District

(Eastern Bronx and Northern Queens—
Astoria, Throgs Neck)

Race and Ethnic Groups. Blacks 13.4 percent. Spanish heritage population 9.4 percent. Italian stock 16.7 percent, Irish stock 5.9 percent, German stock 3.0 percent.
Cities, 1970 Population. Part of New York City 474,745.
Universities, Enrollment. Fordham University (Bronx—part in 20th District, total enrollment 13,841).
Newspapers, Circulation. New York City newspapers circulate throughout district.
Commercial Television Stations, Affiliation. Entire district is located in New York City ADI.

Plants and Offices, Products, Employment.
　　EDO Corp., College Point (Marine and naval signalling and detection equipment—HQ—1,000).

11th District

(Southeast Brooklyn, Southern Queens)

Race and Ethnic Groups. Blacks 16.9 percent. Spanish heritage population 5.7 percent. Italian stock 9.4 percent, Russian stock 8.2 percent, Polish stock 5.7 percent.
Cities, 1970 Population. Part of New York City 469,790.
Newspapers, Circulation. New York City newspapers circulate throughout district.
Commercial Television Stations, Affiliation. Entire district is located in New York City ADI.

12th District †

(Northeastern Brooklyn—
Greenpoint)

Race and Ethnic Groups. Blacks 53.9 percent. Spanish heritage population 19.8 percent. Italian stock 6.4 percent. Polish stock 1.7 percent.
Cities, 1970 Population. Part of New York City 467,726.
Newspapers, Circulation. New York City newspapers circulate throughout district.
Commercial Television Stations, Affiliation. Entire district is located in New York City ADI.
Plants and Offices, Products, Employment.
　　Leviton Manufacturing Co., Brooklyn (Electric socket plugs, switches, wire and wire products—HQ—1,900). Piel Brothers Inc., Brooklyn (Brewery—1,000).

13th District †

(Brooklyn—Coney Island,
Bensonhurst)

Race and Ethnic Groups. Blacks 2.1 percent. Spanish heritage population 2.3 percent. Italian stock 15.7 percent. Russian stock 13.5 percent. Polish stock 9.5 percent. Austrian stock 4.0 percent.
Cities, 1970 Population. Part of New York City 468,726.
Newspapers, Circulation. New York City newspapers circulate throughout district.
Commercial Television Stations, Affiliation. Entire district is located in New York City ADI.

14th District †

(Brooklyn—Williamsburg)

Race and Ethnic Groups. Blacks 46.4 percent. Spanish heritage population 18.3 percent. Italian stock 5.1 percent. Polish stock 2.2 percent.
Cities, 1970 Population. Part of New York City 467,735.

† Based on Census Bureau preliminary figures, Sept. 1974.

Military Installations or Activities. Naval Station, Brooklyn.

Universities, Enrollment. Long Island University, Brooklyn Center (Brooklyn—7,632), Polytechnic Institute of Brooklyn (Brooklyn—3,852), Pratt Institute (Brooklyn—4,530), St. Francis College (Brooklyn—2,624).

Newspapers, circulation. New York City newspapers circulate throughout district.

Commercial Television Stations, Affiliation. Entire district is located in New York City ADI.

Plants and Offices, Products, Employment.

    Robert Hall Manufacturing Co., Brooklyn (Men's and boys' clothing—1,000. **Eagle Clothes Inc.,** Brooklyn (Men's clothing—3,450). **Howard Stores Corp.,** Brooklyn (Men's and boys' apparel—HQ—1,500). **F. and M. Schaefer Brewing Co.,** Brooklyn (Brewery—HQ—2,500). **Caristo Construction Co.,** Brooklyn (General contractor—1,800). **New York News Inc.,** Brooklyn (Newspaper publishing—3,500). **Federated Department Stores,** Brooklyn (Department stores—3,000). **Brooklyn Union Gas Co.,** Brooklyn (Gas utility—3,150). **New York City Transit Authority,** Brooklyn (Transportation—3,500). **Brooklyn Hospital,** Brooklyn (Hospital—1,100). **Pfizer Inc.,** Brooklyn (Pharmaceuticals and chemicals—2,700).

15th District [†]
(Southwestern Brooklyn—Bay Ridge)

Race and Ethnic Groups. Blacks 5.3 percent. Spanish heritage population 8.6 percent. Italian stock 20.6 percent. Irish stock 3.6 percent. Polish stock 2.7 percent. Russian stock 2.2 percent.

Cities, 1970 Population. Part of New York City 466,741.

Military Installations or Activities. Fort Hamilton, Brooklyn.

† Based on Census Bureau preliminary figures, Sept. 1974

Newspapers, Circulation. New York City newspapers circulate throughout district.

Commercial Television Stations, Affiliation. Entire district is located in New York City ADI.

Plants and Offices, Products, Employment.

American Can Co., Brooklyn (Canco Division cans—1,400). Todd Shipyards Corp., Brooklyn (Shipbuilding, offshore oil drilling equipment—1,000). Navy Resale System Office. Brooklyn (General merchandise—HQ—1,000).

16th District

(Central and Southern Brooklyn—Flatbush)

Race and Ethnic Groups. Blacks 22.1 percent. Spanish heritage population 4.3 percent. Russian stock 11.0 percent, Polish stock 6.6 percent, Italian stock 5.5 percent, Austrian stock 2.8 percent, Irish stock 2.7 percent.

Cities, 1970 Population. Part of New York City 466,756.

Universities, Enrollment. Brooklyn College (Brooklyn—29,509).

Newspapers, Circulation. New York City newspapers circulate throughout district.

Commercial Television Stations, Affiliation. Entire district is located in New York City ADI.

17th District

(Staten Island, Southern Manhattan)

Race and Ethnic Groups. Blacks 6.5 percent. Spanish heritage population 7.1 percent. Italian stock 12.0 percent, Polish stock 2.4 percent.

Cities, 1970 Population. Part of New York City 467,656.

Universities, Enrollment. Richmond College (Staten Island—3,133), Pace College (New York—7,621), Wagner College (Staten Island—3,298), College of Insurance (New York—1,572).

Newspapers, Circulation. Staten Island Advance (Ex-Sat—68,762). In addition, New York City newspapers circulate throughout the district.

Commercial Television Stations, Affiliation. Entire district is located in New York City ADI.

Plants and Offices, Products, Employment. (Note: portion of district is located in lower Manhattan business section.)

American Telephone and Telegraph Co., New York (Headquarters—3,500). Western Electric Co. Inc., New York (Headquarters—4,160). Western Union Telegraph Co., New York (Telegraph communications—HQ—1,000). New York Telephone Co., New York (Telephone utility—HQ—3,000). Eastman Dillon, Union Securities and Co., New York (Securities dealers—HQ—1,000). Goldman Sachs and Co., New York (Securities dealers—HQ—1,010). Bache and Co., New York (Securities dealers, underwriters—HQ—1,200). DuPont Glore Forgan Inc., New York (Securities dealers, underwriters—HQ—1,000). Walston and Co., New York (Securities dealers—HQ—1,000). Merrill, Lynch, Pierce, Fenner, and Smith Inc., New York (Securities dealers, underwriters—HQ—4,000). Shearson Hammill and Co. Inc., New York (Securities dealers—2,000). Home Insurance Co. of New York,

New York (Insurance—HQ—2,500). Chubb and Son Inc., New York (Insurance underwriters and managers—HQ—1,000). The State Insurance Fund, New York (Insurance—HQ—1,500). British and Foreign Maritime Fire Insurance Co., New York (Marine casualty insurance—6,650). Johnson and Higgins, New York (Insurance brokers—2,450). Liverpool and London and Globe Insurance, New York (Insurance—2,300). Dun and Bradstreet Inc., New York (Consumer credit and reporting agency—HQ—2,000). Haskins and Sells, New York (Public accounts—HQ—1,000). Price Waterhouse and Co., New York (Public accountants—HQ—3,000). American Stock Exchange, New York (Stock exchange—1,000). New York Stock Exchange Inc., New York (Stock exchange—1,500). American Bank Note Co., New York (Engraving and printing—HQ—1,000). American Express Co., New York (Banking, travelers checks, etc.—HQ—6,000). Ebasco Services Inc., New York (Engineering, construction—HQ—1,900). Liberia Mining Co. Ltd., New York (Mining—2,400). GATX Oswego Corp., New York (Holding company, vessel owner and operator—HQ—4,600). American Transportation Enterprises Inc., New York (Holding company, transportation—5,000). International Terminal Operating, New York (Holding company, cargo handling—5,000). Procter and Gamble Manufacturing Co., Mariners Harbor (Port Ivory Division—soap, shortening—1,100). American Electric Power Service Corp., New York (Electric power systems—HQ—1,100). American Cable and Radio Corp., New York (Holding company, Communications—4,000). Department of Marine and Aviation, New York (NYC transportation—1,000). New York City Department of Public Works, New York. (Municipal public works department—3,000). Pinkertons Inc., New York (Security services—HQ—1,000).

18th District

(Manhattan—East Side, Silk Stocking District)

Race and Ethnic Groups. Blacks 4.3 percent. Spanish heritage population 7.0 percent. Russian stock 7.0 percent, German stock 4.0 percent, Polish stock 3.7 percent, Italian stock 3.6 percent, Irish stock 2.9 percent, British stock 2.9 percent, Austrian stock 2.8 percent.

Cities, 1970 Population. Part of New York City 467,533.

Universities, Enrollment. Bernard M. Baruch College (New York—12,053), City University of New York Graduate School and University Center (New York—2,325), Hunter College (New York—23,465), Cooper Union (New York—1,011), New School for Social Research (New York—3,286), New York University (New York—30,540), John Jay School of Criminal Justice (New York—5,544).

Newspapers, Circulation. New York City newspapers circulate throughout district. They include: New York Daily News (MxSat—2,099,988), New York Post (ExSat—622,883), New York Times (MxSat—874,347), El Diario-LaPrensa (MxSat—75,869).

Commercial Television Stations, Affiliation. Entire district is located in New York City ADI. Stations include: WABC-TV, New York (ABC); WCBS-TV, New York (CBS); WNBC-TV, New York (NBC); WNEW-TV, New York (None); WOR-TV, New York (None); WPIX, New York (None); WNJU-TV, Linden-Newark, New Jersey (None); WXTV, Paterson, New Jersey, (None-Spanish language station).

Plants and Offices, Products, Employment. (Note: Midtown business and office section of city is included in district.)

Standard Oil Company of New Jersey., New York (Headquarters—1,220). **Texaco Inc.**, New York (Headquarters—2,200). **Union Carbide Corp.**, New York (Headquarters—4,000). **Sperry Rand Corp.**, New York (Headquarters—1,500). **Litton Business Systems Inc.**, New York (Business machines—HQ—1,000). **IBM World Trade Corp.**, New York (Headquarters—1,280). **Singer Co.**, New York (Headquarters—1,100). **Pfizer Inc.**, New York (Headquarters—1,000). **Sterling Drug Inc.**, New York (Headquarters—2,300). **Colgate Palmolive Co.**, New York (Headquarters—1,000). **Lever Brothers Inc.**, New York (Headquarters—1,150). **Avon Products Inc.**, New York (Headquarters—1,200). **Revlon Inc.**, New York (Headquarters—1,000). **J. P. Stevens and Co. Inc.**, New York (Headquarters—1,200). **American Broadcasting Company**, New York (Headquarters—2,000). **Columbia Broadcasting Systems**, New York (Headquarters—2,700). **National Broadcasting Co. Inc.**, New York (Headquarters—3,500). **United Artists Corp.**, New York (Motion pictures—HQ—1,200). **Time Inc.** New York (Headquarters—3,000). **Equitable Life Assurance Society of the United States**, New York (Headquarters—7,500). **Hertz Corp.**, New York (Headquarters—1,000). **American Airlines Inc.**, New York (Headquarters—1,500). **Joseph E. Seagram Sons Inc.**, New York (Headquarters—1,200). **Batten, Barton, Durstine and Osborn**, New York (Advertising agency—HQ—1,200). **The Interpublic Group of Companies**, New York (Advertising agencies, holding company—HQ—2,000). **Doyle Dane Berbach Inc.**, New York (Advertising agency—HQ—1,200). **Young and Rubicam Inc.**, New York (Advertising agency—HQ—1,530). **J. Walter Thompson Co.**, New York (Advertising agency—HQ—2,680), **Advertising Distributors of America**, New York (Direct mail advertising services—2,000). **Richards Company Inc.**, New York (Consulting—1,000). **United Medical Services Inc.**, New York (Medical insurance—1,400). **Mutual Life Insurance Co. of New York**, New York (Insurance—HQ—1,800). **Associated Hospital Service of New York**, New York (Hospital and medical service plans—HQ—2,000). **CIT Financial Corp.**, New York (Holding company —HQ—1,200). **Bankers Trust New York Corp.**, New York (Bank, holding company—9,420). **Fairchild Publications Inc.**, New York (Publisher—HQ —1,200). **Harcourt Brace Jovanovich Inc.**, New York (Publishers—HQ—1,000). **Cadence Industries Inc.**, New York (Publishing, holding company—1,660). **W. M. Jackson Inc.**, New York (Book publishing, retailing—2,500). **New York Times Co.**, New York (Publishers—HQ—5,000). **New York News Inc.**,

New York (Publishing—HQ—3,500). **Cowles Communications Inc.**, New York (Publishing—HQ—1,000). **United Press International Inc.**, New York (News agency—4,000). **New York Public Library**, New York (Public library—2,420). **Arcs Industries Inc.**, New York (Engineering, holding company—1,200). **Rissil Construction Associates**, New York (Construction—1,000). **Ibec Housing Co. Inc.**, New York (Building contractor—1,000). **United Merchants and Manufacturers Inc.**, New York (Fabrics —HQ—1,000). **M. Lowenstein and Sons Inc.**, New York (Fabrics—HQ—1,100). **Splentex Inc.**, New York (Design, corsets, etc.—1,000). **Spencer Industries Inc.**, New York (Men's, boys' slacks—2,500).**Yong Industries Inc.**, New York (Men's wear, wigs—3,800). **Alexander's Department Stores**, New York (Department stores—2,000). **Gimbel Brothers Inc.**, New York (Department stores—HQ—4,000). **Associated Dry Goods Corp.**, New York (Department stores—HQ—1,000). **R. H. Macy and Co. Inc.**, New York (Department stores—HQ—5,000). **B. Altman and Co.**, New York (Department stores —HQ—1,000). **J. C. Penney Co. Inc.**, New York (Department stores, holding company—HQ—4,000). **Ohrbachs Inc.**, New York (Women's wear—HQ—1,200). **National Shirt Shops Inc.**, New York (Men's clothing—1,250). **Allied Stores Corp.** New York (Department stores, holding company—HQ—2,000). **American Yvette Co. Inc.**, New York (Beauty supplies—2,500). **Glemby Co. Inc.**, New York (Beauty products—7,500). **Servomation Corp.**, New York (Holding company, food service machines—13,000). **Frank G. Shattuck Co.**, New York (Schrafft's restaurant chain—HQ—1,000). **National Restaurants Inc.**, New York (Child's Restaurants, Calico Kitchen—restaurants, holding company—1,000). **Consolidated Edison Co. of New York Inc.**, New York (Electric and gas utility—HQ—6,700). **Allegheny Power System Inc.**, New York (Holding company, electric utilities—6,300). **Middle South Utilities Inc.**, New York (Holding company, utilities—HQ—total employment 9,140). **National Fuel Gas Co.**, New York (Holding company, gas—3,850). **Meyer Brothers Parking System Inc.**, New York (Holding company, parking systems—1,000). **Carol Management Co.**, New York (Building operators —1,000). **Holmes Protection Inc.**, New York (Protective alarm systems—HQ—1,000). **Prudential Building Maintenance**, New York (Holding company, building maintenance—HQ—2,500). **Owners Maintenance Corp.**, New York (Janitorial services—2,000). **Overseas Shipholding Group Inc.**, New York (Holding company, ship operator—1,000). **Hilton International Co.**, New York (Hotels—HQ—at least 1,000). **Hotel Waldorf Astoria Corp.**, New York (Hotel operator—HQ—2,000).

19th District

(Manhattan—Harlem)

Race and Ethnic Groups. Blacks 58.7 percent. Spanish heritage population 17.3 percent. Italian stock 1.5 percent, Russian stock 1.4 percent.

Cities, 1970 Population. Part of New York City 466,876.

Universities, Enrollment. City College (New York—21,181), The Juilliard School (New York—1,121).

Newspapers, Circulation. New York City newspapers circulate throughout district.

Commercial Television Stations, Affiliation. Entire district is located in New York City ADI.

Plants and Offices, Products, Employment.
Empire Mutual Insurance Co. Inc., New York (Insurance—1,000). **Flower Fifth Avenue Hospital**, New York (Hospital—3,700).

20th District

(Western Manhattan and Bronx— West Side, Riverdale)

Race and Ethnic Groups. Blacks 15.3 percent. Spanish heritage population 9.3 percent. Russian stock 5.5 percent, German stock 5.1 percent, Irish stock 4.1 percent, Polish stock 3.5 percent.

Cities, 1970 Population. Part of New York City 468,667.

Universities, Enrollment. Columbia University (New York—15,124), Barnard College (New York—1,930), Columbia University Teachers College (New York—5,280), Fordham University (New York—part in 10th District, total enrollment 13,841), Yeshiva University (New York—3,891).

NASA Facilities. Goddard Institute for Space Studies, New York.

Newspapers, Circulation. New York City newspapers circulate throughout district.

Commercial Television Stations, Affiliation. Entire district is located in New York City ADI.

Plants and Offices, Products, Employment.
McGraw-Hill Inc., New York (Publishers—HQ—2,100). **Deluxe General Inc.**, New York (Motion pictures—1,200). **Otis Elevator Co.**, New York (Elevators—HQ—1,000). **Central Coat, Apron and Linen Service**, New York (Linen service, etc.—1,000). **Interstate Stores Inc.**, New York (Discount department stores—HQ—1,000). **Holly Stores Inc.**, New York (Women's wear—at least 1,000). **Sears, Roebuck and Co.**, New York (Mail order house—1,820). **Associated Lerner Shops of America**, New York (Women's wear, accessories—1,000). **Bell Transportation System Inc.**, New York (Taxicabs—1,400). **United Parcel Service of America**, New York (Holding company, delivery service—at least 1,000). **Port of New York Authority**, New York (Port authority—8,000).

21st District

(South Bronx—Mott Haven, Morrisania)

Race and Ethnic Groups. Blacks 41.7 percent. Spanish heritage population 43.8 percent. Russian stock 1.1 percent, Italian stock 1.1 percent.

Cities, 1970 Population. Part of New York City 462,030.

Newspapers, Circulation. New York City newspapers circulate throughout district.

Commercial Television Stations, Affiliation. Entire district is located in New York City ADI.

Plants and Offices, Products, Employment.
American Bank Note Co., Bronx (Engraving and printing—1,100). **Eden Transportation System Inc.**, Bronx (Taxi operation and maintenance—HQ—2,000).

22nd District

(Bronx—University Heights, Co-op City)

Race and Ethnic Groups. Blacks 17.6 percent. Spanish heritage population 14.1 percent. Russian stock 8.5 percent, Irish stock 6.2 percent, Polish stock 5.6 percent, Italian stock 5.0 percent, Austrian stock 2.9 percent.

Cities, 1970 Population. Part of New York City 466,931.

Universities, Enrollment. Herbert H. Lehman College (Bronx—13,078).

Newspapers, Circulation. New York City newspapers circulate throughout district.

Commercial Television Stations, Affiliation. Entire district is located in New York City ADI.

Plants and Offices, Products, Employment.
Montefiore Hospital, Bronx (Hospital—4,500).

23rd District

(North Central Bronx, Western Westchester County—Williamsbridge, Yonkers)

Race and Ethnic Groups. Blacks 12.5 percent. Italian stock 13.2 percent, Russian stock 3.2 percent, Irish stock 3.8 percent, German stock 2.9 percent, Polish stock 2.6 percent.

Cities, 1970 Population. Part of New York City 159,779, part of Yonkers 146,433, Eastchester 23,769, Hartsdale 12,330.

Universities, Enrollment. Manhattan College (Bronx—4,572), Marymount College (Tarrytown—1,007), Mercy College (Dobbs Ferry—1,583), College of Mt. St. Vincent (Bronx—1,061).

Newspapers, Circulation. New York City newspapers circulate throughout district.

Commercial Television Stations, Affiliation. Entire district is located in New York City ADI.

Plants and Offices, Products, Employment.
USV Pharmaceutical Corp., Tuckahoe (Pharmaceuticals—1,000). **Ciba-Geigy Corp.**, Ardsley (Chemicals, pharmaceuticals—HQ—1,700). **Technicon Corp.**, Tarrytown (Research and scientific laboratory—HQ—1,700). **General Motors Corp.**, Tarrytown Auto bodies—6,000). **Phelps Dodge Copper Products Corp.**, Yonkers (Insulated wire cables—1,200). **Otis Elevator Co.**, Yonkers (Elevators, moving stairs—1,620).

24th District

(Central and Southeastern Westchester County)

Race and Ethnic Groups. Blacks 12.7 percent. Italian stock 13.4 percent, Russian stock 3.2 percent, German stock 3.0 percent, Irish stock 2.7 percent, British stock 2.5 percent.

Cities, 1970 Population. New Rochelle 75,530, Mount Vernon 72,914, part of Yonkers 58,477, White Plains 50,158.

Universities, Enrollment. College of New Rochelle (New Rochelle—1,400), Iona College (New Rochelle—4,140), Manhattanville College (Purchase—1,518).

Newspapers, Circulation. New York City newspapers circulate throughout district.

Commercial Television Stations, Affiliation. Entire district is located in New York City ADI.

Plants and Offices, Products, Employment.

Pepsico Inc., Purchase (Headquarters—1,250). General Foods Corp., White Plains (Headquarters—3,300). International Business Machines Corp. Armonk (Headquarters—1,600). Readers Digest Association Inc., Chappaqua (Headquarters—3,400). P. Carlin Construction Inc., New Rochelle (General contracting, real estate—at least 1,500). Peter Pan Enterprises Corp., Pelham (Holding company—1,000). County of Westchester, White Plains (County government—5,000).

25th District

(Hudson Valley—Poughkeepsie)

Race and Ethnic Groups. Blacks 4.8 percent. Italian stock 6.0 percent, German stock 3.9 percent.

Cities, 1970 Population. Poughkeepsie 32,018, Kingston 25,535, Peekskill 19,276, Beacon 13,246.

Universities, Enrollment. Marist College (Poughkeepsie—1,796), Vassar College (Poughkeepsie—2,130).

Newspapers, Circulation. New York City newspapers circulate throughout district.

Commercial Television Stations, Affiliation. Almost entire district is located in New York City ADI. Small portion of district is located in Albany-Schenectady-Troy ADI.

Plants and Offices, Products, Employment.

International Business Machines Corp., Poughkeepsie (Electronic computers—11,000). International Business Machines Corp., Hopewell Junc-

tion (Electronic computers—6,000). Western Publishing Co. Inc., Poughkeepsie (Printing and publishing—1,100).

26th District

(Lower Hudson Valley—New City, Newburgh)

Race and Ethnic Groups. Blacks 6.0 percent. Italian stock 5.7 percent, German stock 3.3 percent, Russian stock 2.6 percent, Irish stock 2.6 percent.

Cities, 1970 Population. New City 27,344, Newburgh 26,219, Middletown 22,607, Spring Valley 18,096.

Universities, Enrollment. United States Military Academy (West Point—4,000).

Military Installations or Activities. West Point Military Reservation.

Newspapers, Circulation. New York City newspapers circulate throughout district.

Commercial Television Stations, Affiliation. Entire district is located in New York City ADI.

Plants and Offices, Products, Employment.

Stauffer Chemical Co. Inc., Newburgh (Coated

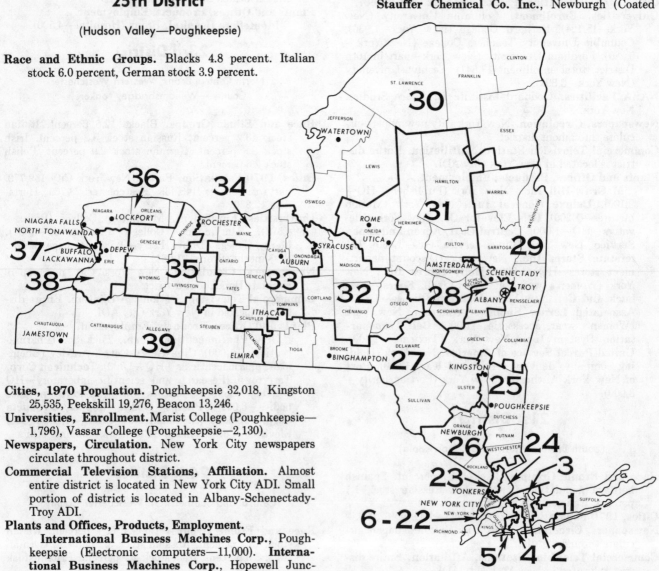

fabrics—1,000). **American Cyanamid Co.**, Pearl River (Biological products, pharmaceuticals—7,000). **Avon Products Inc.**, Suffern (Cosmetics, toiletries—1,000). **R. H. Macy and Co.**, Nanuet (Department store—1,000). **Orange and Rockland Utilities**, Spring Valley (Electric and gas utility—1,300). **Middletown State Hospital**, Middletown (State mental hospital—1,300).

27th District

(Southern Tier—Binghamton)

Race and Ethnic Groups. Italian stock 3.0 percent, German stock 2.4 percent.
Cities, 1970 Population. Binghamton 64,111, Ithaca 26,221, Johnson City 18,021, Endicott 16,553.
Universities, Enrollment. Cornell University (Ithaca—16,144), Ithaca College (Ithaca—4,038), State University of New York at Binghamton (Binghamton—7,182), State University College of Arts and Sciences (New Paltz—8,027).
Newspapers, Circulation. Binghamton Press (Eve—76,725).
Commercial Television Stations, Affiliation. Majority of district is located in Binghamton ADI. Parts of district are located in New York City ADI, Syracuse ADI, and Elmira ADI. Binghamton stations include: WBJA-TV, Binghamton (ABC); WICZ-TV, Binghamton (NBC); WNBF-TV, Binghamton (CBS).
Plants and Offices, Products, Employment.
International Business Machines Corp., Endicott (Systems Manufacturing Division—business machines, typewriters—10,000). **International Business Machines Corp.**, Owego (Federal Systems Division—data processing equipment—5,100). **General Electric Co.**, Johnson City (Aircraft Equipment Division—aircraft equipment—3,000). **Borg-Warner Corp.**, Ithaca (Morse Chain Division—power transmission equipment—1,500). **GAF Corp.**, Vestal (Industrial Products Division—duplicating equipment, supplies—3,500). **Endicott Johnson Corp.**, Endicott (Footwear—HQ—1,000).

28th District

(Hudson-Mohawk Valleys—Albany, Schenectady, Amsterdam)

Race and Ethnic Groups. Blacks 4.0 percent. Italian stock 7.2 percent, Polish stock 3.8 percent, German stock 2.6 percent, Canadian stock 2.5 percent.
Cities, 1970 Population. Albany 115,835, Schenectady 77,832, Amsterdam 25,515, Rotterdam 25,214.
Universities, Enrollment. Siena College (Loudonville—1,821), State University of New York at Albany (Albany—13,288), Union College and University (Schenectady—4,656).
AEC-Owned, Contractor-Operated Facilities. Knolls Atomic Power Laboratory, Schenectady.
Military Installations or Activities. Watervliet Arsenal, Watervliet.
Newspapers, Circulation. Albany Times-Union (Morn—72,512), Knickerbocker News-Union Star, Albany (Eve—71,444), Schenectady Gazette (Morn—63,661).
Commercial Television Stations, Affiliation. Entire district is located in Albany-Schenectady-Troy ADI. Stations include: WAST, Albany (ABC); WRGB, Schenectady (NBC); WTEN, Albany (CBS).
Plants and Offices, Products, Employment.
General Electric Co., Schenectady (Gas, steam turbines—26,000). **General Electric Co.**, Schenectady (Large steam turbine generators—at least 1,010). **General Electric Co.**, Schenectady (Carbon, graphite products—at least 1,000). **General Electric Co.**, Schenectady (Gas turbines—at least 1,000). **General Electric Co.**, Schenectady (Gas turbines—at least 1,000). **Allegheny Ludlum Industries**, Watervliet (Stainless steel—1,600). **Norton Co.**, Watervliet (Behr-Manning Division—abrasive products—2,300). **Mohasco Industries Inc.**, Amsterdam (Rugs, carpets, furniture—HQ—1,000). **Williams Press Inc.**, Albany (Offset letter press—HQ—1,000). **Niagara Mohawk Power Corp.**, Albany (Electric utility—1,050). **Delaware and Hudson Railway Co.**, Albany (Railroad—total employment 2,350). **State of New York**, Albany (State government—total employment 32,000).

29th District

(Upper Hudson Valley—Saratoga Springs, Troy)

Race and Ethnic Groups. Italian stock 3.5 percent, Canadian stock 2.5 percent, German stock 2.5 percent.
Cities, 1970 Population. Troy 62,943, Saratoga Springs 18,851, Glens Falls 17,228, Rensselaer 10,213.
Universities, Enrollment. Rensselaer Polytechnic Institute (Troy—4,737), Russell Sage College (Troy—3,404), Skidmore College (Saratoga Springs—1,868).
Military Installations or Activities. Saratoga Air Force Station, Saratoga Springs.
Newspapers, Circulation. Albany and Schenectady papers circulate in portions of district.
Commercial Television Stations, Affiliation. Nearly entire district is located in Albany-Schenectady-Troy ADI. Small portion of district is located in Burlington (Vermont)-Plattsburgh ADI.
Plants and Offices, Products, Employment.
General Electric Co., Waterford (Silicone materials—1,000). **General Electric Co.**, Hudson Falls (Capacitors—1,000). **Ford Motor Co.**, Troy (Green Island Plant—auto radiators—1,000). **International Paper Co.**, Corinth (Paper mill—1,300). **Hercules Inc.**, Glens Falls (Dyes and pigments—1,050). **Sterling Drug Inc.**, Rensselaer (Winthrop Laboratories—pharmaceuticals—1,320). **Cluett Peabody and Co.**, Troy (Arrow-Troy—men's and boys' shirts—1,420).

30th District

(North—Plattsburgh, Watertown)

Race and Ethnic Groups. Canadian stock 7.4 percent, Italian stock 1.6 percent.

Cities, 1970 Population. Watertown 30,793, Oswego 23,841, Plattsburgh 18,719, Ogdensburg 14,546.

Universities, Enrollment. Clarkson College of Technology (Potsdam—2,608), St. Lawrence University (Canton—2,508), State University College of Arts and Sciences (Oswego—8,044), State University College of Arts and Sciences (Plattsburgh—5,220), State University College of Arts and Sciences (Potsdam—4,568).

Military Installations or Activities. Plattsburgh Air Force Base, Plattsburgh; Watertown Air Force Station, Watertown.

Newspapers, Circulation. Syracuse papers circulate in portions of district.

Commercial Television Stations, Affiliation. District is divided between Watertown ADI and Burlington (Vermont)-Plattsburgh ADI. Small portion of district is located in Syracuse ADI. Plattsburgh station: WPTZ, Plattsburgh (NBC). Watertown station: WWNY-TV, Watertown-Canton (CBS primary, ABC secondary).

Plants and Offices, Products, Employment.
　　Aluminum Company of America, Massena (Aluminum—3,500). **General Motors Corp.,** Massena (Chevrolet Motor Division—castings—1,100). **General Signal Corp.,** Watertown (New York Air Brake Division—air brakes, hydraulic equipment—1,900). **International Paper Co.,** Ticonderoga (Paper—1,050). **Nestle Co. Inc.,** Fulton (Chocolate—1,500).

31st District

(Mohawk Valley—Utica)

Race and Ethnic Groups. Italian stock 6.4 percent, Polish stock 3.5 percent.

Cities, 1970 Population. Utica 91,671, Rome 50,140, Gloversville 19,681, Johnstown 10,047.

Military Installations or Activities. Griffis Air Force Base, Rome.

Commercial Television Stations, Affiliation. District is divided between Utica ADI, Albany-Schenectady-Troy ADI and Syracuse ADI. Utica stations include: WKTV, Utica (NBC, ABC per program basis); WUTR-TV, Utica (ABC).

Plants and Offices, Products, Employment.
　　General Electric Co., Utica (Radio Receiver Division—radio receivers—2,000). **General Electric Co.,** Utica (Aircraft Equipment Division—aircraft electrical systems—6,000). **General Electric Co.,** Utica (Aircraft Equipment Division—aircraft parts—4,000). **Kelsey-Hayes Co.,** Whitesboro (Utica Turbine Parts Division—forgings—1,400). **Kelsey-Hayes Co.,** Utica (Forged jet engine parts—1,400). **Chicago Pneumatic Tool Co.,** Utica (Electric and hydraulic tools—at least 1,500). **Cyprus Mines Corp.,** Rome (Rome Cable Division—wires and cables—1,000). **Revere Copper and Brass Inc.,** Rome (Rome Manufacturing Co. Division—cooking utensils—2,000). **Mohawk Data Sciences Corp.,** Herkimer (Data processing equipment—HQ—2,600). **Sperry Rand Corp.,** Ilion (Remington Rand Univac Divsion—computer equipment—3,200). **Remington Arms Co. Inc.,** Ilion (Firearms—1,700). **Squibb Beechnut Inc.,** Canajoharie (Chewing gum—

1,400). **General Telephone Co., Upstate New York,** Johnstown (Telephone company—HQ—1,100).

32nd District

(Central—Syracuse)

Race and Ethnic Groups. Italian stock 4.4 percent, Canadian stock 2.4 percent.

Cities, 1970 Population. Part of Syracuse 102,530, Cortland 19,635, Oneonta 16,041, Oneida 11,666.

Universities, Enrollment. Colgate University (Hamilton—2,329), Hartwick College (Oneonta—1,687), LeMoyne College (Syracuse—1,713), State University College of Arts and Sciences (Cortland—5,130), State University College of Arts and Sciences (Oneonta—5,435), Syracuse University (Syracuse—18,727).

Newspapers, Circulation. Syracuse Post-Standard (MxSat—91,909), Syracuse Herald Journal (Eve—125,948).

Commercial Television Stations, Affiliation. Nearly entire district is located in Syracuse ADI. Small portions of district are located in Utica ADI and Binghamton ADI. Syracuse stations include: WHEN-TV, Syracuse (CBS); WNYS-TV, Syracuse (ABC); WSYR-TV, Syracuse (NBC).

Plants and Offices, Products, Employment.
　　Chrysler Corp., East Syracuse (New Process Gear Division—auto transmissions—2,400). **General Motors Corp.,** Syracuse (Fisher Body Ternstedt Division—auto equipment, accessories—1,900). **General Electric Co.,** Syracuse (Radar apparatus—3,500). **Carrier Corp.,** Syracuse (Air conditioning, heating equipment—HQ—6,500). **Crouse-Hinds Co.,** Syracuse (Conduit connectors—HQ—2,500). **Eltra Corp.,** Syracuse (Presto-Lite Division—DC motors—1,000). **Bendix Corp.,** Sidney (Electrical components—4,800). **SCM Corp.,** Cortland (Smith Corona Division—typewriters, business equipment—4,000). **Norwich Pharmacal Co.,** Norwich (Pharmaceuticals—HQ—1,300). **Bristol-Myers Co.,** Syracuse (Drugs—2,000). **Oneida Ltd.,** Oneida (Silverware—HQ—2,740). **Carrols Development Corp.,** Syracuse (Holding company, movie theaters, restaurants—3,000). **Victory Markets Inc.,** Norwich (Supermarkets—1,500). **Crouse-Irving Memorial Hospital,** Syracuse (Hospital—1,300). **United Parcel Service Inc.,** East Syracuse (Parcel delivery—1,200).

33rd District

(Central—Syracuse, Canandaigua)

Race and Ethnic Groups. Blacks 4.0 percent. Italian stock 4.8 percent, Canadian stock 2.2 percent.

Cities, 1970 Population. Part of Syracuse 94,860, Auburn 34,616, Geneva 16,801, Fairmount 15,512.

Universities, Enrollment. Hobart and William Smith Colleges (Geneva—1,695).

Military Installations or Activities. Seneca Army Depot, Romulus.

Newspapers, Circulation. Syracuse papers circulate in portions of district.

Commercial Television Stations, Affiliation. Most of district is located in Syracuse ADI. Small portions of district are located in Rochester ADI and Buffalo ADI.

Plants and Offices, Products, Employment.

General Electric Co., Auburn (Semiconductors —1,000). **SCM Corp.,** Groton (Power communications systems—1,250). **Goulds Pumps Inc.,** Seneca Falls (Water systems, pumps—HQ—1,040). **Lipe-Rollway Corp.,** Syracuse (Clutches, industrial machinery—1,150). **Colt Industries Inc.,** Syracuse (Crucible Special Metals Division—special metals —2,100). **Allied Chemical Corp.,** Solvay (Industrial Chemicals Division—soda ash—1,840). **E. W. Edwards and Son,** Syracuse (Department stores— HQ—1,100). **P and C Food Markets Inc.,** Syracuse (Groceries—1,700). **New York Telephone Co.,** Syracuse (Telephone company—2,660).

34th District

(West—Rochester)

Race and Ethnic Groups. Blacks 6.1 percent. Italian stock 7.1 percent, German stock 3.3 percent, Canadian stock 3.0 percent.

Cities, 1970 Population. Part of Rochester 176,242, Newark 11,648.

Universities, Enrollment. Nazareth College of Rochester (Rochester—1,348), Saint John Fisher College (Rochester—1,356), University of Rochester (Rochester—8,461).

Newspapers, Circulation. Rochester Democrat and Chronicle (Morn—138,777), Rochester Times-Union (Eve—140,964).

Commercial Television Stations, Affiliation. Entire district is located in Rochester ADI. Rochester stations include: WHEC-TV, Rochester (CBS); WOKR, Rochester (ABC); WROC-TV, Rochester (NBC).

Plants and Offices, Products, Employment.

Eastman Kodak Co., Rochester (Films, cameras, photo supplies, etc.—HQ—67,000). **Xerox Corp.,** Rochester (Xerographic equipment—1,600). **Xerox Corp.,** Rochester (Copying, duplicating equipment —2,200). **Xerox Corp.,** Webster (Xerographic equipment—8,850). **Bausch and Lomb Inc.,** Rochester (Optical goods—HQ—5,000). **Stromberg Carlson Corp.,** Rochester (Communications equipment—HQ—4,100). **Mobil Oil Corp.,** Macedon (Polyethylene bags—1,200). **Garlock Inc.,** Palmyra (Mechanical Products Division—mechanical packing seals—2,000). **Gleason Works,** Rochester (Machine tools, industrial machinery—2,500). **R. T. French Co.,** Rochester (Food products—HQ—1,000). **Bond Stores Inc.,** Rochester (Clothing—1,700). **Hickey-Freeman Co. Inc.,** Rochester (Apparel— HQ—1,500). **Sarah Coventry,** Newark (Costume jewelry—3,000). **Gannett Co. Inc.,** Rochester (Holding company, newspaper publishing—1,400). **Rochester General Hospital,** Rochester (Hospital— 1,700). **City of Rochester,** Rochester (City government—5,000).

35th District

(West—Rochester, Batavia)

Race and Ethnic Groups. Blacks 6.2 percent. Italian stock 6.2 percent, Canadian stock 3.1 percent, German stock 2.6 percent.

Cities, 1970 Population. Part of Rochester 120,045, Batavia 17,337.

Universities, Enrollment. State University College of Arts and Sciences (Geneseo—5,278), Rochester Institute of Technology (Rochester—10,436).

Newspapers, Circulation. Rochester newspapers circulate in portions of district.

Commercial Television Stations, Affiliation. Most of district is located in Rochester ADI. Small portion of district is located in Buffalo ADI.

Plants and Offices, Products, Employment.

Eastman Kodak Co., Rochester (Kodak Apparatus Division—cameras—9,460). **Eastman Kodak Co.,** Rochester (Kodak Part Division—films, cameras, photo supplies—27,300). **Bausch and Lomb Inc.,** Rochester (Ophthalmic Division—eyeglass frames—1,150). **Itek Corp.,** Rochester (Photo copying machinery—1,200). **GTE Sylvania Inc.,** Batavia (Radio, TV tubes, receivers—1,300). **General Motors Corp.,** Rochester (Delco Products Division— electric motors—3,500). **General Motors Corp.,** Rochester (Rochester Products Division—welded steel tubing—4,000). **General Signal Corp.,** Rochester (General Railway Signal Co. Division—signal equipment—1,090). **Foster Wheeler Corp.,** Dansville (Fabricated plate works—1,000). **Interpace Corp.,** Leroy (Lapp Insulator Division—porcelain insulation—1,500).

36th District

(West—Niagara Falls)

Race and Ethnic Groups. Blacks 2.7 percent. Canadian stock 6.5 percent, Italian stock 5.3 percent, Polish stock 3.5 percent, British stock 3.0 percent, German stock 2.9 percent.

Cities, 1970 Population. Niagara Falls 85,707, North Tonawanda 36,051, part of Buffalo 31,841, Lockport 25,426.

Universities, Enrollment. Niagara University (Niagara Falls—3,336), State University College of Arts and Sciences (Brockport—8,302).

Military Installations or Activities. Lockport Air Force Station, Lockport.

Newspapers, Circulation. Buffalo newspapers circulate throughout most of district.

Commercial Television Stations, Affiliation. Entire district is located in Buffalo ADI.

Plants and Offices, Products, Employment.

General Motors Corp., Tonawanda (Chevrolet Motor Division—automotive parts—10,000). **General Motors Corp.,** Lockport (Harrison Radiator Division—auto radiators, defrosters, heaters—7,500). **Textron Inc.,** Niagara Falls (Bell Aerospace Division—helicopters, rocket engines—7,800). **Hooker Chemical Corp.,** North Tonawanda (Durez Plastics

Division—plastics—1,000). **Hooker Chemical Corp.**, Niagara Falls (Industrial Chemicals Division—industrial chemicals—2,500). **Carborundum Co.**, Niagara Falls (Abrasives, electric components, etc.—HQ—4,000). **Dunlop Tire and Rubber Co.**, Buffalo (Tires and sporting goods—HQ—1,600). **Western Electric Co. Inc.**, Buffalo (Communications equipment—2,550). **Union Carbide Corp.**, Tonawanda (Linde Air Products Division—special machinery—1,360). **Spaulding Fibre Co. Inc.**, Tonawanda (Fibres, plastic products—HQ—1,600). **TRW Inc.**, Buffalo (J. H. Williams and Co. Division—hand tools, forgings—1,050). **Kimberly-Clark Corp.**, Niagara Falls (Paper products—1,010). **E. I. duPont de Nemours and Co.**, Niagara Falls (Elastomen chemicals—1,810). **Harvest Markets Inc.**, Buffalo (Holding company, supermarkets—2,000).

37th District

(West—Buffalo)

Race and Ethnic Groups. Blacks 20.7 percent. Polish stock 7.5 percent, Italian stock 6.4 percent, German stock 3.3 percent, Canadian stock 2.7 percent.

Cities, 1970 Population. Part of Buffalo 430,205, Lackawanna 28,606.

Universities, Enrollment. Canisius College (Buffalo—4,162), D'Youville College (Buffalo—1,205), State University of New York at Buffalo (Buffalo—23,723), State University College of Arts and Sciences (Buffalo—10,182).

Newspapers, Circulation. Buffalo Courier-Express (Morn—132,110), Buffalo Evening News (ExSat—276,520).

Commercial Television Stations, Affiliation. Entire district is located in Buffalo ADI. Buffalo stations include: WBEN-TV, Buffalo (CBS); WGR-TV, Buffalo (NBC); WKBW-TV, Buffalo (ABC); WUTV, Buffalo (None).

Plants and Offices, Products, Employment.

Bethlehem Steel Corp., Lackawanna (Steel products—18,500). **Republic Steel Corp.**, Buffalo (Iron, steel—3,000). **General Motors Corp.**, Buffalo (Chevrolet Buffalo Division—auto parts—3,300). **Ford Motor Co.**, Lackawanna (Stampings—5,000). **Trico Products Corp.**, Buffalo (Auto accessories—HQ—1,500). **Trico Products Corp.**, Buffalo (Auto equipment—1,000). **Worthington Corp.**, Buffalo (Pumps, machinery—at least 1,800). **Buffalo Forge Co.**, Buffalo (Heating, ventilating, air conditioning equipment, etc.—HQ—1,800). **Allied Chemical Corp.**, Buffalo (Dyes, intermediaries—1,700). **National Gypsum Co.**, Buffalo (Gypsum products, cement, tile, etc.—HQ—5,000). **M. Wile and Co.**, Buffalo (Men's apparel—HQ—1,200). **Service Systems Corp.**, Buffalo (Food service, building maintenance—5,000). **Associated Dry Goods Corp.**, Buffalo (William Hengerer Co. Division—department stores—1,000). **Acme Markets Inc.**, Buffalo (Groceries—1,600). **Niagara Frontier Transit System**, Buffalo (Motor carrier—1,100). **Niagara Mohawk Power Corp.**, Buffalo (Electric utility—2,800).

38th District

(West—Buffalo Suburbs)

Race and Ethnic Groups. Polish stock 5.2 percent, German stock 3.9 percent, Italian stock 3.5 percent, Canadian stock 3.3 percent.

Cities, 1970 Population. Depew 22,114, Lancaster 13,375, Hamburg 10,222.

Universities, Enrollment. Rosary Hill College (Buffalo —1,249).

Newspapers, Circulation. Buffalo newspapers circulate throughout district.

Commercial Television Stations, Affiliation. Entire district is located in Buffalo ADI.

Plants and Offices, Products, Employment.

Moog Inc., East Aurora (Electrohydraulic servovalves, machine tools, etc.—HQ—1,000). **Westinghouse Electric Corp.**, Buffalo (Motor generators —6,500). **Cornell Aeronautical Laboratory**, Buffalo (Aeronautical engineering—1,300). **Dresser Industries Inc.**, Depew (Transportation Equipment Division—castings—1,370). **American Optical Corp.**, Buffalo (Optical equipment—1,300). **Quaker Oats Co.**, East Aurora (Fisher-Price Toys Division —toys—at least 1,200). **Arcata Graphics Corp.**, Depew (Commercial, lithographic printing—1,800). **Unexcelled Inc.**, Depew (Holding company, general merchandise—3,000).

39th District

(Southern Tier—Chautauqua, Elmira)

Race and Ethnic Groups. Italian stock 3.1 percent, Swedish stock 2.0 percent.

Cities, 1970 Population. Elmira 39,931, Jamestown 39,781, Olean 19,162, Dunkirk 16,849.

Universities, Enrollment. Alfred University (Alfred—2,364), Elmira College (Elmira—3,266), Houghton College (Houghton—1,210), St. Bonaventure University (Olean—2,637), State University College of Arts and Sciences (Fredonia—4,768).

Newspapers, Circulation. Buffalo newspapers circulate in major portions of district.

Commercial Television Stations, Affiliation. Most of district is located in Buffalo ADI. Portion of district is located in Elmira ADI. Elmira station: WENY-TV, Elmira (ABC).

Plants and Offices, Products, Employment.

Corning Glass Works, Corning (Glass products—HQ—8,000). **Dart Industries Inc.**, Elmira (Glass bottles, containers—1,300). **Westinghouse Electric Corp.**, Elmira (Electron tubes—1,000). **Sperry Rand Corp.**, Elmira (Typewriters, business machines —2,200). **Allegheny Ludlum Industries.**, Dunkirk (Bar Products Division—steel bars—1,000). **Dresser Industries Inc.**, Olean (Clark Turbo Compressor Division—electric, gas, steam compressors—1,500). **Blackstone Corp.**, Jamestown (Auto parts, machinery, malleable iron foundries—HQ—1,000). **Bendix Corp.**, Elmira (Motor Components Division—fuel pumps, automatic starters—1,270). **TRW Inc.**,

Jamestown (Marlin Rockwell Co. Division—auto and aeronautical parts—2,000). **Air Preheater Co. Inc.**, Wellsville (Heating equipment—HQ—1,020). **Cooper Industries Inc.**, Jamestown (Crescent Division—tools—1,000). **Ingersoll-Rand Co.**, Painted Post (Compressors—1,800). **Great Atlantic and Pacific Tea Co. Inc.**, Horseheads (Ann Page Division—confectionaries, jams, jellies—2,000).

NORTH CAROLINA: ELEVEN HOUSE SEATS, NO CHANGE

North Carolina passed a relatively simple redistricting bill, shifting only 10 of the state's 100 counties and avoiding the crossing of county lines. *(Map p. 145)*

Originating in the Senate, the bill passed by voice vote Feb. 24, 1971; the House concurred April 28 also by voice vote. The bill then became law, as redistricting bills do not need the governor's signature in North Carolina.

An earlier, more complex plan would have combined two Democratic incumbents—former Rep. Alton Lennon of the 7th District and Rep. David N. Henderson of the 3rd District—but this proposal was abandoned for the simpler version.

The only major change produced by redistricting occurred in the 4th District, which lost Orange County to the 2nd District. Orange County contains the liberal campus community surrounding the University of North Carolina at Chapel Hill. It gave former 4th District Rep. Nick Galifianakis (D) half his margin of 4,500 votes in 1970 and almost his entire 4,400-vote margin in 1968. Galifianakis ran for the U.S. Senate in 1972 but the district remained in Democratic hands by a narrow margin.

In addition, the transfer of Orange County broke up the "research triangle" consisting of Chapel Hill, Durham and Raleigh, all of which had been in the 4th District.

District	Member Elected 1972	Winning Percentage	1970 Population	Percent Variance
1	Walter B. Jones (D)	68.8	459,543	—0.5328
2	L. H. Fountain (D)	71.6	457,601	—0.9532
3	David N. Henderson (D)	100.0	458,000	—0.8668
4	Ike F. Andrews (D)	50.4	467,046	+ 1.0911
5	Wilmer Mizell (R)	64.8	462,401	+ 0.0857
6	Richardson Preyer (D)	93.9	457,354	—1,0666
7	Charles G. Rose III (D)	60.4	467,476	+ 1.1841
8	Earl B. Ruth (R)	60.2	454,275	—1.6731
9	James G. Martin (R)	58.9	459,535	—0.5346
10	James T. Broyhill (R)	72.5	471,777	+ 2.1151
11	Roy A. Taylor (D)	59.6	467,051	+ 1,0921

1970 State Population: 5,082,059
Ideal District Population: 462,005

Election Results, 1968-1972

Vote for U.S. Representative
(Adjusted to new district boundaries)

District	1968	1970	1972
1	86,629 D (66.8%)	48,313 D (70.4%)	77,438 D (68.8%)
	43,113 R (33.2%)	18,886 R (28.1%)	35,063 R (31.2%)
2	102,993 D (92.4%)	45,794 D (90.8%)	88,798 D (71.6%)
	8,483 R (7.6%)	4,425 R (8.8%)	35,193 R (28.4%)
3	61,183 D (56.3%)	40,346 D (59.6%)	56,968 D (100.0%)
	47,503 R (43.7%)	27,328 R (40.4%)	—
4	66,900 D (50.0%)	43,612 D (51.3%)	73,072 D (50.4%)
	66,829 R (50.0%)	41,409 R (48.7%)	71,972 R (49.6%)
5	85,255 R (54.6%)	67,410 R (57.5%)	101,375 R (64.8%)
	70,925 D (45.4%)	49,900 D (42.5%)	54,986 D (35.2%)
6	72,204 D (53.1%)	45,322 D (65.5%)	82,158 D (93.9%)
	63,862 R (46.9%)	20,291 R (30.9%)	—
7	70,792 D (100.0%)	35,367 D (71.7%)	57,348 D (60.4%)
	—	13,931 R (28.3%)	36,726 R (38.7%)
8	78,524 R (53.0%)	57,994 R (57.8%)	82,060 R (60.2%)
	69,667 D (47.0%)	42,314 D (42.2%)	54,198 D (39.8%)
9	82,975 R (100.0%)	50,756 R (67.3%)	80,356 R (58.9%)
	—	24,625 D (32.7%)	56,171 D (41.1%)
10	84,480 R (54.3%)	61,975 R (56.6%)	103,119 R (72.5%)
	71,196 D (45.7%)	47,530 D (43.4%)	39,025 D (27.5%)
11	92,576 D (55.5%)	90,782 D (66.2%)	94,465 D (59.6%)
	74,372 R (44.5%)	46,337 R (33.8%)	64,062 R (40.4%)
State	765,065 D (54.6%)	513,905 D (55.3%)	734,627 D (54.4%)
	635,396 R (45.4%)	410,742 R (44.2%)	609,926 R (45.2%)

Voting Age Population

District	Voting Age Population	Voting Age Population 18, 19, 20	Voting Age Population 65 and Over	Median Age of Voting Age Population
1	292,095	28,066 (9.6%)	39,247 (13.4%)	42.1
2	292,016	29,167 (10.0%)	40,362 (13.8%)	42.0
3	295,516	39,802 (13.5%)	31,160 (10.5%)	37.7
4	312,185	31,803 (10.2%)	35,032 (11.2%)	39.3
5	304,551	22,737 (7.5%)	39,219 (12.9%)	41.6
6	302,110	26,352 (8.7%)	36,624 (12.1%)	41.4
7	293,448	38,272 (13.0%)	27,203 (9.3%)	35.9
8	298,954	24,181 (8.1%)	42,700 (14.3%)	43.7
9	296,456	23,137 (7.8%)	32,569 (11.0%)	40.2
10	308,054	26,227 (8.5%)	36,194 (11.7%)	40.9
11	317,583	23,208 (7.3%)	53,939 (17.0%)	44.8
State	3,312,968	312,952 (9.4%)	414,249 (12.5%)	40.9

Income and Occupation

District	Median Family Income	White Collar Workers	Blue Collar Workers	Service Workers	Farm Workers
1	$6,368	36.0%	40.1%	13.1%	10.8%
2	6,550	36.1	41.3	12.9	9.7
3	6,193	33.5	42.9	12.3	11.3
4	8,999	49.6	35.5	12.3	2.6
5	8,191	37.4	50.3	9.1	3.2
6	9,300	43.3	45.3	9.6	1.8
7	6,875	40.1	40.3	13.1	6.5
8	7,872	30.4	56.3	9.9	3.4
9	9,594	50.7	37.4	10.9	1.0
10	8,449	30.3	59.2	9.0	1.5
11	6,857	34.8	51.4	10.5	3.3
State	7,770	38.6	45.8	11.0	4.6

Education: School Years Completed

District	Completed 4 years of High School	Completed 4 years of College	Completed 5 years or less of School	Median School years completed
1	35.3%	6.9%	17.2%	10.2
2	33.0	8.5	20.1	9.8
3	36.4	5.8	15.5	10.4
4	46.3	13.8	11.3	11.5
5	36.7	7.8	13.2	10.3
6	41.2	10.5	11.4	11.0
7	43.7	8.1	13.2	11.2
8	32.1	5.6	15.1	10.0
9	48.5	11.9	9.1	11.8
10	32.7	6.4	14.8	10.0
11	37.7	7.4	13.7	10.5
State	38.5	8.5	14.0	10.6

Housing and Residential Patterns

District	Housing Owner Occupied Units	Housing Renter Occupied Units	Urban	Suburban	Nonmetropolitan
1	61.9%	38.1%	—	—	100.0%
2	56.9	43.1	—	12.6%	87.4
3	59.6	40.4	—	—	100.0
4	61.3	38.7	46.4%	47.3	6.3
5	70.6	29.4	28.8	17.6	53.6
6	66.2	33.8	45.3	17.8	36.9
7	60.6	39.4	21.3	47.0	31.7
8	71.3	28.7	—	17.5	82.5
9	63.4	36.6	52.5	24.7	22.8
10	70.7	29.3	—	—	100.0
11	74.2	25.8	12.3	18.7	69.0
State	65.4	34.6	18.8	18.5	62.7

1st District

(Northeast—Greenville, Kinston)

Race and Ethnic Groups. Blacks 35.8 percent.
Cities, 1970 Population. Greenville 29,078, Kinston 22,309, New Bern 14,660, Elizabeth City 13,903.
Universities, Enrollment. East Carolina University (Greenville—10,106), Elizabeth City State University (Elizabeth City—1,104).
Military Installations or Activities. Naval Facility, Cape Hatteras, Buxton; Marine Corps Air Station, Cherry Point; Naval Air Rework Facility, Cherry Point.
Newspapers, Circulation. Raleigh newspapers circulate in portion of district.
Commercial Television Stations, Affiliation. WCTI-TV, New Bern (ABC); WITN-TV, Washington (NBC); WNCT-TV, Greenville (CBS). District located in Greenville-New Bern-Washington ADI and Norfolk-Portsmouth-Newport News-Hampton (Virginia) ADI.
Plants and Offices, Products, Employment.
Weyerhauser Co., Plymouth (North Carolina Pulp Co. Division—paper mill—2,500). Scovill Manufacturing Co., Washington (Hamilton Beach Division

—electric housewares—1,000). E. I. duPont de Nemours and Co., Kinston (Organic fibers—2,700). Hampton Shirt Co. Inc., Kinston (Shirts and pajamas—1,500). A. C. Monk Co. Inc., Farmville (Wholesale leaf tobacco—1,000).

2nd District

(Northeast Central—Rocky Mount, Wilson)

Race and Ethnic Groups. Blacks 40.1 percent.
Cities, 1970 Population. Rocky Mount 34,315, Wilson 29,347, Chapel Hill 25,534, Henderson 13,802.
Universities, Enrollment. Atlantic Christian College (Wilson—1,794), University of North Carolina at Chapel Hill (Chapel Hill—19,160).
Military Installations or Activities. Roanoke Rapids Air Force Station, Roanoke Rapids.
Newspapers, Circulation. Raleigh newspapers circulate in portion of district.
Commercial Television Stations, Affiliation. Portions of district are located in Greensboro-Winston Salem-High Point ADI, Raleigh-Durham ADI, Greenville-New Bern-Washington ADI and Norfolk-Portsmouth-Newport News-Hampton (Virginia) ADI.
Plants and Offices, Products, Employment.
Collins & Aikman Corp., Roxboro (Upholstery fabrics—1,000). Collins & Aikman Corp., Ca-Vel (Upholstery fabrics—1,000). Hardee's Food Systems Inc., Rocky Mount (Holding company—restaurant franchises—1,600).

3rd District

(Southeast Central—Goldsboro)

Race and Ethnic Groups. Blacks 26.7 percent.
Cities, 1970 Population. Camp Lejeune Central 34,517, Goldsboro 26,821, Jacksonville 16,021, Sanford 11,612.
Universities, Enrollment. Campbell College (Buie's Creek—2,401).
Military Installations or Activities. Marine Corps Air Facility, New River; Marine Corps Base, Camp Lejeune; Naval Hospital, Camp Lejeune; Seymour-Johnson Air Force Base, Goldsboro.
Newspapers, Circulation. Raleigh newspaper circulates in portion of district.
Commercial Television Stations, Affiliation. Portions of district are located in Raleigh-Durham ADI, Wilmington ADI and Greenville-New Bern-Washington ADI.
Plants and Offices, Products, Employment.
G. T. & E. Sylvania Inc., Smithfield (Television receivers—1,400).

4th District

(Central—Raleigh, Durham)

Race and Ethnic Groups. Blacks 23.2 percent.
Cities, 1970 Population. Raleigh 121,128, Durham 95,412, Asheboro 10,797.
Universities, Enrollment. Duke University (Durham—8,338), Meredith College (Raleigh—1,206), North Carolina Central University (Durham—3,723), Saint

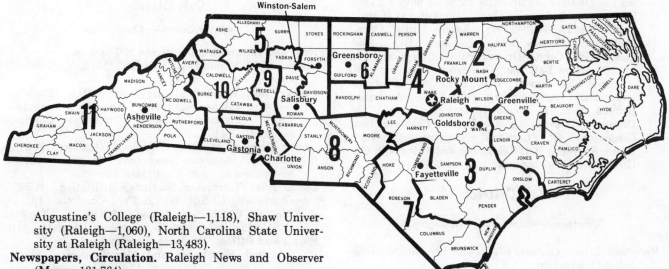

Augustine's College (Raleigh—1,118), Shaw University (Raleigh—1,060), North Carolina State University at Raleigh (Raleigh—13,483).

Newspapers, Circulation. Raleigh News and Observer (Morn—131,764).

Commercial Television Stations, Affiliation. WRAL-TV, Raleigh (ABC); WTVD, Durham (CBS); WRDU-TV, Durham (NBC). Majority of district is located in Raleigh-Durham ADI. Portion of district is located in Greensboro-Winston Salem-High Point ADI.

Plants and Offices, Products, Employment.

Nello L. Teer Co., Durham (Highway, airport construction—HQ—1,500). **Martin Marietta Corp.**, Raleigh (Superior Stone Co. Division—crushed stone —1,000). **Westinghouse Electric Corp.**, Raleigh (Meters—1,250). **International Business Machines Corp.**, Wake County (Computer equipment—2,600). **American Brands Inc.**, Durham (Cigarettes—1,600). **Liggett & Myers Inc.**, Durham (Cigarettes, cigars, other tobacco products—3,010). **Acme-McCrary Corp.**, Asheboro (Hosiery—HQ—1,000). **Burlington Industries Inc.**, Durham (Erwin Mills Division—cotton fabrics—1,700). **Southern Bell Telephone & Telegraph Co.**, Raleigh (Telephone company—1,200). **General Telephone Company of the Southeast**, Durham (Telephone company—HQ—1,200).

5th District

(Northwest—Winston-Salem)

Race and Ethnic Groups. Blacks 14.0 percent.

Cities, 1970 Population. Winston-Salem 132,901, Lexington 17,203, Thomasville 15,230.

Universities, Enrollment. Wake Forest University (Winston-Salem—3,738), Winston-Salem State University (Winston-Salem—1,623).

Newspapers, Circulation. Winston-Salem Journal (Morn —78,492).

Commercial Television Stations, Affiliation. WSJS-TV, Winston-Salem (NBC). Most of district is located in Greensboro-Winston Salem-High Point ADI. Portion of district is located in Charlotte ADI.

Plants and Offices, Products, Employment.

Dombrico Inc., Kernersville (Varco-Pruden Co. Division—prefabricated metal buildings—1,000). **Western Electric Co.**, Winston-Salem (Communications equipment—4,500). **Western Electric Co. Inc.**, Winston-Salem (Offices—2,450). **RJR Archer Inc.**,

Winston-Salem (Filmco Division—aluminum, plastic products—1,000). **Dixie Furniture Co. Inc.**, Lexington (Bedroom furniture—HQ—1,000). **Floyd S. Pike Electrical Contractor**, Mount Airy (Electrical contractor—1,000). **Chatham Manufacturing Co.**, Elkin (Blankets, yarn, upholstery fabrics—3,500). **Spencers Inc. of Mount Airy**, Mount Airy (Infants' sleepwear and underwear—HQ—1,160). **Hanes Corp.**, Winston-Salem (Hosiery, knitted underwear —HQ—4,500). **Holly Farms Poultry Industries**, Wilksboro (Poultry processing—1,400). **Piedmont Aviation Inc.**, Winston-Salem (Airline—HQ—1,250). **North Carolina Baptist Hospital**, Winston-Salem (Hospital—1,600).

6th District

(Central—Greensboro, High Point)

Race and Ethnic Groups. Blacks 20.9 percent.

Cities, 1970 Population. Greensboro 144,245, High Point 63,049, Burlington 36,198, Eden 15,871.

Universities, Enrollment. Elon College (Elon College— 1,862), Guilford College (Greensboro—1,740), High Point College (High Point—1,060), North Carolina Agricultural and Technical State University (Greensboro—4,445), University of North Carolina at Greensboro (Greensboro—6,983).

Newspapers, Circulation. Greensboro News (Morn— 80,617).

Commercial Television Stations, Affiliation. WFMY-TV, Greensboro (CBS); WGHP-TV, High Point (ABC). Entire district is located in Greensboro-Winston-Salem-High Point ADI.

Plants and Offices, Products, Employment.

Western Electric Co. Inc., Burlington (Missile guidance equipment—1,000). **Western Electric Co. Inc.**, Greensboro (Communications and guided missile equipment—1,300). **Washington Mills Co. Inc.**, Mayodan (Knitted underwear—at least 1,200). **Burlington Industries Inc.**, Madison (Madison Throwing Co. Division—commercial throwing plant—1,280). **Burlington Industries Inc.**, Greensboro (Fabric, yarn, hosiery—HQ—2,000). **Adams-Millis Corp.**, High Point (Hosiery, holding company—HQ—1,000). **Cone Mills Corp.**, Greensboro (Cotton cloth—HQ—4,800). **Blue Bell Inc.**, Greensboro (Clothing—HQ—1,500). **Glen Raven Mills**, Burlington (Synthetic and natural yarn, hosiery—HQ—1,000). **American Brands Inc.**, Reidsville (American Tobacco Co. Division—cigarettes—1,700). **Loews Theaters Inc.**, Greensboro (P. Lorrillard Division—cigarettes—2,300). **Southern Bell Telephone and Telegraph Co.**, Greensboro (Telephone company—1,000).

7th District

(Southeast—Fayetteville, Wilmington)

Race and Ethnic Groups. Blacks 25.6 percent. American Indians 6.9 percent.

Cities, 1970 Population. Fayetteville 53,510, Fort Bragg 46,995, Wilmington 46,169, Lumberton 16,961.

Universities, Enrollment. Fayetteville State University (Fayetteville—1,482), Pembroke State University (Pembroke—2,077), University of North Carolina at Wilmington (Wilmington—2,043).

Military Installations or Activities. Fort Bragg, Fayetteville; Sunny Point Military Ocean Terminal, Southport; Pope Air Force Base, Fayetteville; Fort Fisher Air Force Station, Kure Beach.

Commercial Television Stations, Affiliation. WECT, Wilmington (NBC primary); WWAY, Wilmington (ABC). District is divided between Wilmington ADI and Raleigh-Durham ADI.

Plants and Offices, Products, Employment.
B. F. Goodrich Co., Lumberton (Rubber footwear—1,900). **Burlington Industries Inc.**, Raeford (Fabric dyeing and finishing—1,000).

8th District

(South Central—Kannapolis)

Race and Ethnic Groups. Blacks 20.0 percent.

Cities, 1970 Population. Kannapolis 36,236, Salisbury 22,573, Concord 18,464, Monroe 11,282.

Universities, Enrollment. Catawba College (Salisbury—1,133), Pfeiffer College (Misenheimer—1,088).

Newspapers, Circulation. Charlotte newspapers circulate in major portion of district.

Commercial Television Stations, Affiliation. Most of district is divided between Charlotte ADI and Greensboro-Winston-Salem-High Point ADI. Small portion of district is located in Florence (South Carolina) ADI.

Plants and Offices, Products, Employment.
Wiscassett Mills Co. Inc., Albemarle (Yarns, hosiery—3,000). **Springs Mills Inc.**, Wagram (Finished terry towels—1,350). **Fiber Industries Inc.**, Salisbury (Polyester fiber-2,500). **Kayser-Roth Corp.**, Concord (Hosiery—1,000). **U.S. Industries Inc.**, Concord (Pennaco Division—hosiery—2,000). **Seaboard Coast Line Railroad**, Hamlet (Railroad—1,100).

9th District

(West Central—Charlotte)

Race and Ethnic Groups. Blacks 21.7 percent.

Cities, 1970 Population. Charlotte 241,215, Statesville 19,996.

Universities, Enrollment. Davidson College (Davidson—1,089), Johnson C. Smith University (Charlotte—1,036), University of North Carolina at Charlotte (Charlotte—4,676).

Newspapers, Circulation. Charlotte Observer (Morn—175,978), Charlotte News (Eve—70,068). Charlotte newspapers circulate throughout district.

Commercial Television Stations, Affiliation. WBTV, Charlotte (CBS); WCCB-TV, Charlotte (ABC); WRET-TV, Charlotte (None); WSOC-TV, Charlotte (NBC). Entire district is located in Charlotte ADI.

Plants and Offices, Products, Employment.
United Merchants and Manufacturers, Statesville (Langley Processing Division—fiberglass products—1,150). **McDevitt & Street Co. Inc.**, Charlotte (General building contractors—2,000). **Burlington Industries Inc.**, Mooresville (Mooresville Mills Division—cotton blend fabrics—1,900). **Ruddick Corp.**, Charlotte (Holding company—5,000). **Lance Inc.**, Charlotte (Bakery products, confections—2,190). **Family Dollar Stores Inc.**, Charlotte (Holding company—1,000). **Belk Brothers Co.**, Charlotte (Department store—1,000). **Eastern Air Lines Inc.**, Charlotte (Reservation center—1,000). **Duke Power Co.**, Charlotte (Electric utility—HQ—2,000).

10th District

(West—Gastonia)

Race and Ethnic Groups. Blacks 10.7 percent.

Cities, 1970 Population. Gastonia 47,153, Hickory 20,599, Shelby 16,328, Lenoir 14,747.

Universities, Enrollment. Appalachian State University (Boone—8,229), Gardner-Webb College (Boiling Springs—1,528), Lenoir Rhyne College (Hickory—1,395).

Newspapers, Circulation. Charlotte newspapers circulate in major portion of district.

Commercial Television Stations, Affiliation. WHKY-TV, Hickory (None). Hickory has no ADI of its own. Entire district is located in Charlotte ADI.

Plants and Offices, Products, Employment.
General Electric Co., Hickory (Transformers—1,200). **Wix Corp.**, Gastonia (Oil, air, fuel filters—HQ—1,500). **Wix Corp.**, Gastonia (Oil, air filters—1,000). **Firestone Tire & Rubber Co.**, Gastonia (Synthetics, tire cord—1,450). **Pharr Yarns Inc.**, McAdenville (Synthetic and carpet yarns—2,200). **Parkdale Mills Inc.**, Gastonia (Yarn—1,000). **Fiber Industries Inc.**, Shelby (Polyester fibers—2,500). **J. P. Stevens & Co. Inc.**, Hickory (Hosiery—1,300). **Highlander Ltd.**, Morganton (Gastonia Textile Division—knitted outerwear—1,000). **PPG Industries Inc.**, Shelby (Glass fibers—1,500). **Bernhardt Furniture Co.**, Lenoir (Dining room furniture—1,000). **Bernhardt Industries Inc.**, Lenoir (Holding company—2,000). **Akers Motor Lines Inc.**, Gastonia (Long

distance trucking—HQ—1,200). **Carolina Freight Carriers Corp.**, Cherryville (Long distance trucking —HQ—1,600).

11th District

(West—Asheville)

Race and Ethnic Groups. Blacks 5.7 percent.
Cities, 1970 Population. Asheville 57,571.
Universities, Enrollment. Mars Hill College (Mars Hill —1,467), University of North Carolina at Asheville (Asheville—1,107), Western Carolina University (Cullowhee—5,517).
Commercial Television Stations, Affiliation. WLUS-TV, Asheville (ABC). Most of district is located in Greenville (South Carolina)-Spartanburg (South

Carolina)-Asheville ADI. Portions of district are located in Atlanta (Georgia) ADI, Chattanooga (Tennessee) ADI, Knoxville (Tennessee) ADI and Bristol-Kingsport-Johnson City (Tennessee) ADI.
Plants and Offices, Products, Employment. **Olin Corp.**, Pisgah Forest (Ecusta Paper Division —paper—2,800). **U.S. Plywood-Champion Papers**, Canton (Paper coating, glazing—2,300). **Dayco Corp.**, Waynesville (Foam rubber products—1,850). **Stonecutter Mills Corp.**, Spindale (Finished fabrics, fibers—HQ—1,400). **Cone Mills Corp.**, Cliffside (Towels—1,200). **American Thread Co.**, Marion (Cotton thread—1,000). **Akzona Inc.**, Enka (Nylon, rayon, polyester yarns—HQ—4,900). **National Distillers & Chemical Corp.**, Swannanoa (Beacon Manufacturing Co. Division—blankets, bedspreads— 1,700).

OHIO: TWENTY-THREE HOUSE SEATS, LOSS OF ONE

Ohio's Republican legislature faced two main problems in designing new congressional district boundaries: elimination of one district due to reapportionment and designing a plan acceptable to Democratic Gov. John J. Gilligan. *(Maps p. 150, 153)*

As in several other states with different parties in control of the legislature and governor's office (e.g., California, Wisconsin, Minnesota), a compromise was seen as the only solution.

The compromise formula involved creating favorable districts for all incumbents, with the exception of the district that had to be eliminated. The latter problem was solved when Rep. Jackson E. Betts (R) of the old 8th District announced his retirement. His district was then divided among neighboring districts.

Redistricting legislation passed the state House Jan. 5, 1972, 74-22, and the Senate Jan. 13, 25-6. Gilligan signed the bill Jan. 20.

District	Member Elected 1972	Winning Percentage	1970 Population	Percent Variance
1	William J. Keating (R)	70.3	462,725	—0.0876
2	Donald D. Clancy (R)	62.8	463,260	+ 0.0278
3	Charles W. Whalen Jr. (R)	76.2	463,140	+ 0.0019
4	Tennyson Guyer (R)	62.7	463,143	+ 0.0025
5	Delbert L. Latta (R)	72.7	463,727	+ 0.1286
6	William H. Harsha (R)	100.0	463,067	—0.0138
7	Clarence J. Brown (R)	73.3	463,217	+ 0.0185
8	Walter E. Powell (R)	52.2	462,915	—0.0466
9	Thomas L. Ashley (D)	69.1	463,286	+ 0.0334
10	Clarence E. Miller (R)	73.2	463,353	+ 0.0479
11	J. William Stanton (R)	68.2	462,701	—0.0928
12	Samuel L. Devine (R)	56.1	463,120	—0.0023
13	Charles A. Mosher (R)	68.1	464,056	+ 0.1997
14	John F. Seiberling (D)	74.4	464,578	+ 0.3124
15	Chalmers P. Wylie (R)	65.8	462,703	—0.0924
16	Ralph S. Regula (R)	57.3	463,699	+ 0.1226
17	John M. Ashbrook (R)	57.4	462,846	—0.0615
18	Wayne L. Hays (D)	70.2	462,797	—0.0721
19	Charles J. Carney (D)	64.0	463,625	+ 0.1066
20	James V. Stanton (D)	84.3	462,480	—0.1405
21	Louis Stokes (D)	81.1	462,584	—0.1181
22	Charles A. Vanik (D)	63.9	462,271	—0.1856
23	William E. Minshall (R)	49.4	462,724	—0.0878

1970 State Population: 10,652,071
Ideal District Population: 463,131

Election Results, 1968-1972

Vote for U.S. Representative
(Adjusted to new district boundaries)

District	1968	1970	1972
1	110,246 R (67.2%)	97,135 R (68.1%)	119,469 R (70.3%)
	53,884 D (32.8%)	45,536 D (31.9%)	50,575 D (29.7%)
2	117,789 R (68.2%)	80,310 R (55.3%)	109,961 R (62.8%)
	55,008 D (31.8%)	64,260 D (44.2%)	65,237 D (37.2%)
3	112,156 R (78.2%)	86,948 R (73.7%)	111,253 R (76.2%)
	31,229 D (21.8%)	27,469 D (23.2%)	34,819 D (23.8%)
4	137,143 R (92.1%)	93,865 R (71.9%)	109,612 R (62.7%)
	11,616 D (7.8%)	36,730 D (28.1%)	65,216 D (37.3%)
5	122,445 R (72.8%)	98,689 R (73.5%)	132,032 R (72.7%)
	45,822 D (27.2%)	35,667 D (26.5%)	49,465 D (27.3%)
6	121,924 R (74.1%)	88,947 R (66.5%)	128,394 R (100.0%)
	42,528 D (25.9%)	44,232 D (33.1%)	—
7	94,000 R (63.5%)	81,552 R (69.2%)	112,350 R (73.3%)
	53,948 D (36.5%)	36,215 D (30.8%)	—
8	97,689 R (75.7%)	61,107 R (55.2%)	80,050 R (52.2%)
	31,332 D (24.3%)	46,898 D (42.4%)	73,344 D (47.8%)
9	89,365 D (57.2%)	84,597 D (68.6%)	110,450 D (69.1%)
	66,757 R (42.8%)	38,738 R (31.4%)	49,388 R (30.9%)
10	113,269 R (68.8%)	90,310 R (66.6%)	129,683 R (73.2%)
	51,276 D (31.2%)	45,176 D (33.3%)	47,456 D (26.8%)
11	101,695 R (72.2%)	83,236 R (67.7%)	106,841 R (68.2%)
	39,209 D (27.8%)	39,627 D (32.3%)	49,891 D (31.8%)
12	94,823 R (68.2%)	74,106 R (58.3%)	103,655 R (56.1%)
	44,268 D (31.8%)	52,949 D (41.7%)	81,074 D (43.9%)
13	86,139 R (60.9%)	78,067 R (65.7%)	111,242 R (68.1%)
	55,390 D (39.1%)	40,820 D (34.3%)	51,991 D (31.9%)
14	93,666 R (55.7%)	76,938 D (55.2%)	135,068 D (74.4%)
	74,620 D (44.3%)	62,080 R (44.6%)	46,490 R (25.6%)
15	101,888 R (72.1%)	83,343 R (68.1%)	115,779 R (65.8%)
	39,469 D (27.9%)	39,073 D (31.9%)	55,314 D (31.5%)
16	98,273 R (59.3%)	79,735 R (56.3%)	102,013 R (57.3%)
	67,333 D (40.7%)	61,157 D (43.2%)	75,929 D (42.7%)
17	101,537 R (66.7%)	84,891 R (76.0%)	92,666 R (57.4%)
	50,704 D (33.3%)	23,922 D (21.4%)	62,512 D (38.7%)
18	106,398 D (57.5%)	89,850 D (64.8%)	128,663 D (70.2%)
	78,575 R (42.5%)	48,535 R (35.0%)	54,572 R (29.8%)
19	103,798 D (62.1%)	78,492 D (54.9%)	109,979 D (64.0%)
	63,473 R (37.9%)	64,371 R (45.1%)	61,934 R (36.0%)
20	96,548 D (63.4%)	89,300 D (67.6%)	117,302 D (84.3%)
	55,661 R (36.6%)	42,773 R (32.4%)	16,624 R (11.9%)
21	110,026 D (76.5%)	94,389 D (83.2%)	99,190 D (81.1%)
	33,840 R (23.5%)	19,063 R (16.8%)	13,861 R (11.3%)

District	1968	1970	1972
22	101,458 R (52.4%)	105,117 D (61.8%)	126,462 D (63.9%)
	92,229 D (47.6%)	65,029 R (38.2%)	64,577 R (32.6%)
23	100,180 R (55.0%)	100,586 R (61.0%)	98,594 R (49.4%)
	82,022 D (45.0%)	64,344 D (39.0%)	94,366 D (47.3%)
State	2,209,940 R (60.7%)	1,705,205 R (56.1%)	2,071,040 R (54.2%)
	1,429,705 D (39.3%)	1,323,281 D (43.5%)	1,684,303 D (44.0%)

District	Median Family Income	White Collar Workers	Blue Collar Workers	Service Workers	Farm Workers
22	13,427	63.0	28.7	8.1	0.2
23	13,101	60.9	30.0	8.8	0.3
State	10,309	45.4	40.9	12.0	1.7

Voting Age Population

District	Voting Age Population	Voting Age Population 18, 19, 20	Voting Age Population 65 and Over	Median Age of Voting Age Population
1	309,380	25,773 (8.3%)	49,207 (15.9%)	43.6
2	293,381	21,562 (7.3%)	44,750 (15.3%)	43.0
3	306,017	25,262 (8.3%)	39,833 (13.0%)	41.9
4	293,579	21,890 (7.5%)	47,458 (16.2%)	43.6
5	291,614	27,372 (9.4%)	45,265 (15.2%)	42.4
6	292,130	19,385 (6.6%)	47,058 (16.1%)	43.7
7	294,994	24,780 (8.4%)	37,714 (12.8%)	41.0
8	294,345	27,130 (9.2%)	36,473 (12.4%)	40.7
9	303,327	23,169 (7.6%)	49,124 (16.2%)	44.4
10	305,577	29,822 (9.8%)	51,480 (16.8%)	43.2
11	284,112	20,728 (7.3%)	33,536 (11.8%)	41.7
12	291,034	23,545 (8.1%)	30,994 (10.6%)	39.2
13	286,136	22,709 (7.9%)	35,535 (12.4%)	41.7
14	309,317	29,391 (9.5%)	44,336 (14.3%)	42.4
15	314,671	35,666 (11.3%)	41,500 (13.2%)	39.1
16	299,899	23,042 (7.7%)	44,824 (14.9%)	43.3
17	295,950	23,030 (7.8%)	44,493 (15.0%)	42.7
18	306,623	20,168 (6.6%)	54,844 (17.9%)	46.4
19	304,771	22,159 (7.3%)	45,535 (14.9%)	44.7
20	305,961	20,949 (6.8%)	44,358 (14.5%)	44.4
21	304,594	24,841 (8.2%)	46,476 (15.3%)	42.9
22	308,940	19,392 (6.3%)	43,170 (14.0%)	45.2
23	306,083	20,418 (6.7%)	41,111 (13.4%)	44.4
State	6,902,442	552,181 (8.0%)	999,077 (14.5%)	42.8

Education: School Years Completed

District	Completed 4 years of High School	Completed 4 years of College	Completed 5 years or less of School	Median School years completed
1	52.7%	14.2%	5.9%	12.1
2	49.1	11.2	5.9	11.9
3	56.3	12.1	4.7	12.2
4	54.5	6.8	3.4	12.1
5	55.6	6.9	3.4	12.1
6	44.5	5.3	6.2	11.2
7	55.1	8.9	3.7	12.1
8	48.7	7.3	5.3	11.8
9	51.7	9.5	5.7	12.1
10	48.8	6.2	5.5	11.8
11	56.9	9.2	3.5	12.2
12	62.2	11.5	3.3	12.3
13	54.4	7.4	4.8	12.1
14	54.9	10.8	5.1	12.2
15	58.6	16.1	4.8	12.3
16	52.7	7.4	4.4	12.1
17	53.8	6.8	3.6	12.1
18	46.8	4.5	5.7	11.5
19	51.5	7.2	7.0	12.1
20	42.0	3.8	7.4	11.1
21	39.2	5.8	10.8	10.9
22	68.2	19.0	3.4	12.5
23	66.2	14.8	2.9	12.4
State	53.2	9.3	5.1	12.1

Income and Occupation

District	Median Family Income	White Collar Workers	Blue Collar Workers	Service Workers	Farm Workers
1	$10,535	53.4%	32.7%	13.8%	0.1%
2	10,439	53.0	34.1	12.6	0.3
3	11,481	51.1	36.6	12.0	0.3
4	9,710	38.3	45.6	11.8	4.3
5	9,945	37.0	46.4	11.9	4.7
6	8,595	36.9	45.9	11.8	5.4
7	10,132	43.7	41.8	11.5	3.0
8	10,455	40.8	45.4	11.4	2.4
9	10,786	47.6	38.8	13.2	0.4
10	7,894	38.6	45.3	13.2	2.9
11	11,142	40.7	47.1	10.1	2.1
12	10,710	53.7	34.4	11.0	0.9
13	10,795	40.2	46.6	11.6	1.6
14	10,876	48.7	38.3	12.7	0.3
15	10,074	56.7	29.5	12.7	1.1
16	10,197	41.5	44.7	11.7	2.1
17	9,460	38.3	45.7	11.8	4.2
18	8,701	34.3	51.4	11.8	2.5
19	10,311	41.2	46.2	12.1	0.5
20	10,550	41.2	47.3	11.4	0.1
21	8,573	36.9	43.7	18.9	0.5

Housing and Residential Patterns

	Housing		Urban-Suburban-Nonmetropolitan Breakdown		
District	Owner Occupied Units	Renter Occupied Units	Urban	Suburban	Nonmetropolitan
1	53.3%	46.7%	48.3%	51.7%	—
2	59.6	40.4	49.4	50.6	—
3	61.6	38.4	52.6	47.4	—
4	73.9	26.1	11.5	30.8	57.7%
5	76.0	24.0	—	36.8	63.2
6	71.8	28.2	—	37.5	62.5
7	70.0	30.0	17.7	51.6	30.7
8	72.3	27.7	25.2	63.5	11.3
9	68.0	32.0	82.9	17.1	—
10	73.1	26.9	—	12.3	87.7
11	78.0	22.0	—	78.8	21.2
12	67.2	32.8	54.8	40.6	4.6
13	73.9	26.1	28.5	55.4	16.1
14	68.9	31.1	59.3	40.7	—
15	51.8	48.2	61.7	32.2	6.1
16	73.3	26.7	23.7	57.5	18.8
17	73.8	26.2	11.9	16.2	71.9
18	75.8	24.2	6.7	31.6	61.7
19	74.2	25.8	43.8	56.2	—

District	Owner Occupied Units	Renter Occupied Units	Urban	Suburban	Nonmetro-politan
			Urban-Suburban-Nonmetropolitan Breakdown		
20	62.9	37.1	64.5	35.5	—
21	39.3	60.7	86.6	13.4	—
22	72.5	27.5	2.7	97.3	—
23	70.4	29.6	8.6	91.4	—
State	67.7	32.3	32.2	45.5	22.3

1st District

(Hamilton County—Eastern Cincinnati and Suburbs)

Race and Ethnic Groups. Blacks 20.0 percent. German stock 2.5 percent, Russian stock 1.0 percent.

Cities, 1970 Population. Part of Cincinnati 223,641, Norwood 30,343, Kenwood 15,817, Forest Park 15,173.

Universities, Enrollment. University of Cincinnati (Cincinnati—34,552), Xavier University (Cincinnati—5,964).

Newspapers, Circulation. Cincinnati Enquirer (Morn—192,033), Cincinnati Post and Times-Star (Eve—215,818).

Commercial Television Stations, Affiliation. WCPO-TV, Cincinnati (CBS); WKRC-TV, Cincinnati (ABC); WLWT, Cincinnati (NBC); WXIX-TV, Cincinnati-Newport, Kentucky (None). Entire district is located in Cincinnati ADI.

Plants and Offices, Products, Employment.

Procter and Gamble Co., Cincinnati (Headquarters—2,000). **General Electric Co.**, Cincinnati (Aircraft Engine Operating Division—gas turbine jet engines—15,000). **General Motors Corp.**, Cincinnati (Chevrolet Norwood Division—auto assembly—3,700). **General Motors Corp.**, Cincinnati (Fisher Body Division—auto bodies—2,950). **Ford Motor Co.**, Cincinnati (Fairfax Works Division—automatic transmissions—1,600). **Ford Motor Co.**, Cincinnati (Sharon Plant—automotive transmissions—4,400). **RCA Corp.**, Cincinnati (Electronic components and tubes—1,300). **Scovill Manufacturing Co.**, Cincinnati (NuTone Division—electrical appliances and equipment—1,250). **Avco Corp.**, Cincinnati (Electronics Division—electronic components—1,550). **Cincinnati Milacron Inc.**, Cincinnati (Machine tools, plastic products—HQ—12,000). **Allis-Chalmers Corp.**, Cincinnati (Industrial Pumps Division—motors and pumps—1,300). **American Standard Inc.**, Cincinnati (Plumbing and Heating Division—plumbing fixtures, heating equipment—1,000). **Senco Products Inc.**, Cincinnati (Staple machines and staples—HQ—1,000). **Stearns and Foster Co.**, Cincinnati (Cotton wadding material, bedding and box springs—HQ—1,000). **Panacon Corp.**, Cincinnati (Asbestos, asphalt, building and industrial materials—HQ—1,000). **Sterling Drug Inc.**, Cincinnati (Hilton-Davis Chemical Co. Division—dyes—1,000). **Formica Corp.**, Cincinnati (Evendale Plant—plastic laminate—1,400). **Richardson-Merrell Inc.**, Cincinnati (William S. Merrell Division—pharmaceuticals—1,360). **United States Playing Card Co.**, Cincinnati (Playing cards—HQ—1,040). **Keebler Co.**, Cincinnati (Cincinnati Bakery—biscuits, cookies, crackers—1,000). **Federated Department Stores**, Cincinnati (Department stores—HQ—1,500). **Associated Dry Goods Corp.**, Cincinnati (H. and S. Pogue Division—department store—1,300). **Western Southern Life Insurance**, Cincinnati (Insurance—HQ—1,900). **Brunswick Corp.**, Cincinnati (MacGregor Brunswick Division—sporting goods—1,200). **Cincinnati Gas and Electric Co.**, Cincinnati (Gas and electricity—HQ—1,250). **City of Cincinnati**, Cincinnati (City government—6,000).

2nd District

(Hamilton County—Western Cincinnati and Suburbs)

Race and Ethnic Groups. Blacks 11.4 percent. German stock 3.4 percent, Italian stock 0.9 percent.

Cities, 1970 Population. Part of Cincinnati 228,925, Bridgetown 13,398, North College Hill 12,362, Cheviot 11,134.

AEC-Owned, Contractor-Operated Facilities. Feed Materials Production Center, Fernald (part also in 8th District).

Newspapers, Circulation. Cincinnati newspapers circulate throughout district.

Commercial Television Stations, Affiliation. Entire district is located in Cincinnati ADI.

Plants and Offices, Products, Employment.

William Powell Co., Cincinnati (Valves, gauges, etc.—HQ—1,350). **Consolidated Foods Corp.**, Cincinnati (E. Kahns Sons Co. Division—meat packing—1,000). **National Distillers and Chemical Corp.**, Cincinnati (Alcoholic beverages—1,250).

3rd District

(Southwest—Dayton)

Race and Ethnic Groups. Blacks 16.1 percent. German stock 1.7 percent, British stock 0.8 percent.

Cities, 1970 Population. Dayton 243,491, Kettering 69,641, Huber Heights 18,923, Shiloh 11,377.

Universities, Enrollment. University of Dayton (Dayton—8,713), Wright State University (Dayton—12,199).

Military Installations or Activities. Gentile Air Force Station, Dayton.

Newspapers, Circulation. Dayton Journal Herald (Morn—113,615), Dayton News (Eve—150,938).

Commercial Television Stations, Affiliation. WHIO-TV, Dayton (CBS); WKEF, Dayton (ABC); WLWD, Dayton (NBC). Entire district is located in Dayton ADI.

Plants and Offices, Products, Employment.

National Cash Register Co., Dayton (Calculating and accounting equipment—HQ—20,000). **General Motors Corp.**, Dayton (Delco Moraine Division—auto parts—3,800). **General Motors Corp.**, Dayton (Delco Products Division—motors, shock absorbers—4,100). **General Motors Corp.**, Dayton (Delco Products Division—electric motors, shock absorbers—7,000). **General Motors Corp.**, Dayton (Frigidaire Division—major appliances—12,000). **General Motors Corp.**, Dayton (Frigidaire Division—automobile air conditioners, compressors—4,000). **Chrysler Corp.**, Dayton (Airtemp Division—heating and air conditioning equipment—5,800). **Firestone Tire and Rubber Co.**, Dayton (Dayton Tire and Rubber Co. Division—tires—2,150). **Bendix Corp.**, Dayton (Automation and Measurement Division—machine tool gauges—1,000). **Duriron Co. Inc.**, Dayton (Chemical plant equipment—HQ—1,000). **Standard Register Co.**, Dayton (Business forms, form handling equipment—HQ—1,800). **Monarch Marking Systems Co.**, Dayton (Tickets, tags, labels—HQ—1,000). **McCall Corp.**, Dayton (Publishing—4,800). **Dayton Newspapers Inc.**, Dayton (Newspaper publishing—1,130). **Dayton Power and Light Co.**, Dayton (Electric utility—HQ—1,800). **Miami Valley Hospital Society of Dayton**, Dayton (Hospital—1,900). **City of Dayton**, Dayton (Municipal government—3,000).

4th District

(West—Lima, Findlay)

Race and Ethnic Groups. Blacks 2.8 percent. German stock 1.2 percent, British stock 0.5 percent.
Cities, 1970 Population. Lima 53,453, Findlay 35,780, Piqua 20,669, Troy 17,168.
Universities, Enrollment. Findlay College (Findlay—1,175), Ohio Northern University (Ada—2,450), Ohio State University, Lima Campus (Lima—1,197).
Commercial Television Stations, Affiliation. WLIO, Lima (NBC, ABC). District is divided between Lima ADI, Dayton ADI, Toledo ADI, and Columbus ADI.
Plants and Offices, Products, Employment.
Westinghouse Electric Corp., Lima (Motors, aeronautical systems—3,320). **Westinghouse Electric Corp.**, Lima (Aeronautical systems—1,520). **RCA Corp.**, Findlay (Electronic components—1,400). **Ford Motor Co.**, Fostoria (General Parts Division—spark plugs—1,400). **Ford Motor Co.**, Lima (Lima Engine Plant—auto engines—3,000). **Sheller-Globe Corp.**, Lima (Superior Coach Division—bus, ambulance bodies—1,800). **Clark Equipment Co.**, Lima (Construction equipment—1,640). **Goodyear Tire and Rubber Co.**, St. Marys (Fabricated rubber products—1,800). **Cooper Tire and Rubber Co.**, Findlay (Tires, tubes—HQ—1,200). **Timken Co.**, Bucyrus (Roller bearings—1,000). **Avco Corp.**, Coldwater (Farm equipment—2,000). **Union Carbide Corp.**, Fostoria (National Carbon Co. Division—industrial carbons—1,000). **Marathon Oil Co.**, Findlay (Production, refining and marketing of oil products—HQ—1,760). **Copeland Refrigeration Corp.**, Sidney (Refrigeration and air conditioning equipment—HQ—3,000). **A. O. Smith Corp.**, Tipp City (Electric motors—1,200). **Hobart Brothers Co.**, Troy (Welding equipment—HQ—1,600). **Hobart Manufacturing Co.**, Troy (Food machines—HQ—1,800).

5th District

(Northwest—Bowling Green)

Race and Ethnic Groups. German stock 2.2 percent, British stock 0.6 percent.
Cities, 1970 Population. Tiffin 21,590, Bowling Green 21,546, Fremont 18,485, Defiance 16,236.
Universities, Enrollment. Defiance College (Defiance—1,049), Heidelberg College (Tiffin—1,240), Bowling Green State University (Bowling Green—18,874).
Newspapers, Circulation. Toledo newspapers circulate in portion of district.
Commercial Television Stations, Affiliation. Most of district is located in Toledo ADI. Small portion of district is located in Fort Wayne (Indiana) ADI.
Plants and Offices, Products, Employment.
General Motors Corp., Defiance (Grey malleable iron and aluminum—3,000). **Chrysler Corp.**, Perrysburg (Toledo Machining Plant—auto parts—1,800). **General Electric Co.**, Tiffin (Hermetic motor parts—1,000). **GTE Sylvania Inc.**, Ottawa (TV picture tubes—1,600). **Whirlpool Corp.**, Clyde (Clyde Porcelain Division—laundry equipment—1,000). **Aro Corp.**, Bryan (Portable air tools, pumps—HQ—1,100). **Libbey-Owens-Ford Co.**, Rossford (Plate glass—2,500). **Campbell Soup Co.**, Napoleon (Cannery—at least 1,800).

6th District

(South Central—Portsmouth, Chillicothe)

Race and Ethnic Groups. German stock 0.8 percent, British stock 0.4 percent.
Cities, 1970 Population. Portsmouth 27,633, Chillicothe 24,842, Washington 12,495, Circleville 11,687.
AEC-Owned, Contractor-Operated Facilities. Portsmouth Gaseous Diffusion Plant, Piketon.
Newspapers, Circulation. Cincinnati newspapers circulate in portions of district.
Commercial Television Stations, Affiliation. Most of district is divided between Cincinnati ADI and Columbus ADI. Portion of district is located in Charleston (West Virginia)-Huntington (West Virginia) ADI.
Plants and Offices, Products, Employment.
Empire-Detroit Steel, Portsmouth (Steel—2,000). **Wear-Ever Aluminum Inc.**, Chillicothe (Aluminum cooking utensils—HQ—1,000). **Mead Corp.**, Chillicothe (Chillicothe Paper Co. Division—paper and research laboratory—3,550). **Goodyear Atomic Corp.**, Piketon (Industrial inorganic chemicals—1,170). **E. I. duPont de Nemours and Co.**, Circleville (Films—1,300). **Williams Manufacturing Co.**, Portsmouth (Women's and children's shoes—HQ—1,000).

7th District

(West Central—Springfield, Marion)

Race and Ethnic Groups. Blacks 5.7 percent. German stock 1.1 percent, British stock 0.7 percent.

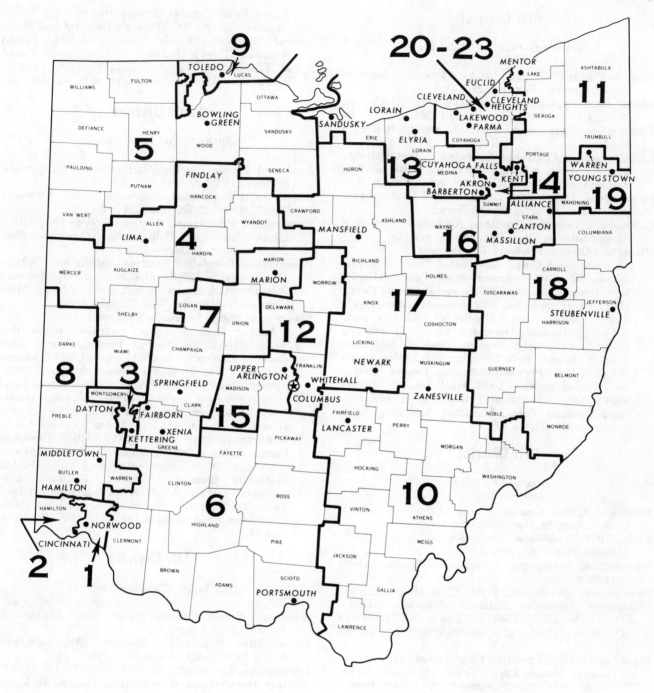

Cities, 1970 Population. Springfield 81,902, Marion 38,705, Fairborn 32,299, Xenia 25,389.

Universities, Enrollment. Antioch College (Yellow Springs—2,275), Central State University (Wilberforce—2,421), Wilberforce University (Wilberforce—1,291), Wittenberg University (Wilmington—3,121).

Military Installations or Activities. Wright-Patterson Air Force Base, Dayton.

Newspapers, Circulation. Dayton newspapers circulate in portion of district.

Commercial Television Stations, Affiliation. WSWO-TV, Springfield (None). Springfield has no ADI of its own. Majority of district is located in Dayton ADI. Portion of district is located in Columbus ADI.

Plants and Offices, Products, Employment.
International Harvester Co., Springfield (Springfield Works—motor trucks—2,700). **Kelsey-Hayes Co.**, Springfield (Speco Division—aircraft and missile parts—1,000). **Robbins and Myers Inc.**, Springfield (Electric motors, hoists, cranes—HQ—2,200). **Marion Power Shovel Co. Inc.**, Marion (Construction machinery and equipment—HQ—1,970). **Tecumseh Products Co.**, Marion (Refrigeration and air conditioning equipment—2,000). **Whirlpool Corp.**, (Dryers, ranges—1,310).

8th District

(Southwest—Hamilton, Middletown)

Race and Ethnic Groups. Blacks 4.4 percent. German stock 1.1 percent, British stock 0.4 percent.

Cities, 1970 Population. Hamilton 67,601, Middletown 48,795, Oxford 15,864, Miamisburg 14,754.

Universities, Enrollment. Miami University (Oxford—17,724).

AEC-Owned, Contractor-Operated Installations. Mound Laboratory, Miamisburg; Feed Materials Production Center, Fernald (part also in 2nd District).

Newspapers, Circulation. Cincinnati and Dayton newspapers circulate in portions of district.

Commercial Television Stations, Affiliation. District is divided between Cincinnati and Dayton ADIs.

Plants and Offices, Products, Employment.

Armco Steel Corp., Middletown (Steel, iron products—HQ—7,800). **Armco Steel Corp.**, Middletown (Steel products—6,800). **General Motors Corp.**, Hamilton (Fisher Body Division—auto stampings—3,200). **Aeronca Inc.**, Middletown (Aircraft parts—1,000). **Monsanto Research Corp.**, Miamisburg (Mound Laboratory Division—research laboratory—1,850). **Mosler Safe Co.**, Hamilton (Safes, vaults—1,750). **U.S. Plywood-Champion Papers**, Hamilton (Coated papers—2,400). **Ohio Security Insurance Co.**, Hamilton (Insurance—HQ—1,000). **Ohio Casualty Corp.**, Hamilton (Insurance, holding company—HQ—3,100).

9th District

(Northwest—Toledo)

Race and Ethnic Groups. Blacks 11.7 percent. Polish stock 3.2 percent, German stock 3.0 percent.

Cities, 1970 Population. Toledo 384,110, Oregon 16,433, Maumee 15,961, Sylvania 12,014.

Universities, Enrollment. University of Toledo (Toledo—14,887).

Newspapers, Circulation. Toledo Blade (Eve—172,876).

Commercial Television Stations, Affiliation. WDHO-TV, Toledo (ABC); WSPD-TV, Toledo (NBC); WTOL-TV, Toledo (CBS). Entire district is located in Toledo ADI.

Plants and Offices, Products, Employment.

General Motors Corp., Toledo (Chevrolet Motor Division—auto transmissions—3,000). **Jeep Corp.**, Toledo (Motor vehicles—4,700). **Jeep Corp.**, Toledo (Motor vehicles—at least 1,000). **Champion Spark Plug Co.**, Toledo (Spark plugs, spraying equipment—HQ—2,200). **Champion Spark Plug Co.**, Toledo (Spraying equipment, atomizers—1,300). **Dana Corp.**, Toledo (Motor vehicle parts, metal stampings—HQ—3,300). **Owens-Illinois Inc.**, Toledo (Glass, plastic, paper products—HQ—5,020). **Owens-Illinois Inc.**, Toledo (Libbey Glass Division—glass tableware—1,400). **NL Industries Inc.**, Toledo (Die castings—2,000). **Midland-Ross Corp.**, Toledo (Steel castings—1,670). **Reliance Electric Co.**, Toledo (Weighing scales, elevators—1,950). **Standard Oil Co. of Ohio**, Toledo (Petroleum refining—

1,200). **Penn Central Transportation Co.**, Toledo (Railroad—2,100). **St. Vincent's Hospital and Medical Building**, Toledo (Hospital—1,300). **Toledo Hospital**, Toledo (Hospital—1,800). **Toledo Board of Education**, Toledo (Education—4,500). **Toledo Blade Co.**, Toledo (Newspaper publishing—1,030).

10th District

(Southeast—Lancaster, Zanesville)

Race and Ethnic Groups. German stock 0.7 percent, British stock 0.5 percent.

Cities, 1970 Population. Zanesville 33,044, Lancaster 32,910, Athens 23,395, Marietta 16,860.

Universities, Enrollment. Marietta College (Marietta—1,913), Muskingum College (New Concord—1,358), Ohio University (Athens—23,918).

Commercial Television Stations, Affiliation. WHIZ-TV, Zanesville (NBC). District is divided between Columbus ADI, Zanesville ADI, and Charleston (West Virginia)-Huntington (West Virginia) ADI.

Plants and Offices, Products, Employment.

Anchor Hocking Corp., Lancaster (Glass products—HQ—3,900). **Anchor Hocking Corp.**, Lancaster (Glassware, molded caps—1,100). **Anchor Hocking Corp.**, Lancaster (Glass tableware—2,000). **Sperry Rand Corp.**, Marietta (Remington Rand Office Systems Division—filing cabinets, safes—1,000). **Goodyear Tire and Rubber Co.**, Logan (Plastic crash pads—1,000). **Union Carbide Corp.**, Marietta (Ferrous alloys—1,500). **Allied Chemical Corp.**, South Point (Agricultural Nitrogen Division—nitrogen, river transportation—1,060). **Dayton Malleable Iron Co.**, Ironton (Malleable iron, aluminum casting—1,160). **Essex International Inc.**, Zanesville (Electric, mechanical equipment—1,500). **Broughton Food Service Inc.**, Marietta (Food service—1,000).

11th District

(Northeast—Cleveland Suburbs)

Race and Ethnic Groups. Italian stock 2.2 percent, British stock 1.6 percent.

Cities, 1970 Population. Mentor 36,901, Ashtabula 24,339, Stow 19,927, Willoughby 18,662.

Universities, Enrollment. Hiram College (Hiram—1,284).

Military Installations or Activities. Youngstown Municipal Airport, Vienna.

Newspapers, Circulation. Cleveland and Youngstown newspapers circulate in portions of district.

Commercial Television Stations, Affiliation. Most of district is located in Cleveland ADI. Portion of district is located in Youngstown ADI.

Plants and Offices, Products, Employment.

General Motors Corp., Hudson (Earthmoving Equipment Division—heavy construction and mining equipment—2,400). **General American Transportation**, Masury (Railroad tank cars—1,800). **Towmotor Corp.**, Mentor (Industrial lift trucks—1,730). **Microdot Inc.**, Hubbard (Valley Mould and Iron Division—ingot moulds, smelting equipment—1,370).

IRC Fibers Co., Painesville (Rayon polyester fiber —2,400). **Eagle-Pitcher Industries Inc.**, Willoughby (Ohio Rubber Co.—rubber products—1,200). **Diamond Shamrock Corp.**, Painesville (Sodium alkalies—1,500).

12th District

(Central—Eastern Columbus and Suburbs)

Race and Ethnic Groups. Blacks 10.5 percent. German stock 1.3 percent, Italian stock 1.0 percent.
Cities, 1970 Population. Part of Columbus 253,852, Whitehall 25,249, Delaware 15,017, Bexley 14,898.
Universities, Enrollment. Capital University (Columbus —2,276), Ohio Wesleyan University (Delaware— 2,543), Otterbein College (Westerville—1,356).
Military Installations or Activities. Defense Construction Supply Center, Columbus; Lockbourne Air Force Base, Columbus.
Newspapers, Circulation. Columbus newspapers circulate throughout district.
Commercial Television Stations, Affiliation. Entire district is located in Columbus ADI.
Plants and Offices, Products, Employment.
Western Electric Co. Inc., Columbus (Telephone equipment—12,600). **Owens-Illinois Inc.**, Columbus (Consumer and Technical Products Division—television tube envelopes—1,200). **North American Rockwell Corp.**, Columbus (Aircraft and missiles —4,500). **Buckeye International Inc.**, Columbus (Steel castings, plastic products—HQ—1,700). **Federal Paper Board Co. Inc.**, Columbus (Federal Glass Division—glass products—1,800). **Nationwide Mutual Insurance Co.**, Columbus (Insurance—HQ —3,000). **Kroger Co.**, Columbus (Grocery stores— 2,800). **American Education Publications**, Columbus (School text books—1,000).

13th District

(North—Sandusky, Lorain)

Race and Ethnic Groups. Blacks 5.1 percent. Spanish heritage population 2.5 percent. German stock 2.1 percent, Hungarian stock 1.7 percent.
Cities, 1970 Population. Lorain 78,432, Elyria 53,600, Barberton 33,032, Sandusky 32,645.
Universities, Enrollment. Oberlin College (Oberlin— 2,710).
NASA Facilities. Plum Brook Station, Sandusky.
Newspapers, Circulation. Cleveland and Akron newspapers circulate in portions of district.
Commercial Television Stations, Affiliation. Entire district is located in Cleveland ADI.
Plants and Offices, Products, Employment.
Ford Motor Co., Lorain (Motor vehicles—5,500). **Ford Motor Co.**, Sandusky (Auto parts—2,500). **General Motors Corp.**, Elyria (Fisher Body Divison —automotive hardware—2,350). **General Motors Corp.**, Sandusky (New Departure-Hyatt Bearing Division—ball bearings, motor vehicle parts—2,320). **Fruehauf Corp.**, Avon Lake (Truck and trailer bodies—at least 1,500). **Koehring Co.**, Lorain

Thew-Lorain Division—construction machinery and equipment—1,100). **Firestone Tire and Rubber Co.**, Barberton (Seiberling Tire and Rubber Co.—tires and tubes—1,500). **United States Steel Corp.**, Lorain (National Tube Division—semifinished steel— 8,000). **Babcock and Wilcox Co.**, Barberton (Boilers, furnaces, heaters—5,000). **Ohio Brass Co.**, Barberton (Porcelain, ceramic products—1,020).

14th District

(Northeast—Akron)

Race and Ethnic Groups. Blacks 10.7 percent. Italian stock 2.2 percent, German stock 1.5 percent.
Cities, 1970 Population. Akron 275,450, Cuyahoga Falls 49,666, Kent 28,255, Tallmadge 15,320.
Universities, Enrollment. Kent State University (Kent— 20,794), University of Akron (Akron—19,674).
Newspapers, Circulation. Akron Beacon Journal (Eve— 176,200).
Commercial Television Stations, Affiliation. WAKR-TV, Akron (ABC). Akron has no ADI of its own. Entire district is located in Cleveland ADI.
Plants and Offices, Products, Employment.
Goodyear Tire and Rubber Co., Akron (Rubber, rubber products, chemicals—HQ—20,000). **B. F. Goodrich Co.**, Akron (Rubber, rubber products, chemicals—HQ—9,100). **General Tire and Rubber Co.**, Akron (Rubber products, chemicals—HQ— 3,700). **Firestone Tire and Rubber Co.**, Akron (Rubber, rubber products, chemicals—HQ—9,500). **Goodyear Aerospace Corp.**, Akron (Aircraft parts, radar—HQ—4,800). **Alside Inc.**, Cuyahoga Falls, (Aluminum products—1,000). **Allied Stores of Ohio Inc.**, Akron (A. Polsky Co.—department store— 1,200). **Akron General Hospital**, Akron (Hospital 1,200).

15th District

(Central—Western Columbus and Suburbs)

Race and Ethnic Groups. Blacks 12.7 percent. German stock 1.2 percent, Italian stock 0.9 percent.
Cities, 1970 Population. Part of Columbus 285,506, Upper Arlington 38,514, Worthington 15,483, Grove City 13,833.
Universities, Enrollment. Ohio State University (Columbus—50,804).
Newspapers, Circulation. Columbus Citizen-Journal (Morn—117,441), Columbus Dispatch (Eve—222,926).
Commercial Television Stations, Affiliation. WBNS-TV, Columbus (CBS); WLWC, Columbus (NBC); WTVN-TV, Columbus (ABC). Entire district is located in Columbus ADI.
Plants and Offices, Products, Employment. (Note: Downtown business section of city is located in district.)
State of Ohio, Columbus (State government— 60,000). **Franklin County**, Columbus (County government—3,000). **City of Columbus**, Columbus (City government—5,820). **Columbus Board of Education**, Columbus (Educational system—6,000). **First Bank Group of Ohio Inc.**, Columbus (Bank

Cuyahoga, Medina
and Summit Counties

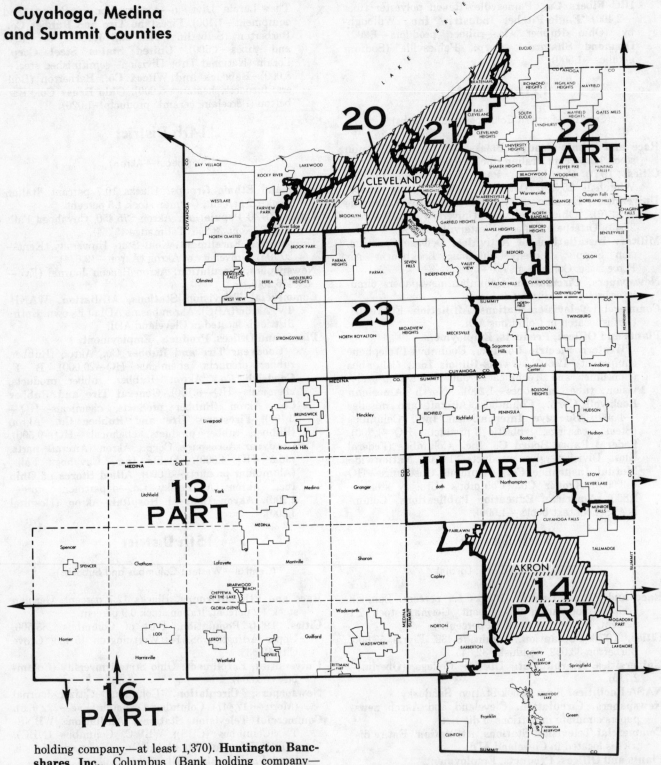

holding company—at least 1,370). **Huntington Bancshares Inc.**, Columbus (Bank holding company—1,700). **Bancohio Corp.**, Columbus (Bank holding company—2,710). **Ohio Bell Telephone Co.**, Columbus (Telephone company—2,500). **General Motors Corp.**, Columbus (Automobile hardware—4,000). **Westinghouse Electric Corp.**, Columbus (Major appliances—5,000). **Timken Co.**, Columbus (Roller bearings—2,400). **Jeffrey Galion Inc.**, Columbus (Bulk material handling equipment—1,800). **Borden**

Inc., Columbus (Columbus Coated Fabrics Co. Division—plastics products—1,200). **Dispatch Printing Co.**, Columbus (Newspaper publishing—1,300). **Federated Department Stores**, Columbus (Department stores—4,160). **Battelle Memorial Institute**, Columbus (Scientific research—HQ—2,350). **Grant Hospital**, Columbus (Hospital—1,100). **Children's Hospital**, Columbus (Hospital—1,000).

16th District

(Northeast—Canton)

Race and Ethnic Groups. Blacks 4.9 percent. Italian stock 2.0 percent, German stock 1.5 percent.

Cities, 1970 Population. Canton 100,017, Massillon 32,623, Alliance 26,566, Wooster 18,716.

Universities, Enrollment. College of Wooster (Wooster—1,881), Mount Union College (Alliance—1,325).

Newspapers, Circulation. Canton Repository (Eve—74,395).

Commercial Television Stations, Affiliation. WJAN-TV, Canton (None). Canton has no ADI of its own. Entire district is located in Cleveland ADI.

Plants and Offices, Products, Employment.
Republic Steel Corp., Canton (Steel mill, metal fabrication—4,500). **Republic Steel Corp.**, Canton (Berger Manufacturing Division—steel mill, metal fabrication—1,000). **Republic Steel Corp.**, Massillon (Union Drawn Steel Co. Division—pig iron, steel billet—4,000). **Timken Co.**, Canton (Bearings, steel bars—HQ—12,000). **TRW Inc.**, Minerva (Precision castings—1,500). **Amsted Industries Inc.**, Alliance (Foundry—1,000). **Standard Alliance Industries**, Alliance (Transue and Williams Steel Forging Division—iron and steel forging, metal stamping—1,000). **White Engines Inc.**, Canton (Hercules Engine Division—internal combustion engines—1,100). **Ford Motor Co.**, Canton (Canton Forge Division—forgings—1,500). **Hoover Co.**, Canton (Electric appliances, etc.—HQ—4,000). **Diebold Inc.**, Canton (Banking systems—HQ—1,600). **Rubbermaid Inc.**, Wooster (Rubber household specialties—2,270). **Teledyne Mid-American Corp.**, Hartville (Teledyne Monarch Rubber Co. Division—fabricated rubber products—1,080). **Packaging Corp. of America**, Rittman (Boxboard—1,250). **Sugardale Foods Inc.**, Canton (Meat packer, slaughterhouse—1,100).

17th District

(Central—Mansfield, Newark)

Race and Ethnic Groups. Blacks 2.6 percent. German stock 1.2 percent, British stock 0.7 percent.

Cities, 1970 Population. Mansfield 55,023, Newark 41,839, Ashland 19,880, Coshocton 13,771.

Universities, Enrollment. Ashland College (Ashland—2,686), Denison University (Granville—2,132), Kenyon College (Gambier—1,300), Ohio State University, Mansfield Campus (Mansfield—1,113).

Commercial Television Stations, Affiliation. District is divided between Columbus and Cleveland ADIs.

Plants and Offices, Products, Employment.
The Tappan Company, Mansfield (Household appliances—HQ—1,200). **The Tappan Company**, Mansfield (O'Keefe and Merritt Division—household appliances—2,000). **Therm-O-Disc Inc.**, Mansfield (Thermostats—1,000). **Westinghouse Electric Corp.**, Mansfield (Mansfield Appliance Division—electric appliances—3,600). **North Electric Co.**, Galion (Communications equipment—HQ—2,730). **General Motors Corp.**, Mansfield (Fisher Body Division—automobile body stamping—3,350). **North American Rockwell Corp.**, Newark (Automobile axles and transmissions—at least 2,400). **Flxible Co.**, Loudonville (Buses, aircraft parts—HQ—1,000). **Cooper Industries Inc.**, Mount Vernon (Cooper Bessemer Division—engines and compressors—2,000). **Cyclops Corp.**, Mansfield (Empire Detroit Steel—steel mill—1,450). **Ohio Brass Co.**, Mansfield (Electric supplies, truck bodies, valves—HQ—1,300). **Mansfield Tire and Rubber Co.**, Mansfield (Tires, tubes, plastic products—HQ—1,770). **Owens-Corning Fiberglass Corp.**, Newark (Mineral wool—3,000). **PPG Industries Inc.**, Mount Vernon (Glass—1,000). **Roper Corp.**, Newark (Newark Division—outdoor equipment—1,100). **R. R. Donnelley and Sons Co.**, Willard (Willard Manufacturing Division—job printing—1,000). **Newark Hospital**, Newark (Hospital—1,000).

18th District

(East—Steubenville)

Race and Ethnic Groups. Italian stock 2.6 percent, British stock 1.6 percent.

Cities, 1970 Population. Steubenville 30,792, East Liverpool 20,115, New Philadelphia 15,185, Salem 14,187.

Universities, Enrollment. College of Steubenville (Steubenville—1,304).

Commercial Television Stations, Affiliation. WSTV-TV, Steubenville (CBS, ABC). Most of district is located in Wheeling (West Virginia)-Steubenville ADI. Small portions of district are located in Cleveland ADI and Pittsburgh (Pennsylvania) ADI.

Plants and Offices, Products, Employment.
Wheeling-Pittsburgh Steel Corp., Yorkville (Steel wire, strips, pipe—1,200). **Wheeling-Pittsburgh Steel Corp.**, Steubenville (Steel—5,100). **Wheeling-Pittsburgh Steel Corp.**, Mingo Junction (Steel—2,000). **Wheeling-Pittsburgh Steel Corp.**, Martins Ferry (Galvanized steel strip, wire—1,250). **Wheeling-Pittsburgh Steel Corp.**, Martins Ferry (Steel—1,100). **Consolidation Coal Co.**, Cadiz (Hanna Coal Co. Division—mining—1,800). **Olin Corp.**, Hannibal (Aluminum plate—1,000). **Ornet Corp.**, Hannibal (Aluminum—HQ—2,000). **National Cash Register Co.**, Cambridge (Electronic systems—2,400). **NRM Corp.**, Columbiana (Rubber Machinery Division—machine shop and foundry—1,050).

19th District

(Northeast—Youngstown, Warren)

Race and Ethnic Groups. Blacks 10.6 percent. Italian stock 5.7 percent, Czechoslovakian stock 2.8 percent.

Cities, 1970 Population. Youngstown 139,715, Warren 63,478, Boardman 30,863, Austintown 29,366.

Universities, Enrollment. Youngstown State University (Youngstown—14,588).

Newspapers, Circulation. Youngstown Vindicator (Eve—102,947).

Commercial Television Stations, Affiliation. WFMJ-TV, Youngstown (NBC); WKBN-TV, Youngstown (CBS); WYTV, Youngstown (ABC). Entire district is located in Youngstown ADI.

Plants and Offices, Products, Employment.

Youngstown Sheet and Tube Co. Inc., Youngstown (Steel, steel products—HQ—12,000). **Youngstown Sheet and Tube Co. Inc.**, Youngstown (Steel —6,000). **Youngstown Sheet and Tube Co. Inc.**, Warren (Van Huffel Tube Division—tubed and rolled steel—1,100). **Youngstown Sheet and Tube Co. Inc.**, Campbell (Steel—10,000). **United States Steel Corp.**, McDonald (McDonald Mills—steel— 2,400). **Republic Steel Corp.**, Warren (Steel— 5,000). **Republic Steel Corp.**, Youngstown (Steel products—7,700). **Republic Steel Corp.**, Youngstown (Iron and steel rails and pipe—5,200). **Copperweld Steel Co.**, Warren (Aristalloy Steel Division —steel—1,000). **Wean Industries Inc.**, Youngstown (Steel, aluminum industry equipment—HQ—1,200). **United Engineering and Foundry Co.**, Youngstown (Rolling mill machinery—1,300). **Commercial Shearing and Stamping Co.**, Youngstown (Pumps, motors, valves, cylinders, steel products—HQ— 1,300). **McKay Machinery Co.**, Youngstown (Weldments—1,200). **General Motors Corp.**, Warren (Chevrolet Division—auto assembly—4,400). **General Motors Corp.**, Warren (Electric cable, plastic products—10,000). **North American Rockwell Inc.**, Newton Falls (Rockwell Standard Division—auto bumpers—1,000).

20th District

(Cleveland—Central, West, Suburbs)

Race and Ethnic Groups. Blacks 2.5 percent. Polish stock 6.1 percent, Czechoslovakian stock 4.1 percent, Italian stock 3.7 percent, German stock 3.4 percent.

Cities, 1970 Population. Part of Cleveland 298,455, Garfield Heights 41,408, Maple Heights 34,058, Brook Park 30,730.

Universities, Enrollment. Cleveland State University (Cleveland—15,201).

NASA Facilities. Lewis Research Center, Cleveland; Space Nuclear Systems Office, Cleveland.

Newspapers, Circulation. Cleveland Plain Dealer (Morn —405,541), Cleveland Press (Eve—370,469).

Commercial Television Stations, Affiliation. WEWS, Cleveland (ABC); WJW-TV, Cleveland (CBS); WKBF-TV, Cleveland (None); WKYC-TV, Cleveland (NBC); WUAB-TV, Parma (None). Entire district is located in Cleveland ADI.

Plants and Offices, Products, Employment. (Note: District includes downtown business section of Cleveland.)

Republic Steel Corp., Cleveland (Headquarters —1,200). **Republic Steel Corp.**, Cleveland (Iron and steel—8,100). **Republic Steel Corp.**, Cleveland (Bolts and nuts—1,200). **Jones and Laughlin Steel Corp.**, Cleveland (Rolled steel products—4,250). **United States Steel Corp.**, Cleveland (Lorain Works —metal, wire—2,000). **Ford Motor Co.**, Cleveland (Iron castings—4,320). **Ford Motor Co.**, Cleveland (Engine parts assembly—1,600). **Ford Motor Co.**, Cleveland (Engine parts assembly—4,000). **Aluminum Company of America Inc.**, Cleveland (Aluminum forging—3,000). **Lear Siegler Inc.**, Cleveland (Power Equipment Division—electric generators, motors—1,150). **Union Carbide Corp.**, Cleveland (Batteries—1,100). **Midland-Ross Corp.**, Cleveland (Midland Frame Division—automobile frames— 1,700). **Otis Elevator Co.**, Cleveland (Materials handling equipment—1,200). **Cleveland Pneumatic Co.**, Cleveland (Aircraft landing gears—1,280). **Gould Inc.**, Cleveland (Torpedoes, hydrophones— 1,100). **Wyle Laboratories Inc.**, Cleveland (Angle Products Division—cabinets, tanks, accessories— 1,000). **American Greetings Corp.**, Cleveland (Greeting cards—HQ—1,300). **Bobbie Brooks Inc.**, Cleveland (Women's wear—HQ—1,200). **Joseph and Feiss Co.**, Cleveland (Men's clothing—HQ— 2,000). **Higbee Co.**, Cleveland (Burrow Brothers Stores Division—department store—2,800). **Chesapeake and Ohio Railway Co.**, Cleveland (Railroad —HQ—16,000). **Cleveland Electric Illuminating Co.**, Cleveland (Electric utility—HQ—3,000). **East Ohio Gas Co.**, Cleveland (Natural gas distribution —3,500). **City of Cleveland**, Cleveland (City government—12,400).

21st District

(Cleveland—East)

Race and Ethnic Groups. Blacks 66.3 percent. Yugoslavian stock 2.4 percent, Italian stock 1.9 percent.

Cities, 1970 Population. Part of Cleveland 400,542, East Cleveland 39,569, Warrensville Heights 18,933.

Universities, Enrollment. Case Western Reserve University (Cleveland—9,172).

Newspapers, Circulation. Cleveland newspapers circulate throughout district.

Commercial Television Stations, Affiliation. Entire district is located in Cleveland ADI.

Plants and Offices, Products, Employment.

Standard Oil Co. of Ohio, Cleveland (Oil exploration, production—HQ—1,800). **Acme-Cleveland Corp.**, Cleveland (Machine tools, foundry equipment, electrical controls—HQ—2,000). **Cleveland Twist Drill Co.**, Cleveland (Drilling and cutting tools—HQ—1,700). **Warner and Swasey Co.**, Cleveland (Machine tools and equipment—HQ— 2,400). **Eaton Yale and Towne Inc.**, Cleveland (Eaton Axle Division—automobile parts—2,450). **White Motor Corp.**, Cleveland (Trucks—3,300). **General Motors Corp.**, Cleveland (Fisher Body Division—automobile trim—2,900). **A. O. Smith Corp.**, Cleveland (Clark Controllers—electric controls and switches—1,200). **General Electric Co.**, Cleveland (Lamps—1,400). **Richman Brothers Co.**, Cleveland (Men's and boys' clothing—HQ—1,500). **May Department Stores Co.**, Cleveland (Department stores—2,200). **Forest City Publishing Co.**, Cleveland (Newspaper publishing—2,150). **E. W. Scripps Co.**, Cleveland (Newspaper publishing— 1,400). **Ohio Bell Telephone Co.**, Cleveland (Telephone company—HQ—2,000). **Cleveland Clinic Foundation**, Cleveland (Hospital—3,000).

22nd District

(Cleveland Suburbs—Cleveland Heights, Euclid)

Race and Ethnic Groups. Italian stock 4.7 percent, Russian stock 3.2 percent, Polish stock 2.8 percent, German stock 2.7 percent, Yugoslavian stock 2.7 percent.

Cities, 1970 Population. Euclid 71,485, Cleveland Heights 60,745, Shaker Heights 36,275, South Euclid 29,588.

Universities, Enrollment. John Carroll University (Cleveland—3,964).

Newspapers, Circulation. Cleveland newspapers circulate throughout district.

Commercial Television Stations, Affiliation. Entire district is located in Cleveland ADI.

Plants and Offices, Products, Employment.

Chrysler Corp., Twinsburg (Automotive stampings —5,000). **General Motors Corp.**, Cleveland (Fisher Body Division—automobile bodies—1,210). **TRW Inc.**, Cleveland (Missiles, aircraft, industrial products—HQ—4,800). **TRW Inc.**, Cleveland (Valves, stampings—at least 1,000). **Clevite Corp.**, Cleveland (Bearings, industrial parts, batteries—HQ—3,300). **Picker Corp.**, Cleveland (X-ray equipment —HQ—1,200). **Addressograph-Multigraph Corp.**, Cleveland (Office duplicating machines, appliances —HQ—3,350). **Chase Brass and Copper Co.**, Cleveland (Chase Cleveland Mills—rolled, drawn and extruded copper—1,500). **Lincoln Electric Co.**, Cleveland (Arc welding equipment and supplies— HQ—1,720). **Borg Warner Corp.**, Cleveland (Pesco Products Division—hydraulic pumps—1,200). **Lubrizol Corp.**, Wickliffe (Chemicals, petroleum additives —HQ—1,050). **Bailey Meter Co.**, Wickliffe (Fluid meters—HQ—3,200). **Hatfield Electric Co.**, Cleveland (Contractor—1,400). **Anchor Motor Freight Inc.**, Cleveland (Long distance carrier—2,300). **Fabri-Centers of America Inc.**, Cleveland (Cleveland Fabric Shops—retail fabrics, notions—1,000). **Campus Sweater and Sportswear Co.**, Cleveland (Knit outerwear—HQ—4,400).

23rd District

(Cleveland Suburbs)

Race and Ethnic Groups. Czechoslovakian stock 3.6 percent, German stock 3.4 percent, Polish stock 2.9 percent, Italian stock 2.6 percent.

Cities, 1970 Population. Part of Parma 74,837, Lakewood 70,216, part of Cleveland 39,617, North Olmsted 34,851.

Universities, Enrollment. Baldwin-Wallace College (Berea—2,982).

Newspapers, Circulation. Cleveland newspapers circulate throughout district.

Commercial Television Stations, Affiliation. Entire district is located in Cleveland ADI.

Plants and Offices, Products, Employment.

General Motors Corp., Cleveland (Chevrolet Motor Division—automobile transmissions—8,630). **Ford Motor Co.**, Cleveland (Auto parts stamping— 4,200). **MTD Products Inc.**, Cleveland (Power mowers, tools, dies, metal stampings—HQ—1,500). **Erie Lackawanna Railway Co.**, Cleveland (Railroad—HQ—1,000).

OKLAHOMA: SIX HOUSE SEATS, NO CHANGE

With the Oklahoma Legislature and governorship in Democratic hands, an attempt to maintain the four-to-two Democratic advantage in redistricting legislation was a foregone conclusion. But it took 19 months of wrangling in the 1971 and 1972 legislative sessions before a redistricting bill was adopted. *(Map p. 159)*

Two areas of controversy held up enactment of a redistricting bill. In the northeast, there was resistance from the small counties surrounding Tulsa County to being attached to the 1st Congressional District, which is dominated by the city of Tulsa. Legislators from these counties—regardless of party—fought against their counties' being included in the 1st District, because they felt they would be submerged by Tulsa voters.

The other problem was in Oklahoma County, which includes Oklahoma City. The county had enough population for one whole congressional district, plus about 100,-000 to be divided among other districts. How to divide these extra people was one of the problems that occupied the legislators for nearly a year.

A final solution was reached by a conference committee in cooperation with Gov. David Hall (D). The decision split Oklahoma County three ways, giving parts of it to the 4th, 5th and 6th Districts. The Tulsa County district acquired Pawnee County and parts of Wagoner, Washington and Osage Counties. The four Democratic districts remained predominantly Democratic, while the Republican margin in the 6th District was cut.

The conference committee bill passed the state House March 21 by a vote of 63-25 and the Senate March 27 by a vote of 29-18. The governor signed it April 3.

Despite the nominal Republican edge in the 1st District, the Democrats picked up the seat in November 1972.

District	Member Elected 1972	Winning Percentage	1970 Population	Percent Variance
1	James R. Jones (D)	54.5	425,620	—0.2161
2	Clem Rogers McSpadden (D)	71.1	426,778	+ 0.0553
3	Carl Albert (D)	93.4	426,596	+ 0.0126
4	Tom Steed (D)	71.3	426,330	—0.0497
5	John Jarman (D)	60.4	426,484	—0.0135
6	John N. Happy Camp (R)	72.7	427,445	+ 0.2117

1970 State Population: 2,559,253
Ideal District Population: 426,542

Election Results, 1968-1972

Vote for U.S. Representative
(Adjusted to new district boundaries)

District	1968	1970	1972
1	Not Available	No Available	91,864 D (54.5%)
			73,786 R (43.7%)
2	NA	NA	105,110 D (71.1%)
			42,632 R (28.9%)
3	NA	NA	101,732 D (93.4%)
			—
4	NA	NA	85,578 D (71.3%)
			34,484 R (28.7%)
5	NA	NA	69,710 D (60.4%)
			45,711 R (39.6%)
6	NA	NA	113,567 R (72.7%)
			42,663 D (27.3%)
State	444,995 D (54.9%)	316,248 D (56.2%)	496,657 D (60.8%)
	364,866 R (45.1%)	245,216 R (43.6%)	310,180 R (38.0%)

Voting Age Population

District	Voting Age Population	Voting Age Population 18, 19, 20	Voting Age Population 65 and Over	Median Age of Voting Age Population
1	278,793	17,976 (6.4%)	38,770 (13.9%)	42.3
2	286,828	20,188 (7.0%)	58,754 (20.5%)	47.3
3	292,373	18,264 (6.2%)	68,119 (23.3%)	49.8
4	281,486	31,597 (11.2%)	37,513 (13.3%)	38.8
5	283,879	21,673 (7.6%)	40,150 (14.1%)	42.1
6	295,509	26,306 (8.9%)	57,115 (19.3%)	45.2
State	1,718,825	135,980 (7.9%)	300,371 (17.5%)	44.2

Income and Occupation

District	Median Family Income	White Collar Workers	Blue Collar Workers	Service Workers	Farm Workers
1	$9,527	54.7%	31.4%	13.2%	0.7%
2	6,567	40.4	39.3	15.0	5.3
3	5,846	38.6	39.9	15.1	6.4
4	7,569	48.8	31.6	14.6	5.0
5	9,305	56.3	30.4	12.8	0.5
6	7,593	45.1	28.7	14.8	11.4
State	7,720	47.9	33.2	14.2	4.7

Education: School Years Completed

District	Completed 4 years of High School	Completed 4 years of College	Completed 5 years or less of School	Median School years completed
1	60.4%	12.4%	4.9%	12.3
2	43.1	7.4	11.1	10.9
3	38.5	6.2	13.4	10.2
4	54.0	10.4	7.0	12.1
5	60.1	13.4	4.8	12.3
6	55.0	10.8	5.2	12.2
State	51.6	10.0	7.8	12.1

Housing and Residential Patterns

	Housing		Urban-Suburban-Nonmetropolitan Breakdown		
District	Owner Occupied Units	Renter Occupied Units	Urban	Suburban	Nonmetro-politan
1	68.0%	32.0%	77.8%	17.6%	4.6%
2	72.1	27.9	—	21.5	78.5
3	70.8	29.2	—	7.5	92.5
4	66.6	33.4	20.2	41.2	38.6
5	66.5	33.5	78.6	21.4	—
6	70.9	29.1	4.6	10.0	85.4
State	69.2	30.8	30.2	19.9	49.9

1st District

(North Central—Tulsa)

Race and Ethnic Groups. Blacks 8.5 percent. American Indians 2.8 percent.

Cities, 1970 Population. Tulsa 331,115, Broken Arrow 11,670, Sand Springs 11,495.

Universities, Enrollment. University of Tulsa (Tulsa—6,194), Oral Roberts University (Tulsa—1,334).

Newspapers, Circulation. Tulsa World (Morn—115,441), Tulsa Tribune (Eve 80,072).

Commercial Television Stations, Affiliation. KOTV, Tulsa (CBS); KTEW, Tulsa (NBC); KTUL, Tulsa (None). Entire district is located in Tulsa ADI.

Plants and Offices, Products, Employment.
Seismograph Service Corp., Tulsa (Seismographic surveys—1,880). **Cities Service Oil Co.**, Tulsa (Headquarters—1,000). **Sun Oil Co.**, Tulsa (Oil production, refining—1,800). **Amoco Production Co.**, Tulsa (Oil, gas production—HQ—2,000). **United Rigging & Equipment Co.**, Tulsa (Oil field equipment—1,100). **Combustion Engineering Inc.**, Tulsa (Oil field equipment—1,000). **CCI Corp.**, Tulsa (Crane Carrier Co. Division—aircraft components, heavy vehicles—2,500). **McDonnell Douglas Corp.**, Tulsa (Air frames—1,500). **North American Rockwell Corp.**, Tulsa (Aircraft, space systems—2,000). **Public Service Co. of Oklahoma**, Tulsa (Electric utility—2,140). **American Airlines**, Tulsa (Airline—4,500).

2nd District

(Northeast—Muskogee)

Race and Ethnic Groups. Blacks 6.3 percent. American Indians 8.2 percent.

Cities, 1970 Population. Muskogee 37,344, part of Bartlesville 27,444, Sapulpa 15,261, Okmulgee 15,222.

Universities, Enrollment. Northeastern State College (Tahlequah—5,520).

Newspapers, Circulation. Tulsa newspapers circulate in portion of district.

Commercial Television Stations, Affiliation. Major portion of district is located in Tulsa ADI. Small portion of district is located in Joplin (Missouri)-Pittsburg (Kansas) ADI.

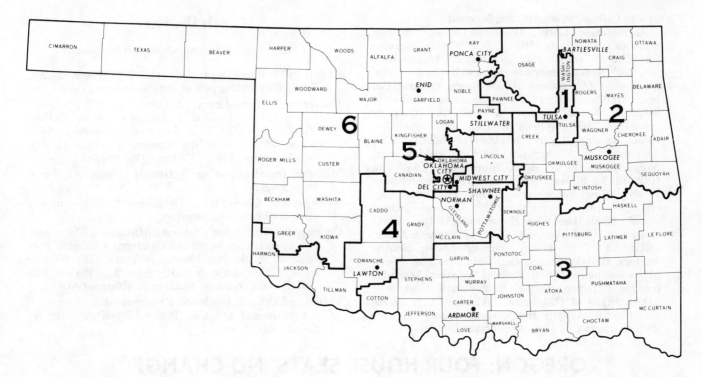

Plants and Offices, Products, Employment.

Phillips Petroleum Co., Bartlesville (Headquarters—5,000). **B. F. Goodrich Co.**, Miami (Tires—2,000).

3rd District

(Southeast—Ardmore)

Race and Ethnic Groups. Blacks 5.9 percent. American Indians 4.5 percent.

Cities, 1970 Population. Ardmore 20,879, Duncan 19,775, McAlester 18,800, Ada 14,858.

Universities, Enrollment. East Central State College (Ada—3,092), Langston University (Langston—1,236), Southeastern State College (Durant—3,793).

Military Installations or Activities. Naval Ammunition Depot, McAlester.

Commercial Television Stations, Affiliation. KTEN, Ada (ABC; NBC on per program basis); KXII, Ardmore (NBC). Portions of district are located in Oklahoma City ADI, Tulsa ADI, Ardmore-Ada ADI, Wichita Falls (Texas)-Lawton ADI, Fort Smith (Arkansas) ADI, and Shreveport (Louisiana)-Texarkana (Texas) ADI.

Plants and Offices, Products, Employment.

Halliburton Co., Duncan (Oil field equipment—2,200). **Naval Ammunition Depot,** McAlester (Ammunition—1,010).

4th District

(South Central—Lawton, Norman)

Race and Ethnic Groups. Blacks 5.8 percent. American Indians 3.3 percent. Spanish heritage population 2.7 percent.

Cities, 1970 Population. Lawton 74,640, Norman 52,138, Midwest City 48,230, Shawnee 25,136.

Universities, Enrollment. Oklahoma Baptist University (Shawnee—1,588), Oklahoma College of Liberal Arts (Chickasha—1,015), University of Oklahoma (Norman—21,586).

Military Installations or Activities. Fort Sill, Lawton; Altus Air Force Base, Altus.

Newspapers, Circulation. Oklahoma City newspapers circulate in portion of district.

Commercial Television Stations, Affiliation. Most of district is divided between Oklahoma City ADI and Wichita Falls (Texas)-Lawton ADI. Small portion of district is located in Tulsa ADI.

5th District

(Oklahoma City)

Race and Ethnic Groups. Blacks 11.2 percent.

Cities, 1970 Population. Part of Oklahoma City 335,070, Del City 27,074, Edmond 16,670, The Village 13,787.

Universities, Enrollment. Bethany Nazarene College (Bethany—1,704), Central State University (Edmond—10,678), Oklahoma City University (Oklahoma City—2,471), Oklahoma Christian College (Oklahoma City—1,140).

Military Installations or Activities. Tinker Air Force Base, Oklahoma City; Oklahoma City Air Force Station, Oklahoma City.

Newspapers, Circulation. Oklahoma City Journal (MxSat—52,396), Oklahoma City Oklahoman (MxSat—189,392), Oklahoma City Times (ExSat—101,266).

Commercial Television Stations, Affiliation. KOCO-TV, Oklahoma City (ABC); KWTV, Oklahoma City (CBS); WKY-TV, Oklahoma City (NBC). Entire district is located in Oklahoma City ADI.

Plants and Offices, Products, Employment.

    Kerr-McGee Corp., Oklahoma City (Oil, gas, minerals, chemicals—HQ—1,230). **Cities Service Gas Co.**, Oklahoma City (Natural gas transmission —1,230). **North American Rockwell Corp.**, Oklahoma City (Aircraft—1,000). **Western Electric Co. Inc.**, Oklahoma City (Communications equipment —8,200). **Woods Corp.**, Oklahoma City (Holding company—1,600). **Wilson & Co.**, Oklahoma City (Meat packing—1,350). **Oklahoma Publishing Co.**, Oklahoma City (Newspaper publishing, holding company—1,800). **T. G. & Y. Stores Co.**, Oklahoma City (Butler Stores Division—general merchandise— 1,400). **Allied Supermarkets Inc.**, Oklahoma City (Humpty Dumpty Supermarkets Division—grocery stores—1,880). **Lee Way Motor Freight Inc.**, Oklahoma City (Trucking—HQ—1,200). **Transcon Lines**, Oklahoma City (Heavy hauling—1,600). **Southwestern Bell Telephone Co.**, Oklahoma City (Telephone company—2,400). **Federal Aviation Administration**, Oklahoma City (U.S. government agency— 4,000). **State of Oklahoma**, Oklahoma City (State government—20,000). **Independent School District 89**, Oklahoma City (City school system—1,800).

6th District

(West—Enid, Stillwater, Oklahoma Panhandle)

Cities, 1970 Population. Enid 44,666, Stillwater 31,208, Ponca City 26,009, part of Oklahoma City 19,479.

Universities, Enrollment. Northwestern State College (Alva—2,258), Oklahoma Panhandle State College (Goodwell—1,268), Oklahoma State University (Stillwater—21,297), Phillips University (Enid—1,361), Southwestern State College (Weatherford—5,482).

Military Installations or Activities. Vance Air Force Base, Enid.

Newspapers, Circulation. Oklahoma City newspapers circulate in portion of district.

Commercial Television Stations, Affiliation. Major portion of district is located in Oklahoma City ADI. Portions of district are located in Tulsa ADI, Wichita Falls (Texas)-Lawton ADI, Amarillo (Texas) ADI and Wichita (Kansas)-Hutchinson (Kansas) ADI.

Plants and Offices, Products, Employment.

    Continental Oil Co., Ponca City (Petroleum refining—4,000).

OREGON: FOUR HOUSE SEATS, NO CHANGE

Oregon missed gaining a fifth representative by only 235 persons. Some thought was given by state officials to filing a suit to gain the extra representative by including in Oregon's population count the state's servicemen and servicewomen stationed in other states and counted as residents of those states, even though they vote and pay taxes in Oregon. *(Map p. 162)*

But nothing developed along these lines in 1972 and the state held elections for four representatives in November 1972.

Redistricting legislation passed the state Senate June 9, 1971, by a vote of 18-12 and the state House June 10 by a vote of 41-18. Gov. Tom McCall (R) signed it July 1.

For the first time in the state's history, counties besides populous Multnomah (Portland) were divided between more than one congressional district.

No major political changes were made as a result of the shift in boundaries. All four incumbents won reelection in 1972 with more than 60 percent of the vote.

District	Member Elected 1972	Winning Percentage	1970 Population	Percent Variance
1	Wendell Wyatt (R)	68.6	523,428	+ 0.1113
2	Al Ullman (D)	99.9	522,898	+ 0.0099
3	Edith Green (D)	62.4	522,258	—0.1124
4	John Dellenback (R)	62.5	522,801	—0.0086

1970 State Population: 2,091,385
Ideal District Population: 522,846

Election Results, 1968-1972

Vote for U.S. Representative
(Adjusted to new district boundaries)

District	1968	1970	1972
1	160,196 R (81.0%)	123,596 R (72.6%)	166,476 R (68.6%)
	37,540 D (19.0%)	46,676 D (27.4%)	76,307 D (31.4%)
2	112,161 D (59.4%)	100,815 D (66.2%)	178,537 D (99.9%)
	76,768 R (40.6%)	51,415 R (33.7%)	—
3	140,181 D (66.2%)	122,809 D (70.0%)	141,046 D (62.4%)
	71,590 R (33.8%)	52,457 R (29.9%)	84,697 R (37.5%)
4	108,533 R (57.5%)	87,216 R (56.4%)	138,965 R (62.5%)
	80,154 D (42.5%)	67,546 D (43.6%)	83,134 D (37.4%)
State	417,107 R (53.0%)	337,846 D (51.8%)	479,024 D (55.1%)
	370,036 D (47.0%)	314,657 R (48.2%)	390,138 R (44.9%)

Voting Age Population

District	Voting Age Population	Voting Age Population 18, 19, 20	Voting Age Population 65 and Over	Median Age of Voting Age Population
1	335,006	32,011 (9.6%)	56,250 (16.8%)	43.1
2	339,666	23,515 (6.9%)	57,301 (16.9%)	45.1
3	354,460	25,187 (7.1%)	62,240 (17.6%)	45.0
4	342,311	26,815 (7.8%)	51,326 (15.0%)	43.4
State	1,391,451	107,532 (7.7%)	227,120 (16.3%)	44.1

Income and Occupation

District	Median Family Income	White Collar Workers	Blue Collar Workers	Service Workers	Farm Workers
1	$10,430	54.4%	29.9%	12.5%	3.2%
2	8,821	42.9	34.2	13.9	9.0
3	10,001	51.4	33.6	14.3	0.7
4	8,854	43.4	40.1	13.1	3.4
State	9,487	48.3	34.3	13.4	4.0

Education: School Years Completed

District	Completed 4 years of High School	Completed 4 years of College	Completed 5 years or less of School	Median School years completed
1	66.2%	17.5%	2.7%	12.5
2	58.4	9.7	3.8	12.2
3	59.4	9.8	3.5	12.3
4	56.1	10.3	3.1	12.2
State	60.0	11.8	3.3	12.3

Housing and Residential Patterns

	Housing		Urban-Suburban-Nonmetropolitan Breakdown		
District	Owner Occupied Units	Renter Occupied Units	Urban	Suburban	Nonmetropolitan
1	63.4%	36.6%	15.4%	47.8%	36.8%
2	68.2	31.8	12.1	28.9	59.0
3	65.2	34.8	58.7	41.3	—
4	67.7	32.3	14.6	26.2	59.2
State	66.1	33.9	25.2	36.1	38.7

1st District

(Northwest—Portland and Suburbs, Corvallis)

Race and Ethnic Groups. Canadian stock 3.0 percent, German stock 2.1 percent.

Cities, 1970 Population. Part of Portland 75,401, Corvallis 35,136, Beaverton 18,494, Hillsboro 14,668.

Universities, Enrollment. Lewis and Clark College (Portland—2,443), Linfield College (McMinnville—1,085), Oregon College of Education (Monmouth—3,975), Oregon State University (Corvallis—15,483), Pacific University (Forest Grove—1,235), Portland State University (Portland—14,497).

Newspapers, Circulation. Portland Oregonian (Morn—241,636), Portland Oregon Journal (ExSat—129,825). Portland newspapers circulate throughout district.

Commercial Television Stations, Affiliation. KATU, Portland (ABC); KGW-TV, Portland (NBC); KOIN-TV, Portland (CBS); KPTV, Portland (None). Entire district is located in Portland ADI.

Plants and Offices, Products, Employment.

Esco Corp., Portland (Metal casting, construction and timber industry equipment—HQ—1,400). **Guy F. Atkinson Co.**, Portland (Bingham-Willamette Co. Division—saw mill machinery, ship repair, pumps—at least 1,200). **Freightliner Corp.**, Portland (Trucks—HQ—1,000). **Tektronix Inc.**, Beaverton (Oscilloscopes—HQ—7,990). **GAF Corp.**, Beaverton (Photographic equipment—1,600). **Castle and Cooke Inc.**, Astoria (Bumble Bee Sea Food Division—canning, freezing seafood—at least 2,400). **Oregonian Publishing Co.**, Portland (Newspaper publishing—1,000). **Montgomery Ward and Co. Inc.**, Portland (Department store—1,400). **May Department Stores Co.**, Portland (Meier & Frank Co. Division—department store—1,600). **Southern Pacific**

Transportation Co., Portland (Railroad—1,350). **Burlington Northern Inc.**, Portland (Railroad—2,500). **Union Pacific Railroad Co.**, Portland (Railroad—1,200). **Pay Less Drug Stores Northwest**, Portland (Holding company—2,000). **Multnomah County**, Portland (County government—2,500). **Board of Hospital Trustees, Diocese of Oregon**, Portland (Hospital and medical center—1,200).

2nd District

(East—Salem)

Race and Ethnic Groups. Canadian stock 1.9 percent, German stock 1.9 percent.

Cities, 1970 Population. Part of Salem 62,976, Albany 18,186, Klamath Falls 15,779, Altamont 15,750.

Universities, Enrollment. Eastern Oregon College (La Grande—1,628), Oregon Technical Institute (Klamath Falls—1,038), Willamette University (Salem—1,713).

Military Installations or Activities. Umatilla Army Depot, Hermison; Keno Air Force Station, Keno; Kingsley Field, Klamath Falls.

Newspapers, Circulation. Portland newspapers circulate in portion of district.

Commercial Television Stations, Affiliation. KOTI-TV, Klamath Falls (CBS, NBC); KVDO-TV, Salem (None). Major portion of district is located in Portland ADI. Smaller portions are located in Klamath Falls ADI, Yakima (Washington) ADI, Spokane (Washington) ADI and Boise (Idaho) ADI.

Plants and Offices, Products, Employment.

Weyerhaeuser Co., Klamath Falls (Lumber and hardwood—1,100). **U.S. Plywood-Champion Papers**, Lebanon (Plywood and hardboard—1,000). **Castle and Cooke Inc.**, Salem (Dole Co. Division—fruit and vegetable canning—1,000). **Ore-Ida Foods Inc.**, Ontario (Quick-frozen potatoes—1,200).

3rd District

(Portland and Suburbs)

Race and Ethnic Groups. Blacks 4.1 percent. Canadian stock 3.0 percent, German stock 2.2 percent.

Cities, 1970 Population. Part of Portland 306,449, part of Milwaukie 14,336.

Universities, Enrollment. Reed College (Portland—1,318), University of Portland (Portland—1,945).

Military Installations or Activities. Portland International Airport, Portland.

Newspapers, Circulation. Portland newspapers circulate throughout district.

Commercial Television Stations, Affiliation. Entire district is located in Portland ADI.

Plants and Offices, Products, Employment.

Freightliner Corp., Portland (Trucks—1,190). **Hyster Co.**, Portland (Trucks, tractor trailers—HQ—1,260). **Bonneville Power Administration**, Portland (Hydroelectric power—HQ—1,300). **Jantzen Inc.**, Portland (Swim suits, sportswear—HQ—1,500). **Safeway Stores Inc.**, Portland (Grocery stores—3,300). **Emanuel Lutheran Charity Board**, Portland (Hospital—1,050).

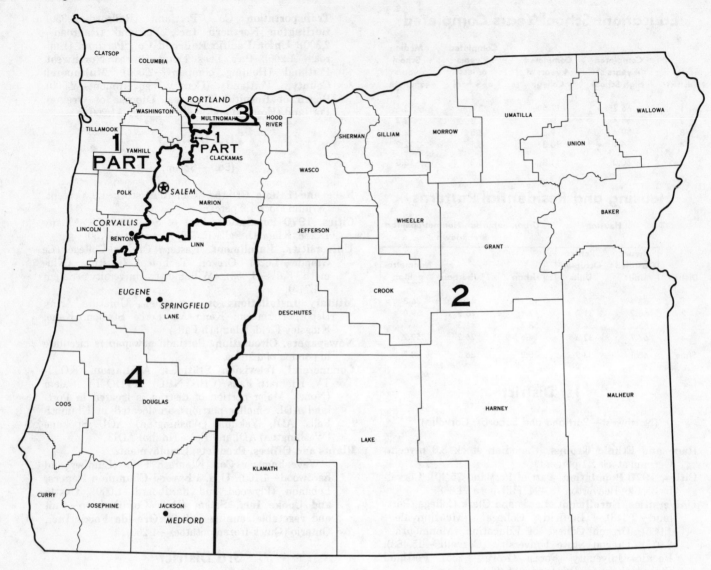

4th District

(Southwest—Eugene, Medford)

Race and Ethnic Groups. Canadian stock 2.2 percent, German stock 1.5 percent.

Cities, 1970 Population. Eugene 76,355, Medford 28,459, Springfield 27,135, Roseburg 14,464.

Universities, Enrollment. Southern Oregon College (Ashland—4,766), University of Oregon (Eugene—15,249).

Military Installations or Activities. Naval Facility, Coos Head; North Bend Air Force Station, North Bend.

Newspapers, Circulation. Eugene Register-Guard (ExSat —56,032). Portland newspapers circulate in portion of district.

Commercial Television Stations, Affiliation. KMED-TV, Medford (NBC, ABC); KOBI-TV, Medford (CBS, ABC); KEZI-TV, Eugene (ABC); KVAL-TV, Eugene (NBC). Major portion of district is located in Eugene ADI. Smaller portions are located in Medford ADI, Portland ADI and Eureka (California) ADI.

Plants and Offices, Products, Employment.

Georgia-Pacific Corp., Eugene (Paper and paper products—1,100). **Weyerhaeuser Co.**, Springfield (Rilco Laminated Products—lumber, plywood, pulp, paperboard—2,850). **Weyerhaeuser Co.**, North Bend (Lumber, pulp, plywood—1,650). **Roseburg Lumber Co.**, Dillard (Plywood, sawmill—1,400). **Teledyne Industries Inc.**, Albany (Metals—1,200). **Southern Pacific Transportation Co.**, Eugene (Railroad terminal—1,500).

PENNSYLVANIA: TWENTY-FIVE HOUSE SEATS, LOSS OF TWO

For the fifth time in a row, Pennsylvania lost seats in the House as a result of the decennial census. The state has 25 seats in the 93rd Congress, down from its previous 27 and from the 36 it held before 1932.

Although the Democrats were in control of both houses of the state legislature and the governorship, they were not able to enact a redistricting plan to their advantage. *(Maps p. 165, 169, 173)*

Such a plan was drawn up and adopted by the House. It provided for a 15-10 Democratic advantage, costing the Republicans three seats. But Democratic factionalism in the Senate prevented that body from approving the House plan. Instead, the Senate adopted a bill more acceptable to the Republicans. The House concurred one day before the deadline—the first day for candidates to file nomination papers. The plan yielded a 13-12 Democratic margin, a loss of one for each party in the 1972 elections.

The vote in the state Senate, on Jan. 22, 1972, was 48-1. The House vote, on Jan. 24, was 155-34. Gov. Milton J. Shapp (D) signed the legislation Jan. 25.

District	Member Elected 1972	Winning Percentage	1970 Population	Percent Variance
1	William A. Barrett (D)	66.1	478,310	+ 1.3892
2	Robert N. C. Nix (D)	70.1	470,267	—0.3156
3	William J. Green (D)	63.3	472,041	+ 0.0604
4	Joshua Eilberg (D)	55.9	474,684	+ 0.6206
5	John Ware (R)	64.7	474,435	+ 0.5678
6	Gus Yatron (D)	64.5	473,574	+ 0.3853
7	Lawrence G. Williams (R)	60.6	470,714	—0.2208
8	Edward G. Biester Jr. (R)	64.4	475,406	+ 0.7737
9	E. G. Shuster (R)	61.8	468,008	—0.7944
10	Joseph M. McDade (R)	73.6	472,007	+ 0.0532
11	Daniel J. Flood (D)	68.3	470,457	—0.2753
12	John P. Saylor (R)	68.1	469,999	—0.3724
13	R. Lawrence Coughlin (R)	66.6	473,179	+ 0.3016
14	William S. Moorhead (D)	59.3	470,537	—0.2583
15	Fred B. Rooney (D)	60.8	469,672	—0.4417
16	Edwin D. Eshleman (R)	73.5	467,811	—0.8362
17	Herman T. Schneebeli (R)	72.2	476,141	+ 0.9295
18	H. John Heinz III (R)	72.8	472,074	+ 0.0674
19	George A. Goodling (R)	57.5	467,999	—0.7963
20	Joseph M. Gaydos (D)	61.5	468,959	—0.5928
21	John H. Dent (D)	62.0	473,040	+ 0.2721
22	Thomas E. Morgan (D)	60.8	469,778	—0.4192
23	Albert W. Johnson (R)	56.5	469,717	—0.4322
24	Joseph P. Vigorito (D)	68.8	472,171	+ 0.0879
25	Frank M. Clark (D)	55.8	472,929	+ 0.2486

1970 State Population: 11,793,909
Ideal District Population: 471,756

Election Results, 1968-1972

Vote for U.S. Representative
(Adjusted to new district boundaries)

District	1968	1970	1972
1	131,101 D (69.0%)	95,138 D (63.0%)	118,953 D (66.1%)
	58,794 R (31.0%)	55,305 R (36.6%)	59,807 R (33.2%)
2	136,035 D (75.3%)	94,247 D (73.0%)	107,509 D (70.1%)
	44,638 R (24.7%)	34,777 R (26.9%)	45,753 R (29.9%)
3	116,480 D (66.6%)	86,105 D (62.6%)	101,144 D (63.3%)
	58,406 R (33.4%)	50,874 R (37.0%)	57,787 R (36.2%)

District	1968	1970	1972
4	132,596 D (60.9%)	115,337 D (60.5%)	129,105 D (55.9%)
	85,161 R (39.1%)	75,262 R (39.5%)	102,013 R (44.1%)
5	106,750 R (62.8%)[1]	83,794 R (61.0%)	121,346 R (64.7%)
	60,474 D (35.6%)[1]	52,263 D (38.0%)	66,329 D (35.3%)
6	98,705 D (51.6%)	101,270 D (64.9%)	119,557 D (64.5%)
	90,648 R (47.4%)	51,281 R (32.9%)	64,076 R (34.6%)
7	113,623 R (57.9%)[1]	94,170 R (58.7%)	122,622 R (60.6%)
	80,838 D (41.2%)[1]	66,294 D (41.3%)	79,578 D (39.4%)
8	93,295 D (58.0%)	72,460 D (56.6%)	115,799 D (64.4%)
	59,457 R (37.0%)	50,615 D (39.5%)	64,069 D (35.6%)
9	109,791 R (68.3%)	85,331 R (64.6%)	95,913 R (61.8%)
	48,688 D (30.3%)	43,088 D (32.6%)	59,386 D (38.2%)
10	132,318 R (65.1%)	106,586 R (63.3%)	143,670 R (73.6%)
	69,451 D (34.1%)	58,797 D (34.9%)	51,550 D (26.4%)
11	131,970 D (68.4%)	150,106 D (93.7%)	124,336 D (68.3%)
	57,904 R (30.0%)	4,781 R (3.0%)[2]	57,809 R (31.7%)
12	111,649 R (59.0%)	91,681 R (57.9%)	122,628 R (68.1%)
	77,598 D (41.0%)	65,271 D (41.2%)	57,314 D (31.9%)
13	125,675 R (60.1%)	89,259 R (58.2%)	139,085 R (66.6%)
	81,755 D (39.1%)	61,490 D (40.1%)	69,728 D (33.4%)
14	118,727 D (60.2%)	92,390 D (65.4%)	106,158 D (59.3%)
	75,178 R (38.1%)	47,473 R (33.6%)	72,275 R (40.4%)
15	100,892 D (59.2%)	87,049 D (66.9%)	99,937 D (60.8%)
	65,678 R (38.5%)	41,130 R (31.6%)	64,560 R (39.2%)
16	101,695 R (66.2%)	75,841 R (63.5%)	112,292 R (73.5%)
	46,535 D (30.3%)	40,816 D (34.2%)	40,534 D (26.5%)
17	114,773 R (67.4%)	84,430 R (59.2%)	120,214 R (72.2%)
	51,580 D (30.3%)	54,633 D (38.3%)	44,202 D (26.5%)
18	123,554 R (62.5%)	90,400 R (59.4%)	144,521 R (72.8%)
	70,228 D (35.5%)	59,218 D (38.9%)	53,929 D (27.2%)
19	90,616 R (57.8%)	69,317 R (53.9%)	93,536 R (57.5%)
	63,963 D (40.8%)	56,560 D (44.0%)	67,018 D (41.2%)
20	114,695 D (58.7%)	93,883 D (64.8%)	117,933 D (61.5%)
	78,055 R (39.9%)	47,913 R (33.1%)	73,817 R (38.5%)
21	105,589 D (57.9%)	87,482 D (63.3%)	104,203 D (62.0%)
	75,988 R (41.7%)	48,113 R (34.8%)	63,812 R (38.0%)
22	104,668 D (58.7%)	88,680 D (63.6%)	100,918 D (60.8%)
	69,063 R (38.7%)	48,255 R (34.6%)	65,005 R (39.2%)
23	94,156 R (61.2%)	75,877 R (58.3%)	90,615 R (56.5%)
	58,942 D (38.3%)	54,136 D (41.6%)	69,813 D (43.5%)
24	106,869 D (61.1%)	94,029 D (66.8%)	122,092 D (68.8%)
	66,429 R (38.0%)	44,395 R (31.5%)	55,406 R (31.2%)
25	109,078 D (61.5%)	95,793 D (67.9%)	97,549 D (55.8%)
	66,100 R (37.3%)	41,983 R (29.8%)	77,123 R (44.2%)
State	2,286,683 D (50.0%)[3]	1,944,690 D (53.8%)	2,281,484 R (51.1%)
	2,230,076 R (48.7%)[3]	1,610,688 R (44.6%)	2,172,844 D (48.7%)

1 Estimated.
2 No candidate in this district as constituted before redistricting.
3 Includes absentee votes not distributed on a district-by-district basis.

Voting Age Population

District	Voting Age Population	Voting Age Population 18, 19, 20	Voting Age Population 65 and Over	Median Age of Voting Age Population
1	330,957	26,663 (8.1%)	53,066 (16.0%)	44.3
2	321,572	22,392 (7.0%)	58,984 (18.3%)	45.4
3	319,094	22,353 (7.0%)	56,599 (17.7%)	46.0
4	328,688	18,911 (5.8%)	53,251 (16.2%)	45.8
5	312,335	28,037 (9.0%)	40,200 (12.9%)	42.4
6	330,782	20,593 (6.2%)	58,884 (17.8%)	47.4
7	311,473	20,933 (6.7%)	46,442 (14.9%)	45.1
8	292,372	19,648 (6.7%)	29,617 (10.1%)	41.4
9	310,100	23,972 (7.7%)	51,724 (16.7%)	44.7

District	Voting Age Population	Voting Age Population 18, 19, 20	Voting Age Population 65 and Over	Median Age of Voting Age Population
10	321,197	22,939 (7.1%)	59,387 (18.5%)	46.9
11	332,344	22,907 (6.9%)	60,570 (18.2%)	47.9
12	313,750	26,991 (8.6%)	54,210 (17.3%)	46.5
13	319,973	20,764 (6.5%)	50,878 (15.9%)	45.8
14	339,530	29,197 (8.6%)	65,455 (19.3%)	47.1
15	323,861	22,724 (7.0%)	50,965 (15.7%)	45.4
16	305,959	22,548 (7.4%)	47,419 (15.5%)	43.6
17	323,134	22,798 (7.1%)	54,366 (16.8%)	45.3
18	318,940	19,162 (6.0%)	51,599 (16.2%)	46.6
19	309,208	21,962 (7.1%)	46,274 (15.0%)	43.6
20	313,472	20,095 (6.4%)	46,197 (14.7%)	46.1
21	310,230	19,597 (6.3%)	44,038 (14.2%)	45.0
22	313,634	22,842 (7.3%)	50,818 (16.2%)	46.2
23	314,400	33,611 (10.7%)	48,733 (15.5%)	42.9
24	306,531	26,343 (8.6%)	47,640 (15.5%)	44.5
25	309,063	23,505 (7.6%)	45,604 (14.8%)	44.8
State	7,932,551	581,490 (7.3%)	1,272,947 (16.0%)	45.3

District	Completed 4 years of High School	Completed 4 years of College	Completed 5 years or less of School	Median School years completed
7	57.5	11.4	4.5	12.2
8	60.2	12.7	2.9	12.3
9	46.1	5.5	4.6	11.4
10	50.6	6.5	6.1	12.0
11	47.2	5.4	8.2	11.6
12	45.3	5.4	7.2	11.2
13	64.8	19.4	4.2	12.4
14	49.4	11.1	7.1	11.9
15	47.7	8.4	5.4	11.7
16	45.8	7.9	3.8	11.4
17	52.2	7.3	4.5	12.1
18	58.4	12.8	4.8	12.2
19	50.1	8.8	4.3	12.0
20	52.9	8.3	6.0	12.1
21	54.6	8.1	5.8	12.1
22	48.2	7.1	7.4	11.7
23	53.8	8.9	4.4	12.1
24	57.6	8.3	3.6	12.2
25	51.7	6.8	5.6	12.1
State	50.2	8.7	6.1	12.0

Income and Occupation

District	Median Family Income	White Collar Workers	Blue Collar Workers	Service Workers	Farm Workers
1	$ 8,690	42.9%	39.7%	17.1%	0.3%
2	8,670	48.8	33.0	17.8	0.4
3	8,368	39.5	45.0	15.3	0.2
4	11,069	56.8	33.1	10.0	0.1
5	12,148	53.6	34.9	9.4	2.1
6	9,009	34.6	53.4	10.4	1.6
7	11,383	56.4	33.1	10.2	0.3
8	11,807	52.0	38.4	8.8	0.8
9	8,124	34.3	49.6	11.6	4.5
10	8,318	37.7	47.3	11.4	3.6
11	8,161	35.3	53.1	10.5	1.1
12	8,030	35.4	49.5	12.4	2.7
13	13,251	63.6	26.9	9.3	0.2
14	8,952	53.2	29.1	17.6	0.1
15	10,171	40.8	47.6	10.7	0.9
16	9,905	37.7	46.3	11.5	4.5
17	8,933	43.9	42.3	12.1	1.7
18	10,770	56.9	31.8	11.1	0.2
19	10,107	44.3	43.1	10.3	2.3
20	9,937	49.5	38.4	11.9	0.2
21	9,645	45.2	42.8	11.1	0.9
22	8,396	39.6	46.8	12.3	1.3
23	8,272	41.0	43.9	13.3	1.8
24	9,215	41.6	44.8	11.5	2.1
25	9,208	38.8	48.0	11.6	1.6
State	9,554	45.1	41.6	11.9	1.4

Education: School Years Completed

District	Completed 4 years of High School	Completed 4 years of College	Completed 5 years or less of School	Median School years completed
1	35.1%	5.0%	11.8%	10.4
2	44.6	10.8	9.9	11.4
3	29.6	4.7	12.1	9.9
4	48.8	6.3	5.3	11.9
5	62.2	17.2	4.1	12.4
6	43.3	5.4	7.0	11.0

Housing and Residential Patterns

District	Housing Owner Occupied Units	Housing Renter Occupied Units	Urban	Suburban	Nonmetro-politan
1	59.9%	40.1%	100.0%	—	—
2	47.6	52.4	100.0	—	—
3	55.2	44.8	100.0	—	—
4	77.1	22.9	100.0	—	—
5	73.8	26.2	—	100.0%	—
6	72.8	27.2	18.5	44.1	37.4%
7	71.2	28.8	—	100.0	—
8	75.3	24.7	—	100.0	—
9	73.2	26.8	13.4	25.8	60.8
10	69.6	30.4	21.9	35.0	43.1
11	68.6	31.4	19.0	53.8	27.2
12	72.4	27.6	9.0	46.9	44.1
13	69.9	30.1	11.2	88.8	—
14	48.1	51.9	83.4	16.6	—
15	70.9	29.1	45.2	54.8	—
16	69.4	30.6	12.3	72.4	15.3
17	67.1	32.9	14.2	32.8	53.0
18	71.5	28.5	12.9	87.1	—
19	72.8	27.2	10.8	89.2	—
20	70.6	29.4	14.2	85.8	—
21	76.1	23.9	—	100.0	—
22	71.7	28.3	—	59.4	40.6
23	73.0	27.0	—	—	100.0
24	73.4	26.4	27.3	28.5	44.2
25	76.1	23.9	—	50.2	49.8
State	68.8	31.2	28.6	50.8	20.6

1st District

(Philadelphia—South)

Race and Ethnic Groups. Blacks 39.2 percent. Italian stock 12.8 percent, Russian stock 1.8 percent.
Cities, 1970 Population. Part of Philadelphia 478,310.

Philadelphia

2

4

13
PART

3

RIVER

SCHUYLKILL

RIVER

1

DELAWARE

Universities, Enrollment. Drexel University (Philadelphia—8,602), University of Pennsylvania (Philadelphia—19,548).

Military Installations or Activities. Philadelphia Naval Shipyard, Philadelphia Naval Station, Philadelphia Naval Hospital, Philadelphia Naval Air Engineering Center, Philadelphia Marine Corps Supply Activity, Philadelphia Army Defense Personnel Support Center, all in Philadelphia.

Newspapers, Circulation. Philadelphia newspapers circulate throughout district.

Commercial Television Stations, Affiliation. Entire district is located in Philadelphia ADI.

Plants and Offices, Products, Employment.
Bluebird Inc., Philadelphia (Meat packing—1,150). **Fairmount Foods Co.** Philadelphia (Dairy products—1,200). **General Electric Co.,** Philadelphia (Power circuit breakers—8,000). **General Electric Co.,** Philadelphia (Signaling, transmitting equipment—4,500). **E. I. du Pont de Nemours & Co.,** Philadelphia (Paints, varnish—1,120). **Atlantic Richfield Co.,** Philadelphia (Pe-

troleum products—3,000). **Chilton Co.,** Philadelphia (Books, periodicals—1,000).

2nd District

(Philadelphia—West, Central)

Race and Ethnic Groups. Blacks 65.0 percent. Russian stock 4.2 percent, Italian stock 1.7 percent.

Cities, 1970 Population. Part of Philadelphia 470,267.

Universities, Enrollment. Chestnut Hill College (Philadelphia—1,128), LaSalle College (Philadelphia—6,565). St. Joseph's College (Philadelphia—6,897), Philadelphia College of Art (Philadelphia—1,088).

Newspapers, Circulation. Philadelphia newspapers circulate throughout district.

Commercial Television Stations, Affiliation. Entire district is located in Philadelphia ADI.

Plants and Offices, Products, Employment. (Note: 2nd District includes portion of downtown business district of Philadelphia.)

Insurance Company of North America, Philadelphia (Insurance—HQ—2,960). Reliance Insurance Co., Philadelphia (Insurance—HQ—1,200). Tasty Baking Co., Philadelphia (Baked goods—1,800). Fairmount Foods Co., Philadelphia (Dairy products—1,650). Best Markets Inc., Philadelphia (Groceries and meats—1,000). United Engineers and Constructors Inc., Philadelphia (General engineering and constructing—HQ—1,200). Catalytic Inc., Philadelphia (Engineering and construction—HQ—1,000). H. Daroff & Sons Inc., Philadelphia (Manufacturers of men's clothing 2,500). Penn Central Transportation Co., Philadelphia (Railroad—3,000). Smith, Kline and French Laboratories, Philadelphia (Pharmaceuticals—HQ—3,660). Sun Oil Co., Philadelphia (Sunoco Division—Oil production and refining—HQ—1,500). William J. Burns International Detective Agency, Philadelphia (Detective agency—1,000). Philadelphia School District, Philadelphia (Public school system—28,000). City of Philadelphia, Philadelphia (Municipal government—29,500). Bell Telephone Company of Pennsylvania, Philadelphia (Telephone company—HQ —2,000). Bulletin Co., Philadelphia (Publishing—Philadelphia Bulletin—2,500).

3rd District

(Philadelphia—East and Central)

Race and Ethnic Groups. Blacks 28.5 percent. Spanish heritage population 4.8 percent. Polish stock 4.2 percent, Italian stock 2.8 percent, Russian stock 2.7 percent.

Cities, 1970 Population. Part of Philadelphia 472,041.

Universities, Enrollment. Temple University (Philadelphia—28,902).

Military Installations or Activities. Frankford Arsenal, Philadelphia.

Newspapers, Circulation. Philadelphia newspapers circulate throughout district. They include: Philadelphia Bulletin (ExSat—619,113), Philadelphia Inquirer (MxSat—444,489), Philadelphia News (ExSat—242,920).

Commercial Television Stations, Affiliation. Entire district is located in Philadelphia ADI. Philadelphia stations include: KYW-TV, Philadelphia (NBC); WCAU-TV, Philadelphia (CBS); WPVI-TV, Philadelphia (ABC); WPHL-TV, Philadelphia (NBC on alternate basis); WTAF-TV, Philadelphia (None); WKBS-TV, Philadelphia (None).

Plants and Offices, Products, Employment. (Note: District includes portion of downtown business district of Philadelphia.)

Potomac Insurance Co., Philadelphia (Insurance—HQ—1,200). General Accident, Fire, & Life Assurance Corp. Ltd., Philadelphia (Insurance—HQ—1,000). LCA Corp., Philadelphia (Lighting fixtures, houseware—HQ—1,000). Walter Kidde & Co. Inc., Philadelphia (Lighting Corp. of America Division—lighting fixtures—1,000). Philco Ford Corp., Philadelphia (Radios, TVs,

phonographs—HQ—9,000). McCloskey & Co. Inc., Philadelphia (General contractor—at least 1,400). Rohm & Haas Co., Philadelphia (Chemicals—2,650). Rohm & Haas Co., Philadelphia (Chemicals—HQ—1,270). Atlantic Richfield Co., Philadelphia (Arco Chemical Co. Division—whole petroleum products—1,000). SKF Industries Inc., Philadelphia (Nice Ball Bearing Co. Division—ball bearings—HQ—2,000). Midvale-Heppenstall Co., Philadelphia (Steel products—1,400). Villager Industries Inc., Philadelphia (Women's clothing—2,680). Gimbel Bros. Inc., Philadelphia (Department store—2,100). Spiegel Inc. of Philadelphia, Philadelphia (General merchandise store—2,000). Strawbridge & Clothier, Philadelphia (Clover Discount Stores Division—HQ—Department store—3,000). John Wanamaker (Philadelphia) Inc., Philadelphia (Department store—HQ—2,500). Cuneo Eastern Press Inc. of Pennsylvania, Philadelphia (Commercial printing—1,350). Fairmount Foods Co., Philadelphia (Dairy products—2,100). Bayuk Cigars Inc., Philadelphia (Holding company, cigars—HQ—1,550). C. Schmidt & Sons Inc., Philadelphia (Valley Forge Brewing Co.—Brewers—HQ—1,000). Philadelphia Electric Co., Philadelphia (Electric, gas utility—HQ—3,000). Rentex Services Corp., Philadelphia (Holding company—1,600). Thomas Jefferson Hospital, Philadelphia (Hospital—2,800). Rapid American Corp., Philadelphia (Joseph H. Cohen & Sons Division—men's clothing—2,400). Budd Co., Philadelphia (Railroad cars, industrial plastics, etc—HQ—6,000). Philco-Ford Corp., Philadelphia (Communications equipment—1,000). Triangle Publications Inc., Philadelphia (Publishing—1,200). Philadelphia Newspapers Inc., Philadelphia (Publishing-Philadelphia Inquirer—3,000).

4th District

(Philadelphia—Northeast)

Race and Ethnic Groups. Blacks 5.2 percent. Russian stock 7.8 percent, Italian stock 3.9 percent, German stock 3.7 percent, Polish stock 3.3 percent, Irish stock 2.8 percent, British stock 2.8 percent.

Cities, 1970 Population. Part of Philadelphia 474,-684.

Military Installations or Activities. Naval Publications and Forms Center, Naval Aviation Supply Office, both in Philadelphia.

Newspapers, Circulation. Philadelphia newspapers circulate throughout district.

Commercial Television Stations, Affiliation. Entire district is located in Philadelphia ADI.

Plants and Offices, Products, Employment.

International Telephone & Telegraph, Philadelphia (Nesbitt Division—Heating and air conditioning equipment—1,000). Eaton Corp., Philadelphia (Industrial Truck Division—Trucks and hoists—2,500). Kelsey-Hayes Co., Philadelphia (Heintz Division—cold extrusions—1,250). Nabisco, Philadelphia (Biscuits, crackers—1,700). Pet Inc., Philadelphia (Steven F. Whitman & Son Division—confectionary products—1,000).

5th District

(Philadelphia Suburbs—Western Delaware County, Central and Southern Chester County, Western Montgomery County)

Race and Ethnic Groups. Blacks 4.3 percent. Italian stock 3.4 percent.

Cities, 1970 Population. Pottstown 25,345, West Chester 19,293, Phoenixville 14,817.

Universities, Enrollment. Cheyney State College (Cheyney—2,162). Haverford College (Haverford—712). Ursinus College (Collegeville—1,869). Villanova University (Villanova—9,993). West Chester State College (West Chester—8,151).

Military Installations or Activities. Valley Forge General Hospital, Phoenixville.

Newspapers, Circulation. Philadelphia newspapers circulate in major portions of district.

Commercial Television Stations, Affiliation. Entire district is located in Philadelphia ADI.

Plants and Offices, Products, Employment.

   Firestone Tire & Rubber Co., Pottstown (Firestone Plastic Division—synthetic rubber and products—3,000). **B.F. Goodrich Co.,** Oaks (Tires, tubes—3,000). **NL Industries,** Pottstown (Doehler-Jarvis Division—aluminum, zinc die castings—1,200). **Bethlehem Steel Corp.,** Pottstown (Fabricated products—1,300). **Stanley G. Flagg & Co.,** Pottstown (Malleable iron—1,000). **Phoenix Steel Corp.,** Phoenixville (Blast furnaces, steel works, rolling mills—1,050). **Dana Corp.,** Pottstown (Spicer Manufacturing Division—universal joints—1,100). **Allegheny Corp.,** Spring City (Johns Motor Co. Division—motor carrier—1,500). **Wyeth Laboratories Inc.,** Malvern (Pharmaceuticals—1,150). **Triangle Publications Inc.,** Wayne (Publishers, radio, TV stations—HQ—1,000).

6th District

(Southeast—Reading)

Race and Ethnic Groups. Polish stock 2.7 percent, Italian stock 2.4 percent.

Cities, 1970 Population. Reading 87,621, Pottsville 19,715.

Universities, Enrollment. Albright College (Reading—1,593), Kutztown State College (Kutztown—4,928).

Commercial Television Stations, Affiliation. Major portion of district is located in Philadelphia ADI. Remainder is located in Wilkes-Barre-Scranton ADI.

Plants and Offices, Products, Employment.

   Berkshire International Corp., Reading (Women's hosiery—HQ—1,500). **North American Rockwell Corp.,** Reading (Textile machinery—4,400). **Aluminum Co. of America,** Cressona (Aluminum extrusions—1,380). **Birdsboro Corp.,** Birdsboro (Steel castings, industrial machinery—HQ—1,250). **Carpenter Technology Corp.,** Reading (Steel Division—specialty steels—HQ—2,900). **Dana Corp.,** Reading (Parish Pressed Steel Division—auto, truck frames—3,200). **Western Electric Co. Inc.,** Reading (Electronic components—3,000). **Atlas Chemical Industries Inc.,** Tamaqua (Explosives—1,500). **Ludens Inc.,** Reading (Cough drops, confectionaries—HQ—1,000).

7th District

(Philadelphia Suburbs—Chester)

Race and Ethnic Groups. Blacks 8.4 percent. Italian stock 5.6 percent, Irish stock 3.0 percent, British stock 2.8 percent.

Cities, 1970 Population. Chester 56,310, Lansdowne 14,086, Darby 13,725, Yeadon 12,133.

Universities, Enrollment. Widener College (Chester—1,574. Includes Pennsylvania Military College for men and coeducational civilian Penn Morton College), Swarthmore College (Swarthmore—1,170).

Newspapers, Circulation. Philadelphia newspapers circulate throughout district.

Commercial Television Stations, Affiliation. Entire district is located in Philadelphia ADI.

Plants and Offices, Products, Employment.

   Scott Paper Co., Chester (Paper products—2,400). **FMC Corp.,** Marcus Hook (American Viscose Division—cellophane 1,400). **Reynolds Metals Co.,** Chester (Aluminum extrusions—1,500). **Sun Oil Co.,** Marcus Hook (Petroleum refining—3,000). **Westinghouse Electric Corp.,** Lester (Large Turbine Division—turbines—at least 8,000). **Franklin Mint Inc.,** Media (Minting of coins—1,000). **Bell Telephone Co. of Pennsylvania,** Upper Darby (Telephone company—1,000).

8th District

(Philadelphia Suburbs—Bucks County)

Race and Ethnic Groups. German stock 2.9 percent, Italian stock 2.6 percent, British stock 2.5 percent.

Cities, 1970 Population. Hatboro West 13,441, Bristol 12,085, Morrisville 11,316.

Universities, Enrollment. Delaware Valley College of Science and Agriculture (Doylestown—1,278).

Military Installations or Activities. Naval Air Development Center, Johnsville; Naval Air Station, Willow Grove; Naval Air Facility, Johnsville.

Newspapers, Circulation. Bucks County Courier Times, Levittown (Eve—56,452). In addition, Philadelphia newspapers circulate throughout the district.

Commercial Television Stations, Affiliation. Entire district is located in Philadelphia ADI.

Plants and Offices, Products, Employment.

   Rockower Brothers Inc., Langhorne (Men's, boys' clothing—2,100). **United States Steel Corp.,** Fairless Hills (Iron, steel products—9,000). **Strick Corp.,** Fairless Hills (Truck trailers—HQ—1,800). **Ameteck Inc.,** Sellersville (U.S. Gauge—pressure guages—1,700). **Rohm & Haas Co.,** Bristol (Plastics, resins—2,800). **Fischer & Porter Co.,** Warminster (Industrial instruments—HQ—3,650).

9th District

(South Central—Altoona, Chambersburg)

Race and Ethnic Groups. Italian stock 1.1 percent, German stock 1.0 percent.

Cities, 1970 Population. Altoona 62,892, Chambersburg 17,313, Lewistown 10,988, Waynesboro 10,010.

Universities, Enrollment. Juniata College (Huntingdon —1,222), Shippensburg State College (Shippensburg—4,059), Susquehanna University (Selinsgrove —1,501).

Military Installations and Activities. Letterkenny Army Depot, Chambersburg.

Commercial Television Stations, Affiliation. WFBG-TV, Altoona (CBS). Most of district is located in Johnstown-Altoona ADI. Portion of district is located in Harrisburg-York-Lancaster-Lebanon ADI.

Plants and Offices, Products, Employment.

Penn Central Transportation Co., Altoona (Railroad shop—4,300). **Penn Central Transportation Co.,** Hollidaysburg (Railroad shop—1,400). **Baldwin-Lima-Hamilton Corp.,** Burnham (Standard Steel Division—steel forgings—2,100). **Grove Manufacturing Co. Inc.,** Shadygrove (Mobile hydraulic cranes, machinery and equipment—HQ—1,200). **FMC Corp.,** Lewiston (American Viscose Division—rayon, synthetic fibers—2,600). **Litton Industries Inc.,** Waynesboro (Landis Tool Co. Division—machine tools—1,200). **Sylvania Electric Products Inc.,** Altoona (Altoona Tube Plant—electronic tubes—1,100). **J. Schoeneman Inc.,** Chambersburg (Stanley Manufacturing Co. Division—men's suits—2,000). **Puritan Sportswear Corp.,** Altoona (Men's sportswear, shirts—HQ—1,500).

10th District

(Northeast—Scranton)

Race and Ethnic Groups. Italian stock 4.5 percent, Polish stock 3.6 percent.

Cities, 1970 Population. Scranton 103,494, Dunmore, 17,300, Carbondale 12,808.

Universities, Enrollment. East Stroudsburg State College (East Stroudsburg—3,400), Mansfield State College (Mansfield—3,097), Marywood College (Scranton—2,214), University of Scranton (Scranton—3,258).

Military Installations and Activities. Tobyhanna Army Depot, Tobyhanna.

Newspapers, Circulation. Scranton Times (Eve—56,523).

Commercial Television Stations, Affiliation. WDAU-TV, Scranton (CBS). Major portion of district is located in Wilkes-Barre-Scranton ADI. Other portions of district are located in Binghamton (New York), Elmira (New York), New York (New York) and Philadelphia ADIs.

Plants and Offices, Products, Employment.

Chamberlain Manufacturing Corp., Scranton (Shell casings—1,760). **GTE Sylvania Inc.,** Towanda (Chemical and Metallurgical Division—

chemical and metallurgical products—1,170). **RCA Corp.,** Dunmore (Television and picture tube division—TV picture tubes—1,000). **Charmin Paper Products Co.,** Mehoopany (Paper mill—2,400). **International Textbook Co.,** Scranton (Haddon Craftsmen Division—book printing—1,070).

11th District

(Northeast—Wilkes-Barre)

Race and Ethnic Groups. Polish stock 6.2 percent, Italian stock 4.1 percent, Austrian stock 2.7 percent.

Cities, 1970 Population. Wilkes-Barre 58,817, Hazleton 30,426, Kingston 18,333, Nanticoke 14,641.

Universities, Enrollment. Bloomsburg State College (Bloomsburg—4,949), King's College (Wilkes-Barre—2,669), Wilkes College (Wilkes-Barre—3,436).

Military Installations or Activities. Benton Air Force Station, Red Rock.

Newspapers, Circulation. Times-Leader, Wilkes-Barre (Eve—55,499).

Commercial Television Stations, Affiliation. WBRE-TV, Wilkes-Barre (NBC); WNEP-TV, Wilkes-Barre (ABC). Most of district is in Wilkes-Barre-Scranton ADI. Portions of district are in Philadelphia and Binghamton (New York) ADIs.

Plants and Offices, Products, Employment.

Lehigh Valley Anthracite Inc., Pittston (Coal preparation—HQ—1,200). **New Jersey Zinc Co.,** Palmerton (Mining and smelting zinc, zinc products—1,800). **Whitaker Corp.,** Berwick (Berwick Forge Fabricating Division—steel forging, fabricating—1,000). **Magee Carpet Co.,** Bloomsburg (Rugs, carpets—HQ—1,300). **Elkay Industries Inc.,** Wilkes-Barre (Girls', children's wear—3,100). **RCA Corp.,** Mountaintop (Electronic Components Division—transistors, photocells—2,700). **Borden Inc.,** Berwick (Wise Foods Division—potato chips—1,100). **American Brands Inc.,** Mountaintop (American Cigar Division—cigars—1,000).

12th District

(West Central—Johnstown)

Race and Ethnic Groups. Italian stock 3.0 percent, Czechoslovakian stock 2.4 percent.

Cities, 1970 Population. Johnstown 42,482, Indiana 16,102.

Universities, Enrollment. Indiana University of Pennsylvania (Indiana—10,206), St. Francis College (Loretto—1,554).

Newspapers, Circulation. Johnstown Tribune-Democrat (All day—57,446).

Commercial Television Stations, Affiliation. WARD-TV, Johnstown (CBS primary, ABC); WJAC-TV, Johnstown (NBC primary, ABC). District is divided between Johnstown-Altoona and Pittsburgh ADIs.

Plants and Offices, Products, Employment.

Allegheny Ludlum Industries, Leechburg (Blast furnaces, steel works, rolling mills—2,300). **Bethlehem Steel Corp.,** Johnstown (Beth Elkhorn Di-

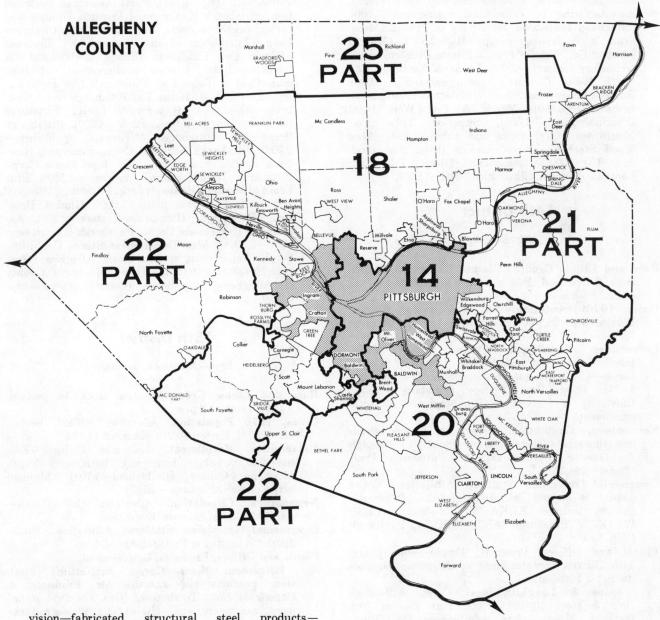

ALLEGHENY COUNTY

vision—fabricated structural steel products—12,500). **United States Steel Corp.**, Johnstown (Steel—1,000). **Penn Central Transportation Co.**, Cherry Tree (Railroad yard—at least 1,010). **Brockway Glass Co.**, Crenshaw (Glass containers—3,000).

13th District

(Philadelphia Suburbs—Eastern Montgomery County)

Race and Ethnic Groups. Blacks 4.1 percent. Italian stock 5.7 percent, Russian stock 3.4 percent, British stock 3.0 percent, German stock 2.6 percent.

Cities, 1970 Population. Norristown 38,181, Penn Square-Plymouth Valley 19,962, Lansdale 18,457, Roslyn 18,297. In addition, district contains 53,160 from city of Philadelphia.

Universities, Enrollment. Bryn Mawr College (Bryn Mawr—1,421), Philadelphia College of Textiles and Science (Philadelphia—2,130). Beaver College (Glenside—1,020).

Newspapers, Circulation. Philadelphia newspapers circulate throughout district.

Commercial Television Stations, Affiliation. Entire district is located in Philadelphia ADI.

Plants and Offices, Products, Employment.

Honeywell, Fort Washington (Industrial Division—industrial instruments—3,500). **Narco Scientific Industries,** Fort Washington (Narco Avionics Division—medical and communications equipment—HQ—1,000). **American Electronic Laboratories**, Lansdale (Electronic instruments—HQ—1,000). **Philco-Ford Corp.,** Lansdale (Audio-video Division—TV tubes, radios—1,950). **Sperry Rand Corp.,**

Blue Bell (Univac Division—research, development, manufacturing of calculators, typewriters—3,000). **Safeguard Industries Inc.**, King of Prussia (Measuring & dispensing pumps—HQ—2,850). **General Electric Co.**, King of Prussia (Space Division—space technology research—3,000) **Leeds & Northrup Co.**, North Wales (Scientific instruments—HQ—3,000). **Rorer-Amchem Inc.**, Fort Washington (Pharmaceuticals—HQ—2,800). **Merck & Co.**, West Point (Pharmaceuticals—1,600). **Superior Tube Co.**, Norristown (Steel pipes and tubes—1,160). **Alan Wood Steel Co.**, Conshohocken (Iron, steel products—HQ—3,000). **American Olean Tile Co.**, Lansdale (Ceramic tile division—HQ—1,000).

14th District

(Pittsburgh)

Race and Ethnic Groups. Blacks 21.3 percent. Italian stock 5.0 percent, Polish stock 3.0 percent, German stock 2.8 percent.

Cities, 1970 Population. Part of Pittsburgh 392,631, Wilkinsburg 26,756, Brentwood 13,758, Dormont 12,854.

Universities, Enrollment. Carlow College (Pittsburgh—1,045), Carnegie-Mellon University (Pittsburgh—4,540), Duquesne University (Pittsburgh—8,427), Point Park College (Pittsburgh—2,584), University of Pittsburgh (Pittsburgh—30,587 total enrollment).

Newspapers, Circulation. Pittsburgh papers circulate throughout district. They include: Pittsburgh Post-Gazette (MxSat—211,254), Pittsburgh Press (ExSat—298,270).

Commercial Television Stations, Affiliation. Entire district is located in Pittsburgh ADI. Pittsburgh stations include: KDKA-TV, Pittsburgh (CBS); WTAE-TV, Pittsburgh (ABC); WIIC-TV, Pittsburgh (NBC).

Plants and Offices, Products, Employment. (Note: 14th District contains most of downtown business district of Pittsburgh.)

Jones & Laughlin Steel Corp., Pittsburgh (Iron & steel—10,400). (Note: Part also in 20th District). **Mine Safety Applicances Co.**, Pittsburgh (MSA Research Division—mine safety equipment—HQ—2,100). **Wean United Inc.**, Pittsburgh (Steelmill equipment—HQ—7,500, total employment). **Blaw-Knox Co.**, Pittsburgh (Rolling mills—HQ—8,000, total employment). **Blaw-Knox Chemical Plants Inc.**, Pittsburgh—HQ—1,500, total employment). **Gulf Oil Corp.**, Pittsburgh (Production, refining, marketing of oil—HQ—1,000). **Aluminum Co. of America**, Pittsburgh (Production, fabricating aluminum—HQ—1,000). **Koopers Co. Inc.**, Pittsburgh (Construction materials, plants, equipment, etc.—HQ—1,300). **Pullman Inc.**, Pittsburgh (Swindell Dressler Co. Division—industrial engineering—1,000) **Westinghouse Air Brake Co.**, Pittsburgh (Signal & Communications Division—HQ—railroad equipment—1,000). **Rockwell Manufacturing Co.**, Pittsburgh (Measuring & controlling instruments, power tools,

valves, etc.—HQ—1,350). **North American Rockwell Inc.**, Pittsburgh (Commercial Products Group—steel springs, metal products, etc.—1,250). **Allis-Chalmers Corp.**, Pittsburgh, (Transformers—2,000). **Emerson Electric Co.**, Pittsburgh (Edwin L. Wiegand Co. Division—electric heating appliances—1,500). **Hillman Coal & Coke Co.**, Pittsburgh (Air conditioning—2,000). **H. J. Heinz Co.** Pittsburgh (Food products—HQ—1,000). **Papercraft Corp.**, Pittsburgh (Gift wrappings, ribbons, cards—4,500). **Pittsburgh Press Co.**, Pittsburgh (Newspaper publishers—2,200). **Pittsburgh National Corp.**, Pittsburgh (One-bank holding company—2,720). **Equi-Mark Corp.**, Pittsburgh (Bank holding company—1,530). **Blue Cross of Western Pennsylvania**, Pittsburgh (Hospital and medical service plans—1,000). **Gimbel Bros. Inc.**, Pittsburgh, (Department store—2,000). **Associated Dry Goods Corp.**, Pittsburgh (Department store—2,000). **May Department Stores Co.**, Pittsburgh (Department stores—4,500). **Allegheny General Hospital**, Pittsburgh (Hospital—1,580). **County of Allegheny**, Pittsburgh (County government—6,000).

15th District

(East—Allentown, Bethlehem)

Race and Ethnic Groups. Italian stock 3.0 percent, Austrian stock 3.0 percent.

Cities, 1970 Population. Allentown 109,521, Bethlehem 72,731, Easton 30,210, Emmaus 11,514.

Universities, Enrollment. Lafayette College (Easton—2,212), Lehigh University (Bethlehem—5,474), Moravian College (Bethlehem—1,709), Muhlenberg College (Allentown—1,785).

Newspapers, Circulation. Allentown Call (Morn—100,653), Easton Express (Eve 53,548).

Commercial Television Stations, Affiliation. Entire district is located in Philadelphia ADI.

Plants and Offices, Products, Employment.

Bethlehem Steel Corp., Bethlehem (Steel, steel products—HQ—22,000). **Air Products & Chemicals Inc.**, Trexlertown (Gas, chemical equipment, machinery, etc.—HQ—1,500). **Western Electric Co. Inc.**, Allentown (Electric components, equipment—4,300). **General Electric Co.**, Allentown (Portable appliances—1,250). **Pennsylvania Power & Light**, Allentown (Electric utility—HQ—1,100) **Mack Trucks Inc.**, Allentown (Motor trucks—3,600). **Rapid-American Corp.**, Northampton (Cross Country Clothes—men's suits—1,100). **Genesco Inc.**, Allentown (Phoenix Clothes—men's suits, raincoats—1,400). **Hess's Inc.**, Allentown (Department store—1,300). **American Can Co.**, Easton (Dixie Products—paper containers—1,300).

16th District

(Southeast—Lancaster)

Race and Ethnic Groups. Blacks 3.0 percent. German stock 1.3 percent, Italian stock 1.0 percent.

Cities, 1970 Population. Lancaster 57,632, Lebanon 28,593, Coatesville 12,340, Columbia 11,245.

Universities, Enrollment. Elizabethtown College (Elizabethtown—1,751), Franklin and Marshall College (Lancaster—2,608), Millersville State College (Millersville—4,729).

Newspapers, Circulation. Lancaster New Era (Eve 59,224).

Commercial Television Stations, Affiliation. WLYH-TV, Lebanon (CBS); WGAL-TV, Lancaster (NBC). Most of district is located in Harrisburg-York-Lancaster-Lebanon ADI. Small portion is located in Philadelphia ADI.

Plants and Offices, Products, Employment.
    Sperry Rand Corp., New Holland (New Holland Machine Division—farm equipment—at least 2,300). **Raybestos Manhattan Inc.,** Manheim (Asbestos products—1,600). **Armstrong Cork Co.,** Lancaster (Linoleum, resilient flooring, insulation, etc.—HQ—5,800). **Bethlehem Steel Corp.,** Lebanon (Steel products—2,000). **Lukens Steel Co.,** Coatesville (Iron, steel products—HQ—5,020). **Bethlehem Mines Corp.,** Cornwall (Mining—1,000). **RCA Corp.,** Lancaster (Radio, TV tubes—4,400). **Schick Electric Inc.,** Lancaster (Electric shavers—at least 1,500). **Burroughs Corp.,** Downingtown (Electronic computing equipment—1,200). **Grinnell Corp.,** Columbia (Malleable iron—1,500).

17th District

(Central—Harrisburg, Williamsport)

Race and Ethnic Groups. Blacks 6.0 percent. Italian stock 1.5 percent, German stock 1.0 percent.

Cities, 1970 Population. Harrisburg 67,880, Williamsport 37,918, Sunbury 13,025, Shamokin 11,719.

Universities, Enrollment. Bucknell University (Lewisburg—2,962), Lebanon Valley College (Anniville—1,307), Lycoming College (Williamsport—1,635).

Newspapers, Circulation. Harrisburg News (ExSat—72,882).

Commercial Television Stations, Affiliation. WHP-TV, Harrisburg (CBS); WTPA-TV, Harrisburg (ABC). District is divided between Harrisburg-York-Lancaster-Lebanon ADI and Wilkes-Barre-Scranton ADI.

Plants and Offices, Products, Employment.
    Avco Corp., Williamsport (Aircraft engines—2,500). **TRW Inc.,** Harrisburg (Aircraft engines—2,000). **Philco-Ford Corp.,** Watsontown (Radio, TV cabinets—1,000). **GTE Sylvania Inc.,** Montoursville (Photoflash bulbs—1,000). **AMP Inc.,** Harrisburg (Electrical connectors—HQ—1,600). **Bell Telephone Company of Pennsylvania,** Harrisburg (Telephone company—2,210). **American Home Foods Inc.,** Milton (Food products—1,600). **Hershey Estates,** Hershey (Department store, dairy products—HQ—1,490). **Hershey Foods Corp.,** Hershey (Chocolate, cocoa—HQ—3,600). **Montgomery Mills Inc.,** Montgomery (Narrow fabrics—1,300). **Bethlehem Steel Corp.,** Steelton (Steel bars, rails—4,000). **Commonwealth of Pennsylvania,** Harrisburg (State government—150,000, total employment). **State of Pennsylvania Liquor Control Board,** Harrisburg (Liquor control and sale—1,800, total employment). **Pennsylvania Turnpike Commission,** Harrisburg (Highway authority—2,000, total employment).

18th District

(Pittsburgh—Northern and Southwestern Suburbs)

Race and Ethnic Groups. Italian stock 4.5 percent, German stock 3.2 percent, Polish stock 3.1 percent.

Cities, 1970 Population. Part of Pittsburgh 61,084, Castle Shannon 11,920, McKees Rocks 11,902, Bellevue 11,595.

Newspapers, Circulation. Pittsburgh newspapers circulate throughout district.

Commercial Television Stations, Affiliation. Entire district is located in Pittsburgh ADI.

Plants and Offices, Products, Employment.
    Shenango Incorporated, Pittsburgh (Pig iron, ingots, molds—1,800). **Allegheny Ludlum Industries,** Brackenridge (Stainless steel—4,000). **Bethlehem Steel Corp.,** Leetsdale (Steel works—1,100). **Pittsburgh-Des Moines Steel Co.,** Pittsburgh (Structural steel fabrication, etc.—HQ—1,000). **Cyclops Corp.,** Bridgeville (Stainless steel, bars, wire—1,700). **Westinghouse Electric Corp.,** Cheswick (Nuclear reactor equipment—1,100). **PPG Industries,** Creighton (Glass—1,500). **Dravo Corp.,** Pittsburgh (Heavy construction machinery and equipment—3,000).

19th District

(South Central—York)

Race and Ethnic Groups. German stock 0.8 percent, British stock 0.7 percent.

Cities, 1970 Population. York 50,340, Carlisle 18,081, Hanover 15,624.

Universities, Enrollment. Dickinson College (Carlisle—1,621), Gettysburg College (Gettysburg—1,887), York College of Pennsylvania (York—2,321).

Military Installations and Activities. Carlisle Army Barracks, Carlisle; New Cumberland Army Depot, New Cumberland; Naval Ships Parts Control Center, Mechanicsburg.

Commercial Television Stations, Affiliation. WSBA-TV, York (CBS). Entire district is located in Harrisburg-York-Lancaster-Lebanon ADI.

Plants and Offices, Products, Employment.
    AMC Inc., York (Industrial machinery—2,000). **Allis-Chalmers Corp.,** York (Hydraulic turbines—1,300). **Borg Warner Corp.,** York (Refrigeration, air conditioning equipment—3,200). **Caterpillar Tractor Co.,** York (Industrial equipment—2,100). **Triumph Hosiery Mills Inc.,** York (Hosiery, leotards—1,320). **C. H. Masland & Sons,** Carlisle (Carpets—HQ—1,100). **Motor Freight Express Inc.,** York (Common carrier—HQ—1,400).

Penn Central Transportation Co., Enola (Railroad—2,000). **American Chain & Cable Co. Inc.**, (Malleable iron, wire products—1,000). **Litton Business Systems Inc.**, York (Cole Steel Equipment Co. Division—metal office furniture—1,250). **P. H. Glatfelter Co.**, Spring Grove (Paper—1,130). **Dentsply International Inc.**, York (L.D. Caulk Co. Division—dental products—HQ—1,790).

20th District

(Southeast Allegheny County—Duquesne, McKeesport)

Race and Ethnic Groups. Blacks 6.6 percent. Italian stock 4.0 percent, Czechoslovakian stock 3.6 percent, Polish stock 2.7 percent, British stock 2.5 percent.

Cities, 1970 Population. Part of Pittsburgh 66,413, McKeesport 38,106, Bethel Park 34,753, Monroeville 29,010.

Newspapers, Circulation. Pittsburgh newspapers circulate throughout district.

Commercial Television Stations, Affiliation. Entire district is located in Pittsburgh ADI.

Plants and Offices, Products, Employment.

United States Steel Corp., McKeesport (National Works—steel—9,200). **United States Steel Corp.**, McKeesport (National-Duquesne Works—steel form composition—3,500). **United States Steel Corp.**, Dravosburg (Irvin Works—steel forms—4,000). **United States Steel Corp.**, Clairton (Clairton Works—steel forms—5,000). **United States Steel Corp.**, Homestead (Homestead Works—steel castings—9,000). **United States Steel Corp.**, McKeesport (Christy Park Works—steel forms—1,500). **Jones & Laughlin Steel Corp.**, Pittsburgh (Iron and steel—10,400) (Note: Part also in 14th District.) **Copperweld Steel Co.**, Glassport (Wire and Cable Division—wires, cables—1,100). **Westinghouse Electric Corp.**, East Pittsburgh (Power generators—10,900). **Westinghouse Air Brake Co.**, Wilmerding (Air brake systems—4,000). **General Motors Corp.**, McKeesport (Auto body assembly—1,500). **Mesta Machine Co.**, Homestead (Mill equipment—HQ—2,700). **Continental Can Co. Inc.**, Homestead (Metal containers—1,100).

21st District

(Southeast—Westmoreland County)

Race and Ethnic Groups. Italian stock 5.9 percent, Polish stock 2.3 percent.

Cities, 1970 Population. Plum 21,919, New Kensington 20,313, Greensburg 15,837, Jeannette 15,277.

Universities, Enrollment. St. Vincent College (Latrobe—1,027).

Newspapers, Circulation. Pittsburgh newspapers circulate throughout district.

Commercial Television Stations, Affiliation. Entire district is located in Pittsburgh ADI.

Plants and Offices, Products, Employment.

Pittsburgh Steel Co., Monessen (Steel—3,000). **Latrobe Steel Co.**, Latrobe (Dies, specialty steels—HQ—1,610). **Carrier Corp.**, Jeannette (Elliott Co. Division—generators, steam turbines—2,700). **Westinghouse Electric Corp.**, Trafford (Power circuit breakers—1,000). **Westinghouse Electric Corp.**, Youngwood (Transisters—1,600). **Robertshaw Controls Co.**, Youngwood (Temperature controls—1,400). **Edgewater Corp.**, Oakmont (Steel forgings, wires, etc.—2,160). **Jeannette Corp.**, Jeannette (Pressed and blown glassware—HQ—1,000). **Ryder Truck Lines Inc.**, Irwin (Common carrier—1,000).

22nd District

(Southwest—Washington, Uniontown)

Race and Ethnic Groups. Blacks 3.5 percent. Italian stock 4.6 percent, Czechoslovakian stock 2.6 percent.

Cities, 1970 Population. Washington 19,864, Uniontown 16,278, Carnot-Moon 13,090, Connellsville 11,640.

Universities, Enrollment. California State College (California—2,703), Washington and Jefferson College (Washington—1,094), Waynesburg College (Waynesburg—1,081). Robert Morris College (Coraopolis—4,349).

Military Installations and Activities. Facilities at Greater Pittsburgh Airport, Coraopolis.

Newspapers, Circulation. Pittsburgh newspapers circulate in portions of district.

Commercial Television Stations, Affiliation. Entire district is located in Pittsburgh ADI.

Plants and Offices, Products, Employment.

United States Steel Corp., Greensboro (Bituminous coal mining—2,400). **Wheeling-Pittsburgh Steel Corp.**, Allenport (Steel—2,600). **Jessop Steel Co.**, Washington (Specialty steels—HQ—1,300). **Anchor Hocking Corp.**, Connellsville (Plastics, glass, metal stampings—2,400). **RCA Corp. of America**, Meadow Lands (Transmitting equipment—1,000). **McGraw-Edison Co.**, Canonsburg (Heavy electrical equipment—3,000). **Corning Glass Works**, Charleroi (Glass, glass products—1,100).

23rd District

(Northwest, Central)

Race and Ethnic Groups. Italian stock 2.0 percent, British stock 1.0 percent.

Cities, 1970 Population. State College 33,773, Oil City 15,031, Warren 12,996, Bradford 12,670.

Universities, Enrollment. Clarion State College (Clarion—4,371), Lock Haven State College (Lock Haven—2,387), Pennsylvania State University (University Park, State College—59,598 total enrollment).

Commercial Television Stations, Affiliation. Major portion of district is located in Johnstown-Altoona

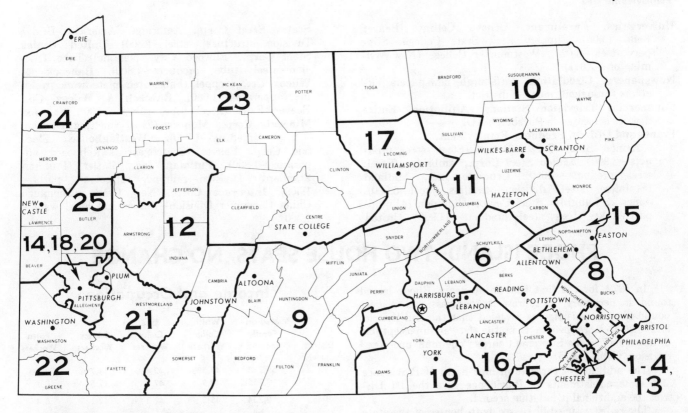

ADI. Other portions are located in Erie, Pittsburgh and Buffalo (New York) ADIs.

Plants and Offices, Products, Employment.

GTE Sylvania Inc., Emporium (Radio, TV tubes—1,370). GTE Sylvania Inc., Warren (Radio, TV tubes, photographic equipment—1,250). Cerro Corp., Bellefonte (Brass rods, bars, shapes—1,400). National Forge Co., Irvine (Steel, steel products—HQ—1,200). Stackpole Carbon Co., St. Marys (Carbon products—HQ—2,500). Air Reduction Co. Inc., St. Marys (Carbon & graphite—1,040). Piper Aircraft Corp., Lock Haven (Aircraft—HQ—2,010). Hammermill Paper Co., Lock Haven (Paper mill—1,310). Owens-Illinois Inc., Clarion (Glass containers—1,000). Joy Manufacturing Co., Franklin (Mining machinery, equipment—1,300). New Process Co., Warren (General merchandise, mail order house—1,000).

24th District

(Northwest—Erie)

Race and Ethnic Groups. Blacks 3.2 percent. Italian stock 3.1 percent, Polish stock 2.7 percent.

Cities, 1970 Population. Erie 129,221, Sharon 22,651, Meadville 16,573, Farrell 11,022.

Universities, Enrollment. Allegheny College (Meadville—1,792), Edinboro State College (Edinboro—7,155), Gannon College (Erie—3,568), Grove City College (Grove City—2,114), Thiel College (Greenville—1,354).

Commercial Television Stations, Affiliation. WICU-TV, Erie (NBC); WJET-TV, Erie (ABC); WSEE-TV, Erie (CBS). Most of district is located in Erie

ADI. Portion of district is located in Youngstown (Ohio) ADI.

Plants and Offices, Products, Employment.

Midland-Ross Corp., Sharon (National Castings Division—steel castings—1,000). Cooper Industries Inc., Grove City (Gray castings—1,600). National Forge Co., Erie (Heavy forged steel castings—1,000). Cyclops Corp., Titusville (Universal-Cyclops Specialty Steel Division—steel alloys—1,250). Sharon Steel Corp., Farrell (Roemer Works—steel, steel products—6,000). Sharon Steel Corp., Sharon (Steel, steel products—5,800). Greenville Steel Car Co., Greenville (Freight cars—1,000). Singer Co. Inc., Corry (Corry Jamestown Division—metal office furniture—1,000). Textron Inc., Meadville (Talon Division—slide fasteners—1,400). Westinghouse Electric Corp., Sharon (Transformers—6,500). Erie Technological Products, Erie (Electronic components, assemblies—HQ—1,100). FMC Corp., Meadville (American Viscose Division—acetates, yarns, synthetic resins, etc.—1,800). Lord Corp., Erie (Hughson Chemical Co. Division—bonded rubber products, vibration, noise and shock control mountings and systems, etc.,—HQ—1,300). Hammermill Paper Co., Erie (Pulp and paper products—HQ—2,100).

25th District

(West—New Castle)

Race, Ethnic Groups. Blacks 3.2 percent. Italian stock 5.5 percent, Polish stock 2.0 percent.

Cities, 1970 Population. New Castle 38,568, Aliquippa 22,230, Butler 18,696, Beaver Falls 14,327.

Universities, Enrollment. Geneva College (Beaver Falls—1,605), Slippery Rock State College (Slippery Rock—6,020), Westminster College (New Wilmington—2,011).

Newspapers, Circulation. Pittsburgh newspapers circulate throughout much of district.

Commercial Television Stations, Affiliation. Entire district is located in Pittsburgh ADI.

Plants and Offices, Products, Employment.

Armco Steel Corp., Butler (Steel, steel products—3,900). **Armco Steel Corp.,** Ambridge (Steel, steel products—1,650). **Crucible Inc.,** Midland (Stainless steel division—stainless steel—6,000). **Jones & Laughlin Steel Corp.,** Aliquippa (Aliquippa Works—steel, steel products—11,900) **United States Steel Corp.,** Ambridge (American Bridge Division—structural steel—1,800) **United States Steel Corp.,** Ellwood City (National Tube Division—steel tube products—1,800). **Babcock & Wilcox Co.,** Koppel (Fabricated plate work, welding apparatus—1,000). **Babcock & Wilcox Co.,** Beaver Falls (Steel pipe, tubes—5,600). **St. Joe Minerals Corp.,** Monaca (Zinc Smelting Division —zinc smelting—1,300). **Westinghouse Electric Corp.** Beaver (Switchgear, switchboard apparatus—1,800). **Pullman Inc.,** Butler (Pullman Standard Division—railroad, streetcar parts— 1,500). **Interpace Corp.,** New Castle (Shenango China Consumer Division—dinner and hotel ware— 1,300).

RHODE ISLAND: TWO HOUSE SEATS, NO CHANGE

In 1972, for the first time in 40 years, Rhode Island found it necessary to redraw its congressional district boundaries. Census figures revealed that the 2nd District had 93,000 more people than the 1st, an unacceptable difference since the Supreme Court's "one-man, one-vote" decision. *(Map p. 175)*

The addition of three townships north of Providence and some adjustments in Providence gave the 1st District the additional population needed.

The redistricting bill passed both houses of the state legislature unanimously—the House on Jan. 27, 1972, and the Senate on Jan. 28. Gov. Frank Licht (D) signed the bill Jan. 31.

District	Member Elected 1972	Winning Percentage	1970 Population	Percent Variance
1	Fernand J. St Germain (D)	62.3	475,441	+0.1219
2	Robert O. Tiernan (D)	63.1	474,282	+0.1221

1970 State Population: 949,723
Ideal District Population: 474,862

Election Results, 1968-1972

Vote for U.S. Representative
(Adjusted to new district boundaries)

District	1968	1970	1972
1	110,643 D (60.6%)	98,294 D (61.1%)	120,705 D (62.3%)
	70,125 R (38.4%)	60,215 R (37.4%)	67,125 R (34.7%)
2	111,346 D (61.1%)	109,693 D (66.6%)	122,739 D (63.1%)
	70,771 R (38.9%)	54,566 R (33.1%)	71,661 R (36.9%)
State	221,989 D (60.9%)	207,987 D (63.9%)	243,444 D (62.7%)
	140,896 R (38.6%)	114,781 R (35.3%)	138,786 R (35.8%)

Voting Age Population

District	Voting Age Population	Voting Age Population 18, 19, 20	Voting Age Population 65 and Over	Median Age of Voting Age Population
1	325,531	28,181 (8.7%)	51,926 (16.0%)	43.7
2	322,259	27,666 (8.6%)	52,534 (16.3%)	44.4
State	647,796	55,848 (8.6%)	104,460 (16.1%)	44.0

Income and Occupation

District	Median Family Income	White Collar Workers	Blue Collar Workers	Service Workers	Farm Workers
1	$9,713	45.5%	42.4%	11.7%	0.4%
2	9,755	44.9	42.2	12.5	0.4
State	9,734	45.2	42.3	12.1	0.4

Education: School Years Completed

District	Completed 4 years of High School	Completed 4 years of College	Completed 5 years or less of School	Median School years completed
1	45.8%	10.2%	8.6%	11.4
2	46.9	8.6	6.4	11.6
State	46.4	9.4	7.5	11.5

Housing and Residential Patterns

	Housing		Urban-Suburban-Nonmetropolitan Breakdown		
District	Owner Occupied Units	Renter Occupied Units	Urban	Suburban	Nonmetropolitan
1	55.2%	44.8%	27.7%	55.7%	16.6%
2	60.6	39.4	44.0	42.1	13.9
State	57.9	42.1	35.8	48.9	15.3

1st District

(East—Eastern Providence, Pawtucket)

Race and Ethnic Groups. Blacks 2.5 percent. Canadian stock 8.9 percent, Portuguese stock 5.1 percent, Italian stock 5.0 percent, British stock 3.8 percent.

Cities, 1970 Population. Pawtucket 76,965, part of Providence 54,468, East Providence 48,118, Woonsocket 46,804.

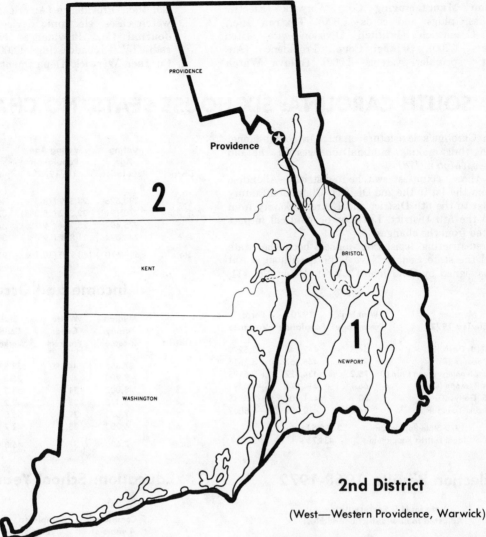

2nd District

(West—Western Providence, Warwick)

Universities, Enrollment. Brown University (Providence—6,206), Roger Williams College (Bristol—1,539).

Military Installations or Activities. Naval Communications Station, Newport; Naval Hospital, Newport; Naval Schools Command, Newport; Naval Station, Newport; Naval Supply Center, Newport; Naval Underseas Research and Development Center, Newport; Public Works Center, Newport.

Newspapers, Circulation. Providence newspapers circulate in portion of district.

Commercial Television Stations, Affiliation. Entire district is located in Providence ADI.

Plants and Offices, Products, Employment.

Raytheon Co., Portsmouth (Submarine Signal Division—electronic equipment, oceanographic instruments—1,900). **American Insulated Wire,** Pawtucket (Insulated wire—1,070). **Davol Inc.,** Providence (Medical and surgical rubber and plastic goods—1,100). **Dart Industries Inc.,** Woonsocket (Tupperware Division—Plastic household containers—1,200). **Hasbro Industries Inc.,** Pawtucket (Toys, games, school supplies—HQ—at least 1,100). **Narragansett Racing Assn. Inc.,** Pawtucket (Race track—1,000).

Race and Ethnic Groups. Blacks 2.8 percent. Italian stock 10.4 percent, Canadian stock 5.0 percent, British stock 3.4 percent.

Cities, 1970 Population. Part of Providence 125,011, Warwick 83,864, Cranston 73,190, Westerly Center 13,652.

Universities, Enrollment. Bryant College (Providence—3,767), Providence College (Providence—3,507), Rhode Island College (Providence—7,534), Rhode Island School of Design (Providence—1,276), University of Rhode Island (Kingston—15,450).

Military Installations or Activities. Naval Air Station, Quonset Point; Naval Construction Batallion Center, Davisville; Naval Air Rework Facility, Quonset Point.

Newspapers, Circulation. Providence Bulletin (Eve—146,936), Providence Journal (Morn—64,301).

Commercial Television Stations, Affiliation. WJAR-TV, Providence (NBC); WPRI-TV, Providence (CBS). Entire district located in Providence ADI.

Plants and Offices, Products, Employment.

Leesona Corp., Warwick (Textile winding and twisting machinery—HQ—2,300). **Brown and Sharpe Manufacturing Co.,** North Kingstown (Machine cutting tools, hydraulic products—HQ—2,000).

Leviton Manufacturing Co., Warwick (Electric switches, plugs and cords—1,800). **Textron Inc.,** East Greenwich (Bostitch Division—wire stitch staplers—1,200). **Grinnel Corp.,** Providence (Automatic sprinkler systems—2,000). **Bulova Watch** **Co. Inc.,** Providence (American Standard Division— watch cases, electronic devices—1,000). **Providence Journal Co.,** Providence (Newspaper publishing, radio-TV broadcasting—1,200). **Jordon Marsh Co. Inc.,** Warwick (Department store—1,000).

SOUTH CAROLINA: SIX HOUSE SEATS, NO CHANGE

South Carolina's legislature enacted a congressional redistricting bill making minimal changes in the old district lines. *(Map p. 178)*

Only three counties switched districts—Allendale County from the 1st to the 2nd District, Clarendon County from the 1st to the 6th District and Laurens County from the 4th to the 5th District. Little or no political impact was expected from the changes.

The redistricting legislation passed both the state House and the state Senate Nov. 4, 1971, without a roll call. It was signed by Gov. John C. West (D) on Nov. 11, 1971.

District	Member Elected 1972	Winning Percentage	1970 Population	Percent Variance
1	Mendel J. Davis (D)	54.5	442,646	+ 2.5229
2	Floyd Spence (R)	99.9	446,267	+ 3.3616
3	William Jennings Bryan Dorn (D)	75.2	434,427	+ 0.6193
4	James R. Mann (D)	66.1	414,270	—4.0493
5	Tom S. Gettys (D)	60.9	441,907	+ 2.3518
6	Edward L. Young (R)	54.4	410,999	—4.8069

1970 State Population: 2,590,516
Ideal District Population: 431,753

Election Results, 1968-1972

Vote for U.S. Representative
(Adjusted to new district boundaries)

District	1968	1970	1972
1	87,453 D (100.0%)	58,437 D (100.0%)	61,625 D (54.5%)
	—	—	51,469 R (45.5%)
2	63,877 R (56.1%)	48,093 R (52.1%)	83,543 R (99.9%)
	49,914 D (43.9%)	43,669 D (47.3%)	—
3	74,104 D (66.1%)	60,708 D (75.2%)	82,579 D (75.2%)
	35,463 R (31.6%)	19,981 R (24.7%)	27,173 R (24.8%)
4	61,247 D (61.1%)	45,431 D (100.0%)	64,989 D (66.1%)
	39,062 R (38.9%)	—	33,363 R (33.9%)
5	79,995 D (73.4%)	50,486 D (69.1%)	66,343 D (60.9%)
	25,624 R (23.5%)	21,911 R (30.0%)	42,620 R (39.1%)
6	63,418 D (60.3%)	50,756 D (65.9%)	63,527 R (54.4%)
	39,876 R (37.9%)	25,546 R (33.1%)	53,324 D (45.6%)
State	416,131 D (66.3%)	309,487 D (72.5%)	328,860 D (52.2%)
	203,902 R (32.5%)	115,531 R (27.1%)	301,695 R (47.8%)

Voting Age Population

District	Voting Age Population	Voting Age Population 18, 19, 20	Voting Age Population 65 and Over	Median Age of Voting Age Population
1	270,689	31,168 (11.5%)	25,586 (9.5%)	36.9
2	288,661	40,105 (13.9%)	31,099 (10.8%)	37.7
3	280,626	23,339 (8.3%)	36,856 (13.1%)	42.1
4	270,191	22,382 (8.3%)	32,785 (12.1%)	41.5
5	275,409	25,124 (9.1%)	34,485 (12.5%)	41.2
6	243,094	21,852 (9.0%)	30,693 (12.6%)	42.0
State	1,628,670	163,970 (10.1%)	191,504 (11.8%)	40.3

Income and Occupation

District	Median Family Income	White Collar Workers	Blue Collar Workers	Service Workers	Farm Workers
1	$7,355	44.3%	38.8%	14.5%	2.4%
2	7,900	47.2	35.3	14.1	3.4
3	8,002	31.9	55.5	10.3	2.3
4	8,416	38.9	49.2	10.8	1.1
5	7,623	29.8	55.8	12.0	2.4
6	6,203	33.5	42.7	13.2	10.6
State	7,620	37.3	46.8	12.3	3.6

Education: School Years Completed

District	Completed 4 years of High School	Completed 4 years of College	Completed 5 years or less of School	Median School years completed
1	45.3%	9.5%	14.6%	11.4
2	45.0	12.6	14.2	11.4
3	33.9	7.9	16.0	10.1
4	39.3	9.5	13.5	10.8
5	32.3	7.3	18.9	9.8
6	31.6	7.0	22.0	9.7
State	37.8	9.0	16.4	10.5

Housing and Residential Patterns

District	Housing Owner Occupied Units	Renter Occupied Units	Urban	Suburban	Nonmetro-politan
1	62.3%	37.7%	15.1%	53.5%	31.4%
2	66.0	34.0	25.5	46.9	27.6
3	70.9	29.1	—	34.5	65.5
4	67.2	32.8	14.8	43.3	41.9
5	66.7	33.3	—	—	100.0
6	62.6	37.4	—	—	100.0
State	66.1	33.9	9.4	29.9	60.7

1st District

(South—Charleston)

Race and Ethnic Groups. Blacks 34.0 percent.

Cities, 1970 Population. Charleston 66,934, Charleston Yard 13,620.

Universities, Enrollment. Baptist College at Charleston (Charleston—1,839), The Citadel (Charleston—2,768).

Military Installations or Activities. Charleston Army Depot, North Charleston; Marine Corps Air Station, Beaufort; Marine Corps Recruit Depot, Parris Island; Charleston Naval Shipyard, Charleston; Naval Hospital, Charleston; Naval Hospital, Beaufort; Naval Station, Charleston; Naval Supply Center, Charleston; Naval Weapons Station, Charleston; Navy Fleet Ballistic Missile Submarine Training Center, Charleston; Polaris Missile Facility-Atlantic, Charleston; Charleston Air Force Base, Charleston; North Charleston Air Force Station, North Charleston.

Newspapers, Circulation. Charleston News & Courier (Morn—65,998).

Commercial Television Stations, Affiliation. WCBD-TV, Charleston (ABC primary); WCIV, Mt. Pleasant (NBC); WCSC-TV, Charleston (CBS). Most of district is located in Charleston ADI. Small portion is located in Savannah (Georgia) ADI.

Plants and Offices, Products, Employment.
Westvaco Corp., North Charleston (Kraft Division —paper, pulp—1,600). **Avco Corp.,** Charleston (Aircraft engines—3,500). **General Electric Co.,** Ladson (Turbine hoods—1,000). **Westinghouse Electric Corp.,** Hampton (Copper-clad laminants—1,000).

2nd District

(Central—Columbia)

Race and Ethnic Groups. Blacks 33.8 percent.

Cities, 1970 Population. Columbia 113,542, Orangeburg 13,252.

Universities, Enrollment. Benedict College (Columbia—1,405), South Carolina State College (Orangeburg—2,148), University of South Carolina (Columbia—16,615).

Military Installations or Activities. Fort Jackson, Columbia.

Newspapers, Circulation. The State, Columbia (Morn—108,312). Columbia newspaper circulates throughout district.

Commercial Television Stations, Affiliation. WIS-TV, Columbia (NBC); WNOK-TV, Columbia (CBS); WOLO-TV, Columbia (ABC). Most of district is located in Columbia ADI. Small portion is located in Augusta (Georgia) ADI.

Plants and Offices, Products, Employment.
M. Lowenstein and Sons Inc., Columbia (Pacific Columbia Mills Division—cotton textiles—2,000). **Allied Chemical Corp.,** Columbia (Nylon fibers —1,200). **State-Record Co.,** Columbia (Newspaper publishing, television broadcasting, holding company —1,000).

3rd District

(West—Anderson)

Race and Ethnic Groups. Blacks 22.6 percent.

Cities, 1970 Population. Anderson 27,556, Greenwood 21,069, Aiken 13,436, North Augusta 12,883.

Universities, Enrollment. Clemson University (Clemson—7,965).

AEC-Owned, Contractor-Operated Installations. Savannah River Facilities, Aiken.

Newspapers, Circulation. Anderson Independent (Morn —52,067). Greenville newspaper circulates in portion of district.

Commercial Television Stations, Affiliation. Most of district is located in Greenville-Spartanburg-Asheville (North Carolina) ADI. Portion is located in Augusta (Georgia) ADI.

Plants and Offices, Products, Employment.
Duke Power Co., Seneca (Keowee Toxaway Hydro Station—heavy construction—1,250). **Singer Co.,** Pickens (Power tools, motors—1,400). **Sangamo Electric Co.,** Pickens (Capacitors, transformers—1,000). **Sangamo Electric Co.,** West Union (Electric meters—1,050). **Parke Davis & Co.,** Greenwood (Medical, surgical supplies—1,010). **E.I. du Pont de Nemours and Co.,** Aiken (Industrial inorganic chemicals—5,200). **Monsanto Co.,** Greenwood (Synthetic organic chemicals—2,800). **Owens-Corning Fiberglas Corp.,** Aiken (Fiberglass—2,000). **Owens-Corning Fiberglass Corp.,** Anderson (Textile glass fiber—1,750). **Alice Manufacturing Co.,** Easley (Print cloth—2,500). **J.P. Stevens and Co. Inc.,** Clemson (Utica Mohawk Cotton Mills—broad woven fabrics—1,900). **Greenwood Mills,** Greenwood (Textiles —HQ—3,000). **Riegel Textile Corp.,** Ware Shoals (Textiles—2,500). **M. Lowenstein & Sons Inc.,** Anderson (Orr-Lyons Mills—cotton goods—1,300). **Dow Badische Co.,** Anderson (Synthetic fibers—1,100). **Kendall Co.,** Pelzer (Cotton goods—1,100). **Graniteville Co.,** Graniteville (Broad woven cloth finishing—HQ—2,000).

4th District

(Northwest—Greenville, Spartanburg)

Race and Ethnic Groups. Blacks 18.4 percent.

Cities, 1970 Population. Greenville 61,208, Spartanburg 44,546, Wade-Hampton 17,056, Gantt 11,404.

Universities, Enrollment. Furman University (Greenville—2,246), Wofford College (Spartanburg—1,030).

Newspapers, Circulation. Greenville News (Morn—90,162).

Commercial Television Stations, Affiliation. WFBC-TV, Greenville (NBC); WSPA-TV, Spartanburg (CBS). Entire district is located in Greenville-Spartanburg-Ashville (North Carolina) ADI.

Plants and Offices, Products, Employment.
Daniel International Corp., Greenville (General building contractor—HQ—3,000). **Daniel Construction Co. International,** Greenville (General building contractor—1,000). **Davis Electrical Construc-**

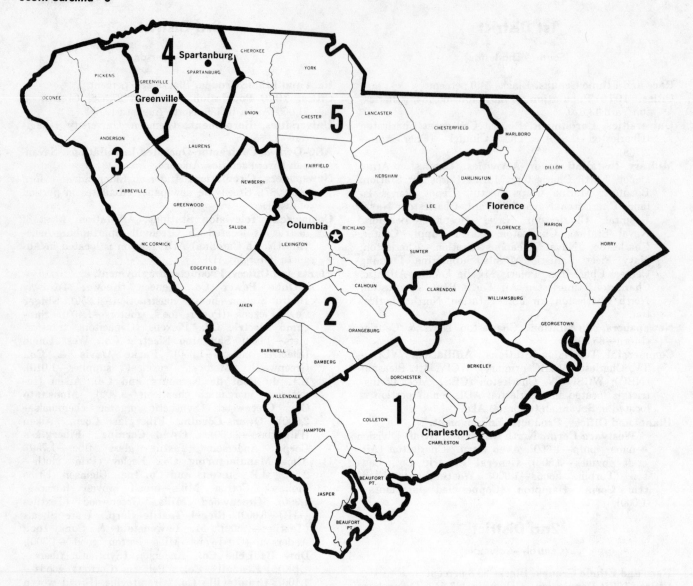

tors, Greenville (Contractor—2,000). **W.R. Grace and Co.**, Simpsonville (Croyovac Division—food products machinery—1,000). **Union Carbide Corp.**, Simpsonville (Capacitors—1,000). **General Electric Co.**, Greenville (Gas turbines—1,000). **Deering Milliken Inc.**, Drayton (Drayton Mills Division—synthetic fabrics—1,000). **Deering Milliken Inc.**, Pacolet Mills (Pacolet Mills Division—fabrics—1,000). **Deering Milliken Inc.**, Greenville (Judson Mills Division—synthetic fabrics—1,000). **Spartan Mills**, Spartanburg (Cotton fabrics, knits—HQ—1,100). **Spartan Mills,** Startex (Startex Mills—cotton fabrics—1,000). **Jonathan Logan Inc.**, Spartanburg (Butte Knitting Mills Division—women's knitwear—2,000). **Fiber Industries Inc.**, Greenville (Nylon fiber—1,620). **J.P. Stevens and Co. Inc.**, Taylors (Tufted carpet—1,000). **J.P. Stevens and Co. Inc.**, Greenville (Woven fabric—1,000). **Abney Mills**, Greenville (Textiles—1,400). **Stone Manufacturing Co. Inc.**, Greenville (Women's, children's wear—HQ—1,800). **Dan River Inc.**, Greenville (Fabrics,

carpets, hosiery—HQ—9,500). **Spartanburg General Hospital**, Spartanburg (Hospital—1,000).

5th District

(North Central—Rock Hill)

Race and Ethnic Groups. Blacks 31.6 percent.

Cities, 1970 Population. Rock Hill 33,846, Sumter 24,435, Gaffney 13,253, Union 10,775.

Universities, Enrollment. Winthrop College (Rock Hill —3,879).

Military Installations or Activities. Shaw Air Force Base, Sumter.

Commercial Television Stations, Affiliation. Most of district is located in Charlotte (North Carolina) ADI and Columbia ADI. Small portion is located in

Greenville-Spartanburg-Asheville (North Carolina) ADI.

Plants and Offices, Products, Employment.

Torrington Co., Clinton (Bearings—1,000). **Uniroyal Inc.**, Winnsboro (Tire cord—1,500). **Campbell Soup Co.**, Sumter (Canning, freezing—1,840). **M. Lowenstein and Sons Inc.**, Rock Hill (Rock Hill Finishing and Printing—finishing and printing yarn —3,250). **M. Lowenstein and Sons Inc.**, Gaffney (Limestone Manufacturing Division—cotton fabric —1,000). **Celanese Corp.**, Rock Hill (Synthetic fibers—2,300). **Springs Mills Inc.**, Fort Mill (Cotton, synthetic wool—HQ—1,800). **Springs Mills Inc.**, Lancaster (Cotton fabric—1,280). **Springs Mills Inc.**, Lancaster (Cotton fabric finishing—3,670). **United Merchants & Manufacturers Inc.**, Union (Union-Buffalo Mills Division—synthetic textiles— 1,500). **Joanna Western Mills Co.**, Joanna (Kaywood Division—cotton fibers—1,000). **E.I. du Pont de Nemours and Co.**, Camden (Synthetic yarns— 1,750). **Greenwood Mills**, Joanna (Joanna Cotton Mill—window shade cloth—1,000).

6th District

(Northeast—Florence)

Race and Ethnic Groups. Blacks 42.2 percent.
Cities, 1970 Population. Florence 25,997, Georgetown 10,449.
Military Installations or Activities. Myrtle Beach Air Force Base, Myrtle Beach.
Commercial Television Stations, Affiliation. WBTW, Florence (CBS; ABC on per program basis). Major portion of district is located in Florence ADI. Smaller portions are located in Columbia ADI, Charleston ADI and Wilmington (North Carolina) ADI.
Plants and Offices, Products, Employment.

International Paper Co., Georgetown (Southern Kraft Division—paperboard—1,600). **Sonoco Products Co.**, Hartsville (Paperboard products—HQ— 2,700). **Emerson Electric Co.**, Bennettsville (Eastern Builder Products Division—light fixtures, fans—1,000). **Electro Motive Manufacturing Co.**, Florence (Electronic components—1,000).

SOUTH DAKOTA: TWO HOUSE SEATS, NO CHANGE

South Dakota legislators had an easy time redrawing the state's congressional district boundaries. There are only two districts in the state, and the variance from the ideal population of each district was only 5 percent before the lines were redrawn. *(Map p. 180)*

Passed by the House on March 3, 1971, by a vote of 71-2, the redistricting received Senate approval on March 16 by a vote of 35-0. The bill was signed by Gov. Richard F. Kneip (D) on March 25.

The bill shifted three counties from the 1st to the 2nd District. No noticeable political change in the districts resulted from these minor changes.

District	Member Elected 1972	Winning Percentage	1970 Population	Percent Variance
1	Frank E. Denholm (D)	60.5%	333,107	—0.0066
2	James Abdnor (R)	54.9%	333,150	+ 0.0063
	1970 State Population:		666,257	
	Ideal District Population:		333,129	

Election Results, 1968-1972

Vote for U.S. Representative
(Adjusted to new district boundaries)

District	1968	1970	1972
1	80,647 R (58.2%)	67,340 D (55.9%)	94,442 D (60.5%)
	57,936 D (41.8%)	53,195 R (44.1%)	61,589 R (39.5%)
2	78,572 R (59.1%)	60,221 D (52.6%)	79,546 R (54.9%)
	54,485 D (40.9%)	54,227 R (47.4%)	65,415 D (45.1%)
State	159,219 R (58.6%)	127,561 D (54.3%)	159,857 D (53.1%)
	112,421 D (41.4%)	107,422 R (45.7%)	141,135 R (46.9%)

Voting Age Population

District	Voting Age Population	Voting Age Population 18, 19, 20	Voting Age Population 65 and Over	Median Age of Voting Age Population
1	216,392	21,407 (9.9%)	42,526 (19.7%)	45.5
2	206,756	15,836 (7.7%)	37,976 (18.4%)	45.1
State	423,142	37,241 (8.8%)	80,500 (19.0%)	45.3

Income and Occupation

District	Median Family Income	White Collar Workers	Blue Collar Workers	Service Workers	Farm Workers
1	$7,695	42.0%	23.4%	15.6%	19.0%
2	7,283	40.2	21.3	14.6	23.9
State	7,490	41.1	22.4	15.1	21.4

Education: School Years Completed

District	Completed 4 years of High School	Completed 4 years of College	Completed 5 years or less of School	Median School years completed
1	54.2%	9.1%	3.4%	12.1
2	52.5	8.1	4.0	12.1
State	53.3	8.6	3.7	12.1

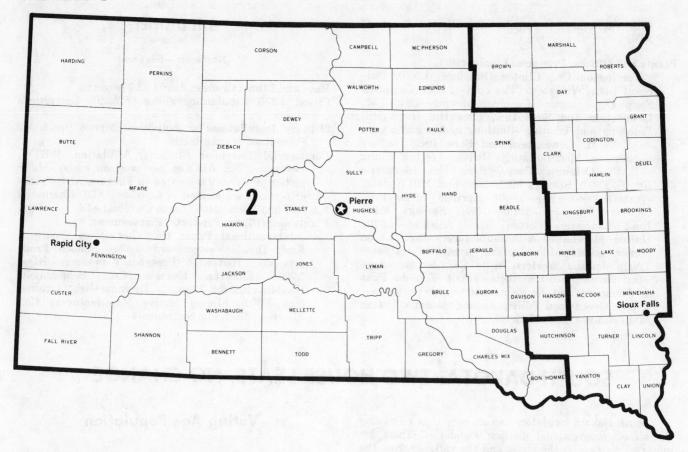

Housing and Residential Patterns

District	Housing		Urban-Suburban-Nonmetropolitan Breakdown		
	Owner Occupied Units	Renter Occupied Units	Urban	Suburban	Nonmetropolitan
1	69.9%	30.1%	21.8%	6.8%	71.4%
2	69.2	30.8	—	—	100.0
State	69.6	30.4	10.9	3.4	85.7

1st District

(East—Sioux Falls)

Race and Ethnic Groups. German stock 4.4 percent.

Cities, 1970 Population. Sioux Falls 72,619, Aberdeen 26,524, Brookings 13,742, Watertown 13,155.

Universities, Enrollment. Augustana College (Sioux Falls—2,078), Dakota State College (Madison—1,208), Northern State College (Aberdeen—3,083), South Dakota State University (Brookings—7,057), University of South Dakota (Vermillion—6,854).

Commercial Television Stations, Affiliation. KELO-TV, Sioux Falls (CBS); KORN-TV, Mitchell (ABC); KSOO-TV, Sioux Falls (NBC). Most of district is located in Sioux Falls-Mitchell ADI. Small portion of district is located in Sioux City (Iowa) ADI.

Plants and Offices, Products, Employment.
John Morrell and Co., Sioux Falls (Meat packing—3,000).

2nd District

(Central and West—Rapid City)

Race and Ethnic Groups. American Indians 7.9 percent. German stock 3.6 percent.

Cities, 1970 Population. Rapid City 43,855, Huron 14,219, Mitchell 13,193.

Universities, Enrollment. Black Hills State College (Spearfish—3,969), South Dakota School of Mines and Technology (Rapid City—1,625), University of South Dakota at Springfield (Springfield—1,061).

Military Installations or Activities. Ellsworth Air Force Base, Rapid City.

Newspapers, Circulation. Sioux Falls Argus-Leader (Eve—50,051).

Commercial Television Stations, Affiliation. KOTA-TV, Rapid City (NBC primary; ABC); KRSD-TV, Rapid City (CBS; ABC on per program basis). Most of district is divided between Rapid City ADI and Sioux Falls-Mitchell ADI. Small portion is located in Minot (North Dakota)-Bismarck (North Dakota) ADI.

Plants and Offices, Products, Employment.
Homestake Mining Co. Inc., Lead (Gold mining—1,800).

TENNESSEE: EIGHT HOUSE SEATS, LOSS OF ONE

Because of reapportionment, Tennessee lost one of its nine seats in the U.S. House. In redrawing congressional district lines, the legislature combined the seats of two Democratic incumbents to reduce the size of the state delegation to eight, and altered two Republican-held districts enough to endanger their incumbents' chances for re-election. The Republicans were Dan Kuykendall of Memphis and LaMar Baker of Chattanooga. (Map p. 183)

Kuykendall's district, the 8th, was drawn to include many more blacks—from 34.2 percent in the old district to 47.5 percent. In addition, the newly drawn district was strongly Democratic in voting habits.

Despite these disadvantages, Kuykendall was re-elected. His Democratic opponent, state senator J. O. Patterson, a black, was unable to attract enough white voters to win.

In the eastern part of the state, Baker's 3rd District was made less Republican by the addition of Democratic voters in Anderson County, which includes Oak Ridge, site of several Atomic Energy Commission installations. Nevertheless, Baker was easily re-elected.

Democratic incumbents William R. Anderson of the old 6th District and Ray Blanton of the old 7th District were thrown together in the new 6th District in west central Tennessee. Blanton ran for the U.S. Senate and was defeated. Anderson was defeated for re-election to the House.

Outside the combining of Blanton's and Anderson's districts, the state's three remaining Democratic representatives—Joe L. Evins of the 4th District, Richard Fulton of the 5th District and Ed Jones of the new 7th District—were not hurt by redistricting.

Redistricting legislation was tied up for more than a year by internal Democratic squabbling. Blacks from Memphis held out for the creation of a predominantly black district in that area, and state senators from central and eastern Tennessee objected to the attachment of relatively small counties in their districts to congressional districts dominated by Nashville and Chattanooga.

After months of negotiating, enough Democrats were reasonably satisfied with a compromise plan to pass the redistricting bill. The House passed the legislation April 5, 1972, by a vote of 55-39, and the Senate concurred the same day, 17-15. Gov. Winfield Dunn (R) vetoed the bill April 12.

Dunn's veto was overridden by the state legislature April 13. The House vote was 55-37; the Senate vote was 19-12. (Only an absolute majority, not a two-thirds vote, is required to override a gubernatorial veto in Tennessee.)

District	Member Elected 1972	Winning Percentage	1970 Population	Percent Variance
1	James H. Quillen (R)	79.4	490,518	—0.0006
2	John J. Duncan (R)	100.0	492,539	+ 0.4113
3	LaMar Baker (R)	55.2	486,363	—0.8476
4	Joe L. Evins (D)	81.1	492,124	+ 0.3267
5	Richard Fulton (D)	62.6	490,178	—0.0699
6	Robin L. Beard Jr. (R)	55.3	472,341	—3.7062
7	Ed Jones (D)	70.5	487,097	—0.6980
8	Dan Kuykendall (R)	55.7	513,004	+ 4.5834

1970 State Population: 3,924,164
Ideal District Population: 490,521

Election Results, 1968-1972

Vote for U.S. Representative
(Adjusted to new district boundaries)

District	1968	1970	1972
1	109,818 R (85.0%)	87,834 R (68.3%)	110,868 R (79.4%)
	19,160 D (14.8%)	40,598 D (31.6%)	28,736 D (20.6%)
2	104,063 R (77.1%)	89,527 R (67.4%)	109,925 R (100.0%)
	27,861 D (20.6%)	42,019 D (31.6%)	—
3	73,874 R (51.4%)	69,805 D (53.4%)	82,561 R (55.2%)
	69,892 D (48.6%)	57,470 R (43.9%)	62,536 D (41.9%)
4	79,665 D (70.3%)	101,524 D (83.8%)	93,042 D (81.1%)
	33,662 R (29.7%)	19,634 R (16.2%)	21,689 R (18.9%)
5	67,011 D (49.7%)	98,525 D (71.7%)	93,555 D (62.6%)
	56,298 R (41.8%)	39,041 R (28.3%)	55,067 R (36.8%)
6	74,110 D (56.5%)	82,899 D (65.7%)	77,263 R (55.3%)
	56,257 R (42.9%)	43,125 R (31.2%)	60,254 D (43.1%)
7	81,626 D (84.6%)	74,463 D (86.5%)	92,419 D (70.5%)
	14,547 R (15.1%)[1]	11,571 R (13.4%)[1]	38,726 R (29.5%)
8	66,508 R (51.3%)	68,898 D (56.2%)	93,173 R (55.7%)
	59,477 R (45.9%)	53,031 D (43.3%)	74,240 D (44.3%)
State	507,996 R (50.1%)	579,783 D (58.6%)[2]	589,272 R (53.5%)
	485,833 D (47.9%)	403,233 R (40.8%)[2]	504,782 D (45.8%)

1 No candidate in this district as constituted before redistricting.
2 Includes absentee votes not included in district-by-district tabulation.

Voting Age Population

District	Voting Age Population	Voting Age Population 18, 19, 20	Voting Age Population 65 and Over	Median Age of Voting Age Population
1	328,000	24,200 (7.4%)	44,591 (13.6%)	42.0
2	333,055	29,755 (8.9%)	49,717 (14.9%)	42.9
3	318,962	23,083 (7.2%)	44,578 (14.0%)	42.8
4	327,558	25,803 (7.9%)	52,912 (16.2%)	43.6
5	327,477	27,795 (8.5%)	44,286 (13.5%)	41.4
6	306,816	24,755 (8.1%)	45,887 (15.0%)	42.9
7	319,894	31,325 (9.8%)	53,469 (16.7%)	43.5
8	329,034	28,820 (8.8%)	49,149 (14.9%)	42.3
State	2,590,815	215,546 (8.3%)	384,611 (14.8%)	42.7

Income and Occupation

District	Median Family Income	White Collar Workers	Blue Collar Workers	Service Workers	Farm Workers
1	$6,820	35.8%	48.9%	10.4%	4.9%
2	7,285	42.8	42.0	12.8	2.2
3	7,940	42.2	44.7	11.7	1.4
4	6,451	33.9	47.5	11.1	7.5
5	9,231	52.5	32.7	13.4	1.4
6	7,151	39.2	44.8	10.5	5.5
7	7,030	37.0	43.6	12.3	7.1
8	7,874	46.6	35.6	17.4	0.4
State	7,447	41.5	42.3	12.5	3.7

Education: School Years Completed

District	Completed 4 years of High School	Completed 4 years of College	Completed 5 years or less of School	Median School years completed
1	37.8%	6.6%	15.1%	9.8
2	43.0	8.6	14.0	10.8
3	45.2	8.9	12.3	11.2
4	34.7	5.8	15.6	9.2
5	49.5	11.4	9.2	11.9
6	40.2	7.6	13.6	10.3
7	38.1	5.7	14.0	10.2
8	45.6	8.6	12.0	11.4
State	41.8	7.9	13.2	10.7

Housing and Residential Patterns

	Housing		Urban-Suburban-Nonmetropolitan Breakdown		
District	Owner Occupied Units	Renter Occupied Units	Urban	Suburban	Nonmetro-politan
1	74.3%	25.7%	—	—	100.0%
2	69.7	30.3	35.4%	33.6%	31.0
3	67.8	32.2	24.6	40.1	35.3
4	72.2	28.8	0.0	18.9	81.1
5	60.5	39.5	91.4	0.0	8.6
6	70.0	30.0	15.0	2.8	82.2
7	66.7	33.3	9.8	16.2	74.0
8	53.3	46.7	98.9	1.1	—
State	66.7	33.3	34.8	14.1	51.1

1st District

(Northeast—Johnson City, Kingsport)

Cities, 1970 Population. Johnson City 33,817, Kingsport 31,965, Morristown 20,346, Bristol 20,092.

Universities, Enrollment. Carson-Newman College (Jefferson City—1,726), East Tennessee State University (Johnson City—9,545).

Commercial Television Stations, Affiliation. WCYB-TV, Bristol (NBC primary); WJHL-TV, Johnson City (CBS primary); WKPT-TV, Kingsport (ABC). District is divided between Bristol-Kingsport-Johnson City ADI and Knoxville ADI.

Plants and Offices, Products, Employment.

Holston Defense Corp., Kingsport (Explosives—at least 1,500). **Mead Corp.**, Kingsport (Paper mill—1,200). **Raytheon Co.**, Bristol (Electronic equipment—1,000). **Sperry Rand Corp.**, Bristol (Univac-Bristol Division—computing equipment—1,400). **Magnavox Co. of Tennessee**, Jefferson City (Radio, television receivers and cabinets—1,900). **North Electric Co.**, Johnson City (Telecom Division—telephone equipment—2,000). **Akzona Inc.**, Morristown (Rayon polyester fiber—4,200). **Eastman Kodak Co.**, Kingsport (Tennessee Eastman Co.—fibers, chemicals, plastics—10,600). **Berkline Corp.**, Morristown (Furniture—1,600). **Kingsport Press Inc.**, Kingsport (Book printing—1,200). **Mason**

& Dixon Lines Inc., Kingsport (Trucking—HQ—1,000).

2nd District

(East Central—Knoxville)

Race and Ethnic Groups. Blacks 5.9 percent.

Cities, 1970 Population. Knoxville 174,587, Maryville 13,808, Athens 11,790.

Universities, Enrollment. Knoxville College (Knoxville—1,039), University of Tennessee at Knoxville (Knoxville—26,620).

Newspapers, Circulation. Knoxville Journal (Morn—63,944), Knoxville News-Sentinel (Eve—106,762).

Commercial Television Stations, Affiliation. WATE-TV, Knoxville (NBC); WBIR-TV, Knoxville (CBS); WTVK, Knoxville (None). Most of district is located in Knoxville ADI. Small portion is located in Chattanooga ADI.

Plants and Offices, Products, Employment.

Aluminum Co. of America, Alcoa (Aluminum production—6,500). **Bowaters Southern Paper Corp.**, Calhoun (Pulp, newsprint—1,250). **Robertshaw Controls Co.**, Knoxville (Fulton Sylphon Division—metal bellows—1,150). **Beaunit Corp.**, Etowah (Fibers, yarn, fabric, underwear—1,100). **Standard Knitting Mills Inc.**, Knoxville (Underwear—2,700). **Levi Strauss & Co.**, Knoxville (Clothing—2,200). **Imperial Reading Corp.**, LaFollette (Imperial Shirt Co.—shirts—1,150). **Tennessee Valley Authority**, Knoxville (Headquarters—2,400). **Millers Inc.**, Knoxville (Department store—1,350). **City of Knoxville**, Knoxville (City government—at least 1,500).

3rd District

(Southeast—Chattanooga, Oak Ridge)

Race and Ethnic Groups. Blacks 11.2 percent.

Cities, 1970 Population. Chattanooga 119,693, Oak Ridge 28,336, East Ridge 21,762, Cleveland 20,616.

Universities, Enrollment. Lee College (Cleveland—1,093), Southern Missionary College (Collegedale—1,414), University of Tennessee at Chattanooga (Chattanooga—4,873).

AEC-Owned, Contractor Operated Installations. Oak Ridge Research and Development and Production Facilities, Oak Ridge.

Newspapers, Circulation. Chattanooga News-Free Press (Eve—66,215), Chattanooga Times (Morn—63,854).

Commercial Television Stations, Affiliation. WDEF-TV, Chattanooga (CBS); WRCB-TV, Chattanooga (NBC); WTVC, Chattanooga (ABC); WRIP-TV, Chattanooga (None). Major portion of district is located in Chattanooga ADI. Portion of district is located in Knoxville ADI.

Plants and Offices, Products, Employment.

Cities Service Co., Copperhill (Copper mining, smelting—2,000). **Atlas Chemical Industries Inc.**, Chattanooga (Explosives—1,100). **Combustion Engineering Inc.**, Chattanooga (Industrial boilers—5,200). **Union Carbide Corp.**, Oak Ridge (Chemicals—16,000). **Magic Chef Inc.**, Cleveland (Electric, gas ranges—HQ—1,700). **Burlington Industries Inc.**, Harriman (Hosiery—1,200). **Burlington Industries Inc.**, Cleveland (Cleveland Woolens Division —woolens—1,000). **Roane Hosiery Inc.**, Harriman (Hosiery—1,800). **Dixie Yarns Inc.**, Chattanooga (Yarn mill—HQ—1,000). **E. I. du Pont de Nemours and Co.**, Chattanooga (Nylon fibers—3,700). **American Uniform Co.**, Chattanooga (Work clothes— HQ—1,020). **Tennessee Valley Authority**, Chattanooga (Electricity, gas—2,430). **South Central Bell Telephone Co.**, Chattanooga (Telephone company —1,100). **Dorsey Corp.**, Chattanooga (Holding company—3,500). **Provident Life and Accident Insurance Co.**, Chattanooga (Insurance—1,000). **City of Chattanooga**, Chattanooga (City government —1,300).

4th District

(Central—Murfreesboro)

Race and Ethnic Groups. Blacks 6.3 percent.
Cities, 1970 Population. Murfreesboro 26,360, Tullahoma 15,382, Cookeville 14,270, Gallatin 13,093.
Universities, Enrollment. Middle Tennessee State University (Murfreesboro—8,646), Tennessee Technological University (Cookeville—6,312).
Military Installations or Activities. Arnold Engineering Development Center, Tullahoma.
Newspapers, Circulation. Nashville newspapers circulate in portion of district.
Commercial Television Stations, Affiliation. Most of district is located in Nashville ADI. Small portions are located in Knoxville ADI and Chattanooga ADI.
Plants and Offices, Products, Employment.
   Heil-Quaker Corp., Lewisburg (Heaters, furnaces —1,150). **Carrier Corp.**, McMinnville (Air conditioning units—1,000). **TRW Inc.**, Lebanon (Ross Gear Division—steering gears—1,000). **Aro Inc.**, Tullahoma (Engineering services—3,000). **Fordham-Bardell Shirt Corp.**, Livingston (Shirts—1,500). **Kayser-Roth Corp.**, Woodbury (Colonial Corp. Division—shirts, outerwear—1,400).

5th District

(Nashville)

Race and Ethnic Groups. Blacks 19.0 percent.
Cities, 1970 Population. Nashville-Davidson 447,888.
Universities, Enrollment. David Lipscomb College (Nashville—2,196), Fisk University (Nashville—1,413), George Peabody College for Teachers (Nashville— 1,993), Tennessee State University (Nashville—4,404), University of Tennessee at Nashville (Nashville— 2,945), Vanderbilt University (Nashville—6,756).
Newspapers, Circulation. Nashville Banner (Eve— 96,333), Nashville Tennessean (Morn—139,159).
Commercial Television Stations, Affiliation. WLAC-TV, Nashville (CBS); WSIX-TV, Nashville (ABC); WSM-TV, Nashville (NBC). Entire district is located in Nashville ADI.
Plants and Offices, Products, Employment.
   Avco Corp., Nashville (Aerostructures Division—

aircraft parts—5,000). **State Stove and Manufacturing Co. Inc.**, Ashland City (Water heaters—HQ —1,000). **Ford Motor Co.**, Nashville (Nashville Glass Plant—glass—2,500). **Aladdin Industries Inc.**, Nashville (Vacuum bottles, lunch boxes—HQ— 1,220). **Louisville and Nashville Railroad**, Nashville (Railroad—11,000). **United Parcel Service Inc.**, Nashville (Trucking—1,010). **South Central Bell Telephone Co.**, Nashville (Telephone company— 2,000). **Newspaper Printing Corp.**, Nashville (Newspaper printing—1,150). **Board of Publications, Methodist Church**, Nashville (Printing and publishing periodicals, books—HQ—1,300). **Sunday School Board, Southern Baptist Convention**, Nashville (Printing and publishing periodicals and books—HQ —1,000). **Malone & Hyde Inc.**, Nashville (Cooper and Martin Division—groceries—1,200). **National Life and Accident Insurance Co.**, Nashville (Insurance—1,600).

6th District

(West Central—Memphis, Clarksville)

Race and Ethnic Groups. Blacks 13.7 percent.
Cities, 1970 Population. Part of Memphis 70,737, Clarksville 31,737, Columbia 21,483.
Universities, Enrollment. Austin Peay State University (Clarksville—3,822).
Newspapers, Circulation. Memphis and Nashville newspapers circulate in portions of district.
Commercial Television Stations, Affiliation. Most of district is located in Nashville ADI. Smaller portions are located in Memphis ADI and Jackson ADI.
Plants and Offices, Products, Employment.
   Arthur G. McKee and Co., Memphis (Heavy construction—1,000). **Trane Co.**, Clarksville (Heating, air conditioning, ventilating equipment—12,000). **Murray Ohio Manufacturing Co.**, Lawrenceburg (Bicycles, children's vehicles—2,600). **Acme Boot Co. Inc.**, Clarksville (Footwear—1,250). **Decaturville Sportswear Inc.**, Decaturville (Sportswear— 1,200). **Kraftco Corp.**, Memphis (Sealtest Food Division—ice cream, milk, edible oils and fats— 1,150).

7th District

(West—Memphis, Jackson)

Race and Ethnic Groups. Blacks 19.3 percent.
Cities, 1970 Population. Part of Memphis 47,610, Jackson 39,861, Millington 21,035, Dyersburg 14,474.
Universities, Enrollment. University of Tennessee at Martin (Martin—4,907).
Military Installations or Activities. Naval Air Station, Memphis; Naval Hospital, Memphis; Naval Air Technical Training Command, Memphis.
Newspapers, Circulation. Memphis newspapers circulate in portion of district.
Commercial Television Stations, Affiliation. WBBJ-TV, Jackson (ABC; CBS on per program basis). Most of district is located in Memphis ADI. Smaller portions are located in Jackson ADI and Paducah (Ken-

tucky)-Cape Girardeau (Missouri)-Harrisburg (Illinois) ADI.

Plants and Offices, Products, Employment.

Harvey Aluminum Sales Inc., Milan (Defense Plant Division—ammunition—4,500). **International Harvester Co.**, Memphis (Farm machinery, equipment—at least 2,300). **Goodyear Tire and Rubber Co.**, Union City (Tires—at least 1,000). **Goodyear Tire and Rubber Co.**, Union City (Tire retreading, manufacturing, retailing—at least 1,010). **International Telephone and Telegraph Co.**, Milan (Communications equipment—2,000). **Henry I. Siegel Co. Inc.**, Bruceton (HIS Sportswear—clothing—at least 1,200). **State of Tennessee**, Jackson (Highway Department—1,150).

8th District

(Memphis)

Race and Ethnic Groups. Blacks 47.5 percent.
Cities, 1970 Population. Part of Memphis 507,289.
Universities, Enrollment. Memphis State University (Memphis—19,701), Southwestern at Memphis (Memphis—1,051), University of Tennessee Medical Units (Memphis—1,784).
Military Installations or Activities. Memphis Army Depot, Memphis.

Newspapers, Circulation. Memphis Commercial Appeal (Morn—223,122), Memphis Press-Scimitar (Eve—129,316).
Commercial Television Stations, Affiliation. WHBQ-TV, Memphis (ABC); WMC-TV, Memphis (NBC); WREC-TV, Memphis (CBS). Entire district located in Memphis ADI.
Plants and Offices, Products, Employment.

Kimberly-Clark Corp., Memphis (Paper products —1,600). **Ambac Industries Inc.**, Memphis (Pace Corp. Division—ammunition—1,000). **General Electric Co.**, Memphis (Lamps, electrical appliances —1,650). **Firestone Tire and Rubber Co.**, Memphis (Xylos Rubber Co. Division—tires, manufacturing, retreading, wholesaling, retailing—3,260). **E. L. Bruce Co. Inc.**, Memphis (Terminix Division—hardwood flooring, wall paneling—2,020). **Memphis Publishing Co.**, Memphis (Newspaper publishing—1,000). **N C C Industries Inc.**, Memphis (Equipment leasing—1,990). **Federated Department Stores**, Memphis (J. Goldsmith and Sons Co. Division—department store—1,420). **ITT Continental Baking Co. Inc.**, Memphis (Wonder Snack Foods Division —bakery—1,080). **South Central Bell Telephone Co.**, Memphis (Telephone company—1,860). **City of Memphis**, Memphis (City government—at least 1,000). **Baptist Memorial Hospital**, Memphis (Hospital—3,000). **Methodist Hospital Inc.**, Memphis (Hospital—2,200).

TEXAS: TWENTY-FOUR HOUSE SEATS, GAIN OF ONE

Texas gained an additional House seat as a result of reapportionment. The redistricting legislation was passed 80-53 by the Texas House on June 4, 1971, and by the Senate the same day, 17-9. Gov. Preston Smith (D) signed the bill June 17. Responding to heavy pressure from cities and suburbs for more districts controlled by urban voters two new urban oriented districts were created, and several other non-metropolitan districts acquired portions of urban counties.

However, on June 18, 1973, the U.S. Supreme Court declared the Texas congressional districts, as redrawn in 1971, unconstitutional because of excessive population variance among districts. The court returned the case to a three-judge federal panel, which adopted a new congressional district plan, effective Oct. 17, 1973.

In general, minor boundary adjustments were sufficient to bring the district populations into closer alignment with each other. However, two districts in the Dallas area—the 5th and 24th—were changed substantially enough to threaten their incumbents with defeat.

The 24th District, created in 1971 when Texas gained a House seat, lost conservative Democratic areas in Denton County and gained liberal Democratic and black areas in Dallas County.

At least one incumbent profited from the court-ordered redistricting. Rep. James M. Collins (R) of the 3rd District saw Republicans and conservatives added, making his seat more secure.

The case began on Oct. 19, 1971, when Dan Weiser, a mathematician, and others, challenged the legislature's congressional redistricting plan as unconstitutional because of unnecessarily large population variances. The challengers submitted two alternate plans—Plan B, which generally followed the redistricting plan set up by the state legislature, and Plan C, which radically altered district lines.

A federal three-judge panel chose Plan C on Jan. 22, 1972, but the U.S. Supreme Court stayed the decision, pending its own consideration of the case. The 1972 elections were held under the legislature's congressional district plan.

The Supreme Court's June 1973 decision agreed that a new plan reducing population variances was needed. But the three-judge panel erred, concluded the Court, in choosing Plan C to replace the legislature's plan. Plan B, to a greater extent than Plan C, adhered to the desires of the state legislature while attempting to achieve population equality among districts. Since redistricting is primarily a state and legislative function, the courts should interfere only to the extent necessary to achieve a satisfactory population variance, and not intrude on the overall nature of the plan, concluded the Court.

District	Member Elected 1972	Winning Percentage	1970 Population	Percent Variance
1	Wright Patmanj)d)	100.0	466,545	+0.0032
2	Charles Wilson (D)	73.8	466,565	+0.0075
3	James M. Collins (R)	73.3	466,266	—0.0565
4	Ray Roberts (D)	70.2	466,234	—0.0634
5	Alan Steelman (R)	55.7	466,620	+0.0192
6	Olin E. Teague (D)	72.6	466,285	—0.0525
7	Bill Archer (R)	82.3	466,336	—0.0415
8	Bob Eckhardt (D)	64.6	466,704	+0.0372
9	Jack Brooks (D)	66.2	466,678	+0.0317
10	J. J. Pickle (D)	91.2	466,313	—0.0465
11	W. R. Poage (D)	100.0	466,258	—0.0583
12	Jim Wright (D)	100.0	466,930	+0.0857
13	Robert Price (R)	54.8	466,663	+0.0285
14	John Young (D)	100.0	466,437	—0.0199
15	Eligio de la Garza (D)	100.0	466,359	—0.0366
16	Richard C. White (D)	100.0	466,663	+0.0285
17	Omar Burleson (D)	100.0	466,432	—0.0210
18	Barbara C. Jordan (D)	80.6	466,520	—0.0021
19	George Mahon (D)	100.0	466,649	+0.0255
20	Henry B. Gonzalez (D)	96.9	466,514	—0.0034
21	O. C. Fisher (D)	56.8	466,753	+0.0477
22	Bob Casey (D)	70.2	466,707	+0.0379
23	Abraham Kazen Jr. (D)	100.0	466,424	—0.0227
24	Dale Milford (D)	65.1	466,875	+0.0739

1970 State Population: 11,196,730
Ideal District Population: 466,530

Election Results, 1968-1972

Vote for U.S. Representative
(Adjusted to new district boundaries)

District	1968	1970	1972
1	100,865 D (100.0%)	77,413 D (79.7%)	94,789 D (99.8%)
	—	18,614 R (19.2%)	206 R (.2%)[1]
2	86,384 D (100.0%)	52,820 D (76.8%)	98,275 D (73.9%)
	—	—	34,788 R (26.1%)
3	65,010 D (40.6%)	54,099 D (42.3%)	58,695 D (30.1%)
	94,973 R (59.4%)	73,804 R (57.7%)	136,244 R (69.9%)
4	92,346 D (92.2%)	68,632 D (93.9%)	101,262 D (73.4%)
	7,832 R (7.8%)[1]	4,435 R (6.1%)[1]	36,648 R (26.6%)

District	1968	1970	1972
5	60,459 D (63.7%)	44,886 D (64.7%)	52,572 D (48.4%)
	34,413 R (36.3%)	24,508 R (35.3%)	55,944 R (51.6%)
6	78,247 D (84.5%)	61,680 D (83.8%)	103,169 D (72.8%)
	14,239 R (15.4%)[1]	11,931 R (16.2%)[1]	38,539 R (27.2%)
7	17,124 D (15.8%)[1]	39,045 D (31.3%)	35,204 D (18.6%)
	90,857 R (84.1%)	85,813 R (68.7%)	154,333 R (81.4%)
8	47,982 D (61.3%)	34,184 D (73.3%)	71,369 D (64.8%)
	30,337 R (38.7%)[1]	11,190 R (24.7%)[1]	37,899 R (34.4%)
9	127,897 D (60.5%)	57,180 D (64.5%)	88,806 D (66.3%)
	77,330 R (39.5%)	31,483 R (35.5%)	45,203 R (33.7%)
10	75,999 D (63.3%)	73,121 D (100.0%)	129,611 D (90.7%)
	44,139 R (36.7%)	—	—
11	88,109 D (95.2%)	66,276 D (100.0%)	89,148 D (100.0%)
	1,810 R (1.9%)[1]	—	—
12	66,582 D (100.0%)	50,337 D (100.0%)	79,432 D (97.3%)
	—	—	2,224 R (2.7%)[1]
13	67,830 D (45.3%)	33,185 D (38.3%)	69,142 D (44.5%)
	81,852 R (54.7%)	53,570 R (61.7%)	85,946 R (55.4%)
14	87,256 D (95.0%)	57,042 D (100.0%)	89,836 D (100.0%)
	4,626 R (5.0%)[1]	—	—
15	72,368 D (100.0%)	65,485 D (79.3%)	75,405 D (100.0%)
	—	17,049 R (20.7%)[1]	—
16	61,426 D (69.2%)	54,257 D (78.9%)	76,515 D (100.0%)
	27,373 R (30.8%)[1]	14,512 R (21.1%)	—
17	96,128 D (92.1%)	76,046 D (94.4%)	89,902 D (98.8%)
	8,264 R (7.9%)[1]	4,529 R (5.6%)[1]	1,138 R (1.2%)[1]
18	39,283 D (58.8%)	34,301 D (64.2%)	84,230 D (82.5%)
	27,486 R (41.2%)	19,158 R (35.8%)	16,679 R (16.3%)
19	81,028 D (80.3%)	52,708 D (82.4%)	93,209 D (100.0%)
	19,832 R (19.7%)[1]	11,248 R (17.6%)[1]	—
20	66,628 D (81.5%)	53,064 D (95.3%)	75,074 D (97.3%)
	15,139 R (18.5%)	2,626 R (4.7%)[1]	—
21	83,674 D (68.3%)	69,502 D (66.4%)	88,285 D (58.6%)
	38,758 R (31.7%)	35,204 R (33.6%)	62,485 R (41.4%)
22	68,701 D (69.5%)	56,298 D (65.4%)	99,274 D (69.9%)
	30,096 R (30.5%)	29,775 R (34.6%)	41,881 R (29.5%)
23	62,133 D (93.5%)	51,967 D (95.4%)	69,514 D (98.6%)
	4,291 R (6.5%)[1]	2,531 R (4.6%)[1]	939 R (1.3%)[1]
24	50,802 D (69.6%)	39,958 D (71.5%)	69,845 D (64.7%)
	22,168 R (30.4%)	15,938 R (28.5%)	38,176 R (35.3%)
State	1,719,937 D (71.8%)	1,339,061 D (73.1%)	2,032,183 D (70.4%)
	672,467 R (28.1%)	476,845 R (26.0%)	835,135 R (28.9%)

1 Winning percentage for member in 1972 in districts as constituted before Oct. 1973 redistricting.

Voting Age Population

District	Voting Age Population	Voting Age Population 18, 19, 20	Voting Age Population 65 and Over	Median Age of Voting Age Population
1	317,678	20,481 (6.4%)	72,419 (22.8%)	49.7
2	306,907	26,150 (8.5%)	54,572 (17.8%)	44.5
3	307,390	19,498 (6.3%)	32,766 (10.7%)	39.7
4	316,217	30,125 (9.5%)	55,812 (17.6%)	43.9
5	297,053	22,993 (7.7%)	30,005 (10.1%)	38.1
6	308,700	26,269 (8.5%)	46,399 (15.0%)	42.4
7	297,881	18,590 (6.2%)	22,655 (7.6%)	38.9
8	279,486	22,659 (8.1%)	23,058 (8.3%)	39.0
9	297,954	23,488 (7.9%)	36,917 (12.4%)	42.6
10	319,186	40,463 (12.7%)	47,883 (15.0%)	39.5
11	322,596	30,913 (9.6%)	61,273 (19.0%)	43.7
12	300,645	22,150 (7.4%)	38,453 (12.8%)	41.2
13	310,500	25,950 (8.4%)	49,087 (15.8%)	43.7
14	283,780	23,524 (8.3%)	36,123 (12.7%)	42.0
15	267,682	28,027 (10.5%)	37,867 (14.1%)	41.4
16	277,914	27,479 (9.9%)	27,129 (9.8%)	38.8
17	317,598	23,449 (7.4%)	64,937 (20.4%)	46.7

District	Voting Age Population	Voting Age Population 18, 19, 20	Voting Age Population 65 and Over	Median Age of Voting Age Population
18	307,636	27,830 (9.1%)	41,805 (13.6%)	39.9
19	288,060	27,491 (9.5%)	31,416 (10.9%)	40.0
20	295,013	40,118 (13.6%)	42,720 (14.5%)	40.1
21	303,953	21,239 (7.0%)	47,111 (15.5%)	43.8
22	287,629	21,755 (7.6%)	23,366 (8.1%)	38.4
23	275,439	23,150 (8.4%)	40,295 (14.6%)	41.5
24	289,997	24,873 (8.6%)	29,214 (10.1%)	37.6
State	7,177,844	618,651 (8.6%)	993,281 (13.8%)	41.5

District	Completed 4 years of High School	Completed 4 Years of College	Completed 5 Years or less of School	Median School Years Completed
11	42.6	8.5	10.6	11.2
12	46.6	8.7	7.8	11.6
13	52.1	9.9	7.0	12.1
14	43.9	8.8	18.6	11.1
15	32.3	7.4	36.8	8.3
16	50.0	10.6	16.7	12.0
17	43.3	7.7	9.6	11.2
18	36.2	7.4	15.2	10.4
19	51.6	12.0	11.4	12.1
20	33.6	5.6	25.0	9.4
21	55.2	14.1	10.3	12.2
22	57.5	14.6	7.2	12.3
23	37.1	6.7	25.2	9.8
24	49.2	9.4	8.0	11.9
State	47.4	10.9	12.3	11.7

Income and Occupation

District	Median Family Income	White Collar Workers	Blue Collar Workers	Service Workers	Farm Workers
1	$ 6,543	36.8%	43.9%	13.5%	5.8%
2	7,259	38.4	43.7	14.0	3.9
3	13,395	74.3	18.6	6.7	0.4
4	8,032	43.7	38.6	14.1	3.6
5	9,480	47.6	37.7	14.4	0.3
6	9,417	53.2	32.4	10.8	3.6
7	13,561	77.0	16.5	5.9	0.6
8	9,555	40.1	46.4	13.2	0.3
9	9,344	44.6	40.1	14.3	1.0
10	7,825	53.3	26.0	15.5	5.2
11	6,755	43.7	33.0	15.3	8.0
12	9,441	46.9	39.2	13.4	0.5
13	8,182	45.4	32.0	14.4	8.2
14	7,683	43.6	36.5	14.5	5.4
15	5,059	40.4	33.7	12.7	13.2
16	7,936	49.0	36.3	13.2	1.5
17	7,144	40.5	34.0	14.5	11.0
18	7,288	39.7	39.7	20.5	0.1
19	8,315	47.0	29.3	13.0	10.7
20	6,566	42.1	39.5	18.0	0.4
21	8,789	56.7	25.7	11.6	6.0
22	11,022	54.1	33.6	10.9	1.4
23	6,512	43.2	34.8	13.0	9.0
24	9,583	48.0	38.0	13.6	0.4
State	8,486	48.5	34.3	13.3	3.9

Housing and Residential Patterns

	Housing		Urban-Suburban-Nonmetropolitan Breakdown		
District	Owner Occupied Units	Renter Occupied Units	Urban	Suburban	Nonmetropolitan
1	73.4%	26.6%	6.5%	8.0%	85.5%
2	72.2	27.8	5.2	27.7	67.1
3	63.0	37.0	54.3	45.7	—
4	68.4	31.6	24.0	44.4	31.6
5	53.4	46.6	63.1	36.9	—
6	71.2	28.8	43.5	36.1	20.4
7	63.0	37.0	77.2	22.8	—
8	70.1	29.9	47.8	48.5	3.7
9	67.9	32.1	59.5	37.9	—
10	61.0	39.0	54.0	9.4	36.6
11	64.9	35.1	20.4	11.2	68.4
12	64.5	35.5	61.0	39.0	—
13	69.1	30.9	48.0	10.2	41.8
14	65.9	35.1	43.8	17.2	39.0
15	69.	30.5	36.8	32.2	31.0
16	61.2	38.8	80.5	9.2	10.3
17	65.3	30.6	19.2	5.2	75.6
18	57.1	62.2	100.0	—	—
19	65.3	34.7	50.1	9.4	40.5
20	57.1	42.9	92.2	7.8	—
21	69.9	30.1	41.7	17.0	41.3
22	68.3	31.7	38.2	61.0	0.8
23	69.2	30.8	34.8	22.5	42.7
24	59.6	40.4	54.3	45.7	—
State	64.7	35.3	48.2	25.3	26.5

Education: School Years Completed

District	Completed 4 years of High School	Completed 4 years of College	Completed 5 years or less of School	Median School years completed
1	38.8%	6.2%	12.2%	10.6
2	36.8	7.5	13.7	10.5
3	74.2	26.2	2.6	12.9
4	46.8	9.7	9.0	11.6
5	46.2	7.7	8.8	11.6
6	50.5	12.4	8.4	12.0
7	75.5	28.7	2.5	13.0
8	39.3	5.7	10.1	10.9
9	45.6	9.3	11.5	11.5
10	48.7	14.5	13.4	11.8

1st District

(Northeast—Texarkana)

Race and Ethnic Groups. Blacks 22.5 percent. Spanish heritage population 0.9 percent. German stock 0.2 percent.

Cities, 1970 Population. Texarkana 30,476, Paris 23,425, Marshall 22,921, Sulphur Springs 10,562.

Military Installations or Activities. Red River Army Depot, Texarkana.

Commercial Television Stations, Affiliation. Most of district is located in Shreveport (Louisiana)-

Texarkana ADI. Portions of district are located in Dallas-Fort Worth and Tyler ADI's.

Plants and Offices, Products, Employment.

Lone Star Steel Co., Lone Star (Steel mill—3,400). **Day and Zimmerman Inc.,** Texarkana (Lone Star Division—ammunition—4,800). **Thiokol Chemical Corp.,** Marshall (Long Horn Division—chemicals—1,500). **Campbell Soup Co.,** Paris (Cannery—1,500).

2nd District
(East—Orange)

Race and Ethnic Groups. Blacks 20.5 percent. Spanish heritage population 2.6 percent. Italian stock 0.4 per cent. British stock 0.2 percent.

Cities, 1970 Population. Orange 24,456, Lufkin 23,048, Nacogdoches 22,543, Huntsville 17,538.

Universities, Enrollment. Sam Houston State University, (Huntsville—11,844), Stephen F. Austin State University (Nacogdoches—9,976).

Commercial Television Stations, Affiliation. Major portion of district is divided between Beaumont-Port Arthur, Houston and Tyler ADI's. Small portions of district are located in Dallas-Fort Worth and Waco-Temple ADIs.

Plants and Offices, Products, Employment.

Levingston Shipbuilding Co., Orange (Shipbuilding—2,000). **Eastex Inc.,** Evandale (Southwestern Timer Co. Division—paperboard—1,150). **Southland Paper Mills Inc.,** Lufkin (Newsprint, Kraft paper—HQ—1,000). **Texas Foundries Inc.,** Lufkin (Malleable iron, steel casting—HQ—1,020). **Lufkin Industries Inc.,** Lufkin (Oil machinery and equipment, truck trailers, steel casting, auto parts—HQ—1,750). **du Pont de Nemours and Co.,** Orange (Plastics 12,300).

3rd District
(North central Dallas, parts of Denton and Collin counties)

Race and Ethnic Groups. Blacks 1.4 percent. Spanish heritage population 4.8 percent. German stock 1.1 percent. British stock 0.8 percent.

Cities, 1970 Population. Dallas (part) 253,363, Richardson 48,636, Irving (part), 40,360, Farmers Branch 27,426.

Universities, Enrollment. Southern Methodist University (Dallas—10,016), University of Dallas (Irving—1,403).

Newspapers, Circulation. Dallas newspapers circulate throughout district.

Commercial Television Stations, Affiliation. Entire district is located in Dallas-Fort Worth ADI.

Plants and Offices, Products, Employment.

Texas Instruments Inc., Dallas (Electronics components and instruments—HQ—12,000). **Texas Instruments Inc.,** Dallas (Government Products Division—military electronic equipment—9,800). **Western Electric Co. Inc.,** Dallas (Distribution, installation, repair of telephone equipment—1,100). **Collins Radio Co.,** Richardson (Communications

equipment—HQ—4,500). **Anderson Industries Inc.,** Dallas (Holding company—1,200). **El Chino Corp.,** Dallas (Mexican restaurants—1,250). **Richardson Independent School District,** Richardson (Public schools—2,100).

4th District
(North central—Denton, Sherman)

Race and Ethnic Groups. Blacks 14.7 percent. Spanish heritage population 2.7 percent. German stock 0.4 percent. British stock 0.3 percent.

Cities, 1970 Population. Tyler 57,832, Longview 45,629, Denton 39,917, Sherman 29,110.

Universities, Enrollment. Austin College (Sherman—1,145), East Texas State University (Commerce—9,759), North Texas State University (Denton—15,579), Texas Woman's University (Denton—5,810).

Newspapers, Circulation. Dallas newspapers circulate in portion of district.

Commercial Television Stations, Affiliation. Most of district is located in Dallas-Forth Worth ADI. Portions of district are located in Tyler and Shreveport (Louisiana)-Texarkana ADI's. KLTV, Tyler (NBC primary, ABC).

Plants and Offices, Products, Employment.

LTV Electrosystems Inc., Greenville (Aircraft modification, overhaul—3,000). **Tyler Pipe Industries Inc.,** Tyler (Cast iron products—2,500). **Kelly Springfield Tire Co.,** Tyler (Tires—1,370). **Eastman Kodak Co.,** Longview (Texas Eastman Co.—industrial and photographic chemicals—1,700). **Texas Instruments Inc.,** Sherman (Subassemblies, electronic components—at least 3,000). **General Electric Co.,** Tyler (Refrigerators, refrigeration machinery—1,350).

5th District
(Northeast—part of Dallas)

Race and Ethnic Groups. Blacks 19.7 percent. Spanish heritage population 7.1 percent. German stock 0.5 percent. British stock 0.4 percent.

Cities, 1970 Population. Dallas (part) 294,271, Garland (part) 76,683, Mesquite 55,159, Irving (part) 11,147.

Newspapers, Circulation. Dallas News (Morn—260,-866), Dallas Times-Herald (ExSat—240,502).

Commercial Television Stations, Affiliation. Entire district is located in Dallas-Fort Worth ADI. KDFW-TV, Dallas (CBS); KDTV, Dallas (None); WFAA-TV Dallas (ABC).

Plants and Offices, Products, Employment.

Electronic Data Systems Corp., Dallas (Computer systems holding company—HQ—1,000). **International Business Machines Corp.,** Dallas (Commercial machines and equipment—at least 1,050). **Recognition Equipment Inc.,** Irving (Optical character recognition equipment—HQ—1,000). **Taylor Publishing Co.,** Dallas (School yearbooks, textbooks—at least 1,000). **Braniff Airways Inc.,** Dallas (Headquarters—5,500).

DALLAS COUNTY

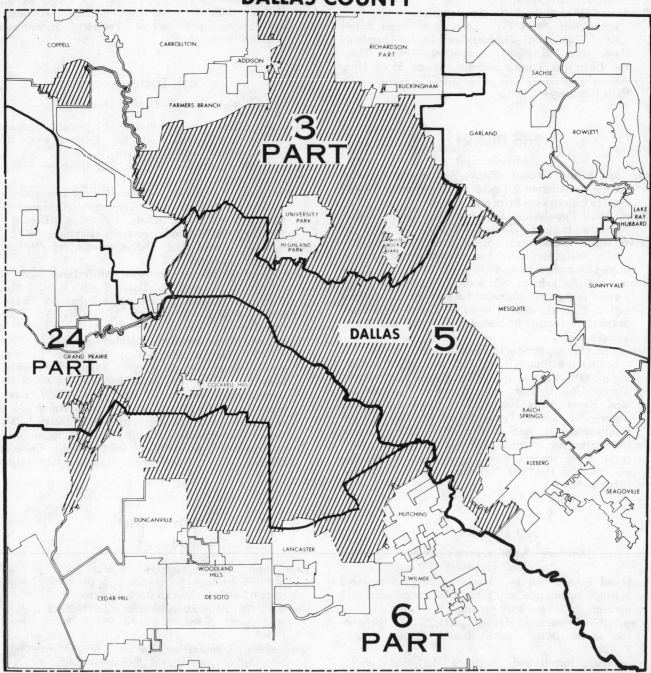

American Airlines Inc., Dallas (Airline—3,010). Steak and Ale Restaurants of America Inc., Dallas (Restaurant management service, holding company—1,720). Dallas County Hospital District, Dallas (Hospital—1,900). Tyler Corp., Dallas (Holding company, cast iron products—3,600). Mobil Oil Corp., Dallas (North American Division—petroleum products, tires, batteries—1,600). Atlantic Richfield Co., Dallas (Oil production—1,650). E Systems Inc., Garland (Radio and television transmitting, signaling and detection apparatus and equipment—1,100). Ling-Temco-Vought Inc., Dallas (Holding company—total employment 96,500). Varo Inc., Garland (Electronic equipment, engineering—1,000). Lone Star Gas Co. Dallas (Natural gas distribution—HQ—1,800). Southwestern Bell Telephone Co., Dallas (Telephone company—at least 5,750). Western Electric Co., Mesquite (Distribution and repair of telephone equipment—1,000). Upjohn Co., Dallas (Wholesale and distribution of pharmaceuticals—5,000). A. H. Belo Corp., Dallas (Newspaper publishing, radio and television broadcasting—1,400). Sammons Enterprises Inc., Dallas (Holding company

—total employment 7,150). **Curtis Mathes Corp.,** Dallas (Holding company—total employment 2,000). **Neiman-Marcus Co.,** Dallas (Department stores—2,250). **Titche-Goettinger Co.,** Dallas (Department stores—HQ—1,100). **United Artists Theatre Circuit,** Dallas (Rowley United Theatre Division—motion picture theatres—1,060). **Dallas Power and Light Co.,** Dallas (Electric utility—2,340). **Texas Utilities Co.,** Dallas (Holding company—total employment 8,000). **Chilton Corp.,** Dallas (Holding company—1,400). **Centex Corp.,** Dallas (Holding company—HQ—2,490). **Group Hospital Service,** Dallas (Insurance—1,700). **Gulf Life Holding Co.,** Dallas (Holding company—total employment 4,100). **Employers Casualty Co.,** Dallas (Insurance—HQ—1,000). **City of Dallas,** Dallas (City government—8,990).

6th District

(East central)

Race and Ethnic Groups. Blacks 9.9 percent. Spanish heritage population 5.3 percent. German stock 0.6 percent. British stock 0.4 percent.

Cities, 1970 Population. Fort Worth (part) 87,616, Dallas (part) 63,820, Bryan 33,739, College Station 17,772.

Universities, Enrollment. Southwestern Baptist Theological Seminary (Fort Worth—1,920), Texas Agricultural and Mechanical University (College Station—14,775). Texas Christian University (Fort Worth—6,537).

Newspapers, Circulation. Dallas and Fort Worth newspapers circulate in portion of district.

Commercial Television Stations, Affiliation. Most of district is located in Dallas-Fort Worth ADI. Portion of district is located in Waco-Temple ADI.

Plants and Offices, Products, Employment.
Atchison, Topeka and Santa Fe Railway, Cleburne (Railroad—1,200). **Army and Air Force Exchange Service,** Dallas (General merchandise stores—1,200).

7th District

(Northwest Harris county)

Race and Ethnic Groups. Blacks 2.0 percent. Spanish heritage population 7.7 percent. German stock 1.2 percent. British stock 1.0 percent.

Cities, 1970 Population. Houston (part) 360,197, Bellaire 19,066, West University Place (part) 7,337.

Universities, Enrollment. Houston Baptist College (Houston—1,126).

Newspapers, Circulation. Houston newspapers circulate throught district.

Commercial Television Stations, Affiliation. Entire district is located in Houston ADI.

Plants and Offices, Products, Employment.
Cameron Iron Works Inc., Houston (Iron and steel forging, oil field machinery, valve and pipe fittings—HQ—3,500). **Federated Department Stores,** Houston (Foley's Department Stores—1,600). 1,600).

8th District

(Northern and eastern Harris county)

Race and Ethnic Groups. Blacks 19.3 percent. Spanish heritage population 10.4 percent. German stock 0.7 percent. British stock 0.3 percent.

Cities, 1970 Population. Houston (part) 223,248, Baytown 44,083, Pasadena (part) 24,722, Deer Park 12,803.

Newspapers, Circulation. Houston newspapers circulate throughout district.

Commercial Television Stations, Affiliation. Entire district is located in Houston ADI.

Plants and Offices, Products, Employment.
Armco Steel Corp., Houston (Steel—6,000). **U.S. Plywood-Champion Papers,** Pasadena (Paper and paperboard—1,500). **Humble Oil and Refining Co.,** Baytown (Enjay Chemical Co. Division—petroleum products—1,900). **Petro-Tex Chemical Corp.,** Houston (Butadiene—1,000). **Shell Oil Co.,** Deer Park (Chemicals—1,500). **Ethyl Corp.,** Pasadena (Tetraethyl lead—1,000). **Brown and Root Inc.,** Houston (Heavy construction, metal fabricating engineers—HQ—7,500).

9th District

(East—Beaumont, Galveston, Port Arthur)

Race and Ethnic Groups. Blacks 22.0 percent. Spanish heritage population 7.2 percent. Italian stock 0.9 percent. German stock 0.8 percent.

Cities, 1970 Population. Beaumont 115,750, Galveston 61,699, Port Arthur 57,274, Texas City 38,753.

Universities, Enrollment. Lamar University (Beaumont—8,942).

Newspapers, Circulation. Beaumont Enterprise (Morn—62,681).

Commercial Television Stations, Affiliation. District divided between Beaumont-Port Arthur and Houston ADIs. KMBT-TV, Beaumont (ABC); KFDM-TV, Beaumont (CBS); KJAC-TV, Port Arthur (NBC).

Plants and Offices, Products, Employment.
Bethlehem Steel Corp., Beaumont (Bethleham Shipbuilding Corp.—fabricated structural steel, shipbuilding and repair—1,800). **Todd Shipyards Corp.,** Galveston (Shipbuilding and repair—1,000). **Texaco Inc.,** Port Arthur (Petroleum refining—4,000). **Texaco Inc.,** Port Neches (Petroleum refining—2,000). **Gulf Oil Corp.,** Port Arthur (Petroleum refining—2,000). **Mobil Oil Corp.,** Beaumont (Petroleum products—at least 1,830). **American Oil Co.,** Texas City (Petroleum refining—1,200). **Union Carbide Corp.,** Texas City (Organic chemicals, plastics—2,570). **Monsanto Co.,** Texas City (Chemicals—1,900). **E. I. du Pont de Nemours and Co.,** Beaumont (Elastic, chemicals and explosives—1,100). **American National Insurance Co.,** Galveston (Insurance—HQ—1,360).

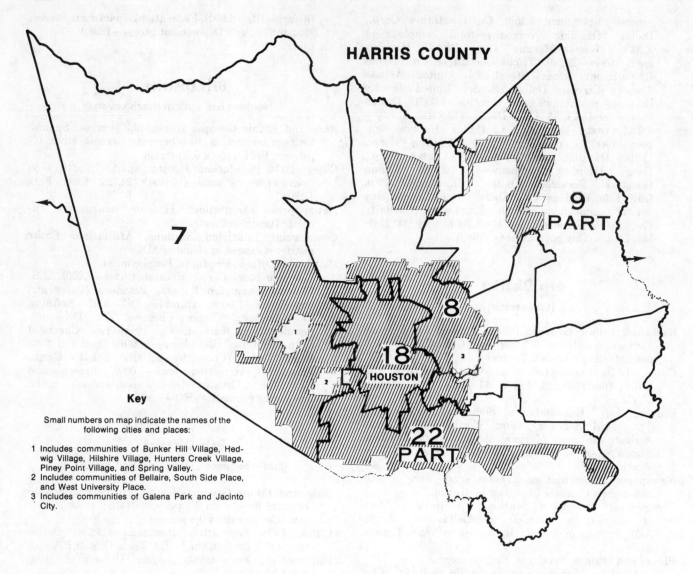

HARRIS COUNTY

7

9 PART

8

18

HOUSTON

22 PART

Key

Small numbers on map indicate the names of the
following cities and places:

1 Includes communities of Bunker Hill Village, Hed-
wig Village, Hilshire Village, Hunters Creek Village,
Piney Point Village, and Spring Valley.
2 Includes communities of Bellaire, South Side Place,
and West University Place.
3 Includes communities of Galena Park and Jacinto
City.

10th District

(East central—Austin)

Race and Ethnic Groups. Blacks 14.1 percent. Spanish
heritage population 14.3 percent. German stock 2.3
percent. Czech stock 1.0 percent.

Cities, 1970 Population. Austin 251,969, San Marcos
18,871.

Universities, Enrollment. Prairie View Agricultural
and Mechanical College (Prairie View—4,000), St.
Edwards University (Austin—1,236), Southwest
Texas State University (San Marcos—11,280). University of Texas at Austin (Austin—45,442).

Military Installations or Activities. Bergstrom Air
Force Base, Austin.

Newspapers, Circulation. Austin American (MxSat—
63,274).

Commercial Television Stations, Affiliation. Most of
district is located in Austin ADI. Portions are located
in Houston, Waco-Temple and San Antonio ADIs.
KHFI-TV, Austin (NBC primary, ABC); KVUE-
TV, Austin (ABC); KTBC-TV, Austin (CBS).

Plants and Offices, Products, Employment.
Tracor Inc., Austin (Timing units, research laboratory—HQ—1,170). **International Business Machines Corp.** Austin (Office machines—1,600). **Texas
Instruments Inc.,** Austin (Government Products Division—computers—1,000). **Kerr-Ban Furniture
Manufacturing Co.,** San Marcos (Bedroom furniture—1,000). **Southwestern Bell Telephone Co.,**
Austin (Telephone company—1,200).

11th District

(East central—Waco)

Race and Ethnic Groups. Blacks 12.2 percent. Spanish
heritage population 8.5 percent. German stock 2.2
percent. Czech stock 0.9 percent.

Cities, 1970 Population. Waco 95,285, Killeen 35,492,
Temple 33,417, Fort Hood 32,663.

Universities, Enrollment. Baylor University (Waco—
7,051).

Military Installations or Activities. Fort Hood, Kil-
len.

Commercial Television Stations, Affiliation. Most of district is divided between Waco-Temple and Dallas-Fort Worth ADI's. Small portions of district are located in Austin and Abilene ADI's. KCEN-TV, Temple (NBC); KWIX-TV, Waco (CBS primary, ABC).

Plants and Offices, Products, Employment.

Aluminum Co. of America, Rockdale (Aluminum production—1,500). **Certain-Teed Products Corp.,** Waco (William Cameron and Co. Division—building materials—at least 1,000). **General Tire and Rubber Co.,** Waco (Tires, tubes—1,550). **Genesco Inc.,** Waco (Haywood Co. Division—clothing—1,100).

12th District

(Central and northern Tarrant county— Fort Worth)

Race and Ethnic Groups. Blacks 15.9 percent. Spanish heritage population 7.4 percent. German stock 0.6 percent. British stock 0.5 percent.

Cities, 1970 Population. Fort Worth (part) 284,637, Halton City 27,947, Hurst 27,232, North Richland Hills 16,569.

Universities, Enrollment. Texas Wesleyan College (Fort Worth—1,874).

Military Installations or Activities. Carswell Air Force Base, Fort Worth.

Newspapers, Circulation. Fort Worth Press (ExSat—53,024), Fort Worth Star-Telegram (Morn—97,592; Eve 137,637).

Commercial Television Stations, Affiliation. Entire district is located in Dallas-Fort Worth ADI. KTVT, Fort Worth (None); WBAP-TV, Fort Worth (NBC).

Plants and Offices, Products, Employment.

General Dynamics Corp., Fort Worth (Convair Aerospace—aircraft, industrial gases—12,600). **Textron Inc.,** Hurst (Helicopters—10,400). **Morrison-Knudsen Co. Inc.,** Fort Worth (Pipeline construction—1,200). **American Manufacturing Co. of Texas,** Fort Worth (Oil well supplies—HQ—1,500). **Swift and Co.,** Fort Worth (Meat packer—1,500). **Montgomery Ward and Co.,** Fort Worth (Deartment store—1,590). **Pier I Imports Inc.,** Fort Worth (Holding company, furniture and other home furnishings stores—1,580).

13th District

(Northwest—Texas Panhandle, Amarillo, Wichita Falls)

Race and Ethnic Groups. Blacks 5.0 percent. Spanish heritage population 6.1 percent. German stock 0.8 percent. British stock 0.4 percent.

Cities, 1970 Population. Amarillo 127,447, Wichita Falls 96,612, Pampa 21,717, Borger 14,240.

Universities, Enrollment. West Texas State University (Canyon—7,351), Midwestern University (Wichita Falls—4,100).

AEC-Owned, Contractor-Operated Facilities. Pantex Plant, Amarillo.

Military Installations or Activities. Sheppard Air Force Base, Wichita Falls.

Newspapers, Circulation. Amarillo News (Morn—50,743).

Commercial Television Stations, Affiliation. Most of district is divided between Amarillo and Wichita Falls-Lawton (Oklahoma) ADI's. Small portion of district is located in Lubbock ADI. KFDA-TV, Amarillo (CBS); KGNC-TV, Amarillo (NBC); KVII-TV, Amarillo (ABC); KAUZ-TV, Wichita Falls (CBS); KFDX-TV, Wichita Falls (NBC).

Plants and Office, Products, Employment.

Diamond Shamrock Corp., Amarillo (Petroleum production, refining—1,000). **Phillips Petroleum Co.,** Borger (Petroleum refining—2,500). **Cabot Corp.,** Pampa (Cabot Machinery Division—Oil and gas guns, carbon black—1,270). **Textron Inc.,** Amarillo (Bell Helicopter Division—helicopter overhaul—1,200). **Mason and Hanger-Silas Mason Co.,** Amarillo (Industrial management, design engineering and construction—1,600). **Atchison, Topeka and Santa Fe Railway Co.,** Amarillo (Railroad—1,400).

14th District

(South gulf coast—Corpus Christi)

Race and Ethnic Groups. Blacks 7.3 percent. Spanish heritage population 36.7 percent. German stock 1.0 percent. Czech stock 0.8 percent.

Cities, 1970 Population. Corpus Christi 204,522, Victoria 41,355, Bay City 11,839, Robstown 11,213.

Military Installations or Activities. Naval Air Station, Corpus Christi; Naval Hospital, Corpus Christi.

Newspapers, Circulation. Corpus Christi Caller (Mx-Sat—69,253).

Commercial Television Stations, Affiliation. Most of district is divided between Corpus Christi and Houston ADI's. Small portion of district is located in San Antonio ADI. KIII, Corpus Christi (ABC); KRIS-TV, Corpus Christi (NBC); KZTV, Corpus Christi (CBS).

Plants and Offices, Products, Employment.

Aluminum Co. of America, Point Comfort (Aluminum—2,100). **Reynolds Metals Co.,** Gregory (Aluminum oxide—1,800). **Union Carbide Corp.,** Port Lavaca (Petrochemicals—1,000). **E.I. du Pont de Nemours and Co.,** Victoria (Chemicals—1,100).

15th District

(South—Brownsville)

Race and Ethnic Groups. Blacks 0.6 percent. Spanish heritage population 74.5 percent. German stock 0.5 percent. Canadian stock 0.2 percent.

Cities, 1970 Population. Brownsville 52,480, McAllen 37,606, Harlingen 33,488, Kingsville 28,582.

Universities, Enrollment. Pan American University, (Edinburg—6,217), Texas Arts and Industries University (Kingsville—8,096).

Military Installations or Activities. Naval Air Station, Kingsville.

Commercial Television Stations, Affiliation. Most of district is divided between Corpus Christi and McAllen-Brownsville ADI's. Small portions of district are located in San Antonio and Laredo ADI's.

TARRANT COUNTY

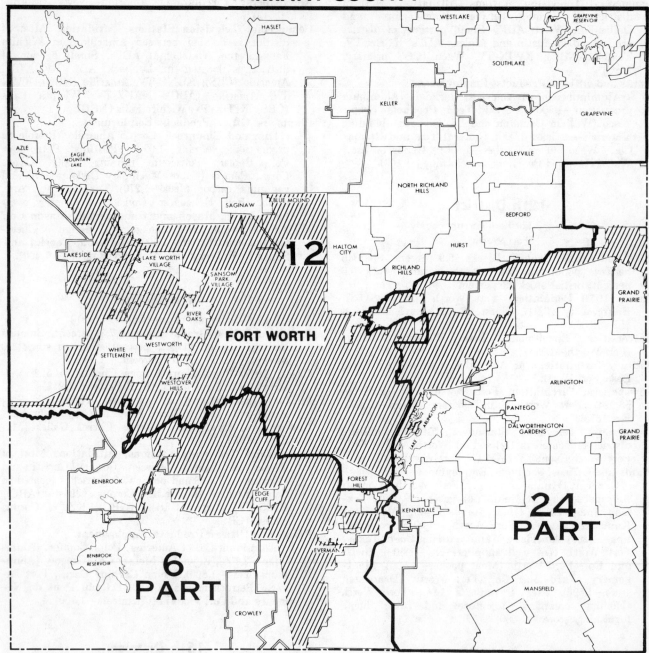

KGBT-TV, Harlingen (CBS, ABC; KRGV-TV, Weslaco (NBC primary, ABC).

16th District

(West—El Paso)

Race and Ethnic Groups. Blacks 3.4 percent. Spanish heritage population 50.0 percent. German stock 1.6 percent. British stock 0.5 percent.

Cities, 1970 Population. El Paso 322,316, Odessa (part) 53,410, Fort Bliss 13,290, Pecos 12,814.

Universities, Enrollment. University of Texas at El Paso (El Paso—11,484).

Military Installations or Activities. Fort Bliss, El Paso.

Newspapers, Circulation. El Paso Times (Morn—61,-231).

Commercial Television Stations, Affiliation. District is divided between El Paso and Odessa-Midland ADI's. KELP-TV, El Paso (ABC); KROD-TV, El Paso (CBS); KTSM-TV, El Paso (NBC); KMOM-TV, Monahans (ABC).

Plants and Offices, Products, Employment.

C.H. Leavell and Co., El Paso (General contractor, heavy construction—1,500). **Phillips Petroleum Co.,** Odessa (Oil production—1,250). **Hortex Inc.,** El Paso (Slacks, dungarees—HQ—1,000). **Blue Bell Inc.,** El Paso (Hicks-Ponder Division—

trousers, dungarees—1,000). **Farah Manufacturing Co. Inc.**, El Paso (Trousers—HQ—3,000). **Safeway Stores Inc.**, El Paso (Grocery stores—1,700). **Mountain States Telephone and Telegraph Co.**, El Paso (Telephone company—1,020).

17th District

(West central—Abilene)

Race and Ethnic Groups. Blacks 3.7 percent. Spanish heritage population 9.3 percent. German stock 0.6 percent. British stock 0.3 percent.

Cities, 1970 Population. Abilene 89,468, Big Spring, 28,818, Mineral Wells 17,517, Gainsville 13,827.

Universities, Enrollment. Abilene Christian College (Abilene—3,290), Hardin-Simmons University (Abilene—1,610), Howard Payne College (Brownwood—1,407), McMurry College (Abilene—1,600), Tarleton State College (Stephenville—3,181).

Military Installations or Activities. Fort Wolters, Mineral Wells; Dyess Air Force Base, Abilene; Webb Air Force Base, Big Springs.

Commercial Television Stations, Affiliation. Major portion of district is located in Abilene-Sweetwater ADI. Small portions of district are located in Lubbock, Wichita Falls-Lawton (Oklahoma), Dallas-Fort Worth and Odessa-Midland ADI's.

Plants and Offices, Products, Employment.

   Southern Airways Co. of Texas, Mineral Wells (Helicopter maintenance—2,700). **Merchants Fast Motor Lines Inc.,** Abilene (Trucking—1,400).

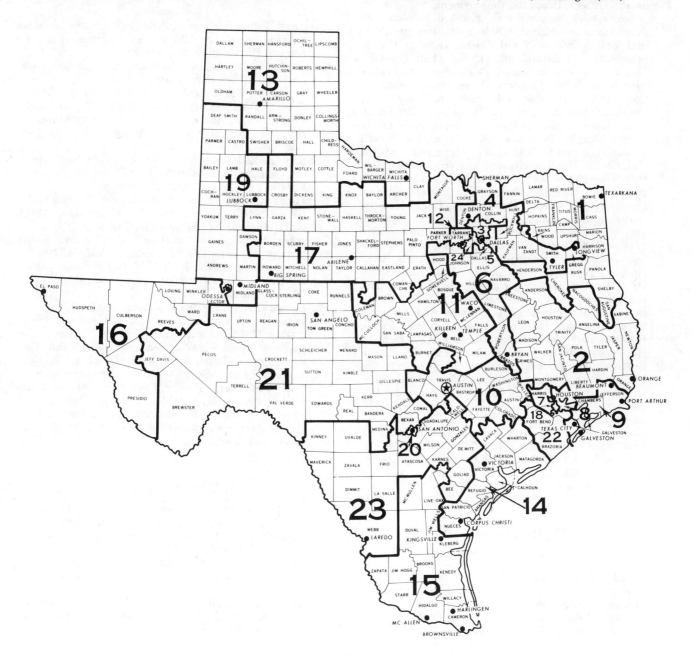

18th District

(Central Houston)

Race and Ethnic Groups. Blacks 44.0 percent. Spanish heritage population 18.6 percent. German stock 0.7 percent. Italian stock 0.5 percent.

Cities, 1970 Population. Houston (part) 466,520.

Universities, Enrollment. Texas Southern University (Houston—6,174), University of Houston (Houston—26,475), University of St. Thomas (Houston—1,510).

Newspapers, Circulation. Houston Chronicle (Ex-Sat—289,062), Houston Post (MxSat 287,024).

Commercial Television Stations, Affiliation. Entire district is located in Houston ADI. KHOU-TV, Houston (CBS); KHTV, Houston (None); KPRC-TV, Houston (NBC); KTRK-TV, Houston (ABC); KVRL-TV, Houston (None).

Plants and Offices, Products, Employment.

Texas Gulf Sulphur Co., Houston (Frasch Sulphur Division—sulphur, crude petroleum and natural gas—1,180). **Gulf Oil Corp.,** Houston (Crude petroleum and natural gas—1,850). **Shell Oil Co.,** Houston (Headquarters—3,000). **Pan American Petroleum Corp.,** Houston (Oil production, exploration—1,400). **Humble Oil and Refining Co.,** Houston (Headquarters—4,200). **Zapata Off-Shore Co.,** Houston (Oil well drilling contractor—1,000). **G. W. Murphy Industries Inc.,** Houston (Oil well drilling equipment—HQ—1,600). **Houston Natural Gas Corp.,** Houston (Natural gas transmission distribution—HQ—3,000). **James J. Flanagan Shipping Corp.,** Houston (Marine cargo handling—4,300). **Houston Chronicle Publishing Co.,** Houston (Newspaper publishing—1,300). **Houston Lighting and Power Co.,** Houston (Electric utility—HQ—1,000). **Southwestern Bell Telephone Co.,** Houston (Telephone company—7,600). **Tennaco Inc.,** Houston (Headquarters—2,500). **Alaska Interstate Co.,** Houston (Holding company, engineering and construction, natural gas transmission and distribution—2,000). **International Systems and Controls Corp.,** (Houston Holding company—at least 2,000). **Houston Belt and Terminal Railway Co.,** Houston (Railroad switching and terminal company—1,450). **Southern Pacific Co.,** Houston (Railroad—at least 1,000). **Kroger Co.,** Houston (Henke and Pilot Division—grocery stores—5,500). **Federated Department Stores,** (Foley's Bros. Dry Goods—department stores—3,420). **American General Insurance Co.,** Houston (Insurance—HQ—2,500). **Prudential Insurance Co. of America,** Houston (Insurance—1,350). **Port of Houston,** Houston (Port operations—1,350). **City of Houston,** Houston (City government—10,000).

19th District

(Northwest—Lubbock, Midland)

Race and Ethnic Groups. Blacks 6.0 percent. Spanish heritage population 18.9 percent. German stock 0.3 percent. British stock 0.2 percent.

Cities, 1970 Population. Lubbock 149,158, Midland 59,712, Odessa (part) 24,988, Plainview 19,103.

Universities, Enrollment. Texas Tech University (Lubbock—21,313).

Military Installations or Activities. Reese Air Force Base, Lubbock.

Newspapers, Circulation. Lubbock Avalanche-Journal (Morn—60,336).

Commercial Television Stations, Affiliation. Major portion of district is located in Lubbock ADI. Small portions of district are located in Odessa-Midland and Amarillo ADI's. KCBD-TV, Lubbock (NBC); KLBK-TV, Lubbock (CBS primary); KMXN-TV, Lubbock (None—Spanish); KSEL-TV, Lubbock (ABC); KDCD-TV, Midland (None); KMID-TV, Midland (NBC).

20th District

(San Antonio)

Race and Ethnic Groups. Blacks 10.9 percent. Spanish heritage population 59.7 percent. German stock 1.2 percent. British stock 0.5 percent.

Cities, 1970 Population. San Antonio 429,973, Lackland 19,076, Fort Sam Houston 10,551.

Universities, Enrollment. Incarnate Word College (San Antonio—1,529), Our Lady of the Lake College (San Antonio—2,018), St. Mary's University (San Antonio—3,977), Trinity University (San Antonio—3,106).

Military Installations or Activities. Fort Sam Houston, San Antonio; Kelly Air Force Base, San Antonio; Lackland Air Force Base, San Antonio.

Newspapers, Circulation. San Antonio Express (Mx-Sat—81,301), San Antonio News (ExSat—66,241), San Antonio Light (ExSat—119,732).

Commercial Television Stations, Affiliation. Entire district is located in San Antonio ADI. KENS-TV, San Antonio, (CBS); KSAT-TV, San Antonio (ABC); KWEX-TV, San Antonio (None—Spanish); WOAL-TV, San Antonio (NBC).

Plants and Offices, Products, Employment.

Finesilver Manufacturing Co., San Antonio (Work clothes—1,000). **Joske Bros. Co.,** San Antonio (Department store—1,000). **Sears Roebuck and Co.,** San Antonio (Department store—1,500). **H. E. Butt Grocery Co.,** San Antonio (Grocery stores—1,500). **Southern Pacific Co.,** San Antonio (Railroad—1,000). **City Public Service Board,** San Antonio (Public electric and gas utility—1,500). **United Services Automobile Assn.,** San Antonio (Insurance—HQ—2,550).

21st District

(South central—San Antonio, San Angelo)

Race and Ethnic Groups. Blacks 1.6 percent. Spanish heritage population 24.3 percent. German stock 1.6 percent. British stock 0.7 percent.

Cities, 1970 population. San Antonio (part) 130,525, San Angelo 63,998, Del Rio 21,395, New Braunfels 17,891.

Universities, Enrollment. Angelo State University (San Angelo—3,892), Sul Ross State University (Alpine—2,537).

Military Installations or Activities. Goodfellow Air Force Base, San Angelo; Laughlin Air Force Base, Del Rio; Medina Air Force Base, San Antonio.

Newspapers, Circulation. San Antonio newspapers circulate in portion of district.

Commercial Television Stations, Affiliation. Most of district is divided between Odessa-Midland, San Angelo and San Antonio ADI's. Small portions of district are located in Austin and Abilene ADIs. KCTV, San Angelo (CBS, ABC).

Plants and Offices, Products, Employment.

Southwest Research Institute, San Antonio (Scientific research—1,020). Ramo Inc., San Antonio (Meyer Machine Co. Division—holding company, motor carrier—3,100).

22nd District

(Southern Harris County—Fort Bend and most of Brazoria county)

Race and Ethnic Groups. Blacks 13.0 percent. Spanish heritage population 10.0 percent. German stock 1.0 percent. British stock 0.6 percent.

Cities, 1970 Population. Houston (part) 178,399, Pasadena (part) 64,650, Lake Jackson 13,340, Rosenberg 12,098.

Universities, Enrollment. Rice University (Houston—3,218).

NASA Facilities. Manned Spacecraft Center, Houston.

Military Installations or Activities. Ellington Air Force Base, Houston.

Newspapers, Circulation. Houston newspapers circulate in district.

Commercial Television Stations, Affiliation. Entire district is located in Houston ADI.

Plants and Offices, Products, Employment.

McDonnell Douglas Corp., Webster (Aircraft engines, parts—38,000). Lockheed Electronics Co. Inc., Houston (Houston Aerospace System Division—electronic parts and equipment, electronics research and development—1,600). Philco-Ford Corp., Houston (Engineering—1,300). Texas International Airlines, Houston (Airline—HQ—1,100). Dow Chemical Co., Freeport (Chemicals—6,500).

23rd District

(South—San Antonio, Laredo)

Race and Ethnic Groups. Blacks 3.4 percent. Spanish heritage population 48.8 percent. German stock 1.7 percent. British stock 0.5 percent.

Cities, 1970 Population. San Antonio (part) 93,835, Laredo 68,858, Seguin 15,916, Eagle Pass 15,581.

Military Installations or Activities. Naval Air Station (Chase Field), Beeville; Brooks Air Force Base, San Antonio; Randolph Air Force Base, San Antonio.

Newspapers, Circulation. San Antonio newspapers circulate in portion of district.

Commercial Television Stations, Affiliation. District is divided between San Antonio and Laredo ADI's. KGNS-TV Laredo (NBC, ABC).

24th District

(Dallas Fort-Worth suburbs)

Race and Ethnic Groups. Blacks 26.3 percent. Spanish heritage population 7.4 percent. German stock 0.5 percent. British stock 0.3 percent.

Cities, 1970 Population. Dallas (part) 232,509, Arlington 91,527, Grand Prairie 46,495, Irving (part) 45,769.

Universities, Enrollment. Bishop College (Dallas—1,651), University of Texas at Arlington (Arlington—14,115).

Military Installations or Activities. Naval Air Station, Grand Prairie.

Newspapers, Circulation. Dallas and Fort Worth newspapers circulate throughout district.

Commercial Television Stations, Affiliation. Entire district is located in Dallas-Fort Worth ADI.

Plants and Offices, Products, Employment.

Ruby Cecil Co. Inc., Dallas (Road construction—1,000). O'Rourke Construction Co., Dallas (General contractor—1,000). LTV Aerospace Corp., Grand Prairie (Aircraft, missiles, space vehicles—12,000). LTV Aerospace Corp., Grand Prairie (Vought Missile & Space Co. Division—missiles, space vehicle assemblies—3,000). General Motors Corp., Arlington (Automobile assembly—4,000). Southwestern Bell Telephone Co., Arlington (Telephone company—4,200).

UTAH: TWO HOUSE SEATS, NO CHANGE

Congressional redistricting in Utah was a relatively simple matter. All that was necessary was the transfer of four sparsely-populated counties in the southern part of the state from the 1st to the 2nd District. (Map p. 196)

The bill passed the state House Jan. 20, 1971, by a vote of 63-2 and the state Senate Feb. 2 by a vote of 21-0. Gov. Calvin L. Rampton (D) signed it Feb. 8.

Neither district was altered significantly by the changes.

District	Member Elected 1972	Winning Percentage	1970 Population	Percent Variance
1	K. Gunn McKay (D)	55.4	529,688	+ 0.0097
2	Wayne Owens (D)	54.5	529,585	—0.0097
	1970 State Population:		1,059,273	
	Ideal District Population:		529,637	

Election Results, 1968-1972

Vote for U.S. Representative
(Adjusted to new district boundaries)

District	1968	1970	1972
1	136,283 R (67.9%)	94,087 D (51.5%)	127,027 D (55.4%)
	64,451 D (32.1%)	87,018 R (47.7%)	96,296 R (42.0%)
2	133,300 R (62.0%)	99,800 R (52.4%)	132,832 D (54.5%)
	81,762 D (38.0%)	88,412 D (46.4%)	107,185 R (44.0%)
State	269,583 R (64.8%)	186,818 R (50.1%)	259,859 D (54.9%)
	146,213 D (35.2%)	182,499 D (48.9%)	203,481 R (43.0%)

(Continued on p. 197)

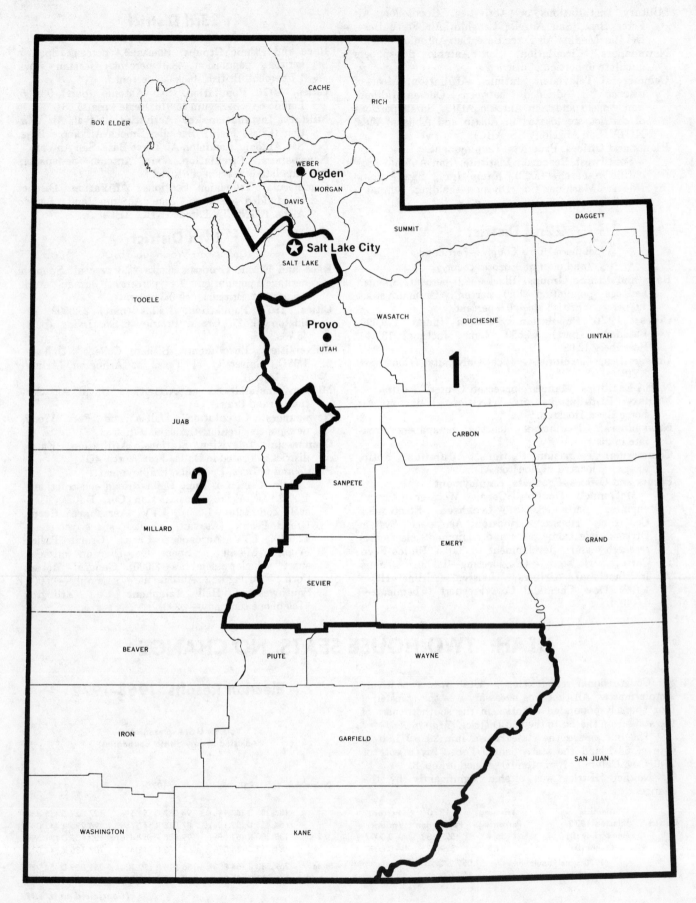

(Continued from p. 195)

Voting Age Population

District	Voting Age Population	Voting Age Population 18, 19, 20	Voting Age Population 65 and Over	Median Age of Voting Age Population
1	313,955	35,455 (11.3%)	36,314 (11.6%)	38.5
2	319,015	28,168 (8.8%)	41,469 (13.0%)	40.1
State	632,973	63,622 (10.1%)	77,784 (12.3%)	39.3

Income and Occupation

District	Median Family Income	White Collar Workers	Blue Collar Workers	Service Workers	Farm Workers
1	$9,080	50.1%	32.7%	12.6%	4.6%
2	9,537	53.5	32.0	12.8	1.7
State	9,320	51.9	32.3	12.7	3.1

Education: School Years Completed

District	Completed 4 years of High School	Completed 4 years of College	Completed 5 years or less of School	Median School years completed
1	67.6%	13.5%	2.9%	12.5
2	66.9	14.5	2.5	12.5
State	67.3	14.0	2.7	12.5

Housing and Residential Patterns

	Housing		Urban-Suburban-Nonmetropolitan Breakdown		
District	Owner Occupied Units	Renter Occupied Units	Urban	Suburban	Nonmetro-politan
1	72.0%	28.0%	28.0%	40.5%	31.5%
2	66.9	33.1	33.2	53.4	13.4
State	69.4	30.6	30.6	47.0	22.4

1st District

(East—Ogden, Provo)

Race and Ethnic Groups. Spanish heritage population 3.6 percent. British stock 2.4 percent.

Cities, 1970 Population. Ogden 69,508, Provo 53,140, Bountiful 27,891, Orem 25,769.

Universities, Enrollment. Brigham Young University (Provo—26,616), Utah State University (Logan—8,842), Weber State College (Ogden—9,818).

Military Installations or Activities. Ogden Defense Depot, Ogden; Hill Air Force Base, Ogden.

Newspapers, Circulation. Salt Lake City newspapers circulate in portion of district.

Commercial Television Stations, Affiliation. Entire district is located in Salt Lake City ADI.

Plants and Offices, Products, Employment.
   United States Steel Corp., Provo (Steel—2,000). **Thiokol Chemical Corp.,** Brigham City (Wasatch Division—rocket propellants—1,660). **Fram Corp.,** Clearfield (Filters—2,000).

2nd District

(West—Salt Lake City)

Race and Ethnic Groups. Spanish heritage population 4.7 percent. British stock 3.0 percent.

Cities, 1970 Population. Salt Lake City 175,755, East Millcreek 26,575, Holladay 23,006, Murray 21,157.

Universities, Enrollment. Southern Utah State College (Cedar City—1,947), University of Utah (Salt Lake City—21,668).

Military Installations or Activities. Dugway Proving Grounds, Dugway; Tooele Army Depot, Tooele.

Newspapers, Circulation. Salt Lake City Deseret News (Eve—80,304), Salt Lake City Tribune (Morn—109,601).

Commercial Television Stations, Affiliation. KCPX-TV, Salt Lake City (ABC); KSL-TV, Salt Lake City (CBS); KUTV, Salt Lake City (NBC). Entire district is located in Salt Lake City ADI.

Plants and Offices, Products, Employment.
   Kennecott Copper Corp., Magna (Copper smelting and refining—2,280). **Kennecott Copper Corp.,** Salt Lake City (Administrative offices—1,500). **Eimco Corp.,** Salt Lake City (Mining machinery and equipment—1,900). **Hercules Inc.,** Bacchus (Chemical Propulsion Division—solid propellants—1,600). **Sperry Rand Corp.,** Salt Lake City (Data processing equipment—2,000). **Union Pacific Railroad Co.,** Salt Lake City (Railroad—2,000). **Mountain States Telephone and Telegraph Co.,** Salt Lake City (Telephone company—3,200). **Health Industries Inc.,** Salt Lake City (Holding company—2,200).

VIRGINIA: TEN HOUSE SEATS, NO CHANGE

Virginia originally enacted a congressional redistricting bill in February 1971, one of the first states to do so. *(Map p. 200)*

The plan provided for combining two sets of Republican representatives in common districts—Reps. Richard H. Poff of the old 6th District and William C. Wampler of the old 9th District, whose homes were placed together in the new 9th District; and Reps. William Lloyd Scott

of the old 8th District and Joel T. Broyhill of the old 10th District, combined in the new 10th.

Poff was appointed to the Virginia Supreme Court in 1972, while Scott made a successful run for the U.S. Senate in November 1972. Both Wampler and Broyhill were re-elected in 1972.

A fifth Republican representative from Virginia—J. Kenneth Robinson of the 7th District—saw his district considerably altered by redistricting, with the addition of large numbers of conservative Democrats and the transfer of Republicans out of the district.

The redistricting bill passed the state House on Feb. 24, 1971, by a vote of 73-25. The state Senate passed the measure Feb. 26 by a vote of 30-4. It was signed March 1 by Gov. Linwood Holton (R).

But the state's redistricting plan was upset March 1, 1972, by a three-judge federal court. A population variance of 7.3 percent between the largest and smallest districts was cited by the court as excessive and clearly in violation of the constitutional requirement of one-man, one-vote.

The state had argued that the large variance was justified by the desire to preserve the seniority of incumbent representatives and to maintain the integrity of political subdivision boundaries.

Faced with drawing new congressional district lines, the state legislature quickly enacted a new bill, reducing the population variance from 7.3 percent to 0.67 percent. The House of Delegates passed the legislation March 6, 1972, by a vote of 84-9; the state Senate followed suit March 10, 34-1. Gov. Holton signed it March 11. Judicial approval was given March 14.

Major changes in the 1971 lines occurred in southern Virginia districts. Five counties were moved from the 4th District to the 5th, including the home county of 4th District Rep. Watkins M. Abbitt (D), Appomattox. Abbitt, finding himself in the same district as Rep. W. C. (Dan) Daniel (D), announced his retirement.

Elsewhere in the state, relatively minor changes were made, although all districts were affected. A total of three counties and one city were divided, compared with only one county (Fairfax) in the 1971 bill.

District	Member Elected 1972	Winning Percentage	1970 Population	Percent Variance
1	Thomas N. Downing (D)	78.1	465,981	+ 0.2435
2	G. William Whitehurst (R)	73.4	464,692	—0.0337
3	David E. Satterfield III (D)	99.8	465,289	+ 0.0946
4	Robert W. Daniel Jr. (R)	47.1	465,738	+ 0.1912
5	W. C. (Dan) Daniel (D)	99.9	462,807	—0.4392
6	M. Caldwell Butler (R)	54.6	464,356	—0.1060
7	J. Kenneth Robinson (R)	66.2	465,342	+ 0.1060
8	Stanford E. Parris (R)	44.4	464,038	—0.1744
9	William C. Wampler (R)	71.9	465,136	+ 0.0617
10	Joel T. Broyhill (R)	56.3	465,115	+ 0.0572

1970 State Population: 4,648,494
Ideal District Population: 464,849

Election Results, 1968-1972

Vote for U.S. Representative
(Adjusted to new district boundaries)

District	1968	1970	1972
1	79,714 D (62.9%)	58,473 D (83.2%)	100,901 D (78.1%)
	16,516 R (25.8%)	11,791 R (16.8%)	28,310 R (21.9%)
2	51,197 D (57.9%)	35,639 D (56.1%)	79,672 R (73.4%)
	32,667 R (36.9%)	27,860 R (43.9%)	28,803 D (26.6%)
3	90,266 D (60.0%)	69,790 D (67.0%)	102,523 D (99.8%)
	60,076 R (40.0%)	34,077 R (32.7%)	—
4	78,036 D (63.8%)	50,224 D (53.6%)	57,520 R (47.1%)
	18,517 R (15.2%)	23,908 R (25.5%)	45,776 D (37.5%)

District	1968	1970	1972
5	88,233 D (58.7%)	68,028 D (72.3%)	83,772 D (99.9%)
	30,590 R (20.4%)	20,302 R (21.6%)	—
6	88,888 R (78.7%)	64,762 R (72.0%)	75,189 R (54.6%)
	16,890 D (15.0%)	25,207 D (28.0%)	53,928 D (39.2%)
7	66,829 R (41.4%)	61,250 R (63.1%)	89,120 R (66.2%)
	62,966 D (39.0%)	35,877 D (36.9%)	45,513 D (33.8%)
8	61,729 R (62.4%)	43,651 R (58.6%)	60,446 R (44.4%)
	37,262 D (37.6%)	30,883 D (41.4%)	51,444 D (37.8%)
9	93,233 R (62.1%)	66,671 R (60.3%)	98,178 R (71.9%)
	54,966 D (36.6%)	43,975 D (39.7%)	36,000 D (26.4%)
10	82,844 R (60.4%)	59,474 R (56.1%)	101,138 R (56.3%)
	54,313 D (39.6%)	46,616 D (43.9%)	78,638 D (43.7%)
State	613,843 D (47.3%)	464,712 D (51.4%)	627,298 D (49.4%)
	551,889 R (42.5%)	413,746 R (45.8%)	589,573 R (46.4%)

Voting Age Population

District	Voting Age Population	Voting Age Population 18, 19, 20	Voting Age Population 65 and Over	Median Age of Voting Age Population
1	302,235	28,188 (9.3%)	36,609 (12.1%)	40.2
2	309,989	37,629 (12.1%)	26,418 (8.5%)	34.5
3	313,655	24,305 (10.9%)	41,447 (13.2%)	42.0
4	295,660	26,645 (9.0%)	35,189 (11.9%)	41.2
5	298,768	23,299 (7.8%)	43,922 (14.7%)	43.2
6	314,562	25,087 (8.0%)	49,522 (15.7%)	43.7
7	308,737	27,054 (8.8%)	46,122 (14.9%)	42.4
8	287,085	21,653 (7.5%)	16,263 (5.7%)	36.2
9	310,012	29,270 (9.4%)	45,309 (14.6%)	42.7
10	311,284	20,518 (6.6%)	26,773 (8.6%)	40.3
State	3,051,904	263,643 (8.6%)	367,492 (12.0%)	40.6

Income and Occupation

District	Median Family Income	White Collar Workers	Blue Collar Workers	Service Workers	Farm Workers
1	$ 8,490	45.4%	37.5%	14.3%	2.8%
2	8,733	55.2	29.5	14.9	0.4
3	9,945	55.4	31.5	12.7	0.4
4	8,294	39.3	43.0	14.6	3.1
5	7,471	31.9	51.8	9.8	6.5
6	8,594	43.3	41.4	13.2	2.1
7	7,952	39.9	42.0	12.7	5.4
8	13,146	68.3	20.9	10.4	0.4
9	6,608	32.6	52.0	10.7	4.7
10	14,457	75.5	15.0	8.8	0.7
State	9,045	49.0	36.2	12.1	2.7

Education: School Years Completed

District	Completed 4 years of High School	Completed 4 years of College	Completed 5 years or less of School	Median School years completed
1	45.9%	10.0%	11.2%	11.5
2	53.4	11.1	7.4	12.1
3	47.6	12.7	8.3	11.7
4	36.8	6.4	14.8	10.4
5	32.7	5.9	17.9	9.4

District	Completed 4 years of High School	Completed 4 years of College	Completed 5 years or less of School	Median School years completed
6	45.0	9.2	11.1	11.3
7	39.8	9.3	13.2	10.5
8	72.1	24.5	3.6	12.7
9	29.4	5.6	19.1	8.8
10	76.9	28.6	2.7	12.9
State	47.8	12.3	11.0	11.7

Housing and Residential Patterns

	Housing		Urban-Suburban-Nonmetropolitan Breakdown		
District	Owner Occupied Units	Renter Occupied Units	Urban	Suburban	Nonmetropolitan
1	65.7%	34.3%	55.6%	7.1%	37.3%
2	51.1	48.9	66.3	33.7	—
3	59.2	40.8	53.6	46.4	—
4	61.2	38.8	34.8	39.2	26.0
5	71.4	28.6	—	12.7	87.3
6	69.7	30.3	31.5	24.8	43.7
7	67.7	32.3	—	8.1	91.9
8	54.7	45.3	—	98.1	1.9
9	72.2	27.8	—	—	100.0
10	48.4	51.6	—	100.0	—
State	62.1	37.9	24.2	37.0	38.8

1st District

(East—Newport News, Hampton)

Race and Ethnic Groups. Blacks 30.1 percent. German stock 0.9 percent, British stock 0.8 percent.

Cities, 1970 Population. Newport News 138,177, Hampton 120,779.

Universities, Enrollment. Christopher Newport College (Newport News—1,768), College of William and Mary (Williamsburg—7,211), Hampton Institute (Hampton—2,313).

Military Installations or Activities. Fort Eustis, Newport News; Fort Monroe, Hampton; Naval Administrative Command—Armed Forces Staff College, Williamsburg; Naval Weapons Laboratory, Dahlgren; Naval Weapons Station, Yorktown; Naval Weapons Station—Skiffes Creek Annex, Yorktown; Cape Charles Air Force Station, Kiptopeke; Langley Air Force Base, Hampton.

NASA Facilities. Langley Research Center, Hampton; Wallops Station, Wallops Island.

Newspapers, Circulation. Newport News Press (MxSat—52,594).

Commercial Television Stations, Affiliation. WVEC-TV, Hampton (ABC). Major portion of district is located in Norfolk ADI. Small portions of district are located in Richmond ADI and Washington, D.C. ADI.

Plants and Offices, Products, Employment.

Newport News Shipbuilding and Drydock Co., Newport News (Shipbuilding—20,000). **Basic Construction Co.**, Newport News (General building contractor—1,500). **Smithfield Foods Inc.**, Newport

News (Holding company, meat packer—1,600). **Colonial Williamsburg Foundation**, Williamsburg (Motels, restaurants, gift shops—at least 2,800).

2nd District

(Norfolk, Virginia Beach)

Race and Ethnic Groups. Blacks 21.6 percent. British stock 1.0 percent. German stock 0.7 percent.

Cities, 1970 Population. Norfolk 307,936, part of Virginia Beach 156,756.

Universities, Enrollment. Norfolk State College (Norfolk—5,678), Old Dominion University (Norfolk—9,666).

Military Installations or Activities. Fleet Anti-Air Warfare Training Center—Dam Neck, Virginia Beach; Operational Control Office—U.S. Atlantic Fleet, Norfolk; Naval Air Station, Norfolk; Naval Air Station—Oceana, Virginia Beach; Naval Amphibious Base—Little Creek, Norfolk; Naval Communications Station, Norfolk; Naval Air Rework Facility, Norfolk; Naval Supply Center, Norfolk; Naval Station, Norfolk; Public Works Center, Norfolk; Naval Degaussing Station, Norfolk.

Newspapers, Circulation. Norfolk Virginian-Pilot (Morn—128,387), Norfolk Ledger-Star (Eve—104,056).

Commercial Television Stations, Affiliation. WTAR-TV, Norfolk (CBS). Entire district is located in Norfolk ADI.

Plants and Offices, Products, Employment.

Norfolk Shipbuilding and Drydock Co., Norfolk (Shipbuilding—2,370). **Tidewater Construction Co.**, Virginia Beach (Heavy construction—1,500). **Landmark Communications Inc.**, Norfolk (Newspaper publishing, radio and television broadcasting—HQ—1,300). **Ford Motor Co.**, Norfolk (Automobiles—1,850). **Colonial Stores Inc.**, Norfolk (Grocery stores—1,000).

3rd District

(Richmond and Suburbs)

Race and Ethnic Groups. Blacks 26.2 percent. German stock 0.7 percent, British stock 0.7 percent.

Cities, 1970 Population. Richmond 249,471, Lakeside 11,130.

Universities, Enrollment. University of Richmond (Richmond—4,992), Virginia Commonwealth University (Richmond—14,892), Virginia Union University (Richmond—1,313).

Military Installations or Activities. Defense General Supply Center, Richmond.

Newspapers, Circulation. Richmond News-Leader (Eve—118,137), Richmond Times-Dispatch (Morn—140,806).

Commercial Television Stations, Affiliation. WTVR-TV, Richmond (CBS); WWBT, Richmond (NBC); WXEX-TV, Richmond (ABC). Entire district is located in Richmond ADI.

Plants and Offices, Products, Employment.

Daniel International Corp., Richmond (Daniel

Construction Co. Division—general building contractor—1,000). **Reynolds Metals Co.**, Richmond (Headquarters—1,000). **Reynolds Metals Co.**, Richmond (North Plant—roll foil—at least 1,010). **E.I. du Pont de Nemours and Co.**, Richmond (Cello acetate film—4,500). **E.I. du Pont de Nemours and Co.**, Richmond (Cello acetate film—1,000). **Philip Morris Inc.**, Richmond (Chewing gum—1,000). **Philip Morris Inc.**, Richmond (Cigarettes—1,100). **American Brands Inc.**, Richmond (American Tobacco Co. Division—tobacco products—1,250). **A.H. Robins Co. Inc.**, Richmond (Pharmaceuticals—HQ—1,350). **Friedman-Marks Inc.**, Richmond (Clothing—1,100). **Southeast Media Inc.**, Richmond (Newspaper publishing—1,000). **Media General Inc.**, Richmond (Holding company, newspaper publishing, broadcasting—HQ—1,600). **Thalhimer Bros. Inc.**, Richmond (Department stores—HQ—1,500). **Garfinckel Brooks Brothers**, Richmond (Miller & Rhodes Division—department stores—2,350). **United Transit Co.**, Richmond (Holding company—2,000). **Seaboard Coast Line Industries Inc.**, Richmond (Holding company, railroad—HQ—2,000). **Virginia Electric and Power Co.**, Richmond (Electric utility—HQ—1,500). **Chesapeake and Potomac Telephone Co.**, Richmond (Telephone company—4,000). **Richmond Corp.**, Richmond (Holding company, life insurance—5,000). **United Virginia Bankshares**, Richmond (Holding company—2,950). **City of Richmond**, Richmond (City government—8,000). **Commonwealth of Virginia**, Richmond (State government—total employment 63,800).

4th District

(Southeast—Portsmouth, Chesapeake)

Race and Ethnic Groups. Blacks 37.1 percent. German stock 0.5 percent, British stock 0.4 percent.

Cities, 1970 Population. Portsmouth 110,968, Chesapeake 89,584, Petersburg 36,105, Hopewell 23,472.

Universities, Enrollment. Virginia State College (Petersburg—3,684).

Military Installations or Activities. Fort Lee, Petersburg; Naval Weapons Station Annex, St. Juliens Creek; Naval Hospital, Portsmouth; Norfolk Naval Shipyard, Portsmouth; Fort Lee Air Force Station, Petersburg.

Newspapers, Circulation. Norfolk newspapers circulate in major portion of district.

Commercial Television Stations, Affiliation. WAVY-TV, Portsmouth (NBC); WYAH-TV, Portsmouth (None). District is divided between Norfolk ADI and Richmond ADI.

Plants and Offices, Products, Employment.

Union Camp Corp., Franklin (Paper products—2,000). **Hercules Inc.**, Hopewell (Chemicals—1,200). **Allied Chemical Corp.**, Hopewell (Industrial gases—1,000). **Firestone Tire and Rubber Co.**, Hopewell (Synthetic rubber—1,250). **Brown and Williamson Tobacco Co.**, Petersburg (Cigarettes—4,400). **General Electric Co.**, Portsmouth (Television receivers—3,000). **Standard Brands Inc.**, Suffolk (Planters Division—nuts—1,500). **ITT Gwaltney Inc.**, Smithfield (Meat packing—1,010).

5th District

(South—Danville)

Race and Ethnic Groups. Blacks 29.0 percent. German stock 0.2 percent, British stock 0.2 percent.

Cities, 1970 Population. Danville 46,419, Martinsville 19,665.

Universities, Enrollment. Longwood College (Farmville—2,363).

Newspapers, Circulation. Richmond newspapers circulate in portion of district.

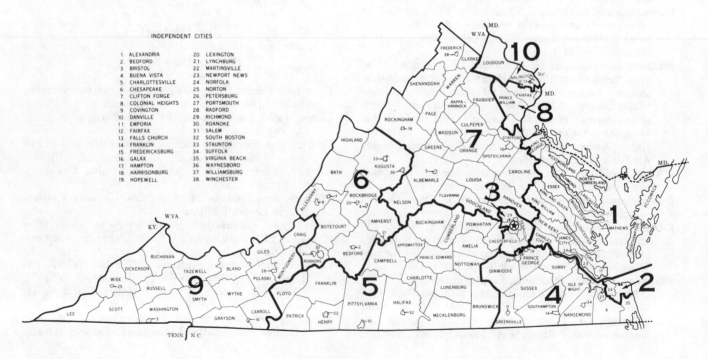

INDEPENDENT CITIES

1.	ALEXANDRIA	20.	LEXINGTON
2.	BEDFORD	21.	LYNCHBURG
3.	BRISTOL	22.	MARTINSVILLE
4.	BUENA VISTA	23.	NEWPORT NEWS
5.	CHARLOTTESVILLE	24.	NORFOLK
6.	CHESAPEAKE	25.	NORTON
7.	CLIFTON FORGE	26.	PETERSBURG
8.	COLONIAL HEIGHTS	27.	PORTSMOUTH
9.	COVINGTON	28.	RADFORD
10.	DANVILLE	29.	RICHMOND
11.	EMPORIA	30.	ROANOKE
12.	FAIRFAX	31.	SALEM
13.	FALLS CHURCH	32.	SOUTH BOSTON
14.	FRANKLIN	33.	STAUNTON
15.	FREDERICKSBURG	34.	SUFFOLK
16.	GALAX	35.	VIRGINIA BEACH
17.	HAMPTON	36.	WAYNESBORO
18.	HARRISONBURG	37.	WILLIAMSBURG
19.	HOPEWELL	38.	WINCHESTER

Commercial Television Stations, Affiliation. Most of district is divided between Roanoke ADI and Richmond ADI. Small portion of district is located in Greensboro (North Carolina) ADI.

Plants and Offices, Products, Employment.

Goodyear Tire and Rubber Co., Danville (Tires—1,120). **Dan River Inc.**, Danville (Dan River Mills—fabric mill—at least 9,000). **Burlington Industries Inc.**, Clarksville (Dyeing, finishing worsted fabric—1,200). **Fieldcrest Mills Inc.**, Fieldale (Bedspreads, blankets, towels—1,470). **Sale Knitting Co. Inc.**, Martinsville (Knit outerwear—HQ—1,800). **E.I. du Pont de Nemours and Co. Inc.**, Martinsville (Synthetic fiber—4,450). **American Furniture Co. Inc.**, Martinsville (Furniture—HQ—2,140). **Bassett Furniture Industries**, Bassett (Furniture—6,000). **Mead Corp.**, Stanleytown (Stanley Furniture Co. Division—furniture—1,600). **Lane Co. Inc.**, Altavista (Furniture—HQ—1,750).

6th District

(West—Roanoke, Lynchburg)

Race and Ethnic Groups. Blacks 12.2 percent. British stock 0.5 percent, German stock 0.3 percent.
Cities, 1970 Population. Roanoke 92,115, Lynchburg 54,083, Staunton 24,504, Salem 21,982.
Universities, Enrollment. Hollins College (Hollins College—1,133), Lynchburg College (Lynchburg—2,044), Roanoke College (Salem—1,355), Virginia Military Institute (Lexington—1,154), Washington and Lee University (Lexington—1,612).
Military Installations or Activities. Bedford Air Force Station, Bedford.
Newspapers, Circulation. Roanoke Times (Morn—64,561), Roanoke World-News (Eve—51,817).
Commercial Television Stations, Affiliation. WLVA-TV, Lynchburg (ABC); WDBJ-TV, Roanoke (CBS); WRFT-TV, Roanoke (ABC); WSLS-TV, Roanoke (NBC). Most of district is located in Roanoke ADI. Small portion of district is located in Richmond ADI.
Plants and Offices, Products, Employment.

Mead Corp., Lynchburg (Lynchburg Foundry Co. Division—gray iron foundry—2,050). **Rubatex Corp.**, Bedford (Fabricated rubber products—1,000). **Westvaco Corp.**, Covington (Paperboard mill, organic chemicals—at least 2,300). **Hercules Inc.**, Covington (Polypropylene fiber—1,600). **E. I. du Pont de Nemours and Co. Inc.**, Waynesboro (Synthetic, organic fibers—2,800). **General Electric Co.**, Salem (Industrial controls—3,450). **General Electric Co.**, Lynchburg (Microwave equipment—1,500). **General Electric Co.**, Lynchburg (Rectifiers—1,750). **General Electric Co.**, Waynesboro (Industrial controls—2,000). **Craddock-Terry Shoe Corp.**, Lynchburg (Shoes—HQ—1,800). **Burlington Industries Inc.**, Glasgow (Lee's Carpet Division—wool rugs—2,000). **Kenrose Manufacturing Co. Inc.**, Roanoke (Dresses—1,500). **Singer Co.**, Roanoke (Johnson-Carper Furniture Division—furniture—1,200). **Philip Morris Inc.**, Staunton (American Safety Razor Products—razors, blades—1,000). **Norfolk and Western Railway Co.**, Roanoke (Railroad—HQ—5,000). **Chesapeake and Ohio Railway Co.**, Clifton Forge (Railroad terminal, freight yard—1,000). **Appalachian Power Co.**, Roanoke (Electric utility—3,700). **Dominion Bankshares Corp.**, Roanoke (Bank holding company—1,100).

7th District

(North—Charlottesville, Winchester)

Race and Ethnic Groups. Blacks 15.0 percent. German stock 0.4 percent, British stock 0.4 percent.
Cities, 1970 Population. Charlottesville 38,952, Winchester 14,670, Harrisonburg 14,632, Fredericksburg 14,477.
Universities, Enrollment. Madison College (Harrisonburg—4,579), University of Virginia (Charlottesville—12,351), Mary Washington College (Fredericksburg—2,111).
Military Installations or Activities. Vint Hill Farm Station (Army), Warrenton.
Commercial Television Stations, Affiliation. WSVA-TV, Harrisonburg (ABC). Most of district is divided between Washington, D.C. ADI and Richmond ADI. Small portion of district is located in Harrisonburg ADI.
Plants and Offices, Products, Employment.

FMC Corp., Front Royal (American Viscose Corp.—nylon, rayon—2,000). **FMC Corp.**, Fredericksburg (American Viscose Corp.—cellophane products—1,700). **Air Control Window Corp. of Va.**, Milford (Aluminum windows, jalousies—1,300). **Sperry Rand Corp.**, Charlottesville (Marine communications systems—1,100). **Stromberg Carlson Corp.**, Charlottesville (Telephone, telegraph apparatus—1,000). **ITT Continental Baking Co. Inc.**, Crozet (Morton Frozen Foods—frozen foods—1,400).

8th District

(Northeast—Washington, D.C. Suburbs, Alexandria)

Race and Ethnic Groups. Blacks 6.6 percent. German stock 1.5 percent, British stock 1.2 percent.
Cities, 1970 Population. Alexandria 110,446, Woodbridge-Marumsco 25,237, Long Branch 21,571, part of Annandale 15,176.
Military Installations or Activities. Fort Belvoir, Alexandria; Cameron Station (Army), Alexandria; Marine Corps Air Station, Quantico; Marine Corps Development and Education Command, Quantico; Naval Hospital, Quantico.
Newspapers, Circulation. Washington, D.C. newspapers circulate throughout district.
Commercial Television Stations, Affiliation. Entire district is located in Washington, D.C. ADI.
Plants and Offices, Products, Employment.

International Business Machines Corp., Manassas (Computer components—1,500). **City of Alexandria**, Alexandria (City government—1,350).

9th District

(Southwest—Bristol)

Race and Ethnic Groups. German stock 0.2 percent, British stock 0.2 percent.

Cities, 1970 Population. Bristol 14,857, Radford 11,596, Pulaski 10,232.

Universities, Enrollment. Radford College (Radford—3,860), Virginia Polytechnic Institute and State University (Blacksburg—14,492).

Newspapers, Circulation. Roanoke newspapers circulate in major portion of district.

Commercial Television Stations, Affiliation. Most of district is divided between Roanoke ADI and Bristol (Tennessee) ADI. Small portion of district is located in Bluefield (West Virginia) ADI.

Plants and Offices, Products, Employment.

Westmoreland Coal Co., Big Stone Gap (Coal mining and shipping—1,030). **Pittston Co.**, Dante (Clinchfield Coal Co.—coal mining—2,900). **Hercules Inc.**, Radford (Radford Ordnance Works—gunpowder, ammunition—4,900). **Mead Corp.**, Radford (Lynchburg Foundry Division—pipe—1,260). **Marion—Harwood Manufacturing Corp.**, Marion (Underwear, pajamas—1,000). **Washington Mills Co. Inc.**, Fries (Broad woven fabric—1,200). **Celanese Corp.**, Narrows (Acetate rayon—2,800). **Brunswick Corp.**, Marion (Billiard tables, furniture—1,220).

10th District

(Northeast—Washington, D.C. Suburbs, Arlington County)

Race and Ethnic Groups. Blacks 4.8 percent. Spanish heritage population 3.0 percent. German stock 1.6 percent, British stock 1.6 percent.

Cities, 1970 Population. Arlington County 174,739, Jefferson 25,488, Fairfax 22,027, McLean 17,765.

Universities, Enrollment. George Mason University (Fairfax—3,140).

Military Installations or Activities. Fort Myer, Arlington County.

Newspapers, Circulation. Washington, D.C. newspapers circulate throughout district.

Commercial Television Stations, Affiliation. Entire district is located in Washington, D.C. ADI.

Plants and Offices, Products, Employment.

Mars Inc., McLean (M & M Mars Division—candy—2,500). **Greyhound Airport Service Inc.**, Arlington (Airport bus and limousine service—1,000). **County of Arlington**, Arlington (County government—at least 3,550). **Fairfax Hospital Assn.**, Falls Church (Hospital—1,450).

WASHINGTON: SEVEN HOUSE SEATS, NO CHANGE

Because of the failure of the Washington legislature to enact new congressional district lines during the year 1971, a three-judge federal panel assumed jurisdiction over the redistricting process. On Feb. 26, 1972, the court appointed a special "master" to draw the new boundaries. He was Dr. Richard L. Morrill, University of Washington geography professor and an expert in economic geography and spatial analysis.

The court laid down a list of instructions to be followed by the master. They were designed to make the process as non-political as possible. Among the directives: "The master shall carefully avoid contacts of any kind—formal or informal—with any incumbent congressman or state legislator, any person who has announced (or plans to announce) his candidacy for public office..." and "any representative of a political party and anyone representing or acting for any of the aforesaid persons...." Furthermore, the master was charged with ignoring precinct borders and voting patterns while drawing the new districts.

Morrill designed an overlapping system of districts—49 state Senate districts, combined in groups of seven to form new congressional districts. Districts were assembled by census tract and other census divisions. The court accepted Morrill's plan April 28, 1972, with a change only in the numbering system.

Despite the non-political nature of the process of drawing the new lines, none of the state's seven districts changed hands politically.

In fact, of the six incumbents who sought re-election in 1972, four increased their percentage of the vote over 1970 (Hansen, Foley, Hicks, Adams) and one was within five-tenths of a percent of his 1970 percentage (McCormack). Only Rep. Lloyd Meeds (D) of the 2nd District saw a sharp decline in his 1970 percentage—and he still won with 60.5 percent of the vote.

In the 1st District, formerly solidly Republican, the retirement of Rep. Thomas Pelly (R) and the challenge of a strong Democratic candidate made the race very close in 1972. The Republicans held it with 50.3 percent of the vote.

District	Member Elected 1972	Winning Percentage	1970 Population	Percent Variance
1	Joel Pritchard (R)	50.3	480,589	—1.3212
2	Lloyd Meeds (D)	60.5	481,041	—1.2284
3	Julia Butler Hansen (D)	66.3	522,755	+ 6.7734
4	Mike McCormack (D)	52.1	478,372	—1.7765
5	Thomas S. Foley (D)	81.3	485,034	—0.4086
6	Floyd V. Hicks (D)	72.1	480,020	—1.4381
7	Brock Adams (D)	85.4	481,358	—1.1633

1970 State Population: 3,409,169
Ideal District Population: 487,024

Election Results, 1968-1972

Vote for U.S. Representative
(Adjusted to new district boundaries)

District	1968	1970	1972
1	Not Available	Not Available	107,581 R (50.3%) 104,959 D (49.1%)
2	NA	NA	114,900 D (60.5%) 75,181 R (39.5%)
3	NA	NA	122,933 D (66.3%) 62,564 R (33.7%)
4	NA	NA	97,593 D (52.1%) 89,812 R (47.9%)
5	NA	NA	150,580 D (81.3%) 34,742 R (18.7%)
6	NA	NA	126,349 D (72.1%) 48,914 R (27.9%)

District	1968	1970	1972
7	NA	NA	140,307 D (85.4%)
			19,889 R (12.1%)
State	623,630 D (51.8%)	608,508 D (59.5%)	857,621 D (65.9%)
	576,072 R (47.8%)	403,946 R (39.5%)	438,683 R (33.7%)

Voting Age Population

District	Voting Age Population	Voting Age Population 18, 19, 20	Voting Age Population 65 and Over	Median Age of Voting Age Population
1	342,536	28,552 (8.3%)	51,826 (15.1%)	42.5
2	307,168	23,921 (7.8%)	42,222 (13.7%)	41.1
3	340,318	36,652 (10.8%)	46,926 (13.8%)	40.9
4	305,387	23,648 (7.7%)	45,650 (14.9%)	44.1
5	322,260	31,766 (9.9%)	52,955 (16.4%)	43.7
6	312,265	23,720 (7.6%)	43,825 (14.0%)	42.2
7	315,043	22,364 (7.1%)	38,816 (12.3%)	41.8
State	2,244,939	190,628 (8.5%)	322,209 (14.4%)	42.3

Income and Occupation

District	Median Family Income	White Collar Workers	Blue Collar Workers	Service Workers	Farm Workers
1	$12,084	64.9%	23.0%	11.9%	0.2%
2	10,563	48.0	36.9	12.3	2.8
3	9,736	42.3	42.3	13.0	2.4
4	9,206	43.6	34.2	12.1	10.1
5	9,164	48.6	28.5	15.7	7.2
6	10,481	50.1	35.6	13.3	1.0
7	11,706	54.3	32.5	12.8	0.4
State	10,404	50.7	32.9	13.1	3.3

Education: School Years Completed

District	Completed 4 years of High School	Completed 4 years of College	Completed 5 years or less of School	Median School years completed
1	72.3%	21.2%	2.0%	12.7
2	63.7	11.1	2.3	12.4
3	58.5	9.1	3.0	12.2
4	57.9	10.2	4.6	12.2
5	63.4	11.9	3.5	12.4
6	62.5	10.7	2.6	12.3
7	65.7	14.3	3.4	12.4
State	63.5	12.7	3.1	12.4

Housing and Residential Patterns

	Housing		Urban-Suburban-Nonmetropolitan Breakdown		
District	Owner Occupied Units	Renter Occupied Units	Urban	Suburban	Nonmetro-politan
1	59.3%	40.7%	67.7%	32.3%	—
2	72.2	27.8	11.2	54.5	34.3%
3	70.8	29.2	0.1	35.6	64.3

	Housing		Urban-Suburban-Nonmetropolitan Breakdown		
District	Owner Occupied Units	Renter Occupied Units	Urban	Suburban	Nonmetro-politan
4	67.2	32.8	—	24.8	75.2
5	67.7	32.3	35.2	24.1	40.7
6	68.9	31.1	32.1	46.7	21.2
7	62.7	37.3	42.8	57.2	—
State	66.8	33.2	26.7	39.3	34.0

1st District

(Northern Seattle and Suburbs)

Race and Ethnic Groups. Canadian stock 5.9 percent, Norwegian stock 3.2 percent, British stock 2.7 percent.

Cities, 1970 Population. Part of Seattle 325,260, part of Bellevue 50,143, part of Mountlake Terrace 14,550.

Universities, Enrollment. Seattle Pacific College (Seattle—1,984), University of Washington (Seattle—33,478).

Newspapers, Circulation. Seattle Post-Intelligencer (MxSat—185,420), Seattle Times (ExSat—231,958).

Commercial Television Stations, Affiliation. KING-TV, Seattle (NBC); KIRO-TV, Seattle (CBS); KOMO-TV, Seattle (ABC). Entire district is located in Seattle-Tacoma ADᵀ.

Plants and Offices, Products, Employment.
Safeco Corp., Seattle (Insurance, holding company—HQ—6,330). **Marine Bancorporation**, Seattle (Holding company—HQ—3,000). **Marshall Field and Co.**, Seattle (Frederick and Nelson—department store—1,500). **Allied Stores Corp.**, Seattle (The Bon Marché—department store—at least 1,500). **Seattle Times Co.**, Seattle (Newspaper publishing—1,200). **United Air Lines Inc.**, Seattle (Airline—2,700). **Loomis Corp.**, Seattle (Trucking, holding company—1,500). **S. Howard Wright Construction Co.**, Seattle (General contractor—1,000). **Pacific Northwest Bell Telephone Co.**, Seattle (Telephone company—at least 1,010). **Seattle City Light**, Seattle (Electric utility—2,010).

2nd District

(Northwest—Bellingham, Everett)

Race and Ethnic Groups. Canadian stock 5.4 percent, Norwegian stock 2.5 percent.

Cities, 1970 Population. Everett 53,721, Bellingham 39,371, part of Edmonds 21,631, Lynnwood 17,024.

Universities, Enrollment. Western Washington State College (Bellingham—10,868).

Military Installations or Activities. Naval Air Station, Whidbey Island, Oak Harbor; Blaine Air Force Station, Blaine.

Newspapers, Circulation. Seattle newspapers circulate in portion of district.

Commercial Television Stations, Affiliation. KVOS-TV, Bellingham (CBS). District is divided between Bellingham ADI and Seattle-Tacoma ADI.

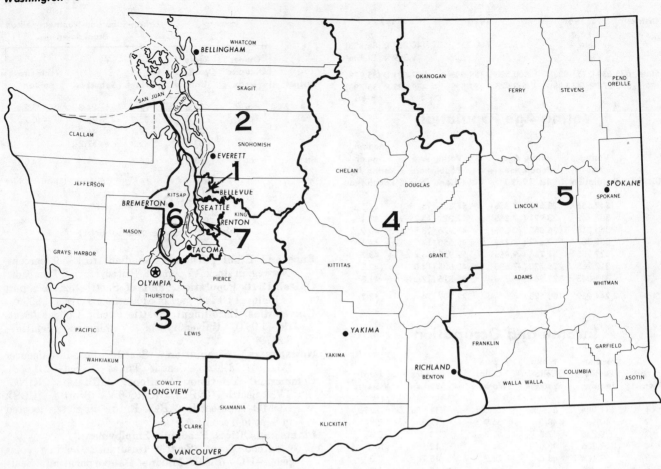

Plants and Offices, Products, Employment.
Scott Paper Co., Everett (Northwest Division—paper products—2,000). **Georgia-Pacific Corp.**, Bellingham (Pulp, paper, paperboard, chemicals—1,200). **Intalco Aluminum Corp.**, Ferndale (Aluminum refinery—1,360). **Boeing Co.**, Everett (747 Division—aircraft—2,000).

paperboard—HQ—1,750). **Weyerhaeuser Co.**, Snoqualmie Falls (Sawmill and logging—1,500). **Simpson Timber Co.**, Shelton (Simpson International Division—plywood, lumber, doors, logs—2,000). **Bechtel Corp.**, Centralia (Heavy construction and engineering—1,000).

3rd District

(Southwest—Olympia)

Race and Ethnic Groups. Canadian stock 2.9 percent, German stock 2.2 percent.

Cities, 1970 Population. Fort Lewis 38,018, Longview 28,347, Olympia 23,089, Parkland 20,992.

Military Installations or Activities. Fort Lewis, Tacoma; Naval Facility, Pacific Beach; Makah Air Force Station, Neah Bay; McChord Air Force Base, Tacoma.

Newspapers, Circulation. Seattle and Tacoma newspapers circulate in portions of district.

Commercial Television Stations, Affiliation. Most of district is located in Seattle-Tacoma ADI. Small portion of district is located in Portland (Oregon) ADI.

Plants and Offices, Products, Employment.
Longview Fibre Co., Longview (Pulp, paper,

4th District

(Central—Yakima, Vancouver)

Race and Ethnic Groups. Spanish heritage population 4.5 percent. Canadian stock 2.6 percent, German stock 1.7 percent.

Cities, 1970 Population. Yakima 45,589, Vancouver 42,461, Richland 26,284, Wenatchee 16,912.

Universities, Enrollment. Central Washington State College (Ellensburg—7,425).

Military Installations or Activities. Yakima Firing Center, Yakima.

AEC-Owned, Contractor-Operated Installations. Hanford Facilities, Richland. (Small portion in 5th District.)

Commercial Television Stations, Affiliation. KAPP-TV, Yakima (ABC); KIMA-TV, Yakima (CBS, ABC); KNDO-TV, Yakima (NBC). District is divided between Yakima ADI, Spokane ADI and Portland (Oregon) ADI.

Plants and Offices, Products, Employment.
    Aluminum Co. of America, Vancouver (Aluminum—1,400). **Aluminum Co. of America**, Wenatchee (Aluminum—1,000). **Douglas United Nuclear Inc.**, Richland (Nuclear reactors—1,000). **Atlantic Richfield Co.**, Richland (Chemical processing—1,500). **Battelle Memorial Institute**, Richland (Pacific Northwest Labs Division—scientific research—1,280). **Crown Zellerbach Corp.**, Camas (Mill Division—paper products—2,700). **Wineberg Properties Inc.**, Vancouver (Logging, real estate holding—1,000).

5th District

(East—Spokane)

Race and Ethnic Groups. Canadian stock 3.5 percent, German stock 2.4 percent.

Cities, 1970 Population. Spokane 170,529, Walla Walla 23,621, Pullman 20,477, Opportunity 16,605.

Universities, Enrollment. Eastern Washington State College (Cheney—6,618), Gonzaga University (Spokane—2,873), Walla Walla College (College Place—1,820), Washington State University (Pullman—14,539), Whitman College (Walla Walla—1,062), Whitworth College (Spokane—1,654).

AEC-Owned, Contractor-Operated Installations. Hanford Facilities, Richland. (Mostly in 4th District; only a small portion in 5th.)

Military Installations or Activities. Mica Peak Air Force Station, Mica; Othello Air Force Station, Othello.

Newspapers, Circulation. Spokane Spokesman-Review (Morn—81,576), Spokane Chronicle (Eve—68,601).

Commercial Television Stations, Affiliation. KHQ-TV, Spokane (NBC); KREM-TV, Spokane (ABC); KXLY-TV, Spokane (CBS). Most of district is located in Spokane ADI. Small portion of district is located in Yakima ADI.

Plants and Offices, Products, Employment.
    Kaiser Aluminum and Chemical Corp., Spokane (Mead Works—aluminum reduction—1,390). **Kaiser Aluminum and Chemical Corp.**, Spokane (Trentwood Works—rolling mill—1,500). **Vinnell-Dravo-Lockheed-Mannix.**, Coulee Dam (Powerhouse construction—1,120). **Spokane Dry Goods Co.**, Spokane (The Crescent—department store—1,170).

6th District

(Puget Sound—Bremerton, Tacoma)

Race and Ethnic Groups. Blacks 3.0 percent. Canadian stock 3.4 percent, German stock 2.6 percent.

Cities, 1970 Population. Part of Tacoma 154,171 (all but 417 residents of Tacoma), part of Lakes District 48,068 (all but 91 residents of Lakes District), Bremerton 35,315, part of Auburn 21,563 (all but 272 residents of Auburn).

Universities, Enrollment. Pacific Lutheran University (Tacoma—3,038), University of Puget Sound (Tacoma—3,652).

Military Installations or Activities. Polaris Missile Facility, Pacific, Bremerton; Naval Hospital, Bremerton; Naval Supply Center, Puget Sound, Bremerton; Naval Torpedo Station, Keyport; Puget Sound Naval Shipyard, Bremerton.

Newspapers, Circulation. Tacoma News Tribune (Eve—97,711). Seattle newspapers also circulate in portions of district.

Commercial Television Stations, Affiliation. KTNT-TV, Tacoma (None); KTVW-TV, Tacoma (None). Entire district is located in Seattle-Tacoma ADI.

Plants and Offices, Products, Employment.
    Weyerhaeuser Co., Tacoma (Headquarters—1,400). **American Smelting and Refining Co.**, Tacoma (Smelting and refining of copper—1,000). **Boeing Co.**, Auburn (Fabrication and Service Division—airplane components—3,500). **W. R. Grace and Co.**, Tacoma (Nalley's Fine Foods—food specialties—1,400).

7th District

(Southern Seattle and Suburbs)

Race and Ethnic Groups. Blacks 7.3 percent. Canadian stock 4.4 percent, British stock 2.3 percent.

Cities, 1970 Population. Part of Seattle 205,970, Renton 25,248, Mercer Island 19,092, part of Kent 17,330.

Universities, Enrollment. Seattle University (Seattle—3,170).

Newspapers, Circulation. Seattle newspapers circulate throughout district.

Commercial Television Stations, Affiliation. Entire district is located in Seattle-Tacoma ADI.

Plants and Offices, Products, Employment.
    Boeing Co., Seattle (Headquarters—1,000). **Boeing Co.**, Renton (Commercial Airplane Division—aircraft—31,000). **Boeing Co.**, Kent (Aerospace Group—missiles, space vehicles, surface transportation—10,000). **Pacific Car and Foundry Co.**, Seattle (Kenworth Motor Truck Division—trucks, special vehicles, railroad cars—1,000). **Pacific Car and Foundry Co.**, Renton (Railroad cars, industrial equipment, forgings—1,980). **Lockheed Shipbuilding and Construction Co.**, Seattle (Colby Crane and Manufacturing Co.—shipbuilding, heavy construction—1,800). **Todd Shipyards Corp.**, Seattle (Shipbuilding and repair—1,200). **Bethlehem Steel Corp.**, Seattle (Steel mill—1,400). **Northwest Airlines Inc.**, Seattle (Airline—1,500). **Seattle Transit System**, Seattle (Bus lines—1,080). **Puget Sound Power and Light Co.**, Renton (Electric utility—at least 1,010).

Glossary and Sources

For a complete explanation of all terms used in this book and a list of source material, consult the details included in the Introduction.

WEST VIRGINIA: FOUR HOUSE SEATS, LOSS OF ONE

West Virginia was one of three states which lost population during the 1960s. The state's population decline cost it a congressional seat. *(Map p. 207)*

A congressional redistricting bill eliminating the old 4th District, represented by Ken Hechler (D), was passed by the state House Feb. 25, 1971, by a vote of 60-39. The measure was approved by the Senate 27-7 on March 6 and received the signature of Gov. Arch A. Moore (R) on March 13, 1971.

At the time of redistricting, all five of the state's incumbent representatives were Democrats in strong Democratic districts. The smallest winning margin in 1970 was 61.5 percent, in the 1st District. Consequently, the Democratic state legislature was faced with the unpleasant task of eliminating one Democrat.

In eliminating the 4th District, the legislature placed its incumbent, Hechler, in the same district (the new 4th) as Rep. James Kee. A majority of the counties in the new district were formerly in Kee's district. But the city of Huntington, the largest in the new district, is Hechler's hometown. Hechler and Kee fought each other in the May, 1972 primary, Hechler emerging the victor by a large majority.

Elsewhere in the state, the incumbents did not find themselves in much trouble as a result of redistricting.

District	Member Elected 1972	Winning Percentage	1970 Population	Percent Variance
1	Robert H. Mollohan (D)	69.4	436,337	+ 0.0637
2	Harley O. Staggers (D)	70.0	436,140	+ 0.0185
3	John M. Slack (D)	63.7	434,165	—0.4343
4	Ken Hechler (D)	61.0	437,595	+ 0.3522

1970 State Population: 1,744,237
Ideal District Population: 436,059

Election Results, 1968-1972

Vote for U.S. Representative
(Adjusted to new district boundaries)

District	1968	1970	1972
1	103,746 D (54.5%)	72,399 D (61.5%)	130,062 D (69.4%)
	86,550 R (45.5%)	45,405 R (38.5%)	57,274 R (30.6%)
2	110,105 D (63.0%)	69,174 D (64.5%)	128,286 D (70.0%)
	64,654 R (37.0%)	38,044 R (35.5%)	54,949 R (30.0%)
3	104,631 D (59.0%)	73,606 D (64.3%)	118,346 D (63.7%)
	72,733 R (41.0%)	40,850 R (35.7%)	67,441 R (36.3%)
4	115,598 D (68.2%)	78,827 D (71.8%)	100,600 D (61.0%)
	53,988 R (31.8%)	28,578 R (28.2%)	64,242 R (39.0%)
State	434,080 D (61.0%)	288,006 D (65.3%)	477,294 D (66.2%)
	277,925 R (39.0%)	152,877 R (34.7%)	243,906 R (33.8%)

Voting Age Population

District	Voting Age Population	Voting Age Population 18, 19, 20	Voting Age Population 65 and over	Median Age of Voting Age Population
1	294,238	21,721 (7.4%)	50,495 (17.2%)	45.6
2	295,549	27,279 (9.2%)	53,305 (18.0%)	45.6
3	284,672	20,593 (7.2%)	44,587 (15.7%)	44.8
4	285,038	23,139 (8.1%)	46,097 (16.2%)	45.3
State	1,159,497	92,732 (8.0%)	194,484 (16.8%)	45.3

Income and Occupation

District	Median Family Income	White Collar Workers	Blue Collar Workers	Service Workers	Farm Workers
1	$8,457	39.1%	47.1%	12.9%	0.9%
2	6,437	36.9	45.3	13.8	4.0
3	7,574	44.3	42.6	12.2	0.9
4	7,039	41.7	45.7	12.0	0.6
State	7,414	40.5	45.2	12.7	1.6

Education: School Years Completed

District	Completed 4 years of High School	Completed 4 years of College	Completed 5 years or less of School	Median School years completed
1	47.6%	6.9%	6.8%	11.6
2	38.1	6.9	11.0	9.9
3	43.3	7.2	10.5	10.8
4	37.2	6.1	14.7	10.1
State	41.6	6.8	10.7	10.6

Housing and Residential Patterns

District	Housing — Owner Occupied Units	Housing — Renter Occupied Units	Urban	Suburban	Nonmetropolitan
1	71.1%	28.9%	17.3%	21.9%	60.8%
2	70.0	30.0	—	—	100.0
3	68.2	31.8	16.5	36.4	47.1
4	66.0	34.0	17.0	16.0	67.0
State	68.9	31.1	12.7	18.6	68.7

1st District

(North Central—Northern Panhandle, Wheeling)

Cities, 1970 Population. Wheeling 48,280, Parkersburg 44,198, Weirton 27,236, Fairmont 25,919.
Universities, Enrollment. Bethany College (Bethany—1,138), Fairmont State College (Fairmont—3,680),

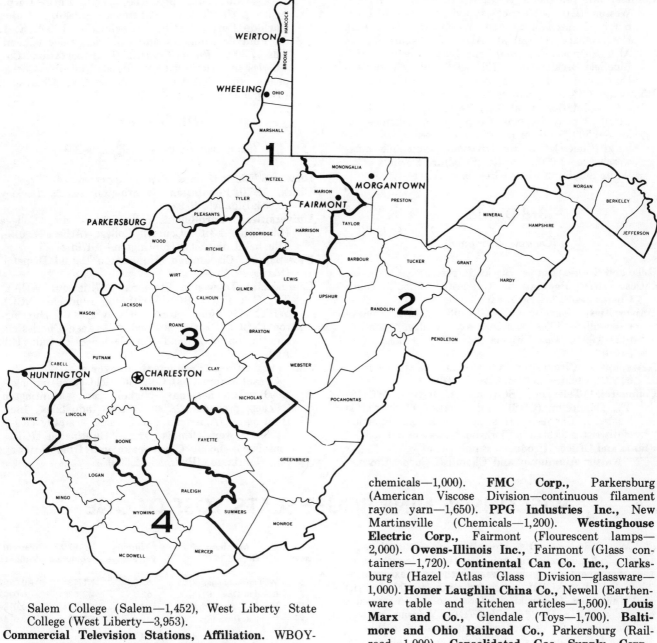

chemicals—1,000). **FMC Corp.**, Parkersburg (American Viscose Division—continuous filament rayon yarn—1,650). **PPG Industries Inc.**, New Martinsville (Chemicals—1,200). **Westinghouse Electric Corp.**, Fairmont (Flourescent lamps—2,000). **Owens-Illinois Inc.**, Fairmont (Glass containers—1,720). **Continental Can Co. Inc.**, Clarksburg (Hazel Atlas Glass Division—glassware—1,000). **Homer Laughlin China Co.**, Newell (Earthenware table and kitchen articles—1,500). **Louis Marx and Co.**, Glendale (Toys—1,700). **Baltimore and Ohio Railroad Co.**, Parkersburg (Railroad—1,000). **Consolidated Gas Supply Corp.**, Clarksburg (Natural gas production, transmission—1,600).

2nd District

(East—Morgantown, Eastern Panhandle)

Race and Ethnic Groups. Blacks 3.5 percent.
Cities, 1970 Population. Morgantown 29,387, Martinsburg 14,602.
Universities, Enrollment. Alderson-Broaddus College (Philippi—1,067), Shepherd College (Shepherdstown—2,054), West Virginia Institute of Technology (Montgomery—2,411), West Virginia University (Morganton—17,941), West Virginia Wesleyan College (Buckhannon—1,675).

Salem College (Salem—1,452), West Liberty State College (West Liberty—3,953).
Commercial Television Stations, Affiliation. WBOY-TV, Clarksburg (NBC); WTAP-TV, Parkersburg (NBC); WTRF-TV, Wheeling (NBC; ABC on per program basis). Most of district is located in Wheeling-Steubenville (Ohio) ADI. Small portions of district are located in Parkersburg ADI and Clarksburg-Weston ADI.
Plants and Offices, Products, Employment.
National Steel Corp., Weirton (Weirton Steel Division—sheet and strip steel, tin plate—12,000). **Wheeling-Pittsburgh Steel Corp.**, Follansbee (Steel—1,000). **McDonough Co.**, Parkersburg (Hand tools, ready mixed cement—HQ—1,000). **E. I. du Pont de Nemours and Co. Inc.**, Parkersburg (Acrylic resin—2,800). **E. I. du Pont de Nemours and Co. Inc.**, Washington (Plastics materials, synthetic resins—2,700). **Borg-Warner Corp.**, Washington (Marbon Division—industrial

Commercial Television Stations, Affiliation. WDTV, Weston (CBS). District is divided between Pittsburgh (Pennsylvania) ADI, Washington, D.C. ADI, Harrisonburg (Virginia) ADI, Clarksburg-Weston ADI, Roanoke (Virginia)-Lynchburg (Virginia) ADI, Bluefield-Beckley-Oak Hill ADI and Charleston-Huntington ADI.

Plants and Offices, Products, Employment.

Consolidation Coal Co., Osage (Coal mining—1,000). **Union Carbide Corp.,** Alloy (Ferrous alloys—1,500). **General Motors Corp.,** Martinsburg (Chevrolet Motor Division—automobile parts warehouse—1,000). **White Sulphur Springs Co.,** White Sulphur Springs (Greenbriar Hotel—1,100).

3rd District

(Central—Charleston)

Race and Ethnic Groups. Blacks 3.1 percent.
Cities, 1970 Population. Charleston 71,505, South Charleston 16,333, St. Albans 14,356.
Universities, Enrollment. Glenville State College (Glenville—1,617), Morris Harvey College (Charleston—3,095), West Virginia State College (Institute—3,590).
Newspapers, Circulation. Charleston Gazette (Morn—60,994), Charleston Mail (Eve—60,378).
Commercial Television Stations, Affiliation. WCHS-TV, Charleston (CBS). Major portion of district is located in Charleston-Huntington ADI. Small portion of district is located in Clarksburg-Weston ADI.
Plants and Offices, Products, Employment.

Kaiser Aluminum and Chemical Corp., Ravens-

wood (Aluminum products—3,550). **FMC Corp.,** South Charleston (Chemicals—1,040). **Union Carbide Corp.,** Institute (Chemicals—2,000). **E. I. du Pont de Nemours and Co. Inc.,** Belle (Chemicals—2,300). **Penn Central Transportation Co.,** Charleston (Railroad—at least 1,010). **Chesapeake and Potomac Telephone Co.,** Charleston (Telephone company—1,000).

4th District

(South and West—Huntington, Beckley)

Race and Ethnic Groups. Blacks 6.9 percent.
Cities, 1970 Population. Huntington 74,322, Beckley 19,884, Bluefield 15,921.
Universities, Enrollment. Bluefield State College (Bluefield—1,316), Concord College (Athens—2,019), Marshall University (Huntington—9,476).
Newspapers, Circulation. Huntington Herald Dispatch (MxSat—52,124).
Commercial Television Stations, Affiliation. WOAY-TV, Oak Hill (ABC); WHIS-TV, Bluefield (NBC); WHTN-TV, Huntington (ABC); WSAZ-TV, Huntington (NBC). District is divided between Charleston-Huntington ADI and Bluefield-Beckley-Oak Hill ADI.
Plants and Offices, Products, Employment.

Consolidation Coal Co., Bluefield (Coal mining—1,000). **International Nickel Inc.,** Huntington (Nickel products—2,750). **ACF Industries Inc.,** Huntington (American Car Division—railway cars—1,400). **Owens-Illinois Inc.,** Huntington (Glass containers—1,650). **Chesapeake and Ohio Railway Co.,** Huntington (Railroad—2,500).

WISCONSIN: NINE HOUSE SEATS, LOSS OF ONE

Wisconsin enacted a bipartisan congressional redistricting bill generally favorable to the re-election of all the incumbent representatives, with one exception—Alvin E. O'Konski (R), whose far northern 10th District was eliminated. O'Konski was forced to run in the same district with Rep. David R. Obey (D) of Wausau and lost.

Because of the divided political situation in Wisconsin—the legislature was split between a Republican senate and a Democratic assembly, while the Governor, Patrick L. Lucey, was a Democrat—neither party was able to gain an advantage. Therefore, a compromise bill was seen as the only one having a realistic chance of enactment and approval by the Governor. *(Map p. 211)*

The bill passed the assembly Oct. 22, 1971, by a vote of 66-32. The Senate concurred Oct. 28, and the Governor signed the bill Nov. 15, 1971.

District	Member Elected 1972	Winning Percentage	1970 Population	Percent Variance
1	Les Aspin (D)	64.4	490,817	—0.0130
2	Robert W. Kastenmeier (D)	68.2	490,941	+ 0.0122
3	Vernon W. Thomson (R)	54.7	491,034	+ 0.0311
4	Clement J. Zablocki (D)	75.7	490,690	—0.0389
5	Henry S. Reuss (D)	77.3	490,708	—0.0352

District	Member Elected 1972	Winning Percentage	1970 Population	Percent Variance
6	William A. Steiger (R)	65.8	490,934	+ 0.0107
7	David R. Obey (D)	62.8	491,030	+ 0.0303
8	Harold V. Froehlich (R)	50.4	490,974	+ 0.0189
9	Glenn R. Davis (R)	61.4	490,805	—0.0154

1970 State Population: 4,417,933
Ideal District Population: 490,881

Election Results, 1968-1972

Vote for U.S. Representative
(Adjusted to new district boundaries)

District	1968	1970	1972
1	90,362 R (51.0%)	88,365 D (60.9%)	122,973 D (64.4%)
	86,866 D (49.0%)	56,665 R (39.1%)	66,665 R (34.9%)
2	103,810 D (56.8%)	97,340 D (64.3%)	148,136 D (68.2%)
	78,830 R (43.2%)	53,413 R (35.3%)	68,167 R (31.4%)
3	115,191 R (62.7%)	72,720 R (51.0%)	112,905 R (54.7%)
	68,644 D (37.3%)	69,564 D (48.8%)	91,953 D (44.6%)
4	126,406 D (65.9%)	111,166 D (73.5%)	149,078 D (75.7%)
	65,270 R (34.0%)	38,073 R (25.2%)	45,003 R (22.8%)
5	100,336 D (60.9%)	86,388 D (71.7%)	127,273 D (77.3%)
	63,488 R (38.6%)	33,243 R (27.6%)	33,627 R (20.4%)

District	1968	1970	1972
6	115,175 R (62.6%)	94,779 R (62.2%)	130,701 R (65.8%)
	66,190 D (36.0%)	55,631 D (36.5%)	63,643 D (32.0%)
7	119,990 R (63.1%)	95,831 D (60.5%)	135,385 R (62.8%)
	70,140 D (36.9%)	61,001 R (38.5%)	80,207 R (37.2%)
8	127,412 R (71.0%)	77,930 R (52.5%)	101,634 R (50.4%)
	52,024 D (29.0%)	69,342 D (46.7%)	97,795 D (48.5%)
9	119,724 R (63.9%)	88,751 R (56.8%)	128,230 R (61.4%)
	67,351 D (35.9%)	66,858 D (42.8%)	76,585 D (36.7%)
State	895,442 R (54.6%)	740,485 D (55.8%)	1,012,821 D (56.2%)
	741,767 D (45.2%)	576,575 R (43.5%)	767,139 R (42.6%)

Voting Age Population

District	Voting Age Population	Voting Age Population 18, 19, 20	Voting Age Population 65 and Over	Median Age of Voting Age Population
1	308,067	26,687 (8.7%)	47,330 (15.4%)	42.4
2	320,073	32,457 (10.1%)	47,750 (14.9%)	40.2
3	319,883	32,217 (10.1%)	62,886 (19.7%)	45.4
4	321,228	21,855 (6.8%)	46,599 (14.5%)	44.2
5	331,186	28,818 (8.7%)	56,890 (17.2%)	42.9
6	315,364	26,935 (8.5%)	57,438 (18.2%)	44.8
7	311,292	24,468 (7.9%)	59,559 (19.1%)	46.4
8	302,289	23,638 (7.8%)	54,318 (18.0%)	45.0
9	298,212	20,893 (7.0%)	40,015 (13.4%)	42.5
State	2,827,584	237,970 (8.4%)	472,782 (16.7%)	43.7

Income and Occupation

District	Median Family Income	White Collar Workers	Blue Collar Workers	Service Workers	Farm Workers
1	$10,478	41.1%	42.2%	13.4%	3.3%
2	10,397	48.8	28.3	14.4	8.5
3	8,485	37.1	32.8	15.1	15.0
4	11,285	47.4	40.0	12.4	0.2
5	10,067	46.6	38.4	14.8	0.2
6	9,727	38.1	41.6	12.8	7.5
7	8,424	38.2	37.5	13.9	10.4
8	9,190	39.4	39.9	12.9	7.8
9	12,479	51.0	35.2	10.6	3.2
State	10,065	43.3	37.3	13.4	6.0

Education: School Years Completed

District	Completed 4 years of High School	Completed 4 years of College	Completed 5 years or less of School	Median School years completed
1	54.4%	8.8%	4.3%	12.1
2	61.9	15.8	3.1	12.4
3	52.0	8.3	4.1	12.1
4	54.7	8.7	4.5	12.1
5	50.3	8.5	5.9	12.0
6	51.7	7.6	4.2	12.1
7	48.9	7.1	5.9	11.8
8	52.0	7.5	5.7	12.1
9	65.0	16.0	2.6	12.4
State	54.5	9.8	4.5	12.1

Housing and Residential Patterns

	Housing		Urban-Suburban-Nonmetropolitan Breakdown		
District	Owner Occupied Units	Renter Occupied Units	Urban	Suburban	Nonmetro-politan
1	70.3%	29.7%	35.5%	23.4%	41.1%
2	64.2	35.8	35.3	23.8	40.9
3	75.7	24.3	10.4	6.0	83.6
4	64.0	36.0	46.2	53.8	—
5	43.0	57.0	100.0	—	—
6	74.6	25.4	11.5	20.8	67.7
7	79.1	20.9	6.6	2.5	90.9
8	77.8	22.2	28.8	27.5	43.7
9	77.7	22.3	—	86.1	13.9
State	69.1	30.9	30.5	27.1	42.4

1st District

(Southeast—Racine, Kenosha)

Race and Ethnic Groups. Blacks 3.3 percent. German stock 4.2 percent, Italian stock 1.8 percent.

Cities, 1970 Population. Racine 95,212, Kenosha 78,832, Janesville 46,435, Beloit 35,736.

Universities, Enrollment. Beloit College (Beloit—1,783), Carthage College (Kenosha—1,807), Kenosha Technical Institute (Kenosha—4,612), University of Wisconsin, Parkside (Kenosha—4,343), University of Wisconsin (Whitewater—8,867).

Commercial Television Stations, Affiliation. District is divided between Milwaukee ADI, Chicago (Illinois) ADI, Rockford (Illinois) ADI and Madison ADI.

Plants and Offices, Products, Employment.
Anaconda American Brass Co., Kenosha (Brass and copper wires and rods—1,100). **General Motors Corp.**, Janesville (GM Assembly Divison—automobile and truck assembly—4,500). **American Motors Corp.**, Kenosha (Automobiles—4,800). **American Motors Corp.**, Kenosha (Automobiles—4,800). **The Bunker Ramo Corp.**, Delevan (Automotive Products Group—automotive products—1,000). **Beloit Corp.**, Beloit (Paper making machinery and equipment—HQ—2,500). **J. I. Case Co.**, Racine (Farm machinery and equipment—HQ—1,150). **J. I. Case Co.**, Racine (Tractors and engines—1,900). **S. C. Johnson and Son Inc.**, Racine (Waxes, polishes, insecticides—HQ—1,100). **Parker Pen Co.**, Janesville (Pens, pencils—1,000). **Western Publishing Co. Inc.**, Racine (Commercial printing, book publishing—HQ—2,280).

2nd District

(South—Madison)

Race and Ethnic Groups. German stock 3.9 percent, Norwegian stock 1.9 percent.

Cities, 1970 Population. Madison 173,164, Beaver Dam 14,213, Monona 10,490.

Universities, Enrollment. University of Wisconsin, Madison (Madison—33,943).

Newspapers, Circulation. Madison Wisconsin State Journal (Morn—73,620).

Commercial Television Stations, Affiliation. WISC-TV, Madison (CBS); WMTV, Madison (NBC). Most of district is located in Madison ADI. Small portions of district are located in Milwaukee ADI and Green Bay ADI.

Plants and Offices, Products, Employment.

Olin Corp., Baraboo (Badger Ordnance Plant—small arms, ammunition—3,500). **Deere and Co.**, Horicon (Farm machinery and equipment—1,000). **Oscar Mayer and Co. Inc.**, Madison (Processed meat products—HQ—3,700).

3rd District

(West—La Crosse, Eau Claire)

Race and Ethnic Groups. Polish stock 3.8 percent, German stock 3.6 percent.

Cities, 1970 Population. La Crosse 51,162, part of Eau Claire 43,669, Menomonie 11,277.

Universities, Enrollment. University of Wisconsin, Stout (Menomonie—5,231), University of Wisconsin (Eau Claire—8,679), University of Wisconsin (La Crosse—7,009), University of Wisconsin (Platteville—4,708), University of Wisconsin (River Falls—4,255).

Military Installations or Activities. Osceola Air Force Station, Osceola.

Commercial Television Stations, Affiliation. WEAU-TV, Eau Claire (NBC); WKBT, La Crosse (CBS primary; ABC). Major portion of district is located in La Crosse-Eau Claire ADI. Small portions of district are located in Minneapolis (Minnesota)-St. Paul (Minnesota) ADI, Cedar Rapids (Iowa)-Waterloo (Iowa) ADI and Madison ADI.

Plants and Offices, Products, Employment.

Uniroyal Inc., Eau Claire (Tires—2,580). **Trane Co.**, La Crosse (Air conditioners, heaters—HQ—3,500). **National Presto Industries Inc.**, Eau Claire (Appliances, holding company—3,120).

4th District

(Southern Milwaukee and Suburbs)

Race and Ethnic Groups. German stock 6.2 percent, Polish stock 6.0 percent.

Cities, 1970 Population. Part of Milwaukee 226,541, West Allis 71,720, Wauwatosa 58,669, Greenfield 24,427.

Universities, Enrollment. Alverno College (Milwaukee—1,101).

Newspapers, Circulation. Milwaukee newspapers circulate throughout district.

Commercial Television Stations, Affiliation. Entire district is located in Milwaukee ADI.

Plants and Offices, Products, Employment.

Babcock and Wilcox Co. Inc., Milwaukee (Tubular Products Division—carbon alloys, stainless steel—1,050). **General Motors Corp.**, Oak Creek (Delco Electronics Division—missile control systems—3,500).

American Motors Corp., Milwaukee (Automobile bodies—1,200). **A-T-O Inc.**, Cudahy (George J. Meyer Manufacturing Co. Division—food products machinery—1,000). **Rex Chainbelt Inc.**, Milwaukee (Handling, packaging, conveyor machinery—HQ—3,000). **Rex Chainbelt Inc.**, Milwaukee (Nordberg Division—engines, machinery and equipment, metal products—2,400). **Harnischfeger Corp.**, Milwaukee (Construction and excavating equipment—HQ—3,300). **Bucyrus-Erie Co.**, South Milwaukee (Excavating machinery—HQ—2,500). **Briggs and Stratton Corp.**, Milwaukee (Gasoline engines, automobile locks, equipment—HQ—5,090). **Allis-Chalmers Corp.**, Milwaukee (Construction machinery, farm machinery—HQ—10,000). **Perfex Inc.**, Milwaukee (Heating, air conditioning, food products machinery—HQ—1,000). **Kearney and Trecker Corp.**, Milwaukee (Machine tools—HQ—1,500). **Louis Allis Co.**, Milwaukee (Electric motors and equipment—HQ—1,900). **Allen-Bradley Co.**, Milwaukee (Electronic industrial controls—HQ—6,420). **General Electric Co.**, Milwaukee (X-Ray equipment—2,000). **Ladish Co.**, Cudahy (Forgings, pipe fittings, valves—HQ—4,700). **Milprint Inc.**, Milwaukee (Commercial printing—HQ—1,200). **St. Lukes Hospital Association**, Milwaukee (Hospital—1,800).

5th District

(Northern Milwaukee)

Race and Ethnic Groups. Blacks 21.3 percent. German stock 7.3 percent, Polish stock 1.7 percent.

Cities, 1970 Population. Part of Milwaukee 490,708.

Universities, Enrollment. Marquette University (Milwaukee—10,295), University of Wisconsin (Milwaukee—22,277), Milwaukee School of Engineering (Milwaukee—2,431).

Newspapers, Circulation. Milwaukee Journal (Eve—356,312), Milwaukee Sentinel (Morn—172,494).

Commercial Television Stations, Affiliation. WISN-TV, Milwaukee (CBS); WITI-TV, Milwaukee (ABC); WTMJ-TV, Milwaukee (NBC), WVTV, Milwaukee (None). Entire district is located in Milwaukee ADI.

Plants and Offices, Products, Employment.

American Motors Corp., Milwaukee (Automobile bodies—3,000). **A. O. Smith Corp.**, Milwaukee (Motor vehicle parts and accessories—HQ—7,500). **Falk Corp.**, Milwaukee (Transmission equipment, steel foundry—HQ—2,600). **American Can Co.**, Milwaukee (Canco Division—metal containers—1,010). **Johnson Service Co.**, Milwaukee (Temperature controls—HQ—1,400). **Cutler-Hammer Inc.**, Milwaukee (Industrial controls and equipment—HQ—1,000). **Master Lock Co. Inc.**, Milwaukee (Locks, padlocks, lockers—1,030). **Miller Brewing Co.**, Milwaukee (Beer—HQ—1,900). **Miller Brewing Co.**, Milwaukee (Beer—at least 1,000). **Joseph Schlitz Brewing Co.**, Milwaukee (Beer—HQ—3,000). **Pabst Brewing Co.**, Milwaukee (Beer—HQ—2,650). **Federated Department Stores**, Milwaukee (Milwaukee Boston Store Division—department store—1,250). **Gimbel Bros. Inc.**, Milwaukee (Department store—4,000). **Journal Co.**, Milwaukee (Newspaper publishing, radio and television broadcasting—HQ—

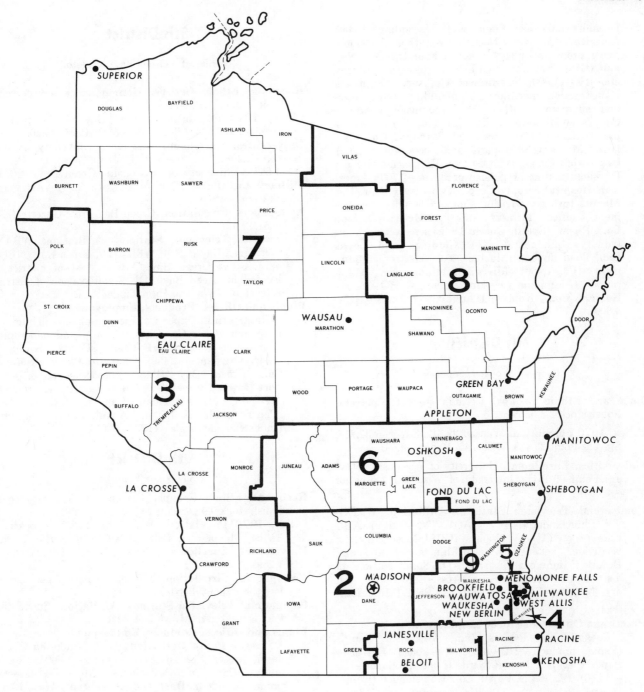

2,000). **Milwaukee and Suburban Transportation,** Milwaukee (Transport company—1,500). **Northwestern Mutual Life Insurance Co.,** Milwaukee (Insurance—HQ—1,500). **City of Milwaukee,** Milwaukee (City government—10,000). **Mount Sinai Medical Center Inc.,** Milwaukee (Hospital—1,100). **Columbus Hospital Inc.,** Milwaukee (Hospital—1,300).

6th District

(East Central—Oshkosh, Sheboygan)

Race and Ethnic Groups. German stock 6.1 percent, Polish stock 0.8 percent.

Cities, 1970 Population. Oshkosh 53,182, Sheboygan 48,549, Fond du Lac 35,716, Manitowoc 33,514.

Universities, Enrollment. Ripon College (Ripon—1,024), University of Wisconsin (Oshkosh—11,811).

Commercial Television Stations, Affiliation. KFIZ-TV, Fond du Lac (None). Fond du Lac has no ADI of its own. Major portion of district is located in Green Bay ADI. Smaller portions of district are located in Milwaukee ADI, Madison ADI, Wausau-Rhinelander ADI, Madison ADI and La Crosse-Eau Claire ADI.

Plants and Offices, Products, Employment.

Kimberly-Clark Corp., Neenah (Paper, cellulose products—HQ—1,000). **Kimberly-Clark Corp.,**

Neenah (Lakeview Plant—creped wadding—1,000). **American Can Co.**, Neenah (Marathon Division—paper products—1,220). **Neenah Foundry Co.**, Neenah (Gray iron and ductile iron castings, patterns, etc.—HQ—1,000). **Manitowoc Co. Inc.**, Manitowoc (Construction machinery, shipbuilding, refrigerators and equipment—HQ—1,250). **Tecumseh Products Co.**, New Holstein (Lauson Engine Division—gasoline engines—1,500). **Rockwell Standard Co.**, Oshkosh (Motor vehicle parts and accessories—1,200). **Brunswick Corp.**, Fond du Lac (Kiekhaefer Mercury Division—marine propulsion products—2,700). **American Hospital Supply Corp.**, Two Rivers (Hamilton Manufacturing Division—home laundry equipment, office furniture—1,600). **McGraw-Edison Co.**, Ripon (Speed Queen Division—electric home laundry equipment—1,300). **Giddings and Lewis Inc.**, Fond du Lac (Machine tools, electronic equipment—HQ—1,450). **Mirro Aluminum Co.**, Manitowoc (Aluminum cooking utensils—HQ—1,400). **Kohler Co.**, Kohler (Plumbing fixtures—HQ—4,600).

7th District

(North—Wausau, Superior)

Race and Ethnic Groups. German stock 5.8 percent, Polish stock 2.3 percent.

Cities, 1970 Population. Wausau 32,812, Superior 32,218, Stevens Point 23,468, Wisconsin Rapids 18,591.

Universities, Enrollment. University of Wisconsin (Stevens Point—9,154), University of Wisconsin (Superior—3,004).

Commercial Television Stations, Affiliation. WAEO-TV, Rhinelander (NBC); WAOW-TV, Wausau (ABC primary); WSAU-TV, Wausau (CBS). Most of district is divided between Wausau-Rhinelander ADI and Duluth (Minnesota)-Superior ADI. Small portions of district are located in La Crosse-Eau Claire ADI and Minneapolis (Minnesota)-St. Paul (Minnesota) ADI.

Plants and Offices, Products, Employment.
    Consolidated Papers Inc., Wisconsin Rapids (Paper products—HQ—4,000). **Nekoosa Edwards Paper Co. Inc.**, Port Edwards (Paper products—HQ—1,500). **St. Regis Paper Co.**, Rhinelander (Rhinelander Paper Co. Division—paper mill—1,000). **Hardware Mutual Casualty**, Stevens Point (Insurance—3,760).

8th District

(Northeast—Green Bay, Appleton)

Race and Ethnic Groups. German stock 4.8 percent, Polish stock 1.2 percent.

Cities, 1970 Population. Green Bay 87,640, part of Appleton 53,574, Allouez 13,746, De Pere 13,370.

Universities, Enrollment. Lawrence University (Appleton—1,456), St. Norbert College (West De Pere—1,647), University of Wisconsin (Green Bay—4,579).

Military Installations or Activities. Antigo Air Force Station, Antigo.

Newspapers, Circulation. Green Bay Press-Gazette (Eve —51,193).

Commercial Television Stations, Affiliation. WBAY-TV, Green Bay (CBS); WFRV-TV, Green Bay (NBC); WLUK-TV, Green Bay (ABC). Most of district is located in Green Bay ADI. Small portion of district is located in Wausau-Rhinelander ADI.

Plants and Offices, Products, Employment.
    Hammermill Paper Co. Inc., Kaukauna (Thilmany Pulp and Paper Co. Division—pulp and paper products—1,600). **Kimberly-Clark Corp.**, Kimberly (Pulp and paper—1,450). **Charmin Paper Products Co.**, Green Bay (Paper products—HQ—1,400). **Fort Howard Paper Co.**, Green Bay (Paper products —HQ—1,900). **American Can Co.**, Green Bay (Paper products—1,200). **Ansul Co.**, Marinette (Industrial chemicals—HQ—1,000).

9th District

(Milwaukee Suburbs)

Race and Ethnic Groups. German stock 5.9 percent, Polish stock 0.9 percent.

Cities, 1970 Population. Waukesha 40,231, Brookfield 32,154, Menomonee Falls 31,701, New Berlin 26,920.

Universities, Enrollment. Carroll College (Waukesha—1,259).

Newspapers, Circulation. Milwaukee newspapers circulate throughout district.

Commercial Television Stations, Affiliation. Entire district is located in Milwaukee ADI.

Plants and Offices, Products, Employment.
    Bangor Punta Operations Inc., Waukesha (Waukesha Motor Co. Division—engines—1,800). **Continental Can Co.**, Milwaukee (Metal containers, products—1,200). **Dart Industries Inc.**, West Bend (Aluminum and stainless steel utensils—2,300). **United Parcel Service**, Elm Grove (Parcel delivery —1,000).

SIX AT LARGE STATES AND THE DISTRICT OF COLUMBIA

Six states and the District of Columbia have only one member of the U.S. House and, therefore, are not divided into congressional districts. *(Maps p. 216-220)*

North Dakota lost its second seat following the 1970 census and elected a single member in 1972 for the first time since 1900.

Alaska, Nevada, Wyoming and the District of Columbia have never had more than one member of the House. In 1970 the District of Columbia was granted the right to elect one non-voting delegate. The election took place in March 1971. The city also had a non-voting delegate in the period 1871-1875.

Delaware has had only one House member since 1823. Vermont was reduced to one member from two in 1933. At one time (1813-23), Vermont had as many as six U.S. Representatives.

State	Member Elected 1972	Winning Percentage	1970 Population	Percent Variance
				Not Applicable
Alaska	Nick Begich (D) [1]	56.2	302,173	
Del.	Pierre S. (Pete) du Pont (R)	62.5	548,104	NA
Nev.	David Towell (R)	52.2	488,738	NA
N.D.	Mark Andrews (R)	72.7	617,761	NA
Vt.	Richard W. Mallary (R)	65.0	444,732	NA
Wyo.	Teno Roncalio (D)	51.7	332,416	NA
D.C.	Walter E. Fauntroy (D)	59.8	756,510	NA

1 Died in plane crash October 1972. Don Young (R) won special election March 6, 1973.

Election Results, 1968-1972

Vote for U.S. Representative

State	1968	1970	1972
Alaska	43,577 R (54.2%)	44,137 D (55.1%)	53,561 D (56.2%)
	36,785 D (45.8%)	35,947 R (44.9%)	41,750 R (43.8%)
Del.	117,827 R (58.7%)	86,125 R (53.7%)	141,237 R (62.5%)
	82,993 D (41.3%)	71,429 D (44.6%)	83,230 D (36.9%)
Nev.	104,136 D (72.1%)	113,496 D (82.5%)	94,113 R (52.2%)
	40,209 R (27.9%)	24,147 R (17.5%)	86,349 D (47.8%)
N.D.	140,076 R (58.8%)	122,056 R (58.1%)	195,360 R (72.7%)
	94,347 D (39.6%)	88,104 D (41.9%)	72,850 D (27.1%)
Vt.	156,956 R (99.9%)	103,812 R (68.0%)	120,924 R (65.0%)
	—	44,417 D (29.1%)	65,062 D (35.0%)
Wyo.	77,363 R (62.7%)	58,456 D (50.3%)	75,632 R (51.7%)
	45,950 D (37.3%)	57,848 R (49.7%)	70,667 R (48.3%)
D.C.	Not Applicable	68,166 D (58.4%) [1]	95,300 D (59.8%)
		29,249 R (25.1%)	39,487 R (24.8%)

1 Election held in March, 1971.

Voting Age Population

State	Voting Age Population	Voting Age Population 18, 19, 20	Voting Age Population 65 and Over	Age of Voting Age Population
Alaska	181,659	17,209 (9.5%)	6,857 (3.8%)	34.0
Del.	350,952	28,693 (8.2%)	43,616 (12.4%)	41.3
Nev.	318,151	21,534 (6.8%)	30,744 (9.7%)	40.5
N.D.	390,141	34,884 (8.9%)	66,363 (17.0%)	44.0
Vt.	287,025	26,665 (9.3%)	47,483 (16.5%)	42.8
Wyo.	212,233	16,914 (8.0%)	30,302 (14.3%)	42.7
D.C.	518,000	46,000 (8.9%)	70,962 (13.7%)	40.2

Income and Occupation

State	Median Family Income	White Collar Workers	Blue Collar Workers	Service Workers	Farm Workers
Alaska	$12,441	55.3%	29.9%	14.4%	0.4%
Del.	10,209	51.0	34.4	12.5	2.1
Nev.	10,687	47.1	26.3	24.7	1.9
N.D.	7,836	42.5	21.0	15.7	20.8
Vt.	8,928	46.3	34.3	14.1	5.3
Wyo.	8,944	46.4	30.3	14.4	8.9
D.C.	9,583	57.9	20.8	21.0	0.3

Education: School Years Completed

State	Completed 4 years of High School	Completed 4 years of College	Completed 5 years or less of School	Median School years completed
Alaska	66.7%	14.1%	7.1%	12.5
Del.	54.6	13.1	5.5	12.2
Nev.	65.2	10.8	2.8	12.4
N.D.	50.3	8.4	5.7	12.0
Vt.	57.1	11.5	3.2	12.2
Wyo.	62.9	11.8	3.5	12.4
D.C.	26.2	8.1	4.1 [1]	12.2

1 1-4 school years completed.

Housing and Residential Patterns

State	Housing		Urban-Suburban-Nonmetropolitan Breakdown		
	Owner Occupied Units	Renter Occupied Units	Urban	Suburban	Nonmetropolitan
Alaska	50.3%	49.7%	—	—	100.0%
Del.	68.0	32.0	14.7%	55.7%	29.6
Nev.	38.5	61.5	40.6	40.1	19.3
N.D.	68.4	31.6	8.6	3.3	88.1
Vt.	69.1	30.9	—	—	100.0
Wyo.	66.4	33.6	—	—	100.0
D.C.	28.2	71.8	100.0	—	—

ALASKA

Race and Ethnic Groups. Blacks 2.9 percent. American Indians 5.4 percent.

Cities, 1970 Population. Anchorage 48,444, Spenard 18,175, Fairbanks 14,943.

Universities, Enrollment. University of Alaska (College —2,958).

Military Installations or Activities. Fort Richardson, Anchorage; Fort Wainwright, Fairbanks; Fort Greely, Big Delta; Naval Communications Station, Adak; Naval Station, Adak; Eielson Air Force Base, Fairbanks; Elmendorf Air Force Base, Anchorage; Galena Airport, Galena; King Salmon Airport, King Salmon; Shemya Air Force Station, Shemya.

Commercial Television Stations, Affiliation. KENI-TV, Anchorage (NBC, ABC); KIMO, Anchorage (ABC); KTVA, Anchorage (CBS); KFAR-TV, Fairbanks (NBC, ABC); KTVF, Fairbanks (CBS); KINY-TV, Juneau (ABC); KIFW-TV, Sitka (CBS). Alaska has no ADIs.

DELAWARE

Race and Ethnic Groups. Blacks 14.3 percent.

Cities, 1970 Population. Wilmington 80,386, Newark 20,681, Dover 17,488, Wilmington Manor-Chelsea-Leedom 10,100.

Universities, Enrollment. Delaware State College (Dover—1,903), University of Delaware (Newark—16,784).

Military Installations or Activities. Naval Facility, Lewes; Dover Air Force Base, Dover.

Newspapers, Circulation. Wilmington Journal (Eve—90,494). Philadelphia (Pa.) newspapers circulate throughout state.

Commercial Television Stations, Affiliation. Most of state is located in Philadelphia (Pennsylvania) ADI. Small portion is located in Salisbury (Maryland) ADI.

Plants and Offices, Products, Employment.
E. I. du Pont de Nemours and Co., Wilmington (Headquarters—8,500). E. I. du Pont de Nemours and Co., Seaford (Nylon fibers—3,000). E. I. du Pont de Nemours and Co., Wilmington (Laboratory—2,300). Hercules Inc., Wilmington (Explosives—HQ—1,500). General Motors Corp., Wilmington (Automobile assembly—3,600). Chrysler Corp., Newark (Automobile assembly—5,000). Phoenix Steel Corp., Claymont (Headquarters—2,300). Electric Hose and Rubber Co., Wilmington (Briggs Rubber Products Division—fabricated rubber products, plastic products—1,300). Joseph Bancroft and Sons Co., Wilmington (Dyeing, bleaching—HQ—1,600). Rapid-American Corp., Clayton (Leeds Travelers Division—luggage—1,000). General Foods Corp., Dover (Jello Division—gelatin products—1,770). Rollins International Inc., Wilmington (Holding company, corporate services—4,200). American Finance Systems Inc., Wilmington (Holding company—HQ—3,570). State of Delaware, Dover (State government—2,000).

NEVADA

Race and Ethnic Groups. Blacks 5.7 percent. Spanish heritage population 5.6 percent.

Cities, 1970 Population. Las Vegas 125,641, Reno 72,863, North Las Vegas 36,216, Paradise 24,459.

Universities, Enrollment. University of Nevada (Reno—7,016), University of Nevada (Las Vegas—4,922).

Military Installations or Activities. Naval Ammunition Depot, Hawthorne; Naval Auxiliary Air Station, Fallon; Fallon Air Force Station, Fallon; Indian Springs Auxiliary Air Field, Indian Springs; Nellis Air Force Base, Las Vegas.

AEC-Owned, Contractor-Operated Installations. Nevada Test Site, Mercury; Nuclear Rocket Development Station, Jackass Flats; Sandia Laboratories, Tonopah.

NASA Facilities. Space Nuclear Systems Office, Jackass Flats.

Newspapers, Circulation. Las Vegas Review-Journal (ExSat—57,525).

Commercial Television Stations, Affiliation. KLAS-TV, Las Vegas (CBS); KORK-TV, Las Vegas (NBC); KSHO-TV, Las Vegas (ABC); KVVU, Henderson (None); KCRL-TV, Reno (NBC); KOLO-TV, Reno (ABC); KTVN-TV, Reno (CBS). Most of state is divided between Reno ADI and Las Vegas ADI. Small portion of state is located in Salt Lake City (Utah) ADI.

Plants and Offices, Products, Employment.
Kennecott Copper Corp., McGill (Copper mining and smelting—1,400). Central Telephone Co., Las Vegas (Telephone company—1,800). Hotel Riviera Inc., Las Vegas (Hotel, casino—1,200). Sahara-Nevada Corp., Las Vegas (Hotel and casino, golf and country club—1,200). Las Vegas International Hotel, Las Vegas (Hotel, casino—2,500). M and R Investment Co. Inc., Las Vegas (Hotel, casino—1,800). Desert Palace Inc., Las Vegas (Hotel, casino—1,600). Harvey's Wagon Wheel Inc., Stateline (Hotel, gambling restaurant—at least 1,800). Harrah's Club, Stateline (Motel, gambling restaurant—at least 2,000). Harrah's Club, Reno (Hotel, gambling bar, restaurant—1,000). Sparks Nuggett Inc., Sparks (Hotel, motel, bar, restaurant—1,300). Harold's Club Inc., Reno (Gambling restaurant—1,000). ALW Inc., Incline Village (Hotel, casino—1,000). International Leisure, Las Vegas (Holding company—4,000). Washoe Medical Center, Reno (Hospital—1,050).

NORTH DAKOTA

Race and Ethnic Groups. Norwegian stock 6.3 percent, Russian stock 5.4 percent.

Cities, 1970 Population. Fargo 53,342, Grand Forks 39,044, Bismarck 34,670, Minot 32,270.

Universities, Enrollment. Dickinson State College (Dickinson—1,412); Minot State College (Minot—3,138), North Dakota State University of Agriculture and Applied Science (Fargo—7,118), University of North Dakota (Grand Forks—8,823), Valley City State College (Valley City—1,200).

Military Installations or Activities. Finley Air Force Station, Finley; Fortuna Air Force Station, Fortuna; Grand Forks Air Force Base, Grand Forks; Minot Air Force Base, Minot.

Newspapers, Circulation. Fargo Forum (All day—61,084).

Commercial Television Stations, Affiliation. KFYR-TV, Bismarck (NBC, ABC); KXMB-TV, Bismarck (CBS); KXMC-TV, Minot (CBS); KDIX-TV, Dickinson (CBS); KTHI-TV, Fargo (ABC); KXJB-TV, Fargo (CBS); WDAY-TV, Fargo (NBC); KCND-TV, Pembina (ABC). Most of state is divided between Minot-Bismarck ADI and Fargo ADI. Small portions of state are located in Dickinson ADI, Pembina ADI and Sioux Falls-Mitchell (South Dakota) ADI.

VERMONT

Race and Ethnic Groups. Canadian stock 10.4 percent.

Cities, 1970 Population. Burlington 38,668, Rutland 19,310, Barre 10,218.

Universities, Enrollment. Castleton State College (Castleton—1,534), Goddard College (Plainfield—1,599), Johnson State College (Johnson—1,123), Middlebury College (Middlebury—1,892), Norwich University (Northfield—1,042), Saint Michael's College (Winooski—1,281), University of Vermont (Burlington—9,064).

Military Installations or Activities. St. Albans Air Force Station, St. Albans.

Commercial Television Stations, Affiliation. WCAX-TV, Burlington (CBS); WVNY-TV, Burlington (ABC). Most of state is located in Burlington-Plattsburgh (New York) ADI. Small portions of state are located in Portland (Maine)-Poland Spring (Maine) ADI, Boston (Massachusetts) ADI and Albany (New York)-Schenectady (New York)-Troy (New York) ADI.

Plants and Offices, Products, Employment.
   General Electric Co., Burlington (Water distillation equipment—3,300). **General Electric Co.**, Rutland (Power transformers—1,200). **International Business Machines Corp.**, Burlington (Electronic components—3,300). **International Business Machines Corp.**, Essex Junction (Electronic computers—3,000).

WYOMING

Cities, 1970 Population. Cheyenne 40,863, Casper 39,484, Laramie 23,019, Rock Springs 11,686.

Universities, Enrollment. University of Wyoming (Laramie—8,546).

Military Installations or Activities. Francis E. Warren Air Force Base, Cheyenne.

Commercial Television Stations, Affiliation. KTWO-TV, Casper (NBC primary; ABC, CBS); KFBC-TV, Cheyenne (CBS primary; ABC); KWRB-TV, Thermopolis (CBS; ABC, NBC on per program basis). State is divided between Casper-Riverton ADI, Cheyenne ADI, Denver (Colorado) ADI, Salt Lake City (Utah) ADI, Rapid City (South Dakota) ADI, Billings (Montana) ADI and Idaho Falls (Idaho)-Pocatello (Idaho) ADI.

DISTRICT OF COLUMBIA

Race and Ethnic Groups. Blacks 72.1 percent. British stock 0.7 percent, German stock 0.7 percent.

Cities, 1970 Population. Washington, D.C. 756,510.

Universities, Enrollment. American University (14,508), Catholic University of America (6,486), District of Columbia Teachers College (2,782), Gallaudet College (1,019), George Washington University (20,969), Georgetown University (4,387), Howard University (10,090), Washington Technical Institute (3,042).

Military Installations or Activities. Army Map Service; Harry Diamond Laboratories; Fort Leslie J. McNair; Walter Reed Army Medical Center; Naval Observatory; Naval Photographic Center; Naval Reconnaissance and Technical Support Center; Naval Research Laboratory; Naval Security Station; Naval Station; Bolling Air Force Base.

Newspapers, Circulation. Washington Post (MxSat—526,432), Washington Star-News (ExSat—302,682).

Commercial Television Stations, Affiliation. WDCA-TV (None); WMAL-TV (ABC); WRC-TV (NBC); WTOP-TV (CBS); WTTG (None). City located in Washington, D.C., ADI.

Plants and Offices, Products, Employment. (Note: federal civilian employment in the District of Columbia as of Dec. 31, 1971, was 171,899.)
   International General Industries (Holding company, automobile parts—1,500). **Publishers Co. Inc.** (Holding company, commercial printing—3,000). **Washington Post Co.** (Newspaper publishing—3,100). **Evening Star Newspaper Co. Inc.** (Newspaper publishing—2,000). **American Telephone and Telegraph Co.** (Communications—5,000). **Peoples Service Drug Stores** (Drug stores—4,000). **Garfinckel Brooks Bros. Inc.** (Department stores—HQ—1,500). **Woodward and Lothrop Inc.** (Department stores—HQ—3,500). **Marriott Corp.** (Motels, restaurants, catering, holding company—HQ—1,500). **Air America Inc.** (Air carrier—4,800). **Pacific Corp.** (Holding company—8,620). **Government Employees Insurance Co.** (Insurance—HQ—2,200). **Peoples Life Insurance Co.** (Insurance—1,780).

Alaska

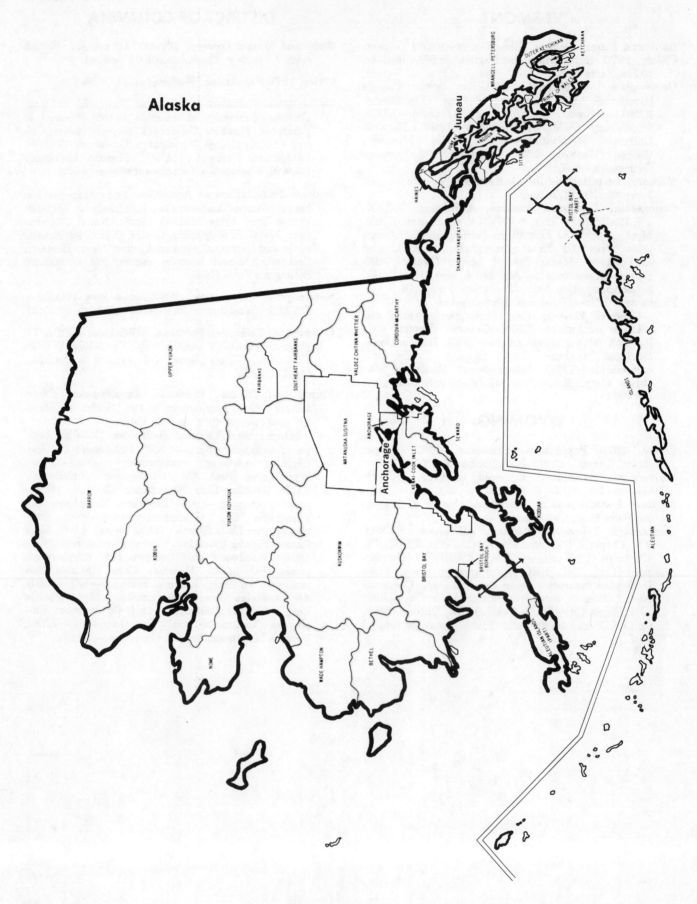

Juneau

Anchorage

OUTER KETCHIKAN
WRANGELL-PETERSBURG
KETCHIKAN
PRINCE OF WALES
ANGOON
JUNEAU
SITKA
SKAGWAY-YAKUTAT
HAINES

BRISTOL BAY (PART)

CORDOVA-McCARTHY
VALDEZ CHITINA WHITTIER
SOUTHEAST FAIRBANKS
FAIRBANKS
UPPER YUKON

ISLANDS

ALEUTIAN

MATANUSKA SUSITNA
ANCHORAGE
KENAI-COOK INLET
SEWARD

BARROW
KOBUK
YUKON KOYUKUK
KUSKOKWIM

KODIAK
BRISTOL BAY BOROUGH

NOME
WADE HAMPTON
BETHEL
BRISTOL BAY

ALEUTIAN ISLANDS (PART)

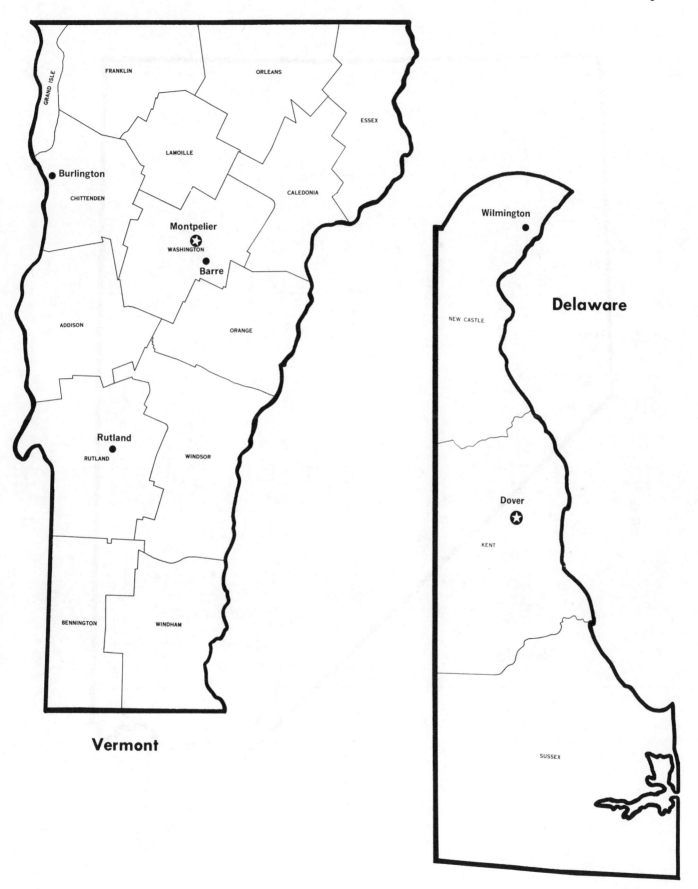

FRANKLIN

GRAND ISLE

ORLEANS

ESSEX

LAMOILLE

● Burlington

CHITTENDEN

CALEDONIA

Montpelier
★
WASHINGTON

● Barre

ADDISON

ORANGE

Rutland
●
RUTLAND

WINDSOR

BENNINGTON

WINDHAM

Vermont

Wilmington
●

Delaware

NEW CASTLE

Dover
★

KENT

SUSSEX

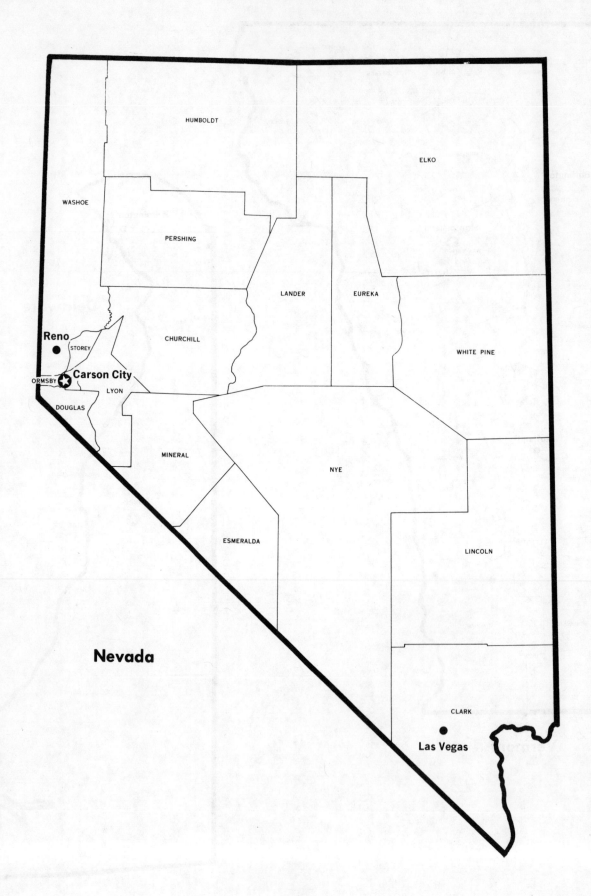

Nevada

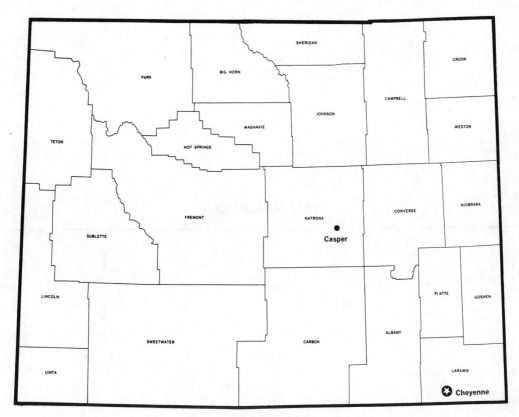

Wyoming

North Dakota

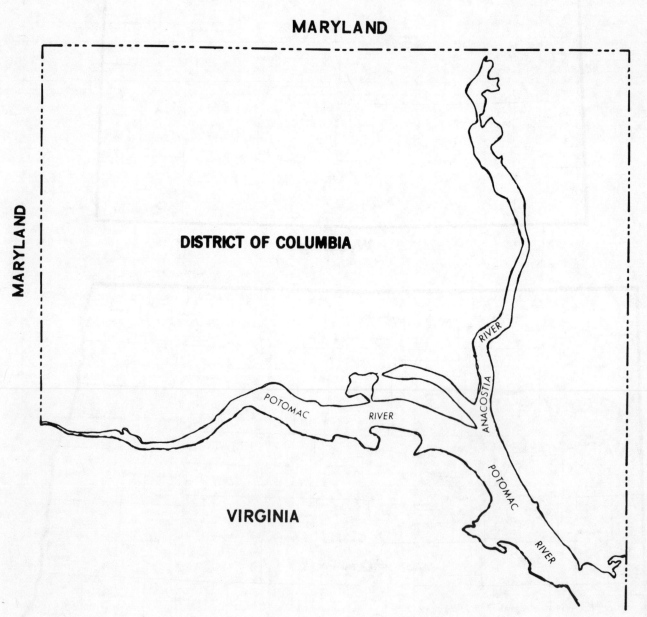

History of

Reapportionment and Redistricting

WHEN the 55 delegates to the Constitutional Convention emerged from their remarkable nation-creating endeavor in September 1787, their work was seen to contain many unique features. Among them was a national legislative body (the House of Representatives) whose membership was to be elected by the people and apportioned on the basis of population. But, as with almost everything in the Constitution, only a few basic rules and regulations were laid down. How to interpret and implement the instructions contained in the document was left to the future. Practical reactions to concrete problems would shape the institutions and create the customs by which the new nation would develop and prosper.

Within this framework, many questions soon arose concerning the lower house of Congress. How large was it to be? What mathematical formula was to be used in calculating the distribution of seats to the various states? Were the Representatives to be elected at large or by districts? If by districts, what standards should be used in fixing their boundaries? The Congress and the courts have been wrestling with these questions for almost 200 years.

Nor were such problems considered to be minor or routine. George Washington's only speech at the Constitutional Convention concerned the question of the ratio of population per Representative in the House. Moreover, his first veto as President—and therefore the first Presidential veto in American history—was of the Reapportionment Bill of 1792. Other such prominent figures in American history as Alexander Hamilton, Thomas Jefferson and Daniel Webster played leading roles in reapportionment and redistricting debates.

Until the mid-twentieth century, such questions generally remained in the hands of the legislators. But with growing concentration of the population in urban areas, variations in population between Congressional districts became more pronounced—and more noticeable. Moves in Congress to redress the grievance of heavily populated but under-represented areas proved unsuccessful. So intent were rural legislators on preventing power from slipping out of their hands that they managed to block reapportionment of the House following the Census of 1920. That census showed urban residents in the majority for the first time in American history.

Before long, the focus shifted to the Supreme Court, where litigants tried to get the Court to order the states to revise Congressional district boundaries in line with population shifts. After initial failure, a breakthrough occurred in 1964 in the case of *Wesberry v. Sanders*. The Court declared that the Constitution required that "as nearly as practicable, one man's vote in a Congressional election is to be worth as much as another's."

BACKGROUND AND EARLY HISTORY

Modern legislative bodies are descended from the councils of feudal lords and gentry which medieval kings summoned for the purpose of raising revenues and armies. These councils did not represent a king's subjects in any modern sense; they represented certain groups of subjects, such as the nobility, the clergy, the landed gentry and town merchants. Thus representation was by interest groups and had no relation to equal representation for equal numbers of people. In England, the king's council became Parliament, with the higher nobility and clergy making up the House of Lords and representatives of the gentry and merchants making up the House of Commons.

Beginning as little more than administrative and advisory arms of the throne, royal councils in time developed into lawmaking bodies and acquired powers which eventually eclipsed those of the monarchs they served. The power struggle in England was climaxed during the Cromwellian period when the Crown gave way, temporarily, to the Commonwealth. By 1800, Parliament was clearly the superior branch of Government.

During the 18th and early 19th centuries, as the power of Parliament grew, Englishmen became increasingly concerned about the "representativeness" of their system of apportionment. Newly developing industrial cities had no more representation in the House of Commons than small, almost deserted country towns. Small constituencies were bought and sold. Men from these empty "rotten boroughs" were often sent to Parliament representing a single "patron" landowner or clique of wealthy men. It was not until the Reform Act of 1832 that Parliament curbed such excesses and turned toward a representative system based on population.

The growth of the powers of Parliament as well as the development of Englishmen's ideas of representation during the 17th and 18th centuries had a profound effect on the colonists in America. Representative assemblies were unifying forces behind the breakaway of the colonies from England and the establishment of the newly independent country.

Colonists in America, generally modeling their legislatures after England's, used both population and land units as bases for apportionment. Patterns of early representation varied. "Nowhere did representation bear any uniform relation to the number of electors. Here and there the factor of size had been crudely recognized," Robert Luce pointed out in his book *Legislative Principles*.

In the New England states, the town was usually the basis for representation. In the Middle Atlantic states, the county was frequently used. Some southern states used the county with extra representation for specified cities. In many areas, towns and counties were fairly equal in population. Thus territorial representation afforded roughly equal representation for equal numbers of people. Delaware's three counties, for example, were of almost equal population and had the same representation in the state legislature. But in Virginia the disparity was enormous (from 951 people in one county to 22,015 in another), and Thomas Jefferson criticized the state's constitution on the ground that "among those who share the representation, the shares are unequal."

The Continental Congress, with representation from every colony, proclaimed in the Declaration of Independence in 1776 that Governments derive "their just powers from the consent of the governed" and that "the right of representation in the legislature" is an "inestimable right" of the people. The Constitutional Convention of 1787 included representatives from all the states. However, in neither of these bodies were the state delegations or voting powers proportional to population.

INTENTIONS OF FOUNDING FATHERS

Andrew Hacker, in his book *Congressional Districting,* said that to ascertain what the framers of the Constitution had in mind when they drew up the section concerning the House of Representatives, it was necessary to study closely (1) the Constitution itself, (2) the recorded discussions and debates at the Constitutional Convention, *(3) The Federalist Papers* (essays written by Alexander Hamilton, John Jay and James Madison in defense of the Constitution) and (4) the deliberations of the state ratifying conventions.

Provisions of Constitution. The Constitution states only that each state is to be allotted a certain number of representatives. It does not state specifically that Congressional districts must be equal or nearly equal in population. Nor does it even require specifically that a state create districts at all. However, it seems clear that the first clause of Article I, Section 2, providing that House Members should be chosen "by the people of the several states," indicated that the House of Representatives, in contrast to the Senate, was to represent people rather than states. "It follows," Hacker believed, "that if the states are to have equal representation in the upper chamber, then individuals are to be equally represented in the lower body."

The third clause of Article I, Section 2, provided that Congressional apportionment among the states must be according to population. But, Hacker argued, "there is little point in giving the states Congressmen 'according to their respective numbers' if the states do not redistribute the members of their delegations on the same principle. For Representatives are not the property of the states, as are the Senators, but rather belong to the people who happen to reside within the boundaries of those states. Thus, each citizen has a claim to be regarded as a political unit equal in value to his neighbors." In this and similar ways, Constitutional scholars have argued the case for single-member Congressional districts deduced from the wording of the Constitution itself.

Constitutional Convention. As for the debates in the Constitutional Convention, the issue of unequal representation arose only once. The occasion was Madison's defense of Article I, Section 4, of the proposed Constitution giving Congress the power to override state regulations on "the times...and manner" of holding elections for United States Senators and Representatives. Madison's argument related to the fact that many state legislatures of the time were badly malapportioned: "The inequality of the representation in the legislatures of particular states would produce a like inequality in their representation in the national legislature, as it was presumable that the counties having the power in the former case would secure it to themselves in the latter."

The implication was twofold: that states would create Congressional districts and that unequal districting was bad and should be prevented.

Provisions of the Constitution on Apportionment and Districting

Article I, Section 2: The House of Representatives shall be composed of Members chosen every second Year by the People of the several States, and the Electors in each State shall have the Qualifications requisite for Electors of the most numerous Branch of the State Legislature....

Representatives and direct Taxes shall be apportioned among the several States which may be included within this Union, according to their respective Numbers, which shall be determined by adding to the whole Number of free Persons, including those bound to Service for a Term of Years, and excluding Indians not taxed, three fifths of all other Persons. The actual Enumeration shall be made within three Years after the first Meeting of the Congress of the United States, and within every subsequent Term of ten Years, in such Manner as they shall by Law direct. The Number of Representatives shall not exceed one for every thirty thousand, but each State shall have at least one Representative....

Article I, Section 4: The Times, Places and Manner of holding Elections for Senators and Representatives, shall be prescribed in each State by the Legislature thereof; but the Congress may at any time by Law make or alter such Regulations, except as to the Place of Chusing Senators....

Article (Amendment) XIV, Section 2: Representatives shall be apportioned among the several States according to their respective numbers, counting the whole number of persons in each State, excluding Indians not taxed. But when the right to vote at any election for the choice of electors for President and Vice President of the United States, Representatives in Congress, the Executive and Judicial officers of a State, or the members of the Legislature thereof, is denied to any of the male inhabitants of such State, being twenty-one years of age, and citizens of the United States, or in any way abridged, except for participation in rebellion, or other crime, the basis of representation therein shall be reduced in the proportion which the number of such male citizens shall bear to the whole number of male citizens twenty-one years of age in such State.

Federalist Papers. Madison made this interpretation even more clear in his contributions to the Federalist Papers. Arguing in favor of the relatively small size of the projected House of Representatives, he wrote in Paper No. 56: "Divide the largest state into ten or twelve districts and it will be found that there will be no peculiar local interests in either which will not be within the knowledge of the Representative of the district."

In the same paper, Madison said: "The Representatives of each State will not only bring with them a considerable knowledge of its laws, and a local knowledge of their respective districts, but will probably in all cases have been members, and may even at the very time be members, of the state legislature, where all the local information and interests of the state are assembled, and from whence they may easily be conveyed by a very few hands into the legislature of the United States." And finally, in the next Federalist Paper (No. 57), Madison made the statement that "...each Representative of the United States will be elected by five or six thousand citizens." In making these arguments, Madison seems to have assumed that all or most Representatives would be elected by districts rather than at large.

State Conventions. In the state ratifying conventions, the grant to Congress by Article I, Section 4, of ultimate jurisdiction over the "times, places and manner of holding elections" (except the places of choosing Senators) held the attention of many delegates. There were differences over the merits of this section, but no justification of unequal districts was prominently used to attack the grant of power. Further evidence that individual districts were the intention of the Founding Fathers was given in the New York ratifying convention, when Alexander Hamilton said: "The natural and proper mode of holding elections will be to divide the state into districts in proportion to the number to be elected. This state will consequently be divided at first into six."

From his study of the sources relating to the question of Congressional districting, Hacker concluded: "There is, then, a good deal of evidence that those who framed and ratified the Constitution intended that the House of Representatives have as its constituency a public in which the votes of all citizens were of equal weight. In the final analysis, the aristocratic pronouncements of Hamilton, Gerry and Morris cannot be regarded as having been written into the document's provisions dealing with the lower chamber of the national legislature. The House of Representatives was designed to be a popular chamber, giving the same electoral power to all who had the vote. And the concern of Madison, King and Pinckney that districts be equal in size was an institutional step in the direction of securing this democratic principle."

The Early Years: 1789-1842

Article I, Section 2, Clause 3, of the Constitution laid down the basic rules for apportionment and reapportionment of seats in the House of Representatives: "Representatives...shall be apportioned among the several states which may be included within this Union, according to their respective numbers, which shall be determined by adding to the whole number of free persons, including those bound to service for a term of years, and excluding Indians not taxed, three-fifths of all other persons. The actual enumeration shall be made within three years after the first meeting of the Congress of the United States, and within every subsequent term of ten years, in such manner as they shall by law direct. The number of Representatives shall not exceed one for every thirty thousand, but each state shall have at least one Representative...."

Until the first census had been taken, the 13 states were to have the following numbers of Representatives: New Hampshire, three; Massachusetts, eight; Rhode Island and Providence Plantations, one; Connecticut, five; New York, six; New Jersey, four; Pennsylvania, eight; Delaware, one; Maryland, six; Virginia, ten; North Carolina, five; South Carolina, five; and Georgia, three. The apportionment of seats—65 in all—thus mandated by the Constitution remained in effect during the First and Second Congresses (1789-93).

Apparently realizing that apportionment of the House of Representatives was likely to become a major bone of contention, the First Congress submitted to the states a proposed constitutional amendment containing a formula to be used in future reapportionments. The amendment, which was not ratified, provided that following the taking of a decennial census there would be one Representative for every 30,000 persons until the House membership reached 100, "after which the proportion shall be so regulated by Congress that there shall be not less than 100 Representatives, nor less than one Representative for every 40,000 persons, until the number of Representatives shall amount to 200, after which the proportion shall be so regulated by Congress, that there shall not be less than 200 Representatives, nor more than one Representative for every 50,000 persons."

FIRST APPORTIONMENT BY CONGRESS

The failure to ratify this amendment made it necessary for Congress to enact apportionment legislation after the first census had been taken in 1790. The first apportionment bill was sent to the President on March 23, 1792. Washington, at the urging of Secretary of State Thomas Jefferson, sent the bill back to Congress without his signature—the first Presidential veto.

The bill had incorporated the constitutional minimum of 30,000 as the size of each district. But the population of each state was not a simple multiple of 30,000. Significant fractions were left over when the number of people in each state was divided by 30,000. Thus, for example, Vermont was found to be entitled to 2.851 Representatives, New Jersey to 5.98 and Virginia to 21.018. Therefore, a formula had to be found that would deal in the fairest possible manner with unavoidable variations from exact equality.

Accordingly, Congress proposed in the first apportionment bill to distribute the Members on a fixed ratio of one Representative per 30,000 inhabitants, and give an additional Member to each state with a fraction exceeding one-half. Washington's veto was based on the belief that eight states would receive more than one Representative per 30,000 people under this formula.

A motion to override the veto was unsuccessful. A new bill meeting the President's objections was introduced April 9, 1792, and approved April 14. The Act provided for a ratio of one Member for every 33,000 inhabitants and fixed the exact number of Representatives to which each state was entitled. The total membership of the House was to be 105. In dividing the population of the various states by 33,000, all remainders were to be disregarded. This was known as the Method of Rejected Fractions; it was devised by Thomas Jefferson.

REAPPORTIONMENT BY JEFFERSON'S METHOD

Jefferson's method of reapportionment resulted in great inequalities between states. A Vermont district would contain 42,766 inhabitants, a New Jersey district 35,911 and a Virginia district only 33,187. Emphasis was placed on what was considered the ideal size of a Congressional district rather than on what the size of the House ought to be. This method was in use until 1840.

The reapportionment act based on the Census of 1800 continued the ratio of 33,000, which provided a House of 141 Members. Debate on the third apportionment bill began in the House on Nov. 22, 1811, and the bill was sent to the President on December 21. The ratio was fixed at 35,000, yielding a House of 181 Members. Following the Census of 1820, Congress approved an apportionment bill providing a ratio of 40,000 inhabitants per district. The sum of the quotas for the various states produced a House of 213 Members.

The Act of May 22, 1832, fixed the ratio at 47,700, resulting in a House of 240 Members. Dissatisfaction with the method in use continued, and Daniel Webster launched a vigorous attack against it. He urged adoption of a method that would assign an additional Representative to each state with a large fraction. His philosophical approach to the reapportionment process was made in a report he submitted to Congress in 1832: "The Constitution, therefore, must be understood not as enjoining an absolute relative equality—because that would be demanding an impossibility—but as requiring of Congress to make the apportionment of Representatives among the several states according to their respective numbers, *as near as may be.* That which cannot be done perfectly must be done in a manner as near perfection as can be... In such a case approximation becomes a rule."

Following the Census of 1840, Congress adopted a reapportionment method similar to that advocated by Webster. The method fixed a ratio of one Representative for every 70,680 persons. This figure was reached by deciding on a fixed size of the House in advance (223), dividing that figure into the total national "Representative population" and using the result (70,680) as the fixed ratio. The population of each state was then divided by this ratio to find the number of its Representatives and assigned an additional Representative for each fraction over one-half.

REDISTRICTING PROBLEMS

Another new feature of the legislation following the Census of 1840 was a redistricting provision that became law on June 25, 1842. Under that provision, Representatives were to be "elected by districts composed of contiguous territory equal in number to the Representatives to which said state may be entitled, no one district electing more than one Representative." This provision climaxed a 50-year struggle to enact some sort of districting legislation. Despite substantial evidence of the intent of Congress, many states had not divided themselves into Congressional districts.

In the first few elections to the House, New Hampshire, Pennsylvania, New Jersey and Georgia elected their Representatives at large, as did Rhode Island and Delaware—the two states with only a single Representative. Districts were used in Massachusetts, New York, Maryland, Virginia and South Carolina. In Connecticut, a preliminary election was held to nominate three times as many persons as the number of Representatives to be chosen at large in the subsequent election. In 1840, 22 of the 31 states elected their Representatives by districts. New Hampshire, New Jersey, Georgia, Alabama, Mississippi and Missouri, with a combined representation of 33 out of a total of 232, elected their Representatives at large; three states, Arkansas, Delaware and Florida, had only one Representative each.

Constant efforts had been made during the early 1800s to lay down national rules, by means of a constitutional amendment, for Congressional districting. The first resolution proposing a mandatory division of each state into districts was introduced in Congress in 1800. In 1802 the Legislatures of Vermont and North Carolina adopted resolutions in support of such action. From 1816 to 1826, 22 state resolutions were adopted proposing the election of Representatives by districts.

In Congress, Sen. Mahlon Dickerson (D N.J.) proposed an amendment regularly almost every year from 1817 to 1826. The resolution embodying the Dickerson amendment was adopted by the Senate three times, in 1819, 1820 and 1822, but each time it failed to reach a vote in the House.

Acceptance by most states of the principle of local representation put an end to Congressional efforts in behalf of a constitutional amendment and led to the enactment of the 1842 law requiring contiguous single-member Congressional districts.

When President Tyler signed the bill, he appended to it a memorandum voicing doubt as to the constitutionality of the districting provisions. The memorandum precipitated a minor constitutional crisis. The House, urged on by Rep. John Quincy Adams (Whig Mass.), appointed a select committee to consider the action of the President. Chaired by the aging ex-President, the committee drew up a resolution protesting the President's action as "unwarranted by the Constitution and laws of the United States, injurious to the public interest, and of evil example for the future; and this House do hereby solemnly protest against the said act of the President and against its ever being repeated or adduced as a precedent hereafter." The House took no action on the resolution; several attempts to call it up under suspension of the rules failed to receive the necessary two-thirds vote.

The action of the Congress in enacting districting legislation along with apportionment legislation did stand as a precedent, however. For the next 80 years, some sort of districting requirements were included in successive reapportionment laws.

Another phenomenon encountered—or perhaps only named—in this era, was the gerrymander. Gerrymandering was the practice of drawing district lines so as to maximize the advantage of a political party or interest group. The name originated from a salamander-shaped Congressional district created by the Massachusetts Legislature in 1812 when Elbridge Gerry was Governor.

The Gerrymander

The practice of "gerrymandering"—the excessive manipulation of the shape of a legislative district to benefit a certain incumbent or party—is probably as old as the Republic, but the name originated in 1812.

In that year, the Massachusetts Legislature carved out of Essex County a district which historian John Fiske said had a "dragonlike contour." When the painter Gilbert Stuart saw the misshapen district, he pencilled in a head, wings and claws and exclaimed: "That will do for a salamander!"—to which editor Benjamin Russell replied: "Better say a Gerrymander"—after Elbridge Gerry, then Governor of Massachusetts.

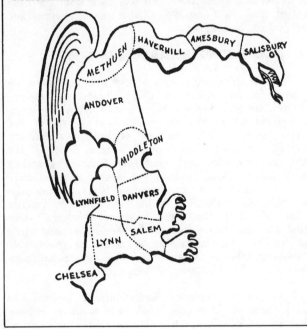

The Middle Years, 1850-1920

The modified reapportionment formula adopted by Congress in 1842 was found more satisfactory than the previous method, but another change was made following the Census of 1850. The new system was proposed by Rep. Samuel F. Vinton (Whig Ohio) and became known as the Vinton method.

VINTON APPORTIONMENT FORMULA

Under this formula, Congress first fixed the size of the House and then distributed the seats. The new method of distribution involved the same procedure as the 1842 system. The total Representative population of the country was divided by the desired number of Representatives and the resulting number became the ratio of population to each Representative. The population of each state was divided by this ratio and each state received the number of Representatives equal to the whole number in the quotient for that state. Then, to reach the required size

of the House, additional Representatives were assigned based on the remaining fractions, beginning with the state having the largest fraction. This procedure differed from the 1842 method only in the last step, which assigned one Representative to every state having a fraction larger than ½. The Vinton method was used from 1850 through 1900.

ADVANTAGES AND DIFFICULTIES

Proponents of the Vinton method pointed out that it had the distinct advantage of making it possible to fix the size of the House in advance and to take into account at least the largest fractions. The concern of the House, grown in size from 65 in 1789 to 240 in 1833, turned from the ideal size of a Congressional district to the ideal size of the House itself. The 1842 legislation resulted in an actual reduction in the size of the House, to 233 Members.

Under the 1842 reapportionment formula, the exact size of the House could not be fixed in advance. If every state with a fraction over ½ were given an additional Representative, the House might wind up with a few more or a few less than the desired number. However, under the Vinton method, only states with the largest fractions were given additional House Members and only up to the desired total size of the House.

Despite the apparent advantages of the Vinton method, certain difficulties began to reveal themselves as the formula was applied. Zechariah Chafee Jr. of the Harvard Law School summarized these difficulties in an article in the *Harvard Law Review* in 1929. The method, he pointed out, suffered from a fatal defect called the "Alabama paradox". Under the paradox, an increase in the total size of the House might be accompanied by an actual loss of a seat by some state, even though there had been no corresponding change in population. This phenomenon first appeared in tables prepared for Congress in 1881, which gave Alabama eight Members in a House of 299 but only seven Members in a House of 300. It could even happen that the state which lost a seat was the one state which had expanded in population, while all the others had fewer people.

Chafee concluded from his study of the Vinton method: "Thus, it is unsatisfactory to fix the ratio of population per Representative before seats are distributed. Either the size of the House comes out haphazard, or, if this be determined in advance the absurdities of the 'Alabama paradox' vitiate the apportionment. Under present conditions, it is essential to determine the size of the House in advance; the problem thereafter is to distribute the required number of seats among the several states as nearly as possible in proportion to their respective populations so that no state is treated unfairly in comparison with any other state."

REAPPORTIONMENTS BY VINTON METHOD

Six reapportionments were carried out under the Vinton method. The 1850 Census Act contained three provisions not included in any previous law. First, it provided not only for reapportionment after the Census of 1850 but also for reapportionment after all subsequent censuses; secondly, it purported to fix the size of the House permanently at 233 Members; and thirdly, it provided in advance for an automatic apportionment by the Secretary of the Interior under the method prescribed in the Act.

Following the Census of 1860, according to the provisions of the Act passed a decade before, an automatic reapportionment was to be carried out by the Interior Department. However, because the size of the House was to remain at the 1850 level, some states faced loss of representation and others would gain less than they expected. To avert these eventualities, an Act was approved March 4, 1862, increasing the size of the House to 241 and giving an extra Representative to eight states— Illinois, Iowa, Kentucky, Minnesota, Ohio, Pennsylvania, Rhode Island and Vermont.

Apportionment legislation following the Census of 1870 contained several new provisions. The Act of Feb. 2, 1872, fixed the size of the House at 283, with the proviso that the number should be increased if new states were admitted. A supplemental Act of May 30, 1872, assigned one additional Representative each to Alabama, Florida, Indiana, Louisiana, New Hampshire, New York, Pennsylvania, Tennessee and Vermont.

Another section of the 1872 Act provided that no state should thereafter be admitted "without having the necessary population to entitle it to at least one Representative fixed by this bill." That provision was found to be unenforceable because no Congress can bind a succeeding Congress.

The Reconstruction era being at its height in the South, the reapportionment legislation of 1872 reflected the desire of Congress to enforce Section 2 of the new 14th Amendment. That section attempted to protect the right of Negroes to vote by providing for reduction of the House representation of a state which interfered with exercise of that right. The number of Representatives of such a state was to be reduced in proportion to the number of inhabitants of voting age whose right to go to the polls was denied or abridged. The reapportionment bill repeated the language of the section, but it was never put into effect because of the difficulty of determining the exact number of persons whose right to vote was being abridged.

The reapportionment Act of Feb. 25, 1882, provided for a House of 325 Members, with additional Members for any new states admitted to the Union. No new apportionment provisions were added. The acts of Feb. 7, 1891, and Jan. 16, 1901, were routine pieces of legislation as far as apportionment was concerned. The 1891 measure provided for a House of 356 Members and the 1901 statute increased the number to 386.

MAXIMUM MEMBERSHIP OF HOUSE

On Aug. 8, 1911, the membership of the House was fixed at 433. Provision was made in the reapportionment Act of that date for the addition of one Representative each from Arizona and New Mexico, which were expected to become states in the near future. Thus, the size of the House reached 435, where it has remained up to the present with the exception of the brief period 1959-63 when the admission of Alaska and Hawaii raised the total temporarily to 437.

Limiting the size of the House amounted to recognition that the body would soon expand to unmanageable proportions if the practice of adding new seats every 10 years, to match population gains without depriving any state of its existing representation, were continued. The limitation to a fixed number made the task of reapportionment all the more difficult when the population not only increased but became much more mobile. Population shifts brought Congress up hard against the politically painful necessity of taking seats away from slow-growing states to give the fast-growing adequate representation.

A new mathematical calculation was adopted for the reapportionment following the Census of 1910. Devised by Prof. W. F. Willcox of Cornell University, the new system established a priority list which assigned seats progressively beginning with the first seat above the constitutional minimum of at least one seat per state. When there were 48 states, this method was used to assign the 49th Member, the 50th Member, and so on, until the desired size of the House was reached. The method was called Major Fractions and was used after the Censuses of 1910, 1930 and 1940 *(There was no reapportionment in 1920. See below).*

DISTRICTING LEGISLATION, 1850-1910

The districting provisions of the 1842 Act were not repeated in the legislation that followed the Census of 1850. But in 1862 an Act separate from the reapportionment Act revived the provisions of the Act of 1842 requiring districts to be composed of contiguous territory.

The 1872 reapportionment Act again repeated the districting provisions and went even further by adding that districts should contain "as nearly as practicable an equal number of inhabitants." Similar provisions were included in the Acts of 1881 and 1891. In the Act of Jan. 16, 1901, the words "compact territory" were added and the clause then read "contiguous and compact territory and containing as nearly as practicable an equal number of inhabitants." This requirement appeared also in the legislation of Aug. 8, 1911.

Attempts to Enforce Redistricting. Several attempts, none of them successful, were made to enforce redistricting provisions. Despite the districting requirements of the Act of June 25, 1842, New Hampshire, Georgia, Mississippi and Missouri elected their Representatives at large that autumn. When the House elected at that time convened for its first session on Dec. 4, 1843, objection was made to seating the Representatives of the four states. The matter was referred to the Committee on Elections. The majority report of the Committee, made by its chairman, Rep. Stephen A. Douglas (D Ill.), asserted that the Act of 1842 was not binding upon the states and that the Representatives in question were entitled to their seats. A minority report by Rep. Garrett Davis (Whig Ky.) contended that the Members had not been elected according to the Constitution and the laws and were not entitled to their seats.

The matter was debated in the House from Feb. 6 to 14, 1844. With the Democratic party holding a majority of more than 60, and with 18 of the 21 challenged Members being Democrats, the House decided to seat the Members. An amendment to the majority report in the form of a substitute deleted all reference to the apportionment law. However, by 1848, all four states had come around to electing their Representatives by districts.

Methods of Apportioning House Seats

Fixed Ratio With Rejected Fractions, 1790-1830

The Method of Fixed Ratio With Rejected Fractions was devised by Thomas Jefferson at the time of the first reapportionment following the Census of 1790. Under this method, a predetermined ratio of inhibitants per Representative (say 33,000) was divided into the population of each state. The result was the quota for the state. A Representative was assigned for every whole number in the quota and the fractions were disregarded. Thus a state with a quota of 3.9 got three Representatives.

This method was subject to the population paradox. With a fixed ratio of representation, an increase in the total population might result in a decrease in the size of the House. An example was constructed by Edward V. Huntington in *Methods of Apportionment in Congress:* A fixed ratio of 250,000 persons per district would result in a House of 435 members if the population totaled 102,750,113 but in a House of only 391 members if the population rose to 102,958,798.

Fixed Ratio With Major Fractions, 1840

The Method of Fixed Ratio With Major Fractions was used only once—after the Census of 1840. It was based on an idea formulated by Daniel Webster. As under the Method of Fixed Ratio With Rejected Fractions, a predetermined ratio of persons per district was selected and divided into the population of each state. But in this case, the fractions were not discarded.

For every fraction over one-half, an additional Representative was assigned. Thus, a state with a quota of 3.51 got four Representatives but a state with a quota of 3.49 got only three. This method also was subject to the population paradox.

Vinton Method, 1850-1900

The Vinton method was based on a fixed ratio and a fixed size of the House. The total population of the country was divided by the number of House members to determine the ratio, or number of persons per district. This ratio was then divided into the population of each state, resulting in the quota for each state. Each state received a Representative for each whole number in its quota (with every state getting at least one Representative, fulfilling the Constitutional requirement). The remaining Representatives were then assigned in order to the states having the highest fractions, until the predetermined size of the House was reached.

The Vinton method was subject to the Alabama paradox, in which a state might lose a Representative even though the size of the House was increased.

Major Fractions, 1910-1940

The Method of Major Fractions, in use after the Censuses of 1910, 1930 and 1940, was based on the same principles as the previous method but some new, complex mathematical formulas were added to make the distribution fairer. Furthermore, a priority list system of ranking states' claims to Representatives was introduced *(See Method of Equal Proportions for explanation of the priority list system).*

SOURCES: Laurence F. Schmeckebier, *Congressional Apportionment;* Edward V. Huntington, *Methods of Apportionment in Congress.*

The next challenge to a Member of the House based on Federal districting laws occurred in 1901. It was charged that the Kentucky redistricting law then in force was contrary to the redistricting provisions of the Federal reapportionment law of Jan. 16, 1901. The specific challenge was to Rep. George G. Gilbert (D) of the eighth Kentucky district. The committee assigned to investigate the matter turned aside the challenge, asserting that the Federal act was not binding on the states. The reasons given were practical and political:

"Your committee are therefore of opinion that a proper construction of the Constitution does not warrant the conclusion that by that instrument Congress is clothed with power to determine the boundaries of Congressional districts, or to revise the acts of a State Legislature in fixing such boundaries; and your committee is further of opinion that even if such power is to be implied from the language of the Constitution, it would be in the last degree unwise and intolerable that it should exercise it. To do so would be to put into the hands of Congress the ability to disfranchise, in effect, a large

body of the electors. It would give Congress the power to apply to all the States, in favor of one party, a general system of gerrymandering. It is true that the same method is to a large degree resorted to by the several states, but the division of political power is so general and diverse that notwithstanding the inherent vice of the system of gerrymandering, some kind of equality of distribution results."

In 1908, the Virginia Legislature transferred Floyd County from the fifth to the sixth Congressional district. As a result, the population of the fifth district was reduced from 175,579 to 160,191 and that of the sixth district was increased from 181,571 to 196,959. The average for the state was 185,418.

When the newly elected Representative from the fifth district, Rep. Edward W. Saunders (D), was challenged by his opponent in the 1908 elections, the majority of the investigating committee upheld the challenge. They concluded that the Virginia law of 1908 was null and void as it did not conform with the Federal law of Jan. 16, 1901, or with the constitution of Virginia, and that the

Malapportionment and Gerrymandering

The prevalence of malapportionment and "gerrymandering" in the creation of U.S. Congressional districts was, to many observers, one of the chief evils in the American system prior to reforms brought about by a Feb. 17, 1964, U.S. Supreme Court decision declaring that "as nearly as is practicable, one man's vote in a Congressional election is to be worth as much as another's."

Malapportionment. Malapportionment involved creating districts of grossly unequal populations—either through actions of state legislatures in establishing new districts or, as was the more frequent practice, simply by failing to redistrict despite major population movements that result in population inequalities. At the time of the 1964 Supreme Court decision, for instance, Louisiana had not redistricted since 1912, nor had Colorado or Georgia since 1931, or South Carolina since 1932.

Examples of great disparity in Congressional district sizes in modern U.S. history: New York (1930) 776,425 in largest district and 90,671 in smallest district; Ohio (1946) 698,650 and 163,561; Illinois (1946) 914,053 and 112,116; Arkansas (1946) 423,152 and 177,476; Texas (1962) 951,527 and 216,371; Michigan (1962) 802,994 and 177,431; Maryland (1962) 711,045 and 243,570; South Dakota (1962) 497,669 and 182,845.

The decennial census and ensuing reapportionment of House seats eventually forced reapportionment in most states, although some resorted to the expedient of electing Members at large (like Texas, Hawaii, Ohio, Michigan and Maryland in 1962) rather than face the process of redrawing district lines.

Gerrymandering. Gerrymandering was the name given to excessive manipulation of the shape of legislative districts. The gerrymander was named after Elbridge Gerry, Governor of Massachusetts in 1812 when the Legislature created a peculiar salamander-shaped district to benefit the Democratic party to which Gerry belonged.

Like malapportionment, gerrymandering was practiced by both political parties. In 1961, for example, Republican redistricters in New York created one gerrymander-like creature stretching across the greater part of upstate New York, his head hanging over Albany in the east and his tail reaching for Rochester in the west. Such salamander, tadpole and fishlike creatures sprang to life on the maps of New York City's boroughs. In California, Democrats in control of the Legislature connected two pockets of strong Republican strength in Los Angeles by a thin strip of land to form an unwieldly district running for miles along the coastline. In North Carolina, Democratic redistricters formed an almost perfect gerrymander shape to throw the state's sole Republican Representative in with a strong Democratic opponent.

The basic intent of practically every gerrymander was political—to create a maximum number of districts which would elect the party candidates or types of candidates favored by the controlling group in the state legislature that did the redistricting. The effect was almost always to increase the political power of the already politically dominant group. Up to the 1950s, this was said to be the Republicans in the North and the Democrats in the South. Growing Democratic strength in many northern states tended to cancel out the Republican advantage in that part of the country, however, and signs of the reverse happening in the South could be detected in the 1950s.

district should be regarded as including the counties which were a part of it before enactment of the 1908 state legislation. In that case the contestant would have had a majority of the votes, so the committee recommended that he be seated. Thus, for the first time, it looked as though the districting legislation would be enforced, but the House did not take action on the committee's report and the contestant was not seated.

Reapportionment Struggle of 1920s

Conflict Over Urban Growth. The results of the 14th decennial census were announced Dec. 17, 1920, just after the short session of the 66th Congress convened. The Census of 1920 showed that, for the first time in history, a majority of Americans were urban residents. Disclosure of this fact came as a profound shock to the many persons who were used to emphasizing the nation's rural traditions and the virtues of life on farms and in small towns. Rural legislators immediately mounted an attack on the census results which postponed reapportionment legislation for almost a decade.

Thomas Jefferson once wrote: "Those who labor in the earth are the chosen people of God, if ever He had a chosen people, whose breasts He had made His peculiar deposit for substantial and genuine virtue....The mobs of great cities add just as much to the support of pure government as sores do to the strength of the human body....I think our governments will remain virtuous for many centuries as long as they are chiefly agricultural; and this shall be as long as there shall be vacant lands in any part of America. When they get piled up upon one another in large cities as in Europe, they will become corrupt as in Europe."

As their power waned throughout the latter part of the 19th century and the early part of the 20th, farmers and their spokesmen clung to the Jeffersonian belief that they were somehow more pure and virtuous than the growing number of urban residents. When finally faced with the fact that they were in the minority, they put up a strong rearguard action to prevent the inevitable shift of Congressional districts to the cities.

In the first place, rural Representatives insisted that, since the census was taken as of Jan. 1, the farm population had been undercounted. Supporting this contention, they argued that many farm laborers were seasonally employed in the cities at that time of year. Furthermore, mid-winter road conditions probably had prevented enumerators from visiting many farms; and other farmers were said to have been counted incorrectly because they were absent on winter vacation trips. The change of the census date to Jan. 1 in 1920 had been made to conform

(Continued on p. 230)

CONGRESSIONAL APPORTIONMENT 1789-1970

YEAR OF CENSUS[x]

	Constitution† (1789)	1790	1800	1810	1820	1830	1840	1850	1860	1870	1880	1890	1900	1910	1930#	1940	1950	1960	1970
Ala.				1*	3	5	7	7	6	8	8	9	9	10	9	9	9	8	7
Alaska																	1*	1	1
Ariz.														1*	1	2	2	3	4
Ark.							1*	1	2	3	4	5	6	7	7	7	6	4	4
Calif.							2*	2	3	4	6	7	8	11	20	23	30	38	43
Colo.										1*	1	2	3	4	4	4	4	4	5
Conn.	5	7	7	7	6	6	4	4	4	4	4	4	5	5	6	6	6	6	6
Del.	1	1	1	2	1	1	1	1	1	1	1	1	1	1	1	1	1	1	1
Fla.							1*	1	1	2	2	2	3	4	5	6	8	12	15
Ga.	3	2	4	6	7	9	8	8	7	9	10	11	11	12	10	10	10	10	10
Hawaii																	1*	2	2
Idaho											1*	1	1	2	2	2	2	2	2
Ill.				1*	1	3	7	9	14	19	20	22	25	27	27	26	25	24	24
Ind.				1*	3	7	10	11	11	13	13	13	13	13	12	11	11	11	11
Iowa							2*	2	6	9	11	11	11	11	9	8	8	7	6
Kan.									1	3	7	8	8	8	7	6	6	5	5
Ky.		2	6	10	12	13	10	10	9	10	11	11	11	11	9	9	8	7	7
La.				1*	3	3	4	4	5	6	6	6	7	8	8	8	8	8	8
Maine				7*	7	8	7	6	5	5	4	4	4	4	3	3	3	2	2
Md.	6	8	9	9	9	8	6	6	5	6	6	6	6	6	6	6	7	8	8
Mass.	8	14	17	13‡	13	12	10	11	10	11	12	13	14	16	15	14	14	12	12
Mich.							1*	3	4	6	9	11	12	13	17	17	18	19	19
Minn.								2*	2	3	5	7	9	10	9	9	9	8	8
Miss.				1*	1	2	4	5	5	6	7	7	8	8	7	7	6	5	5
Mo.					1	2	5	7	9	13	14	15	16	16	13	13	11	10	10
Mont.											1*	1	1	2	2	2	2	2	2
Neb.									1*	1	3	6	6	6	5	4	4	3	3
Nev.									1*	1	1	1	1	1	1	1	1	1	1
N.H.	3	4	5	6	6	5	4	3	3	3	2	2	2	2	2	2	2	2	2
N.J.	4	5	6	6	6	6	5	5	5	7	7	8	10	12	14	14	14	15	15
N.M.														1*	2	2	2	2	2
N.Y.	6	10	17	27	34	40	34	33	31	33	34	34	37	43	45	45	43	41	39
N.C.	5	10	12	13	13	13	9	8	7	8	9	9	10	10	11	12	12	11	11
N.D.											1*	1	2	3	2	2	2	2	1
Ohio			1*	6	14	19	21	21	19	20	21	21	21	22	24	23	23	24	23
Okla.														5*	8	9	8	6	6
Ore.								1*	1	1	1	2	2	3	3	4	4	4	4
Pa.	8	13	18	23	26	28	24	25	24	27	28	30	32	36	34	33	30	27	25
R.I.	1	2	2	2	2	2	2	2	2	2	2	2	2	3	2	2	2	2	2
S.C.	5	6	8	9	9	9	7	6	4	5	7	7	7	7	6	6	6	6	6
S.D.											2*	2	2	3	2	2	2	2	2
Tenn.		1	3	6	9	13	11	10	8	10	10	10	10	10	9	10	9	9	8
Texas							2*	2	4	6	11	13	16	18	21	21	22	23	24
Utah												1*	1	2	2	2	2	2	2
Vt.		2	4	6	5	5	4	3	3	3	2	2	2	2	1	1	1	1	1
Va.	10	19	22	23	22	21	15	13	11	9	10	10	10	10	9	9	10	10	10
Wash.											1*	2	3	5	6	6	7	7	7
W.Va.										3	4	4	5	6	6	6	6	5	4
Wis.							2*	3	6	8	9	10	11	11	10	10	10	10	9
Wyo.											1*	1	1	1	1	1	1	1	1
Total	65	106	142	186	213	242	232	237	243	293	332	357	391	435	435	435	437**	435	435

x Apportionment effective with Congressional election two years after census.
† Original apportionment made in Constitution pending first census.
# No apportionment was made in 1920.
* These figures are not based on any census, but indicate the provisional representation accorded newly admitted states by the Congress, pending the following census.

‡ Twenty Members were assigned to Massachusetts, but seven of these were credited to Maine when that area became a state.
** Normally 435 but temporarily increased two seats by Congress when Alaska and Hawaii became states.

SOURCE: Biographical Directory of the American Congress and Bureau of the Census

(Continued from p. 228)

with recommendations of the Agriculture Department, which had asserted that the census should be taken early in the year if an accurate statistical picture of farming conditions was desired.

Another point raised by rural legislators was that large numbers of unnaturalized aliens were congregated in northern cities, with the result that these cities gained at the expense of constituencies made up mostly of citizens of the United States. Rep. Homer Hoch (R Kan.) submitted a table showing that, in a House of 435 Representatives, exclusion from the census count of persons not naturalized would have altered the allocation of seats to 16 states. Southern and western farming states would have retained the number of seats allocated to them in 1911 or would have gained, while northern industrial states and California would have lost or at least would have gained fewer seats.

A constitutional amendment to exclude all aliens from the enumeration for purposes of reapportionment was proposed during the 70th Congress by Rep. Hoch, Sen. Arthur Capper (R Kan.) and others. During the Senate Commerce Committee's hearings on reapportionment, Sen. Frederic M. Sackett (R Ky.) and Sen. Lawrence D. Tyson (D Tenn.) said they too intended to propose amendments to the same effect. But nothing further came of the proposals.

LACK OF PROGRESS ON BILLS

The first bill to reapportion the House according to the Census of 1920 was drafted by the House Census Committee early in 1921. Proceeding on the theory that no state should have its representation reduced, the Committee proposed to increase the total number of Representatives from 435 to 483. But the House voted 267 to 76 to keep its membership at 435 and passed the bill so amended on Jan. 19, 1921. Under this bill, 11 states would have lost seats and eight would have gained. The Senate sent the bill to a committee where it died when the 66th Congress expired March 4, 1921.

Early in the 67th Congress, the House Census Committee again reported a bill, this time fixing the total membership at 460, an increase of 25. Two states—Maine and Massachusetts—would have lost one Representative each and 16 states would have gained. On the floor of the House an attempt to fix the number at the existing 435 failed, and the House voted to send the bill back to committee, where it remained until that Congress came to an end on March 4, 1923.

During the 68th Congress (1923-25), the House Census Committee failed to report any reapportionment bill, and midway of the 69th Congress (1925-27) it again looked as if no reapportionment measure would come out of the Committee. Accordingly, on April 8, 1926, Rep. Henry E. Barbour (R Calif.) moved that the Committee be discharged from further consideration of a bill identical with that passed by the House in 1921 continuing membership at 435.

Chairman Bertrand H. Snell (R N.Y.) of the House Rules Committee, representing the Republican leadership of the House, raised a point of order against Barbour's motion. The Speaker of the House, Nicholas Longworth (R Ohio), pointed out that decisions of earlier Speakers tended to indicate that reapportionment had been considered a matter of "constitutional privilege,"

and that Rep. Barbour's motion must be held in order if these precedents were followed. But the Speaker said he doubted whether the precedents had been interpreted correctly. He therefore submitted to the House the question of whether the pending motion should be considered privileged. The House sustained the Rules Committee by a vote of 87 to 265.

INTERVENTION BY PRESIDENT COOLIDGE

President Coolidge, who previously had made no reference to reapportionment in his communications to Congress, announced in January 1927 that he favored passage of a new apportionment bill during the short session of the 69th Congress, which would end in less than two months. The House Census Committee refused to act. Its chairman, Rep. E. Hart Fenn (R Conn.) therefore moved in the House on March 2, 1927, to suspend the rules and pass a bill he had introduced authorizing the Secretary of Commerce to reapportion the House immediately after the 1930 census. The motion was voted down 183 to 197.

The Fenn bill was rewritten early in the 70th Congress (1927-29) to give Congress itself a chance to act before the proposed reapportionment by the Secretary of Commerce should go into effect. The bill was submitted to the House, which on May 18, 1928, voted 186 to 165 to recommit it to the Census Committee. After minor changes, the Fenn bill was again reported to the House and was passed on Jan. 11, 1929. No record vote was taken on passage of the bill, but a motion to return it to the Committee was rejected 134-227.

Four days later, the reapportionment bill was reported out of the Senate Committee on Commerce. Repeated efforts to bring it up for floor action ahead of other bills were made in vain. Its supporters gave up the fight on Feb. 27, 1929—five days before the end of the session, when it became evident that Senators from states which would lose representation were ready to carry on a filibuster that would have blocked not only reapportionment but all other measures then awaiting final passage.

INTERVENTION BY PRESIDENT HOOVER

With the time for the next census rapidly approaching, President Hoover listed provision for the 1930 census and reapportionment as "matters of emergency legislation" that should be acted upon in the special session of the 71st Congress that was convened on April 15, 1929. In response to this urgent request, the Senate June 13 passed, 48 to 37, a combined census-reapportionment bill which had been approved by voice vote of the House two days earlier.

The 1929 law established a permanent system of reapportioning the 435 House seats following each census. It provided that immediately after the convening of the 71st Congress for its short session in December 1930, the President should transmit to Congress a statement showing the apportionment population of each state together with an apportionment of Representatives to each state based on the existing size of the House. Failing enactment of new apportionment legislation, that apportionment would go into effect without further action and would remain in effect for ensuing elections to the House of Repre-

(Continued on p. 232)

Method of Equal Proportions

The basic problem in reapportionment is to determine the most equitable distribution of the 435 House seats among the states. There is no way of assigning a fractional Representative to a state or of giving a Representative a fractional vote. Nor is there any way by which two states could share the same Representative. To surmount such difficulties and achieve the fairest possible distribution of seats, Congress in 1941 adopted the Method of Equal Proportions. By this method, the proportional differences in the number of persons per Representative for any pair of states are reduced to a minimum.

Under the Constitution, each state is entitled to at least one seat in the House of Representatives. Thus, the first 50 seats are fixed. The question then becomes how to divide the remaining 385—which states are entitled to a second, third, fourth, etc. seat? To make the computation according to the Method of Equal Proportions, the apportionment population of each state is multiplied by the decimal of the fraction $\frac{1}{\sqrt{n(n-1)}}$

where "n" is the number of seats for the state. The result of this multiplication is a number called a priority value.

For example, for 1970 the priority value for a second seat for California was determined by multiplying the apportionment population (residents plus residents overseas) of the state for that year, 20,-098,863, by $\frac{1}{\sqrt{2(2-1)}}$ (or 0.707 10678). The result of this multiplication was 14,212,042. The same computation was then made for New York, which involved multiplying New York's apportionment population, 18,-287,529, by the same factor, 0.707 10678. The result was 12,931,236. This operation was repeated for every state. The result for the least populous state, Alaska, was 215,008.

To determine the priority value for each state's claim to a third seat, the population of the state is multiplied by $\frac{1}{\sqrt{3(3-1)}}$, or 0.408 24829. The result for California was a priority value of 8,205,326. This process is repeated for every state for any desired number of seats. Thus, to determine the strength of California's claim to a 40th seat, the multiplier was $\frac{1}{\sqrt{40(40-1)}}$ or 0.025 31848. The resulting priority value for the state in 1970 was 508,873.

When the necessary priority values for all the states have been computed, they are arranged in order, largest first. California, with the largest priority value for a second seat in 1970, received that seat, which was number 51 for the entire House. New York came next in line for a second seat, which was number 52.

The first 10 and bottom 10 priority values and the states involved, calculated by the Census Bureau on the basis of the 1970 census, were as follows:

Size of House	State	Size of State Delegation	Priority Value
51	California	2	14,212,042
52	New York	2	12,931,236
53	Pennsylvania	2	8,403,479
54	California	3	8,205,326
55	Texas	2	7,989,449
56	Illinois	2	7,908,509
57	Ohio	2	7,587,397
58	New York	3	7,465,852
59	Michigan	2	6,319,552
60	California	4	5,802,042
426	Michigan	19	483,268
427	Texas	24	480,908
428	South Carolina	6	477,855
429	Ohio	23	477,016
430	South Dakota	2	476,058
431	Illinois	24	476,036
432	New York	39	475,041
433	Florida	15	473,088
434	California	43	472,947
435	Oklahoma	6	472,043

The test of fairness of the Method of Equal Proportions is whether the percentage difference in population per Representative is the smallest possible for any pair of states. Again using the Census Bureau calculations for 1970, states can be compared with each other to test the method.

With six seats for Oklahoma, the average number of persons per Representative was 430,914. The state of Connecticut also was allocated six seats. The average number of persons per seat in Connecticut was 508,-449, 17.99 percent more than the average for Oklahoma. But if a seat were taken from Oklahoma and given to Connecticut, the difference in the number of persons per Representative would have been 18.65 percent.

South Dakota received two seats, North Dakota only one. The difference was 85.2 percent in population of Congressional districts. However, if the situation had been reversed, North Dakota receiving two and South Dakota one seat, the difference would have been 115.72 percent. In each of these comparisons, the test is met: the proportional difference between the numbers per Representative is smaller for the apportionment as computed than would be the case with alternative methods. A similar comparison could be carried out in relation to the number of Representatives per million of the population, and the results would be the same.

SOURCE: Conrad Taeuber (Associate Director, Bureau of the Census), "Reapportionment," *U.S. Department of Commerce News,* Dec. 7, 1970, p. 1-6.

(Continued from p. 230)

sentatives until another census had been taken and another reapportionment made.

Because two whole decades had passed between reapportionments, a greater shift than usual took place following the Census of 1930. California's House delegation was almost doubled, rising from 11 to 20. Michigan gained four seats, Texas three, and New Jersey, New York and Ohio two each. Twenty-one states lost a total of 27 seats: Missouri alone lost three and Georgia, Iowa, Kentucky and Pennsylvania each lost two.

The 1929 Act required the President to report the distribution of seats by two methods, major fractions and equal proportions. This was in the nature of a test to see which method yielded the fairest result. However, pending legislation to the contrary, the method of major fractions was to be used.

The two methods gave an identical distribution of seats based on 1930 census figures. However, in 1940 the two methods gave different results: under major fractions, Michigan would have gained a seat lost by Arkansas; under equal proportions, there would have been no change in either state. The automatic reapportionment provisions of the 1929 Act went into effect in January 1941. But the House Census Committee moved to reverse the result, favoring the certain Democratic seat in Arkansas over a possible Republican gain if the seat were shifted to Michigan. Congress went along, adopting Equal Proportions as the method to be used in reapportionment calculations after the 1950 and subsequent censuses, and making this action retroactive to January 1941 in order to save Arkansas its seat.

While politics doubtless played a part in timing of the action taken in 1941, the Method of Equal Proportions had come to be accepted as the best available. It had been worked out by Prof. Edward V. Huntington of Harvard in 1921. At the request of the Speaker of the House, all known methods of apportionment were considered in 1929 by the National Academy of Sciences Committee on Apportionment. The Committee expressed its preference for Equal Proportions.

This method involves complicated mathematical calculations. In brief, each of the states (now 50) is initially assigned the one seat to which every state is entitled by the Constitution. The population of each state then is multiplied by a series of multipliers. There are 59 of these multipliers, each one decreasing in size. The products of all the multiplications are arranged in order of size, beginning with the largest, to form what is known as the priority list. Seats numbered 51 through 435 are then distributed according to that list. *(For full explanation, see box.)*

Court Action on Apportionment

After the long and desultory battle over reapportionment in the 1920s, those who were unhappy over the inaction of Congress or the state legislatures began taking their cases to court. At first, they had no luck. But as the disparity in both Federal and state legislative districts grew, and the Supreme Court began to show a tendency to intervene, plaintiffs were more successful. Finally, in a series of decisions beginning with *Baker v. Carr* in 1962, the Court intervened massively in the redistricting process, ordering that Congressional districts as well as state and local legislative districts be drawn so that their populations would be as nearly equal as possible.

SUPREME COURT'S 1932 DECISIONS

In 1932 the Supreme Court handed down several important decisions on Congressional redistricting. In each case, petitioners asserted that state legislatures had not complied with the 1911 Act's requirement that districts be separate, compact, contiguous and equally populated. The question was whether that requirement, neither specifically repealed nor reaffirmed in the 1929 Act, was still in effect.

In *Smiley v. Holm* the petitioner also attacked a Minnesota redistricting statute which the Legislature had not repassed over the Governor's veto because it contended that districting legislation was not subject to veto. The Supreme Court, ignoring the question of compliance with the 1911 Act and ruling solely on the issue of the gubernatorial veto, declared that the U.S. Constitution did not exempt districting statutes from a Governor's veto. Two other 1932 Congressional districting cases—*Koenig v. Flynn,* from the New York Court of Appeals, and *Carroll v. Becker,* from the Missouri Supreme Court, were decided by the Supreme Court on similar questions regarding gubernatorial vetoes.

The question of the 1911 Act's applicability was reached in *Wood v. Broom,* a 1932 case challenging the constitutionality of a new Mississippi redistricting law. Speaking for the Court, Chief Justice Charles Evans Hughes ruled that the 1911 Act had, in effect, expired with the approval of the 1929 apportionment Act and that the standards of the 1911 Act were therefore no longer applicable. The Court reversed the decision of a lower Federal court which had permanently enjoined elections under the new Mississippi redistricting act because it violated the standards of the 1911 Act. Later the same year the Court made a similar ruling in *Mahan v. Hume,* a Kentucky Congressional districting case.

Four Members of the Supreme Court—Justices Louis D. Brandeis, Harlan F. Stone, Owen J. Roberts and Benjamin N. Cardozo—while concurring in the majority opinion, said they would have dismissed the Wood suit for "want of equity." The "want-of-equity" phrase in this context suggested a policy of judicial self-limitation with respect to the entire question of judicial involvement in essentially "political" questions.

COURT'S DECISION IN 1946 CASE

Not until 1946, in *Colegrove v. Green,* did the Court again rule in a significant case dealing with Congressional redistricting. The case was brought by Kenneth Colegrove, a political science professor at Northwestern University, who alleged that Illinois' Congressional districts—varying between 112,116 and 914,053 in population—were so unequal that they violated the 14th Amendment's guarantee of equal protection of the laws. A seven-man Supreme Court divided 4-3 in dismissing the suit.

Justice Felix Frankfurter gave the plurality opinion of the Court, speaking for himself and Justices Stanley F. Reed and Harold H. Burton. Frankfurter's opinion cited *Wood v. Broom* to indicate that Congress had deliberately removed the standard set by the 1911 Act. "We also agree," he said, "with the four Justices (Brandeis, Stone, Roberts and Cardozo) who were of the opinion that the bill in *Wood v. Broom* should be 'dismissed for want of equity.' " The issue, Frankfurter said, was "of a peculiarly political nature and therefore not meet for judicial interpretation....The short of it is that the Constitution has conferred upon Congress exclusive authority to secure fair representation by the states in the popular House and has left to that House determination whether states have fulfilled their responsibility. If Congress failed in exercising its powers, whereby standards of fairness are offended, the remedy lies ultimately with the people...To sustain this action would cut very deep into the very being of Congress. Courts ought not to enter this political thicket. The remedy for unfairness in districting is to secure state legislatures that will apportion properly, or to invoke the ample powers of Congress." Frankfurter said, in addition, that the Court could not affirmatively remap Congressional districts and that elections at large would be politically undesirable.

Justice Hugo L. Black, joined in a dissenting opinion by Justices William O. Douglas and Frank Murphy, expressed the belief that the District Court had jursidiction under a section of the U.S. Code giving district courts the right to redress deprivations of constitutional rights occurring through action of the states. Black's opinion also rested on a previous case in which the Court had indicated that Federal constitutional questions, unless "frivolous," fall under the jursidiction of the Federal courts. Black asserted that the appellants had standing to sue, that the population disparities did violate the equal protection clause of the 14th Amendment, and that relief should be granted. Black specifically rejected the view that *Smiley v. Holm* had set a precedent of non-justiciability. *Smiley v. Holm,* he said, merely decided that the 1911 Act was no longer applicable. Only a minority of the Court, he pointed out, had thought the case should be dismissed for "want of equity."

With the Court split 3-3 on whether the Judiciary had or should exercise jurisdiction, the deciding opinion in *Colegrove v. Green* was that of Justice Wiley B. Rutledge. On the question of justiciability, Rutledge agreed with Black, Douglas and Murphy that the issue could be considered by the Federal courts. "But for the ruling in *Smiley v. Holm,*" Rutledge said, he would have thought that the Constitution specifically reserved the regulation of Congressional elections to the states and Congress. Rutledge believed, however, that Smiley "rules squarely to the contrary." Thus a majority of the Court participating in the Colegrove case felt that Congressional redistricting cases were justiciable.

On the other hand, on the question of granting relief in this specific instance, Rutledge agreed with Frankfurter, Reed and Burton that the case should be dismissed. He pointed out that four of the nine justices in *Wood v. Broom* had felt that dismissal should be for want of equity. Rutledge saw a "want-of-equity" situation in *Colegrove v. Green* as well. "I think the gravity of the constitutional questions raised so great, together with the possibility of collision (with the political departments of the Government), that the admonition (against avoidable constitutional decision) is appropriate to be followed here," Rutledge said. Jurisdiction, he thought, should be exercised "only in the most compelling circumstances." He thought that "the shortness of time remaining (before the forthcoming election) makes it doubtful whether action could or would be taken in time to

secure for petitioners the effective relief they seek." Rutledge warned that Congressional elections at large would deprive citizens of representation by districts, "which the prevailing policy of Congress demands." In the case of at-large elections, he warned, "the cure sought may be worse than the disease." For all these reasons he concluded that the case was "one in which the Court may properly, and should, decline to exercise its jurisdiction."

FACTORS LEADING TO NEW COURT POSITION

In the ensuing years, law professors, political scientists and other commentators expressed growing dislike for the Colegrove doctrine and growing impatience with the Supreme Court's position. Yet the membership of the Court was changing, and the new members were more inclined toward judicial action on redistricting. By 1962, only three members of the Colegrove Court remained: Justices Black and Douglas, dissenters in that case, and Justice Frankfurter, aging spokesman for restraint in the exercise of judicial power.

Already in the 1950s, the Court had decided two cases which laid some groundwork for its subsequent reapportionment decisions. The first was *Brown v. Board of Education* (1954), the historic school desegregation case, in which the Court decided that an individual citizen could assert a right to equal protection of the laws under the 14th Amendment, contrary to the "separate but equal" doctrine of public facilities for white and Negro citizens. Six years later, in *Gomillion v. Lightfoot* (1960), the Court held that the Alabama Legislature could not draw the city limits of Tuskegee so as to exclude the Negro community. Justice Frankfurter based his opinion on the 15th Amendment, but Justice Charles E. Whittaker said that the equal protection clause was the proper constitutional basis for the decision. One commentator later remarked that *Gomillion* amounted to a "dragon" in the "political thicket" of Colegrove.

With this groundwork already laid, during the years 1962-64 the Supreme Court rendered a series of four landmark decisions in the politically sensitive area of Congressional and state legislative apportionment and districting. The precedent-breaking decisions all had a common theme—that "as nearly as practicable, one man's vote... is to be worth as much as another's." By entering the "political thicket" of apportionment and redistricting, the Court extended its authority far beyond its previous scope and seemed certain to cause a revolution in the complexion of state government and the bases of Congressional power.

A major element causing the reversal of the Court's previous decision on reapportionment and redistricting was the population migration from country to city, which had been under way ever since the turn of the century. By 1960, there was not a single legislative body in a single state in which there was not at least a 2-1 population disparity between the most and the least heavily populated districts. For example, the disparity was 242 to 1 in the Connecticut House, 223 to 1 in the Nevada Senate, 141 to 1 in the Rhode Island Senate and 9 to 1 in the Georgia Senate. Studies of the effective vote of large and small counties in state legislatures between 1910 and 1960 showed that the effective vote of the large counties had slipped while their percentage of the national population had more than doubled. The most lightly populated counties, on the other hand, advanced from a position of slight over-representation to one of extreme over-representation, holding almost twice as many seats as they would be entitled to by population alone. Predictably, the rural-dominated state legislatures resisted every move toward reapportioning districts to reflect new population patterns.

By no means as gross but still substantial was population imbalance among Congressional districts. In Texas, the Census of 1960 showed the most heavily populated district had four times as many inhabitants as the most lightly populated. Arizona, Maryland and Ohio each had at least one district with three times as many inhabitants as the most lightly populated. In a majority of cases, it was rural areas which benefited from Congressional malapportionment. As a result of the postwar population movement out of central cities to the surrounding areas, the suburbs were the most under-represented.

HISTORIC 1962 DECISION

It was against this background that a group of Tennessee city dwellers successfully broke the long-standing precedent against Federal court involvement in legislative apportionment problems. For more than half a century, since 1901, the Tennessee Legislature had refused to reapportion itself, even though a decennial reapportionment based on population was specifically required by the state's constitution. In the meantime, Tennessee's population had grown and shifted dramatically to urban areas. By 1960, the House legislative districts ranged from 3,454 to 36,031 in population, while the Senate districts ranged from 39,727 to 108,094. Appeals by urban residents to the rural-controlled Tennesee Legislatures proved fruitless. A suit brought in the state courts to force reapportionment was rejected on the ground that the courts should stay out of legislative matters.

The urban interests then appealed to the Federal courts, stating that they had no redress: the Legislature had refused to act for more than half a century; the state courts had refused to intervene; Tennessee had no referendum or initiative laws. The city dwellers charged that there was "a debasement of their votes by virtue of the incorrect, obsolete and unconstitutional apportionment" to such an extent that they were being deprived of their right to "equal protection of the laws" under the 14th Amendment. (The 14th Amendment reads, in part: "No state shall...deny to any person within its jurisdiction the equal protection of the laws.")

The Supreme Court on March 26, 1962, handed down its historic decision in *Baker v. Carr,* ruling in favor of the Tennessee city dwellers by a 6-2 margin. In the majority opinion, Justice William J. Brennan Jr. emphasized that the Federal judiciary had the power to review the apportionment of state legislatures under the 14th Amendment's equal protection clause. "The mere fact that a suit seeks protection as a political right," Brennan wrote, "does not mean that it presents a political question" which the courts should avoid.

In a vigorous dissent, Justice Frankfurter said the majority decision constituted "a massive repudiation of the experience of our whole past" and was an assertion of "destructively novel judicial power." He contended that the lack of any clear basis for relief "catapults

the lower courts" into a "mathematical quagmire." Frankfurter insisted that "there is not under our Constitution a judicial remedy for every political mischief." Appeal for relief, he maintained, should not be made in the courts, but rather "to an informed civically militant electorate."

ONE MAN, ONE VOTE FOR CONGRESSMEN

Shortly after the Baker decision was handed down, James P. Wesberry Jr., an Atlanta resident and a member of the Georgia Senate, filed suit in a Federal court in Atlanta claiming that gross disparity in the population of Georgia's Congressional districts violated 14th Amendment rights of equal protection of the laws. At the time, Georgia districts ranged in population from 272,154 in the rural 9th district in the northeastern part of the state to 823,860 in the 5th district in Atlanta and its suburbs. District lines had not been changed since 1931. The state's number of House seats remained the same in the interim, but Atlanta's district population—already high in 1931 compared with the others—had more than doubled in 30 years, making a 5th District vote worth about one-third that of a vote in the 9th.

On June 20, 1962, the three-judge Federal court divided 2-1 in dismissing Wesberry's suit. The majority reasoned that the precedent of *Colegrove* still controlled in Congressional district cases. The judges cautioned against Federal judicial interference with Congress and against "depriving others of the right to vote" it the suit should result in at-large elections. They suggested that the Georgia Legislature (under court order to reapportion itself) or the U.S. Congress might better provide relief. Wesberry then appealed to the Supreme Court, which heard arguments on the case in November 1963.

On Feb. 17, 1964, the Supreme Court ruled in the case of *Wesberry v. Sanders* that Congressional districts must be substantially equal in population. The Court, which upheld Wesberry's challenge by a 6-3 decision, based its ruling on the history and wording of Article I, Section 2, of the Constitution providing that Representatives shall be apportioned among the states according to their respective numbers and be chosen by the people of the several states. This language, the Court stated, meant that "as nearly as is practicable, one man's vote in a Congressional election is to be worth as much as another's."

The majority opinion, written by Justice Black and supported by Chief Justice Earl Warren and Justices Brennan, Douglas, Arthur J. Goldberg and Byron R. White, said that "While it may not be possible to draw Congressional districts with mathematical precision, that is no excuse for ignoring our Constitution's plain objective of making equal representation for equal numbers of people the fundamental goal for the House of Representatives."

Predictably, the decision referred to the findings of the Baker case to show that districting questions were justiciable and to the *Gray v. Sanders* case to establish the principle of "one man, one vote." (*Gray v. Sanders,* 1963, overturned Georgia's county unit system of voting in statewide and Congressional primary elections.) Unlike those two decisions, however, the Wesberry decision did not attempt to use the 14th Amendment as its justification.

In a strongly worded dissent, Justice John M. Harlan asserted that the Constitution did not establish population as the only criterion of Congressional districting and that the subject was left in the Constitution to the discretion of the states, subject only to the supervisory power of Congress.

Justice Potter Stewart said he found that the Constitution gave "no mandate to this Court or to any court to ordain that Congressional districts within each state must be equal in population," but he disagreed with Harlan in that he thought the matter was justiciable.

Justice Tom C. Clark also found the matter justiciable but rejected the idea that Article I, Section 2, required a "one man, one vote" standard in Congressional elections. Clark said the case should be returned to the lower court for a hearing on the merits based on the 14th Amendment's equal protection requirements set down in the Baker case.

The Wesberry opinion established no precise standards for districting beyond declaring that districts must be as nearly equal in population "as is practicable." In his dissent, Harlan suggested that a disparity of more than 100,000 between a state's largest and smallest districts would "presumably" violate the equality standard enunciated by the majority. On that basis, Harlan estimated, the districts of 37 states with 398 Representatives would be unconstitutional, "leaving a constitutional House of 37 Members now sitting."

Neither did the Court's decision make any reference to gerrymandering, since it discussed only the population, not the shape of districts. In a separate districting opinion handed down the same day as *Wesberry,* the Court dismissed a challenge to Congressional districts in New York City, which had been brought by voters who charged that Manhattan's 17th "silk-stocking" district had been gerrymandered to exclude Negroes and Puerto Rican citizens.

Decision on Variance in Size of Districts

The next step in the Court's districting rulings came on April 7, 1969. On that date, the Court in a 6-3 decision tightened the "one man, one vote" principle by declaring Missouri's redistricting statute unconstitutional. *(Kirkpatrick v. Preisler).* Justice Brennan, speaking for the Court, said that states must strive to create Congressional districts of precisely equal population. Any variance in population, "no matter how small," must be justified by the state or shown to result in spite of a "good-faith effort."

In *Wesberry v. Sanders,* Brennan pointed out, the Court had held that the Constitution required "as nearly as is practicable one man's vote in a Congressional election...be worth as much as another's." Defining the phrase "as nearly as is practicable," Brennan said there was no fixed population variance small enough to be considered negligible. The Wesberry standard directed states to create districts absolutely equal in population. In the Court's words: "Equal representation for equal numbers of people is a principle designed to prevent debasement of voting power and diminution of access to elected Representatives. Toleration of even small deviations detracts from these purposes."

Maximum Population Variations From State Averages

(At time of Wesberry v. Sanders, *February 1964)*

State*	Maximum Variation	Total Districts
Alabama	+ 21.4%	8
Arizona	− 54.3	3
Arkansas	+ 28.8	4
California	+ 42.4	38
Colorado	− 55.4	4
Connecticut	− 37.1	6
Florida	+ 60.3	12
Georgia	+ 108.9	10
Idaho	22.9 #	2
Illinois	− 33.6	24
Indiana	+ 64.6	11
Iowa	+ 12.3	7
Kansas	+ 23.9	5
Kentucky	+ 40.8	7
Louisiana	− 35.2	8
Maine	4.3 #	2
Maryland	+ 83.5	8
Massachusetts	− 12.3	12
Michigan	+ 84.8	19
Minnesota	− 13.2	8
Mississippi	+ 39.7	5
Missouri	+ 17.3	10
Montana	18.7 #	2
Nebraska	− 14.0	3
New Hampshire	9.3 #	2
New Jersey	+ 44.8	15
New York	+ 15.1	41
North Carolina	− 32.9	11
North Dakota	5.4 #	2
Ohio	+ 72.1	24
Oklahoma	+ 42.5	6
Oregon	− 40.0	4
Pennsylvania	+ 31.9	27
Rhode Island	7.0 #	2
South Carolina	+ 33.9	6
South Dakota	46.3 #	2
Tennessee	+ 58.2	9
Texas	+ 118.5	23
Utah	28.6 #	2
Virginia	+ 36.0	10
Washington	+ 25.2	7
West Virginia	− 18.6	5
Wisconsin	+ 3.4	10

Alaska, Delaware, Hawaii, Nevada, New Mexico, Vermont and Wyoming seats were filled at large and therefore are not listed.
#State has only two districts: thus one district is the stated percentage above the average and the other district is the stated percentage below the average.

The only permissible variances in population, the Court ruled, were those unavoidable despite the effort to achieve absolute equality or those which could be legally justified. The variances in Missouri, which amounted to 3.1 percent between Congressional districts on a statewide basis, could have been avoided, the Court said.

None of Missouri's arguments for the plan qualified as "legally acceptable" justifications. The Court rejected the argument that population variance was necessary to allow representation of distinct interest groups. It held acceptance of such variances in order to produce districts with specific interests as "antithetical" to the basic purpose of equal representation.

The Court also rejected the argument that political reality—legislative compromise or the integrity of existing political boundaries—justified population variance. It dismissed arguments that nonvoting military personnel and students inflated census figures for certain districts, that post-1960 population trends were reflected in the new districts, and that geographical compactness dictated the new boundaries and some population inequality.

Dissenting Opinions. Justice White dissented from the Court's opinion, which he characterized as "an unduly rigid and unwarranted application of the Equal Protection Clause which will unnecessarily involve the courts in the abrasive task of drawing district lines." The Justice added that some "acceptably small" population variance could be established. He indicated that considerations of existing political boundaries and geographical compactness could justify to him some variation from "absolute equality" of population.

Justice Harlan, joined by Justice Stewart, objected that "whatever room remained under this Court's prior decisions for the free play of the political process in matters of reapportionment is now all but eliminated by today's Draconian judgments."

As a result of the Court decisions of the 1960s, nearly every state was forced to redraw its Congressional district lines—sometimes more than once. By the end of the decade, 39 of the 45 states with more than one Representative had made the necessary adjustments.

Congress and Redistricting

Several attempts were made during the period of court action to enact new legislation on redistricting. Only one of the efforts was successful—the passage of a measure to rule out at-large elections in states with more than one Representative.

On Jan. 9, 1951, President Truman, upon presentation of the official state population figures of the Census of 1950, asked for changes in the existing law which would tighten Federal control of state redistricting. Specifically, he asked for a ban on gerrymandering, an end to "at-large" seats in states having more than one Representative, and a sharp reduction in the huge differences in size between Congressional districts in each state.

On behalf of the Administration, Chairman Emanuel Celler (D N.Y.) of the House Judiciary Committee introduced a bill to require compact and contiguous Congressional districts which would not vary by more than 15 per cent between districts within a state. The bill also would have eliminated at-large seats and made redistricting mandatory every 10 years in accordance with population changes. But the House Judiciary Committee took no action on the proposals.

Rep. Celler regularly introduced his bill throughout the 1950s and early 1960s, but it made no headway until the Supreme Court handed down the Wesberry decision in 1964. On June 24, 1964, a Celler bill was approved by a House Judiciary Subcommittee. But the full Committee did not act on the bill before adjournment.

On March 16, 1965, the House passed a new Celler bill. It established 15 percent as the maximum percentage by which a Congressional district's population might deviate from the average size of the state's districts; prohibited at-large elections for any state with more than one House seat; required that districts be composed of "contiguous territory in as compact form as practicable;" and forbade more than one redistricting of a state between decennial censuses. A major reason for House approval of Celler's bill appeared to be a desire to gain protection from Court imposition of even more rigid criteria. But the measure encountered difficulties in the Senate Judiciary Committee. After considerable wrangling over its provisions, the committee voted to report the bill without precise agreement on its wording. No actual report was ever filed by the Senate Judiciary Committee.

In 1967, a redistricting bill was passed by both the Senate and the House but not in the same form. And the bill had a different purpose from that of previous bills dealing with the subject. Instead of trying to establish standards of fairness in drawing district lines, the chief purpose in 1967 was to prevent the courts, until after the House had been reapportioned on the basis of the Census of 1970, from ordering redistricting of House seats or from ordering any state to hold elections at large—a procedure that many incumbent Representatives feared.

A combination of liberal Democrats and Republicans in the Senate managed to defeat the conference report Nov. 8, 1967, by a vote of 22-55. Liberals favored court action which they believed would eliminate many conservative rural districts, while Republicans felt that redistricted areas, especially in the growing suburbs, would elect more Republicans than Democrats.

To avoid at-large elections, the Senate added a rider to a House-passed private bill. Under the rider, at-large elections of U.S. Representatives were banned in all states entitled to more than one Representative, with the exceptions of New Mexico and Hawaii. Those states had a tradition of electing their two Representatives at large. Both of them, however, soon passed districting laws—New Mexico for the 1968 elections and Hawaii for 1970.

Following the Census of 1960, an attempt had been made to increase the size of the House to avoid some of the losses of seats that would otherwise be suffered by several states. By a vote of 12-14 the House Judiciary Committee on Sept. 9, 1961, rejected a motion to recommend enlarging the House to 453 seats. And by a vote of 14-15, the same Committee rejected a bill reported by a subcommittee which would have increased the permanent size of the House to 438. In Committee voting, a majority of Democrats favored the House-increase bills while Republicans were almost unanimous in opposition. Republican National Chairman William E. Miller and other Republican leaders reportedly reached the conclusion that any increase in the size of the House was more likely to benefit Democrats than Republicans.